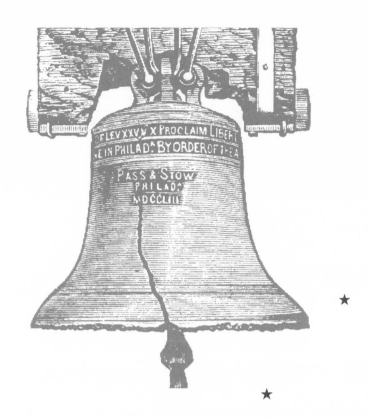

PENNSYLVANIA'S REVOLUTION

Edited by WILLIAM PENCAK

THE PENNSYLVANIA STATE UNIVERSITY PRESS

UNIVERSITY PARK, PENNSYLVANIA

Library of Congress Cataloging-in-Publication Data

Pennsylvania's revolution / edited by William Pencak.
p.   cm.
Includes bibliographical references and index.
Summary: "A collection of essays on the American Revolution in
Pennsylvania. Topics include the politicization of the English- and
German-language press and the population they served; the
Revolution in remote areas of the state; and new historical
perspectives on the American and British armies during the Valley
Forge winter"—Provided by publisher.
ISBN 978-0-271-03579-6 (cloth : alk. paper)
1. Pennsylvania—History—Revolution, 1775–1783.
I. Pencak, William, 1951– .

E263.P4P47 2010
974.8'03—dc22
2009025007

The Pennsylvania State University Press is a member of the
Association of American University Presses.

It is the policy of The Pennsylvania State University Press to
use acid-free paper. Publications on uncoated stock satisfy the
minimum requirements of American National Standard for
Information Sciences—Permanence of Paper for
Printed Library Material, ANSI Z39.48-1992.

This book is printed on Natures Natural, which contains 50%
post-consumer waste.

CONTENTS

CONTENTS

This book emerged out of my graduate seminar on early American history. So I decided to do what I did about a decade ago. When a critical mass of fine graduate students at Penn State produced work on Pennsylvania in the Civil War, I collected the essays, added a few more, and sent them off to Penn State Press. The former book, which William Blair and I edited as *Making and Remaking Pennsylvania's Civil War,* was validated by receiving the Philip S. Klein Prize of the Pennsylvania Historical Association for the best book on Pennsylvania published in 2001–2.

I am proud to say that the referees for the present collection—Paul Douglas Newman and Wayne Bodle—accepted these essays (adding very helpful comments) without knowing who most of the contributors were. I'd also like to thank John Murrin for his excellent comments on three of the papers at a session of the Pennsylvania Historical Association in 2007. The essays by James Bailey, Meredith Lair, Philipp Münch, and Russell Spinney originated in my seminars, whereas I discovered the work of Robert Guy Jr. and Melissah Pawlikowski (who introduced me to Douglas MacGregor) when they applied to Penn State's history program, although they were ultimately unable to attend. At the same time, students I knew from the McNeil Center, Patrick Spero from the University of Pennsylvania and Elizabeth Pardoe and Anthony Joseph from Princeton, had also been doing work on Pennsylvania's experiences during the Revolution. John Frantz not only preceded me in teaching early American history at Penn State, he also replaced me temporarily when I was seriously ill in 2004. Through John and the Pennsylvania Historical Association (another society I have enjoyed and benefited much from for twenty-five years) I met Owen Ireland, whose contributions to the field are always fascinating and seemingly inexhaustible. (P.S. I hope John will someday collect his fine series of essays on the Pennsylvania Germans in a book; this essay was previously published in the *Yearbook of the Pennsylvania German Society* and appears here with its permission.) Karen Guenther, after she received her MA at Penn State, also replaced me at the Berks Campus in the late 1980s, when I was on sabbatical. I met Nathan Kozuskanich when he asked me to read his dissertation, from which his article was taken.

In many respects, this collection symbolizes the work on Pennsylvania history I have been doing for most of my professional life with colleagues and students at my own university—both in the History Department and with the University Press—and elsewhere. Rather than play favorites, permit me to dedicate this book to all the people connected with Penn State, the McNeil Center, and the PHA, past and present, who have allowed me to contribute to the substantial historical legacy they have offered the world. They know who they are, and the respect and affection I feel for them. Special thanks to Patrick Alexander, Kathryn Yahner, and Suzanne Wolk for their help in bringing this complicated manuscript into print.

INTRODUCTION

William Pencak

The noted painting by Benjamin West of "William Penn's Treaty with the Indians" is perhaps the most famous iconic representation of colonial Pennsylvania aside from Benjamin Franklin. It signifies the peaceful relations begun in 1682, when Penn founded the colony, that broke down only in 1755 at the outset of the French and Indian War. But the painting originated as a weapon in a political controversy; it was executed in 1771 by Benjamin West, the history painter to King George III, at the behest of the Penn family proprietors, who wished to contrast the peace that had prevailed in their province to the recent internal strife they sought to blame on their Quaker Party adversaries, who were seeking to transform Pennsylvania into a royal government.

Periodization is an important lens through which history is viewed. If we separate peaceful pre-1755 Pennsylvania from the strife the colony and state endured between that year and 1800, we lose sight of the important fact, brought to significant scholarly attention by James Merrell,[1] that it was the very manner in which Pennsylvania kept the peace that was responsible for the violent reaction against it that followed. By removing Indians through chicanery against their wishes, using the Iroquois as the iron fist behind the velvet glove of treaty presents and payments to compel their southern neighbors to move west, Pennsylvania ensured that smoldering resentments would burst into flames once people on the frontier began ignoring the established boundaries. Similarly, the largely harmonious political system fashioned by the Quakers in the mid-eighteenth century only flourished because Quaker-dominated counties were overrepresented, and in peacetime neither the western settlers nor the Philadelphia artisans had much to complain about.

By the early 1760s Pennsylvania was ruled by an unrepresentative government whose proprietary and Quaker factions were both kowtowing to a British administration that would decide which one would rule the province. They had failed to protect the frontiers, blaming each other (with historians still taking one side or the other) for stalling defense measures to avoid taxes (the proprietors) or make inroads on proprietary power (the Quakers). The province's ruling elite was thus unwilling to lead Pennsylvania in the struggle against British taxes and regulations, as, for example, the Virginia planters and the Massachusetts legislature were. Historians seeking to show that the American Revolution was an internal struggle that produced important social and political change have turned more frequently to Pennsylvania than to any other state. From Charles H. Lincoln's 1901 *Revolutionary Movement in Pennsylvania* and Theodore Thayer and Robert Brunhouse's volumes in the series on Pennsylvania politics published by the State Historical and Museum Commission in 1953 and 1942, respectively, to studies by Gary Nash, Richard Ryerson, Charles Olton, Steven Rosswurm, Billy Smith, and Ronald Schultz written between 1970 and the early 1990s, Pennsylvania's revolutionary turmoil has proved the most fertile American territory for scholars seeking class and sectional struggles.[2] Elisha Douglass, in *Rebels and Democrats,* and Gordon Wood, in *The Creation of the American Republic,* focused especially on the Pennsylvania constitution of 1776 as the most extreme example of this revolutionary transformation.[3] Benjamin Franklin's metamorphosis from the main supporter in the 1760s of changing the province from a proprietary to a royal government, to the state's first president under the new state constitution, to a leading Federalist who sought to supplant it at the Philadelphia Convention in 1787, exemplifies this turbulence.[4]

Studies that concentrated on state-level upheaval have recently been joined by others that examine the equally important events that occurred throughout the commonwealth. *Beyond Philadelphia* looked systematically at the Revolution in various regions of the state, supplementing Jerome Wood's older book on Lancaster. *Friends and Enemies in Penn's Woods,* along with a monograph by Gregory Knouff, deal with the savage frontier warfare and accompanying racial division of society into white and red that accompanied the Revolution in the northeast and far west of Pennsylvania. Owen Ireland has cast the state's political conflict in ethnic and religious terms. Francis Fox has marvelously reconstructed the lives of obscure people in Northampton County to show how the Revolution made and broke fortunes and careers with great rapidity. Gary Nash and Jean Soderlund have recounted the Revolution's impact on its African American population.[5] Three recent monographs greatly enhance our understanding of the violence and social turmoil that accompanied Pennsylvania's revolution: David Preston and Paul Moyer on Native Americans, revolutionaries, and loyalists on the western and northeastern frontiers, respectively, and Terry Bouton on tax resistance and court closings. Paul Douglas Newman is currently preparing a book on westerners' attempts to form a separate state.[6]

The empowerment of new citizens was a major consequence of Pennsylvania's internal revolution. The importance of Nathan Kozuskanich's essay, which opens this collection, lies in his showing the direct connection between the principles of the Paxton Boys—who in 1763 vented their frustration against the province's inability to defend them by massacring innocent Christian Indians who were under provincial protection—and those of the new revolutionary government that emerged in Pennsylvania in 1776. For admirers of the constitution of 1776 as an exercise in democracy that gave power to the western part of the state and Philadelphia's artisans, it is not pleasant to remember that the same constitution was also an exercise in populist authoritarianism that made swearing a Christian oath (in a state still containing many Quakers and other pacifists) to defend the commonwealth the basis of citizenship, and rode roughshod over individual rights by confiscating dissidents' guns and property, and prosecuting as traitors those who criticized it.

Recently, Hermann Wellenreuther has examined the grassroots proceedings of Pennsylvania committees that organized the Revolution in spite of a reluctant provincial government, tracing the process of communications between Philadelphia and the hinterland that made the Revolution possible in the countryside.[7] But private communications were at work as well. Patrick Spero and Philipp Münch examine how almanacs, the most popular secular literature of early America, conveyed revolutionary ideology. What is interesting, though, is how reluctantly and how few of the almanacs in Pennsylvania actually espoused the Revolution openly in a state that was severely divided, and whose capital and "old counties"—Philadelphia, Bucks, and Chester—were heavily loyalist and neutral. But the aged Henry Miller (Heinrich Müller), who was only two years younger than Benjamin Franklin, was crucial as a conduit of revolutionary ideology for the Pennsylvania German speakers—the majority in the counties of Northampton, Berks, Lancaster, and York and a significant minority in Philadelphia—who came into their own as soldiers and officeholders. In an appendix, Jan Logemann reinforces Miller's importance in spreading word of the cause in his pamphlets and newspapers.

Although by no means as important as in early colonial America, when publications that were neither religious nor sanctioned by the government were rare, ministers still played an important role in disseminating ideas from their pulpits. John Frantz demonstrates the active involvement of Pennsylvania German-speaking ministers in the Revolution: although many favored the cause, the presence of pacifists and loyalists among them reflected Pennsylvania's general internal division. Pennsylvania's dozen Anglican preachers, on the other hand, with the exception of Philadelphia's William White, all became loyalists, reflecting both their oath to the king and the fact that most of them were missionaries sent from Britain.

Besides politicizing the hinterland, the Revolution involved new actors in the city and environs of Philadelphia. Esther DeBerdt Reed, as Owen Ireland shows, was one of many women who found themselves drawn into the conflict. As the daughter of a former provincial agent, however, she had well-defined ideas of her own even before the Revolution began and is famous as the first woman to organize American women for a political purpose—to raise money for the impoverished Continental treasury in 1780. Most women who expressed their opinions on the struggle did so only when the war touched their lives directly. Meredith Lair, in her study of British theater in occupied Philadelphia, shows how even loyalists were offended by the arrogant behavior of officers who flouted curfews and lived well during a time of trouble for most inhabitants. Intending to liberate the loyal Americans from a revolutionary minority that it believed was terrorizing the general population, the British army, by exhibiting contempt for their allies, opponents, and civilian population alike, probably made more revolutionaries than all the writings and speeches of the patriots.

The Revolution reached to most remote regions of Pennsylvania. In *Beyond Philadelphia,* Tim Blessing and Frederick Stefon showed that the struggle in the Juniata and Wyoming valleys was more about who would possess the land than about loyalty to either side in the greater cause: Indians and those who became loyalists or revolutionaries took sides as best suited their chances of obtaining title to disputed land. Douglas MacGregor looks at the far western frontier, the area around Pittsburgh, disputed by Indians, Virginians, and Pennsylvanians; here a significant loyalist presence of Virginians who had relied upon that province's loyalist British governor, Lord Dunmore, remained a thorn in the side of the Pennsylvania authorities throughout the war. Russell Spinney demonstrates, however, that on the West Branch of the Susquehanna River the handful of prerevolutionary Euro-Americans retained peaceful ties with Native Americans that had disappeared elsewhere until the war finally reached the valley in 1777, precipitating the "Great Runaway," which required white resettlement (largely in the form of bounty land to veterans) following the war.

The war itself transformed the lives of many Pennsylvanians. Two authors in this collection present the two poles of the revolutionary experience. The Continental Congress looked primarily to the Pennsylvania Riflemen—the most accurate marksmen in the world, with experience in fighting Indians on the frontier—when it sought soldiers to aid New Englanders besieging Boston in the summer of 1775. Robert Guy Jr. tells their story through the eyes of their commander, William Thompson, whose lengthy imprisonment and premature death belie his regiment's major contribution to the outcome of the war. Melissah Pawlikowski, in contrast, focuses on Isaac Craig, a Philadelphia carpenter who rose to become commander of the munitions depots in the Pennsylvania countryside following the Valley Forge winter, and later became one of the leading developers of the infant city of Pittsburgh. James Bailey reconsiders that winter itself and contrasts it in detail with the far colder, yet much less deadly, experience of the Continental army at Morristown in 1779–80. He also examines why we remember the former and have all but forgotten the latter.

The transformation of ideas was also an important part of Pennsylvania's revolutionary experience. Elizabeth Pardoe looks at the convention where Pennsylvania ratified the federal Constitution, and brings to light the fact that James Wilson turned to Pennsylvania's contentious recent history to refute the Anti-Federalists' contention that the states could in any reasonable way represent the people's interests. He anticipated James Madison's insight that a multiple representation of popular interests at local, state, and federal levels was not only a possible but a far superior way of governing a large and diverse republic. Next, Anthony Joseph traces the transformation of Pennsylvanians from "cheerful tax-payers" to supporters of tax resistance in the Whiskey and Fries rebellions of the 1790s. Pennsylvanians did not object to paying taxes, but they reserved the right to judge whether they were fair or unfair and act accordingly. At the same time, as the state efficiently invested its surplus money in bank stocks, Pennsylvanians lost the habit of paying taxes in the early nineteenth century and grumbled when they were required to do so (as we continue to do today).

The volume concludes with Karen Guenther's traversal of the way films have dealt with Pennsylvania's revolutionary experience. Unfortunately, few of these works have gone beyond romanticism, one-dimensional portrayals of characters, or simplistic interpretations of the conflict. We can only hope that someday revolutionary Pennsylvania will be featured in a film similar to the one that depicts the Revolution as experienced by a Connecticut woman, *Mary Silliman's War,* which graphically illustrates the turmoil of the war—its tragedy as well as its triumph. I am no film director, but I hope this volume will help bring to life much of the diversity and reason for the persistent fascination of Pennsylvania's revolution.

Back in the 1920s, a Harvard professor told a young Perry Miller that there was little more to be written about the Puritans. A few years ago, as eighteenth-century Pennsylvania—especially the frontier and the Revolution—was becoming one of the hottest topics in the historical profession, I wondered whether I ought to have warned away the youthful enthusiasts, much as that old-timer warned Miller. I'm glad I didn't. As its natural resources were once deemed, Pennsylvania's revolutionary past seems truly inexhaustible, as do the (mostly young) historians who keep finding more to say about it.

NOTES

1. James Hart Merrell, *Into the American Woods: Negotiators on the Pennsylvania Frontier* (New York: W. W. Norton, 1999).

2. Charles H. Lincoln, *The Revolutionary Movement in Pennsylvania, 1760–1776* (Philadelphia: University of Pennsylvania Press, 1901); Theodore Thayer, *Pennsylvania Politics and the Growth of Democracy, 1740–1776* (Harrisburg: Pennsylvania Historical and Museum Commission, 1953); Robert L. Brunhouse, *The Counter-Revolution in Pennsylvania, 1776–1790* (Harrisburg: Pennsylvania Historical and Museum Commission, 1942); Gary B. Nash, *Urban Crucible: Political Change, Social Consciousness, and the Origins of the American Revolution* (Cambridge: Harvard University Press, 1979); Richard A. Ryerson, *The Revolution Is Now Begun: The Radical Committees of Philadelphia, 1765–1776* (Philadelphia: University of Penn-

sylvania Press, 1978); Charles S. Olton, *Artisans for Independence: Philadelphia Mechanics and the American Revolution* (Syracuse: Syracuse University Press, 1975); Billy G. Smith, *"The Lower Sort": Philadelphia's Laboring People, 1750–1800* (Ithaca: Cornell University Press, 1990); Steven Rosswurm, *Arms, Country, and Class: The Philadelphia Militia and the "Lower Sort" During the American Revolution, 1775–1783* (New Brunswick: Rutgers University Press, 1987); Ronald A. Schultz, *The Republic of Labor: Philadelphia Artisans and the Politics of Class, 1720–1830* (New York: Oxford University Press, 1993).

3. Elisha P. Douglass, *Rebels and Democrats: The Struggle for Equal Political Rights and Majority Rule During the American Revolution* (Chapel Hill: University of North Carolina Press, 1955); Gordon S. Wood, *The Creation of the American Republic, 1776–1787* (Chapel Hill: University of North Carolina Press, 1969).

4. William S. Hanna's *Benjamin Franklin and Pennsylvania Politics* (Stanford: Stanford University Press, 1964) is still a good introduction to the flexible Franklin. The late J. A. Leo Lemay was working on what would have been the most complete biography of Franklin (in seven projected volumes). See Lemay's *The Life of Benjamin Franklin*, 3 vols. (Philadelphia: University of Pennsylvania Press, 2005–2008).

5. John B. Frantz and William Pencak, eds., *Beyond Philadelphia: The American Revolution in the Pennsylvania Hinterland* (University Park: Pennsylvania State University Press, 1998); Jerome H. Wood, *Conestoga Crossroads: Lancaster, Pennsylvania, 1730–1790* (Harrisburg: Pennsylvania Historical and Museum Commission, 1979); William Pencak and Daniel K. Richter, eds., *Friends and Enemies in Penn's Woods: Indians, Colonists, and the Racial Construction of Pennsylvania* (University Park: Pennsylvania State University Press, 2004); Gregory T. Knouff, *The Soldiers' Revolution: Pennsylvanians in Arms and the Forging of Early American Identity* (University Park: Pennsylvania State University Press, 2004); Gary B. Nash and Jean Soderlund, *Freedom by Degrees: Emancipation in Pennsylvania and Its Aftermath* (New York: Oxford University Press, 1991); Francis S. Fox, *Sweet Land of Liberty: The Ordeal of the Revolution in Northampton County, Pennsylvania* (University Park: Pennsylvania State University Press, 2000); Owen S. Ireland, *Religion, Ethnicity, and Politics: Ratifying the Constitution in Pennsylvania* (University Park: Pennsylvania State University Press, 1995).

6. David Preston, *The Texture of Contact: European and Indian Settler Communities on the Iroquoian Borderlands, 1720–1780* (Lincoln: University of Nebraska Press, 2009); Paul Moyer, *Wild Yankees: The Struggle for Independence Along Pennsylvania's Revolutionary Frontier* (Ithaca: Cornell University Press, 2007); Terry Bouton, *"The People," the Founders, and the Troubled Ending of the American Revolution* (New York: Oxford University Press, 2007). Newman's work is tentatively titled *Westsylvania, Watauga, and Western Identity in the Age of Revolution*.

7. Hermann Wellenreuther et al., *The Revolution of the People: Thoughts and Documents on the Revolutionary Process in North America, 1774–1776* (Göttingen: Göttingen University Press, 2006).

"FALLING UNDER THE DOMINATION TOTALLY OF PRESBYTERIANS": THE PAXTON RIOTS AND THE COMING OF THE REVOLUTION IN PENNSYLVANIA

Nathan Kozuskanich

The Quakers in England, wrote Benjamin Franklin in 1765, "dread nothing more than what they see as otherwise inevitable, their Friends in Pennsylvania falling under the domination totally of Presbyterians."[1] Looking at the election results for the Pennsylvania Assembly, it is hard to see why the Quakers and their allies held such fears, since they controlled the House until the 1770s. But when we consider the politics of the streets and the popular leaders of the resistance to Britain, most of whom never set foot in the Assembly, their apprehension is much more understandable. Grafting itself onto the Proprietary Party, the Quaker Party's arch-nemesis, an emerging "Presbyterian Party" led Pennsylvania's opposition to the Stamp Act and the Townshend duties, and eventually brought the province into open rebellion against the Crown. Proprietary Party supporters saw their chance to undermine the Quakers and their conservative stance toward the imperial crisis by letting their Presbyterian allies do most of the dirty work.[2] This fragile but dangerous coalition did not go unnoticed. "Since the Pextang Riots," wrote Quaker James Pemberton of the Presbyterians, the Proprietary Party has "remarkably caressed these people."[3]

The Quakers' fear of total domination by Presbyterian power in the 1760s suggests that we need to consider Pennsylvania's road to the American Revolution in light of the problems of the frontier and the impact they had on constitutional thought and political culture.[4] While the important role the Stamp Act played in bringing about the American Revolution has been widely accepted, the incredible amount of internal squabbling and local partisan politics in Pennsylvania that exploded after 1763 makes it hard to simultaneously keep the imperial crisis in focus.[5] Compounding this problem is the fact that our understanding of the Revolution in Pennsylvania has been largely shaped by studies of Philadelphia and the arrival of Thomas Paine in November 1774.[6] But Franklin's worried letter indicates that perhaps the historiography has been too myopic, and asks us to place more value on the impact of the so-called Presbyterian Party during the imperial crisis, even if it never took control of the Assembly before the Revolution. More important, Pemberton's disgust with the Proprietary Party's attempts to ally with the Presbyterians casts new light on one of Pennsylvania's most infamous events: the Paxton Riots. Long understood as the culmination of frontier racism and hatred toward Indians, the riots have generally been seen as a footnote to the French and Indian War, not the beginning of something new. And yet Pemberton notes the genesis of a new political era, one in which a politicized Presbyterian faction and the frontier would play an increasingly important role.

Since Pennsylvania had a vibrant print culture that fueled both local and imperial crises from the 1760s until the Revolution, it is a perfect place to study the dual legacy of the Revolution, both its top-down ideological impact and the bottom-up social movements that often co-opted elite rhetoric. And, since the debate over establishing a new government in 1776 was inextricably linked to establishing the province's first militia, Pennsylvania offers fertile ground for exploring the interplay between individual liberty and communal rights and responsibilities. Taking a cue from Franklin and Pemberton, this essay maps out a road to 1776 that largely begins in 1763 with the Paxton Boys and focuses on how issues of safety shaped Pennsylvania's political and constitutional culture. As a result of the violence of the French and Indian War, the Paxton rioters challenged the Quaker emphasis on peace through negotiation with Native Americans and articulated a new vision of government that demanded that elected representatives provide safety against all belligerents. They also demanded that all men contribute to the common defense, an ideology that would shape the rise of a Presbyterian political faction through the 1760s and 1770s and become reality in 1776, when Pennsylvanians drafted a new state constitution.

Pennsylvania was unique in that it was the only colony without an established militia tradition or militia laws. Even though the duke of York demanded in 1664 that those living in the lands under his control be "furnished with arms and other suitable provisions," all such militia provisions became void when Charles II granted Quaker spokesman William Penn the lands of Pennsylvania as a Proprietary colony in March 1681.[7] The 1681 royal charter recognized that incursions from Indian nations, "as of other enemies, pirates and robbers, may probably be feared," and thus made provisions for Penn to "muster and train all sorts of men, of what condition soever, or wheresoever borne."[8] However, Penn founded his colony on the Quaker ideals of religious freedom and liberty of conscience, and as such the 1682 "Frame of Government" he drafted made no provisions for defense and did not mandate any sort of militia service.

The Quakers who came to Pennsylvania and controlled its increasingly powerful Assembly were determined to make the colony surpass all others with regard to popular privileges, which meant that they would not coerce any man into militia service if it violated his religious rights. As continental wars spilled over into the colonies, the issue of defense and a provincial militia arose again and again, as frontier residents argued that the Assembly was infringing on their natural rights through its commitment to pacifism. Quakers in the Assembly were able to build an effective popular coalition with non-Quakers who either shared their pacifism, valued individual liberty, or saw no immediate danger that necessitated coerced militia service. The peace the colonies enjoyed with the conclusion of Queen Anne's War in 1714 only served to strengthen this alliance.

By the 1740s and the War of Jenkins' Ear, some Quakers saw that compromise on defense issues might be necessary. James Logan, a Scots-Irish Quaker, argued that a Quaker minority would soon lose power if it did not rule in the interest of the majority. While Logan still considered an offensive war incompatible with biblical principles, a war to defend one's property did not contradict Quaker pacifism. Claiming that the majority of Pennsylvanians now wanted a militia law and that a Quaker minority could therefore not deny it, Logan suggested that "all such who for conscience-sake cannot join in any law for self-defense, should not only decline standing candidates at the ensuing election for representatives themselves, but also advise all others who are equally scrupulous to do the same."[9] When the French joined the war in 1744, the threat of attack and the need to prepare some kind of defense system seemed more pressing to Pennsylvanians.

It was during this debate over defense that Benjamin Franklin published *Plain Truth: Or, Serious Considerations on the Present State of the City of Philadelphia and Province of Pennsylvania.* He argued that the answer to the defense problem lay in the formation of a private volunteer army, but he also condemned the Assembly for putting its religion before its duties as representatives of the people. "*Protection* is as truly due from the government to the people, as *obedience* from the people to the government," he wrote, thus providing the ideological groundwork for future polemics against the Assembly by explicitly stating that the government was *required* to provide protection.[10] In the short term, Franklin's associator movement was a success, with thirty-three companies raised in Lancaster County, twenty-six in Chester, nineteen in Bucks, twelve in Philadelphia City, and eight in Philadelphia County by 1749.[11] Although Franklin had taken a significant step in providing a system of defense for Pennsylvania, his associator movement did not solve the political tensions or constitutional debates that had thwarted previous attempts to form a militia. No one in Pennsylvania was obligated to join an associator company, nor was the Assembly required to supply funds or arms to these units. Although Franklin had side-stepped the recalcitrant Assembly, he had not addressed the constitutional ideology that had caused the problems in the first place. Quakers could still refuse to pass a militia law and appeal to sacred British rights and freedom of conscience under the Pennsylvania constitution.

Pennsylvania had avoided any direct attack from either France or Spain during the 1740s, but when hostilities with France heated up in the Ohio River valley in the early 1750s, Pennsylvania was not so fortunate. When France's Indian allies began to attack the frontier settlements, it became clear that a volunteer force alone could not provide adequate defense. With a very real threat of a land attack on Pennsylvania, an ideology of rights and obligations in which defense was a central concept began to gain credence. Men were bound together by the bonds of civil society and were thus obligated to one another to contribute to the common defense, to "rise up as one man."[12] For Protestants, a defensive war against heathen and Catholic attackers was lawful and necessary to ensure the security of British liberty. Protestants needed to lay aside their theological differences and be "perfectly joined together in the same mind" to ensure the "future peace and happiness" of "religion and liberty."[13] Anglican Thomas Barton explained that "to defend our country, when in danger, is virtuous; and to preserve our religion in her departing moments is—it is more than virtuous! It is divine!"[14] As fears of attack were realized, many looked to the Assembly to contribute its share to the province's protection.

Like their colonial contemporaries, many Pennsylvanians understood civil society in Lockean terms, namely, as a state in which "any number of men are so united into one society, as to quit every one his executive power of the law of nature, and resign it to the public."[15] This power was vested in a popular government, which had "no other end but the preservation of property."[16] The binding together of men into civil society created a community protected by the rule of law to which all men were equally subject.[17] Once a man entered into this community, every man put "himself under an obligation to everyone of that society, to submit to the determination of the majority."[18] As one Pennsylvanian wrote, civil society consisted of men bound together "according to the law of nature, for the safety of the whole; having a common established law and judicature to appeal to; with authority to settle controversies between them, and to punish offenders."[19] Every man was obligated "by the law of nature to preserve his own life, liberty, and property; but also that of others." To neglect the safety of the frontier was thus to violate the very contract that formed the basis of civil society. Pacifism was antithetical to the purpose of government, and many Pennsylvanians believed that "government has no power if it has not the sword."[20] Critics of the Quakers were quick to point out that most people in the province wanted a militia, and that to let a minority faction of pacifists block it was contrary to the very purpose of civil society.

The pressing issue of defense led to the formation of a pragmatic political alliance between Anglican and Presbyterian factions, two groups that had opposed each other in Europe. Anglicans were a minority in Pennsylvania, headed up in the political arena by Reverend William Smith, provost of the College of Philadelphia, and Reverend Richard Peters, head of the governor's council. Relations had soured between the Quakers and the Proprietor (now converted to Anglicanism), and personal friendships and patronage wedded the Anglicans and pro-Proprietary factions together. The most significant of these factions was the Scots-Irish Presbyterians under the leadership of William Allen, Presbyterian merchant and provincial attorney general, and frontier leaders like militia officer and Proprietary land agent John Armstrong of Carlisle.[21] The Quakers had found allies in pietistic Germans who shared their pacifist convictions, and through this alliance were able to control the Assembly up until the American Revolution. Of course, religious denomination or ethnicity was not a guarantee of political affiliation, and many people traversed the province's political divisions over the years. Political unity was fleeting among these tenuous alliances, which were strained to the breaking point by the time Pennsylvania declared independence from Britain.[22]

The Pennsylvania frontier was beset by violence beginning in 1754 but enjoyed relative peace from 1758 until the outbreak of Pontiac's War in May 1763.[23] Confusion and fear once again gripped the backcountry as Forts Venango, Le Boeuf, and Presque Isle fell to Pontiac's confederacy, and by September petitions from the frontier greeted both the Assembly and the governor, asking for money to keep local militia units viable lest the residents be "obliged to abandon their plantations to the savages, to the ruin on themselves, and the great injury of their neighbours."[24] When frontier inhabitants became suspicious that friendly local Indians, such as the Conestoga, had been involved in the murder of local citizens, the issue of protection became more complicated. On September 13, Colonel John Elder wrote to the governor, "I suggest to you the propriety of an immediate removal of the Indians from Conestoga, and placing a garrison in their room."[25] Penn replied that he could not remove the Conestoga without adequate cause, explaining that "the Indians of Conestoga have been represented as innocent, helpless, and dependent upon the Governor for support. The faith of this Government is pledged for their protection."[26]

Penn should have listened to Elder, for on December 14, 1763, fifty-seven men rode under Matthew Smith to Conestoga Manor in Lancaster County and killed and scalped the six Indians they found there, later claiming that those they killed had murdered whites on the frontier.[27] Thirteen days later a second group of men rode to the Lancaster workhouse and murdered the fourteen Indians who had been placed there under government protection after the first massacre.[28]

The violence of the French and Indian War forged a very exclusionary and masculine view of citizenship premised on participation in local voluntary militia units that provided for the security of the community by maintaining a strict boundary between civilization and savagery.[29] Critics scoffed at this idea of masculinity. Franklin declared the Paxton Boys to be "unmanly men" who were "not ashamed to come with weapons against the unarmed, and the bayonet against young children."[30] Above all, the rule of law had to prevail, or the government's ability to govern would be compromised and the people's safety would be threatened. "It is a fundamental law of all *Civil Government*," a pamphleteer argued, "that no person shall put another to death by his own authority."[31] As Franklin concluded in his *Narrative of the Late Massacres in Lancaster County,* the only way to ensure "security for our persons or properties" was through the "support of the laws, and in strengthening the hands of government."[32]

The heated exchange of words in the wake of the Paxton massacres was abruptly halted in early February 1764. A frantic Philadelphia was now rife with credible rumors that hundreds of armed frontiersmen from Paxton and Donegal townships were on the march toward the city. The Assembly quickly drafted and passed a riot act into law, while Governor John Penn asked them for a militia bill. "I think it my duty to his Majesty, and to the good people of this province," he explained, "to recommend to you to frame a militia law, . . . as the only natural and effectual means of preserving the public tranquility, and enabling the civil power to enforce the laws."[33] An already tense situation was compounded when a number of Quakers took up arms and organized themselves into militia companies. The sight of an armed Quaker did not go unnoticed by even the smallest Philadelphians: a group of young boys followed a prominent Quaker down the street, shouting, "Look, look! a Quaker carrying a musket on his shoulder!"[34] Older citizens as well were baffled at the sight of Quakers bearing flintlock muskets and daggers. As Sally Potts wondered to her sister, the Quakers "seem'd as ready as any to take up arms in such a cause to defend the laws and libertys of their country against a parcel of rebels."[35]

Although there was much posturing on both sides, not a single shot was fired during the Paxton Riots. The would-be rioters soon returned home after a delegation of prominent Philadelphians, including Benjamin Franklin, met in Germantown with Matthew Smith and James Gibson of the Paxton Boys and persuaded them to write down their grievances. This meeting produced two important documents, "A Declaration" and "Remonstrance," that reveal the frontier perception of authority in civil society. Insisting that they and their men were loyal subjects of King George III, Smith and Gibson sought to expose how permeable the lines of white civil society had become under Quaker rule. Why, they asked, did the government protect non-British enemies while its own citizens were exposed to the violence these enemies inflicted on the frontier? The Indians, they argued, "pretend themselves Friends, . . . and the publick, that could not be indulged the liberty of contributing to his Majesty's assistance, obliged, as tributaries to savages, to support those villains, those enemies to our king and country."[36] The Quakers had now become subordinates to the Indians, and had been lulled into a false sense of security. The fact that the government had "prostituted" public funds to hire a "mercenary guard to protect his Majesty's worst of Enemies" was particularly repulsive and contrary to the rights afforded them as British subjects.

The meeting at Germantown revealed that the motivation for the Paxton Boys' march was in part constitutional. In their "Remonstrance," Smith and Gibson first attacked the nature of representation in Pennsylvania, pointing out the inequity in allowing the three eastern counties twenty-six representatives, while the five western counties, with about the same population, were permitted only ten. Since men deferred their natural right to protect themselves and their property to their representatives, it was imperative that the Assembly truly represent the population. The "Remonstrance" also echoed the sentiments in the "Declaration" that saw putting enemy Indians under government protection while refusing to protect the frontier as a serious transgression. The Paxton Boys wanted to reestablish the line between civil and savage, which they felt had been damaged by Quaker treaties. "We humbly conceive," they wrote to Penn, "that it is contrary to the maxims of good Policy and extremely dangerous to our frontiers, to suffer any *Indians* of what tribe soever, to live within the inhabited parts of this province, while we are engaged in an *Indian* war." European ancestry and participation in the common defense, in short, determined citizenship.[37]

The deluge of pamphlets that circulated in Pennsylvania in the wake of the riots impelled the Paxton Boys to issue an apology that explained once again the constitutional reasons why they had embarked on their expedition. Along with their declaration and remonstrance, this apology succinctly captures the frontier defense ideology that would later push the radical Whigs to independence in 1776. In language that would be echoed more than ten years later in Pennsylvania's 1776 constitution, the Paxton Boys explained that when they asked the government for relief, "the far greater part of our Assembly were Quakers, some of whom made light of our sufferings & plead conscience, so that they could neither take arms in defense of themselves or their country."[38] As frontier petitioners had asserted throughout the French and Indian War, the Quakers had shirked their civic duty to the common defense. Not only had they refused to bear arms to protect the community, they had neglected to protect the country at large from French incursions.

The Paxton Boys' armed march to Philadelphia forced the issue of defense front and center in the public mind. No longer could the east imagine frontier discontent as mere words or faceless names on a petition; it now appeared in the flesh as mounted and armed men capable of insurrection and violence. The ensuing public debate focused on the qualities of leadership, namely, who should be allowed to sit in the Assembly. While many on the frontier felt that Quakers should not rule because their pacifism would ensure the defeat of any militia bill, eastern Quakers distrusted Presbyterians as a factious lot of rebels who would run roughshod over personal liberties, rule only in their own interest, and jeopardize any future chance of restoring the peaceful relations with the Indians that had distinguished the colony. The outcry against the Paxtonians galvanized the heretofore politically inept Presbyterians to join them in defending their common religion and their desire for safety on the frontier. "The most violent parties, and cruel animosities have hence arisen, that I have ever seen in any country," Franklin lamented, "so that I doubt the year will scarce pass over without some civil bloodshed."[39] Indeed, Pennsylvanians were at one another's throats during the election of October 1764, with a Presbyterian faction and electorate energized by Pontiac's War, the Paxton Riots, and Franklin's new proposal to replace the Proprietors with a royal government.

At the center of the debates during the election of 1764 were two differing interpretations of how to secure colonial liberty and ensure safety: a Quaker vision that sought protection through a royal government, and a Presbyterian vision that pushed for equitable provincial representation.[40] Perhaps nothing better illustrates the complexity of the 1764 election contest than the figures at the center of the public debate. The most prominent individual was Benjamin Franklin, Quaker Party supporter and a firm advocate of voluntary defense associations. His closest ally, Quaker Joseph Galloway, tired of the Proprietors' check on the Assembly, quickly threw his weight behind Franklin's royal campaign. Also joining Franklin's faction was Anglican Isaac Hunt, one of the most vituperative anti-Paxton writers. On the other side of the aisle was John Dickinson, a late convert to the cause who admitted that Proprietary government was not perfect but whose moderate appeals against the royal campaign were based on fear of "the *uncertainties* of the times to come." He was joined by speaker of the House, Isaac Norris, who at first supported a royal government but soon followed Dickinson in speaking out against it. Much more effective at inflaming the public was Presbyterian Hugh Williamson, who interpreted the entire royal campaign as a Quaker smokescreen to hide years of Quaker misrule. Anglican cleric and provost of the College of Philadelphia William Smith joined these men and organized a petition drive in support of the Proprietary Party. Last, and perhaps most baffling, was Israel Pemberton, a prominent Quaker who had been ridiculed mercilessly in pro-Paxton cartoons and accused of having illicit sexual affairs with Native women, yet believed Proprietary government should be preserved.[41]

On March 29, 1764, Franklin issued his "Explanatory Remarks on the Assembly's Resolves" in the *Pennsylvania Gazette,* launching a concerted propaganda campaign for the Quaker Party. Franklin knew which buttons to push to try and sway the western counties to his cause, since he had helped the Paxton Boys draft their grievances only a month earlier. It was Proprietary instructions not to tax the Proprietary estates to support a militia that left the frontier "bleeding in every quarter" and the "unhappy inhabitants reduced to every kind of misery and distress."[42] He also drafted a "Petition of the Pennsylvania Freeholders and Inhabitants to the King," printing one hundred copies on March 31 and another two hundred copies on April 18. Franklin framed his argument in the language of safety, reminding the king that Proprietary stubbornness had led to "mischiefs . . . during the two last wars," and asserting that Pennsylvanians wanted to "partake in that happiness and security which they see all those colonies around them enjoy."[43] Franklin reiterated these claims in a later pamphlet, writing that old disputes between Assembly and Proprietor had been "obstructing the public defense."[44] The problem lay not in Quaker pacifism, as the Paxtonians asserted, but with the nature of a Proprietary government. Since the blame for poor defense lay with Proprietary unwillingness to tax its estate to aid in the common defense, the same obstacles to a militia law would continue to exist under their rule. Franklin pointed to New Jersey as an example, arguing that as soon as it became a royal colony it received "arms, ammunition, cannon, and military stores of all kinds" from Britain, things yet to be given to any Proprietary colony. These were constitutional concerns. As Franklin observed, "religion has happily nothing to do with our present differences, tho' great pains [are] taken to lug it into the squabble."

Unfortunately for Franklin, he was a poor judge of public sentiment, and his royalist campaign ultimately cost him his seat in local government. Perhaps cheered by the sitting Assembly's positive reaction to his campaign ("never was there greater unanimity in any Assembly"), Franklin pushed forward, only to become the focus of many a vituperative and vindictive tirade. "We are now in the utmost confusion," he wrote on March 31 to Richard Jackson, Pennsylvania's agent in London, with "animosities between the Presbyterians and Quakers, and nothing in which we seem generally to agree but the wish for a King's government."[45] This was, of course, an overstatement, and Franklin was far too optimistic in predicting his petition's success in the western counties. In fact, Gilbert Tennent, a pro-Paxton New Light preacher, and Francis Alison, a more conservative Presbyterian Old Light, had sent out a joint letter to Presbyterian churches instructing them not to sign any Quaker petition. The plan for royal government, they argued, was "an artful scheme . . . to *divert* the attention of the injur'd frontier inhabitants."[46] Sympathies for the Paxton Boys, and distaste for the Quaker Party's attempts to shift all the blame for the frontier's problems onto the Proprietors, convinced many not to sign Franklin's petition.

The first response to the campaign for royal government came in early April from Philadelphia Presbyterian Hugh Williamson. "For my part," he wrote, "I am clearly persuaded that Quaker politics, and a Quaker faction, have involved this province into almost all the contentions, and all the miseries under which we have so long struggled."[47] Denouncing the Quakers for not allowing equal representation in the Assembly for the western counties, Williamson attacked them for refusing to provide defense money while opening negotiations with Indians that guaranteed "friendship and trade . . . no matter what miseries we suffered." He pointed out the contradiction of Quakers supporting the push for a royal government: those who had resisted raising money for the king's use during the French and Indian War now wanted royal authority to dictate the workings of the province. This was particularly ironic given the Quakers' pacifism. At the heart of Williamson's argument were Paxtonian constitutional issues. "You have denied us of charter privileges, have made laws for us, and have offered to deprive us of juries," he charged, "so that you might have the power to spare our lives, or take them away, at pleasure." For Williamson, the change the province needed was not from Proprietary-Slavery to Royal-Liberty, but from Quaker-Slavery to British-Liberty.

Seeking to sway the Presbyterians and other frontier peoples to his side, Franklin turned to the issue of defense. "Your present proprietors," he argued, "have never been more unreasonable hitherto, than barely to insist on your fighting in defense of their property, and paying the expense yourselves."[48] Indeed, it was the unwillingness of the Proprietor to tax his estates a single penny for the common defense that had led to the depredations of the French and Indian War and Pontiac's War. Franklin was particularly critical of the Presbyterian-Proprietary alliance and its violent consequences:

> Are there not pamphlets continually written, and daily sold in our streets, to justify and encourage [a spirit of riot and violence]? Are not the mad armed mob in those writings instigated to imbrue their hands in the blood of their fellow citizens, and then representing the Assembly and their Friends as worse than Indians, as having privately stirr'd up the Indians to murder the white people, and arm'd and rewarded them for that purpose? Lies, Gentlemen, villainous as ever the malice of hell invented; and which to do you justice, not one of you believes, tho' you would have the mob believe them.[49]

For all his partisan anger, Franklin was not far off in his assessment of the fragility of Pennsylvania's political friendships. The Paxton Riots and Pontiac's

War had drawn together groups that formerly opposed one another. Old and New Light Presbyterians tried to find common ground and establish committees of correspondence among the western counties while working with Provost Smith to gain the German vote. Smith worked tirelessly in Philadelphia County, urging the governor to appoint German justices of the peace, and ensuring that Anglicans were on the Proprietary ticket for October.[50] All of these political machinations took place within an explosion of pamphleteering and public debate brought on by the Paxton Riots. No fewer than 150 pamphlets, essays, and broadsides were published that year, compared to sixty-five in 1763 and fifty-seven in 1762.[51]

Although ultimately defeated by the Quaker Party's Old Ticket, an emerging Presbyterian faction made inroads in 1764 by grafting itself to the Proprietary Party. Able to overcome internal divisions wrought by the theological earthquake that was the Great Awakening, Old and New Lights found some sense of unity against the Old Ticket. Also, for the first time Germans voted against the Quaker Party in Philadelphia, leading to the defeat of two of the Old Ticket's most prominent figures, Benjamin Franklin and Joseph Galloway. It was no mistake that these gains were made in the months directly after the Paxton Riots. While most leaders in the west condemned the means by which the Paxton Boys hoped to create change, they had no qualms about the call for equitable representation in the Assembly and adequate defense on the frontier. Indeed, the Paxton Boys' view of civil society, which placed a premium on participation in the common defense, provided a common ideology that unified the anti-Quaker coalition. And it was this same ideology that would provide the basis for the Presbyterian faction's navigation through the looming imperial crisis brought on by unprecedented taxation.

Parliament's heavy imperial hand during the Stamp Act crisis posed a problem for both the Quaker and Proprietary parties, the former not wanting to quash their petition for a royal government through civil disobedience, the latter eager to prove its competence to rule. With both established parties supporting the Crown's imperial dictates, dissenters were increasingly attracted to a third faction, now dubbed the "Presbyterian Party" by its opponents. The "party" was not, of course, made up solely of Presbyterians, and it functioned largely as an alternative for those dissatisfied with both the Quaker and the Proprietary parties. As such, its membership was continually in flux. Although many of its leaders were Presbyterians, the major exception to this rule was John Dickinson, who joined because of his resistance to British imperial policy (most famously as the Pennsylvania Farmer) and his personal dislike for the leaders of both the Proprietary and Quaker parties. Those who opposed the Stamp Act were more likely to side with the Presbyterian faction, since the other two parties had become too royalist in their policy. Thus, the Presbyterian "party" found its greatest support among the nonelite of the frontier and among the workingmen of the city. As Galloway confided to Franklin,

A certain sort of people, if I may judge from all their late conduct, seem to look on this as a favorable opportunity of establishing their Republican Principles and throwing off all connection with their Mother Country. Many of their publications justify the thought. Besides I have other reasons to think, that they are not only forming a private union among themselves from one end of the continent to the other, but endeavouring also to bring into their union Quakers and all other dissenters if possible. But I hope this will be impossible. In Pennsylvania, I am confident it will.[52]

But Galloway was wrong.

The Quaker Party had always achieved remarkable electoral success as the champion of individual rights and the foil to executive power. Its refusal to openly oppose the Stamp Act had the potential to tarnish that reputation and allow the Presbyterian faction to make significant political gains. The Proprietary Party wanted to openly resist the Stamp Act and thereby discredit the Quaker Party, but it too had to tread carefully, lest the Crown dissolve the proprietorship for insubordination. As a result, the Proprietary and Quaker factions began to move into a more cooperative relationship. Indeed, all factions in Pennsylvania were able to find common ground in nonimportation, a peaceful form of protest. Most agreed that the Stamp Act was unconstitutional, but they disagreed on a proper course for opposing it. In Philadelphia the Quaker Party was able to keep the public peace, and so the Stamp Act went into effect on November 1, 1765, with only the ringing of muffled bells and other peaceful demonstrations. Although there were no overt protests or mob violence, some did fear that the Presbyterians would galvanize people in the streets. "The dreadful first of November is over," Deborah Franklin wrote to her husband, "and not so much disorder as was dreaded."[53]

Indeed, Franklin had good reason to be fearful. Only a month and a half earlier, emboldened to resist the Stamp Act upon hearing of George Grenville's resignation as prime minister, a group of men had gathered at the London Coffee House and hatched a plan to pull down Franklin and Galloway's houses. Deborah had spent the night holed up in one room, surrounded by guns and ammunition.[54] But now, instead of rioting, city merchants turned to economic coercion to oppose the Stamp Act by quickly forming a nonimportation association. A "very great number of the merchants" signed their names immediately, and supporters had no doubt that the nonimportation articles would soon "be subscribed by all."[55] The nonimportation coalition brought together an odd coalition of political enemies, with Presbyterians like George Bryan and conservative Quakers like Thomas Wharton working in agreement.[56]

Pennsylvanians were able to successfully boycott British goods under the terms of the nonimportation agreement while also preventing the sale of any stamped papers. Newspapers were printed on unstamped paper, and courts refused to print their decrees and pronouncements on the requisite paper.[57] News of the Stamp Act's repeal in the spring of 1766 brought feelings of great joy and vindication, as well as new life, to the Quaker Party. No longer could the act compromise the Quakers' reputation as the champions of popular rights. Their acquiescence in imperial taxation had not gone unnoticed, and one local pamphleteer implored them to "SHAKE off all prejudices" and "exert your usual PUBLIC SPIRIT, and the GOOD SENSE for which you are remarkable."[58] Still seeking to please London, the Quakers discouraged public demonstrations celebrating the act's repeal by patrolling the streets "to prevent any indecent marks of triumph and exultation."[59] Although Philadelphia was "illuminated by the Proprietary Party," Quakers were careful to present a loyal and obedient image to a watchful Britain. Only celebrations that emphasized loyalty and unity were permitted, such as the celebration of the king's birthday in Philadelphia in June, an event carefully crafted by Galloway.

The resolution of the Stamp Act crisis did nothing to ease the Paxtonian tensions that still persisted on the frontier. Superintendent of Indian affairs for the northern colonies, Sir William Johnson of New York, confided to Franklin, "I daily dread a rupture with the Indians occasioned by the licentious conduct of the frontier inhabitants who continue to rob and murder them."[60] In a July 1766 meeting at Fort Pitt, the Iroquois, Shawnee, and Delaware balked at signing a peace treaty "unless some speedy and effectual measures were made use of to restrain [the] frontier people."[61] Like the Paxton Boys who had sought to establish a firm boundary between civil and savage, the Indians asked for a permanent boundary between themselves and the settlers "over which no white man should be suffered to hunt." The Philadelphia merchant firm of Baynton, Wharton & Morgan, already the victims of attacks on their supply trains throughout the frontier, feared that unless a boundary was established, Indians would soon forget the "partial provocation" from frontier settlers and "quickly involve all *white men* in one general predicament." Violence on the frontier would continue into the late 1760s, forcing some settlers to abandon their homes "under an apprehension of a speedy Indian War."[62] In its 1768 instructions to Pennsylvania's agents in London, Benjamin Franklin and Richard Jackson, the Pennsylvania Assembly warned of the "prospect of an immediate rupture with the Natives" as a result of "the late horrid and cruel massacre of the Indians at Conestogoe and Lancaster."[63] The Assembly asked the agents to do what they could to see the establishment of a border between the Indians and the colonies (negotiated by William Johnson three years earlier but never finalized) brought to fruition.

Quaker leaders still believed in 1767 that they could persuade the Crown to establish a royal government.[64] Thus local opposition to the Townshend duties exacerbated tensions between the Quaker and Presbyterian parties. Galloway believed that the duties would be of no consequence. "I don't well see," he wrote to Franklin on October 9, 1767, "how the public weal of the Province can be affected by it."[65] In his view, Pennsylvania only stood to benefit from the revenues generated by the duties, since the king would use the money to appoint and pay officials in the province. Sensible that few Pennsylvanians would see his point of view, he instructed Franklin and Jackson to protest the Townshend Act only if the agents from the other colonies first took the initiative. The Quakers' "protest" stopped there. As with the Stamp Act, they tried to prevent public displays against the acts, and unsuccessfully tried to discourage merchants from signing a nonimportation act. Some Quaker supporters were sure that the Townshend duties would not create as much furor in Philadelphia as the Stamp Act had. "We seem at present very quiet here," wrote one Philadelphian in November 1767, "and I am satisfied that the watchword among the Presbyterians is *moderation.*"[66] The Proprietary Party was no less conservative, preferring to send petitions to the Crown rather than organize overt opposition in the streets. Resistance therefore fell to the Presbyterian Party and John Dickinson.

Opposition to the Townshend duties solidified Dickinson's status as a defender of colonial liberties against royal excess, and as the voice of the Presbyterian Party his writings exhibited the concerns of a post-Paxton Pennsylvania. Although rooted in local concerns, Dickinson's essays still spoke to a larger colonial audience.[67] As such, it is no surprise that one of his foremost arguments was that consent was essential if taxes were to be levied in a constitutional manner. Indeed, the Stamp Act and the new Townshend duties were as "universally detested . . . as slavery itself" because they were passed without the consent of the colonies.[68] Such an idea would have struck a particularly resonant chord with Pennsylvania's western readers, especially those who had agreed with the Paxton Boys' call for equal representation in 1764. Dickinson also warned of the usurpation of rights, which "acquire strength by continuance and thus become irresistible."[69] History had proved that excises and a standing army went hand in hand with the destruction of the people's liberty. "A *standing army* and *excise* have not *yet happened,*" Dickinson warned, "but it does not follow from this that they *will not happen.*"[70] Dickinson expressed fear of what might happen to colonial liberties should the Townshend Act go unopposed.[71] "Let us take care of our *rights,*" he urged his readers in his final installment, for "SLAVERY IS EVER PRECEDED BY SLEEP."[72]

With the publication of Dickinson's final essay on February 15, 1768, a meeting of freeholders in Philadelphia issued a letter to the local papers saluting the "FARMER as the Friend of Americans, and the common benefactor of man-kind."[73] Such letters were the prevailing form of resistance in Pennsylvania, which stayed relatively calm and free of riot. Galloway and the Quaker Party were fairly successful in keeping opposition to the Townshend duties to a mini-mum. But the tide turned in April when the secretary of state for the colonies, Lord Hillsborough, issued a letter ordering colonial governors to keep their assemblies in line or face the dissolution of their governments. Incensed, the Presbyterian Party began to organize a public protest, and Galloway and the Quakers were shocked and offended by such harsh words from London. A ner-vous John Penn wrote to his uncle that "those persons who were the most moderate are now set in a flame and have joined the general cry of liberty."[74]

Presbyterians publicly protested the letter on July 30, while Quakers watched their hopes of a royal government slip through their fingers. How could they promise freedom from Proprietary slavery when the Crown was threatening to dissolve the Assembly? Galloway was unsure what the future would bring, disappointed that the Crown would neglect "a people who wish well to the Mother Country," and certain that "the greatest confusion . . . will assuredly ensue."[75] The Assembly, although affronted by Hillsborough's words, refused to join the Massachusetts legislature's call for intercolonial cooperation. With Galloway at the helm, still holding on to hope that the plan for royal govern-ment would succeed, the Assembly sent a petition to the king asking for his "paternal care and regard" in protecting British liberties in the colonies.[76] But Galloway's hopes were crushed when Franklin's letter to him of August 20, 1768, arrived in Philadelphia in late October. Franklin had met with Lord Hills-borough to discuss the royal petition, but they "parted without agreeing on anything."[77] To Galloway's shock, Franklin had decided that he would no longer press for a royal government "during the administration of a minister that appears to have a stronger partiality for Mr. Penn than any of his predecessors." The petition for a royal government was dead, and with it Franklin and Gallo-way's friendship.

Together, the Stamp Act and the Townshend duties contributed to the rise of an increasingly viable political faction committed to a Paxtonian agenda of equal representation and coherent defense. Although it had yet to achieve much electoral success, as the voice of colonial liberty in times of imperial crisis the so-called Presbyterian Party was able to fashion the local ideologies of the Paxton Riots into coherent responses to unprecedented taxation. Thus issues of defense and representation framed much of Pennsylvania's response to the crisis. Even Joseph Galloway, who had rejected the notion that the Assembly had neglected frontier defense, felt obligated to justify his position in the language of safety. True safety would come from the Crown, he argued, "in whose hands is constitutionally lodged the powers of war and peace, and of the *protection of the people.*"[78]

The rise of popular leaders like the Presbyterian merchant Charles Thomson, who took to the streets to effect change, force us to look beyond the Assembly to understand the contours of Pennsylvania's political culture. Indeed, it was men like Thomson who began to play an increasingly important role in Pennsylvania's growing rebellion against Britain in the American Revolution. Although the Quaker Party was able to secure victories at the polls, the Quakers were wary of the rising Presbyterian faction and feared what would happen should these men actually be able to wield power. Surely it would mean the realization of the Paxtonian agenda and an end to lawful and peaceable Quaker rule. Indeed, Paxton ideology was coming to fruition, as the Presbyterian Party demanded the protection of British liberty and insisted on equal representation, a language of rights forged in the fires of local conflict.

Nonimportation did nothing to quell Pennsylvania's political strife between Quakers and Presbyterians, even though the conservative Quaker Joseph Galloway privately believed that there would never be a "union either of affections or interest between G[reat] Britain and America until justice is done to the latter and there is a full restoration of its liberties."[79] Indeed, the impact of Philadelphia's nonimportation was dubious. The Quakers' failure to publicly support nonimportation as strongly as the Presbyterian Party had done caused a shift in loyalties among Philadelphia's working class, which had begun to experience an economic reinvigoration since the signing of a nonimportation agreement in March 1769. Galloway had opposed economic coercion, writing numerous articles for the *Pennsylvania Chronicle* against nonimportation as a viable solution to the imperial crisis. "As to our election, we are all in confusion," he lamented. "The White Oaks [a fraternity of ship carpenters] and mechanics or many of them have left the Old Ticket and 'tis feared will go over to the Presbyterians."[80] Nonimportation had meant good business for Philadelphia's mechanics, who no longer had to compete with cheaper and higher-quality British goods, and some wondered if their interests were truly being served by their Quaker patrons in the Assembly. Indeed, the Quakers' failure to support the measure cost them the valuable allies who had helped them weather the Stamp Act and Townshend duties.

Although the Presbyterian faction became the voice of popular dissent during the imperial crisis, it was unable to make significant gains in colonial elections or to bend the Quakers to its cause. As such, Pennsylvanians who favored vigorous resistance to Britain soon turned to extralegal committees to effect change. When Paul Revere rode into Philadelphia on May 19, 1774, with a public letter from Boston detailing the passage of the Boston Port Bill, popular leaders realized, as they had during the protest against the Stamp Act, that they could not rely on the Quaker Assembly to support Massachusetts's resistance movement. Presbyterians Charles Thomson and Joseph Reed, and Quaker Thomas Mifflin, the leaders of the increasingly radical Presbyterian faction, immediately got to work. They read the Boston letter that day in the coffee house and again the following evening at City Tavern. Thomson knew that Dickinson's attendance was paramount if public opinion was to be swayed, and he promised not to come to the tavern without Dickinson in tow. The men agreed that Mifflin and Thomson would draft a radical plan of action, leaving it to Dickinson to "moderate that fire by proposing measures of a more gentle nature."[81] Everything worked according to plan. Joseph Reed opened the meeting urging immediate and decisive action, supported by Thomson, who, with the heat of the room and the fervor of his speech, fainted and had to be carried away. Finally Dickinson rose and suggested establishing a committee of correspondence that could write to Boston explaining that "firmness, prudence, and moderation" were in order.[82]

As per Dickinson's suggestion, Pennsylvania joined the other colonies in establishing a Committee of Correspondence, which met in Philadelphia on May 21 under his leadership. Taking its cue from Virginia, the committee asserted that a general congress was needed to "collect the sentiments of the people of the province." It also requested an informal meeting of the Assembly, which had been in recess since late January, to discuss the issues at hand.[83] Not surprisingly, Dickinson did not trust the Quaker Assembly, with Galloway at its head, and thus asked the committee to issue a countywide call for an independent provincial conference. Party fissures opened up once again, but this time with a noticeable difference: Franklin and Galloway, long political allies, were beginning to go their separate ways. The Proprietary Party tried to lie low with the passage of the Intolerable Acts, hoping the political storm would pass quickly, as the controversy over the Stamp Act had. Thus, as with the passage of the Townshend duties, Dickinson took the spotlight in opposition to Parliament's heavy hand. While Galloway hoped that Quaker compliance with imperial dictates would revive the moribund petition for royal government, Franklin had a much more realistic appraisal of the situation. Thus Franklin began to throw his support behind Dickinson, who opposed both Galloway and the Proprietary Party.

When Penn refused to convene the Assembly to discuss Parliament's recent actions at the behest of a petition signed by almost nine hundred freeholders, Thomson and his compatriots felt justified in calling another town meeting. On June 18, nearly eight thousand people packed into the Statehouse yard to discuss the current political situation, under the careful eyes of John Dickinson and the prominent Anglican merchant Thomas Willing. The orderly meeting declared the Boston Port Bill unconstitutional, supported the formation of a continental congress, and elected a committee of forty-three men to carry out further business and correspond with county committees. Indeed, the support of the frontier was crucial to successful opposition to Britain. After the meeting, Dickinson, Mifflin, and Thomson toured the frontier to gauge public sentiment and seek support for a provincial conference.[84] An excited James Wilson wrote from Carlisle that "in the interior parts of the province the public attention is very much engrossed about the late conduct of the Parliament with regard to America, and the steps which the colonies ought jointly to take to maintain their liberties."[85] The quick pace of events and the power of the extralegal committees prompted some to advocate caution. As one local essayist wrote, "let us patiently hear and consider every opinion that is offered with candor."[86] It was a fine line to tread between caution and action, however, as many believed that "in the present exigency of our affairs, every freeman in the British Empire who is not for us, is against us." The shots fired on Lexington Green only heightened such sentiments.

While the Assembly could not bring itself to support a militia in the wake of hostilities in Massachusetts, Pennsylvanians had little compunction about mustering themselves, as they had since the 1740s, without state sanction. Many now saw the Assembly as defunct and illegitimate and the extralegal committees as the voice of the people. Military associations began to play an increasingly important role in Pennsylvania's road to the Revolution, serving as a bridge between Paxtonian frontier ideology and revolutionary action. It was through these associations that men who never sat on committees, or were not prominent enough to get elected to the Assembly, could express their political views. With news of Lexington and Concord filling the pages of Pennsylvania newspapers, military preparations began throughout the province, despite the Assembly's inability to promise any money.[87] When Free Quaker Christopher Marshall went to visit James Cannon on April 29, he found that Cannon "was not there, being gone to the State House Yard to help consult and regulate the forming of a militia."[88] Advertisements in the local papers asked anyone with firearms to "give public notice thereof, and dispose of them at a moderate price to those who want them."[89] The call to arms swept through the province, from young, upper-class Philadelphians (mockingly dubbed the "Silk Stocking Company" and the "Lady's Light Infantry),[90] to elderly Germans in Berks County, who formed the Old Man's Company under the leadership of a ninety-seven-year-old German veteran.[91]

By the autumn of 1775, "committees of privates" had formed in Philadelphia and in other counties to advocate for enlisted men. Opposing the Assembly's moderate stance toward the imperial crisis, these committees pushed for expanded voting rights for enlisted men and demanded that all nonassociators be forced to contribute to the common defense through mandatory fines.[92] In a petition to the Assembly, the Philadelphia Committee of Privates asked for a militia law that would "equally extend to all the good people of this province."[93] Their numbers swelling, the associators were fast becoming a social and political force to be reckoned with. While souring imperial relations forced colonials to evaluate the British government, the Assembly's reluctance to establish a militia law called its legitimacy into question. "What is government," Pennsylvanians were asked to consider, "but a trust committed by all . . . [so] that every one may, with the more security, attend upon his own [affairs]?"[94] If Britain and the Assembly violated that trust, they would have to be replaced.

The same tensions that fueled Pennsylvania's political controversies in the 1750s and '60s exploded once again in the fall of 1775. In response to a Quaker petition to the Assembly asserting the Quakers' liberty of conscience and commitment to pacifism, an exasperated Committee of the City and Liberties of Philadelphia drew up a counterpetition and remonstrance and marched two by two to the Statehouse on October 31 to deliver it by hand. For the members of the committee, the refusal to participate in militia service was "unfriendly to the liberties of America," since the Quakers would enjoy full protection without contributing money or time to the "common safety."[95] Indeed, the Paxton Boys' vision of civil society, in which all citizens contributed to the common defense, was becoming increasingly viable outside the confines of the frontier. Quakers feared that this Paxtonian view would soon become reality if the extralegal committees took complete control of the government. To be sure, the Quakers had much to fear, as radical Whigs demanded a new constitution for Pennsylvania that would ensure equal representation for the west and the unpropertied of the east and proper defense for the province.

When Pennsylvania's provincial Conference of Committees met on June 18, 1776, it reinforced the growing public commitment to defense and safety. Perhaps most telling was the choice of two associator colonels to lead the conference, Thomas McKean as president and Joseph Hart as vice president. The first order of business was to approve the Continental Congress's resolution of May 15, which called for the united colonies to meet in conventions and draft new local governments that could ensure the "happiness and safety of their constituents in particular, and America in general."[96] Exercising its perceived right as the voice of the people, the committee resolved that a provincial convention be called "for the express purpose of forming a new government in this province, on the authority of the people only." The next day, the conference considered a proposal from German associators in Philadelphia asking that they be granted the right to vote by virtue of their military service. On June 20 it was resolved to afford every associator in the province the right to vote for members of the Constitutional Convention, provided that they be at least twenty-one years old and have paid provincial or county taxes. Even associators in Westmoreland, a new county that had been exempt from taxes since it was severed from Bedford County in 1773, were given the right to vote. A truly Paxtonian Pennsylvania was emerging, in which the willingness to defend the community and join an association trumped property qualifications and gave men access to rights previously denied.[97]

The concern for safety and the attempt to determine who could wield political power in Pennsylvania developed simultaneously in the summer of 1776. On June 23 the conference issued an address to the people of Pennsylvania concerning the election of members to the upcoming Constitutional Convention. "Your liberty, safety, [and] happiness . . . will depend on their deliberations," the conference warned; "therefore choose such persons only . . . as are distinguished for wisdom, integrity, and a firm attachment to the liberties of this province."[98] Having already given every associator the right to vote, the convention abolished the £50 property qualification that had disenfranchised both easterners and westerners for decades.

In the wake of Thomas Jefferson's formal Declaration of Independence, county-level committees of safety throughout Pennsylvania continued to organize men into militia units and gather supplies, as they had been doing since Lexington and Concord the previous year. Associators were asked to supply their own firearms, and men who did not join associations were required to surrender their guns to the committee. Those who did not render their guns to the collectors of arms, or who appeared to be "possessed of good firearms, and [did] not deliver them," were given a citation and required to answer for their conduct before the Committee of Safety.[99] Personal firearms became subject to the needs of a community shaped by a commitment to safety and defense. Indeed, there was no room anymore for the pacifist Quaker paradigm that allowed citizens to refuse to take up arms for reasons of religious conscience, nor could individuals escape relinquishing their property to the needs of the community. The men who came to Philadelphia in mid-July 1776 to draft a new constitution at the behest of the Continental Congress founded a new government based on Paxtonian principles.

Who were these men who traveled to Philadelphia in the summer of 1776 to undertake the formidable task of drafting a new government for Pennsylvania? No study has examined the membership of the convention in any significant detail, perhaps because its heterogeneity frustrates the historiographical dichotomies that have been used to explain the constitution.[100] These men are hard to categorize, for they were not all young Presbyterian radicals, nor were they all poor western farmers and eastern mechanics. Benjamin Franklin was the oldest, at seventy years of age, and John Weitzall of Northumberland the youngest, at twenty-four. Approximately three-quarters of the men were born in Pennsylvania or other American colonies, the rest having immigrated from such places as

England, Wales, Ireland, Scotland, France, and Germany. The men ranged in wealth and status; large landholders and speculators sat in the convention with small farmers, millers, and mechanics. Judges, lawyers, magistrates, surveyors, sheriffs, and justices of the peace debated and deliberated with ministers, Indian traders, gunsmiths, and ironworkers. The men's religious beliefs were equally diverse, and Anglicans, Baptists, Lutherans, Moravians, Presbyterians, and Quakers all participated in Pennsylvania's radical experiment in constitution making. What bound these men together was a vision of government premised on the idea of safety and the defense of the community.[101]

The convention quickly established a committee to write a declaration of rights, a document that perhaps best outlines the convention's view of civil society. The best glimpse we have into the deliberations of the committee drafting this declaration, and into the Constitutional Convention itself, lies in comparing the July 29 published draft essay to the final version. Half of the sixteen sections remained untouched, including the opening clause, which stated that "all men are born equally free and independent, and have certain natural, inherent and unalienable rights. Amongst which are the enjoying and defending life and liberty, acquiring, possessing and protecting property, and pursuing and obtaining happiness and safety." This one clause summed up the essence of virtually every frontier petition during the French and Indian War, namely, that every man had a natural right to both safety and the defense of his life and property. The petitioners had insisted, however, that government play a role in protecting these rights, and had begged the Assembly for a militia, forts for protection, and money and supplies. "One would think," the Paxton Boys had written, "that a government might do something to help a bleeding frontier." Indeed, the Paxtonians claimed, the frontier had "no militia in the province to come to our assistance, no stockades or forts to repair for safety." On top of that, the people on the frontier "were unaccustomed to the life of arms . . . so that we were unable to defend ourselves against the first incursions of our savage enemies." Of course, the Quaker Assembly "plead conscience so that they could neither take arms in defense of themselves or their country."[102]

The Declaration of Rights directly addressed the Paxton Boys' concerns. First, it guaranteed the people's "right to bear arms for the defense of themselves and the state."[103] This clause remained untouched from the original draft. Second, it demanded that every member of society contribute to the common defense. This clause underwent significant revision from the original to underscore the idea that because all men had a natural right to protection, all men needed to contribute to that defense.

Government would protect all men's natural rights, but it was every man's civic responsibility to contribute to that defense. Quakers and other objectors could no longer refuse to take part in the common defense. They could be

Original	Final
That all private property, being protected by the state, ought to pay its just proportion towards the expense of that protection; but that no part of a man's property can be taken from him, or applied to public uses, without his own consent, or that of his legal representatives: Nor are the people bound by any laws but such as they have, in a like manner, assented to, for their common good.	*That every member of society hath a right to be protected in the enjoyment of life, liberty and property, and therefore is bound to contribute his proportion towards the expense of that protection, and yield his personal service, when necessary, or an equivalent thereto:* But no part of a man's property can be taken from him, or applied to public uses, without his own consent, or that of his legal representatives: *Nor can any man who is conscientiously scrupulous of bearing arms, be justly compelled thereto, if he will pay such equivalent:* Nor are the people bound by any laws but such as they have in a like manner assented to, for their common good.[104]

excused from bearing arms, but only if they paid an equivalent fine. Thus freedom of religion could not totally excuse anyone from his responsibility to the community.

The Constitutional Convention was trying to define the boundaries of civil society, to define a community and who could belong to it. While that community could be diverse, certain essential requirements had to be met. Contributing to the community's defense was necessary, as was a recognition of God, the author of all natural rights. While the convention agreed that "all elections ought to be free," it wanted all voters to have "common interest with, and attachment to the community."[105] Indeed, the people needed to be careful who they elected to public office, and were encouraged to hold dear "fundamental principles" and adhere to "justice, moderation, temperance, industry and frugality."[106] The sole reason why government existed was to protect the community and remain accountable to the people in it, since it was from them that government derived its power to rule. In two clauses that remained unchanged in the final version, the convention agreed that "the people of this state have the sole exclusive and inherent right of governing and regulating the internal police of the same," and that since government's power was "derived from the people," it was "at all times accountable to them."[107] The Quakers had long been accused of controlling the government for their own ends by denying the western counties equal representation with the eastern. The Paxton Boys considered this inequality "the cause of many of our grievances, and an infringement of our natural privileges of freedom and equality."[108] The convention agreed that government was "instituted for the common benefit, protection and security of the people, nation, or community," adding a new clause to the final version of the declaration that government could not serve the "particular emolument or advantage of any single man, family or set of men who are a part only of that community."[109] Finally, it guaranteed that "the majority of the community" had a right to abolish any government that operated against the "public weal."

The new constitution was a vindication of Paxtonian principles and the natural rights ideology of equal participation forged on the frontier. Under the new militia law, all "the freemen of [the] commonwealth and their sons" were to be "trained and armed for its defense."[110] Property restrictions for the franchise were eliminated, and every freeman twenty-one years of age or older was entitled to be an elector, provided he had lived in the state for a year and had paid public taxes. Also, the sons of freemen, regardless of tax payments, were entitled to vote. Members of the Assembly were to be chosen for their "wisdom and virtue," and were forbidden to hold any other office while they sat in the legislature, "except in the militia."[111] Seeking to prevent entrenched power, representatives were to be chosen annually, and no man could serve more than four years in seven. To ensure accountability, the doors of the legislature were to remain open to "all persons who behave decently, except only when the welfare of this state may require the doors to be shut."[112] Confident that such provisions would make the legislature the voice of the people, the convention did not provide for an executive and elite balance to the Assembly. It was this unicameral body that provoked the harshest criticism.

The new militia law did not escape scrutiny. Presbyterian merchant George Bryan celebrated the fact that "the assembly have not even exempted themselves from military duty," as the Quakers of the past had done.[113] Benjamin Rush, however, objected to the constitution's provision that all officers under the rank of brigadier general be chosen by the people, since "most of the irregularities committed by the militia . . . were occasioned by that laxity of discipline" allowed by officers elected by the people.[114] In addition, more executive discipline was needed, for "above one half of the state have refused or neglected to choose officers, agreeably to the recommendation of the Assembly." Indeed, a poorly disciplined militia and a flawed system of government would spell certain doom for Pennsylvania. "A *good government* is an engine not less necessary to ensure us success . . . than ammunition and *fire-arms,*" Rush argued. Aware of the widespread support for the constitution among the militia, a critic of the new constitution submitted an essay, signed "An Associator," warning his countrymen of "the dangers that now threaten them, from the attempt to establish the government formed by the late Convention."[115] The essay caused "a good deal of noise" in Philadelphia, and an opposing essayist called on all "true Whigs" to meet at Philosophical Hall to debate amending the militia law.[116] Bryan chastised his opponents for trying to prevent the execution of the militia law when Washington was "ordering our militia to hold themselves in readiness," and was saddened to see "some respectable characters countenance such proceedings."[117]

Debate over the 1776 constitution would continue for the next thirteen years, until Pennsylvanians drafted a new frame of government. For the time being, however, the Paxtonians, their Presbyterian successors, and the diverse coalition of regional, ethnic, and economic groups that followed in their footsteps had won a victory. Although condemned as naïve upstarts unqualified to understand the intricacies of government, the men who drafted the 1776 constitution appealed to a coherent ideology that had shaped constitutional discussion and political debate since the 1750s. Indeed, these Pennsylvanians changed the configuration of authority in civil society, rejecting the Quaker paradigm of pacifism and elite rule and placing a premium on safety and equal obligation to the community. Although the delegates to the convention had not ridden to Philadelphia with the Paxton Boys in February 1764, they identified and agreed with the propositions the Paxtonians laid out in their declaration and remonstrance. Smith and Gibson had identified the major constitutional inconsistencies of Quaker rule and had asked that they be redressed. It would take twelve years for their vision of civil society to become reality. Latching onto the independence movement sweeping the colonies, Philadelphia revolutionaries truly did revolutionize who would rule at home. In a way, Pennsylvania had indeed fallen under the domination of Presbyterians.

NOTES

1. Franklin to John Ross, February 14, 1765, in *The Papers of Benjamin Franklin*, ed. Leonard W. Labaree et al., 39 vols. to date (New Haven: Yale University Press, 1959–), 12:68. Hereafter cited as *PBF*.

2. The term "Presbyterian Party" is used in the broadest sense, since it spent most of its existence until the Revolution as the more radical/popular arm of the Proprietary Party (earning its adherents another name, the "Half and Halfs"), and since its membership was never exclusively Presbyterian. Its opponents dubbed it the "Presbyterian Party" and, while problematic, the term is used here to describe the ever-changing coalition of people who resisted imperial taxes and Quaker rule but were never at home in the Proprietary Party.

3. James Pemberton to John Fothergill, Pemberton Papers, Historical Society of Pennsylvania, quoted in James H. Hutson, *Pennsylvania Politics, 1746–1770: The Movement for Royal Government and Its Consequences* (Princeton: Princeton University Press, 1972), 207.

4. The idea that during the Revolution Pennsylvania experienced a dual revolution against imperial British authority and local Quaker power is now more than a century old. See Charles H. Lincoln, *The Revolutionary Movement in Pennsylvania, 1760–1776* (Philadelphia: University of Pennsylvania Press, 1901). Lincoln details the many tensions that permeated the colony in the decades before the Revolution—namely, the ethnoreligious tension between Scots-Irish and German immigrants and the Quaker oligarchy's overrepresentation in the Assembly. Unprotected from Indian raids on the frontier and underrepresented in politics, western rebels capitalized on revolutionary sentiment to redress the wrongs done them over the years. The rebel cause found aid in the growing number of revolutionaries in Philadelphia, as well as in the Continental Congress. These support systems, Lincoln argues, did not cause rebellion in Pennsylvania; they only hastened the inevitable. Lincoln, however, was not interested

in explaining the 1776 state constitution, only in understanding the coming of the Revolution in Pennsylvania.

5. Ethnocultural analysis has dominated Pennsylvania's historiography. The best example is Owen S. Ireland's *Religion, Ethnicity, and Politics: Ratifying the Constitution in Pennsylvania* (University Park: Pennsylvania State University Press, 1995), which views the Revolution in Pennsylvania as the product of a Presbyterian-led ethnoreligious alliance bent on destroying its enemies. But, as Steven Rosswurm argues, evidence for ethnoreligious studies consists "almost entirely of an analysis of the assembly's membership roll-call divisions and random quotes from the 1750s to the 1790s, [and] is so weak that one hesitates to call the ethnic-religious argument an interpretation." See Rosswurm, *Arms, Country, and Class: The Philadelphia Militia and the "Lower Sort" During the American Revolution, 1775–1783* (New Brunswick: Rutgers University Press, 1987), 4.

6. For example, see Eric Foner, *Tom Paine and Revolutionary America* (New York: Oxford University Press, 1976); and Richard A. Ryerson, *The Revolution Is Now Begun: The Radical Committees of Philadelphia, 1765–1776* (Philadelphia: University of Pennsylvania Press, 1978).

7. *The Statutes at Large of Pennsylvania in the Time of William Penn: Compiled Under the Authority of the Act of May 19, 1887, as Supplemented,* ed. Gail McKnight Beckman (New York: Vantage Press, 1976), 71. Each man was to have a serviceable gun "kept in constant fitness," along with four pounds of bullets, a pound of powder, and four flints. A "sword, bandeleer, or horne" finished the list of requirements, along with the order that military captains send yearly reports to the governor detailing "how the inhabitants are furnished and provided, that due supply may be ordered."

8. 1681 Charter of Pennsylvania, in *A Collection of Charters and Other Public Acts Relating to the Province of Pennsylvania* (Philadelphia: Franklin, 1740), 8.

9. James Logan, *To Robert Jordan, and Others* (Philadelphia, 1741), 4.

10. Benjamin Franklin, *Plain Truth: Or, Serious Considerations on the Present State of the City of Philadelphia and Province of Pennsylvania* (Philadelphia: Franklin, 1747), 14.

11. Samuel J. Newland, *The Pennsylvania Militia: The Early Years, 1669–1792* (Annville, Pa.: Pennsylvania Department of Military and Veterans Affairs, 1997), 42. Bucks, Chester, Philadelphia City and County, and Lancaster were the only organized counties in 1749. Cumberland would be created from western Lancaster in 1750, and Berks and Northampton would be created in 1752.

12. Philip Reading, *The Protestant's Danger, and the Protestant's Duty* (Philadelphia: Franklin & Hall, 1755), 6.

13. Thomas Barton, *Unanimity and Public Spirit* (Philadelphia: Franklin & Hall, 1755), 1.

14. Ibid., 5–6. Although Barton personally despised Presbyterians and New Side evangelicals, the need for pan-Protestant solidarity and Barton's ties with the Proprietor forced him to become a frontier spokesman against the Quakers throughout the French and Indian War. See Kerby Miller et al., eds., *Irish Immigrants in the Land of Canaan* (Oxford: Oxford University Press, 2003), 488.

15. John Locke, *Two Treatises of Government,* ed. Mark Goldie (London: Everyman, 1993), par. 89, p. 159.

16. Ibid., par. 94, p. 162.

17. Use of the phrase "civil society" was quite infrequent in Pennsylvania texts in the 1750s. When it was employed, it was used to denote the space protected and defined by law. Thus, when the law-abiding Reverend Thomas Arthur died, the *Pennsylvania Gazette* could report on February 19, 1751, that "civil society is deprived of one of its brightest ornaments." Likewise, an essayist in the September 5, 1754, issue of the *Gazette,* who had not bothered with the debates of the political arena before, could consider himself "a peaceable member of civil society." Pennsylvania readers could also nod in assent to the words of Jonathan Belcher, chief justice of Nova Scotia, whose inaugural speech was reprinted in the December 12, 1754, edition of the *Gazette:* "be assured the authority of government shall be ready to support the law; for the law, gentlemen, is the firm and solid basis of civil society."

18. Locke, *Two Treatises of Government,* par. 97, p. 164.

19. John Goodlet, *A Vindication of the Associate Synod* (Philadelphia: D. Hall & W. Sellers, 1767), 8–9.

20. John Carmichael, *A Self-Defensive War* (Philadelphia: Dean, 1775), 11.

21. See Miller et al., *Irish Immigrants in the Land of Canaan,* 490.

22. The Anglican-Presbyterian alliance was often an uneasy one, not just because of European animosities but owing to provincial politics as well. Thomas Barton and Armstrong disliked each other and were competitors for Proprietary favors in Carlisle. When Barton accepted an offer to serve as spiritual

advisor to John Forbes's men on the expedition to Fort Duquesne, it is quite possible that Armstrong, one of Forbes's three colonels, led the charge of the predominately Scots-Irish regiment to reject Barton's appointment. Consequently, Barton was able to serve only as a volunteer to the Anglicans in the regiment, and he complained to Peters about the insults he had suffered. See ibid., 492.

23. The Assembly did pass a militia bill in 1755, only to have it vetoed by the Crown. The Assembly passed another militia bill in 1757, but a protracted debate with the governor over amending that bill meant that it was never signed into law.

24. "A Petition from the Inhabitants of the Great Cove," September 17, 1763, *Pennsylvania Archives,* 8th ser., ed. Gertrude MacKinney and Charles F. Hoban, 8 vols. (Harrisburg: Pennsylvania Bureau of Publications, 1931–35) (hereafter *Pennsylvania Archives*), 6:5438.

25. John Elder to John Penn, September 13, 1763, quoted in John Raine Dunbar, ed., *The Paxton Papers* (The Hague: Martinus Nijhoff, 1957), 22. Elder was also a Presbyterian clergyman, ordained pastor of Paxtang and Derry Presbyterian churches. During the French and Indian War, Elder captained a company of his own parishioners, and for two years every man in the church, including Elder, carried a rifle. See Hiram H. Shenk, ed., *Encyclopedia of Pennsylvania* (Harrisburg: National Historical Association, 1932), 163–64.

26. John Penn to John Elder, quoted in Dunbar, *Paxton Papers,* 22.

27. C. Hale Sipe, *The Indian Wars of Pennsylvania,* 2d ed. (Harrisburg: Telegraph Press, 1931), 463. Sipe identifies Matthew Smith as the ringleader, although contemporaries did not mention him by name until after the meeting in Germantown.

28. Ibid., 465. Sipe credits Lazarus Stewart with the leadership of the second massacre, but his name is not mentioned in the correspondence with the Assembly or governor.

29. As John Smolenski argues, the vision of public order and citizenship that emerged in the backcountry by 1764 was "martial, white, masculine, [and] virulently anti-Quaker." Smolenski, "Friends and Strangers: Religion, Diversity, and the Ordering of Public Life in Colonial Pennsylvania, 1681–1764" (PhD diss., University of Pennsylvania, 2001).

30. Benjamin Franklin, *A Narrative of the Late Massacres in Lancaster County* (Philadelphia, 1764), 29. Perhaps something can be made as well of the fact that the rioters were dubbed "boys."

31. *A Serious Address, to Such of the Inhabitants of Pennsylvania, as Have Connived at, or Do Approve of, the Late Massacre of the Indians at Lancaster; or the Design of Killing Those Who Are Now in the Barracks at Philadelphia* (Philadelphia: Steuart, 1764), 4.

32. Franklin, *Narrative of the Late Massacres,* 29.

33. Governor Penn to the Assembly, February 4, 1764, *Pennsylvania Archives,* 7:5540–41. The Assembly did not see the letter until the tenth, for the rumors that the Paxtonians were coming came true and threw the city into disarray. The Assembly finally drafted and passed a militia bill on February 28, 1763. Penn rejected it, however, because it gave the governor very limited powers in either commissioning officers or controlling the militia's movements. As Franklin speculated correctly in early February, "The jealousy of the addition of power to the proprietary government, which is universally dislik'd here, will prevail with the House not to leave the sole appointment of the militia officers in the hands of the governor; and he, I suppose, will insist upon it, and so the bill will probably fall through." Franklin to Richard Jackson, *PBF,* 11:78.

34. Henry Melchior Mühlenberg, *The Journals of Henry Melchior Muhlenberg,* trans. and ed. Theodore G. Tappert and John W. Doberstein, 3 vols. (Philadelphia: Muhlenberg Press, 1942–58), 2:20.

35. Quoted in Dunbar, *Paxton Papers,* 40n2.

36. The two documents were later published together as a single pamphlet. Matthew Smith and James Gibson, *A Declaration and Remonstrance of the Distressed and Bleeding Frontier Inhabitants of the Province of Pennsylvania* (Philadelphia: Bradford, 1764), 6.

37. Ibid., 15.

38. *The Apology of the Paxton Volunteers Addressed to the Candid and Impartial World,* reprinted in Dunbar, *Paxton Papers,* 185. The Pennsylvania Declaration of Rights that opened the 1776 state constitution guaranteed in its thirteenth clause that the people of Pennsylvania had the right to "bear arms for the defense of themselves and the state." A digital copy of the first page of the handwritten apology can be found at the Historical Society of Pennsylvania's Web site, http://www.hsp.org/files/apology.jpg.

39. Franklin to Richard Jackson, June 25, 1764, *PBF,* 11:239.

40. As Alan Tully argues, "unquestionably, Presbyterian rhetoric had a significant impact on public affairs" in Pennsylvania. Tully, *Forming American Politics: Ideals, Interests, and Institutions in Colonial*

New York and Pennsylvania (Baltimore: Johns Hopkins University Press, 1994), 203. Tully is comfortable with using a Presbyterian versus Quaker dichotomy in order to show the primacy of civil Quakerism in Pennsylvania politics. I argue that Pennsylvania's political alliances were more complicated and nuanced, while tracing the persistence of Presbyterian rhetoric in the public dialogue.

41. See ibid.; Theodore Thayer, *Pennsylvania Politics and the Growth of Democracy, 1740–1776* (Harrisburg: Pennsylvania Historical and Museum Commission, 1953); and Ryerson, *Revolution Is Now Begun*, for accounts of elite factional and personal allegiance at this time. See also John Dickinson, *A Reply to a Piece Called the Speech of Joseph Galloway* (Philadelphia: Bradford, 1764), 17.

42. Franklin, "Explanatory Remarks on the Assembly's Resolves," March 29, 1764, *PBF*, 11:137.

43. "Petition of the Pennsylvania Freeholders and Inhabitants to the King," March 29, 1764, *PBF*, 11:147.

44. Benjamin Franklin, *Cool Thoughts on the Present Situation of our Public Affairs* (Philadelphia: Steuart, 1764), 3, 7, 14.

45. Franklin to Richard Jackson, March 31, 1764, *PBF*, 11:150.

46. Copy of a Circular Letter, March 30, 1764, in *A Looking Glass, &c., Number II* (Philadelphia, 1764), reprinted in Dunbar, *Paxton Papers*, 311–12.

47. Hugh Williamson, *The Plain Dealer, Number I* (Philadelphia: Andrew Steuart, 1764), 3–4.

48. Joseph Galloway and Benjamin Franklin, *The Speech of Joseph Galloway* (Philadelphia: William Dunlap, 1764), iii, vii.

49. Ibid., xxxii.

50. For a more detailed look at the two men at the center of the debate over a royal government, and of the political machinations at work, see J. Phillip Gleason, "A Scurrilous Colonial Election and Franklin's Reputation," *William and Mary Quarterly* 18 (1961): 68–84; and David L. Jacobson, "John Dickinson's Fight Against Royal Government, 1764," *William and Mary Quarterly* 19 (1962): 64–85.

51. These numbers come from a search of Evans Digital Edition (http://infoweb.newsbank.com/) for anything published in 1764 in Pennsylvania.

52. Galloway to Franklin, January 13, 1766, *PBF*, 13:37.

53. Deborah Franklin to Franklin, November 3, 1765, *PBF*, 12:350.

54. As Deborah wrote to Benjamin, she "made one room [of her house] into a magazine," and prepared to "show a proper resentment" to anyone who dared threaten her. Deborah Franklin to Franklin, September 22, 1765, *PBF*, 12:271.

55. Thomas Wharton to Franklin, November 7, 1765, *PBF*, 12:357.

56. The resolutions were printed by Franklin and David Hall as *Remarkable Occurrences* (Philadelphia: Franklin & Hall, 1765), and in *The Merchant Traders of the City* (Philadelphia: William Bradford, 1765).

57. Rumors spread around the city that Galloway had opposed the courts' refusal to use stamped paper, so he issued a broadside in December "to put a stop to the further progress of this calumny." Joseph Galloway, "Advertisement" (Philadelphia: Franklin & Hall, 1765), Early American Imprints, series 1, Evans (1639–1800), microfilm, no. 9977.

58. "Friends, Brethren, and Countrymen" (Philadelphia, 1765).

59. Galloway to Franklin, May 23, 1766, *PBF*, 13:285.

60. Sir William Johnson to Franklin, July 10, 1766, *PBF*, 13:330.

61. Baynton, Wharton, and Morgan to Franklin, August 28, 1766, *PBF*, 13:397.

62. *Pennsylvania Chronicle*, February 8, 1768.

63. Pennsylvania Assembly, Committee of Correspondence, to Richard Jackson and Benjamin Franklin, January 19, 1768, *PBF*, 15:21.

64. In their instructions to provincial agents Franklin and Jackson, the new Assembly revived the instructions of the previous four Assemblies to petition for a change in government "with all convenient speed." Pennsylvania Assembly, Committee of Correspondence, to Richard Jackson and Benjamin Franklin, October 17, 1767, *PBF*, 14:286.

65. Galloway to Franklin, October 9, 1767, *PBF*, 14:277.

66. Thomas Wharton to Franklin, November 17, 1767, *PBF*, 14:307.

67. Dickinson's letters were printed in nearly every paper in the colonies. See Carol Lynn H. Knight, *The American Colonial Press and the Townshend Crisis, 1766–1770* (Lewiston, N.Y.: E. Mellen Press, 1990), 94.

68. John Dickinson, "Letter II," reprinted in Forrest McDonald, ed., *Empire and Liberty* (Engle-

wood Cliffs, N.J.: Prentice Hall, 1962), 12. In his fourth installment, Dickinson quoted New York's resolves against the Townshend duties, which stated in the third clause that "it is *inseparable essential to the freedom of a people, and the undoubted right of Englishmen,* that NO TAX be imposed on them, *except with their own consent.*" "Letter IV," ibid., 23.

69. "Letter III," ibid., 16. In his seventh installment, Dickinson argued that allowing the duties to pass because they were small and insignificant was "a fatal error" because it would "establish a precedent for future use." "Letter VII," ibid., 43.

70. Dickinson, "Letter XI," ibid., 73.

71. Dickinson would use the same fear of futurity in his opposition to the proposal for a colonial bishopric in 1768.

72. Dickinson, "Letter XII," in McDonald, *Empire and Liberty,* 81.

73. *Pennsylvania Chronicle,* March 28, 1768.

74. John Penn to Thomas Penn, quoted in Hutson, *Pennsylvania Politics, 1746–1770,* 225.

75. Galloway to Franklin, October 17, 1768, *PBF,* 14:231.

76. "The Petition of the Representatives of the Freemen of the Province of Pennsylvania," September 22, 1768, *Pennsylvania Archives,* 7:6273, 6277.

77. Franklin to Galloway, August 20, 1768, *PBF,* 14:189.

78. Galloway to Franklin, July 18, 1765, *PBF,* 12:218.

79. Galloway to Franklin, June 21, 1770, *PBF,* 17:177–78.

80. Galloway to Franklin, September 27, 1770, *PBF,* 17:228. For more on the White Oaks, see James H. Hutson, "An Investigation of the Inarticulate: Philadelphia's White Oaks," *William and Mary Quarterly* 28 (1971): 3–25.

81. Joseph Reed, "Narrative," *New York Historical Society Collections* (1878): 271, quoted in J. Paul Selsam, *The Pennsylvania Constitution of 1776* (Philadelphia: University of Pennsylvania Press, 1936), 50–51.

82. *Pennsylvania Gazette,* June 8, 1774.

83. "A Letter from the Committee of the City of Philadelphia to the Committee of Boston, Sent by Mr. Paul Revere, May 21st, 1774," *Pennsylvania Packet,* June 6, 1774.

84. Charles Thomson to W. H. Drayton, quoted in Charles J. Stillé, ed., *The Life and Times of John Dickinson, 1732–1808* (Philadelphia: Historical Society of Pennsylvania, 1891), 346.

85. James Wilson to Arthur St. Clair, July 7, 1774, in William Henry Smith, ed., *The St. Clair Papers,* 2 vols. (New York: Da Capo Press, 1971), 1:324.

86. "A Few Political Reflections Submitted to the Consideration of the British Colonies, by a Citizen of Philadelphia," *Pennsylvania Packet,* 20 June 1774.

87. The *Pennsylvania Gazette* printed "Extract of a Letter from Boston, April 19," in the April 27, 1775, issue, detailing the march of British regulars to Lexington and Concord.

88. *Extracts from the Diary of Christopher Marshall, 1774–1781,* ed. William Duane (Albany, N.Y.: J. Munsell, 1877), entry for 29 April 1775, 21. The Free Quakers renounced their pacifism and joined the Revolution, and as a result were expelled from the Quaker meeting. In 1783, around two hundred Free Quakers established their own meetinghouse on Arch Street in Philadelphia.

89. *Pennsylvania Evening Post,* May 4, 1775.

90. Rosswurm, *Arms, County, and Class,* 50.

91. *Pennsylvania Evening Post,* June 1, 1775.

92. In Pennsylvania, only resident men over the age of twenty-one with either fifty acres or an estate worth £50 could vote. Gregory T. Knouff, *The Soldiers' Revolution: Pennsylvanians in Arms and the Forging of Early American Identity* (University Park: University of Pennsylvania Press, 2004), 15.

93. "A Petition from the Committee of Privates," *Pennsylvania Evening Post,* October 26, 1775.

94. From Cato's Letters, no. 38, *Pennsylvania Evening Post,* March 28, 1775.

95. *Pennsylvania Gazette,* November 8, 1775.

96. Proceedings of the Provincial Conference of Committees, *Journals of the House of Representatives of the Commonwealth of Pennsylvania* (Philadelphia: Dunlap, 1782), June 19, 1776, 36.

97. For more on Philadelphia's mobilization for war, see Rosswurm, *Arms, Country, and Class.*

98. Proceedings of the Provincial Conference of Committees, *Journals of the House,* June 23, 1776, 42.

99. "In Committee, Bucks County," *Pennsylvania Gazette,* July 17, 1776.

100. It is also difficult to piece together biographies of the men at the convention because of the

paucity of records left behind. The most comprehensive accounts of these men appear in William H. Egle, "The Constitutional Convention of 1776: Biographical Sketches of Its Members," *Pennsylvania Magazine of History and Biography* 3 (1879): 96–101, 194–201, 319–30, 438–46; and 4 (1880): 89–98, 225–33, 361–72, 483–84. Military information was taken from the Pennsylvania State Archives' Revolutionary War Military Abstract Card File (series no. 13.50) and the Militia Officers Index Cards, 1775–1800 (series no. 13.36), available online at http://www.digitalarchives.state.pa.us/archive.asp.

101. The only study to look at all of the men of the Constitutional Convention in any detail is Nathan R. Kozuskanich, "For the Security and Protection of the Community: The Frontier and the Makings of Pennsylvanian Constitutionalism" (PhD diss., Ohio State University, 2006). See in particular 321–30.

102. *The Apology of the Paxton Boys* (Philadelphia, 1764), reprinted in Dunbar, *Paxton Papers,* 187.

103. *Constitution of the Commonwealth of Pennsylvania,* clause 13 (Philadelphia: Dunlap, 1776).

104. Ibid., clause 8. The "original" clauses are taken from *An Essay of a Declaration of Rights* (Philadelphia: John Dunlap, 1776), and the "final" clauses are taken from *Constitution of the Commonwealth of Pennsylvania.* I have italicized the changes.

105. *Constitution of the Commonwealth of Pennsylvania,* chapter 1, "A Declaration of the Rights of the Inhabitants of Pennsylvania," clause 7.

106. Ibid., clause 16.

107. Ibid., clauses 3–4.

108. Smith and Gibson, *Declaration and Remonstrance.*

109. *Constitution of the Commonwealth of Pennsylvania,* chapter 1, clause 5.

110. Ibid., chapter 2, "Plan or Frame of Government," sec. 5.

111. Ibid., sec. 7.

112. Ibid., sec. 13.

113. George Bryan, "Letter II to Ludlow," *Pennsylvania Gazette,* June 4, 1777.

114. Benjamin Rush, "Letter III," *Pennsylvania Journal,* May 28, 1777.

115. An Associator, "For the *Pennsylvania Journal,*" *Pennsylvania Journal,* May 21, 1777.

116. A Citizen, "For the *Pennsylvania Evening Post,*" *Pennsylvania Evening Post,* May 24, 1777.

117. George Bryan, "Letter III to Ludlow," *Pennsylvania Packet,* June 10, 1777.

$\mathscr{2}$

THE AMERICANIZATION OF THE PENNSYLVANIA ALMANAC

Patrick Spero

Every fall during the colonial era dozens of advertisements in Philadelphia news-papers heralded the printing of new almanacs.[1] Traders and individual readers descended on the printing shops in the city to acquire the latest editions.[2] Every year, for instance, Jasper Yeates, a prominent attorney in Lancaster, sixty miles west of Philadelphia, would make a trip to the city to buy almanacs for himself and his neighbors.[3] The American Revolution did little to upset this annual custom, but it did much to change the purpose and content of the almanacs. Throughout the colonial period, the almanac provided pleasure, entertainment, and useful information for the upcoming year, as well as various material that conveyed the colony's heritage as part of the British Empire. Independence not only erased the symbols in the almanacs that expressed a common British iden-tity, it also Americanized content that had once been playful and entertaining, turning the almanac into a venue for the cultivation of a new national identity.[4]

Between 1765 and 1800 at least seven different almanacs competed annually in the Greater Philadelphia market.[5] In addition to the traditional octavo almanacs, numerous Philadelphia printers produced smaller, utilitarian "pocket alma-nacs."[6] Some printers also tried to enter distant markets, such as South Carolina, where presses did not or could not produce adequate numbers of almanacs for the populace.[7] With such robust production, Philadelphia printers accounted for almost 30 percent of all almanacs produced in British North America, mak-ing the city the largest producer of almanacs in the colonies.[8]

The prominence of almanacs in Pennsylvania's print culture was characteris-tic of most British printing centers. Indeed, almanacs were perhaps the most widely read genre in the Atlantic world. The almanac was the only piece of printed material many Britons—on both sides of the Atlantic—purchased every year.[9] In the colonies, the most popular almanac was Nathaniel Ames's, pub-lished in Massachusetts, which sold as many as fifty thousand copies a year. The Philadelphia-produced *Poor Richard's Almanack* had circulation runs of more than ten thousand.[10] This phenomenal popularity was not confined to the shores of British North America. Indeed, it was a tradition imported, much like the genre of the almanac itself, from Britain. Annual print runs of almanacs in Britain topped four hundred thousand in the 1760s, and the profit from their sale made almanacs the largest source of income for the Stationers' Company, which printed nearly all of them.[11]

Colonial printers also found almanacs the surest source of profit, after the printing of official government documents. Benjamin Franklin recounted that he "reap'd a considerable profit" for *Poor Richard's Almanack;* Virginia printers reported profit margins upward of 300 percent on almanacs; and Boston's Margaret Draper claimed that the almanac produced a profit of £50, a handsome sum by eighteenth-century standards.[12] Indeed, the almanac was often one of the first nongovernmental texts a new printer produced because of its reliable profitability.[13]

While the popularity and profitability of almanacs as a genre were shared throughout the British Atlantic world, structural differences in local production created texts that varied widely between metropolis and provinces. In Britain, the Stationers' Company had a virtual monopoly on almanac production.[14] While the company produced a number of different almanacs, all ostensibly penned by seventeenth-century almanac makers long dead, their content had, as Maureen Perkins observed, reached "a period of stagnation," with "the Stationers' Company . . . producing almost the same titles and content at the end of the century as it had done at the beginning."[15] In the colonies, the lack of legal impediments such as the copyright led to greater competition in the almanac market, particularly in Philadelphia, which by 1765 had become the largest printing center in North America.[16]

In order to compete successfully in an open market, almanac makers in Philadelphia aimed to make their products, in Franklin's words, both "entertaining and useful."[17] Unlike Britain, where production was controlled by a single, centralized organization, virtually every reputable printer in Philadelphia produced an almanac for market. By the 1760s, printers in Philadelphia produced almanacs more than fifty pages long, far longer than the almanacs in neighboring colonies and sometimes longer than those produced by the Stationers' Company in London.[18] Philadelphia almanacs, mimicking their British peers, often credited a pseudonymous author with compiling the almanac, such as Richard Saunders (a seventeenth-century English almanac maker in England), Andrew Aguecheek (a character from Shakespeare's *Twelfth Night*), or Father Abraham Weatherwise.[19]

Competition among printers in Philadelphia led to both more accurate and more interesting products. Instead of poor, handed-down astronomical calculations, as in England, Philadelphia-based Pennsylvania printers employed talented mathematicians such as David Rittenhouse to calculate the astronomical data. Philadelphia almanac makers filled their pages with amusing biographical information about fictitious authors, playful stories, and jokes, alongside more mundane and serious items, such as political maxims, histories, and agricultural and medicinal advice. All of this ephemeral material created a dynamic text or, as one Philadelphia almanac styled itself, a "yearly magazine," in stark contrast to the staid English almanacs.[20]

Such pleasurable and entertaining pieces filled every major Philadelphia almanac. The content, as Arthur Schlesinger observed dismissively, was "edifying pabulum."[21] For instance, *The Universal Almanack for 1766* contained "a strange and wonderful Relation of a HEN that spoke at a certain ancient Borough in Staffordshire, on Shrove-Tuesday; together with her dying speech."[22] *Father Abraham's Almanack for 1767* continued a multiyear autobiographical depiction of Abraham Weatherwise's travails, along with other items both useful and entertaining.[23] *The American Almanack* included poetry and other items meant to amuse in its 1768 issue.[24]

In addition to "entertaining" content, other parts of the almanac provided the "useful" items. *Poor Richard's* almost always followed Franklin's formula of including poetry, agricultural advice, and a plethora of other items. The printer of the *American Almanac* for 1768 included poetry, along with cures for asthma, sore throat, and rheumatism. Generally, most almanacs contained the same useful information. One other piece found in the opening pages of virtually every almanac was a zodiac. The zodiac reflected the astrological origins of the almanacs, a tradition that was also conveyed through a number of prognostications in the almanac meant to help people plan for the year ahead.[25] The last few pages of Philadelphia almanacs frequently contained information on roads between cities in North America and within the colony, as well as a list of important meetings in the colony. The calendar, however, served as the primary conveyor of "useful" information. Taking up at least a quarter of the pages of most almanacs, the calendar gave the times of sunrise and sunset, the stations of the moon, the tides, information on the convening of courts and markets, as well as important political holidays.

Readers of almanacs found ways to make their pages even more useful. Many extant almanacs show that consumers adapted the pages to serve their own ends. Many almanacs contain readers' marginalia. These annotations served a variety of purposes. Some kept track of financial transactions on the calendar days, while others noted the day's weather or local events. Some users even interleaved their almanacs with blank pages so that they had more room to write. Such usage speaks to the almanacs' regular and heavy use and explains why a common subtitle for an almanac was "diary."

Philadelphia was a highly literate colony when compared to other regions, but the almanac was accessible even to those without the benefits of learning.

The almanacs' most utilitarian section—the calendar—was adapted to reach the broadest audience possible through the use of symbols to convey information. Someone with a marginal level of literacy would, through time and study, be able to read the calendars even if he or she could not read the accompanying anecdotes.[26]

The utilitarian purpose of the almanac not only made it widely popular but also limited its potential market reach. The almanac by its very nature was a local text. The calendar conveyed data important to a wide array of people—the farmer concerned with the sun's rotation, the trader concerned with the dates of markets, the lawyer worried about the convening of courts, the merchant and mariner who needed to know the rhythm of the tides. But such information was only locally applicable. Harvard University's commencement, a date marked in New England almanacs, was of no concern to Pennsylvanians.[27] The sun rose and set, just as the tides ebbed and flowed, at different times in Philadelphia than they did in northern and southern settlements. Thus, local Philadelphia astronomers—David Rittenhouse was the most prominent—made many of the calculations for Pennsylvania almanacs, while Nathaniel Ames and other Bostonians made similar calculations for New England.[28]

Yet one piece of information was conveyed in virtually every almanac in the British Atlantic world. The political holidays commemorated in all the calendars, regardless of place, linked otherwise local texts to a broader imagined community by evoking a sense of a shared British heritage. By 1765, all calendars in British North America listed the same historic dates—Charles I's beheading, the Restoration, the birth and ascension of the current monarch, and the Gunpowder Plot. The printers of almanacs in British North America arrived at this shared calendar at different times, but on the verge of the imperial crisis, all almanacs in British North America and England itself had settled on the same important dates. Collectively, the calendar conveyed a specific royalist interpretation of British history centered on the perseverance of and reverence for the monarchy. Such an understanding of history embodied both a shared British heritage and the general Anglicization of British North America in the latter half of the eighteenth century. While all producers of almanacs in Britain and its North American colonies adopted these central dates, Philadelphia almanacs were inclined to expand the political commemorations to include the births of the entire royal family, making the Philadelphia political calendar more conservative than the already royalist almanacs produced in other printing centers.[29]

Rarely before 1765 did overt political material appear in the almanacs except in the calendar. What may seem the political nature of the calendar to historians today probably seemed unremarkable and apolitical to a loyal British subject in the 1760s. The Stamp Act, however, brought Pennsylvania almanacs into the imperial conflict. Benjamin Franklin, retired from printing and living in London, observed that with the act's passage, "every . . . almanack will be severely tax'd."[30] Almanacs would be taxed four pence per item (unless they were only one sheet long, in which case the tax was two pence), which placed a heavy proportional burden on an item that sold for a few pennies at most and whose large circulation meant that many people of small means bought either one or several varieties. David Hall, Franklin's former partner and current printer of *Poor Richard's Almanack,* used the opening pages of his almanac, the most popular printed text in the colony, for a critique of the proposed Stamp Act in 1764. He argued that the tax would take precious specie from colonists, thus removing their ability to purchase imported manufactures from England and causing them to begin to manufacture goods locally. This development, he argued, would be deleterious to the interests of the British Empire. The following year, after the act's passage, he published the entire Stamp Act in the pages of the almanac. Thus, in addition to the protests in the streets, essays in newspapers, and printed protests, the almanac, at least for these two years, served as a political pamphlet that conveyed arguments against the proposed act and probably reaching a broader market than any single speech, protest, or other singular pamphlet. Indeed, the owner of a copy of *Poor Richard's Almanack* for these two years was reminded of the act for the entire year if it hung, as was usual, by the fireplace for easy consultation and the incineration of pages month by month.

The Stamp Act also spurred William Bradford, one of Hall's competitors, to politicize his almanac. Although he did not take the kind of action that Hall did, he marked the date of the Stamp Act's repeal (March 13) in his calendars from 1767 to 1772. This addition placed this act's repeal alongside other historic British events, equal in importance to such monumental occurrences as the Restoration of the monarchy. Yet even if Bradford's inclusion of the single date suggests a radical (or at least a politicized) position in his almanac, he offset it by including an extended list of the births of all the royal family in addition to the traditional dates. In his almanac for 1774, the last almanac he ever printed, he did not include the date of the repeal at all.[31]

Such politicization was as rare for Philadelphia almanacs as it was short-lived. Hall's two-year exercise in politicization receded with the Stamp Act's repeal, and Bradford was the only printer in the market to alter his calendar in any substantive way before American independence. When Bradford stopped printing almanacs in 1773, the market lost the only almanac that gave the faintest hint of the rancorous politics of the imperial crisis.

The conservatism of the Philadelphia almanacs may seem unremarkable, and if viewed as a self-contained segmented market, perhaps it is. But when viewed within the broader British North American almanac trade, the hesitancy with which Philadelphia producers approached the imperial crisis casts new light on the political culture of the city and perhaps of the colony of Pennsylvania as a whole. The Stamp Act politicized every New England almanac, much as it had done in Philadelphia. Essays decrying the act filled the opening pages of almanacs, and calendars marked its repeal. The difference lies in the prevalence of such sentiments in New England almanacs and how much longer the trend persisted. The Stamp Act provided the catalyst for ever-increasing politicization in New England almanacs. As the imperial crisis played out, the almanacs contained increasing numbers of essays, political cartoons, and dates that symbolized continued colonial defiance of imperial prerogatives. Whereas only one almanac in Philadelphia included the Stamp Act's repeal, which evoked colonial defiance of parliamentary imperatives, every almanac in New England did, and continued to add new dates relative to colonial protests and British outrages as they occurred. Whereas only one almanac in Philadelphia contained two consecutive items in its ephemera expressing opposition to the Stamp Act, every New England almanac did so, and continued to do so long after the act's repeal.

New York was similar to Philadelphia in that there was never the same adamant and sustained politicization common in New England, but at least three different printers at various times politicized their almanacs in reaction to the Stamp Act by including the repeal in their calendars or using the almanac to express their opposition to the act. New York almanac makers, like their New England counterparts, also reacted to other events during the imperial crisis, by recounting the Battle of Concord and Lexington, for example. After the Continental Congress ordered citizens to arm themselves, a New York almanac included instructions on how to make saltpeter, an ingredient in gunpowder.[32] Virginia almanacs also included instructions on saltpeter, although they appear to have steered clear of other political content prior to 1776.[33] South Carolina almanacs contained scattered references to the imperial crisis, including Congress's declaration to take up arms in 1775, a letter of admiration addressed to John Wilkes in 1770, and an essay opposed to taxation in 1771.[34]

Thus Philadelphia's complete lack of politicization after the repeal of the Stamp Act stands in stark contrast to other colonial markets. Most markets seemed to express uncertainty about politicizing almanacs but also a willingness to experiment in that direction. Not every almanac contained political items, and some that did might print a political essay one year but not the following year. The only exceptions to this trend were New England and Philadelphia, where almanacs appear to have taken positions on opposite ends of the political spectrum. Every New England almanac included political content, and as the imperial crisis dragged on, as the Boston Massacre enraged Bostonians, and as Thomas Hutchinson became a lightning rod for mobilizing crowds, the almanacs expressed increasingly radical stands, including a political cartoon implying that Hutchinson should be executed and consigned to eternity in hell.[35]

As the most popular and profitable item a printer sold, the decision whether to politicize an almanac had to be based in part on economic calculations. In Boston, printers surveyed their audience and the larger print and political culture of the local market and realized that people accepted and perhaps even desired some political content. That this was more an economic than a political decision is suggested by the case of Margaret Draper. Draper was an avowed loyalist who eventually fled from Boston to London, but her almanacs never revealed her political leanings. Instead, she regularly published almanacs with patriotic content.

Philadelphia, on the other hand, was similar to New England in its market's uniformity, but completely different in what this uniformity meant. Philadelphia printers surveyed their market and saw a far more divided populace; the easiest and safest course was thus to maintain the status quo. Indeed, even the slightest hint of direct politicization—the continued commemoration of the Stamp Act's repeal in Bradford's almanacs—was erased by 1772. Philadelphia almanacs maintained virtual silence on the imperial crisis, emphasizing instead playful jokes, histories, and other material. The only almanac that waded, although ambivalently, into the imperial crisis was John Dunlap's *Father Abraham's Almanack,* and even that was a far cry from the direct political content found in other colonies' almanacs. Dunlap used his "political maxims" to publish sayings in which anyone could find solace, regardless of his or her political beliefs. In 1772, for instance, the almanac contained a passage stating that Britons "know better than any other people on earth how to value, at the same time, these three great advantages, religion, commerce, and liberty." The nature of such "maxims" meant that almost every reader could concur with advice and knowledge so vague and uncontextualized.

Philadelphia's conservative almanacs reflected the city's conservative stance vis-à-vis other cities in the decade prior to the Revolution. Other historians, many of whom focus on specific social sectors, have drawn similar conclusions about Pennsylvania society. Thomas Doerflinger, for instance, chronicled how Philadelphia merchants expressed extreme wariness of radical action until the mid-1770s. Richard Ryerson, who studied the Committees of Correspondence in Philadelphia, similarly found that radical elements did not take hold until the 1770s. Anne Ousterhout, in *A State Divided,* argues that Pennsylvania society was deeply conflicted about the Revolution and that a growing proportion of the populace became "disaffected" with the Revolution as the war wore on.[36]

On top of these social considerations, Pennsylvania's political institutions also contained conservative elements that for a variety of reasons expressed reverence for the monarchy. The Quaker Party tried to prove its loyalty to the Crown in order to replace the proprietary Penn family; similarly, the Proprietors' supporters hoped to show that they had done nothing to merit royal disfavor. Only when extralegal committees authorized by the Continental Congress took control of resistance to Britain beginning in late 1774 did Pennsylvanians who favored more vigorous resistance, and who also sought to restructure their unresponsive provincial government, begin to seize power. Collectively, the almanacs offer new evidence to support these conclusions about Philadelphia society and perhaps reflect a broader division within Pennsylvania society writ large.[37]

Outside Philadelphia, the story is slightly different. Francis Bailey established the first and only English-language commercial printing press in Lancaster, Pennsylvania, in 1774. In his first year of operation, unsurprisingly, Bailey produced an almanac. Bailey's almanacs, in contrast to those produced in more politically diverse Philadelphia, were similar to New England almanacs. Printed in the fall of 1774, his calendar included the event that had enraged the colonists most recently: the British attempt to shut the port of Boston in March. Additionally, Bailey included an explicitly political message in the maxims, declaring, "Oh American Liberty! To barter thee for gold! And rather toil endure; and pain than let their rights be sold!"[38] The almanac also contained a rather detailed woodcut of John the duke of Argyll and celebrated his willingness to defy the monarch.

Unlike Philadelphia, where loyalties were divided and it made sense for almanac makers to keep their material neutral to attract the largest possible readership, Lancaster was far more politically mobilized in the 1770s. Support for the Revolution was widespread and very public. During the nonimportation movement of the late 1760s and early 1770s, merchants in Philadelphia commented with some surprise on Lancaster's adamant support of the measure.[39] The Lancaster Committee of Safety was headed by such elite figures as Edward Shippen and Jasper Yeates, and many men in town supported the militia. Later in life, Lancastrian Rhoda Barber remembered watching the militia muster in Lancaster during the imperial crisis. The militiamen were so enthusiastic that many of them drilled using broomsticks and other devices in lieu of muskets that they had not yet received.[40] Eventually, the militia became a venue for radical—or at least disruptive—political action in the town. After the Committee of Safety decided that it could not make pacifists join the militia, the militia mustered in the middle of town, marched through the streets in protest, and then strung up the handbills that announced that decision and used them for target practice.[41]

Bailey's press operated within this culture. In addition to the politicized almanac, he also published sermons and other items in support of the patriotic cause. Eventually he was named the official printer for the Committee of Correspondence in Lancaster. In Philadelphia, however, where society was far more divided, printers often had to walk a fine line on their best-selling publication.[42]

Not even American independence, declared first in Philadelphia, led to a commitment to independence in the city's almanacs. Instead, Philadelphia almanac makers took a far more hesitant approach to creating a new American calendar that reflected the political implications of independence. In this sense, the almanacs continued to reflect the divided city, in which the conservative provincial assembly continued to meet, ineffectually, side by side with the Continental Congress and state Constitutional Convention into late 1776. For instance, *The Universal Almanack* for 1777, published in 1776, still honored Charles I as a martyr, commemorated the ascension of George III, and listed George's birthday along with those of other royals. In the two years following independence, all Philadelphia calendars excised dates that referred to the current monarch and added no new dates, but kept dates like Charles's beheading and the 1605 Gunpowder Plot.[43]

These moderate changes are indicative of printers' search for a middle ground that would appease as many as possible. On one hand, one could read a calendar with only "Charles's Beheading" and the "Powder Plot" as celebrations of rebellions against the monarch. Then again, a loyalist could read these dates as marking the failure of unpopular rebellions. In New England, on the other hand, almanacs celebrated independence by erasing all traditional dates except Charles's beheading or execution (as it was often called) and adding a number of new "American" dates that commemorated battles for liberty fought throughout the new states.[44]

It was not until 1778, after the British army had occupied and left Philadelphia, that the city's printers began altering the calendars, and the almanacs more generally, by distancing themselves from a British past. In so doing, they created calendars embodying a new national history. In 1778 both *Poor Richard's* and *Father Abraham's* included both Charles's beheading and Independence Day. By removing the Gunpowder Plot, the narrative clearly framed Charles's beheading as a precedent to the only other date commemorated, independence. In other words, the English Civil War was radically reinterpreted, now providing historic precedent for the current British rebels.[45]

The transformation of John Dunlap's almanacs illustrates the slow transition in Philadelphia to adopting a calendar that commemorated the new nation. Dunlap was a captain in the Philadelphia militia and had to evacuate Philadelphia during its occupation because of his patriotic sympathies. He published a number of radical tracts throughout the imperial crisis, yet his almanacs did not immediately become a venue for his personal views. Only after the British left did he adopt new dates on the New England model, and only then did he and other almanac makers begin to express a sense of national identity. In his almanac for 1776 he had included the following dates: "Charles Beheaded, Queen Charlotte Birth date observed,[46] Charles II Restored, King George III Born, Princess Amelia Born, Prince of Wales Born, King George III Crowned, King

George III Proclaimed, Prince Edward Born, Powder Plot, Duke of Cumberland, Princess Amelia Sophia, Duke of Gloucester."

In the fall of 1777, with the British in Philadelphia, Dunlap's almanacs for 1778 commemorated only Charles's beheading, an evocation of the last time subjects overthrew an English monarch in a civil war. At the time, Dunlap had relocated to Lancaster to be away from British-occupied Philadelphia, but he still chose not to politicize his almanac. Although he consciously excised all the previous dates, he did not replace these historical/political events with new national ones.[47] In 1778, back in the recently evacuated Philadelphia, he added independence for almanacs to be used throughout 1779, which continued in the following year's almanac.[48] Finally, in the fall of 1780, after the state had experienced the ravages of war, Dunlap included an Americanized list of dates, including the "Battle of Trenton, Battle of Princeton, Alliance with France, Battle of Lexington, Congress first met, Charleston Surrenders, Bunker Hill, Philadelphia Evacuated, Battle of Monmouth, Independence, Stoney Point, Battle of Camden, Battle of Long Island, Battle of Brandywine, New York Taken, Arnold's Plot, Philadelphia Taken, Burgoyne Taken, Battle of Red Bank, Battle of White Plains, Mifflin Evacuated, Fort Washington taken, Fort Lee, Newport burnt."[49]

By 1780 an Americanized calendar that commemorated a variety of battles both local and distant became the norm in the Philadelphia market and beyond. Although no two calendars were ever identical, the intent was the same. After experiencing war, the Pennsylvania readership had become radicalized, and printers no longer felt the need to maintain an ambivalent stance. Instead, they realized that they needed to begin reflecting a larger sense of national unity. Pennsylvania almanacs commemorated battles from Georgia to Massachusetts, linking local experiences with similar recent events in a land now united in a common cause. Other new American states followed a similar pattern; as soon as war passed through a state and the British had left, they began depicting battles throughout the new nation as worthy of commemoration, creating in this way an imagined national community bound by war. Indeed, virtually every month, and frequently more often, readers were reminded of the war as they used the almanac in the usual ways.

Dunlap's transition from an apolitical almanac to one explicitly supportive of the Revolution is symbolic of a larger transition. As Stephen Botein argues, the Revolution profoundly changed most printers' self-perceived role in society. Before the Revolution, most saw themselves as tradesman rather than as actors within the broader public sphere. During the Revolution, however, printers came under social pressure to express their political loyalties, and at a time when neutrality was synonymous with loyalism, most began to become active political agents who expressed support for the Revolution. The almanacs provide a window onto this transformation. Dunlap, for instance, though a militia captain, continued to express neutrality in his almanacs until well after independence was declared. In Boston, by contrast, printers made this transition much sooner. Such variations may expose differences in social mores. In Boston, a more strident reading public forced printers—even loyalists—to publish almanacs with patriotic content well before independence, while Philadelphia printers did not experience similar pressures until after war passed through the region.[50]

More broadly, however, the change in the dates commemorated between the colonial and early Republic periods signifies the larger cultural shift from a heritage of a hierarchical monarchy to a republic resting on citizenship and popular sovereignty. Colonial and early Republican calendars both instilled and reflected a sense of common national identity. The way they accomplished this, however, was different. The colonial calendar commemorated a common heritage rooted in a distant metropolis and events with which few if any of the readers had any direct experience. Monarchy bound individual colonial subjects together, and its history and their loyalty faced east across the Atlantic, toward London.

The new national calendar, by contrast, linked citizens in a new polity who had not previously felt connected.[51] Although almanacs in different states came to this common sense of national unity at different times, that they all ultimately produced a common calendar reflects much about popular concepts of national identity in the context of the War of Independence. Indeed, when "half the free population experienced the loss of either a brother or nephew, or first cousin," and bands of militia and armed troops roamed much of the country, shared wartime experiences were formative events for many citizens.[52] In Pennsylvania, where militia duty was mandatory for all free adult males, numerous men voluntarily joined the Continental army, and many others made wartime sacrifices. The war helped embody this new sense of nationhood. Wartime experiences were so widely shared that they came to symbolize a more egalitarian society, one that rested not on deference to a monarch but on the ideals of popular sovereignty and shared citizen sacrifice for the common good.

The content of these almanacs, particularly the calendars, both reinforces and challenges the conclusions about colonial society recently put forth by Brendan McConville in *The King's Three Faces*. McConville argues that historians have largely overlooked and underestimated the reverence of colonists toward the monarch, even in the face of the imperial crisis. The calendar certainly suggests a monarchical bent, but at the same time the staggered and uneven erasure of this British calendar suggests regional variations and peculiarities. In Boston, printers changed this calendar far sooner and with greater ease than in Philadelphia, where printers held on to the monarchical calendar longer and adopted new dates only hesitantly.[53]

In addition to commemoration in the calendars, revolutionary events were frequently listed in the extended chronologies found in the last pages of the almanac. The chronology was common in British almanacs and particularly commonplace in early New England almanacs, but it had largely fallen out of favor in colonial almanacs by the mid-eighteenth century. Many postrevolutionary almanacs reintroduced chronologies and used them as reminders of the numerous battles and other events of the Revolution. Some were more than six pages long and contained an exhaustive list of dates important to the Revolution—almost all of which dealt with battles fought.[54]

The almanac's title page also shed its monarchical heritage. Prior to the Revolution, many title pages contained the name of the monarch and the year of his reign; *The Universal Almanack for 1773,* for instance, added below its title the words "The Thirteenth Year of the Reign of King George III."[55] With a new regime in place, the title pages erased the commemoration of a single political figure and instead commemorated the number of years the American nation had been in existence. As with the changes in the calendar and chronology, although the form stayed the same, its meaning changed. The title page of the almanac registered both the Christian year and the number of years the current regime had been in power; before the Revolution the latter signified a monarch, whose name was replaced by the phrase the "American Empire." Many of the titles also began to change, as did the authorship of the almanac's contents. New almanac titles like *Father Tammany's Almanack, The Continental Almanack, The Federal Almanack,* and *Columbian Almanack,* reflected the new American identity.[56]

The Americanization of the Pennsylvania almanac was not confined to forms of remembrance. After the war had passed through the region but before the Republic was secured, political images began to complement the new, nationally oriented calendars. These images conveyed a clear political message, castigating both Tories and the British. One depicted a Tory hanging from a rope, executed, it implied, for returning to Pennsylvania to claim his property. Another depicted a cross-dressed Cornwallis suckling a babe, a British soldier portrayed as his mistress.[57] While images and woodcuts were often found in Pennsylvania almanacs before the Revolution, they usually complemented the written content; an essay on agriculture, for example, might have been accompanied by a drawing of a man tilling his fields. These stock images were elaborately drawn and frequently reused. Like his calendar, Bailey's political images stand out for their early and explicit politicization, another similarity between Bailey's almanacs and those of New England. But, like the changes to the calendar that eventually came to all Philadelphia almanacs, such images did become common in Philadelphia almanacs of the early Republic.

The study of the almanac complements the work of other historians in this volume. Meredith Lair, in exploring drama in Philadelphia during the British occupation, has shown how even loyalist society was fractured and increasingly disaffected with the British army because of soldiers' behavior during the occupation. Philipp Münch's essay on German-language almanacs reveals similarities with English-language almanacs. While German-language almanacs seemed to be far more varied in their content, owing in part to the rapid turnover of almanac makers, they show a similar transition from a British orientation to a new national focus. Collectively, these works show how varied the American Revolution was in Pennsylvania, and the ambivalence and anxiety of different social groups as they tried to come to terms with the meaning of the Revolution as it unfolded.

As soon as the war ended, printers replaced the playful ephemera that had filled almanacs with material that conveyed a deep sense of nationhood. Bailey's images of Cornwallis and the Tory, printed before independence was clearly secured, were not positive expressions of nationhood but explicitly anti-Tory and anti-British cartoons. Soon, images and other content began to express a positive sense of national being. One of the first to make this switch was, again, Bailey, in the *Lancaster Almanack* and in his subsequent *Continental Almanack*. The latter had an image of thirteen pillars, each representing a state that collectively supported the new nation. The image also evoked a sense of the ancient republic, the symbol and basis for the new American government.

Other forms of ephemera began appearing in almanacs. Many disseminated news about the new nation that also conveyed a sense of national strength and legitimacy.[58] New census data on the nation appeared following the first federal census of 1790, helping citizens of the new nation imagine themselves as part of a whole.[59] Others contained descriptions of Kentucky and other western lands that promised to be the future of America.[60] One included the most recent laws passed by the new U.S. Congress, including the Northwest Ordinance, while another contained the most recent laws enacted by the Pennsylvania Assembly.[61] Many listed the names of prominent officeholders as well, and most also contained depreciation pages for the Continental currency, further reminding citizens of their connection through a shared currency linked by markets and economic behavior.[62] Others included copies of constitutions, both federal and state, thus cementing readers' sense of belonging to the new polity.[63]

The changes in Pennsylvania almanacs mirrored similar changes in almanacs throughout these new states. New England almanacs contained extended chronologies in their ephemera as well as maps of the new nation. New York almanacs featured an extended description of America, a list of all the framers of the Constitution, and the extended chronology of the Revolution.[64] One New York almanac styled itself the *United States Almanack*. New Jersey and Maryland, both colonies in which almanacs were published infrequently, began to produce them more regularly, and some contained an extended chronology of the Revolutionary War.[65] South Carolina and Georgia almanacs also contained national information, such as a copy of the Articles of Confederation.[66]

Collectively, these changes reoriented readers away from Britain and directed them inward. Colonial almanacs, oriented to British tradition, explicitly mimicked British precedents in their use of titles and pseudonyms. Many copied stories and descriptions of Britain. With the Revolution, the length of the almanac did not change drastically, and the number of almanacs in the market stayed fairly constant. Other aspects did change, however, in ways that took the almanac and its reader away from an imagined British community and began creating a new community of readers.

Almanacs of the new nation helped make politics and government part of everyday experience, thus serving an important civic function, as new political institutions needed authority, especially in a republic founded upon popular sovereignty. Informing citizens of new laws, census data, and faraway places that were nevertheless part of the new nation helped to create this authority, while also providing citizens with information necessary for their political lives. In a British colony subservient to a king and unrepresentative Parliament, such information was unnecessary. Indeed, only once, in protest against a law that taxed almanacs themselves heavily, did political machinations occurring in the imperial core make it into a Pennsylvania almanac. After the Revolution, such information became commonplace. The new content reflected the principles of the new nation and its states, which rested on the principles of popular sovereignty and an informed citizenry.

As time wore on, the War of Independence faded from the calendars. Its result—the nation—assumed and maintained a prominent place. The calendars that had so intensively commemorated revolutionary battles increasingly—but by no means exclusively—celebrated only Independence Day, which stood alone as the critical date for the new nation. Memories of the death, destruction, and division of war were allowed to fade, displaced by celebrations of victory and national unity.

New events that affected both the nation and Philadelphia also appeared in Pennsylvania almanacs. The text of the Constitution, not surprisingly, was featured in later almanacs. Later, the 1790 Pennsylvania constitution was also reprinted, and in 1794 accounts of the yellow fever in Philadelphia were featured.[67] In short, throughout the early Republic the changes wrought by the Revolution continued to inform the content of the almanac. Although it still contained useful and entertaining features, the things considered useful and entertaining had changed. Where useful information in colonial times generally dealt with readers' livelihoods, such as medicinal and agricultural advice, almanacs in the new nation added information on laws and other governmental actions. Content now included accounts of Kentucky or the history of the printing press in the United States. Such a reorientation reflected the changed political reality.

In some respects the almanac was a uniquely provincial and colonial product that, like so much else, was altered permanently by the changing economic, political, and social realities of the early Republic. The almanac's importance peaked in the context of colonial America's economic and political dependence. Imperial regulations, trade within the empire, and lack of local industry reduced the ability of printers to produce the variety of genres found in Britain. In the colonial era, paper and other supplies cost more in America; it was cheaper to import books from Britain than to produce them at home, and most printers relied on a variety of job printing for income. In this environment, the almanac in Pennsylvania filled a niche as a catchall, a "yearly magazine" for a market that had no other printed magazines, and it was no surprise that the almanac was the most popular publication in the colonies. By the nineteenth century, the almanac had become only one product among many, and certainly not the most important. As the almanac's importance declined, so too did its reputation. Whereas, in the colonial era, an almanac was often the only printed item residents of the hinterland bought annually, the explosion of printing presses in the late eighteenth and early nineteenth centuries brought newspapers and other competitive forms to the market.

Indeed, changes in the content of almanacs reflected not only the changed political reality but perhaps also printers' strategic repositioning of the product in an attempt to keep the almanac viable in the new marketplace. Dropping entertaining content, which the burgeoning number of newspapers, books, and magazines could provide more regularly, printers began to emphasize the compendious aspects of the almanac. Reference information, previously only one part of the almanac, became its primary focus. Now, in purchasing a handy almanac, one could have a copy of the Constitution, the previous year's laws, and the ever-useful currency depreciation tables. The Pennsylvania almanac thus underwent a process of Americanization throughout its history in the colonial and early republican periods. It was shaped by its local context within British North America before the Revolution, and only became more Americanized as the Revolution reshaped the economic and political landscape of Pennsylvania and the new nation.

NOTES

1. For a few examples, see the *Pennsylvania Chronicle,* September 25 and October 2, 1769, and the *Pennsylvania Gazette,* September 28, 1769.

2. James Green discusses how Benjamin Franklin would regularly sell "wholesale to a number of country storekeepers in the surrounding region who came to town regularly to restock the small assort-

ments of Bibles, school books, almanacs, and stationery . . . they kept," in "English Books and Printing in the Age of Franklin," in *The Colonial Book in the Atlantic World,* ed. Hugh Amory and David D. Hall (Worcester, Mass.: American Antiquarian Society, 2000), 264.

3. Jasper Yeates Diary, 1764–69, AM, 1962, Historical Society of Pennsylvania, Philadelphia (hereafter HSP). Yeates often served as an intermediary between the print cultures of Philadelphia and Lancaster, frequently going to Philadelphia to acquire books from sellers and at auctions as well as to borrow them from friends. He would then lend them out to friends and acquaintances in Lancaster. For Yeates, who moved to Lancaster in 1764, this unofficial book trade inevitably helped him make important contacts in town, frequently exchanging books with the Shippen and Burd families and other lawyers in town. For instance, when he went to get almanacs in 1765, Reverend Thomas Barton, head of the local Anglican church, asked him to buy a copy of Delaney's now famous pamphlet opposing the Stamp Act.

4. American historians have tended to focus on almanacs for their astrological content. See, for example, Jon Butler, *Awash in a Sea of Faith: Christianizing the American People* (Cambridge: Harvard University Press, 1990), esp. 79–81. Butler argues that the persistence of occult belief conveyed through the almanac shows the syncretism present in popular religious belief. An alternative view can be found in Peter Eisenstadt, "Almanacs and the Disenchantment of America," *Pennsylvania History* 65, no. 2 (1998): 143–69. Eisenstadt argues that the sign of the man was an expendable piece of ephemera that was increasingly erased in an age in which scientific reason was on the rise. A few articles have explored the political content of almanacs. See, for example, William Pencak, "Politics and Ideology in Poor Richard's Almanack," *Pennsylvania Magazine of History and Biography* 116, no. 2 (1992): 183–211. For an analysis of the rhymes and prefaces in New England almanacs, primarily, during the American Revolution, see Allan Raymond, "'To Reach Men's Minds': Almanacs and the American Revolution, 1760–1777," *New England Quarterly* 51, no. 3 (1978): 370. Most recently, David Waldstreicher has analyzed almanac calendars and images in the new nation in his *In the Midst of Perpetual Fetes: The Making of American Nationalism, 1776–1820* (Chapel Hill: University of North Carolina Press, 1997) 45–50.

5. This number includes pocket almanacs but excludes almanacs published for markets other than Philadelphia and German-language almanacs; the latter are discussed in Philipp Münch's essay in this volume.

6. For examples, see Richard Saunders [Benjamin Franklin], *A Pocket Almanack for the Year 1768* (Philadelphia, 1767), which sold approximately two thousand copies. See also Marion Barber Stowell, *Early American Almanacs: The Colonial Weekday Bible* (New York: Burt Franklin, 1977), x; and Hugh Amory, "Reinventing the Colonial Book," in Amory and Hall, *Colonial Book,* 52.

7. For Greater Philadelphia almanacs destined for other areas, see John Tobler, *The South-Carolina Almanack, for the year of our Lord 1758* (Germantown, Pa., 1757). After the Revolution this occurred more frequently, as the volume of printing and transportation increased. See, for example, Benjamin Banneker, *Benjamin Bannaker's Pennsylvania, Delaware, Maryland and Virginia almanac, for the year of our Lord 1795* (Philadelphia, 1794), and *The Pennsylvania, New-Jersey, Delaware, Maryland and Virginia almanac for 1795–1801* (Philadelphia, 1795–1801).

8. Between 1764 and 1783, Pennsylvania produced 29.43 percent of all almanacs. The Philadelphia printers reached a high of twenty-one different almanacs in 1779 but on average produced fifteen almanacs a year. Massachusetts was the second-largest producer, with 18.5 percent of the market. G. Thomas Tanselle, "Some Statistics on American Printing, 1764–1783," in *The Press and the American Revolution,* ed. Bernard Bailyn and John B. Hench (Worcester, Mass.: American Antiquarian Society, 1980), 344. For more on almanac production in the Atlantic world, especially Boston and Philadelphia, see Patrick Spero, "The Revolution in Popular Publications: The Almanac and New England Primer, 1750–1800," in *Early American Studies,* special issue, ed. James Green and Rosalind Remer (forthcoming, January 2010).

9. Marion Barber Stowell hypothesizes that "the average New England home's library consisted of a Bible, an almanac, the New England Primer, and perhaps a few sermons." Stowell, *Early American Almanacs,* 273. This hypothesis is given greater weight by Hugh Amory in "Reinventing the Colonial Book," esp. 51–52.

10. The estimate of 50,000 almanacs per annum is based on the popular Nathaniel Ames almanacs published in Boston. Estimates on Ames's sales figures range as high as 70,000 copies. I have chosen the more conservative estimate. In his doctoral dissertation, "Colonial American Almanacs: A Study in Non-institutional Education" (Rutgers University, 1965), Robert Sidwell takes a conservative annual estimate of 50,000 for Ames's almanacs. Margaret Draper, in a report to the British Audit Office, estimated that her press in Boston produced 60,000 to 70,000 Ames almanacs per year, a figure that, for a variety of

reasons, is likely to be inflated. Most other historians have generally accepted the former figure, although occasionally Draper's numbers are used. Hugh Amory also accepted the 50,000 number in "Reinventing the Colonial Book," 52. Franklin estimated that he sold "near ten Thousand" annually. Benjamin Franklin, *The Autobiography and Other Writings* (New York: Penguin Books, 1986), 106. In the 1760s, after Franklin had retired, *Poor Richard's Almanack* sold on average 10,000 quarto editions and 2,000 smaller "pocket almanacs." Stowell, *Early American Almanacs,* x.

11. Cyprian Blagden has done the best work on the circulation of almanacs in England. See his "Distribution of Almanacks in the Seventeenth Century," *Studies in Bibliography* 11 (1958): 107–16, and "Thomas Carnan and the Almanack Monopoly," *Studies in Bibliography* 14 (1961): 23–43. A table with almanac circulation for 1760 and 1761 can be found in the latter article. Blagden also determined that for the years 1673–82, 38 percent of all stock went to making almanacs. Whether this number continued to be so high throughout the eighteenth century is uncertain. In *English Almanacs, 1500–1800: Astrology and the Popular Press* (Ithaca: Cornell University Press, 1979), Bernard Capp accepted most of Blagden's numbers, though he often used four hundred thousand as the annual circulation of the almanac. Blagden's number is based on the official Stationers' Company ledger.

12. Franklin, *Autobiography and Other Writings,* 106. See Cynthia Z. Stiverson and Gregory A. Stiverson, "The Colonial Retail Book Trade: Availability and Affordability of Reading Material in Mid-Eighteenth-Century Virginia," in *Printing and Society in Early America,* ed. William L. Joyce, David D. Hall, Richard D. Brown, and John B. Hench (Worcester, Mass.: American Antiquarian Society, 1983), 143–51, 165–68. For the New England profit, see especially Mary Ann Yodelis, "Who Paid the Piper? Publishing Economics in Boston, 1763–1775," *Journalism Monographs* 38 (February 1975): 32–33. To put the £50 profit in perspective, the average property-owning New Englander could expect to die with a lifetime fortune of £160. Thomas Purvis, *Almanac of American Life: Revolutionary America, 1763 to 1800* (New York: Facts on File, 1995), 113.

13. Examples of printers making almanacs one of their first publications date from the very first press opened in the colonies. The second item ever printed at the Cambridge Press was an almanac. In Delaware, the first nongovernmental tracts published were a spelling book, an advice manual, and an almanac. Later, when Kentucky was settled, the first document ever printed was an almanac. Lawrence Wroth, *The Colonial Printer* (New York: Dover, 1994), 16, 37–38, 58–59. In this essay, *Poor Richard's Almanack* is referred to as such, as this is its best-known title, even though its actual title varied and was most often *Poor Richard Improved.*

14. Details on the Stationers' Company monopoly run throughout the work of Cyprian Blagden but are perhaps best expressed in "Thomas Carnan and the Almanack Monopoly." The best recent analysis of the monopoly and its effects on the almanac can be found in Maureen Perkins, *Visions of the Future: Almanacs, Time and Cultural Change, 1775–1870* (Oxford: Oxford University Press, 1996), 13–46, and Capp, *English Almanacs, 1500–1800,* 240–41. Perkins argues that the monopoly on almanacs was not absolute in legal terms prior to 1775 but that a series of stamp acts and maneuvers by the company allowed the monopoly to exist in practice. For instance, according to Blagden, the Stationers paid universities £1,000 annually not to produce any almanacs, and they advocated for laws that required almanacs to be taxed, which meant that the Stationers' Company, because of its size and organization, was the only group that could afford to pay the tax. Thus, Perkins concludes, "the only competitors were those who dared to publish unstamped almanacs, risking three months imprisonment or a fine. The company continued to behave as if its monopoly existed, issuing warnings to other printers not to issue unauthorized, that is, unstamped, almanacs." After the court decision that formally ended any implied monopoly rights, the Stationers' Company adopted the next-best method of stamping out competition: they wielded their enormous capital to buy up all the popular competing almanacs. Perkins, *Visions of the Future,* 18–21.

15. Perkins, *Visions of the Future,* 12.

16. Philadelphia became the largest printing center in British North America after a pamphlet war erupted in 1763–64 over a rebellion in Lancaster, Pennsylvania, and a movement spurred by the Assembly to convert the proprietary colony to a royal colony. Details on the episode and growth of the printing industry can be found in Alison Olson, "The Pamphlet War over the Paxton Boys," *Pennsylvania Magazine of History and Biography* 123, nos. 1–2 (1999): 31–55.

17. Franklin, *Autobiography and Other Writings,* 106.

18. All English almanacs were forty-eight pages long. Boston almanacs ranged from sixteen to twenty-four pages, with a few reaching forty pages. In 1760, for instance, two Boston almanacs were

sixteen pages and one, twenty-four. In Philadelphia, however, the shortest was thirty-six pages, two were forty pages long, and the longest was fifty-six pages. For more on the regional variations in almanac production, see Spero, "Revolution in Popular Publications."

19. Richard Saunders was Franklin's pseudonym in *Poor Richard's Almanack,* Aguecheek was the putative author of *The Universal Almanack,* and Benjamin Weatherwise was Father Abraham.

20. *Father Abraham's Almanack,* for instance, serialized his biography, reprinting a new episode in his life every year. For Abraham's biography, see *Father Abraham's Almanack for 1766* (Philadelphia, 1765).

21. Arthur Schlesinger, *Prelude to Independence: The Newspaper War on Britain, 1764–1776* (New York: Knopf, 1958), 41–42.

22. Timothy Aguecheek [pseud.], *The Universal Almanack for 1766* (Philadelphia, 1765).

23. Abraham Weatherwise [pseud.], *Father Abraham's Almanack for 1767* (Philadelphia, 1766).

24. Philo Copernicus [pseud.], *The American Almanack for 1768* (Philadelphia, 1767).

25. Peter Eisenstadt argues in "Almanacs and the Disenchantment of America" that Pennsylvania almanacs became less inclined in the eighteenth century to include the zodiac. Others, such as Jon Butler in *Awash in a Sea of Faith,* use the prevalence of the zodiac to argue for the importance of the occult in early American life. Even if Eisenstadt is correct that the Zodiac became less prominent, it was still included more often than not, as were other unscientific prognostications.

26. Lawrence Cremin estimates that literacy rates ranged from 70 to 100 percent in colonial America. Cremin, *American Education: The Colonial Experience, 1607–1783* (New York: Harper and Row, 1970), esp. 539–46.

27. For an example of Harvard's commencement, see Samuel Stearns, *North American Almanack for 1772,* and Nathaniel Ames, *An Astronomical Diary for 1772* (Boston, 1771). Commencement was held on July 21.

28. Biographies of Ames can be found in Stowell, *Early American Almanacs,* and in Samuel Briggs, *The Essays, Humor, and Poems of Nathaniel Ames, Father and Son, of Dedham, Massachusetts, from their Almanacks, 1726–1775, with notes and comments* (New York: Johnson Reprints, 1970). Rittenhouse frequently compiled calculations for a number of almanacs in Philadelphia. In 1773, for instance, he provided calculations for *The Virginia Almanack, The Universal Almanack,* and *Father Abraham's Almanack.* It appears that he provided the calculations for eight almanacs, or virtually every almanac published in 1774.

29. Expanded birth dates can be found in several almanacs. See, for example, Richard Saunders [pseud.], *Poor Richard's Almanack for 1767* (Philadelphia, 1766), Abraham Weatherwise [pseud.], *Father Abraham's Almanack for 1769* (Philadelphia, 1768), William Andrews [pseud.] *Poor Will's Almanack for 1772* (Philadelphia, 1771).

30. Benjamin Franklin to John Ross, February 14, 1765, Read Manuscripts, HSP.

31. Philo Copernicus [pseud.], *An American Calendar for 1767* (Philadelphia, 1766), *Pennsylvania Pocket Almanack for 1769* (Philadelphia, 1768), *Pennsylvania Pocket Almanack for 1773* (Philadelphia, 1772), *An American Calendar for 1770* (Philadelphia, 1769), *An American Calendar for 1771* (Philadelphia, 1770), and *An American Calendar for 1772* (Philadelphia, 1771). Bradford stopped including the repeal of the Stamp Act in his *Pocket Almanack for 1774* (Philadelphia, 1773).

32. For some New York examples of politicization, see *Hutchins Improved for 1766* (New York, 1765), which states the Stamp Act is "very disagreeable to the printer." In the same year, the *American County Almanack* (New York, 1765) included an essay opposing the act. *Poor Roger's Almanack for 1767* (New York, 1766) celebrated the act's repeal. *Poor Roger's* continued to include essays in the almanacs for 1768, and in the 1770 edition it stated that the comet that had passed through the sky the previous year portended English oppression.

33. The Virginia almanac did address political matters, but hesitantly. *The Virginia Almanack for 1776* (Williamsburg, 1775) included instructions for making saltpeter but also contained a poem that called for restraint and peace by asking the king to "restrain the hand of Civil War." Note also that David Rittenhouse compile the astronomical calculation for this almanac.

34. John Tobler, *South Carolina and Georgia Almanac for 1767* (Charleston, 1766), Thomas Moore [pseud.], *Poor Tom Revised, for 1770* (Charleston, 1769), *Georgia Almanack for 1771* (Charleston, 1770).

35. For the powerful image of Hutchinson's execution, see Ezra Gleason, *The Massachusetts Calendar for 1774* (Boston, 1773).

36. See Thomas Doerflinger, *A Vigorous Spirit of Enterprise: Merchants and Economic Development in Revolutionary Philadelphia* (Chapel Hill: University of North Carolina Press, 1986), and Doerflinger's

essay "Philadelphia Merchants and the Logic of Moderation, 1760–1775," *William and Mary Quarterly* 80 (1983): 197–226; Richard A. Ryerson, *The Revolution Is Now Begun: The Radical Committees of Philadelphia, 1765–1776* (Philadelphia: University of Pennsylvania Press, 1978); Anne M. Ousterhout, *A State Divided: Opposition in Pennsylvania to the American Revolution* (New York: Greenwood Press, 1987).

37. The political history of the province is told in almost every account of revolutionary Pennsylvania. See, for instance, John B. Frantz and William Pencak, eds., *Beyond Philadelphia: The American Revolution in the Pennsylvania Hinterland* (University Park: Pennsylvania State University Press, 1998), ix–xxv.

38. Anthony Sharp, *The Lancaster Almanack for 1775* (Lancaster, Pa., 1774).

39. [Thomas?] Clifford to Lancelot Cowper, June 21, 1770, Clifford Family Papers, Clifford Correspondence, Thomas and John Clifford Letterbooks, vol. 28, HSP.

40. Rhoda Barber, "Journal of Settlement at Wright's Ferry on Susquehanna River, 1830," HSP.

41. Shippen to Delegates in Philadelphia, June 3, 1775, Jasper Yeates Papers, HSP.

42. Lancaster Committee of Correspondence to the Pennsylvania delegates in Congress, Lancaster, Pa., June 3, 1775, ibid.

43. For the slow and uncertain changes to Philadelphia almanacs, see *The Universal Almanack for 1777* (Philadelphia, 1776), which included a traditional calendar. That same year, *Poor Richard's Almanack* included only Charles's beheading, the Restoration, and the Gunpowder Plot.

44. For examples of these changes to New England almanacs, see Benjamin West, *Bickerstaff's Boston Almanack for 1778* (Boston, 1777), and *Nathaniel Low, An Astronomical Diary for 1778* (Boston, 1777).

45. Abraham Weatherwise [pseud.], *Father Abraham's Almanack for 1779* (Philadelphia, 1778).

46. Philadelphia almanacs often included the celebration of the queen's birthday in early January.

47. Abraham Weatherwise [pseud.], *Father Abraham's Almanack for 1778* (Lancaster, Pa., 1777).

48. Weatherwise [pseud.], *Father Abraham's Almanack for 1779.*

49. Abraham Weatherwise [pseud.], *Father Abraham's Almanack for 1781* (Philadelphia, 1780).

50. Stephen Botein, " 'Meer Mechanics' and an Open Press: The Business and Political Strategies of Colonial American Printers," *Perspectives in American History* 9 (1975): 127–225.

51. In his essay "Identity in Early America: Unease in Eden," in *Colonial Identity in the Atlantic World, 1500–1800,* ed. Nicholas Canny and Anthony Pagden (Princeton: Princeton University Press, 1987), Michael Zuckerman argues that most colonists faced east. New work in the field of Atlantic studies has largely supported Zuckerman's conclusions over time. See also Benedict Anderson, *Imagined Communities: Reflections on the Origin and Spread of Nationalism* (London: Verso, 1995), for a discussion on how printed sources help create national identity and unity.

52. Statistics on the death rates can be found in Purvis, *Almanac of American Life,* 234.

53. Brendan McConville, *The King's Three Faces: The Rise and Fall of Royal America, 1688–1776* (Chapel Hill: University of North Carolina Press, 2006).

54. For a chronology, see *The American Almanac for 1781* (Philadelphia, 1780). The almanac also includes an extended list of all the new offices in the federal, state, and local governments. *Poor Richard's Almanack for 1782* (Philadelphia, 1781) also included a remarkable page of dates. A later example can be found in *Father Tammany's Almanack for 1787* (Philadelphia, 1786) and in *Poulson's Town and Country Almanack for 1791* (Philadelphia, 1790).

55. Father Abraham also included such information on the title page. See, for instance, Abraham Weatherwise, *Father Abraham's Almanack for 1774* (Philadelphia, 1773).

56. A great many almanacs added to their title pages the number of years since independence had been declared; for example, *Father Abraham's Almanack* for 1781 included the phrase "the Sixth Year of American Independence." *Father Abraham's* was the first Philadelphia almanac to institute this practice, in the 1779 edition, the same year it first included Independence Day in the calendar.

57. *The Continental Almanack* (Philadelphia, 1781 and 1782).

58. *The New Pennsylvania Almanack for 1787* (Philadelphia, 1786) contained all the laws passed in Pennsylvania from 1765 to 1786. *The Pennsylvania Almanac for 1789* (Philadelphia, 1788) included the Pennsylvania laws passed the previous year.

59. Many almanacs included this type of data. See, for instance, *McCulloch's Pocket Almanack for 1792* (Philadelphia, 1791), and *Father Abraham's Almanack for 1792* (Philadelphia, 1791). Both probably relied on the recent federal census data.

60. See, for example, *Father Tammany's Almanac* (Philadelphia, 1786 and 1788). An alternative view was offered in *Poulson's Town and Country Almanac for 1789* (Philadelphia, 1788), which argued that

Pennsylvania was a better place to live than the west because it had more to offer settlers, such as schools and established laws.

61. The Northwest Ordinance can be found in *Father Tammany's Almanack for 1786* (Philadelphia, 1785). Other almanacs reprinted documents like the Treaty of Paris (*The American Almanac for 1785*) and the Pennsylvania legislature's act regulating goods (*The Columbian Almanack for 1790*).

62. See, for example, *McCulloch's Pocket Almanac for 1792* and *Poulson's Town and Country for 1793* (Philadelphia, 1792).

63. Pennsylvania's constitution can be found in *Father Tammany's Almanac for 1791,* and copies of the U.S. Constitution were printed in his almanac for 1788.

64. One of the descriptions of the new nation can be found in *Stoddard's Diary for 1787* (Hudson, N.Y., 1786). A chronology can be found in *Poor Will's Almanack for 1785* (New York, 1784). For the list of framers, see *Stoddard's Diary for 1788* (Hudson, N.Y., 1787).

65. See, for example, the *New Jersey Almanack for 1788* (Trenton, 1787), and the *Maryland, Delaware, Pennsylvania, Virginia, North Carolina Almanac for 1781* (Baltimore, 1780).

66. *South Carolina and Georgia Almanac for 1777* (Charleston, 1776).

67. Accounts of yellow fever items appear in *The Colombian Almanac for 1795, Father Abraham's Almanack for 1795,* and *Banneker's Almanac for 1795* (Philadelphia, 1794). The Pennsylvania constitution was printed in *Father Tammany's Almanack for 1791* (Philadelphia, 1790).

3

GERMAN-LANGUAGE ALMANACS IN
REVOLUTIONARY PENNSYLVANIA

Philipp Münch

From the beginning, German-language printing accompanied the events of the American Revolution. The very first report on the Declaration of Independence was printed in a German-language newspaper, and the first complete German translation was published as a broadside a few days later.[1] Works of the Revolution's intellectual fathers and agitators, such as Thomas Paine, were issued in German as well.[2]

Recent scholarship on early American history has increasingly paid attention to the role of Pennsylvania's German-speaking population on the eve of and during the Revolution.[3] However, it is still difficult to examine German speakers as a common group within Pennsylvania's diverse society. Not only did they come from German-language areas in Europe as different as Switzerland's cantons and Prussia's Silesian provinces, but German-speaking immigrants also had diverse religious backgrounds. Although much attention has been paid to marginal German-speaking sectarian groups, most German speakers were Lutheran or Reformed Protestants.[4] As with all other groups of immigrants, class divisions could be found among those from German-language areas. But they shared a common language in a foreign country. The pull of a common language and shared interests led many recently arrived German-speaking immigrants to settle in ethnically homogenous communities. Intermarriage and the use of German place names, as well as periodical literature and books in German, characterized these communities.[5]

By the time of the Revolution, German speakers constituted approximately a third of Pennsylvania's population.[6] Despite their large numbers, certain factors made it difficult and gave few incentives for most German speakers to participate in politics. As comparatively late arrivals in America, most of them were concerned with establishing themselves in the New World and getting an income at first. They typically engaged in politics only when immediate interests were at stake. Since most of them arrived in the middle of the eighteenth century, they lacked a deep-rooted tradition of active political commitment on the eve of the Revolution.[7] Even if they wanted to engage in politics, they had to wait until they were naturalized. Although German-speaking immigrants had been allowed to vote and to run for office, their often precarious economic situation and inability to speak English posed a barrier to holding office. German speakers often settled on the frontier, where land was still available. But the frontier counties were underrepresented in Pennsylvania's assemblies, and the government was in Philadelphia, which contributed to a general misrepresentation of German speakers in political affairs.[8]

Although not very active in politics, German-speaking voters quickly became a crucial factor in Pennsylvanian politics as their numbers increased with new waves of immigration. Like the Scots-Irish, German-speaking immigrants passively resisted Thomas Penn's land policy of 1732 by simply not paying the mandated rents, relying on the vast size of the country and the lack of government officials to enforce the rule. The Penn proprietors' efforts to gather support for a militia in the late 1740s was also opposed by German-speaking voters, who therefore supported the Quakers. This constellation changed with the French and Indian War. German-speaking backcountry farmers now demanded protection from Indian raids, and a large group of German-speaking farmers marched to Philadelphia in 1755 and achieved the immediate approval of a bill to support the colony's defense. Many still supported the Quakers, however, in their opposition to Penn's land policy.[9]

Rising numbers of naturalized Germans mirrored German speakers' growing engagement in politics. An outstanding example of this was the appearance of twenty-six hundred German speakers, who in 1764 traveled to Philadelphia to become naturalized and vote for the Assembly. In Philadelphia, emerging German institutions like the Patriotic Society of the City and County of Philadelphia provided a platform for political discussion and a means of putting pressure on the government.[10]

Despite obstacles to their political participation, many German speakers eventually developed an understanding of the issues of the Revolution and took an active part in it. By the eve of the Revolution, as A. G. Roeber has established, German Lutherans and Reformed from the Palatinate especially—the largest groups among German-speaking immigrants—had learned that liberty and property ownership went hand in hand, and they took the side of those who agitated against British taxation without representation. This adaptation was due not merely to the process of Anglicization but to the translation of English legal terms into words comprehensible to German speakers. The German-language press, which could rely on a high level of literacy among German speakers, contributed significantly to this politicization by translating and explaining legal terms, but also by consciously agitating for political activity among German speakers.[11]

The first German printer of note, and the first of a dynasty of printers, was Christoph Saur I (sometimes spelled Sauer or Sower, 1695–1758),[12] who in 1738 started printing in Germantown. He was the first to print a Bible in America and was the editor and printer of an almanac and a newspaper.[13] His primary competitor was the Swiss-born John Henry Miller (also Heinrich Möller or Henrich Miller, 1702–1782), who in 1762 began to publish a Philadelphia newspaper.[14] Miller's and the Saurs' newspapers addressed different readerships. While the Saurs appealed more to sectarian German speakers in the backcountry, Miller's periodicals were more likely to be read by educated German speakers in Philadelphia.[15]

Saur started an almanac in 1738 and a newspaper the following year. He provided his readers with an introduction to English legal terms and an education in the issues of liberty and property. When Miller entered the newspaper business in 1762, he was able to rely on the groundwork Saur had laid in the preceding decades.[16] While the Saurs pretended to be independent—but in fact supported Quaker rule—Miller tried more openly to make German speakers take sides in politics, and his newspapers focused heavily on political events and policies, both domestic and international. Despite growing interest in current political matters among German speakers, however, most of them had little use for lengthy and comprehensive discussions of political issues. The Saurs' periodicals, which concentrated more on local politics and the practical issues of daily life, were thus more popular than Miller's newspaper.[17]

Although the German-language press in general did not emphasize politics, it was seen as a crucial means of influencing the opinion and actions of the largest non-English-speaking group in Pennsylvania. Benjamin Franklin edited the first German-language newspaper in America to gain political currency in his fight with the ruling Quakers. From 1747 until 1748, Christoph Saur battled Franklin over the question of an institutionalized defense in Pennsylvania—a fight that Saur, thanks to his more popular newspaper, won, in the opinion of most German speakers.[18] The emphasis of Franklin's German newspaper on public affairs was another reason for its failure.[19] Miller, who stood on Franklin's side, and Christoph Saur II, Saur's son, continued this battle after Saur I's death in 1758.[20]

The Saur-Miller competition is well documented.[21] Less attention has been paid to the almanacs of other German-language printers, though almanacs were the primary reading matter of the average man in early America.[22] How did publishers appeal to average German speakers during the War of Independence, and what does this say about the attitude of German-speaking immigrants toward the Revolution? What can be said about the printers themselves? In endeavoring to answer these questions, this study looks at Pennsylvania's German-language almanacs—the second-most widely read medium in early America, after the Bible.

Usually consisting of fewer than fifty pages, early American almanacs could be produced in relatively large numbers and sold cheaply.[23] At the time of the Revolution, editions sometimes reached five to ten thousand copies and thus clearly outnumbered the editions of contemporary newspapers.[24] Forty years before large paper mills were built in New England, William Rittenhouse (originally Ryttinghauser) established one in Germantown in 1690. Although the paper was of comparatively poor quality, it was sufficient for newspapers and almanacs, which were usually thrown away quickly. In the following decades, Pennsylvania remained the center of paper production in the New World and became increasingly independent, relying less and less on imported paper.[25] In addition to the fact that Philadelphia was the largest and most cosmopolitan city in British North America, the local supply of paper was another reason why Pennsylvania still published the majority of American newspapers during the Revolution.[26]

As in the case of newspapers, the printers of almanacs usually acted as editors, too, and therefore influenced content significantly.[27] When there were separate printers and authors, conflicts between them were not uncommon. But printers usually wrote most of the content of their almanacs, typically under a pseudonym, like Benjamin Franklin's "Richard Saunders." Since there was no legal copyright protection before 1790, some printers copied whole almanacs from other editors. Reprinting articles from other periodicals was even more common.[28]

Eighteenth-century American almanacs followed a common format, containing, in addition to the all-important calendar, astronomical and astrological data, the cycle of the tides, medical advice for both people and animals, and agricultural and household information. They also included schedules for currency conversion—a necessity in a society where several kinds of money were used—and dates of court hearings, fairs and markets, lists of roads, chronologies of historical events, the birthdays of monarchs, essays (mostly religious or historical, but during the Revolution also political), poems, funny stories, jokes, and articles on recent events.[29] Since the sixteenth century, German-speaking areas within the Holy Roman Empire of the German Nation had seen the spread of periodical printings, accompanied by an increasing politicization of the press. As in America, calendars were the primary reading material for common people.[30] Therefore, American printing culture was not alien to German-speaking immigrants.

For purposes of this study I have examined ten almanacs from the revolutionary era, with thirty-four issues altogether. Of these, thirteen issues contained articles, poems, or essays that can be considered "patriotic" propaganda.[31] This constitutes almost all of the known issues of German-language almanacs from 1775 until 1783.[32] According to the publication information given in the almanacs, three were at least temporarily printed in Lancaster, one in Frederickstown (now Frederick, Maryland), one in Germantown, and the rest in Philadelphia. The salesmen named—except those in these cities and towns—were located in Reading, Lebanon, Yorktown, Hagerstown, New Germantown, and Ephrata, Pennsylvania; Baltimore, Maryland; and, less frequently, Albany, New York; Rheinbeck, New York; Annapolis, Maryland; Easton; and "grocers in New Jersey, Maryland, and Virginia." Places of sale were not limited to these towns and cities, as many almanacs also added "et al." to the list of places where the almanacs were sold.

Revolutionary-era almanacs still focused overwhelmingly on the practical needs and the entertainment of their readers. However, on the first pages of almost every almanac, one could find a list of birthdays of European monarchs and an account of the most important historical events, usually beginning with the creation of the world. As in English-language almanacs, George III nearly always took the first place in the list of monarchs, both before and at the outset of the Revolution. Because he was German, people from German-language territories could often accept him as their king, too.[33] But as the Revolutionary War progressed, he lost his first place in the list, and his name was moved somewhere between the kings of Poland and Denmark. The historical events also mirrored the colonists' struggles with Great Britain. Even in Saur II's more pro-British calendar, the repeal of the "unbearable" (unerträglichen) Stamp Act in 1766 was considered a major historical event.[34] But nearly all other almanacs, whose editors were obviously on the patriots' side, listed the beginning of the Revolution and the Declaration of Independence, while Saur II did not mention them at all.

Christoph Saur II

Saur II's *Der Hoch-deutsch-americanische Calender* was the only German-language almanac that appeared to be pro-British. His title pages, beginning in 1775, bore the motto "Sorrowful Times" (kümmerliche Zeiten), and George III was the first monarch in the list. To underline the king's importance, his name was written in capital letters, as usually only "GOD" was. His wife and children were named beneath.[35] During this time, Saur II continued a series about England's kings. With up to ten pages per issue, the series was extraordinarily thorough for an almanac. It obviously reminded the reader of the historical might and dignity of the royal family.[36] Saur II also attempted to teach German speakers the English language and to make them familiar with the British legal system. Beginning with the 1775 issue he began a series of lessons, printed in roman font and designed to teach children and adults how to read and write English, explaining to his readers that this was useful "in a country that belongs to the English crown."[37] Examples of legal contracts were included, too.

Saur's stories about Britain's monarchs and English lessons came to an abrupt end after his 1776 issue (although the English-language series remained), which may indicate growing pressure put on Saur II by American patriots. His only account of the Revolution, published in the 1778 edition of the almanac, the year after the Battle of Germantown, was a poem entitled "Salutation of a Con-templating American to his Fellow Citizens," which lamented the awful griev-ances of the current war but gave no clear political statement. Instead, the poem complained about war profiteering and the sinfulness of the people, the result of their lack of piety and lavish way of life that had led to the turmoil, which was God's punishment.[38] During the Battle of Germantown, Saur II escaped for a short visit to Philadelphia, where his sons Christoph III and Peter printed a Tory paper. When he returned he was temporarily detained by patriots, his press and other belongings were sold, and his Germantown printing business came to an end.[39]

Henry Miller

Miller was the first printer in America to publish a report on the Declaration of Independence.[40] He had produced many other patriotic pieces since the begin-ning of the war[41] and decided to flee Philadelphia on September 25, 1777, as the British army approached.[42] Aware of Miller's role, the British confiscated his printing material and gave it to Christoph Saur II. It is likely that Saur or his sons published Miller's almanac for 1778 under his name.[43] Though it contained nothing that could be called radical loyalist propaganda, its content was modi-fied. The Stamp Act, which had been mentioned in Miller's prewar issues, disap-peared from the list of historical events, George III was listed as the first monarch, and the Revolution was not mentioned at all.[44]

Although Miller's prewar almanacs contained fewer political discussions than his famous newspaper did, he had at least touched on crucial aspects of the struggles with Britain. In his 1771 almanac he admired the courage of New Englanders, who had given "obvious proof of their love of liberty in the present days."[45] Even more unequivocal was an essay on pride under the byline "Mr. von Loen," which he printed in 1772 and which contained the assertion that "monarchs rose through pride, and men, created equal by nature, were sent to servitude."[46] However, he still saw German speakers in America as subjects of the British king.[47] George III was therefore still mentioned first in the lists of monarchs before the war.

Miller returned in 1778—copies of his newspaper were issued again on August 5, 1778—and accused Saur II of having profited from his expropriation.[48] Probably to signify that he, a supporter of the Revolution, had returned, he renamed his almanac *The Newly Positioned and Improved American State Calendar*.[49] In his almanac for 1780 he averred that the "senselessness, injustice, and infinite pride of Great Britain's rulers" had laid Philadelphia low.[50] Furthermore, after the "British soldiers, Hessians, and other auxiliary peoples" had marched in, about twenty thousand inhabitants fled.[51] He also incorporated the Declaration of Independence into his list of important historical events, gave the emperor of the Holy Roman Empire of the German Nation, Joseph II, first place in the list of monarchs, and listed the French ruler Louis XVI as the first king, while George III lost his position. Whereas he had referred to George III as "his majesty" before the Revolution, he now called him simply "this king."[52] Being almost eighty years old, Miller decided to cease printing in 1779.[53] The almanacs of 1778 and 1779 were his last.[54]

Francis Bailey

Printers outside Philadelphia, who were thus more distant from British authorities, were less cautious in their patriotic statements. Francis Bailey (1735?–1815) was trained by the German printer Peter Miller at Ephrata and later moved to the town of Lancaster, where he established a press in 1772.[55] At the beginning of the Revolution he joined the Continental army and later became a major in the state militia at Valley Forge.[56] Though he still listed George III as the first monarch in his almanac for 1778, he also depicted the Dutch jurist Hugo Grotius as a hero who "preferred his fatherland's liberty to . . . the court's grace," a clear allusion to the patriotic cause.[57] Grotius was one of the founders of natural law theory and an advocate of the Dutch revolution, which many American patriots saw as an example. Bailey admired the ancient Greeks for their love of liberty and their military abilities. His description of Alexander the Great, who had fought against a (Persian) king who fell prey to his selfish and corrupt advisors, was probably intended as a parallel to George Washington's efforts against George III, whose bad decisions were usually blamed on his advisors.[58] Bailey's next almanac was much more explicit. Its first page showed an angel holding a medallion engraved with Washington's face; the accompanying text read, "The Country's Father—Washington" (Landes Vater—Washington).[59] Among the European monarchs, the French king Louis XVI was now listed first. Bailey's was also one of the first almanacs to mention the members of

Congress. He provided a thorough but balanced account of the war's battles. One article dealt with the extraordinarily high British debts and anticipated their rise in the future, implying the end of widespread British rule overseas.[60]

In the following years, Bailey's almanacs became less politically radical and more religious.[61] After the 1778 edition, his almanacs were probably edited and printed by someone else, because he moved in 1778 or 1779 to Philadelphia to publish a newspaper, while his almanacs continued to be printed in Lancaster.[62] In Philadelphia he began publishing the short-lived patriotic *Freeman's Journal,* edited by Philip Freneau, in April 1781.[63]

"God's Intentions in War" (Gottes Absichten beym Krieg) was the title of an article in Bailey's almanac for 1781. It described the necessity of war as a means of self-defense and concluded that the reason for suffering in war is man's sinfulness.[64] The following almanacs did not mention the Revolution at all, except in the list of historical events. In 1782 the title page carried the same slogan that Saur's had done since 1775: "Sorrowful Times." The angel on the title page for 1784 simply announced "Peace" (Friede).[65] After the war, Bailey was appointed official printer for the U.S. Congress and the Commonwealth of Pennsylvania.[66]

Matthias Bartgis

Another Lancaster printer was Matthias Bartgis (originally Bärtgis, 1759–1825), who in 1777 printed an almanac there and later, probably beginning in 1778, several in Frederickstown, Maryland.[67] His almanacs included the highlights of the Revolution among important historical events, but beyond that had no political content. A poem from his 1777 Lancaster almanac included a prayer for peace in the coming year and expressed the wish "that the enemy will do us no harm." Still, in that issue's historical account, a British naval attack was characterized as an "enemy" attack.[68] Despite the martial name of his Frederickstown almanac (*The Very Newest, Improved, and Reliable American Empire, State, War, Victory, and History Calendar*), there were no comparable accounts.[69]

Theophilus Cossart

The title of Theophilus Cossart's first almanac, published in Lancaster, was *The Republican Calendar* (Der Republikanische Calender). It promised a radical attitude and it kept its promise. Its first issue was printed in 1778 and in the foreword Cossart proudly claimed that his new almanac was "the first new German calendar which dares to come to birth since the American states have formed a republic; it can therefore rightfully be called *Republican Calendar.*"[70]

In this first almanac Cossart listed the members of Congress above a short list of monarchs. Under the headline "Several strange incidents . . . Heaven and Earth Gave Signs of Felicitation," he reported, among other things, that the sky was most beautifully illuminated when General Burgoyne surrendered his troops to the Americans at the Battle of Saratoga and while negotiations with France were progressing.[71] The report on this strange coincidence obviously underlined the divine meaning of the Revolution. Astonishingly, the next issue did not include anything political—there was neither a list of congressmen or monarchs nor an account of historical events. These omissions were probably related to a new business partner, since Cossart had informed the reader in his first almanac that his enterprise could easily fall apart if he did not find a partner.

Cossart most probably moved to Philadelphia in 1780 or 1781. Some identical print settings indicate that he might have worked with Melchior Steiner and Carl Cist there. Only parts of the 1780 almanac have survived, so it is not possible to know with certainty where it was printed.[72] It does contain a long account of Benedict Arnold's treason in Philadelphia. Arnold had ordered a disguised British major, John Andrie, to Washington's camp to capture him and his staff. But the major was exposed by two incorruptible camp guards from West-Chester County, New York, who rejected his bribery attempt "with Republican virtue" (mit Republicanischer Tugend). Unfortunately, Arnold could not be captured. Major Andrie was executed by the Americans, despite threats from Arnold that he would execute American hostages in retaliation. That the Americans executed Andrie—"one of the most skillful . . . British officers"—anyway "showed that we are not frightened by threats but only more determined to vanquish our enemies until our country gains peace again."[73]

The Arnold report was one of the most radical pieces of patriotic propaganda to appear in a revolutionary almanac. Cossart's following two issues were more temperate, however. His almanac for 1782 contained only a poem that admired independence as a general value in human life. For 1783 he printed—now in Philadelphia—a catalogue of political questions and answers, stating sarcastically that they were taken from the British *Gentleman's Magazine.*[74] Its first part listed relatively positive questions and answers, such as, "What kind of people are the English? Answer. A magnanimous, brave, restless, unsettled, and generous nation."[75] But most of the essay consisted of anti-British propaganda: What was needed to be an English patriot? "An unrestrained infamy . . . an iron forehead to lie . . . and eventually he has to be resistant against every kind of bribery— which is not high enough."[76] What was the predominant religion in England? "Manifest faithlessness" (der offenbare Unglaube). Did the English admire some ideals? "Yes . . . fashion and selfishness" (mode und eigennutz). What were the most important English laws? "To prefer French Haches to English beef and pudding, to be in raptures over an Italian opera, or to learn the most popular arias of an opera within a short period of time."[77] What was the English constitution? "A thing that many people mention and few know."[78] Several other questions followed. This sequence of questions thoroughly maligned the British state and society. It should have been obvious to the almanac's readers that the values of the new American nation were the opposite of the British: American virtue, faith in God, the simple pragmatism of the frontier, and a just legal system based on the U.S. Constitution countered British insincerity, selfishness, corruption, atheism, decadence, and disregard of the importance of rule of law. Throughout all of his almanacs, Cossart used the German language in a remarkable way: in contrast to German rules of grammar followed by all other German printers, he used initial capital letters only for words that were capitalized in English, too.

John Dunlap

A similarly patriotic almanac was John Dunlap's (1747–1812). Dunlap was born in Northern Ireland and in 1766 took over his uncle William's printing business in Philadelphia. After he started the *Pennsylvania Packet* in 1771, which was known for its patriotic attitude, in 1775 he became a captain in a militia cavalry. Congress appointed him printer of its journals in 1778, a position he held for five years.[79] In the same year, he bought the confiscated press of Christoph Saur II and continued his almanac.[80]

Dunlap, although Scots-Irish, printed a good deal in German. He did not mention King George III at all among the monarchs, and in his first issue he printed a five-page German translation of Thomas Paine's *The American Crisis, No. 6*. Paine focused on the new alliance with France, defending its legitimacy and anticipating that Great Britain would soon be defeated.[81] The title page of the almanac for 1780 stated, "Loving Will Have Its Time" (Lieben hat seine Zeit), a reminder to readers that the war would have to be waged before the new nation could begin a peaceful existence. The issue also contained dubious advice for soldiers in the field. A certain type of stone put in the mouth would make a soldier invincible and prevent thirst, and a special ointment would protect guns from rust for thirty years. With a mirror, the text promised, a soldier could observe enemy troops even if they were half a mile away.[82] "Peace Will Have Its Time" (Frieden hat seine Zeit) was the motto of the 1781 almanac. But the only political pronouncement was a very short poem that disdained nobility:

The origins of nobility:
As GOD created the earth,

She was without stain;
But she became bad
Then began nobility's reign.[83]

Melchior Steiner and Carl Cist

Melchior Steiner (d. 1807?) and Carl Cist (pseudonym of Charles Jacob Sigis-
mund Thiel, 1738?–1805) were both German apprentices of Henry Miller. In
1776 they started a business together and published the first complete copy of
the Declaration of Independence in German and a translation of Thomas
Paine's *Common Sense*.[84] They fled with Miller when the British approached
Philadelphia. After their return, Miller decided to cease printing and turned his
business over to them. Together they printed two almanacs from 1779 to 1780.[85]

Their almanacs' content was clearly patriotic but not as radical as Dunlap's
or Cossart's. An article for 1780 described very colorfully the cruelties, destruction, and atrocities of war, adding that God was responsible for war's outcome,
though he did not approve its cruelties. But the reader needed to keep in mind
that everything God did made sense, even the destruction of the property, which
in wartime is usually the property of people who own too much. Eventually the
editors appealed directly to the reader, urging him not to despair but to keep
his faith in God and in a good outcome of the war. They referred the reader to
a story from "Herr Henry Moore" printed next to the article. This story
described a wanderer who met a stranger who joined him on his journey. On
their way, the stranger committed several crimes, each one more ghastly than
the last. The wanderer at first refused to interfere, but eventually he confronted
the stranger about his actions. All of a sudden, the stranger turned into an angel
and explained to the man that everything he had done was actually good,
because all the seemingly good people he had treated badly were indeed evil.
The wanderer had just not been able to see the hand of the angel behind his
own actions. Without referring to ideology or "higher causes," both texts simply
appealed to the reader's faith in good to make him stay the course. The righ-
teousness of the Revolution was not explicitly expressed but was implied by the
confident assertion that God would make sure that the right side, the revolutionaries, won the war.

Again in 1780 Steiner and Cist used religion to justify the patriots' cause.
That General Arnold's treason had been discovered, they wrote, was a "new
proof for God's support of the United States."[86] In this almanac one also finds
the same story about Arnold that appeared in Cossart's almanac for 1781, a
report, accompanied by an illustration, of a Philadelphia procession burning a
two-faced effigy of Arnold.[87] Arnold is depicted as someone who has made a

pact with the devil and will eventually be sent to hell. Symbolically, the Arnold effigy was burned on the march. The description of the procession was a translation of a broadside from Philadelphia.[88] The almanac also contained a thorough account of the previous year's battles.

In 1781 Steiner and Cist parted company and began to print almanacs individually, each man calling his almanac *Americanischer Haus- und Wirthschafts-Calender*.[89] Steiner's almanacs for 1782 and 1783 featured the same comprehensive accounts of recent battles that had appeared in their almanac for 1781. The account for 1782 noted that Pennsylvania troops had mutinied in 1780 but that the uprising had been put down "through wise measures" (durch weise Anstalten).

Cist's almanacs were the same as Steiner's up until the year 1782, which indicates that both printers still used the same press. Cist printed an individual almanac in 1783. It contains no information about the war, but there is a significant article for postwar Pennsylvania. The editor states that he has been urged by several readers to report on the state's land office. He notes that the land office had been suspended during the war and had thus received no payments since 1776. These payments were now due, and there would be no further land distribution until the outstanding debts were paid and veterans had received their share of land.

Joseph Crukshank

In 1782 Joseph Crukshank (1746?–1836) printed a German almanac for the first time in which he revived the title of Miller's first almanac.[90] Crukshank printed Philadelphia's *Poor Will's Almanack* as well.[91] His German almanac was identical to Cossart's, and its next known issues were printed after the Revolution.[92]

In about half of the almanacs from the revolutionary period that I examined, the Revolution figured little if at all. Practical matters of daily life clearly dominated. Even in the issues free of patriot propaganda, however, all of the publishers except Saur quietly took a patriotic stance by including the events of the Revolution in their list of major events in human history and by removing George III from the first position in the list of monarchs. But because this meant altering only a few lines of an almanac's text, it did not mean that someone who bought the almanac was necessarily on the patriots' side. Rather, the character of the almanacs during the revolutionary period seems to mirror the split among German speakers. Many were content with British rule or were indifferent and tried to stay neutral.[93] It is therefore not surprising that the only instance in which a printer explicitly responded to readers' requests is Carl Cist's report on the state of land distribution in Pennsylvania shortly after the end of the war. Furthermore, although the German-language press tried to inform readers about politics, a considerable number of German speakers still had trouble understanding the key issues of the Revolution.[94]

Although it seems that a large group of German speakers were not committed to the Revolution, there were also many German Americans—in some instances including even sectarian pacifists—who joined the revolutionaries in their fight against the British and thereby made a significant contribution to America's independence. Though clearly not all of them joined the Continental army for patriotic reasons—some joined in order to shorten their time as redemptioners, gain land after their service, or evade taxes—German speakers made up about 12 percent of Washington's army.[95] Strong support for the Revolution in Pennsylvania's heavily German backcountry indicates that a majority of German speakers were on the patriots' side. The counties of Berks, Cumberland, Lancaster, and York formed the core of support for the Revolution—Berks and Lancaster had majorities of German speakers, were highly taxed before the war, and had been politically underrepresented—and in fact supplied the majority of the first troops, the famed Pennsylvania Rifles, to join the Continental army in 1775.[96] It is therefore not surprising that most radical almanacs were printed in the heavily pro-patriot town of Lancaster, in the center of Pennsylvania German country, which was also the place of refuge for the revolutionary government and for at least one political printer after the British took Philadelphia.[97] Patriotic almanacs must have attracted a significant number of these German-speaking readers, for they purchased almanacs with a relatively high proportion of political propaganda and less practical advice and entertainment.

Since the German-language market for almanacs in Philadelphia was dominated by Henry Miller and his two apprentices, Melchior Steiner and Carl Cist, the printing products from this part of Pennsylvania were clearly pro-patriot, while Philadelphia's English-language almanacs—at least until 1780—were more equivocal by this time.[98] Outside the city, the German-speaking printer Matthias Bartgis was also on the patriots' side but did not print explicit propaganda. Besides Miller and his apprentices, only English-speaking printers produced overtly propagandistic almanacs in German. The commitment of those printers—among them prominent supporters of the Revolution like John Dunlap and Francis Bailey—shows how much importance was given to efforts to persuade German speakers to join the Revolution or stay the course.[99] Not surprisingly, their major propaganda efforts, and those of Miller and his apprentices, were undertaken in the years 1778, 1779, and 1780, when the patriots were in a precarious position, after several losses in the south, and when Benedict Arnold's treason showed that support for the Revolution was probably not as stable as had been assumed. Consequently, when victory seemed to be close after the American success at Yorktown, most English-speaking printers ceased producing German almanacs.[100]

Concerning the content of Pennsylvanian almanacs, a significant difference between those printed by German and English speakers can be observed. While before the Revolution, English-language printers tried to construct a British American identity by giving the monarch a prominent position and presenting a royalist interpretation of British history, they changed this practice over the course of the Revolution. Henceforth, symbols of the new American Republic replaced those of the British monarchy. In the case of German-language almanacs, one could find the same British interpretation of history, but accompanied by German events, like the foundation of the Holy Roman Empire of the German Nation, in an attempt to promote a British-German American identity. George III was given the first position in the list of monarchs—followed by the emperor of the Holy Roman Empire of the German Nation and rulers of the largest German states—but, in contrast to English-language almanacs, George's portrait never appeared on the cover of a German one. The British king therefore did not receive such a prominent role as in English-language almanacs.[101]

After the Revolution began, Emperor Joseph II took the first position in every almanac produced by a German-speaking printer, while George III—at the same time ruler of the German state Hanover—was moved to a minor position among the other kings. Miller and his apprentices even extended the list of monarchs, which eventually encompassed two pages, to include a large number of landgraves and other rulers of smaller German states. English-speaking printers who produced German-language almanacs did not abandon the list of monarchs, either, but after the treaty with France put Louis XVI in first place. Obviously, German-speaking printers assumed that monarchs still constituted an important part of the identity of many German speakers in America. In this context, monarchs were not seen as representatives of a certain form of political rule but as symbols of the native land to which one had originally belonged. Therefore, by listing as many monarchs of the vast number of German states as possible, Miller and his apprentices tried to give symbols of identification to as many German speakers as possible. They believed that German speakers in America would find it relatively easy to reject George III as the American sovereign, but still problematic—and for the generation of short-term support for the Revolution also unnecessary—to reject monarchs in general as symbols of identity. The connection of former British "subjects" to the motherland across the Atlantic, however, had to be cut by patriot ideologues.[102]

The wariness of German-speaking printers about severing their readers' feelings of identity is evident in the way they treated the issue of Hessian mercenaries who fought for the British. With the exception of Miller, who was probably personally angered about the destruction of his property during the occupation of Philadelphia by British and Hessian forces, only English-speaking printers mentioned the German mercenaries—and particularly their defeat at Trenton—at all.[103]

German- and English-speaking printers also differed significantly in their assumptions about the symbolic order that shaped their readership's mentality. Whether a publisher saw a certain kind of propaganda as appropriate for his German-speaking readers was shaped by his assumption about their level of cultural assimilation. These assumptions differed widely. On the one side, Christoph Saur II still saw in 1777 the necessity to teach German speakers English legal practice and the English language. His pro-British articles were cautious and implicit, reminding the reader only that monarchs deserved a certain level of obedience. Though probably shaped by threats of patriots in Germantown, Saur II's criticism of the Revolution had a clear general character: rather than criticize the revolutionaries directly, he demanded stricter godly behavior from everyone.

German pro-Revolution printers Bartgis, Steiner, and Cist printed less radical propaganda—if it was propaganda at all—than their English colleagues did. Their almanacs were mostly accompanied by religious injunctions as well. Even Steiner and Cist, who produced translations of English-language propaganda during the Revolution, saw this kind of propaganda as questionable for their more widely read almanacs, which were certainly distributed in the backcountry as well. Though the majority of German speakers were not members of sects, they were probably more attracted by religious themes than by secular English-style propaganda.[104]

On the contrary, English-speaking German-language printers (Cossart, Crukshank, Dunlap, Bailey) already assumed a full understanding of the Revolution's key issues or intentionally applied the same radical propaganda to German as to English speakers. Their historical analogies, reports on recent events, and poems were frequently mere translations of English originals, like Paine's letters or the report on Arnold's treason. German-language printers had indeed already adapted English terms like "fair [market]," "court," and even "prison," though German equivalents existed. Yet the most radical printer, Theophilus Cossart, went one step further and replaced German-language rules with English ones.

It seems that the almanacs of German-language printers were more popular with their linguistic cohort. Most original English-language printers had to retreat from the German-language market in the years following the Revolution: Cossart probably turned his business over to Crukshank, who ceased his German-language business two years after the war ended, and Dunlap did not issue his almanac after 1784.[105] The difference between sharing similar political goals, as in the Revolution, and sharing the exact culture probably became evident in the development of Pennsylvania's eighteenth-century German-language almanacs.

NOTES

1. W. M. Verhoeven, "'A Colony of Aliens': Germans and the German-Language Press in Colonial and Revolutionary Pennsylvania," in *Periodical Literature in Eighteenth-Century America,* ed. Mark L. Kamrath and Sharon M. Harris (Knoxville: University of Tennessee Press, 2005), 77; Russell Earnest, Corinne Earnest, and Edward L. Rosenberry, *Flying Leaves and One-Sheets: Pennsylvania German Broadsides, Fraktur, and Their Printers* (New Castle, Del.: Oak Knoll Books, 2005), 138.

2. Karl John Richard Arndt and Reimer C. Eck, eds., *The First Century of German Language Printing in the United States of America: A Bibliography Based on the Studies of Oswald Seidensticker and Wilbur H. Oda,* comp. Gerd-J. Bötte and Werner Tannhoff, vol. 1, *1728–1807* (Göttingen: Niedersächsische Staats-und Universitätsbibliothek Göttingen, 1989), 490.

3. Aaron Spencer Fogleman, *Hopeful Journeys: German Immigration, Settlement, and Political Culture in Colonial America, 1717–1775* (Philadelphia: University of Pennsylvania Press, 1996); John B. Frantz and William Pencak, eds., *Beyond Philadelphia: The American Revolution in the Pennsylvania Hinterland* (University Park: Pennsylvania State University Press, 1998); A. G. Roeber, *Palatines, Liberty, and Property: German Lutherans in Colonial British America* (Baltimore: Johns Hopkins University Press, 1993).

4. Roeber, *Palatines, Liberty, and Property,* ix.

5. Fogleman, *Hopeful Journeys,* 81, 86, 99. Susan M. Johnson has criticized the notion of a common eighteenth-century Pennsylvania German identity. She refers to the ethnic mixture of the middle colonies and denies the existence of a Pennsylvania German identity before the nineteenth century. However, she also refers to the tendency of German speakers to live apart from other settlers. Johnson, "Pennsylvania's Social History and Pennsylvania German Studies: A Look at the Eighteenth Century," *Yearbook of German-American Studies* 32 (1997): 47–62, 55.

6. Roeber, *Palatines, Liberty, and Property,* 98–99.

7. As several studies have shown, however, political rule in the Holy Roman Empire of the German Nation was often scrutinized in day-to-day life. It seems that the reach of authorities differed vastly from place to place and was dependent on its social acceptance. See the overview of current research on German early modern history in Anette Völker-Rasor, *Frühe Neuzeit* [Early Modern History], with a foreword by Winfried Schulze (Munich: R. Oldenbourg Verlag, 2000), 347–52.

8. Marianne S. Wokeck, "German Settlements in the North American Colonies: A Patchwork of Cultural Assimilation and Persistence," in *In Search of Peace and Prosperity: New German Settlements in Eighteenth-Century Europe and America,* ed. Hartmut Lehmann, Hermann Wellenreuther, and Renate Wilson (University Park: Pennsylvania State University Press, 2000), 212–13.

9. Fogleman, *Hopeful Journeys,* 135–36, 140–42.

10. Ibid., 135, 132; Roeber, *Palatines, Liberty, and Property,* 291–92, 298.

11. Roeber, *Palatines, Liberty, and Property,* 5, 7, 60, 176–77, 284, 293, 303–4, 311. Based on signature rates on naturalization oaths, Roeber assumes that literacy among German speakers had reached nearly 100 percent at the time of the Revolution. It should be noted, however, that the level of literacy varied widely, from the basic ability to write one's name to fluency in reading and writing complicated texts. By the latter standard, about 70 percent of the rural population in Germany was illiterate by the second half of the eighteenth century. It does not seem likely that literacy rates of German speakers in America were a great deal higher. See Reinhard Wittmann, "Der lesende Landmann: Zur Rezeption aufklärerischer Bemühungen durch die ländliche Bevölkerung im 18. Jahrhundert" [The Reading Peasant: The Reception of the Enlightenment by the Eighteenth-Century Rural Population], in Wittmann, *Buchmarkt und Lektüre im 18. und 19. Jahrhundert: Beiträge zum literarischen Leben, 1750–1880* [Book Market and Reading in the Eighteenth and Nineteenth Centuries: Contributions to Literary Life, 1750–1880] (Tübingen: Max Niemayer Verlag, 1982), 4. See also Eckart Hellmuth and Wolfgang Piereth, "Germany, 1760–1815," in *Press, Politics, and the Public Sphere in Europe and North America, 1760–1820,* ed. Hannah Barker and Simon Burrows (Cambridge: Cambridge University Press, 2002), 71. Hellmuth and Piereth

estimate the literacy rate of people in Germany in the last third of the eighteenth century as 15 percent at most.

12. To avoid confusion, I follow the spelling of German names, with the exception of Henry Miller, used in Arndt and Eck, *German Language Printing.*

13. Marion Barber Stowell, *Early American Almanacs: The Colonial Weekday Bible* (New York: Burt Franklin, 1977), 114–18.

14. Verhoeven, "'Colony of Aliens,'" 87.

15. Ibid., 78–79; A. G. Roeber, "Henry Miller's *Staatsbote:* A Revolutionary Journalist's Use of the Swiss Past," *Yearbook of German-American Studies* 25 (1990): 63.

16. Roeber, *Palatines, Liberty, and Property,* 175–76, 201.

17. Roeber, "Henry Miller's *Staatsbote,*" 57–58, 62–63.

18. Verhoeven, "'Colony of Aliens,'" 78–79.

19. Roeber, *Palatines, Liberty, and Property,* 178–79.

20. Roeber, "Henry Miller's *Staatsbote,*" 64–65.

21. For an account of the Saurs, see also Donald F. Durnbaugh, "The Sauer Family: An American Printing Dynasty," *Yearbook of German-American Studies* 23 (1988): 31–40; and Heinz G. F. Wilsdorf, *Early German-American Imprints* (New York: Peter Lang, 1999), 39–71. On Miller, see Roeber, "Henry Miller's *Staatsbote,*" and the Appendix to this volume, translated by Jan Logemann, with notes by William Pencak.

22. Stowell, *Early American Almanacs,* ix–x.

23. Ibid., 14.

24. Ibid., x; Hugh Amory, "Reinventing the Colonial Book," in *The Colonial Book in the Atlantic World,* ed. Hugh Amory and David D. Hall (Worcester, Mass.: American Antiquarian Society, 2000), 51. Verhoeven ("'Colony of Aliens,'" 79) gives a figure of 120,000 copies per year for Saur's almanac, which is probably too high.

25. Wilsdorf, *Early German-American Imprints,* 12. See also Patrick Spero's essay in this volume.

26. Philip Davidson, *Propaganda and the American Revolution, 1763–1783* (Chapel Hill: University of North Carolina Press, 1941; reprint, 1966), 393–94, 397–98.

27. James N. Green, "English Books and Printing in the Age of Franklin," in Amory and Hall, *Colonial Book in the Atlantic World,* 266. According to Stowell, almanacs were "the only American literature to be so much influenced by the printer." Stowell, *Early American Almanacs,* 13–14, 25.

28. Stowell, *Early American Almanacs,* 26–27, 31, 137.

29. Ibid., xv, 17, 20, 63–64, 135–36. All of Stowell's characteristics of an almanac's content could be found in Pennsylvania's almanacs of the revolutionary period.

30. Thomas Schröder, "The Origins of the German Press," in *The Politics of Information in Early Modern Europe,* ed. Brendan Dooley and Sabrina A. Baron (London: Routledge, 2001), 130, 146; Wittmann, "Lesende Landmann," 19.

31. In this study I follow Leonard W. Doob's definition of propaganda, also followed by Davidson: "Intentional propaganda is a systematic attempt by an interested individual (or individuals) to control the attitudes of groups of individuals through the use of suggestion and, consequently, to control their actions." Quoted in Davidson, *Propaganda and the American Revolution,* xiii.

32. See the thorough work of Arndt and Eck, *German Language Printing.*

33. Even Miller mentioned the British king—with all his spouses (!)—see Henrich Miller, *Der Neueste, verbessert- und zuverlässige americanische Calender 1771* (Philadelphia, 1770); *Der Neueste americanische Calender 1772* (Philadelphia, 1771); *Der Neueste americanische Kalender 1773* (Philadelphia, 1772); and *Der Neueste americanische Calender 1774* (Philadelphia, 1773). See also Roeber, *Palatines, Liberty, and Property,* 292. Copies of all of the almanacs I examined were taken from the digital database Early American Imprints, series 1, Evans (1639–1800), microfilm.

34. Christoph Saur, *Der Hoch-deutsch-americanische Calender 1776* (Germantown, Pa., 1775); *Der Hoch-deutsch-americanische Calender 1777* (Germantown, Pa., 1776); *Der Hoch-deutsch-americanische Calender 1778* (Germantown, Pa., 1777). Saur had already attacked every form of taxation before the Revolution; see Roeber, "Henry Miller's *Staatsbote,*" 59. The Stamp Act hit German speakers—especially printers—harder than others, since non-English-language printing products were taxed at twice the usual rate; see Benedikt Kaukler, *Die deutschen Auswanderer und die Amerikanische Revolution: Die Haltung der deutschsprachigen Gruppen während der Amerikanischen Revolution in Pennsylvania, 1763–1790* [German

Immigrants and the American Revolution: The Attitude of German-Speaking Groups During the American Revolution in Pennsylvania, 1763–1790] (PhD diss., Albert-Ludwigs-Universität, 1993), 97.

35. See Saur's *Der Hoch-deutsch-americanische Calender* for 1776, 1777, and 1778.

36. Ibid., 1776 and 1777.

37. Ibid., 1776 ("in einem Lande welches unter die Englische Krone gehört"). All translations are my own.

38. "Anrede eines nachdenkenden Americaners an seine Mit Bürger," in ibid., 1778. The poem was also printed in his newspaper *Der Hoch-Deutsch Pennsylvanische Geschicht-Schreiber.* John Joseph Stoudt translated it in part in his "German Press in Pennsylvania and the American Revolution," in *The German Language Press of the Americas,* vol. 3, *German-American Press Research from the American Revolution to the Bicentennial,* ed. Karl J. R. Arndt and Mary E. Olson (Munich: K. G. Saur, 1980), 302–3.

39. Verhoeven, " 'Colony of Aliens,' " 86.

40. Roeber, *Palatines, Liberty, and Property,* 283.

41. Arndt and Eck, *German Language Printing,* 462, 466, 469–70, 484.

42. Verhoeven, " 'Colony of Aliens,' " 90.

43. See John B. Frantz's essay in this volume.

44. Henrich Miller, *Der Neue, Verbessert- und Zuverlässige Americanische Calender 1778* (Philadelphia, 1777). I did not examine Miller's almanacs for 1776 and 1777 for purposes of this essay. Note the title change of his almanacs after 1777. Arndt and Eck, *German Language Printing,* 485, 502.

45. Miller, *Der Neueste americanische Calender 1772* ("ihre Freiheitsliebe in diesen gegenwärtigen Zeiten deutlich bewiesen").

46. Ibid. ("durch den Hochmuth sind die Monarchen aufgekommen, und die Menschen, welche die Natur gleich erschaffen hat, in die Knechtschaft gerathen").

47. Roeber, "Henry Miller's *Staatsbote,*" 64.

48. Verhoeven, " 'Colony of Aliens,' " 90.

49. *Der Neugestellete und verbesserte americanische Staats-Calender.* I did not examine the 1779 almanac. See Arndt and Eck, *German Language Printing,* 519.

50. Ibid., 1780 edition ("die Unsinnigkeit, Ungerechtigkeit und der grenzenlose Stolz der Regenten Großbrittaniens").

51. Ibid. ("die Brittischen Soldaten, Hessen, und andere ihre Hülfsvölker").

52. Ibid.

53. Verhoeven, " 'Colony of Aliens,' " 90.

54. See Arndt and Eck, *German Language Printing,* 526.

55. Isaiah Thomas, *The History of Printing in America, with a Biography of Printers in Two Volumes, Second Edition with the Author's Corrections and Additions and a Catalogue of American Publications previous to the Revolution of 1776,* 2 vols. (New York: Burt Franklin, 1874; reprint, 1972), 1:286–88. I did not examine Thomas's almanacs for 1776 and 1777 in researching this essay. See Arndt and Eck, *German Language Printing,* 458, 482. On Bailey, see also Patrick Spero's essay in this volume.

56. Earnest, Earnest, and Rosenberry, *Flying Leaves and One-Sheets,* 308.

57. Francis Bailey, *Der Gantz neue verbesserte nord-americanische Calender 1778* (Lancaster, Pa., 1777) ("die freyheit seines Vaterlandes . . . der gunst der Hofes vorzog").

58. Ibid.

59. According to the Earnests and Rosenberry, Bailey was the first to call Washington the country's father. Earnest, Earnest, and Rosenberry, *Flying Leaves and One-Sheets,* 308.

60. Bailey, *Der Gantz neue nord-americanische Calender 1779.*

61. The issue for 1780 I examined was only partly preserved. Bailey, *Der Gantz neue nord-americanische Calender 1780.*

62. Thomas, *History of Printing in America,* 1:286.

63. Davidson, *Propaganda and the American Revolution,* 398.

64. Bailey, *Der Gantz neue nord-americanische Calender 1779.*

65. Bailey, *Der Gantz neue nord-americanische Calender 1781,* and *Der Gantz neue nord-americanische Calender 1782.*

66. Earnest, Earnest, and Rosenberry, *Flying Leaves and One-Sheets,* 308.

67. For a short account of Bartgis, see also A. G. Roeber, "German and Dutch Books and Printing," in Amory and Hall, *Colonial Book in the Atlantic World,* 310; Wilsdorf, *Early German-American Imprints,*

126. Though no copy was found, Arndt and Eck assumed that Bartgis printed the first issue of his almanac as early as 1776. Arndt and Eck, *German Language Printing*, 483.

68. Matthias Bartgis, *Der Hinckend- und stolpernd- doch eilfertig- fliegend- und laufende americanische Reichs-Bott 1778* (Lancaster, Pa., 1777) ("das uns der Feind nicht schade").

69. *Der Allerneuste, verbesserte, und zuverlässige americanische Reichs- Staats- Kriegs- Siegs und Geschichts-Calender 1780* (Fredericksburg, Md., 1779).

70. Theophilus Cossart, *Der Republikanische Calender 1779* (Lancaster, Pa., 1778) ("der erste, neue Deutsche Calender, der sich in die Welt wagt, seitdem die Americanischen Staaten sich in eine Republic formiert haben; er kann also füglich den Namen des *Republicanischen Calenders* führen").

71. Ibid. ("Verschiedene merkwürdige Begebenheiten . . . Himmel und Erde gaben Zeichen eines Glückwunsches"). Cossart used a title page showing Mercurius and a shining sun, very similar—but not identical—to Saur's.

72. According to Arndt and Eck, the most complete surviving copy has thirty-six pages, in contrast to the forty pages of the preceding issue. *German Language Printing*, 523, 517.

73. Cossart, *Der Republikanische Calender 1781* ("eines der geschicktesten . . . Officiers," "zeiget, daß wir uns nicht durch grosse drohungen schreken lassen, sondern entschlossen sind, unsere feinde einen nach dem andern auszurotten, bis unser land wieder den Frieden erhält").

74. It is not known whether he meant the famous British magazine, founded in 1732, which was also popular in America, or the American version. Charles E. Clark, "Periodicals and Politics, Part One: Early American Journalism, News and Opinion in the Popular Press," in Amory and Hall, *Colonial Book in the Atlantic World*, 360; Elizabeth Carrol Reilly and David D. Hall, "Customers and the Market for Books," ibid., 390.

75. Cossart, *Der Republikanische Calender 1783* ("Was für eine Art volck sind die Engelländer? Antwort. Eine großmüthige, tapfre, rastlose, unbeständige und großzügige nation").

76. Ibid. ("Eine zügellose unverschämtheit . . . eine eiserne stirne zum lügen . . . und endlich muß er fest seyn, gegen eine jede bestechung—die nicht wichtig genug ist").

77. Ibid. ("die Französischen Haches dem Englischen Beef und Pudding vorzuziehen, in einer Italienischen Opera vor vergnügen entzückt zu seyn, oder . . . in kurzer zeit die beliebtesten arien aus einer opera zu lernen").

78. Ibid. ("Ein ding, welches viele nennen, und wenige kennen").

79. Thomas, *History of Printing in America*, 1:258–59, 2:139. On Dunlap, see also Patrick Spero's essay in this volume.

80. Stowell, *Early American Almanacs*, 121.

81. John Dunlap, *Der Hoch-deutsch-americanische Calender 1779* (Philadelphia, 1778). Steiner and Cist had printed a German translation of Paine's *Common Sense* in 1776. Arndt and Eck, *German Language Printing*, 490.

82. The title page of the 1778 almanac has not survived. Dunlap, *Der Hoch-deutsch-americanische Calender 1780*.

83. Dunlap, *Der Hoch-deutsch-americanische Calender 1782* ("Der Ursprung des Adels: Als GOtt die welt erschuf, da war sie ohne tadel / Allein sie wurde schlimm, / hernach entstund der adel").

84. Roeber, *Palatines, Liberty, and Property*, 283; Wilsdorf, *Early German-American Imprints*, 141; Arndt and Eck, *German Language Printing*, 490; Earnest, Earnest, and Rosenberry, *Flying Leaves and One-Sheets*, 138.

85. Verhoeven, "'Colony of Aliens,'" 90; Earnest, Earnest, and Rosenberry, *Flying Leaves and One-Sheets*, 138.

86. Steiner and Cist, *Americanischer Haus- und Wirthschafts-Calender 1781* ("Neuer Beweis für die göttliche Vorsorge für die Vereinigten Staaten").

87. Arndt and Eck, *German Language Printing*, 540.

88. The broadside is reprinted in Davidson, *Propaganda and the American Revolution*, 388.

89. Thomas, *History of Printing in America*, 1:269–70.

90. Joseph Crukshank, *Der Neue, verbessert- und zuverlässige americanische Calender 1783* (Philadelphia, 1782); Arndt and Eck, *German Language Printing*, 568.

91. Stowell, *Early American Almanacs*, 104–6.

92. Arndt and Eck, *German Language Printing*, 568.

93. John B. Frantz and William Pencak, "Introduction: Pennsylvania and Its Three Revolutions," in Frantz and Pencak, *Beyond Philadelphia*, xix–xx.

94. Roeber, *Palatines, Liberty, and Property,* 308.

95. Charles Patrick Neimeyer, *America Goes to War: A Social History of the Continental Army* (New York: New York University Press, 1996), 48, 51, 63–64.

96. Frantz and Pencak, "Introduction: Pennsylvania and Its Three Revolutions," xix–xx; Kaukler, *Deutschen Auswanderer,* 292, 352.

97. During the British occupation of Philadelphia, John Dunlap printed his patriotic *Pennsylvania Packet* in Lancaster. Davidson, *Propaganda and the American Revolution,* 398.

98. See Patrick Spero's essay in this volume.

99. Numerous other propaganda measures were aimed at German speakers. Davidson, *Propaganda and the American Revolution,* 354.

100. Cossart started to print his radical almanac in 1778 and ceased printing it in 1782. Also in 1778, Dunlap started to print in German after purchasing Saur's confiscated press. No German-language sources identifying him as the printer after 1781 have been discovered. Also, Crukshank printed in German only briefly, beginning in 1782.

101. See Patrick Spero's essay in this volume.

102. Ibid.

103. For examples of the mention of the Hessian defeat at Trenton, see Bailey, *Der Gantz neue verbesserte nord-americanische Calender 1778;* Crukshank, *Der Neue, verbessert- und zuverlässige americanische Calender 1783;* Cossart, *Der Republikanische Calender 1783.*

104. See John B. Frantz's essay in this volume.

105. Arndt and Eck, *German Language Printing,* 567, 568, 636, 549.

RELIGION, THE AMERICAN REVOLUTION,
AND THE PENNSYLVANIA GERMANS

John B. Frantz

By the outbreak of the American Revolution, Pennsylvania's population was approximately three hundred thousand. William Penn had advertised his colony as a land of economic opportunity and freedom of worship. So many German speakers responded that Benjamin Franklin could inform a committee of the British House of Commons that one-third of the population consisted of emigrants from Germany and Switzerland.[1] Although some settled in the original counties of Bucks, Philadelphia, and Chester, most moved on to the interior Northampton, Berks, Lancaster, and York counties, where they may have constituted 90 percent of the inhabitants. In time, others moved southwest into western Maryland and the Shenandoah Valley of Virginia.[2]

The Germans and Swiss helped to make Pennsylvania the most religiously diverse colony in British America. Lieutenant Governor George Thomas charged that German-speaking settlers had brought with them "all the religious whimsies of their homelands" and had subdivided further after they arrived in Pennsylvania. In early Germantown there were Quakers, the pietistic "Hermits of the Wissahickon," Mennonites, Lutherans, and Reformed. Later arrivals shared their backgrounds and affiliations. Add to those groups Roman Catholics; Amish; German Baptist Brethren, popularly known as Dunkers; Seventh Day Baptists, who established cloisters at Ephrata; Schwenkfelders; Moravians, formally called the Unitas Fratrum; and also small numbers of Universalists; Inspired; New Born; and New Mooners.[3]

Actually, the diversity was more apparent than real. The vast majority of the Pennsylvania Germans, possibly 90 percent, were of Lutheran and Reformed background. They were the "church people," sometimes called the "Gay Dutch" because of their allegedly worldly ways.[4] Virtually pastorless in their early years of settlement, by the time of the American Revolution they had several capable and articulate leaders. They had formed large congregations in the city of Philadelphia and in the towns of Lancaster, Reading, and York. They had organized supervisory and administrative bodies to assign clergy and mediate disputes.[5] The people of other denominations, except for the Moravians, were sectarians who had withdrawn from Europe's state-sponsored churches. They were the pacifistic "Plain Dutch," who tried to follow biblical injunctions literally.[6]

What follows is an explanation of how the Pennsylvania Germans' religious beliefs influenced their involvement or noninvolvement in the American Revolution and the ways in which the War of American Independence affected the Pennsylvania Germans' religious practices (using the term loosely). No written history is comprehensive, and this one is no exception. The names and denominational affiliations of many have not survived.

Regardless of ecclesiastical ties, the Pennsylvania Germans initially allied politically with the colony's Quaker Party. It dominated the colony's legislature and kept taxes low and prevented military action. Many German-speaking settlers had suffered from excesses of both prior to their departure from Europe. The outbreak of the French and Indian War undermined the German-Quaker alliance. As the Native Americans attacked the outlying settlements during the mid-1750s, many of the Lutheran and Reformed residents demanded protection. Indeed, in late November 1755 they approached Philadelphia and a "delegation from the 'Dutch mob' entered the Assembly hall" to urge "immediate passage of a defense bill." Their objection to the military previously had been economic, not theological. The Mennonites, Amish, Schwenkfelders, Dunkers, and Seventh Day Baptists did not resist the Indian attacks. Seventh Day Baptist leader Conrad Beissel claimed that God had promised him that no harm would come to his people.[7] This division between pacifists and other Germans became obvious during the War of Independence.

The American Revolution was an "aftermath of the Great War for the Empire," known in America as the French and Indian War. By the time that the Treaty of Paris officially ended the conflict in 1763, the British national debt had doubled, and the cost of administration and defense of the empire had increased fivefold. Consequently, the British Parliament revised its colonial policy by passing a series of measures, including several intended to recoup recent expenditures in America from the colonists. Many English-speaking colonists resisted vigorously. In opposition to the Stamp Act, they held a Congress in 1765, organized nonimportation agreements to protest the 1767 Townshend Duties, and after the Tea Act of 1773 threw tea into the Boston harbor and forced the return of the tea ships when they tried to land it at other ports.[8]

The revolutionary movement began more slowly among the Pennsylvania Germans. Partially because of the language barrier and their location in the hinterlands, their response to the British measures was mild. The Stamp Act attracted the attention of Germans mostly in Philadelphia. The Moravian printer Johann Heinich Müller temporarily suspended his Philadelphia newspaper, *Der Wochentliche Philadelphische Staatsbote,* in reaction against its double tax on non-English-language material. When he resumed publication, he vigorously promoted the preservation of the "old constitutional arrangement." He protested the British Parliament's revenue measures, use of admiralty courts, and the presence of British troops in Boston. Christoph Saur II, a Dunker bishop, also defended the colonial "rights" in his newspaper until 1775. These papers circulated widely among the largely literate German-speaking settlers from Maine to Georgia. In 1775 Müller published in German an "Appeal" from Philadelphia's Lutheran and Reformed church councils and the German Society of Pennsylvania to the German-speaking residents of New York and North Carolina. A year later, he published the first non-English edition of the Declaration of Independence.[9]

Nevertheless, even a leading Pennsylvania German in Philadelphia was reluctant to become involved in the protests. When asked to ring the church bells to celebrate the repeal of the Stamp Act in 1766, Lutheran pastor Heinrich Melchior Mühlenberg advised the Germans to "remain quiet" and have nothing to do with politics.[10] Mühlenberg not only served what probably was the largest Lutheran congregation of the largest German denomination in colonial Pennsylvania, he was the "patriarch" of German Lutheranism in British America. Sent by the German Halle Missionary Society in 1742, his specific call was to serve congregations in Philadelphia; Providence, now known as Trappe; and New Hanover. Nevertheless, he ministered to Lutherans wherever he found them—in the interior of Pennsylvania, in the neighboring colonies of New York and Maryland, as well as in faraway Maine and Georgia. He was their leader, and his position on issues was crucial. His European Lutheran background emphasized the "separate but equal nature of the two swords, the church and state," and the church's willingness to defer to the ruler in secular matters. He was mindful of the Apostle Paul's admonition to be "subject to the higher powers, for there is no power but of God." Mühlenberg's motto was "fear God, honor the king." Whether he was aware of Martin Luther's repudiation for rebellion is not certain. Upon arriving in Pennsylvania, he took an oath of loyalty to George II, who not only was king of Great Britain but also ruled his native province of Hanover, where Lutheranism was the established church. He was grateful for the opportunity that Germans had to settle under "the protection of the glorious Protestant King of Great Britain" and to enjoy "the precious liberty of conscience" under the "honorable Penns." A practical reason for his reluctance to become involved was that he feared that the side that he did not support would harm his Lutheran Church if it won. In 1775 he left Philadelphia and moved with his ailing wife to what he hoped would be the quiet countryside at Trappe, where he hoped that he could remain officially neutral. "War," he wrote, "is an unspeakable tragedy and sin. . . . Singing a Te Deum after a military victory is like doing so after a man commits adultery without being caught."[11]

Unlike Mühlenberg, Pennsylvania Germans who lived "beyond Philadelphia" were aroused by the Coercive Acts, which Americans labeled "intolerable," especially the Boston Port Act.[12] In mid-May 1774, Paul Revere rode into Philadelphia to describe the plight of the Bostonians, whose commerce had been cut off by the closing of the harbor, whose provincial government was suspended, whose town meetings were prohibited, and among whom four thousand British troops were stationed.[13] The news spread rapidly into the interior, where the inhabitants responded promptly.

In July 1774 Berks County leaders assembled and declared the "Intolerable Act" "unjust and tyrannical" and agreed to provide supplies and money to the people of Boston. They organized a committee to correspond with "leaders of other colonies." By the end of the year this committee included a majority of Germans and Swiss. When Berks County formed a militia, four German Reformed with the surname Hiester became officers. The Reading Reformed congregation "furnished two colonels, Peter Nagle, and Nicholas Lutz."[14]

Northampton County formed committees of observation and safety that contained Pennsylvania Germans, including David Dresher and Peter Rhoades, members of the Allentown area's Reformed congregation, and the leading elder of Easton's Reformed congregation, Peter Kichlein. Kichlein later commanded a regiment at the Battle of Long Island, was captured, and was eventually released. As the committees began to discuss military actions, sectarian members withdrew, leaving only church people, Lutherans and Reformed.[15]

Of Lancaster's twelve most important revolutionary leaders, three were Lutheran and two were Reformed. (The others were Anglican and Presbyterian.) Lutheran innkeeper Adam Reigart, "long Lancaster's most radical agitator," hosted protest meetings in his own home in the months following the "tea act crisis." After the April 1775 clash of Minutemen and British regulars at Lexington and Concord, Reigart's Grape Tavern "bustled with activity as visitors came and went inquiring about the latest news from Massachusetts." On May 1, a large crowd that taxed the "Grape's physical capacity" assembled and resolved to "defend and protect the religious and civil rights of this and our sister colonies with our lives and fortunes." The group passed resolutions providing for the formation of militia companies. Lutheran Mathias Slough was elected colonel and the Lutheran John Hubley and Reformed Casper Schaffner were named majors. In response to requests for supplies, Slough donated his supply of gunpowder to the developing military units. He later became one of Lancaster County's "largest suppliers of war provisions." Reigart and Reformed Casper Schaffner served on the county's six-member committee of safety.[16]

Across the Susquehanna River in York County, in 1774 Michael Swope, a member of Yorktown's Reformed church, presided over a meeting at which residents organized a committee of correspondence. On December 16 of that year the freeholders elected three Reformed churchmen, Baltzer Spangler, Peter Reel, and George Eichelberger, to the committee of safety. Eichelberger then was sent as the county's delegate to the state provincial convention. In the fall of 1774, even before the Continental Congress advised that a colonial militia be organized, Michael Doudell became captain of a company for which both Scots-Irish and Germans volunteered. In early July 1775 the troops attended services in York's German Reformed Church, where they were encouraged by Pastor Daniel Wagner "to keep God before their eyes" during the expedition and then they would "be assured of his protection," ate a "farewell meal," and marched off to join the Continental army "carrying a banner that proclaimed Liberty or Death." Swope became a colonel in the Continental army's Flying Camp. Eichelberger and Spangler were among the organizers of the local militia, which included "at least twenty members of York's Reformed congregation." In western York County, Conewago's Pennsylvania German Roman Catholics joined the revolutionary forces, among them Peter Brichner, Henry Eckenroth Jr., Christian Hemler, and Peter Kehler, who was stationed at Valley Forge during the winter of 1777–78.[17]

Of course, Pennsylvania Germans in the Philadelphia area were active in the revolutionary movement. Philadelphia Lutheran and Reformed soldiers quickly formed military units after Lexington and Concord. The "field officers who were elected in May, 1775, included [Lutherans] Francis Hasenclever: George Laib: Heinrich Keppele's son, John Keppele." On Sundays, Lutheran and Reformed soldiers, "accompanied by fife and drum," marched to Zion Lutheran Church on Cherry Street and to the Reformed Church on Race Street. "The accompanying music was deemed so execrable that the fifers and drummers were told to practice more diligently." A company of German schoolboys also marched for muster at the Lutheran Church. A year later, Lutheran Christopher Ludwick, while delivering baked goods, scouted Hessian positions around Trenton. He passed on his information to General George Washington, who led his troops across the Delaware River to attack the Hessian mercenaries on Christmas night, 1776. Among them was a "picked force of Pennsylvania soldiers" led by German Reformed Daniel Hunter from Berks County. Helping to protect Philadelphia from a British counterattack was the Northern Liberties Militia Battalion, commanded by Colonel William Will, a member of the city's Reformed Church. Guarding upper Philadelphia County was "Moravian Frederick Antes who organized local units of the Pennsylvania Militia."[18]

Support for the Revolution also developed among Pennsylvania Germans outside Pennsylvania. Significant numbers of Pennsylvania Germans had moved into western Maryland. "On the eve of the Revolution, there were fifteen

Lutheran, fourteen Reformed," and an undetermined number of Mennonite and Dunker congregations in that province. They were unhappy because in Maryland all colonists, regardless of their denominational affiliations, had to pay taxes to the legally established Church of England. "The Germans constituted the largest group of immigrants who remained outside the official church." They were a "strong, active, relatively closed group of dissenters who had long demanded equal rights" with the Anglicans.[19]

The church tax was an "explosive" issue that hastened the Germans toward Revolution. Churchmen "Weller, Koontz, Hoover, Westfall [and] Nead attended a protest meeting in the town of Frederick." In 1775, Reformed Jonathan Hager, founder of Hagerstown, became a member of Frederick County's "committee of observation," as did members of Frederick's Reformed congregation Peter Hoffman, Elias Brunner, Frederick Kemp, John Ramsbaugh, Jacob Miller, and Nicolas Hower. Pacifistic Mennonites, Dunkers, and other sectarians were "sympathetic with the Patriots . . . though they could not bear arms" and "supported the American cause with money."[20]

Rebellion was developing also in Dunmore County (now Shenandoah) in the "Valley" of Virginia, where 60 percent of the population was of Pennsylvania German background. There, Pastor Mühlenberg's oldest son, John Peter Gabriel, served the heavily German Beckford Parish. Peter's father had instructed him to go to London for Anglican ordination so that he could receive his salary from the civil government of Virginia, which had legally established the Church of England. Unlike his father, Peter entered fully into public life. Already a magistrate in 1773, in the following year he was elected chairman of the Mullerstadt, now called Woodstock, freeholders. They gathered "to consider the best mode . . . to secure their liberties and properties." Residents then named him chairman of their committee of correspondence and resolutions committee.[21]

When Virginia's governor, John Murray, earl of Dunmore, dissolved the colony's House of Burgesses in 1774, young Mühlenberg became one of Dunmore County's two representatives to Virginia's extralegal convention. The convention appointed him colonel of a regiment of Virginia troops. When he returned to Woodstock to recruit, he is said to have concluded a worship service by announcing that "in the language of Holy Writ, there was a time for all things, a time to preach and a time to pray," and that "there was a time to fight and that time had now come!" He subsequently recruited several hundred men to serve in his regiment and marched them to join the Continental army at Cambridge. His brother Frederick disapproved of his action and wrote, "You have become too involved in matters with which as a preacher you have nothing whatsoever to do." Peter's father felt likewise. He had worried about Peter when he was a boy who liked to hunt and fish rather than study and pray. In time,

Peter Mühlenberg rose to the rank of major general in the Continental army. He served with distinction at Charleston, Brandywine, Monmouth, and Yorktown and became the most visible Pennsylvania German in America's revolutionary armed forces.[22]

Other Pennsylvania Germans also achieved fame in the Continental army. Lutheran Christopher Ludwick became "Baker-General of the Army," and Bodo Otto became the "senior surgeon," treating both American and Hessian wounded. They supervised numerous subordinates in various units. Although their names and denominational backgrounds have survived, there were several thousand Pennsylvania German soldiers about whom such information is not readily available. Some Pennsylvania Germans began their service in German regiments, but most eventually were placed in units of mixed ethnic identity.[23]

Some military units had Pennsylvania German chaplains. Peter Mühlenberg's Lutheran friend Christian Streit served his Eighth Virginia Regiment. In Pennsylvania, Northampton County's Reformed pastor Abraham Blumer and Philadelphia's Reformed Casper Dietrich Weyberg served their units' spiritual needs. Unlike many militia chaplains who served only briefly, the unordained Reformed Philip Jacob Michael was the chaplain of Berks County Militia's First Battalion from 1777 until early 1781. Unordained Lutheran pastor Henry Moeller was appointed in 1777 to serve the Pennsylvania State Regiment and in 1778 "was appointed chaplain to the Germans in the main army." The German-speaking Swiss Reformed John Conrad Bücher became chaplain to Pennsylvania's German Regiment and to the Second Battalion of the Lancaster County Militia. (Presbyterian and Congregational chaplains far outnumbered those from the German churches.)[24]

Pastors on the home front also were supportive. When, in 1775, the troops were about to leave Lancaster for service in New England, Reformed pastor John Albert Conrad Helfenstein advised them that when they stood on the "field of conflict," heard "the booming of the cannon," and saw the "dead and dying lying around" them, they should "be of good courage, and shout, 'if God be for us who can be against us.'" Later, after the Battle of Trenton, to the Hessian prisoners who were confined to barracks in Lancaster, he quoted the prophet Isaiah, informing them, "Ye have sold yourselves for naught and will be redeemed without money." In Philadelphia, Reformed minister Caspar Weyberg preached to large numbers of Hessians during the British occupation of the city in 1777 and 1778, and "so boldly asserted the justice of the American cause" and the "wickedness of the oppressors that the British began to feel the effects of his fearless appeals in the daily desertions of their . . . mercenaries." To silence him, the British imprisoned him and "threatened his life." According to Isaac Potts, whose Valley Forge home General Washington used as his headquarters, German Reformed John Christian Runkel was a "most devout Christian and true Patriot," whose "presence among Washington's men was always attended with good results." As General Friedrich von Steuben struggled to make the English-speaking troops understand his commands, he noticed the bilingual Runkel and used him effectively as a translator. Runkel was awaiting ordination, permission for which was granted by the Reformed ministerium. He was ordained by Daniel Wagner and William Hendel in 1778.[25]

Possibly in retaliation for the German clergymen's support of the Revolution, the British used their church buildings for their own purposes. Weyberg complained that during the British occupation of Philadelphia, "my beautiful church was torn up." When the British left the city in 1778 and the congregation returned to the building, he preached on Psalm 79, "O God the heathen are come into Thine inheritance; thy holy temple they have defiled." H. M. Mühlenberg noted that Zion Lutheran in Philadelphia was so devastated that worshippers had to bring their own chairs to sit on. At the Lutheran Church in Barren Hill, near Germantown, the British tore off the doors and shutters, removed the pews and altar, and burned them, probably for heat. They used the building as a stall for their horses. During the Battle of Germantown, the British occupied the Lutheran Church there, "planted cannons in it, and fired from the windows." H. M. Mühlenberg confided to his journal, "one can just imagine what the building looks like." The revolutionaries too usurped some German churches. The Lutheran church in Lebanon and the Moravian church at Hebron were transformed into prisons for captured Hessian soldiers. The German Reformed congregation in Frederick, Maryland, fared better. It purchased from the state a parcel of loyalist Daniel Dulany's confiscated land for the expansion of its burying ground.[26]

Also rendering church property unsuitable for normal activities was its use as hospitals. After the Battle of Trenton in 1776, wounded soldiers were treated in Easton's and Allentown's Reformed churches and in the Moravian buildings at Bethlehem. Twice between 1776 and 1778, the "general hospital" of the American army was located in Bethlehem. The single Brethren's house contained seven hundred, and more were placed elsewhere. The Moravian settlement at Lititz also housed the wounded, and "120 died there." After the Battle of Brandywine in 1777, wounded soldiers were treated in Chester County's East Vincent Reformed Church. Lutheran church buildings at Reading, Lebanon, and elsewhere also provided housing for the casualties.[27]

Whether pastors and people willingly provided facilities and care for the wounded soldiers is open to question. Pastor H. M. Mühlenberg "protested vigorously against the proposed conversion" of his Trappe church building to a hospital. "Such confiscations of church property," he wrote, "are hardly to be found among the Turks and Persions. Much less is it customary in Christian Kingdoms and States, . . . except the degenerated Britons who of late have spared the Popish Chappels and Quaker Meetings in Philadelphia and profaned our churches." (Note Mühlenberg's hostility to Roman Catholics and Quakers.) When General Washington ordered Moravian John Ettwein, soon to be come a bishop, to receive wounded soldiers after the Battle of Long Island in 1776, Moravians at Lititz considered it "disagreeable news" and objected, but to "no avail." They complained that on December 20, "15 wagons full of sick soldiers" arrived and filled all of the rooms and halls. "It certainly is not easy to reconcile ourselves to this enforced surrender of our houses for such use," they said. By the end of August 1778, "110 soldiers [had died and] were buried there.[28]

In contrast, when General Washington ordered five hundred wounded troops to be transported to the Ephrata Cloisters, the "Brethren and Sisters immediate mobilized as nurses, orderlies, and provisioners." Their effort cost them dearly as they contracted the "camp fever," scarlet fever, and typhus that the soldiers brought with them. Approximately 28 percent of the cloisters' residents died and were buried with the soldiers in "God's acre."[29]

After it was used as a hospital, the revolutionaries commandeered the Reformed Church in Allentown for a different reason. As the British approached Philadelphia in September 1777, members of the Continental Congress fled to Lancaster and then to York. Before leaving, they ordered that Philadelphia's bells to be taken to safe locations. They feared that the British would melt them and use the metal for cannon and cannon balls. Farmers' wagons carried many to Easton and others to Allentown. The one now known as the Liberty Bell was placed in an excavation under the floor of Allentown's German Reformed church. Pastor Blumer's sermon record indicates that no services were held in the building until June 1778, when the bell was carried back to Philadelphia. The Continental Congress provided funds to repair the building.[30]

Although not used for any purpose other than worship, Hain's (St. John's) German Reformed Church, in Berks County, near what is now Wernersville, revised the inscription over the door. When it was constructed in 1766, the builders carved in stone the words, "All who go in and out must be true to God and King." After the war, someone "climbed up to it and cut out the word 'King.'" To this day, the "mutilated" stone remains where it was as a reminder of the members' sentiments.[31]

Several pastors' homes required changes too. While Continental troops camped near Fegleysville in northwestern Philadelphia County in 1777, General Anthony Wayne took over Falkner Swamp Reformed Church pastor Nicolas Pomp's parsonage and used it as his headquarters. He left it undamaged when the troops moved out. The British plundered the Chestnut Hill home of Reformed pastor Michael Schlatter. He had been sent by the Dutch Reformed Church in 1746 to supervise German Reformed congregations in Pennsylvania and surrounding colonies and to organize an administrative body. Possibly because news of his immoral behavior in Switzerland before he came to Pennsylvania had reached his colleagues, he was excluded by the ministerium that he had organized. Subsequently, he became a chaplain to the Royal American Regiment in the British army during the French and Indian War and "may have served as a chaplain to a Pennsylvania unit during the Henry Bouquet expedition into the Ohio country against the Indians" in 1764. He resigned his commission and supported the Revolution. Two of his sons served in the American army. During the British occupation of Philadelphia, they imprisoned Schlatter for approximately five months, during which he was reported to have been "reduced to hunger and misery." The British destroyed not only his house but also his eight hundred books, papers, maps, and household items. Like Jacob Duché, the Anglican rector of Philadelphia's prestigious Christ Church and chaplain of the Continental Congress, Schlatter changed his allegiance for reasons that never became known. Shortly after he was released, he asked British general William Howe for permission to renew his oath to Great Britain. The general forwarded Schlatter's request to officials in London as he was preparing to take his army to New York in the spring of 1778, but none responded. Unlike Duché, who went to England and later returned to the United States, much reduced in status, Schlatter remained in Pennsylvania and lived more or less happily ever after.[32]

The home of the Germantown Reformed pastor Samuel Dubendorf received similar attention from the British. He was caught in a crossfire. Because he had come to America with the Hessians in 1776, had served as their chaplain, and had spent four months in British-held New York before coming to Pennsylvania, some of his parishioners suspected him of being a loyalist and forced him to leave. He went to the Lykens Valley, east of the Susquehanna River, between present-day Harrisburg and Sunbury, where he was in danger from both British and Indian attacks. Armed men accompanied him to his services. Nevertheless, he was fortunate to have avoided the fate of the Cumberland County Anglican missionary David Batwell, whom local rebels "tossed into an icy river" for his alleged Toryism.[33]

Occasionally, the opposite occurred. Despite what Pastor John Christian Stahlschmidt called his efforts to "avoid" the disaffected in his York-area congregations, he claimed that those who "vented their rage against the Congress were dissatisfied with me." Under the circumstances, he decided to resign and return to Europe. York County lieutenant Richard McAllister reported to the Executive Council of Pennsylvania that "two hundred German opponents to militia duty agreed they would neither muster nor pay the fine and that they would kill anyone who tried to make them." John William Weber had a similar problem with the "disaffected" in his charge near Wind Gap in Northampton County. He had to leave there because his parishioners claimed that "he preached too much about the war," and went to southwestern Pennsylvania, where he became the first "regularly ordained clergyman in that area." His baptismal register eventually included thirty-eight hundred names.[34]

Under such circumstances, church activities changed. Weyberg lamented that during the British occupation of Philadelphia in 1777, his congregation "scattered," as members, with many other Philadelphians, sought refuge elsewhere. Mühlenberg's daughter-in-law, Peggy Kunze, complained in 1776 that so many of the militiamen from Trappe had gone to New York that "next Sunday, we shall have very few men in our church." The pastors too had difficulty in assembling. Weyberg could not attend the 1776 meeting of the Reformed group because of the danger of a British attack. Lutheran pastor Christopher Emanuel Schultze wrote that the "sad condition caused by the war and the difficulty of providing travel expenses" would prevent him from attending the ministerium's meeting in 1778. He predicted that attendance by the preachers would be "meagre." Attendance at both the Lutheran and Reformed meetings was so low in that year that the pastors could not conduct important business.[35]

After the hostilities ended, however, some Pennsylvania German churches added to their rolls in unusual ways. Four of the communicants on April 27, 1782, at Christ Reformed Church in Middletown, Maryland, were identified as "prisoners of war." The records of Reading's Lutheran congregation contain the names of "some of the mercenary soldiers who had been imprisoned and remained in the town." "A prisoner of war chaplain captured at Trenton," Henry Giesy, stayed in America and served Reformed congregations in the Shenandoah Valley of Virginia and later in Pennsylvania. Frederick Melshimer, chaplain of "a Dragoon Regiment of the Brunswick Auxiliaries" was captured at the Battle of Bennington in 1777. Exchanged for an American chaplain, he resigned his commission, married a Pennsylvania German wife, and "assumed charge of several Lutheran congregations in Lancaster County."[36]

The Amish experience was different. "The social pressure to conform was just too much for some Amish young people. A number left (or just never joined) the church and cast their futures with the patriot Committees." Some even joined the armed forces. "After the war, there was a steady flow of converts to the Tunkers or Brethren, German Baptists, and even to the Lutherans as well as the Moravians." "To the Amish community the Revolutionary War was more disruptive than the assaults of the Indians" during the French and Indian War.[37]

The Amish were among the Pennsylvania German pacifistic sectarians, including in this context the Moravians, whose outward religious lives were most affected by the Revolution. They were nonconformists. Their ancestors had suffered martyrdom in Europe rather than conform to the legally established Roman Catholic, Lutheran, or Reformed churches. They took seriously the scriptural admonition to beat their "swords into ploughshares and their spears into pruning hooks, and know of no war." They could not fit a theory of revolution into their theology. Furthermore, like H. M. Mühlenberg, they believed that they owed a debt of loyalty to the British kings to whom their fathers had affirmed allegiance.[38]

The sectarians' beliefs brought them into conflict with Pennsylvania's revolutionary government. In 1776 the state convention required all voters to take an oath to support the new state constitution. When the voluntary associations, formed in 1776, failed to provide sufficient manpower for military defense, the legislature made service in the militia mandatory for all adult men, "except conscientious objectors who were to pay fines based on property assessments" or to hire substitutes. Although these acts were modified slightly, the basic provisions remained in effect until 1789.[39]

The Mennonites, Amish, Dunkers, Schwenkfelders, and Moravians refused to obey the most important articles of the Test Acts. Like the Quakers, they did not swear oaths in general or this one in particular. When the Continental Congress declared a "day of fasting and prayer" for July 20, 1775, Moravians at Lititz prayed for "our whole country and for George III." They asked how they could "forever renounce a King who was our great benefactor?" Moravians who took the oath of allegiance to the state, as required by the Test Act of 1776, were denied the sacrament of Holy Communion and excluded from the community. The Dunkers, at their annual meeting in 1779, also determined to exclude members who took the oath of allegiance to the state, claiming, "we can not know whether God has rejected the king and chosen the [American] state, while the king had the government; therefore we could not with a good conscience, repudiate the king and give allegiance to the state."[40]

The law produced numerous protests. In 1777, fifteen hundred "Schwenkfelders, Separatists, and many others" from Philadelphia, Northampton, and Berks counties signed a petition that they intended to present to the Pennsylvania Assembly. The petition never reached the Assembly, which had fled to York because of the British advance on the state capital. Later, John Ettwein petitioned the Pennsylvania Assembly and the Continental Congress to have the Moravians excused from taking the oath and gained his objective in 1779.[41]

Pacifists also refused to bear arms. It was difficult for recruiters to fill battalions in Lancaster County's Mennonite townships. Mennonite constable John Newcomer would not even provide a list of eligible men in Hempfield Township. Mennonites, Amish, Dunkers, and Moravians of Earl Township declined to drill or to hire substitutes. The Moravians' diarist at Lititz observed that the young people hid in the woods to avoid the militia draft. Benjamin Franklin, no friend of the Pennsylvania Germans, proposed that those who would not fight be fined. Ettwein persuaded leading Americans, including Washington,

Henry Laurens, Samuel Adams, and John Hancock, to understand and tolerate the Moravians' position on military service.[42]

Payment of wartime taxes was another problem, especially for the pacifists. Mennonites and Dunkers decided that they would pay what was demanded by the state in accord with Christ's command to Peter to "render unto Caesar that which is Caesar's." Some rationalized that their payments went to "feed the hungry and give the Thirsty Drink." It was more likely that they went to the military. A petition from sectarians in Frederick County, Maryland, asked for permission to comply in "produce instead of cash." Mennonite farmers in Lancaster County did provide "Conestoga wagons" and the "powerful draft horses that drew them."[43]

The revolutionaries made the pacifists suffer for their beliefs. A "Schwenkfelder chronicler" complained that rebellious Americans insisted that anyone who "did not actively join their cause was against them and was to be treated accordingly." The Pennsylvania Assembly raised the fines on those who would not drill. Ettwein directed his people in the Bethlehem area to withhold payment until the amount was actually seized. A York County Mennonite "who talked about the folly of mustering at a barn raising . . . was sentenced to be tarred and feathered." In 1777 the Assembly required that those who had not taken the oath turn over their rifles "to designated collectors." Revolutionaries sometimes demanded other possessions as well. A Berks County farmer refused to surrender his horse, for which he was labeled a "Tory" and imprisoned. Those who could not pay their taxes and fines had their goods impounded. The Northampton County Court even ordered nonjurors to leave the state within thirty days and confiscated their belongings, including their "Beds, Bedding, linen, Bibles, and Books" and sold them for about forty thousand pounds. Inevitably, the proceedings became corrupt, as some auctioneers sold items at less than their appraised value and as some officials lined their own pockets with the proceeds. Vice president of Pennsylvania George Bryan mildly and ineffectively rebuked Northampton County lieutenant John Wetzell for his excessive zeal in prosecuting Mennonite violators of the Test Act. In June 1778, ten Northampton County Mennonites were jailed for refusal to take the oath. Also in 1778, the Assembly declared that those who had not sworn allegiance to the new government were to be denied all "rights and privileges enjoyed by freemen . . . and forfeit all legal rights; schoolmasters, merchants, apothecaries, doctors, surgeons were not to be allowed to carry on their professions," apparently regardless of whether they had paid their fines and taxes. Those who did not cooperate fully with the rebels would have agreed with Conrad Bücher, the secretary of the Reformed ministerium, who wrote, "We live in precarious times."[44]

The harassment that pacifistic Pennsylvania Germans experienced during the Revolution caused some to seek homes elsewhere. Until that conflict, they had prospered and lived peacefully with their neighbors. Their failure to support the War of American Independence led to hostility and discrimination against them. Again, as in Europe, they considered themselves "a people apart." The strict enforcement of Pennsylvania's wartime measures caused them to look back nostalgically to the government of the British kings, which had provided a "milder climate for pacifists." In 1786 a group of Mennonites left Bucks County to form their own community on the Niagara peninsula in Ontario, Canada. Another thirty families were reported by the *Pennsylvania Gazette* in 1789 to be ready to go from Lancaster County to the Niagara country. A decade later, other Bucks County Mennonites purchased a thousand more acres of land in Ontario. So many Mennonites and Amish settled there that that the area came to resemble southeastern Pennsylvania in the culture of its people and its place names.[45]

Some churchmen also were reluctant to pay the war taxes or to serve in the military forces. Possibly because of the rampant inflation, some Berks County farmers in 1780 could not afford to pay the high levies assessed that year. Consequently, residents of Bern, Bethel, and Tulpehocken townships—heavily Lutheran and Reformed territory—conducted a "tax revolt," and numerous township officials refused even to try to collect taxes and militia fines. The state supreme court showed them no mercy and fined them for their "treasonous and seditious" actions. Also in Berks County, William Reeser, a member of Reading's Reformed congregation, explained that he and his group "opposed taking up arms" and implied that they did not intend to do so. In Cumberland County, where most German-speaking settlers were Lutheran and Reformed, the Scots-Irish, "who loved both Johns—Calvin and Barleycorn," provided more defense of the area than the "more taciturn Germans."[46]

Despite the hesitation of some Pennsylvania Germans to support the Revolution wholeheartedly, few were loyalists, or, as such people were commonly called, "Tories." The best known was the Dunker publisher Christoph Saur II. Following in the footsteps of his father, he had published a popular German-language newspaper and almanac that "had a wide circulation up and down the seaboard." The Saurs had published numerous books, including German editions of the Bible. They were benefactors of the Germantown Academy and the Philadelphia Hospital, but the Revolution ruined the Saurs. Because of Christoph Saur's religious pacifism, submission "to the powers that be," and "devotion to the English monarchy," he was labeled "an enemy of American liberty." During the British occupation of Philadelphia, General Howe gave him Henrich Müller's print shop and chose him as his German printer. When he continued to publish pro-British material after the Americans returned to the city in 1778, he was "stripped of his estate, his possessions, and his very clothes." General Peter Mühlenberg intervened on Saur's behalf and effected his release, but Saur was not permitted to remain in his Germantown home or to resume his career as a publisher. His son, Christoph Saur III, left Philadelphia with the British troops and went to England to obtain compensation for his loyalty to England, and later became the king's printer in New Brunswick, where many loyalists had settled.[47]

The Pennsylvania Germans welcomed the end of the fighting in 1781. No doubt the pacifists were especially pleased, but the church people expressed their gratitude more obviously. Pastor H. M. Mühlenberg's son Frederick reported from Philadelphia to his father that the United States Congress, the Pennsylvania Assembly, and the state's Supreme Executive Council were to meet in Zion Lutheran Church for a service of thanksgiving. The now elderly pastor was thankful for peace, for during the war he complained that he was "caught between two fires" because of his refusal to take sides publicly. As the war proceeded, however, Mühlenberg seemed "almost by imperceptible stages to have become somewhat reconciled" to the Revolution, perhaps having recognized that liberty and property were worth fighting for. Shortly after the British surrendered, he held a service of thanksgiving for his family that included the familiar hymn "Praise the Lord, O My Soul." At the Reformed ministerium's annual meeting in 1783, the secretary, Frederick Dallicker, noticed a "special joy and cheerfulness of spirit in the ministers, and also in the faithful elders, on account of the blessed times of peace." Moravians at Lititz celebrated the return of peace by illuminating their houses and playing their trombones.[48]

The Revolution changed the attitudes of many Americans, including the Pennsylvania Germans. Their deference to authority waned. A Hessian officer observed that they were "steeped in the idea of American liberty." Lutherans paid less attention to the Halle Missionary Society that had guided and supplied them during the colonial period. Reformed pastors began to ordain candidates without waiting for permission from their ecclesiastical superiors in Europe. In 1793 they severed their ties to their European superiors and organized themselves as an American denomination. Philadelphia's German Catholics organized their own ethnic parish, Holy Trinity, and in 1787 elected a German priest in defiance of their bishop, John Carroll.[49]

Politically, the American Revolution emancipated the Pennsylvania German church people. Having broken their ties with the Quakers, they began to exert political influence more consistent with their proportion of the state's population. In 1783, traveler David Shoeph wrote, "Not until this last war have Germans been seized with a passion to appear in a better light, by going after posts of honor." Although both sectarians and churchmen had held local offices in the prewar period, they increased their share thereafter. In Berks County, for example, "more than eighty percent of the justices of the peace elected between 1777 and 1780" were Germans. They moved into state and national offices as well. Approximately 25 percent of the revolutionary assemblymen from 1776 to

1778 were German churchmen—Lutherans and Reformed. Frederick Mühlenberg abandoned what he considered an unsuccessful Lutheran ministry and entered politics. He became speaker of the Pennsylvania Assembly in 1783 and was elected president of the Pennsylvania convention that ratified the federal Constitution in 1787. In 1788 he was Pennsylvania's top vote getter in the congressional elections, representing his southeastern Pennsylvania district, and served as the Speaker of the House of Representatives in the first and third United States Congresses. Peter Mühlenberg also was elected to the House in 1788, 1792, and 1798, and to the Senate in 1800. He resigned in 1801 to hold appointive positions in the national government.[50] In addition to the Mühlenberg brothers, Berks County Reformed Joseph Hiester and Nicholas Lutz, as well as Northampton County's Reformed David Dresher, John Arndt, and Stephen Balliet, served in Pennsylvania's ratifying convention in 1787. Philadelphia's Reformed-turned-Anglican Michael Hillegas was appointed treasurer of the Continental Congress in 1788.[51]

In Maryland also, the "revolutionary cause was the vehicle upon which the Germans rose into the previously forbidden territory of local and state politics. The German immigrants who had formerly been entirely unpolitical became political-minded through the Revolution."[52] Few if any of these men would have achieved these positions in the colonial government. Pastor H. M. Mühlenberg charged that the Germans were being used by the "English Presbyterian politico-theologians," who depended on the Germans' votes for their power in the new government. He complained that "hitherto they compared us Germans with sauerkraut and foul cheese."[53]

In summary, the American Revolution transformed the Pennsylvania Germans' religious lives. Although English-speaking colonists had protested vigorously since 1765, Pennsylvania Germans did not become involved significantly in the protests against Britain until 1774. Even then, there is little evidence that the Pennsylvania German "church people" or sectarians cared about issues that concerned English-speaking religious groups, such as the appointment of a bishop that Anglicans advocated and Presbyterians opposed. The Quebec Act's recognition of Roman Catholicism in Canada that so alarmed the descendents of New England Puritans did not seem to interest them. Neither did they believe that the American Revolution would initiate the millennium, as did some English-speaking churchmen.[54]

Most supportive of the Revolution were the "church people," both pastors and parishioners. Reformed pastors were more involved than Lutheran pastors, most of whom were reticent concerning the Revolution and attempted to remain neutral.[55] The pacifistic sectarians did not support the war. They reluctantly did what they could not avoid doing for the revolutionary movement. Nevertheless, with few exceptions, they were not loyalists. Both "church people" and sectarians experienced disruption of their normal patterns because of the war. Some pacifists were marginalized for their refusal to cooperate, and based their stand on religious beliefs. They and their English-speaking allies, the Quakers, lost whatever political influence they had exercised. The discrimination that they suffered was a factor in the decision of some to move to Canada, where they hoped to experience greater acceptance from a government that tolerated their beliefs and practices.

During and after the war, Pennsylvania German churchmen became more independent and relied less on European authorities. Those that had binding ties broke them; others distanced themselves. In local, state, and national governments, churchmen became more prominent than they had been in the prewar period. The American Revolution enabled the "church people" to enter more fully into American life if they desired.

The Pennsylvania Germans' theological interpretation of the American Revolution is more difficult to summarize. While Presbyterians and Congregationalists left hundreds of sermons that they preached and published,[56] Pennsylvania Germans left only a few indicators of their theological understanding of the revolt and the war that it engendered. Nevertheless, several agreed that the war was God's punishment for the Americans' sins. H. M. Mühlenberg was typical, explaining that "God who rules over all things, is first using the motherland as a rod" to chastise the American colonists. The remedy, according to Reformed pastors, was humble penitence. Whether the Americans, including the Pennsylvania Germans, were sufficiently remorseful is not a matter of record. In any case, they concluded that the "Lord had crowned [with victory] the physical and spiritual struggle" that they had survived during the American Revolution.[57]

NOTES

1. Evarts B. Greene and Virginia D. Harrington, *American Population Before the American Revolution of 1790* (New York: Peter Smith, 1932), 116; Jean R. Soderlund, ed., *William Penn and the Founding of Pennsylvania, 1680–1684: A Documentary History* (Philadelphia: University of Pennsylvania Press, 1983), 58–66; and *The Papers of Benjamin Franklin*, ed. Leonard W. Labaree et al., 39 vols. to date (New Haven: Yale University Press, 1959–), 13:132.

2. Alfred F. Buffington and Preston A. Barba, *A Pennsylvania German Grammar* (Allentown: Pennsylvania German Folklore Society, 1965), reprinted in Charles H. Glatfelter, *The Pennsylvania Germans: A Brief Account of Their Influence on Pennsylvania* (University Park: Pennsylvania Historical Association, 2000), vi; Dieter Cunz, *The Maryland Germans: A History* (Princeton: Princeton University Press, 1948), 49, 56, 58–61; Klaus Wust, *The Virginia Germans* (Charlottesville: University Press of Virginia, 1969), 28–41; and John W. Wayland, *The German Element in the Shenandoah Valley* (1907; reprint, Bowie, Md.: Heritage Books, 2000), 20–57.

3. Wilbur Zelinsky, "Religion," in *The Atlas of Pennsylvania*, ed. David J. Cuff et al. (Philadelphia: Temple University Press, 1989), 88, 91; Glatfelter, *Pennsylvania Germans*, 8; Gottlieb Mittelberger, *Journey to Pennsylvania*, ed. and trans. Oscar Handlin and John Clive (1756; reprint, Cambridge: Harvard University Press, 1960), 21, 41; William J. Hinke, ed., *Life and Letters of the Reverend John Philip Boehm . . .* (Philadelphia: Publication and Sunday School Board of the Reformed Church in the United States,

1916), 161; Sally Schwartz, *A Mixed Multitude: The Struggle for Toleration in Colonial Pennsylvania* (New York: New York University Press, 1987), 113; Stephanie Wolf, *Urban Village: Population, Community, and Family Structure in Germantown, Pennsylvania, 1680–1800* (Princeton: Princeton University Press, 1976), 9, 32–33; Karen Guenther, "'A Garden for the Friends of God': Religious Diversity in the Oley Valley," *Pennsylvania Folklife* 33, no. 3 (1984): 138–44; Frederic Klees, *The Pennsylvania Dutch* (New York: Macmillan, 1951), 2–3; and John B. Frantz, "The Awakening of Religion Among the German Settlers in the Middle Colonies," *William and Mary Quarterly* 33 (April 1976): 268.

4. Klees, *Pennsylvania Dutch*, 3–4.

5. Henry Melchior Mühlenberg, *The Journals of Henry Melchior Muhlenberg*, trans. and ed. Theodore G. Tappert and John W. Doberstein, 3 vols. (Philadelphia: Muhlenberg Press, 1942–58), 1:68, 154; William J. Hinke, *Ministers of the German Reformed Congregations in Pennsylvania and Other Colonies in the Eighteenth Century*, ed. George W. Richards (Lancaster, Pa.: Historical Commission of the Evangelical and Reformed Church, 1951), 293–95, 288–90, 255–65; John B. Frantz, "John Philip Boehm: Pioneer Pennsylvania Pastor," *Pennsylvania Folklife* 31, no. 3 (1982): 130–31; Abdel Ross Wentz, *A Basic History of Lutheranism in America* (Philadelphia: Muhlenberg Press, 1955), 42, 46–47; Adolph Spaeth et al., eds., *Documentary History of the Evangelical Lutheran Ministerium of Pennsylvania and Adjacent States: Proceedings of the Annual Conventions from 1748 to 1821* (Philadelphia: General Council of the Evangelical Lutheran Church in North America, 1898), 8–12; William J. Hinke et al., eds., *Minutes and Letters of the Coetus of Pennsylvania, 1734–1792 . . .* (Philadelphia: Reformed Church Publication Board, 1903), 256; and Charles H. Glatfelter, *Pastors and People: German Lutheran and Reformed Congregations in the Pennsylvania Field, 1717–1793*, 2 vols. (Breinigsville: Pennsylvania German Society, 1980–81), 2:117–23.

6. Klees, *Pennsylvania Dutch*, 2.

7. William T. Parsons, *The Pennsylvania Dutch: A Persistent Minority* (Boston: Twayne, 1976), 77–79, 99–100; Arthur D. Graeff, *The Relations Between the Pennsylvania Germans and the British Authorities, 1750–1776* (Norristown, Pa.: Norristown Herald, 1939), 135–39; and Lamech and Agrippa, *Chronicon Ephratense: A History of the Seventh Day Baptist Community at Ephrata. . . ,* trans. J. Max Hart (Lancaster, Pa.: S. H. Zahm, 1889), 236–37.

8. Lawrence Henry Gipson, "The American Revolution as an Aftermath of the Great War for the Empire," *Political Science Quarterly* 68 (March 1950): 86–104; Lawrence Henry Gipson, *The Coming of the American of the Revolution, 1763–1775* (New York: Harper Torchbooks, 1962), 95–100, 187–88; Benjamin Woods Labaree, *The Boston Tea Party* (New York: Oxford University Press, 1964), 141–44, 153, 156, 158–59; and Robert Middlekauff, *The Glorious Cause: The American Revolution, 1763–1789* (New York: Oxford University Press, 1982), 70–93, 124–25, 149–51, 179–85, 219–27.

9. Willi Paul Adams, "The Colonial German-Language Press and the American Revolution," in *The Press and the American Revolution,* ed. Bernard Bailyn and John B. Hench (Worcester, Mass.: American Antiquarian Society, 1980), 162–200, 214 (quotations on 200 and 214). See also William T. Parsons, *Another Rung Up the Ladder: German Reformed People in American Struggles, 1754–1783* (Collegeville, Pa.: Institute on Pennsylvania Dutch Studies, 1976), 7; and Parsons, *Pennsylvania Dutch,* 140, 145.

10. Mühlenberg, *Journals of Muhlenberg,* 2:273. See also Glatfelter, *Pastors and People,* 2:363.

11. Leonard R. Riforgiato, *Missionary of Moderation: Henry Melchior Muhlenberg and the Lutheran Church in English America* (Lewisburg: Bucknell University Press, 1980), 201–14; Paul A. W. Wallace, *The Mühlenbergs of Pennsylvania* (Philadelphia: University of Pennsylvania Press, 1950), 106–9 (quotations on 107); Theodore G. Tappert, "Henry Melchior Mühlenberg and the American Revolution," *Church History* 11 (1942): 300–301; and Roland H. Bainton, *Here I Stand: A Life of Martin Luther* (Nashville: Abingdon Press, 1950), 243, 246.

12. Karen Guenther, "Berks County," in *Beyond Philadelphia: The American Revolution in the Pennsylvania Hinterland,* ed. John B. Frantz and William Pencak (University Park: Pennsylvania State University Press, 1998), 72; Eugene R. Slaski, "The Lehigh Valley," ibid., 49–50; Paul E. Doutrich, "York County," ibid., 91.

13. Esther Forbes, *Paul Revere and the World He Lived In* (Cambridge: Riverside Press, 1942), 215–17; and Middlekauff, *Glorious Cause,* 229–31.

14. Guenther, "Berks County," 72–73 (quotations on 72). See also James I. Good, *History of the Reformed Church in the United States* (Reading, Pa.: Daniel Miller, 1899), 613.

15. Slaski, "Lehigh Valley," 50–51; Jean Stauffer Hudson, "A History of Allentown, 1762–1810," in *Allentown, 1762–1987: A Two-Hundred-Twenty-Five-Year History,* ed. Mahlon Hellerich (Allentown: Lehigh Valley Historical Society, 1987), 22; and Good, *History of the Reformed Church,* 612–13.

16. G. Terry Madonna, *The Revolutionary Leadership* (Lancaster, Pa.: Lancaster County Bicentennial Committee, 1776), 6, 8, 5, 20, 15–16, 20 (quotations on 20).

17. Doutrich, "York County," 91–92; Benjamin T. Griffen, *The Americanization of a Congregation: A History of Trinity United Church of Christ, York, Pennsylvania* (York: Trinity United Church of Christ, 1984), 11–12; and Edmund Adams and Barbara Brady O'Keefe, *Catholic Trails West: The Founding Catholic Families of Pennsylvania,* 2 vols. (Baltimore: Gateway Press, 1989), 2:349.

18. "Addenda to Watson's *Annals of Philadelphia*: Notes by Jacob Mordicai, 1836," ed. Whitefield J. Bell, *Pennsylvania Magazine of History and Biography* 98 (April 1974): 146; A. G. Roeber, *Palatines, Liberty, and Property: German Lutherans in British Colonial America* (Baltimore: Johns Hopkins University Press, 1993), 306; Parsons, *Another Rung Up the Ladder,* 13–17; and Good, *History of the Reformed Church,* 613.

19. Cunz, *Maryland Germans,* 131; and James B. Ranck et al., *A History of the Evangelical Reformed Church, Frederick, Maryland* (Frederick, 1964), 49.

20. Cunz, *Maryland Germans,* 131; and Wallace, *Mühlenbergs of Pennsylvania,* 111.

21. Freeman H. Hart, *The Valley of Virginia in the American Revolution, 1763–1789* (Chapel Hill: University of North Carolina Press, 1942), 34n3; and Carl Bridenbaugh, *Myths and Realities: Societies of the Colonial South* (New York: Atheneum, 1963), 121.

22. Middlekauff, *Glorious Cause,* 232; Wallace, *Mühlenbergs of Pennsylvania,* 111–30, 202–45 (quotations on 111, 115, and 118, respectively). See also Glatfelter, *Pastors and People,* 2:388–89.

23. Parsons, *Pennsylvania Dutch,* 144, 153; Richard K. MacMaster et al., *Conscience in Crisis: Mennonites and Other Peace Churches in America, 1739–1789* (Scottdale, Pa.: Herald Press, 1979), 340; and Henry Melchior Muhlenberg Richards, "The Pennsylvania-Germans in the Revolutionary War, 1775–1783," *Pennsylvania German Society: Proceedings and Addresses* 17 (1908): 369–72, 390–91.

24. Mühlenberg, *Journals of Muhlenberg,* 2:736; Parsons, *Pennsylvania Dutch,* 141; Henry Harbaugh, *Fathers of the German Reformed Church in the United States,* 4 vols. (Lancaster, Pa.: Springer and Westhaeffer, 1857, 1872), 2:197–200, 100–108; Parsons, *Another Rung Up the Ladder,* 17; Glatfelter, *Pastors and People* 1:92–93, 2:389; and David H. Rapp, "Philip Jacob Michael: Ecclesiastical Vagabond or 'echt Reformirte' Pastor?" *Pennsylvania Folklife* 28, no. 3 (1979): 18. English-speaking denominations provided many more chaplains than did the German churches. See Jon Butler, *Awash in a Sea of Faith: Christianizing the American People* (Cambridge: Harvard University Press, 1990), 209–11.

25. Harbaugh, *Fathers of the Reformed Church,* 2:225, 102–3, 286; Good, *History of the Reformed Church,* 627n; and Hinke et al., *Minutes and Letters of the Coetus,* 366–67.

26. Harbaugh, *Fathers of the Reformed Church,* 2:103; Mühlenberg, *Journals of Muhlenberg,* 3:82, 167–68; Wallace, *Mühlenbergs of Pennsylvania,* 165; and Daniel Zacharias, *A Centenary Sermon Preached on Whit Monday, 1847, on the Centennial Festival of the German Reformed Congregation of Frederick City, Maryland* (Frederick: Turner and Young, 1847), 9. British troops destroyed churches of the English and Scots-Irish also. See Butler, *Awash in a Sea of Faith,* 208.

27. Slaski, "Lehigh Valley," 57, 67; Good, *History of the Reformed Church,* 610–11; and Parsons, *Pennsylvania Dutch,* 146.

28. Tappert, "Mühlenberg and the American Revolution," 296–97; "Extracts from the Brethren's House and Congregation Diaries of the Moravian Church at Lititz, Pa., Relating to the Revolutionary War," trans. Abraham Reinke Beck, *Penn Germania,* old ser., 13 (November–December 1912): 854–55, 858 (quotations on 854 and 858). See also J. Taylor Hamilton and Kenneth G. Hamilton, *History of the Moravian Church: The Renewed Unitas Fratrum, 1722–1957* (Bethlehem: Interprovincial Board of Christian Education, Moravian Church in America, 1967), 226; and John W. Jordan, "The Military Hospitals at Bethlehem and Lititz During the American Revolution," *Pennsylvania Magazine of History and Biography* 20 (1896): 139.

29. E. G. Alderfer, *The Ephrata Commune: An Early American Counterculture* (Pittsburgh: University of Pittsburgh Press, 1985), 164–65; and MacMaster, *Conscience in Crisis,* 294. See also Michael Showalter, "The Good Samaritan Reconsidered: The Revolutionary War Hospital at Ephrata Cloister," *Der Reggeboge: Journal of the Pennsylvania German Society* 36 (2002): 28–40.

30. Hudson, "History of Allentown," 19; Slaski, "Lehigh Valley," 59; Parsons, *Another Rung Up the Ladder,* 21; and Good, *History of the Reformed Church,* 616.

31. Glatfelter, *Pastors and People,* 2:338.

32. George W. Roth, *History of the Falkner Swamp Reformed Church, 1720–1904* (Lebanon: Report Print, 1904), 34; Henry Harbaugh, *Life of Reverend Michael Schlatter, With a Full Account of his Travels*

and Labors Among the Germans . . . (Philadelphia: S. R. Fisher, 1857), 336–38; and Glatfelter, *Pastors and People,* 1:118–19, 31–32 (quotation on 118). See also Hinke, *Ministers of the German Congregations,* 198–99; and Kevin J. Dellape, "Jacob Duché: Whig-Loyalist?" *Pennsylvania History* 62, no. 2 (1995): 293, 300–301; and Robert G. Crist, "Cumberland County," in Frantz and Pencak, *Beyond Philadelphia,* 128.

33. Good, *History of the Reformed Church,* 605–6; Hinke, *Ministers of the German Congregations,* 186–90; and Crist, "Cumberland County," 128.

34. Good, *History of the Reformed Church,* 606; Anne M. Ousterhout, *A State Divided: Opposition in Pennsylvania to the American Revolution* (New York: Greenwood Press, 1987), 168–69; and Hinke, *Ministers of the German Congregations,* 190.

35. Wallace, *Mühlenbergs of Pennsylvania,* 127; Hinke et al., *Minutes and Letters of the Coetus,* 353, 336; and Spaeth, *Documentary History of the Evangelical Lutheran Ministerium,* 151.

36. Paul Elsworth Fogle, *A History of Christ Reformed Church* . . . , *Middletown, Maryland* (Middletown: Mick's American Printing, 1995), 25; Guenther, "Berks County," 79; Parsons, *Another Rung Up the Ladder,* 20; Hinke, *Ministers of the German Congregations,* 402–3; and Glatfelter, *Pastors and People,* 1:87.

37. Steven M. Nolt, *A History of the Amish* (Intercourse, Pa.: Good Books, 1992), 73–74; and John A. Hostetler, *Amish Society,* 3d ed. (Baltimore: Johns Hopkins University Press, 1980), 63.

38. Harold S. Bender, "The Anabaptist Vision," *Church History* 13 (1944): 3–24 (quotation on 21). See also John C. Wenger, *Even unto Death: The Heroic Witness of the Sixteenth-Century Anabaptists* (Richmond, Va.: John Knox Press, 1961), 22–30, 50, 54–55, 101–10, 112–15; and Donald F. Durnbaugh, ed., *A Source Book on the Transplantation and Development of the Church of the Brethren in the Eighteenth Century* (Elgin, Ill.: Brethren Press, 1967), 342.

39. Robert L. Brunhouse, *The Counter-Revolution in Pennsylvania, 1776–1790* (Harrisburg: Pennsylvania Historical and Museum Commission, 1942), 16–39, 180–81, 197–99 (quotation on 36).

40. Durnbaugh, *Source Book,* 344, 352, 359; and Richard C. MacMaster, *Land, Piety, and Peoplehood: The Establishment of Mennonite Communities in America, 1683–1790* (Scottdale, Pa.: Herald Press, 1985), 264; and Beck, "Extracts from the Brethren's Diaries," 861.

41. Durnbaugh, *Source Book,* 347; Hamilton and Hamilton, *History of the Moravian Church,* 226.

42. MacMaster, *Conscience in Crisis,* 315, 288, 261–62, 292; Hamilton and Hamilton, *History of the Moravian Church,* 426.

43. Durnbaugh, *Source Book,* 341 (quotation), 344, 361–62. See also MacMaster, *Conscience in Crisis,* 267, 340, 298 (quotations on 267 and 298).

44. Durnbaugh, *Source Book,* 341 (quotation), 342, 344, 348, 350, 399–400. See also MacMaster, *Conscience in Crisis,* 303, 315–16; Guenther, "Berks County," 81; Slaski, "Lehigh Valley," 61–62; Doutrich, "York County," 93–94; Francis S. Fox, *Sweet Land of Liberty: The Ordeal of the Revolution in Northampton County, Pennsylvania* (University Park: Pennsylvania State University Press, 2000), 82, 90–91; MacMaster, *Land, Piety, and Peoplehood,* 259, 265; and Hinke et al., *Minutes and Letters of the Coetus,* 352.

45. MacMaster, *Land, Piety, Peoplehood,* 249, 278–79; MacMaster, *Conscience in Crisis,* 449; and Arthur D. Graeff, "The Pennsylvania Germans in Ontario, Canada," *Pennsylvania German Folklore Society* 11 (1946): 11, 13, 22, 30.

46. Guenther, "Berks County," 81–82, 75–76; Crist, "Cumberland County," 118 (quotation), 116, 115.

47. Durnbaugh, *Source Book,* 377–422 (quotations on 368). See also Donald F. Durnbaugh, *Fruit of the Vine: A History of the Brethren, 1708–1995* (Elgin, Ill.: Brethren Press, 1997), 153–63; and Stephen L. Longenecker, *The Christopher Sauers: Courageous Printers Who Defended Religious Freedom in Early America* (Elgin, Ill.: Brethren Press, 1981), 125–40.

48. Mühlenberg, *Journals of Muhlenberg,* 3:454; Tappert, "Mühlenberg and the American Revolution," 301; Hinke et al., *Minutes and Letters of the Coetus,* 362; Beck, "Extracts from the Brethren's Diaries," 851, 858.

49. Parsons, *Another Rung Up the Ladder,* 19; Roeber, *Palatines, Liberty, and Property,* 326; Hinke et al., *Minutes and Letters of the Coetus,* 301, 451, 449; H. M. J. Klein, *The History of the Eastern Synod of the Reformed Church in the United States* (Lancaster, Pa.: Eastern Synod, 1943), 80–89; and Dale B. Light, *Rome and the New Republic: Conflict and Community in Philadelphia* (Notre Dame: Notre Dame University Press, 1996), 5–9.

50. Glatfelter, *Pastors and People,* 2:361, 420; Guenther, "Berks County," 84; Owen S. Ireland, "The Internal Revolution," *Pennsylvania History* 41, no. 1 (1974): 150; J. Paul Selsam, *The Pennsylvania*

Constitution of 1776 (Philadelphia: University of Pennsylvania Press, 1936), 187–88; Gordon S. Wood, *The Radicalism of the American Revolution* (New York: Vintage Books, 1993), 260–61; Wallace, *Mühlenbergs of Pennsylvania,* 276–82, 291; and Owen S. Ireland, *Religion, Ethnicity, and Politics: Ratifying the Constitution in Pennsylvania* (University Park: Pennsylvania State University Press, 1995), 245–47, appendix 2, "The German Vote and the Election of 1788," 283–84.

51. Parsons, *Pennsylvania Dutch,* 155, 180–81; Hudson, "History of Allentown," 22; and Parsons, *German Reformed People,* 113.

52. Cunz, *Maryland Germans,* 133–34.

53. Mühlenberg, *Journals of Muhlenberg,* 3:551.

54. Carl Bridenbaugh, *Mitre and Sceptre: Transatlantic Faiths, Ideas, Personalities, and Politics, 1689–1775* (New York: Oxford University Press, 1962); Charles H. Metzger, *The Quebec Act: A Primary Cause of the American Revolution* (New York: United States Catholic Historical Society, 1936); Melvin B. Endy, "Just War, Holy War, and Millennialism in Revolutionary America," *William and Mary Quarterly* 42 (January 1985): 3–25.

55. Tappert chides early Lutheran historians for claiming, without studying the sources, that Mühlenberg and other Lutheran pastors supported the Revolution. See Tappert, "Mühlenberg and the American Revolution," 284–85n1.

56. See Alan Heimert, *Religion and the American Mind: From the Great Awakening to the Revolution* (Cambridge: Harvard University Press, 1966), 339–515.

57. Mühlenberg, *Journals of Muhlenberg,* 2:701; Hinke et al., *Minutes and Letters of the Coetus,* 352, 383 (quotation on 383).

✳   *5*   ✳

OUT OF MANY, ONE:
PENNSYLVANIA'S ANGLICAN LOYALIST CLERGY
IN THE AMERICAN REVOLUTION

William Pencak

With the exception of the Reverend William White, who became the first bishop of Pennsylvania and was instrumental in founding the American Episcopal Church, the other ten Anglican clergymen preaching in Pennsylvania when the American Revolution broke out became loyalists. They faced a unique problem once the Americans declared independence. Upon their ordination, they had to swear to adhere faithfully to the church liturgy, which obliged them to pray for their sovereign and maintain that "it is unlawful upon any pretence whatever to take up arms against the king," and to "abhor that traitorous position." Five Anglican missionaries, supported by the British Society for the Propagation of the Gospel (in addition to one based in New Jersey), served two to four congregations each throughout the state. In Philadelphia the congregations chose and supported their own priests: St. Paul's had one, the united parish of St. Peter's and Christ Church, four; and Provost William Smith of the College of Philadelphia was an ordained cleric who sometimes preached. Between 1778 and 1781, however, only White remained in his pulpit.[1]

That outcome was not inevitable. All of the Anglican priests in Pennsylvania underwent their own odysseys and personal soul searching. They had to weigh not only the physical consequences of allegiance to self and family and political ideology, like most of their contemporaries, but also the possible eternal as well as the earthly consequences of violating an oath of loyalty that almost no other British Americans before the Revolution had to take. The stories of these men exemplify both the complexity of the development of resistance and revolutionary allegiance in Pennsylvania—a state whose prewar elite largely opposed independence—and the agony and diversity of experiences occurring in a state that underwent a fierce internal struggle over who was to rule at home.[2]

With the exception of college provost William Smith—an ardent controversialist in matters of politics, education, and religion since he arrived in the province in 1753—who served as a moderate on numerous committees to resist British policy, the Pennsylvania clergy in both Philadelphia and the hinterland initially refrained from playing any political role in the severely divided province. On June 1, 1774, after "the cruel act for blocking up Boston Harbor took effect," Christopher Marshall of the Committee of Observation and Inspection reported, Christ Church's "muffled bells rung a solemn peal at intervals, from morning till night." Yet Rector Richard Peters published a newspaper article that this had been done without his approval, and unlike other churches in town, the Anglicans held no special services, although Jacob Duché mourned the "dreadful event."[3]

But on September 7, when the first Continental Congress met, Samuel Adams, the arch-Puritan from Massachusetts, suggested that Duché open the session with a prayer, a "prudent" move Adams deliberately made—and boasted of in the *Boston Gazette*—to court some of "our warmest friends," the Anglican delegates, most of whom were from the south. Pennsylvania's Joseph Reed, like Adams an ardent patriot, bragged, "we were never guilty of a more masterly stroke of polity." Duché's reputation as a fine speaker had preceded the prayer— because he was so nearsighted, he preached and prayed without notes. The other Massachusetts Adams, John, reported to his wife, Abigail, that Duché's prayer was "as pertinent, as affectionate, as sublime, as devout as ever I heard offered up to Heaven." He described Duché himself as "one of the most ingenious men and best characters and greatest orators in the Episcopalian order upon this continent; yet a zealous friend to the liberty of the country." Congress then chose Duché as its chaplain.[4]

Shortly after war broke out the following spring, Philadelphia's other Anglican ministers, with one exception, spoke publicly on behalf of the patriot cause. The exception, ironically, was the young William White, who in the end turned out to be the only priest who remained true to the Revolution to the end. White told Timothy Matlack, one of Philadelphia's most ardent revolutionaries, that although he shared his "sentiments, I would never beat the ecclesiastical drum," his objection being "the making of the ministry instrumental to the war." Only after he took the oath of allegiance to the new nation, which he thought "was exposing his neck to great danger . . . on account of my being a clergyman of the church of England"—having violated his oath he might have been executed by the British—did White preach for the cause, and thereafter he remained faithful to it.[5]

Following the hostilities, however, the other three priests at Christ's and St. Peter's—the aged Richard Peters retired in 1775 and died in 1776—had no qualms about supporting resistance to Britain, although they were careful to tell their British correspondents that they only entered the fray reluctantly. William Smith wrote to the Society for the Propagation of the Gospel that "our people have all taken up Arms . . . we see nothing in our churches but men in their uniforms." The committees that had seized control of the city and much of Pennsylvania from a conservative government that still courted royal favor were "everywhere requesting occasional sermons on the present situation of things." Smith noted that Philadelphia's military associators demanded these talks so as to win recruits and inspire resistance if possible—if not, then to force disloyal Anglican priests to show their true colors. All six Philadelphia clergymen justified their resistance activities in a letter to the bishop of London, while they prayed that "the unhappy controversy between the Parent Country and these Colonies might be terminated upon Principles honorable and advantageous to both." They argued that if they did not support "our congregations [in which] people of all ranks have associated themselves, determined never to submit to the Parliamentary claim of taxing them at pleasure," they might "irritate the tempers of the people . . . , and even [see] our religious usefulness destroyed."[6]

William Smith was the first to speak out. "A Sermon on the Present State of American Affairs," delivered on June 23, 1775, showed him, the *London Magazine* commented in August, "to be as zealous a friend to the Liberties of America, and as warm a person against the measures of administration, as any person whatsoever." Translated into Swedish and Welsh, and reprinted numerous times in the colonies and Britain—where the sympathetic Chamberlain of London issued ten thousand copies—Smith's sermon was a stirring call to liberty. "Animated with the purest zeal for the mutual interests of Great-Britain and the colonies; ardently panting for the return of those Halcyon-days of harmony," Smith "thought it his duty, with the utmost impartiality, to attempt a state of the unhappy controversy that rends the empire in pieces." Claiming that "the idea of independence upon the parent-country, or the least licentious opposition to its just interests, is utterly foreign" to the Americans, Smith insisted "that our rightful sovereign has nowhere more loyal subjects." At the same time, he maintained that "the people of this country know their rights," which they held by "a plain original contract, entitling us to all the natural and improvable advantages of our situation." It was Britain that, through "unconstitutional exactions, violated rights, and mutual charters," called them "to worship [the] idols of Dignity and supremacy," whereas "true Dignity is to govern Freemen, not slaves, and true supremacy is to excel in Doing Good." Condemning the "doctrine of absolute non-resistance" as "fully exploded among every virtuous people," Smith called on his countrymen to "with reverence look back to the mighty purpose which your fathers had in view . . . their labors, their toils, their perseverance," and to "look forward also to distant posterity," and "figure to yourselves millions and millions to spring from your loins, who may be born freemen or slaves." He predicted that "Heaven has great and gracious purposes towards this continent, which no human power or human device shall be finally able to frustrate," and that America would be "for ages to come, a chosen seat of Freedom, Arts, and heavenly Knowledge, which are now either drooping or dead in most countries of the old world." America as a continent, a divinely chosen refuge for freedom in a world dominated by tyranny—all the basic ideas of Thomas Paine's *Common Sense* are here except the deduction that independence was the logical conclusion.[7]

Smith was a Latitudinarian whose theology verged on deism—the belief that there was an omnipotent God but that humankind worked out its own destiny—and who rested his case largely on the Lockean argument that occupation and development of the land gave Americans the natural right to rule themselves.[8] Two weeks later, when Jacob Duché, whose theology veered more toward the mystical, preached to the First Battalion of Philadelphia a sermon entitled "The Duty of Standing Fast in Our Spiritual and Temporal Liberties," he stressed instead that "civil liberty is as much the gift of God" as religious liberty. Choosing as his text Galatians 5:1, "stand fast in the liberty whereby Christ hath made us free," Duché dedicated his text to George Washington, whom he knew well from his service as chaplain of the Continental Congress, out of respect "for his many amiable virtues in his private as in public life."[9]

On July 20, when Congress proclaimed a fast day, Duché changed his tone to suit the occasion. "An unnatural war burst forth in the bowels of our nation," he chided his hearers at Christ Church, because it was "carried away by the streams of prosperity." "Cherish not an overweening fondness for gaiety and pleasure," he warned the audience, "if we wish the God of hosts to return to look down from heaven and visit our American vine."[10] The same day, Thomas Coombe preached from St. Peter's in a similar vein: "The last remains of uncorrupted liberty" in the world "are committed to your care," and "forbid it heaven that the glorious inheritance of millions yet unborn should ever perish in our hands, or be violated by our national iniquity." If the American struggle for freedom was not accompanied by moral as well as civic virtue, Coombe foretold that a "continent . . . with all the bounties of existence" would "become once more the dreary haunt of savages." He dedicated his sermon to a pew holder of the United Churches, "that illustrious citizen and philosopher, Benjamin Franklin of America, to whose dignified character titles are no addition."[11]

Although they had tried to advocate both spirited resistance and the restoration of harmony, the Anglican clergy had to make their choice after independence was proclaimed. Would they continue, as required by their oaths, to pray for the king as their lawful ruler? At the United Churches, recently chosen rector Jacob Duché called a meeting of the vestry on July 4, 1776, and asked them whether it was best "for the peace and welfare of the congregation, to shut up the churches or to continue the service, without using the prayers for the royal family." The vestry responded that "for the peace and well being of the churches," the prayers should be omitted.[12]

None of the Anglican ministers, however, supported the intolerant constitution of 1776 that proclaimed Pennsylvania a Christian republic and required a Christian oath for office holding and voting. Henry Melchior Mühlenberg, the leading minister of the German Lutheran Church in America, first proposed these measures. Mühlenberg had been absent from Pennsylvania for several months. After he returned in 1776, he was displeased that in the proposed constitution "the Christian religion is paid scant or no respect, but is rather considered [in] an indifferent, arbitrary manner." On September 16 he approached several of the town's ministers and warned them that without a religious test it would seem "as if a Christian people were ruled by Jews, Turks, Spinozists, Deists, and perverted naturalists." Duché made light of Mühlenberg's fears, commenting that an oath not limited to Christians "was well suited to the present time and conditions, for, after all, in God's forbearance there must be one corner in the world where practical atheists, so-called deists, perverted naturalists, and similar genteel rabble could have their place of abode"—that is, Pennsylvania. William Smith, for his part, "expressed the opinion that it was sufficient if members of the new government merely confessed faith in the Supreme Being as creator and upholder of all things." Philadelphia's Old Light Presbyterian minister Francis Alison backed them up.

Mühlenberg next turned to the German Reformed and Swedish ministers—a Swedish church survived from the days of New Sweden—who were far more amenable to his suggestion. On September 26 a letter appeared in the *Pennsylvania Gazette* warning against the toleration of Turks, Jews, and infidels. Benjamin Franklin, president of the Constitutional Convention, presented the test oath on the ministers' behalf. Although personally tolerant, he complained that he "was overpowered by numbers" and was lucky to achieve a compromise whereby "no further or more Extended profession of faith" than mere Christianity "should ever be exacted." Franklin at this point was the titular head of Pennsylvania's radical revolutionaries.[13]

Although they seemed to support independence at first by permitting the loyalty oath to be omitted in their services, three of Philadelphia's Anglican clergy changed their minds. Coombe, Duché, and Stringer ultimately affirmed their allegiance to the Crown and went into exile. In so doing, they revealed the personal anxieties that came from being forced to take a political stand requiring them to forsake either their community or their church. William Smith took his own path, which may best be described as watchful waiting to see which side came out on top before he left the province for Maryland.

Smith was actually the first of the ministers to feel the patriots' wrath. Even before independence was declared, as early as January 6, 1776, the Philadelphia

Council of Safety prepared to "enquire respecting the conduct of Parson Smith and Christ Church parishioner Tench Francis, they having, as reported, spoken and acted very disrespectfully of the Congress and all our proceedings." On February 14, 1776, Smith confirmed these suspicions when he preached a funeral oration to honor General Richard Montgomery, a former major in the British army, and the American soldiers who had been killed in the attempt to conquer Canada that winter. In a city alive with talk of independence and the recent publication of Thomas Paine's *Common Sense,* Smith dwelled instead on Montgomery's "principles of loyalty to his sovereign," which "remained firm and unshakeable." Smith prayed "most ardently" that "Heaven may speedily reunite us in every bond of affection and interest, and that the British Empire may again become the envy and admiration of the universe." A Congress in which many if not most members already supported independence refused to publish the sermon, and John Adams termed it "an insolent performance." Smith published it at his own expense.[14]

Smith's main difficulty seems to have been that although he believed America's cause was just, he also thought it unwinnable given Britain's wealth and strength. On March 15, 1776, in conversation with Timothy Matlack and James Cannon, two of Philadelphia's radical leaders, he referred to Britain's hiring foreign troops and willingness to spend whatever it took to win the war: "Great Britain would mortgage America for as much money as would enable her to conquer it." Between March 13 and April 24, 1776, under the name "Cato"—the Roman patriot who warned of the destruction of his country—Smith published eight letters in the *Pennsylvania Gazette* opposing independence.

Until the British army approached in December 1776, Philadelphia-area committees tended to leave people alone who remained neutral. That month they arrested Smith when he refused to "sign an association in favor of the rebellion." They released him after the Battle of Trenton, but once again, when the British approached the city in August 1777, he was one of a number of Philadelphians singled out and made to promise not to do anything "injurious to the United Free States of America." After he complied, like much of the city's population, Smith left town, retiring to family property near Valley Forge. While there, he sometimes preached at St. Peter's in the Great Valley and St. David's in Radnor. Yet he returned to enemy lines at least once during the British occupation, for he showed Ambrose Serle, Lord Howe's secretary, David Rittenhouse's orrery, or miniature planetarium, at the college.[15]

When Smith returned to Philadelphia after the British left, the state legislature and President Joseph Reed especially began to question the government of the college. On November 28, 1779, it passed an act dissolving the college's board of trustees and faculty on the grounds that the present, Anglican-dominated institution had "departed from the plan of the original founders, and narrowed the foundation of said institution." The revolutionary government waited until 1779 to do so, both because the college's principal founder, Benjamin Franklin, remained in the city until December 1776, and because the British occupied the city from 1777 to 1778. Franklin had packed the board of trustees with Anglicans, as he believed that only they could guarantee a liberal education free from religious bigotry. Smith, who was hired as the college's vice provost and had raised more money and interested himself more in the college's governance and welfare over the past thirty years than anyone, left Philadelphia for Maryland early in 1780, after the Pennsylvania government took over the college, promptly granting an honorary degree to Thomas Paine in the bargain.[16] Smith vented his spleen by publishing there "The Candid Retrospect; or The American War Examined, by Whig Principles," in which he deplored the Revolution and the misery the war had brought, concluding, "Miserable Americans! Say now who are your foes."[17]

Yet it is hard to say, in short, whether Smith had real problems making up his mind or whether he opportunistically catered to both sides as suited his immediate situation. Later in 1780 Smith began to salvage his reputation with the patriots. On December 28 he delivered a talk to the Pennsylvania Masons in Christ Church, with George Washington, the nation's most prominent Mason, in attendance. Comparing Washington to Cincinnatus, he told the assembled audience that they could "describe virtue from his example." Smith's admiration for Washington seemed boundless. He successfully proposed him for membership in the American Philosophical Society, and in November 1782, when the school he established in Maryland was incorporated as a college, he named it after the general. In 1790 Smith would celebrate the removal of the national capital from New York, and with it the arrival of President Washington. On July 4 he returned to Philadelphia to preach before the Cincinnati, a society of former Revolutionary War officers named after the ancient Roman hero to whom he had compared Washington. Here he praised "the rising American states" and urged them to "the support of freedom and virtue." Given his lifelong connection with colleges, he thought the best way to ensure that America would become "a free and happy land" was through "wise establishments for the instruction of youth, the advancement of the arts and sciences, the encouragement of industry, and the maintenance of religion and morality."[18]

Thomas Coombe also ran afoul of the patriots. Like his counterparts at the Society for the Propagation of the Gospel, Coombe objected to omitting the prayers for the king of England, which he was still including as late as June 1776. That month, Charles Willson Peale, the famous painter and a fervent revolutionary, "hissed the minister" when he made the prayer. Coombe continued to preach, omitting the prayers after independence was declared but refusing to swear allegiance to the Commonwealth of Pennsylvania. As he later wrote when he resigned his pulpit, he would have been guilty of "the most criminal duplicity" as long as "the Sovereign still keeps up his claim of right upon this country, and every inhabitant is called upon by the late test law to renounce all allegiance to him, I had only to choose between my duty and my interest." Coombe's biographer, Walter High, has questioned this dilemma. He notes that Coombe loved and admired Britain when he went there to study and be ordained, and frequently complained about the stinginess of American congregations, especially the United Churches, considering all their wealthy parishioners, compared to the secure livings of British prelates.

Coombe's opinions and lack of support for the Revolution caused the Supreme Executive Council of Pennsylvania to list him, in early September 1777, after the British approached the city having won the Battle of Brandywine, as one of those inimical to the American cause. These suspected loyalists and neutrals, mostly Quakers, were being sent into exile in Winchester, Virginia, to prevent them from aiding the British. Coombe and some others whose cases were ambiguous were allowed to remain in their homes if they promised "to refrain from doing anything injurious to the United free States of America." Coombe did not so promise, and efforts by Jacob Duché and the vestry of the United Churches failed to persuade the council of Coombe's loyalty, objecting that "the removal of a Minister upon a general charge, without suffering him to know his accusers, or being heard in his own defense, cannot but be deem'd an infringement of religious as well as civil liberty." George Bryan, the president of the council, responded that "his case was wholly political," and warned the churches that they would be "very sorry your corporation should draw imputations on them, by this application"—that is, their own loyalty would be suspect as well. The unmistakably revolutionary William White and Colonel John Cadwalader were more successful in persuading the council, however, and prevented Coombe's removal when he gave his word that he would leave the state for the West Indies. But the British arrived before Coombe could leave, so he remained in the pulpit until the Americans returned on June 18, 1778. Then, when he once again refused to take the oath, the patriot authorities permitted him to leave for the British lines in New York. He soon moved to Britain, where he lived until 1822, serving as rector of various London parishes and as one of forty-eight chaplains to the king.[19]

Duché himself proclaimed his loyalty to the Crown only a month later than Coombe. Jailed by the British when they entered Philadelphia, Duché changed his allegiance after one night in a cell. Alexander Graydon, a prominent Philadelphia revolutionary, commented that "Reverend Duché was a whig before and I believe after the Declaration of Independence; but being in Philadelphia when the British army took possession of it, and thinking, probably, that his country was in a fair way of being subdued, he changed sides." Not only did

Duché change sides, but he wrote a letter to George Washington urging that he do likewise. Duché claimed to have been "surprised and distressed" by his appointment as chaplain of Congress on July 8, 1776, and to have "rashly accepted the post, as he thought "the churches in danger" and hoped to use his position to protect them. After October 1776, he further claimed to have been "opposed to all their measures," but kept his post for safety's sake. He wondered why Washington would continue to lead a rebellion from whose Congress "the most respectable characters have withdrawn themselves, and are succeeded by a great majority of illiberal and violent men." The army, "a set of undisciplined men and officers, many of whom have been taken from the lowest of the people, without principle and without course," was no better. He urged Washington to bypass Congress, abandon independence, and "NEGOTIATE for AMERICA at the head of your ARMY."

Washington did not reply to Duché, but he informed the latter's brother-in-law, Francis Hopkinson, about the "unmerited and illiberal abuse" Duché had given him before he laid the letter before Congress, fearing that had he not disclosed it, "might it not have been said, that I had betrayed my country." It was Hopkinson who wrote to Duché, "what infatuation could influence you to offer to his Excellency an address filled with gross misrepresentation, illiberal abuse, and sentiments unworthy of a man of character?" As for a negotiated peace, "would not the blood of the slain in battle rise against such perfidy!" To the president of Congress, Washington called the letter "ridiculous"; copies of it were made and spread throughout the nation, much to Duché's consternation. Even Ambrose Serle, private secretary to General William Howe, who commanded the British troops occupying Philadelphia, termed the letter "a performance which does but little honor either to the head or the heart of its author."[20]

But the Reverend Henry Melchior Mühlenberg was somewhat more sympathetic and explained that Duché had a good reason for his action. General Howe was deciding whether or not to try him by court martial—which could have resulted in a death sentence—for his pro-revolutionary activities but instead released him from imprisonment on parole, "with the condition that he journey to England, surrender to the archbishop or ecclesiastical court, and submit to their judgment and punishment." "The good man probably thought [that with the letter to Washington] he would extricate himself from a precarious position with one side and also mitigate his expected punishment in England, but it only increased bitterness on the other side and it probably would have been better if he published nothing." In any event, Duché's ship was driven off course and wound up in Antigua, a wealthy sugar island that offered him the sum of £600 per year to serve as its priest (double his salary as rector in Philadelphia), but his parole and the fact that his name appeared on the "registry of traitors" induced him to return to the mother country, where he was pardoned.[21]

Although Duché never did anything else that smacked of loyalism, the Commonwealth of Pennsylvania sentenced him to treason in absentia while he remained behind British lines, confiscating his property when the British left Philadelphia. Thomas McKean, revolutionary and future governor of the state, moved into his beautiful mansion on South Third Street. Humiliated by the circulation of his letter and the contempt with which the patriots treated it, Duché resigned his Philadelphia post on December 9, 1778, hoping to vindicate himself before the archbishop of Canterbury. In 1783 he begged Washington to help him return to his home and family, which he had left behind. He asked pardon for his "mere political error," explaining that he had not advised "an act of base treachery" but wanted Washington to "negotiate with Britain for our constitutional rights." Washington, for his part, replied cordially that if it were up to him, he would be glad to welcome Duché home, but that it was his "duty" not to interfere with the civil authorities, a position he had taken consistently throughout the war. Only in 1793 did Pennsylvania allow Duché to return; he died five years later.[22]

Like Thomas Coombe and Jacob Duché, William Stringer of St. Paul's initially expressed sympathy for the resistance; he joined his fellow priests in signing the letter of July 20, 1775, to the bishop of London. He continued to preach, omitting the king's prayer, in 1776 and 1777. His turning point, like Duché's, came when the British troops occupied Philadelphia. The Sunday after they arrived, in October 1777, Stringer preached a sermon on Ezekiel 20:38, "I will purge out the rebels from among you and those that transgress." The revolutionaries at St. Paul's, angered that he was referring to them, compelled him to shut his church.[23] Although not possessing many men of great wealth and nationwide prominence like the United Churches, which boasted Benjamin Franklin, Robert Morris, William Bingham, James Wilson, and Thomas Willing among its members, St. Paul's did have several notable revolutionaries. Blair McClenachan was a founder of the Bank of North America, leader of the Pennsylvania Anti-Federalists, and president of the Democratic Society of Philadelphia, inaugurated in 1793. Colonel Thomas Proctor was the Continental army's chief of artillery. Stephen Girard, although not a communicant, attended St. Paul's and was married there in 1777.[24]

Outside of Philadelphia and Chester and Bucks counties, where there was a substantial loyalist presence, Anglican clergy found themselves nearly alone in a sea of ardent revolutionaries. Congregations were overwhelmingly patriotic. These British-born and Society for the Propagation of the Gospel–supported clergy were all loyalists, with the exception of the Lutheran Reverend Illing on the Juniata frontier, who alone continued to officiate during the war and afterward. While the Reverend Thomas Barton of Lancaster was clearly exaggerating when he wrote that the Anglican "missionaries suffered beyond experience or beyond the records in any of history in this time of trial," he was not off the mark when he mourned that "most of them have lost their all. . . . Many of them are in a melancholy state of pilgrimage and poverty."[25]

The senior Anglican priest in Pennsylvania was William Currie. Since 1737, St. David's in Radnor, St. Peter's in the Great Valley, and St. James's at Perkiomen had been under his care. Currie was born in Glasgow in 1709, educated at the university there, and licensed as a Presbyterian preacher before being admitted to Anglican orders in 1736 by the bishop of London. Currie had frequently complained that his parishioners, although wealthy, left him "extremely destitute"—his income from three parishes amounted to less than £20 sterling per year—and his residence was but "a little ruinous house." Somehow, despite these complaints, he managed to accumulate an estate of more than £3,000 by the time of his death in 1793.[26]

Currie had no problem deciding which side to take in the American Revolution. In May 1776, when colonists everywhere were clamoring for independence, when he included the prayer for "thy servant George, our most gracious King and Governor" mandated by the liturgy. Instead of the congregation's usual response, "We beseech thee to hear us, good Lord," there was silence except for one voice in the gallery, which shouted out, "Good Lord, deliver us—from the king!" Later that month Currie resigned his posts, penning an eloquent letter. Just like the revolutionaries, who sometimes compared themselves to the biblical Hebrews chafing under Egyptian bondage, Currie invoked the image of the Jews hiding from the plague that struck the firstborn of Egypt to describe those who remained loyal to the Crown. "When flashes of judgment burst upon other persons, 'tis calm in the prayer room; when the destroying Angel had overrun every house in Egypt with death, when there was nothing but carcasses and crying in each dwelling, there was not one shriek in all the land of Goshen." There, as God released "Inundations of Tempests upon a careless, lukewarm, and backsliding people, yet even then his face shines in the closets of devotion; there he breaks in and reveals his comforts and is so as his Angel was at that time, a pillar of light to the one and a cloud to the other." Calm and secrecy were Currie's watchwords during the Revolution. He prayed with the faithful and performed baptisms, weddings, communion services, and funerals in private, urging his parishioners to remain apart from the Revolution shaking the land: "Let the Devotion chamber be your sanctuary till these troublesome times be overpassed."[27]

As with many people in Bucks and Chester counties, Currie's parishioners were sharply divided.[28] The most notable loyalist was Judge William Moore, a cantankerous man who had removed himself from the St. Peter's vestry in 1749 rather than consent to a levy the vestry placed on all graves in the churchyard. Moore was also tried before the Pennsylvania Assembly for his ardent criticism of its failure to defend the province adequately during the French and Indian War. He transferred to St. David's in Radnor, where he served on the vestry from 1765 to 1767. Although the revolutionaries left him in peace—some of Washington's officers even visited his mansion, located near Valley Forge, and enjoyed his hospitality during the winter of 1777–78, which the army spent there—any mention of an independent United States "threw him into a state of apoplexy." He split his treasured sword in half rather than surrender it to the patriots. Moore died in 1783 and is buried in St. David's churchyard in Radnor, near General Anthony Wayne, the church's leading revolutionary, who served on the vestry of St. David's from 1770 to 1785.[29]

Unlike most other loyalist clergymen who went into exile or were persecuted, Currie remained undisturbed throughout the Revolution. His son and wife died of "camp fever" during the Valley Forge winter, leaving him with three grand-children under the age of seven to raise. Despite his allegiance, in September 1777 loyalist raiders robbed him, he wrote, of all his "cabbage, bacon, cheese, and butter, a bushel of fine salt," and also his "fine sheets, table linen, fine shirts, head dresses, stockings, and table silver spoons to the value of 20 pounds," not to mention £200 of Continental money. They came back the following day for his wagons of oats and wheat and a saddle. Three of Currie's sons fought for the Revolution, which may have been the reason for these depredations.[30]

While Currie performed rites and comforted those who requested them in private, visiting preachers of various denominations spoke at his churches. Most notable was the Baptist David Jones of Tredyffrin in the Great Valley. Politically, Jones was at the opposite extreme from Currie. During one sermon he wore an American army uniform under his cloak, which he dramatically revealed, point-ing his finger at some young men who had not enlisted and exclaiming to the St. Peter's congregation, "I'm not afraid to go—They can't hurt me; they may kill me, if they like, and make a drum-head of my old hide, but they'll beat a tattoo that will carry the British out of the country."

The most frequent visitor, however, was "a wandering Lutheran clergy-man."[31] Who this Lutheran was is uncertain. He certainly was not the leading minister of that church in America, Henry Melchior Mühlenberg. Mühlenberg, who lived near Valley Forge and frequently cooperated with and aided the local Anglicans, demonstrated the sort of interchurch cooperation that the different denominations routinely practiced in an age when clergymen had to cover mul-tiple congregations and were not always on hand for their own flock. On Sep-tember 23, 1777, he vouched for an "old neighbor" as an "honest man" who had been a member of the Anglican Church for more than thirty years to a patriot general who had him arrested as a spy. On April 6, 1778, he comforted and prayed with a member of the Perkiomen Anglican church who was suffering from a "burning fever." On June 2 he accepted an invitation to preach at St.

James's, Perkiomen, but it was raining was so hard that he could not cross the creek of that name to reach it. Yet, while Anglicans were interested in uniting with Lutherans, even Mühlenberg spurned these efforts, fearing that his denomination would become subordinate to what was the established church in England and several colonies.[32]

Mühlenberg's sympathy for the Anglicans even extended to trying to help them secure a priest. In August 1779 the Perkiomen congregation, "left destitute of a regular faithful officiating minister since the present civil war, and the members thereby neglected and scattered abroad as sheep having no shepherd," asked that Mühlenberg examine John Wade, a candidate for the post, and give his opinion as to whether he could serve the congregation. After finding Wade "sound in doctrine agreeable with the 39 articles of the church and tolerably well-versed in reading and explaining part of the New Testament in Greek," Mühlenberg recommended "that in the present emergency" the congregation could accept the candidate on "probation" and believed that "the further examination may be easily obtained, if not by a bishop yet by a regular Protestant ministry, which is nearest to the Episcopal Church." Wade also served the Swedish Episcopal Church at Molatton vacated by Alexander Murray, for on February 28, 1781, the church's members, declaring themselves "pleased with his abilities . . . as a proper candidate for clerical ordination, and waiving or setting aside our former prejudices in favor of the mode of ordination by bishops," asked that Mühlenberg ordain Wade himself. Mühlenberg referred this "difficult and doubtful matter to two Lutheran ministers in Philadelphia "who know most about the English church affairs." They responded, however, that in addition to a call from the congregation, he not only had to take "the oath of allegiance to be a true member and citizen of the United Independent States of America"—as did all males in Pennsylvania, on pain of exile—but also to "undergo . . . an examination . . . concerning the Augustan Confession . . . the mode of ordination established within our German protestant Lutheran church, from the which we dare not deviate."[33]

When Wade was offered yet a third post in Delaware on August 26, 1782, Mühlenberg could only ask him how "could it be proper for a Lutheran or a Presbyterian minister to examine and ordain a candidate for an English Episcopal congregation?" Regretting "that various Episcopal congregations are left so deserted and wounded," Mühlenberg concluded that "this matter probably can never be solved until the church of Christ upon earth again becomes one flock with the shepherd." As late as April 1783, however, Wade, who was serving three congregations in Chester County, was "still insisting upon ordination by our Lutheran ministerium." Mühlenberg prepared a form that he thought acceptable whereby the congregations, as "there is no opportunity to get a minister ordained by Episcopal rites and ceremony," could choose him as their minister "by our primitive inherent right and liberty of conscience." Someone finally did ordain Wade before Samuel Seabury arrived as America's first Episcopal bishop in 1785; he is listed as "the Reverend" John Wade, priest of the church in New London, Chester County, in 1784.[34]

At the conclusion of the war, Currie resumed his duties under self-imposed conditions. He continued to receive a salary from the Society for the Propagation of the Gospel, telling its members in 1785, "I have officiated to a crowded audience and baptized a great number of children, there being no Episcopal minister within twenty miles of me by myself, for which services I make it a point to receive no lucrative emolument having made a firm resolution when I laid down my charge at the declaration of independence never to take wages of subjects of a government to which I cannot give my test of allegiance." The St. Peter's congregation, perhaps glad that they could save on expenses, thanked the SPG for paying Currie's salary and prayed that God would bless its activities in other lands, a hint that its work was about finished in America. The year before, Currie attended the first convention of what became the Episcopal Church in Philadelphia, although as the representative of St. Paul's Church in Chester County, following a specific invitation from William White and the other delegates. The St. Peter's congregation sent vestry member John Francis to represent it. He retired in 1785 and died in 1793, being replaced in 1788 by Slator Clay, who supported the Revolution.[35]

George Craig of Chester County was a more vehement loyalist than Currie, but he too escaped the war with relatively little damage. He had first come to Pennsylvania as a missionary in 1751, covering the dispersed parishes at Lancaster, Carnaervon, Huntington (York Springs), and Carlisle on a rotating basis. Craig frequently complained about his parishioners, who he claimed were "more inclined to build churches than they are to make any certain provision for the maintenance of a minister." "The canons [of the church] are of no more avail here than the Alcoran of Mahomet," he wrote of his Lancaster parish, where a "juncto" made the "odious" choice of two church wardens over his opposition. He argued to the SPG far more insistently than his fellow Pennsylvanians, and more like their colleagues in New England, New Jersey, and New York, that an American bishop who could ordain clergy might remedy Pennsylvania's "unhappy [ecclesiastical] constitution . . . which leaves everyone to follow their own unhappy humor which they think they may change as often as their clocks."[36]

Also grousing about the large territory he was obliged to cover, Craig was finally settled by the SPG in 1758 at St. Paul's in Chester County, whence he also presided at St. John's in Concord and St. Martin's in Marcus Hook. Even after being settled, Craig remained unhappy. Following two years' residence at St. Paul's, he was angry that "not one farthing of the subscription is collected to this day" toward his support, concluding that "when a clergyman becomes an object of some people's charity, instead of their relieving him, he instantly becomes an object of their contempt." In 1762 he objected to the "unbounded liberty" of religion in Pennsylvania, in 1769 of the "ruinous condition" of the churches and the "few members" to whom he ministered. Predictably, he ceased preaching in 1776, although he continued to administer the sacraments and comfort those in private who sought his help until his death in 1783. He was buried under St. Martin's Church at Marcus Hook. Only in 1788 did James Conner succeed him.[37]

Craig's and Currie's sufferings were mild compared to those of the other Anglican clergymen in Pennsylvania, all of whom were missionaries whose salaries were largely paid for by England's Society for the Propagation of the Gospel. The rector at Bristol was the famous loyalist satirist Reverend Jonathan Odell. He was based primarily in Burlington, New Jersey, across the Delaware River, where he served as rector, although William Smith and Jacob Duché also preached there. Son-in-law of Jonathan Dickinson and a former president of the College of New Jersey (later Princeton), Odell converted to Anglicanism after serving as a chaplain in the British army. Ordained in 1767, he became rector of the parishes of St. Ann's Burlington and St. Andrew's, Mt. Holly, in New Jersey, along with St. James's, Bristol, in Pennsylvania, although he lived in Burlington. A fervent loyalist, he wrote numerous satires criticizing the American cause, fled to British lines, spent the war in Philadelphia and New York, served as an intermediary between Benedict Arnold and John André when the former was planning treason, and was rewarded for his services to the Crown by appointment as provincial secretary of New Brunswick, Canada. Located in heavily loyalist and Quaker Bucks County, St. James's suffered destruction by the revolutionaries, who quartered their soldiers there. The building was reconstructed only in 1808, when services finally resumed.[38]

Batwell, Barton, and Murray, unlike Odell, found themselves in the midst of one of the most fervently revolutionary areas in America. Berks, York, Lancaster, and Cumberland counties were the first outside New England to send forces—the famed Pennsylvania Riflemen—to join the emerging Continental army near Boston in 1775. They also led Pennsylvania's own internal revolution. Angered that the eastern-dominated Assembly had failed to defend them during the French and Indian War and Pontiac's Rebellion, westerners considered themselves victims of taxation without representation within the colony. In the mid-1770s they joined with Philadelphia's working class—many of whom could not vote—to overthrow a legislature that had spent most of the late 1760s and 1770s trying to replace the Penn family proprietors with a royal government.[39]

The Reverend David Batwell's principal parish was St. John's in York, but he also officiated at St. John's in Carlisle and the church in Huntington near what is now York Springs. Arriving in York in 1774 at the "Church of St. John the Baptist in the Wilderness," whose church edifice was only nine years old, Batwell initially pleased English-speaking "Protestants of all denominations," whom York Anglicans welcomed to their church in a predominantly German-speaking area. He had replaced John Andrews, who presided from 1769 to 1772, at an "elegant church" made of brick, fifty-four by thirty-six feet, that had been funded by "a few families" who were "more liberal" than Andrews had ever seen "upon like occasions." Few indeed were these families, for in 1774, of the three parishes (Huntington, York, and Carlisle) Batwell covered, "only Huntington has a vestry, neither York nor Carlisle affording 12 heads of families whereof to compose one." Like the other SPG missionaries, Batwell insisted on praying for the king after the Revolution broke out. Earlier, as had his colleagues in Philadelphia, he expressed sympathy for the patriot grievances while urging reconciliation in his own fast day sermon on July 20, 1775. His last service in York occurred in April 1776. According to the Anglican lawyer, county prothonotary, and vestryman Samuel Johnston—a member of the SPG whom Andrews considered in "great measure" responsible for the enthusiastic Anglicanism of some York inhabitants—"the times carried everything before them and since that time we have had no church service here."[40]

Batwell removed to Huntington, where he had it better—at first. In this remote parish of Christ's Church, he ministered to a group of Anglicans who were surrounded by Quakers and Germans who took little interest in the Revolution. He boasted that his congregation had not a "single associator." But his continued support of the Crown, along with three of his parishioners, John Curry, James Bracken, and John Wilson Jr.—the first distilled whiskey; the other two were wealthy farmers—"soon brought upon them annoyance from without." They were looked upon with a jealous eye both at York and at Carlisle and were distinguished by the name of "Bermudian Creek Tories." In September 1776 Batwell took a chance and made a trip back to York to obtain supplies for his family. Discovered by ethnically German revolutionaries, he was pelted with sticks and stones, dragged from his horse, which they claimed he had stolen, and "with more than savage cruelty" led to the river that flowed through the town, where "they soused him several times." He was forced to ride away (he got his horse back) and could not find dry clothes for twelve miles. Johnston added that "the better sort of people greatly disapprove[d] of this assault," but Batwell could not bring his persecutors to justice as the courts were all closed. Johnston concluded that "what Mr. Batwell had done those wicked people could not say themselves but it was because he was a Tory as they thought proper to call him, as almost all the Church people are, and every other person who is against the most violent measures is sure of the same Epithet."[41] Johnston was mistaken about at least some of the best people. Three vestrymen of St.

John's, Thomas Hartley, Henry Miller, and John Clark, led the region's armed forces in the Revolution and were prominent in its political life thereafter.

From the patriots' point of view, Batwell deserved his fate. In July or August 1777 he was one of three men to plan a "conspiracy," as the patriots called it, to destroy the revolutionaries' arsenals at Carlisle, York, and Lancaster, vital to the Continental army's supply of rifles, cannon, and ammunition. Headed by James and William Rankin of York, and communicating via Martin Weaver of Northampton County and Christoph Saur III of Germantown (whose father was Pennsylvania's leading German-language printer) with General William Howe and Colonel John Graves Simcoe of the Queen's Rangers, this backcountry Pennsylvania movement claimed two thousand supporters and was in touch with the British from September 1777 until 1781. Batwell and his parishioners' plot against the arsenals was found out, however. He was arrested on September 30, 1777. After a month in jail, he pleaded with Congress to be released, presenting a doctor's certificate that he "was so emaciated by a complication of his disorders, that his life was endangered unless he was removed from the said jail." He was released in February 1778, placed in a wagon with his family, and sent to British lines in Philadelphia over ice-covered roads, following a journey that left him "well nigh blind" and unable to walk because of "the severity with which he has been treated." Batwell returned to England, where the Loyalists' Claims Commissions denied his request for £1,250 in compensation; he continued to be supported by the SPG.[42]

With Batwell removed, York enjoyed the services of Philadelphia's William White, who was one of the two chaplains of Congress who fled Philadelphia along with that body in 1777–78. White's genial personality and religious toleration showed in the fact that he lived at first with the Reverend Kurtz, pastor of the town's Lutheran church. St. John's only regained a permanent rector, the Reverend John Campbell, in 1784. Campbell served for twenty years, during which time he lost many of the congregation to the Presbyterian Church, forcing the Episcopal academy formed in York in 1787 to be taken over by the Commonwealth of Pennsylvania.[43]

Except for the absence of physical violence, Thomas Barton fared no better than Batwell. Although his main parish was St. James's in Lancaster, his other charges being St. John's in Pequa and the church in Caernarvon (now Churchtown), before Reverend John Andrews came on the scene in 1769, Barton had also handled the churches in York and Carlisle. He complained in 1764 that "my itinerancy also bears heavy upon me in the present state of health," not to mention that he had to support a wife, two servants, and seven children, which he claimed he could not do for less than £150 sterling per year, far more than his income. Born in Ireland in 1730, Barton was no newcomer to Pennsylvania. He was a member of the American Philosophical Society, a scientific gardener, a community leader who had accompanied soldiers in battle in the French and Indian War, an (anonymous) defender of the Paxton Boys' massacre of peaceful Conestoga Indians in 1763, and (under his own name) a booster in 1772 for a road to connect Philadelphia with Wright's Ferry on the Susquehanna River, passing naturally through his hometown of Lancaster, Pennsylvania's largest inland city. His first wife, Esther, was the sister of the astronomer and revolutionary leader David Rittenhouse.[44]

Barton resumed his travels after Andrews, who had been educated at the College of Pennsylvania, returned to his native Maryland in 1772. Like Batwell, Barton found himself standing almost alone when the Revolution broke out. His parish included George Ross, a signer of the Declaration of Independence; Edward Shippen, head of Lancaster's Committee of Correspondence; Mathias Slough, innkeeper and business partner of the town's leading Jewish merchant, Joseph Simon, and his relatives, the Gratz brothers of Philadelphia; William Henry, a leading manufacturer of the Pennsylvania rifle; and Edward Hand, adjutant general of the Continental army. They had begun to mobilize support for Boston as early as June 1774 and voted, on May 1, 1775, to send troops to Massachusetts within two weeks of the Battle of Lexington. That August, the staunchly loyalist but still politically quiet Barton wrote to the SPG that "matters have now got to such a crisis that it is neither prudent nor safe to write or speak one's sentiments—would to God an accommodation could take place! Everything here, at present, wears a dreadful aspect, religion, and all the arts of peace, are lost amidst the horrid apparatus of war."[45]

Barton preached for the last time on June 23, 1776. Once Congress adopted the Declaration of Independence, he closed his churches so as "to avoid the fury of the populace who would not suffer the Liturgy to be used unless the Collects and Prayers for the King were omitted." In November he reported to the SPG that he had been confined to his house, where he remained until 1778, by "those who usurped authority and rule and exercised the severest tyranny over us . . . my life and property have been threatened upon mere suspicion of being unfriendly to what is called the American cause." James Graham, the schoolmaster who presided over the classroom Barton had established in 1771 to teach blacks and poor children—about a dozen scholars in all—resigned on Christmas Day 1777 to serve in the revolutionary government. In 1778, upon the recommendation of revolutionary leader Jasper Yeates, Barton was allowed to move to the British lines in New York City, where he died on May 30, 1780. Yeates commented that Barton deserved his freedom because "his private deportment as a Christian hath been exemplary; that he hath ever evinced himself a zealous minister . . . and that his public preaching here has given general satisfaction."[46]

Yet on the other hand, in 1779 the Pennsylvania Supreme Executive Council credited Barton with being "very instrumental in poisoning the minds of his parishioners who are generally of very disaffected disciples as to the present contest." It is interesting that Barton would receive such backhanded credit, as by this time disaffection throughout the commonwealth with the constitutionalist government was rampant. They were probably searching for scapegoats, as Barton did not preach publicly after 1776, and even before that year had "not intermeddled with any matters inconsistent with our callings and functions."[47]

The year before his death, Barton wrote an eloquent summary of the fate of Anglican clergy in America. Calling on the British nation to "deliver us from the tyranny that has scourg'd us so long," he predicted that thousands of "martyrs," who "have clung round the neck of their parent state and only wait for some security to evince their zeal and unshaken attachment," would surface. After a renewed, vigorous British war effort, he hoped to "have the pleasure to see the church of England flourish in America, with increasing luster." Unable to understand why the revolutionaries persecuted him and most of Pennsylvania's other Anglican clergy, for they had gone out of their way to take no part in political affairs until compelled to reject or take oaths of allegiance, he concluded that "we have obey'd the laws and government now in being, as far as our consciences and prior obligations would permit. We know of no crime that can be alleg'd against us, except an honest avowal of our principles can be deemed such." Barton failed to understand the new nation's republican consciousness, which mandated active participation in war and government rather than mere passive, law-abiding good behavior of its citizens. Also, in times of revolution, liberty rarely extends to the right of individuals to speak their minds but usually means the collective right of a people to seek self-government. Lancaster had no Episcopal priest until 1784, when Joseph Hutchins arrived.[48]

John Andrews, Barton's successor at York, Carlisle, and Huntington, remained there only from 1769 to 1772. Born in Cecil County, Maryland, in 1736, and graduated from the College of Philadelphia in 1765, he was ordained in 1767. He left his Pennsylvania parishes to take a more lucrative position as rector of St. John's parish in Queen Anne's County, Maryland, but his conscience forbade him to omit the prayers for the king once independence was declared, and his congregation would not allow him to keep them in. So he returned to York, where he began a successful academy that later became York College. In 1779, however, Pennsylvania officials approached him and insisted on enforcing the law of 1778, requiring him to leave the state or take an oath of allegiance. He chose the latter option, writing to Reverend William White that if the church insisted on retaining its bishops, "she will no longer if the states should be able to maintain their independence, have an existence in America." He placed the "great" good of supporting his wife and children over "the uncertain . . . good that might arise from my refusing to conform." He described taking the oath as a "surrender, after having stood a pretty siege of about three years." In 1782 he returned again to Maryland, this time to St. Thomas's parish, before moving to Philadelphia in 1785 to head the Episcopal Academy.[49]

Philip Reading, who presided over St. Augustine's parish in Maryland and Apoquiniminick in Delaware, acted in consort with the Pennsylvania clergy. "Much industry has been used to render me obnoxious to popular resentment," he wrote in one of many frequent and lengthy missives he sent to the SPG. Someone scribbled "*No more passive obedience and non resistance*" on his church door, he wrote on March 18, 1776, and a local militia captain "lugged his company to church on the day of a public fast to hear *that old wretch* (meaning myself) *preach*." But he insisted that he could not "dispense with these solemn obligations" and pray for the king. Despite threats, once independence was declared, Reading informed his parishioners, "as I had no design to resist the authority of the new government on one hand and as I was determined on the other not to incur the heavy guilt of perjury," he planned to shut up his Delaware church for six weeks. More than two years later, the church was still closed: shortly before his death, on September 20, 1778, "laboring under a nervous atrophy which has been brought upon me by the anxiety, disappointment, and distress I have suffered during the present contest betwixt America and the parent state," Reading asked the SPG to continue to support him, as he insisted on "sturdily adhering to and not in the least violating the oaths, vows, and obligations I entered into when I took upon me the ministerial office."[50]

Alexander Murray, born in 1727 and a graduate of the University of Aberdeen in Scotland, also found that his entire congregation in Reading (about forty-five families), with one exception, supported the Revolution. Murray did double duty at St. Mary's Church in Reading (now Christ Church, not the current St. Mary's in that city) and St. Gabriel's in Morlattan, now Douglassville, a Swedish Lutheran Church that had joined the Anglican Communion as it could not pay a minister of its own. He had been a successful preacher. Between his arrival in 1763 and the Revolution, his flock had increased from six or seven families and included Quakers, Baptists, and Presbyterians who were bereft of clergy in this overwhelmingly German-speaking area. Murray praised his "parishioners" as "orderly and quiet amidst the clamor and noise, contention and foul speaking of the German colonists." Most notable of those who were not orderly was the lawyer Edward Biddle, who handled more cases in Reading than all the other lawyers together. The Anglican Biddle chaired the first meeting Reading citizens held in July 1774 to protest the Coercive Acts, and went on to serve in the Continental Congress. Ironmasters John Patton and Mark Bird, whose forges were crucial to the Continental army's supply when it wintered at Valley Forge and afterward, were also Reading Anglicans who joined the cause. On July 20, 1775, Murray decided to mark the fast day mandated by Congress with a sermon that described "the fatal cause and effects of civil war" instead of praying for American success in the war. The community's response was to boycott Murray's church, which was completely vacant the following Sunday. Murray continued to preach to his congregation of former Swedish Lutherans at Morlattan (Douglassville) until 1778, when a mob attacked his house, destroyed his furniture, books, and papers, and threatened to tar and feather him. The Reading vigilance committee, however, permitted him to escape to British lines, from which he went to England. Anglican services ceased in Reading until 1826. Murray returned to Pennsylvania in 1790 and lived in Philadelphia, commuting to his still faithful Morlattan Swedes. He died in the yellow fever epidemic of 1793.[51]

Historian Rodney Miller described Joseph Andrews and Philip Reading as "passive loyalists." The same may be said of Stringer, Currie, Barton, and Murray—although definitely not of the militant Odell and conspiring Batwell. They took no steps to further the loyalist cause or dissuade patriots from their course but wished to continue services with the proper loyalty to the Crown even in an independent, revolutionary society. That they all retained their posts unmolested until independence was either declared or became imminent is proof that they were not behaving obnoxiously to the patriots. But as Barton's plaintive lament indicates, passivity was no longer an option in revolutionary times. The radical constitutionalists, like the English king, insisted on a loyalty oath, and with the exception of John Andrews, none of the rural clergy could take it.[52]

The Philadelphia clergy, except for William White, on the other hand, switched from active supporters of the resistance to active opponents of the Revolution or, in Smith's case, a passive observer. Stringer and Duché appeared to favor the Revolution as well but became convinced when the British occupied Philadelphia (as Smith had even before) that the colonies could not win. Coombe, on the other hand, while opposing taxation and British efforts to curtail colonial freedom, appears to have made his decision when independence was declared, if not before. But whether passive or active loyalists, no prerevolutionary Pennsylvania Anglican cleric supported the Revolution, with the exception of William White.

It was thus White's task to reconstitute a discredited church once the war ended, as new priests for the commonwealth's other congregations assumed their posts only in the 1780s (in Bristol not until 1808 and in Reading not until 1826). That White had to save his faith first in his own state—his call for a convention in 1784 led to the creation of the diocese of Pennsylvania—prepared him well to become the principal founder of a united American Episcopal Church that freed its Anglican predecessor from its strong taint of disloyalty and colonial subservience.

NOTES

1. The oath appears in William E. Hannum, *The Story of St. John's: Being an Historical Sketch of St. John's Episcopal Church, Concord, Delaware County, Pennsylvania* (Concord: St. John's Episcopal Church, 1959), 17. I discuss these issues more fully in "From Anglicans to Episcopalians: The Revolutionary Years," in *History of the Episcopal Diocese of Pennsylvania*, ed. David Contosta (University Park: Pennsylvania State University Press, 2010), and a forthcoming biography of Bishop William White.

2. John Frantz and I summarize the literature and issues in the introduction and afterword to our edited volume, *Beyond Philadelphia: The American Revolution in the Pennsylvania Hinterland* (University Park: Pennsylvania State University Press, 1998).

3. Christopher Marshall, *Passages from the Remembrancer*, ed. William Duane Jr. (Philadelphia: James Crissy, 1839), 6; Deborah Mathias Gough, *Christ Church, Philadelphia: The Nation's Church in a Changing City* (Philadelphia: University of Pennsylvania Press, 1995), 130; Horace Wemyss Smith, *Life and Correspondence of the Rev. William Smith, D.D.*, 2 vols. (Philadelphia: A. S. George, 1879), 1:491–505.

4. Kevin J. Dellape, "Jacob Duché: Whig-Loyalist?" *Pennsylvania History* 62, no. 2 (1995): 296; C. P. B. Jeffreys, "The Provincial and Revolutionary History of St. Peter's Church, 1753–1783," *Pennsylvania Magazine of History and Biography* 48 (1924): 188–89.

5. Bird Wilson, *Memoir of the Life of the Right Reverend William White, D.D., Bishop of the Protestant Episcopal Church in the State of Pennsylvania* (Philadelphia: James Kay Jr. and Bro., 1839), 50–51.

6. William Smith to Society for the Propagation of the Gospel (hereafter SPG), July 10, 1775, in Williams Steven Perry, ed., *Historical Collections Relating to the American Colonial Church*, 5 vols., vol. 2, *Papers Relating to the History of the Church in Pennsylvania* (Hartford, Conn., 1879), 475–80; Philadelphia Clergy to Bishop of London, June 30, 1775, ibid., 470–42.

7. Much of the sermon is reprinted in Albert Frank Gegenheimer, *William Smith, Educator and Churchman, 1727–1803* (Philadelphia: University of Pennsylvania Press, 1943), 163–70.

8. Herbert M. Morais, *Deism in Eighteenth-Century America* (New York: Columbia University Press, 1934), 73–74.

9. Jacob Duché, preface, "The Duty of Standing Fast in Our Spiritual and Temporal Liberties" (Philadelphia, 1775), Early American Imprints, series 1, Evans (1639–1800), microfilm, no. 14459.

10. Jacob Duché, "The American Vine," ibid., no. 14012, 22–24, 33.

11. Thomas Coombe, "A Sermon Preached Before the Congregation of Christ Church and St. Peter's Philadelphia, on Thursday, July 23 recommended by the Honorable Continental Congress for a general fast throughout the twelve united colonies of North America," ibid., no. 13893, 19–20.

12. Jeffreys, "St. Peter's"; Gough, *Christ Church*, 138.

13. Henry Melchior Mühlenberg, *The Journals of Henry Melchior Muhlenberg*, trans. and ed. Theodore G. Tappert and John W. Doberstein, 3 vols. (Philadelphia: Muhlenberg Press, 1942–58): 2:739–41; "Letter of Henry Melchior Muhlenberg, October 2, 1776," *Pennsylvania Magazine of History and Biography* 22 (1898): 129–31.

14. Marshall, *Passages from the Remembrancer*, 61; Smith, *Life and Correspondence of Smith*, 1:544–60.

15. Marshall, *Passages from the Remembrancer*, 71; Smith, *Life and Correspondence of Smith*, 2:9–10; Gegenheimer, *William Smith*, 178–80; Ambrose Serle, *The American Journal of Ambrose Serle, Secretary to Lord Howe, 1776–1778*, ed. Edward H. Tatum Jr. (San Marino, Calif.: Huntington Library, 1940), 289.

16. Smith, *Life and Correspondence of Smith*, 2:17–29; Gegenheimer, *William Smith*, 178–80; Deborah Mathias Gough, "Pluralism, Politics, and Power Struggles: The Church of England in Colonial Philadelphia, 1695–1789" (PhD diss., University of Pennsylvania, 1978), 558–60; vestry minutes of the United Churches (annual vestry elections held in late March or April, 1775–90), microfilm, reel 1, Historical Society of Pennsylvania, Philadelphia (hereafter HSP).

17. William Smith, "The Candid Retrospect" (Charlestown, Md., 1780), 11.

18. Smith, *Life and Correspondence of Smith*, 2:39–82; Gegenheimer, *William Smith*, 180–82; William West to William White, October 31, 1786, Episcopal Archives of Maryland, Office of the Cathedral of the Incarnation, Baltimore, Maryland.

19. J. Walter High, "Thomas Coombe, Loyalist," *Pennsylvania History* 62 (1995): 284–86; Christ Church vestry minutes, September 6–10, 1777, microfilm, HSP.

20. Alexander Graydon, *Memoirs of a Life Chiefly Passed in Pennsylvania* (Edinburgh: W. Blackwood, 1822), 99, appendix, 429–39; Serle, *American Journal*, 269.

21. Mühlenberg, *Journals of Muhlenberg*, 3:160–61 (June 4, 1778).

22. Jeffreys, "St. Peter's," 260–61; Dellape, "Jacob Duché," 299–301; Graydon, *Memoirs*, 439–42.

23. Perry, *Historical Collections*, 2:471; Norris S. Barratt, *Outline of the History of Old St. Paul's, Philadelphia* (Philadelphia: Colonial Society of Pennsylvania, 1917), 29–34; Gough, *Christ Church*, 81.

24. Barratt, *History of Old St. Paul's*, 94, 117.

25. Quoted in R. Chester Ross, *Two Hundred Years of Church History: The History of St. John's, Pequa, Protestant Episcopal Church Located at Compass, Chester County, Pa.* (n.p., 1929), 27.

26. Quoted in Harold Donaldson Eberlein and Cortlandt van Dyke Hubbard, *The Church of St. Peter in the Great Valley, 1700–1940* (Richmond, Va.: August Dietz and Son, 1944), 26, 64, 76–77, 87.

27. Ibid., 80–82.

28. See the chapters on Bucks and Chester counties by Owen S. Ireland and Rosemary Warden, respectively, in *Beyond Philadelphia: The American Revolution in the Pennsylvania Hinterland*, ed. John B. Frantz and William Pencak (University Park: Pennsylvania State University Press, 1998).

29. Eberlein and Hubbard, *Church of St. Peter*, 36, 69–70, 75, 78–79, 84–85; Henry Pleasants, *The History of Old St. David's Church, Radnor, in Delaware County, Pennsylvania* (Philadelphia: John Winston and Co., 1907), 151.

30. Eberlein and Hubbard, *Church of St. Peter*, 86; Currie quoted in Pleasants, *History of Old St. David's*, 153, 83.

31. Eberlein and Hubbard, *Church of St. Peter*, 84–87.

32. Mühlenberg, *Journals of Muhlenberg*, 3:79, 140, 159, 161; Gough, "Pluralism, Politics, and Power Struggles," 385–87.

33. Mühlenberg, *Journals of Muhlenberg*, 3:254–55; 405–6, 408–9.

34. Ibid., 3:450, 503, 534; minutes of May 25, 1784, meeting, in "Journals of Meetings that Led to the Formation of the Diocese of Pennsylvania in 1784," Archives of the Episcopal Diocese of Pennsylvania, on deposit at the Lutheran Theological Seminary of Philadelphia.

35. Eberlein and Hubbard, *Church of St. Peter*, 86–88; *Journal of the Meetings Which Led to the Institution of a Convention of the Protestant Episcopal Church in the State of Pennsylvania . . .* (Philadelphia: Hall and Sellers, 1790), 5.

36. For his complaints before settling at Chester and then the need for a bishop, see George Craig to SPG, June 30, 1754, August 5, 1757, September 30, 1759, June 25, 1766, October 14, 1772, Craig Papers, HSP.

37. George Craig to SPG, July 17, 1760, June 25, 1762, July 11, 1763, November 10, 1769, ibid.; William Shaler Johnson, *The Story of St. Paul's "the Delaware," 1703–1903* (n.p., 1903), 4–6; Arthur Chilton Powell, *Historic St. John's: Centennial Sermon Preached in St. John's Episcopal Church, York, Pennsylvania* (York: Gazette Printing, 1887), 17–19.

38. J. Wesley, *A History of the Diocese of Pennsylvania of the Protestant Episcopal Church in the U.S.A., 1784–1968* (Philadelphia: Diocese of Pennsylvania, 1969), 117–23; for Odell, see the biography by Robert M. Calhoon, at American National Biography Online, ed. John A. Garrity and Michael Carnes (2000), http://www.anb.org/articles/01/01-00680.html; for St. James's, see John T. Faris, *Old Churches and Meeting Houses in and Around Philadelphia* (Philadelphia: Lippincott, 1926), 220–21.

39. See Frantz and Pencak, *Beyond Philadelphia*, chapters on Berks (Karen Guenther), York (Paul Doutrich), and Cumberland (Robert G. Crist) counties; for Lancaster, see Jerome H. Wood, *Conestoga Crossroads: Lancaster, Pennsylvania, 1730–1790* (Harrisburg: Pennsylvania Historical and Museum Commission, 1979).

40. W. Walter van Banaam, *A Brief History of St. John's [the Baptist, York, Pennsylvania, 1755–1955]* (n.p., 1955?), no page numbers (approximately 9–12 pages into text); Powell, *Historic St. John's*, 6–7.

41. Samuel Johnston to SPG, November 25, 1776; see also Thomas Barton to SPG, November 25, 1776, both in Perry, *Historical Collections*, 2:487–90; James P. Myers Jr., "The Bermudian Creek Tories," *Adams County History* 3 (1997): 4–40. Myers's use of British military documents proves the existence of the conspiracy and the identity of its leaders.

42. Myers, "Bermudian Creek Tories," 25–36; Powell, *Historic St. John's*, 11–15.

43. Powell, *Historic St. John's*, 8–10.

44. For Barton's early career, see ibid., 5–6; James P. Myers Jr., "Thomas Barton's *Unity and Public Spirit* (1744): Controversy and Plagiarism on the Pennsylvania Frontier," *Pennsylvania Magazine of History and Biography* 119 (1995): 125–48; Myers, "The Rev. Thomas Barton's Authorship of *The Condition of the Paxton Men, Impartially Represented*," *Pennsylvania History* 61 (1994): 155–84; Marvin F. Russell,

"Thomas Barton and the Pennsylvania Colonial Frontier," *Pennsylvania History* 46 (1979): 313–34; Theodore W. Jeffries, "Thomas Barton (1730–1780): Victim of the American Revolution," *Journal of the Lancaster County Historical Society* 81 (1977): 39–74; H. M. J. Klein and William F. Diller, *The History of St. James' Church (Protestant Episcopal), 1744–1944* (Lancaster, Pa.: Vestry of St. James' Church, 1944), 41–57.

45. Klein and Diller, *History of St. James' Church,* 49–54.

46. Ibid., 46–47, 54–57.

47. Jeffries, "Thomas Barton," 61; Edgar Legaré Pennington, "Anglican Clergy of Pennsylvania in the American Revolution," *Pennsylvania Magazine of History and Biography* 63 (1939): 401–31.

48. Thomas Barton to SPG, January 8, 1779, quoted in Jeffries, "Thomas Barton," 58–60.

49. Rodney K. Miller, "The Political Ideology of the Anglican Clergy," *Historical Magazine of the Protestant Episcopal Church* 45 (1976): 227–36, esp. 232; Van R. Baker, "The 'Sterling Honesty' of John Andrews," ibid., 31–45, esp. 31–34; William Stevens Perry, "The Alleged 'Toryism' of the Clergy of the United States at the Breaking Out of the War of the Revolution: An Historical Examination," ibid., 133–44; Charles Latham Jr., *The Episcopal Academy, 1785–1984* (Devon, UK: William T. Cooke, 1984), 19; and David M. Dean, ed. "The End of a Siege: A Silent Loyalist Becomes a Reluctant Patriot; a Letter from John Andrews to William White, December 14, 1779," *Pennsylvania History* 37 (1970): 381–86.

50. Miller, "Political Ideology," 232–33; Perry, *Historical Collections,* 2:480–87, 494–95. Reading's detailed letters are moving and give a clear picture of a man fighting to retain his conscientious beliefs in the face of great adversity.

51. Karen Guenther, "'A Faithful Soldier of Christ': The Career of the Reverend Dr. Alexander Murray, Missionary to Berks County, Pa., 1762–1778," *Historical Magazine of the Protestant Episcopal Church* 55 (1986): 5–20; William DuHamel, *Historical Annals of Christ Church [formerly called St. Mary's], Reading, Pa.* (Douglassville, Pa.: Church Press, 1927), 13–14, 16–18.

52. Miller, "Political Ideology."

★   *6*   ★

THE SONS OF THE OLD CHIEFS:
SURVEYING IDENTITY AND EUROPEAN-AMERICAN RELATIONSHIPS
IN THE "NEW PURCHASE" TERRITORY (CENTRE COUNTY,
PENNSYLVANIA, 1769–1778)

Russell Spinney

> *Great Island November 8th, 1769*
> *The Indians answer to James Parr conserning some of their Brother Indians*
> *being sent from Genl. Johnston to The Great Island in Order to meet the*
> *Surveyors to see the Boundery Lines of the New Purchase run. Was there had*
> *not been any there yet Neither did they know anything about it.*

> JOHN SECCALEMUS
>
> JOSEPH NEWTEMUS
>
> JOHN LOGAN, JOHN PETTY

> *John Seccalemus further says if any Indians should come on that business he*
> *desires to be acquainted there with as he intends going with them.*

In 1769, the Great Island below present-day Lock Haven stood along the shifting lines of European colonial and American Indian regional politics.[1] For many years the island had been an important meeting place between different American Indian tribes in the mid-Atlantic region, although few scholars have paid this seemingly isolated region any attention in the wake of the French and

I would like to thank my father, Ralph W. Spinney, for inspiring me with his love of history and good books. Dr. Amy Schutt, Dr. David Hsiung, Phil Hnatkovich, and Matthew Padron have provided me with many helpful comments and suggestions. My research would not have been possible without the assistance of Joyce Adgate at the Pennsylvania Room Collection of the Centre County Library and Historical Museum and the archivists at the Pennsylvania State Archives in Harrisburg. I would also like to thank Doug MacGregor and Fred Threlfall at the Fort Pitt Museum for the maps that appear in this chapter. Finally, I am very grateful for the questions and comments of those before whom I presented this research at the McNeil Center for Early American Studies at the University of Pennsylvania in November 2004, and before the Centre County Historical Society in February 2006.

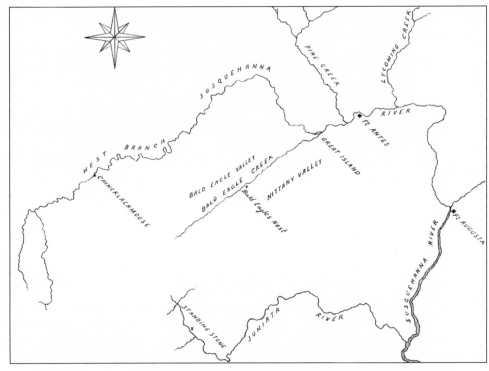

Detail of the Susquehanna River tributary system. The Bald Eagle Creek area was one of the first three "New Purchase" tracts surveyed for sale in Philadelphia. It was also the home to Chief Bald Eagle and the location of the Great Island, an important meeting place in the region. Courtesy of Fred Threlfall.

Indian War and the advent of the American War of Independence.[2] The sons of the region's old chiefs, who gathered there that fall and composed this letter for the colonial surveyors coming up from Philadelphia, wanted to make sure that when the powers of the world decided the boundaries of Pennsylvania's new territorial acquisition, they would be part of that process.

In examining the frontier of the "New Purchase" territory of Pennsylvania in present-day Centre and Clinton counties, I revisit an important historiographical question about the sort of frontier that characterized early American society.[3] Scholars such as Richard White have envisioned the frontier experience as a "middle ground," where Europeans and American Indians mediated their interactions using terms developed in common through language, diplomacy, trade, sexual relationships, violence, and coexistence.[4] Others, such as James H. Merrell, have used the notion of "going into the woods" to illuminate how both American Indians and Europeans viewed one another's worlds as places of both peril and opportunity, in need of go-betweens who kept these different worlds linked. When Europeans went into the woods, however, this meant transforming the wilderness in ways that would inevitably map its space, establish civilization, and displace other worlds in the process.[5] From the perspective of the old chiefs' sons, then, it appears as if they knew that other groups of American Indians and Europeans were supplanting their authority and that time was running out for their world.

The French and Indian War (1754–63) and Pontiac's War (1763–65) increased the level of violence all along the English colonial frontier, and thereby accelerated the redefinition of space and place between American Indians and European Americans. Source materials verify the increasing level of racial tensions between the two populations along the frontier of the Pennsylvania "New Purchase" territory. Other source materials, however—the letter from the sons of local American Indian leaders, the diary of the Presbyterian supply minister, Philip Vickers Fithian, Pennsylvania colonial records, surveyors' correspondence, and other local accounts—indicate that a high level of peaceful interaction persisted at least on the Susquehanna's West Branch at the time of the Revolution. As violence redefined this diverse matrix of place, space, and peoples, alternative forms of European and American Indian identity and settlement—alternative in relation to those predicated on racial separation—appear to have vanished. But appearances can be deceiving. Having reviewed the available archival materials for this region of the frontier, I want to make the case for local history research as a way of documenting the persistence of interracial coexistence despite the violence of the frontier experience. In other words, the middle ground never totally disappeared.

Race as the Defining Character of Frontier Space

Despite the thriving settlements of colonial Pennsylvania, much of the land between British Philadelphia and French Fort Duquesne still remained an isolated backcountry to European colonists in the mid-eighteenth century. Supply ministers (itinerant ministers sent to serve frontier communities) like George Brainerd, along with traders who left few records, provide some of the earliest accounts of the region up the branches of the Susquehanna and Juniata rivers. Until the 1750s, the boundaries of Penn's Woods had marked off a relatively peaceful place of European and American Indian relations. Gregory T. Knouff identifies four key reasons why Pennsylvania sustained a peaceful alternative to other English colonies' use of violence and exterminatory strategies: (1) the engagement of the Quaker Society of Friends in promoting harmony; (2) later European colonization that avoided the frontier conflicts of New England, Virginia, and the Carolinas; (3) the noninvolvement of Pennsylvania in British imperial wars; and (4) the lack of an organized colonial militia.[6]

As French and British imperial leaders relied on their American Indian allies to harass each other's settlements, imperial conflict reshaped the Pennsylvania frontier.[7] French alliances with the Chippewas, Tawas, Tightwees (Miamis), Notowas, Lenni Lenape, and Shawnees made places like Kitanning, Chincklaca-moose (Clearfield), and the Great Island, below present-day Lock Haven, staging grounds for attacking Pennsylvania's backcountry. The construction of Fort Augusta in 1756 (at present-day Sunbury) created an opposing staging ground for British power up the North and West branches of the Susquehanna, from which its commander, Colonel William Clapham, ordered Captain John Ambright to strike up the West Branch of the Susquehanna against Indian settlements like the Great Island and Chincklacamoose. The resulting new form of violence, as Matthew C. Ward contends, tended to erode the spread-out, isolated farm pattern that had characterized much of Pennsylvania's frontier settlement and create more consolidated communities in response to the violence of the 1750s and 1760s.[8]

The end of the French and Indian War brought British dominance to much of eastern North America as far as the Mississippi River. Coupled with French leaders' territorial concessions to Great Britain, the Iroquois Confederacy's strategy of playing imperial and colonial powers against each other by trading away the land rights of people to the south, who were dependent upon them, yielded much of the ground below the feet of American Indians in north-central Pennsylvania to the authority of leaders in London and Philadelphia.[9] Pontiac's alliances with other tribes drew upon the resulting animosities among these dispossessed Indians, and in the process heightened tensions between Europeans and Indians in the band of western settlement. Knouff asserts that settlers such as the Paxton Boys used the vilification of Native Americans resulting from these conflicts to justify a type of "total war," that is, the violent extermination of all Native Americans in the region, which led to the massacre of Conestoga Indians living peacefully in and around Lancaster in December 1763.[10] Krista Camenzind argues that this racialized violence and distrust resulted from a crisis of gender that was the consequence of the destruction of homes, the taking of hundreds of captives, and the destabilization of patriarchal identities during the French and Indian War. Coupled with the failure of the patriarchal assembly to defend them, Camenzind contends that these men resorted to violent extralegal solutions or, in her words, "acts of cowardice" that gave the Paxton Boys a compensatory sense of male valor.[11]

The start of the Pennamite Wars in 1769, which would continue into the early national period between competing Pennsylvania and Connecticut settlement companies in the Wyoming Valley and contiguous areas, became a further cause of alarm for American Indians and European Americans.[12] As a result, English colonial authorities sought to establish clear legal and racial boundaries to stabilize the frontier and maintain peaceful relations. Pennsylvania's negotiation of its "New Purchase" territory with British, colonial, and Native American authorities in 1768, as part of the Fort Stanwix Treaty, attempted to fix the broader frontier boundaries of the British Empire.

The New Purchase Frontier Through the Letters of the Surveyor

According to the Pennsylvania surveyors' records, the lines of the New Purchase ran as follows:

> Beginning in the said Boundary Line, on the East side of the East Branch of the River Susquehanna, at a place called Owegy, and running with the said Boundary Line down the said Branch, on the East side thereof, till it comes opposite the mouth of a Creek called by the Indians Awandae, and across the River, and up the said Creek on the south side thereof, and along the Range of Hills called Burnett's Hills by the English, and by the Indians on the north side of them to the Head of a Creek which runs into the West Branch of the Susquehanna, which Creek is by the Indians called Tiadaghton, and down the said Creek on the south side thereof, to the

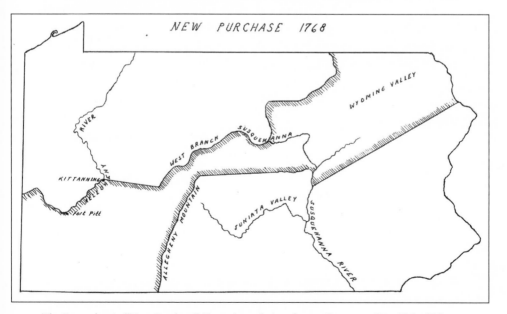

The Pennsylvania "New Purchase" Treaty boundaries of 1768. Courtesy of Fred Threlfall.

said West Branch of Susquehanna; then, crossing the said River and running up the same, on the South side thereof, the Several Courses thereof, to the Fork of the same River, which lies nearest to a place on the River Ohio, called Kittanning, and from the said Fork by a strait Line to Kittanning aforesaid, and then down the said River Ohio, by the several Courses thereof, to where the western Bounds of the said Province of Pennsylvania crosses the same River; and then, with the said Western Bounds to the south Boundary thereof, and with the south Boundary aforesaid, to the East side of the Alleghany Hills.[13]

Surveying played a key role in shaping the frontiers of colonial state building, settlement, and social relationships.[14] Heading deep into the woods, the surveyors not only mapped and shaped an empire but at times functioned as intermediaries, conversing with those Europeans and American Indians who lived in the backcountry. In the process, they were able to describe the initial contacts between the peoples as no one else could.

The letter from Seccalemus, Newtemus, Logan, and Petty quoted in the epigraph to this chapter, found in the correspondence of Charles Lukens to his father, John, the Pennsylvania surveyor-general, provides as clear a window as we have onto the lives of those people who considered places like the Great Island, below Lock Haven on the West Branch of the Susquehanna, one of their settlements, the realm of their fathers and sacred ground. Except for Newtemus, they were probably the sons of Shikellamy, chief of the Oneida Nation, who had represented the interests of the Six Nations in the Susquehanna Valley and kept watch over the Shawnee and Lenni Lenape Indians from 1728 until his death in 1748. As tensions and conflicts arose between various groups in the region, Shikellamy's sons became known for their attempts to mediate between the various peoples and their representatives and to keep the peace. Historian Harry E. Swanger suspects that Logan had settled in the Kishacoquillas Valley, near present-day Reedsville, in 1765, when the early surveyors came into that valley, but there is no mention of him after this except for a sighting at Standing Stone in the early 1770s.[15]

Joseph Newtemus was probably the son of the Chief Nutimus involved in the Walking Purchase Treaty. Nutimus was a chief of a Lenni Lenape clan who opposed the acceptance of that treaty in 1737. Nutimus settled on the Great Island after the French and Indian War. The last record of Nutimus comes from 1763.[16]

This letter indicates that the sons of Shikellamy and Nutimus were still present in 1769 in territory deeded away at Fort Stanwix the previous year. Their description of the encounter with another group of Indians also seems to suggest that other groups of Native Americans were already acting as representatives to the colonial authorities. With this letter the sons of Shikellamy and Nutimus were most probably declaring their continued presence in the area of the Great Island and possibly attempting to assert their rights as local leaders who would want to meet formally with other Indian delegates and by extension with representatives of Pennsylvania. That the letter is in English proves their ability to speak the tongues necessary to navigate different worlds, perhaps even their intention to negotiate a new middle ground.

Comparison with the diaries of German Moravian missionaries like David Zeisberger shows that the Great Island, located within the boundaries of Native American territory, would remain an important meeting place for Native Americans and German Moravian missionaries passing through the region as late as the Revolutionary War.[17] But the reference in their letter to Indians sent from General Johnston, who was probably Sir William Johnston, the British superintendent of Indian affairs for the northern colonies (1755–74), suggests that British authorities had supplanted local Indian authority with the appointment of new, probably nonlocal Indian agents. With no further record of the sons of Shikellamy and Nutimus in the Pennsylvania State Archives, it appears that their bid for maintaining or recovering their fathers' political influence had failed.

Charles Lukens, son of the surveyor-general, also sent reports of Native and European American relations to his father in Philadelphia out of concern with how those relations might affect the speculation in and sale of land. Lukens's reports indicate that emerging conflict between Pennsylvania and Connecticut settlers in the Wyoming Valley was increasing tensions among both Indian and European American settlers along the New Purchase frontier. For instance, Charles wrote to his father from Fort Augusta on June 6, 1770, that "the indians seem extreamly uneasy" because of the Connecticut settlements up the North Branch of the Susquehanna, "and by the advice of some of them given to their friends here, I am apprehensive there will be War this Summer or fall. It is also the Opinion of some People here who understand their Manners & Customs."[18]

Lukens's letter is remarkable in several respects. The violent attacks along the North Branch of the Susquehanna, in what became known as the First Pennamite War (1769–71), were increasing the concerns among the adjoining regions' populations of Native and European Americans that intercolonial and interracial violence there would spill over into their settlements. His report also suggests a high level of communication between groups of Native and European Americans. Intermediaries tended to keep the lines of communication open between groups on both sides, who did not know how to communicate with one another but wanted to maintain peaceful relations.

A set of related sources comes from property documents. Pennsylvania awarded tracts of land to veterans of the French and Indian War in lieu of hard currency and to land speculators in Philadelphia who hoped to profit from the sale of these tracts to the first actual settlers. Pennsylvania opened the New Purchase territory for applications in 1769. Soon thereafter, Pennsylvania authorities incorporated the territory into Northumberland County, and perhaps as early as 1773 organized the growing settlements of the region into Bald Eagle and Potter townships. The first to purchase land in the Bald Eagle tract were Andrew and Margery Boggs, whom the supply minister Philip Vickers Fithian would later visit on his journey through the region. They moved that same year into the territory, near present-day Milesburg, that is, to a place remote even for the New Purchase territory.[19]

The earliest surviving assessment of Bald Eagle Township is a list from 1774 of one female (a widow named Dewitt) and thirty male proprietors, which records the size of their property in acres, the number of acres they had improved, and the number of horses and cattle they owned.[20] Most names on the list appear to be of Scots-Irish and English descent, although at least two men, Gershom Hoff and Anthony Saltsman, were probably German.[21] At least seven of the men share one of two family names, Fleming or Wilson, and are related either as brothers or fathers and sons. One man, Abraham Dewitt, was a tenant of John Fleming, Esq. The average size of an individual's landholdings was approximately three hundred acres, although one was as small as fifty acres. Several had holdings consisting of 100, 150, or 200 acres, and John Fleming, Esq., had more than a thousand acres. On average, these property holders had improved about eighteen acres of their individual properties, which indicates that most farms were designed for subsistence. Property improvement could mean as little as a mark on a tree or as much as land cultivation or home construction. In several cases the owners had improved five or fewer acres. John Fleming had improved 143 acres. Twenty-eight of the listed settlers had on average two horses and two cattle.

Through the Eyes of the Preacher

Philip Vickers Fithian (1747–1776) provides an account of the New Purchase region in the manuscripts of his supply ministry, which extended from the Shenandoah Valley up through Mercersburg and Sunbury in Pennsylvania along the West Branch of the Susquehanna River. Trained at Princeton from 1770 to 1772, Fithian began his journey on May 9, 1775, three weeks after the battles of Lexington and Concord, and passed along the West Branch of the Susquehanna to the home of John Fleming, Esq., on July 25, 1775.[22] Although a bit melodramatic at times, or perhaps influenced by his prejudices against the Native Americans, his affinities for the colonial cause, and his disdain for backcountry living,

Fithian's selective observations offer interesting details for the study of this part of the frontier and the nature of its settlement.[23]

When Fithian passed through the region, he found a land and its diverse peoples in transition, somewhat foreign to him, and not fully understood. He followed the West Branch of the Susquehanna to where it meets Pine Creek and noted the long clearing on either side of the creek, where he had been told Indian towns once existed. In their place Fithian found the cattle and horses of European settlers grazing on what he called a common. At John Fleming's place, Fithian found the largest tract in the region, which included all the land between the Bald Eagle and Susquehanna to more than two miles upstream, where the Fleming house stood along the riverbank. Upon inspection, Fithian suspected that Fleming's property included the site of the former Native American settlement across from the Great Island and a clearing of more than one hundred acres that the Indians had made long before the arrival of the European Americans.

Fithian also made note of various people he met on his journey. On the way to "Squire Fleming's" at dusk on July 25, 1775, Fithian met an "Indian Trader" and his companion, who were passing over Pine Creek. The man rode on horseback armed with a "bright rifle," followed by a horse with packs and "his Man" with their luggage. Fithian also saw two Native Americans on the first full day of his stay with the Fleming family. He experienced an unpleasant feeling when he viewed "these heathenish Savages," but he also noted that they carried "clean Riffles" and were headed downriver with skins (probably for trade with the European settlements).[24]

Fithian kept notes on the nature of the homesteads, which provide insights into the nature of the household, the division of labor, the situation of the home in relation to the surrounding settlements, and the political, regional, and even global connections implied. Squire Fleming went to work in the fields well before 7:00 A.M., when the women began working in the same room where Fithian slept, waking him up in the process. Fleming's daughter helped with the milking and his niece helped with the reaping. The Flemings' home was also a way station for people traveling through the region and a place where settlers' families could socialize. On the second day of his stay, Fithian recorded Squire Fleming's hope that the sparse settlement would "soon form to society." That evening, Fleming's brother and his family joined them all for dinner.

On the fourth evening of his stay, July 28, 1775, Fithian described his visit with the family of William Read, where he ate a dish of huckleberries and drank coffee, which Fithian noted was a rare commodity for the region. The same evening Fithian returned to the Flemings' home to meet a Mr. Gilaspee, who had just arrived from the town of Northumberland with the latest gossip about a local couple's infidelity. On the evening of the next day Fithian recorded his conversation with a young gentleman, Mr. Waggoner, who had arrived at the Flemings' from Philadelphia on his way upriver with a surveyor. In the late afternoon William Read's daughter, Jenny, joined Fithian, John Fleming's daughter, Betsey, and Mr. Gilaspee for a trip over the river and up the mountain to collect huckleberries. On their return across the river, Mr. Gilaspee purposely overturned the canoe in a "rare Diversion," throwing the women and the fruit into the shallow current. Their diversion became a water fight that ended in Mr. Gilaspee's submission, as many people watched from the shore. In the "Squire's Library" Fithian also noted John Dickinson's *Letters from a Farmer in Pennsylvania to the Inhabitants of the British Colonies* (1767–68), which criticized British colonial policy and suggested resistance, though not necessarily independence.[25] In his journal entry for July 28, 1775, Fithian also expressed his concern for "poor distressed Boston, to the Eastward."

On Sunday, July 30, at 11:00 A.M., Fithian held a worship service for approximately 140 people on the "Indian Land" along the north side of the Susquehanna River, opposite the Great Island. He stood at the base of a large tree and his congregation sat on the grass and in the bushes around him. In his journal he recorded three points that he stressed in his sermon: observation of the Sabbath, regular attendance, and the establishment of a more permanent ministry. Fithian provided no further information about the nature of the people gathered at this worship service. It is interesting to note that he held the service outside the officially designated territory of the Pennsylvania New Purchase. Most people were probably of European descent, although it is not at all clear how many were officially settled on the New Purchase tract and how many were squatters. It is also likely that Native Americans were present, given Fithian's description of another service he held later at the Boggs homestead further up the Bald Eagle Valley. This suggests a greater level of interaction between Native Americans and Europeans, centered around the Christian religion, for this time and place than the current historiography, which stresses sharp racial divisions, suggests.

On the following Monday, Fithian traveled with Mr. Gilaspee up the Bald Eagle Creek. Before leaving, John Fleming paid Fithian twenty shillings for his "Supply." On this part of his journey Fithian provided further descriptions of the Native Americans living within the New Purchase boundaries. On an approximately twenty-mile stretch of the creek Fithian noted no signs of European settlement and many "Indian Camps." He described the dwellings as "small crotched Sticks covered with thick Bark" and noted that some of them were no longer occupied. Fithian also recorded finding a fire near a brook where Native Americans had camped the night before, and the warm hindquarters of a deer hanging over the road, which Mr. Gilaspee took down and wrapped in leaves. A little farther up the creek Fithian heard "Whoop! Whoop!" and saw two Native Americans lying in a tent, which must have signaled an invitation, for Fithian and Gilaspee rode up to meet them. Fithian noted that the Native Americans were very kind, and afterward he and Gilaspee continued on to Andrew Boggs's house.[26]

On Monday, July 31, Fithian described his visit at the Boggs homestead:

> Mr. Andrew Bogg's lives here 25 Miles from 'Squire Flemings. We dined on Fish, Suckers, Chups, & on Venison—It is a level, rich, pleasant Spot the broad Creek running by the Door.
>
> Many of the Trees on this Road are cut, by the Indians, in strange Figures; in Diamond's—Deaths Heads—Crowned Heads—Initial Letters—Whole Names—Dates of Years—Blazes.
>
> Soon after we had dined, two Indian Boys bolted in / they never knock or speak at the Door / with seven large Fish—One would weigh two Pound!—In Return Mr. Boggs gave them Bread, & a Piece of our Venison; down they sat in the Ashes before the Fire, stirred up the Coals, & laid on their Flesh—when it was a little roasted, they bit it off in great Mouthfuls, and devoured it with the greatest Rapacity. When they were gone Gilaspee threw himself on a Blanket & is now asleep; I sat me down on a three-legged Stool, to writing—This House looks & smells like a Shambles; raw Flesh & Blood in every Part—Mangled, wasting Flesh on every Shelf—Hounds licking up the Blood from the Floor—An open Landlady—Naked Indians & Children—Ten hundred thousand Flies—O! I fear there are as many—Fleas.

Andrew Boggs owned approximately three hundred acres of land and had improved ten of them, according to the 1774 assessment.[27] His property was probably a subsistence farm at this point. According to Boggs, his homestead was one of the two farthest west on the Bald Eagle tract. Fithian's description suggests a much poorer homestead than the Flemings' (Fithian stayed only one night with the Boggs family and did not record receipt of payment from Andrew Boggs for his ministerial services), but his sketch of the place suggests that Native Americans and solitary European American drifters interacted with one another there.[28] That evening, for example, "six large Indians" came to the house, each carrying a large knife and tomahawk. The next morning, Tuesday, August 1, Fithian held morning prayers at the Boggses' house; three Native Americans, who remained motionless, attended, along with one "irreverent Hunter," a white man who lay on a deerskin during prayers.

Later that morning Fithian headed south through the gap of the Muncy ridge along eighteen miles of unsettled woods. Along the way he ate huckleberries and found wild cherries ripening. Just before sunset he arrived at the home of Captain James Potter in Penn's Valley. Fithian described the Potter house as similar to the Flemings', noting that he had an elegant supper and slept in a bed (things that the Boggs family lacked). The house was neat and devoid of fleas. Captain Potter took him on a tour of his property, which encompassed several thousand acres of good farmland. His improvements included fields of unripened wheat and rye. Potter reported to Fithian that twenty-eight families lived in Penn's Valley. Twenty-two of them were subscribers who had raised £40 to pay for supply ministers. In the afternoon Fithian rode his horse five miles down the valley to a smith, who charged him nothing to shoe his horse. Along the way Fithian noticed that Native Americans also lived in this part of the New Purchase territory. On the return journey that night, Fithian passed ten of them gathered around a campfire, "hollowing, & in frantic Screams, not less fearful than inebriated Demons, howling, til' we were out of Hearing."[29]

James Potter's household included four adult male servants and two boys. When Fithian awoke on Sunday morning, August 6, 1775, he found a "Negro Girl" in the house, awake before anyone else, and a dripping, muddy dog sleeping among his freshly washed clothes.[30] Among James Potter's books Fithian noted Justice William Blackstone's *Commentaries,* Alexander Pope's *Works,* Charles Harvey's *Meditations,* and many "Theological Tracts." At 1:00 in the afternoon and despite a violent storm, Fithian held a service for eight men in the Potter family house. He preached two sermons, separated by a ten-minute intermission, and noted that William Linn had been the last supply minister to pass through the valley two Sabbaths prior to his own. For his services James Potter gave Fithian twenty-five shillings.[31]

The descriptions in Fithian's journal reveal the varied forms of settlement in the New Purchase territory, which ranged from small subsistence farms to large cash-crop tracts and households with domestic African American slaves. The details of his worship services in the settlers' homes and the "Indian" territory suggest the permeable, even shifting boundaries and interrelationships beyond those laid down by the British, Pennsylvania, and Iroquois authorities, even intersecting with spaces considered domestic, sacred, and private, with both whites and American Indians going "into the woods" yet also constituting a "middle ground."[32] Fithian's notes on the Native Americans he saw traveling downriver with pelts, and Reverend John Harris Boggs's recollections about his grandparents (presented below), demonstrate the importance of trade and material goods as motivating factors and central elements in European and Native American relationships, including the presence of traders at Fithian's worship services. Yet Fithian's supply ministry also suggests the importance of religion in connecting various peoples and framing their interactions on this part of the frontier.

Through the Recollections of Widow Boggs

Several records involving members of Andrew Boggs's family look back on the time of settlement before the Great Runaway of 1778, when warfare with American Indians compelled Pennsylvania settlers to leave the valley for the duration of the war. In the Centre County court case of *Richard Fenn Lessee of Lydia Wallis . . . vs. John Denn with notice to John Holt* (April 1800), James Harris asked Andrew Boggs's widow, Margery Boggs, to recall the settlement in the Bald Eagle Valley before Judge Petrikin, in order to clarify the exact lines of the Christopher Cottenton property involved in John Holt's attempt to purchase a tract from the Wallis family.[33] In this case, James Harris asked Margery Boggs to recall events that had occurred more than thirty years earlier. This raised the problem of Margery Boggs's memory, but her testimony also provides information that allows us to reconstruct the nature of settlement.[34]

When James Harris asked Margery Boggs if she had ever been to the house of Christopher Cottenton when he lived there, she told the court that she had been there many times during the sickness of Cottenton's wife and for her death and burial. When asked how long Cottenton had lived there, she said she believed that it was no less than three years, but perhaps more. Questioned about whether she could recall Cottenton's improvements to his property, the amount, type, and location, Boggs remembered visiting Cottenton's wife with a group of neighboring women. She testified that Cottenton's wife told them that her husband was working with his sons to clear the bottomland on the lower end of his property, but she could not tell the court how much land he had improved. When asked to describe Cottenton's improvements around his house or on the island in the Bald Eagle Creek, Margery Boggs answered that Cottenton had cleared a piece of land to the side of the house and land on the island. She remembered that Cottenton had horses, cows, a yoke of oxen, one wagon, and various farming utensils. He had raised a large hemp crop and stored it before the Great Runaway. When asked to describe Cottenton's character, she responded, "He was a very industrious man and in pretty good circumstances[.] [He] had a parcel of good working boys."

When asked about Cottenton's actions during the Great Runaway, when Europeans abandoned their settlements in the area after Native American attacks in 1777 and 1778, Margery Boggs noted that the Cottenton family had left the area before the Boggses had, and that when the Boggs family left, only three families remained in the valley. She remembered too that Cottenton had often told her husband that he was supposed to buy the land from Samuel Wallis. When asked what happened to Cottenton after he left, she told the court that she had heard he had died on the road. To the best of her knowledge, she said, two other men resided on the same property. One, John Kerr, was known more for his drinking and carousing with the Native Americans than for his industry. He left of his own accord before Cottenton. The other, John Turner, also left during the Great Runaway. After the Revolutionary War, John Holt moved onto the Cottenton tract, which led to the court case with the original owners, the heirs of Samuel Wallis.

The historian John B. Linn also provides another account of Margery Boggs, in his *History of Centre and Clinton Counties,* that shows how American Indian and European American women possibly played a very important role in maintaining peaceful, even friendly relations with one another on the frontier. Linn writes, "Mrs. Boggs related that when her husband was away one occasion, the squaws came to her and told her the men were having a carouse and they meant to hide themselves, and cautioned her to leave her doors open that night in case they came to search for them. She did so, and long after nightfall the drunken band entered the house, searched it for their wives, and not finding them went off without molesting her or the family."[35]

Through the Recollections of the Grandson

More evidence of the region's commercial and social networks comes from a letter of Andrew Boggs's grandson, Reverend John Harris Boggs, of Boone, Iowa, to John B. Linn dated September 12, 1882. According to the recollections of Reverend Boggs, his grandfather and the other settlers of the Bald Eagle Valley crossed the Muncy, Nittany, and Seven Mountains to take their grain to a flour mill on the Juniata River. They then transported their flour to market at Northumberland town via canoe and returned with the supplies they would need for the following year.[36] In another letter, dated September 18, 1882, according to John Linn, Reverend Boggs relates a story of his grandparents' relations with two Native Americans, John Logan and his wife, before the wife's murder in April 1774. While his grandfather and Logan were traveling to Philadelphia "to recruit his stock of goods," Logan's wife stopped by the Boggs homestead on her way back from having her corn ground at the mill on the Juniata. She suspected that Mrs. Boggs was in need and gave Boggs's daughter, who was home alone, about half of her corn meal.[37]

Through the Committee of Safety and the Great Runaway of 1778

With the advent of hostilities between the colonies and the British authorities, European American settlers began to organize committees of safety in the New

Purchase territory in the summer of 1775. Both Bald Eagle and Potter townships settlers elected representatives to the Northumberland Committee of Safety. In the backcountry, these committees tended to fill the void of authority and order that had persisted since the aftermath of the French and Indian War. The committees also strengthened the political links to Philadelphia and helped articulate a new political identity in response to the American Revolution. Alongside the regulation of the salt trade and grain prices, compliance with the rules of the Sabbath, hearings of conspirators, and (after July 1776) administration of an oath of loyalty to the new "United States of America," this committee in the Pennsylvania backcountry provided companies of armed men and American Indian scouts for the defense of the frontier against Indian and Connecticut Yankee attacks and for service in the Continental army.[38]

The committee's reports to the General Committee of Safety in Philadelphia indicate that the demands of the Continental army and the defense of the frontier against both Native American and Connecticut attacks created a set of conflicting problems for the Northumberland committee. Other counties in the province had sent agents into Northumberland County to recruit able-bodied men for their own militia companies.[39] Committee members expressed their concern that as a result they could not provide enough men for the defense of the frontier and the "business of agriculture." They also conveyed their concern about the "poverty of the people" and expressed growing uncertainty over relations with the American Indians in the region. They acknowledged that their "enemies" were "tampering" with the natives and voiced concern over the local interventions of the Connecticut colony.[40]

In July 1776 the Continental Congress ordered the raising of a Pennsylvania regiment of seven companies to protect the Allegheny Valley, when it became clear to leaders like General George Washington that the Six Nations would side with the British. On September 12, 1776, the Northumberland Committee of Safety reported to the members of the Pennsylvania convention in Philadelphia that peaceful relations between Native and European Americans had broken down along the frontier and that tensions were escalating toward open conflict:

> That the exposed situation of the north-western Frontier of this County has engaged this Committee to turn a watchful eye towards every motion of the Indians in our Neighborhood; It is with grief we learn That the Sentiments of the Indians in general inimical, and those of them who were lately conversant among Us, having suddenly [sic] withdrawn themselves to their towns, leaves us little Room to Doubt, that our next interview with them, will be as Enemys—A strong (and as we believe) well founded Expectation. That some Men would be raised for the Defense of this County, has hitherto supported in some measure the Spirits of the People;

disappointed as they now consider themselves, in this Expectation, we are not able to keep the single and disengaged Men in the County, they consider fighting as inevitable, and choose rather, under pay, to have to do with a humane Enemy, than at their own expense to encounter merciless Savages. Strongly actuated as we are with a Just Sense of the General Calamity, yet we cannot remain insensible of our own eminent [*sic*] danger, and tho' it is with Reluctance, that we would divert your attention, from matters of greater magnitude, yet we cannot help imploring the assistance of this Convention, and that our situation may be taken into their serious consideration, and such Relief granted, as may in some measure be adequate to our circumstances, either by taking men into Pay for the Protection and support of that part of the Frontier when the enemy may attempt to make an inroad, and to pursue them to their Retreats and Towns—or by granting such sum of Money as will enable the Inhabitants to secure themselves in Forts or Places of safety, in Case of any sudden Invasion, and your Committee as in Duty bound will pray.[41]

In the view of the Northumberland committee, the prospect of war with the Native Americans had begun to weaken the resolve of some of the younger and unmarried men in the region and was leading to the depletion of a supply of able-bodied men needed for defense. Fears of "merciless savages" caused many to choose service against the British, but those fears also informed a specific kind of warfare along the territorial boundaries. The threat of war with the Indians, despite connections with those "conversant among us," logically led the committee to request the colonial convention's support in terms of men, arms, places of refuge, and fortification. The logic of this threat also led the committee to call explicitly for a "total" form of war, such as had developed in the wake of the French and Indian War, to pursue the Indians to their retreats and towns and to eliminate their presence well beyond the bounds of the established frontier.

At the end of January 1777, a delegation of Native American leaders, including chiefs from the Cayuga, Seneca, Munsee, Nanticoke, Conoy, and Mohawk tribes, met at Easton, Pennsylvania, with a Continental congressional commission.[42] The delegation reaffirmed its neutrality in the colonial war, but by the spring of 1777 attacks by various groups of Native Americans and their British agents against settlements along the Pennsylvania frontier signaled an end to the truce. The Big Spring massacre near Standing Stone on June 19, 1777, for example, where a party of Native Americans destroyed the local plantations, must have reconfirmed the frontier's European American leaders' fears of a war of extermination.[43]

The launching of Indian raids against the frontier settlements in the New

Purchase territory in the spring of 1777 led to the flight of most settlers down into the Juniata Valley and along the West Branch of the Susquehanna to safety at Fort Augusta. This became the first exodus of what is known as the Great Runaway, as noted above. From the available accounts, it appears that word of the attacks and the nature of the violence directed against the settlers and their homes spread through express correspondence between militia and government leaders and the stories settlers told upon their arrival at a safe haven. The total warfare that ensued more or less ended any attempts at peaceful coexistence on the Pennsylvania frontier. In the report of Lieutenant Samuel Hunter at Fort Augusta to Thomas Wharton, president of the Supreme Executive Council of the Commonwealth of Pennsylvania in Lancaster, on October 27, 1777, the militia of Northumberland County was clearing the region within fifty miles of the Great Island of "any Enimy indians," and helping to provide for the defense of more than five hundred men, women, and children who had assembled at the mouths of the "Bald Eagle, Antis's mill & Leacoming." Interestingly, Lieutenant Hunter also noted that "there is some friend Indians with their familys come in to our people whome I allow provisions while they stay."[44]

Until the Great Runaway, the possibility of a middle ground still existed in the mid-1770s. Then the logic of racial violence, coupled with the frontier notion of secure space, worked together to destabilize this space and signal its loss. Yet some evidence suggests that, even so, the interactions and experiences of American Indian and European American settlers across the lines of colonial and Indian territories were still capable of producing friendships and loyalties between them—so much so that recurring hostilities between their more racially defined groupings could not easily tear them apart. That Hunter would provide for the care of "friend Indians with their familys" also speaks to the investments of some European settler families in helping their native friends and their attempts to keep alternative forms of relationship intact despite the return of racialized violence and total warfare.

Remaining Questions

The racial definition of Pennsylvania's territorial boundaries was part of a more complex set of political relations involving the strategies of British leaders, the Continental Congress, the Six Nations, disgruntled and dispossessed members of American Indian societies along the frontier, and European Americans invested in settlement of the New Purchase territory. Even with these forces at work, this part of the Pennsylvania frontier still exhibited a high degree of diversity in its forms of settlement and relationships between Europeans and American Indians. Going into the woods did not necessarily mean crossing between completely divided worlds, one disappearing and one being displaced. The middle ground still existed. For example, there were the words of the sons of the old chiefs, which amounted to a fleeting call for continued recognition of their authority in the region and their involvement in the decision-making processes of expanding states and empires. There were American Indians who still went downstream to trade and share goods and hospitality with neighboring European families on their way back. There were still go-betweens, such as the unknown merchants making their way into the woods to trade with American Indians, and surveyors seeking information on the land and the relations of its inhabitants for land speculators back in Philadelphia. Finally, there was the Boggs family, whose home was open to the Indian families on the other side of the creek.

Despite the attempts to redefine the frontier in very clear political, cultural, and racial terms, European and Native Americans continued to cross those boundaries out of necessity, for the exchange of commodities, the practice of religion, and, I suspect, out of simple curiosity and friendship. This part of the New Purchase territory still occupied an important set of spaces of intersection, travel, meeting, commerce, and communication in the region. Enough people like the Boggs family moved out to this frontier who were at least able to put aside preconceptions and prejudices, interact peacefully with the Indians, carve out various forms of shared domestic and sacred space, and develop a common language with a mixture of symbols and gestures that visitors such as the supply minister Fithian could not always read.

Even with the war that followed, these forms of middle ground and "going into the woods" were still possible; they were tenuous but not necessarily doomed. Historian Gregory Knouff argues that high-ranking officers still tended to differentiate between hostile, neutral, and friendly American Indians on the frontier. Despite their prejudices, they generally preferred to make alliances with the Indians, securing their neutrality or establishing personal relationships for strategic purposes rather than eradicating the Indian presence on the frontier.[45]

But the Revolution brought together several conflicts, which regenerated racial violence and destabilized patterns of peaceful coexistence on the New Purchase frontier. This frontier phenomenon coincided with European settlers' identification with the new United States and with their willingness to apply for the aid of the new Pennsylvania government and the Continental Congress, thereby ensuring the termination of older dialogical relationships between regional American Indian authorities and authorities in Philadelphia. This part of the frontier experience included establishing greater control and order. Whether out of necessity or because of ideology, settlers elected representatives from their newly established townships to the committees of safety in order to regulate commerce, identify possible political threats and conspirators, cement political loyalties, maintain public law and order, provide for the defense of the frontier, and expand a protective zone fifty miles beyond the settled boundaries of Pennsylvania. In this respect the history of the New Purchase territory is not dissimilar to the earlier colonial and later U.S. history of the frontier, but its development during the Revolutionary War signaled the end of the older, more peaceful and tolerant vision of Penn's Woods.

During the Revolution, violence once again became the dominant form of expression on this part of the frontier, which subsequently reduced the range of alternative social practices and the political possibilities for a middle ground. The representatives of the Northumberland Committee of Safety and their enemies, the dispossessed Indian leaders, responded to the increasing sense of threat with exterminatory forms of warfare, which resulted from a logic that had grown out of the experiences of the French and Indian and Pontiac's wars. Necessity also drove the region's European American leaders to appeal to the new Pennsylvania and U.S. representative bodies for support, and in turn created a democratic experience on this part of the frontier by the way they established authority and decision making and by replicating colonial administrative and judicial institutions on the frontier.[46] These findings demonstrate a much more ambiguous frontier experience, including settlers' involvement in state building, democratic self-government, and an exterminatory form of conflict. "Going into the woods" for purposes of settlement and taming the wilderness also provided a feeling of security for European American settlers. General John Sullivan's expedition against the tribes of the Six Nations and their allies in north-central Pennsylvania and New York in 1779 wiped out American Indian settlements within reach of the U.S. frontier and, as Paul Moyer argues, inculcated a new generation of European Americans, the first generation of U.S. citizens, in the experience of a total and racial form of warfare.[47] In his discussion of the story of John Struther's refusal to participate in the Gnadenhütten expedition of 1782 and the subsequent destruction of Indian communities, Knouff suggests that participation in the indiscriminate eradication of all Native American settlement resulted in a revolutionary experience of fraternal military violence.[48]

Interestingly, Lieutenant Hunter's report that "friend Indians" remained also raises important questions about what really happened. Where did those American Indian families and their European friends end up? We know that despite total racial warfare, some Native Americans, such as Joab Chillaway and Shawnee John, who had aided American military expeditions against hostile native tribes, were able to return to their homesteads and live out the remainder of their lives in Pennsylvania after the Revolution.[49] Their continued presence within European American society suggests that even with the advancement of a racially defined frontier, alternative forms of coexistence persisted. Did those people remain close to each other? Did they return to their former homes? Did they go their separate ways? Did they intermarry? Did groups of angry settlers hunt down American Indians in their places of refuge and force them out, and did they terrorize European Americans who would have supported their American Indian friends, as the Paxton Boys had done fifteen years earlier in Lancaster? Or did those friendly relationships, that middle ground, persist in the new United States of America, only to fall outside the purview of official sources and ways of reading the frontier? When I presented this paper at the meeting of the Centre County Historical Society in the late winter of 2006, one local resident told the story of her family's mixed European and American Indian heritage. She claimed descent from Chief Logan, which suggests the need to collect the region's oral history accounts and look again.

NOTES

1. The epigraph is from "Lukens-Lenox Papers, Land Office Papers, John Lukens Correspondence, 1768–1772," Manuscript Group 489, Pennsylvania State Archives, Harrisburg.

2. For literature on the Pennsylvania hinterland, see C. Hale Sipe, *The Indian Wars of Pennsylvania* (Lewisburg, Pa.: Wennawoods, 1995); and J. F. Meginness, *Otzinachson: A History of the West Branch Valley of the Susquehanna* (Williamsport, Pa.: Gazette and Bulletin Printing House, 1889). See also Tim H. Blessing, "The Upper Juniata Valley," in *Beyond Philadelphia: The American Revolution in the Pennsylvania Hinterland,* ed. John B. Frantz and William Pencak (University Park: Pennsylvania State University Press, 1998), 153–70; David C. Hsiung, *Two Worlds in the Tennessee Mountains: Exploring the Origins of Appalachian Stereotypes* (Lexington: University Press of Kentucky, 1997); and Hsiung, "Death on the Juniata: Delawares, Iroquois, and Pennsylvanians in a Colonial Whodunit," *Pennsylvania History* 65, no. 4 (1998): 445–77.

3. Literature on the problem of space and place since Turner's "frontier thesis" in U.S. history includes Stephen Aron, *How the West Was Lost: The Transformation of Kentucky from Daniel Boone to Henry Clay* (Baltimore: Johns Hopkins University Press, 1996); and Stanley Elkins and Eric McKitrick, "A Meaning for Turner's Frontier Thesis, Part 1: Democracy in the Old Northwest," *Political Science Quarterly* 69, no. 3 (1954): 321–53.

4. See Richard White, *The Middle Ground: Indians, Empires, and Republics in the Great Lakes Region, 1650–1815* (Cambridge: Cambridge University Press, 1991), 1–93. Compare Daniel K. Richter, "Whose Indian History?" *William and Mary Quarterly,* 3d ser., 50, no. 2 (1993): 379–93.

5. James Hart Merrell, *Into the American Woods: Negotiators on the Pennsylvania Frontier* (New York: W. W. Norton, 1999).

6. Gregory T. Knouff, "Soldiers and Violence on the Pennsylvania Frontier," in Frantz and Pencak, *Beyond Philadelphia,* 172–73.

7. Compare Sipe, *Indian Wars of Pennsylvania,* 299–300; and Meginness, *Otzinachson,* 296–301. See *Pennsylvania Colonial Records* (Harrisburg: Theo Fenn & Co., 1852), 7:299–302; and *Pennsylvania Archives,* 8th ser., ed. Gertrude MacKinney and Charles F. Hoban, 8 vols. (Harrisburg: Pennsylvania Bureau of Publications, 1931–35), 3:41–42.

8. See Matthew C. Ward, *Breaking the Backcountry: The Seven Years' War in Virginia and Pennsylvania, 1754–1765* (Pittsburgh: Pittsburgh University Press, 2003). Compare James Lemon, *The Best Poor Man's Country: A Geographical Study of Early Southeastern Pennsylvania* (Baltimore: Johns Hopkins University Press, 1972).

9. See Fred Anderson, *Crucible of War: The Seven Years' War and the Fate of Empire in British North America, 1754–1766* (New York: Vintage Books, 2001).

10. Knouff, "Soldiers and Violence on the Pennsylvania Frontier," 176–77.

11. Krista Camenzind, "Violence, Race, and the Paxton Boys," in *Friends and Enemies in Penn's*

Woods: Indians, Colonists, and the Racial Construction of Pennsylvania, ed. William Pencak and Daniel K. Richter (University Park: Pennsylvania State University Press, 2004), 204–7.

12. See Paul Moyer, "'Real' Indians, 'White' Indians, and the Contest for the Wyoming Valley," ibid., 231–35.

13. See *Pennsylvania Colonial Records,* 9:551–53; and Kenneth D. McCrea, *Pennsylvania Land Applications,* vol. 2, *New Purchase Applications, 1769–1773* (Philadelphia: Genealogical Society of Pennsylvania, 2003). Compare *Pennsylvania Colonial Records,* 9:554–55, for the description of the treaty boundaries.

14. In her examination of the role that mapping played in imagining national communities on the Indian subcontinent, Sumathi Ramaswamy views cartography as a product of European influence. Drawing on the work of David Harvey, Ramaswamy notes that European "modernity" was predicated on the "domination of nature as a necessary condition of human emancipation." She contends that cartographers systematically and scientifically produce maps through empirical observation, survey, and measurement. Mapmaking functions as a technology for the rational organization of geographic space and helps facilitate the imagination of a community, state, or nation. See Ramaswamy, "Catastrophic Cartographies: Mapping the Lost Continent of Lemuria," *Representations* 67 (Summer 1999): 92–129. For early America, compare Martin Brueckner, *The Geographic Revolution in Early America: Maps, Literacy, and National Identity* (Chapel Hill: University of North Carolina Press, 2006).

15. Compare C. Hale Sipe, *Indian Chiefs of Pennsylvania* (Lewisburg, Pa.: Wennawoods, 1994), 151–64; and Harry E. Swanger, *The Logans, Sons of Shikellamy* (Sunbury, Pa.: Northumberland County Historical Society, 1996).

16. Compare Sipe, *Indian Chiefs of Pennsylvania,* 165–76; and Paul A. W. Wallace, *Indians in Pennsylvania* (Harrisburg: Pennsylvania Historical and Museum Commission), 179.

17. See David Zeisberger, *Herrnhuter Indianermission in der amerikanischen Revolution: Die Tagebücher von David Zeisberger, 1772–1781,* ed. Hermann Wellenreuther and Carola Wessel (Berlin: Akademie Verlag, 1995), esp. the entries for July 7, 1772, September 9 and October 9, 1773; and September 14 and November 12, 1774.

18. "Lukens-Lenox Papers," Pennsylvania State Archives. The involvement of some of the "Paxton Boys" on the side of the Connecticut settlers in January 1770 could possibly have exacerbated the fear of a racially violent conflict among some of the Native Americans in the region.

19. George W. Neible found a listing for Andrew Boggs in his "Account of Servants": "James Mitchell assigns *John Cairus* (a servant from Ireland in the snow Happy Return) to Andrew Boggs of Lancaster County yeoman, for four years from May 21st 1746. Consideration £12:10 / customary dues." Neible, "Account of Servants, Bound and Assigned Before James Hamilton, Mayor of Philadelphia," *Pennsylvania Magazine of History and Biography* 31 (1907): 461–73.

20. John B. Linn, *History of Centre and Clinton Counties, Pennsylvania* (Waynesville: County Heritage, 2000), 14–15.

21. Compare Michael C. O'Laughlin, *The Book of Irish Families Great and Small* (Kansas City: Irish Genealogical Foundation, 1997); George F. Jones, *German-American Names* (Baltimore: Genealogical Publishing, 1990).

22. The more developed urban centers of the colonies had few vacant positions for trained ministers, so many ministers traveled as missionaries to the frontier, where they ministered to the settlers and received food, lodging, and some money in return. In his journal entry for Friday, July 28, 1775, Fithian wrote that John Fleming had told him he was the first "orderly" preacher to visit that settlement. A church clergymen, Mr. Page, and a Mr. Hog, who came to view some land, had visited, but not by appointment of the synod or presbytery. For a biography of Fithian, see *Philip Vickers Fithian: Journal, 1775–1776,* vol. 2, ed. Robert Albion and Leonidas Dodson (Williamsburg, Va.: Colonial Williamsburg, 1934), vii–xviii.

23. I base this study on Fithian's journal entries from July 25 to August 8, 1775. See ibid., 69–92.

24. Compare Peter Mancall, *Valley of Opportunity: Economic Culture Along the Upper Susquehanna, 1700–1800* (Ithaca: Cornell University Press, 1991), 39–59. Mancall asserts that as the Native Americans accepted the introduction of the "new economy" based on the procurement of sought-after natural resources, the western European commercial system helped to destabilize the Native American exchange system and communities in the region with far-reaching and disastrous ecological and environmental effects.

25. See William Pencak, "The Promise of Revolution," in *Pennsylvania: History of a Commonwealth,* ed. Randall Miller and William Pencak (University Park: Pennsylvania State University Press, 2002), 116.

Dickinson aimed his *Letters from a Pennsylvania Farmer* at the rural colonial audience; he argued that the British had no right to tax the colonies.

26. Compare Mancall, *Valley of Opportunity,* 48–52. Mancall argues that a code of hospitality existed in the region that called on hosts to offer their guests food, and that travelers should reciprocate with a gift if possible. From Fithian's description and what he omits, it is not clear how well he understood forms of communication and patterns of hospitality with the Native Americans in the region.

27. See note 19.

28. There is no record of Andrew Boggs's last will and testament at the Northumberland County courthouse in Sunbury, or of the exact date of his death, although some sources put his death around 1776. See, for example, the assessment of Bald Eagle Township from May 1, 1778, which lists Margery Boggs as "Widow Boggs." Compare Linn, *History of Centre and Clinton Counties,* 19.

29. Fithian, *Philip Vickers Fithian: Journal,* 86.

30. In his will, James Potter bequeathed "one Negro man named Hero and one Mulatto boy named Adam, whom I value at one hundred pounds, to have and to hold to my son James, his heirs and assigns forever," and to Martha Gregg, Potter's daughter, "one Negro woman named Dauphine, one Mulatto girl, her daughter, named Sal, and one Mulatto boy, her son, named Bob, whom I value at sixty pounds to have and to hold . . . forever." See Rich Kerstetter, "On Hallowed Ground? Potters Mills May Be Home to a Slave Cemetery," *Centre Daily Times,* http//:www.pnafoundation.org/Contest/Keystone/Div%20IV/Kerstetter.htm (accessed March 11, 2004); and Kerstetter, "Ground Forces: Group Uses State-of-the-Art Equipment to Gather Evidence of Slave Cemetery's Existence," *Centre Daily Times,* April 13, 2003.

31. William Linn (1752–1808) graduated from Princeton in 1772. He was pastor at Big Spring, Pennsylvania, from 1777 to 1784 and received his doctoral degree from Columbia University in 1789. Linn went on to hold several important posts, including associate minister of the Collegiate Dutch Church in New York City from 1786 to 1805, trustee of Rutgers College from 1787 to 1808, and chaplain to the U.S. House of Representatives from 1789 to 1791. He also published several works, among them *The Blessings of America* and *Serious Considerations on the Election of a President.*

32. Nancy Stover has found an interesting case of Native American and European interaction on this part of the frontier in her genealogical research on Robert Moore (1753–1831). Moore served as a ranger on the frontier. In his obituary in the *Centre Democrat* on May 7, 1831, an "Early Settler" recalled that Moore was also an adopted son in a local Indian tribe, well versed in the ways of both Europeans and Native Americans, and an important go-between for those living in the region. It was Moore who found the first victims of Native American attacks in the region in the fall of 1777 (actually the Jacob Stanford family, massacred in May 1778). Moore helped spread the word and aided in conducting the safe passage of other settlers. See Nancy Stover, "In Search of Robert Moore," *Centre County Roots: The Newsletter of the Centre County Genealogical Society* 29, no. 3 (2004): 1, 4; and Sipe, *Indian Wars of Pennsylvania,* 541.

33. The name "Christopher Cottington" appears on an assessment of Bald Eagle Township from May 1, 1778, shortly before the Great Runaway, but it does not list any assessment of property. John Holt first appears on the assessment of new territory in the valley from 1785, with no indication of property ownership. It becomes clear through the line of questioning in the court case that Holt is interested in determining the chain of deed, and the extent of improvement to the land originally owned by Samuel Wallis, in order to purchase it. See Linn, *History of Centre and Clinton Counties,* 19, 22.

34. Ibid., 14.

35. Linn does not provide the source of this account. It does not appear in Mrs. Boggs's court deposition and it is not listed in the John B. Linn Collection of the Centre County Library Historical Museum. However, it is an interesting anecdote, if true, about European and Native American interaction. Compare ibid., 14.

36. This letter is located in the John B. Linn Collection of the Centre County Library Historical Museum.

37. Linn cites this letter of September 18, 1882, which includes Reverend Boggs's story as told in the letter of September 12. The John B. Linn Collection contains no letter from Boggs dated September 18, 1882. The letter of September 12 also does not contain Boggs's story about his grandmother and John Logan's wife. Another letter from Reverend Boggs, dated October 3, 1882, can be found in the Linn Collection. In that letter, Boggs recalls the family story about their plight during the Great Runaway. It also appears in Linn's *History of Centre and Clinton Counties* (13), but is not dated there.

38. See the case of William Read of Bald Eagle Township, who was taken into custody and brought before the committee for his refusal to bear arms on behalf of the United States. Because he had been arrested in a riot against the English in Ireland, known as the "Hearts of Steel" riot, Read had taken an oath of allegiance to the king as the condition for his acquittal, obligating him never to bear arms against the king. The committee asked him to swear an oath of allegiance to the United States: "I do swear to be true to the United States of America, and do renounce and disclaim all allegiance to the King of Great Britain, and promise that I will not either directly or indirectly speak or act any thing in prejudice to the cause or safety of the States, or lift arms against them, or be any way assistant to their declared enemies in any case whatsoever." *Pennsylvania Archives*, 2d ser., ed. J. B. Linn and W. H. Egle, 19 vols. (Harrisburg: E. K. Myers, 1874–90), 14:363–64. For a history of the Committee of Safety of Northumberland County, see John H. Carter, "The Committee of Safety of Northumberland County," in *Early Events in the Susquehanna Valley* (Millville, Pa.: Precision Printers, 1981), 163–76. For documents relating to the committee, see *Pennsylvania Archives*, 2d ser., 14:337–64.

39. *Pennsylvania Archives*, 2d ser., 14:341–42.

40. Ibid., 14:343–44. On February 13, 1777, Bald Eagle Township sent John Fleming, James Hughes, and John Walker to the Committee of Safety meeting in Northumberland. Potter Township sent John Livingston and John McMillan. Ibid., 14:358–60.

41. Ibid., 14:350.

42. Sipe, *Indian Wars of Pennsylvania*, 509–11.

43. For a list of the frontier conflicts involving the New Purchase territory and contiguous regions between 1777 and 1783, see ibid., 509–684.

44. *Pennsylvania Archives*, 1st ser., ed. Samuel Hazard, 12 vols. (Philadelphia: Joseph Severns, 1851–62), 5:717–18. Compare Linn, *History of Centre and Clinton Counties*, 18–20.

45. Knouff, "Soldiers and Violence on the Pennsylvania Frontier," 191–92.

46. For example, on July 15, 1776, the convention for the first constitution of Pennsylvania appointed Henry Antes and James Potter, at that time Northumberland County's representative to the convention, as justices of the courts in Northumberland County. On April 5, 1777, the Continental Congress commissioned General James Potter as a brigadier general; Potter then actively served around Philadelphia. On June 9, 1777, the Northumberland Committee of Safety appointed John Livingston a justice of the courts for the county.

47. Sullivan's expedition eradicated almost all of the Native American settlements in north-central Pennsylvania and New York, but some managed to return. It is also unclear how many of the settlers who had enlisted in the Northumberland County militia companies took part in total warfare. Most served in the ranger battalions and Colonel Cookson Long's company of the Second Battalion, Northumberland County Militia, on the frontier, or against the British in units of the Continental army. William Pencak has found the accounts of George Long and Daniel Livingston in the U.S. Revolutionary War Pension Records, which indicate that Colonel Long's company, for example, served mostly in defense of the local frontier and experienced smaller-scale skirmishes with attacking Native Americans. Lieutenant Hunter's accounts suggest that some may have participated in the clearing of the region around the Great Island, but this requires further research. See Moyer, " 'Real' Indians, 'White' Indians," 231–35; Nancy Lee Stover, *Revolutionary War Soldiers, Centre County* (Boalsburg, Pa.: self-published, 2004); Sipe, *Indian Wars of Pennsylvania*, 599–606; *Pennsylvania Archives*, 2d ser., 14:318–36; *Pennsylvania Archives*, 5th ser., ed. Thomas L. Montgomery, 8 vols. (Harrisburg: State Printer, 1906), 8:670; and U.S. Revolutionary Pension Records, microfilm, reel 1573, no. 522361, and reel 1580, no. 9139, David Library of the American Revolution, Washington Crossing, Pennsylvania.

48. Knouff, "Soldiers and Violence on the Pennsylvania Frontier," 188.

49. See Sipe, *Indian Wars of Pennsylvania*, 548. Zeisberger notes in his diary entry for August 8, 1778, that "Job Challowey's" wife arrived at the Moravian mission at Gnaddenhütten on the Muskingum River in Ohio, in flight from the European American counterattacks in the vicinity of the Great Island. Zeisberger relates that Chillaway's wife believed that her children and husband had also been killed, like all the other Native Americans, by the white people. Compare Zeisberger, *Herrnhuter Indianermission in der amerikanischen Revolution*, 458: "Von Gros Eyland an der West Branch der Susquehanna kam Job Challoweys Frau unsers Samuel Moor Schwester her, die ihr Leben mit der Flucht gerettet, denn alle Indianer daselbst, wie auch ihr Mann und ihre Kinder, sagte sie, wären von den weissen Leuten umgebracht."

7

DOUBLE DISHONOR:
LOYALISTS ON THE MIDDLE FRONTIER

Douglas MacGregor

Just as Dante found traitors worthy of his vision of the lowest level of hell, many Americans relegated loyalists to the same depths. Writing more than 150 years after the Revolution, Stephen Vincent Benet populated hell with loyalists Walter Butler and Simon Girty, who kept company with Benedict Arnold and the famed American Indian leader King Philip.[1] Although many of these loyalists found new homes north of the U.S. border in Canada, Americans pictured their eternal homes well south of heaven. Many loyalists along the American frontiers suffered a double damnation. Butler and Girty were considered not only betrayers of their "American brethren" but betrayers of their race. Their associations with American Indians before the war had been viewed with a suspicious eye, but their decision to join the Indians in a war against Americans had crossed distinct cultural lines. Many of the loyalists of western Pennsylvania had close ties to the native tribes of the Ohio country and would bequeath the legacy of alleged treachery to their race as well as their country.

The war in the west did not end with the American victory at Yorktown in October 1781. Many of the loyalists who fled western Pennsylvania would maintain their alliances with Ohio country Indian nations and resist the westward movement of the United States in the decades that followed, further cementing their fate in the American psyche. Land was the determining factor in the loyalist uprisings in western Pennsylvania and the decision to remain loyal to the British government. For some it was their own land, but for others it was the American sentiment and policy toward American Indians and their land that would drive loyalists away from the American cause. By abandoning their country and joining the British in leading Indian war parties against their former countrymen, the loyalists incurred a double dishonor.

By the time the "shot heard around the world" was heard in Pittsburgh in May 1775, the contest for loyalties between the mother country and their "American brethren" had acquired another layer of complexity in a region already divided. Tension between Pennsylvania and Virginia over possession of the region had split residents into two groups vying for control. Conflict between Virginians and Indian nations of the Ohio country had resulted in Lord Dunmore's War and subsequent peace negotiations scheduled for the summer of 1775 that would have major implications for the war between Britain and the American colonies. Now that war had erupted on Lexington Green, loyalties in the American Revolution would take precedence over provincial differences.

The imperial presence in the region at Fort Pitt evaporated in 1772 when General Thomas Gage, commander-in-chief of the king's forces in North America, ordered the fortress abandoned, creating a power vacuum. The province of Pennsylvania had begun selling land in the region following the Fort Stanwix purchase in 1768. As settlers flowed westward, Pennsylvania created new western counties—Bedford in 1771 and Westmoreland in 1773—to govern them. Virginia had tried to grant lands beyond the Appalachians but was unsuccessful. The Privy Council, fearing another war with Native Americans, had denied almost all of its grants following the Fort Stanwix purchase. With the arrival of Lord Dunmore as governor, Virginia made more creative attempts to claim western lands. Dunmore evaded royal instructions prohibiting the creation of new counties out west by claiming that the area about Fort Pitt lay in the district of West Augusta, a division of Augusta County. Dunmore appointed John Connolly "Captain Commandant of the Militia of Pittsburgh and its Dependencies." Connolly ordered the Virginia militia to muster on January 25. Arthur St. Clair, a Westmoreland County Pennsylvania magistrate, led the Pennsylvania defense of the region by keeping Governor John Penn informed of the situation and arresting Connolly. Connolly was eventually released, but this marked the beginning of civil, and often violent, disturbances that would last until the final settlement of the boundary between Pennsylvania and Virginia in 1780 and bitterly divide the region during the Revolutionary War, when the two colonies' cooperation was desperately needed.[2]

Conflict was not limited to provincial competition for Pittsburgh. Lord Dunmore had expressed great interest in the region as a land speculator and had promised John Connolly a large tract at the falls of the Ohio (Louisville, Kentucky) in return for his services in Pittsburgh. Dunmore had hoped to increase his personal wealth by driving the Shawnee out of Kentucky and then selling their valuable land. The general peace that had existed between colonists and the American Indian nations of the upper Ohio River valley was shattered in April 1774, after a series of killings took place along the river involving colonists and the Shawnee. Among the victims was the family of Logan, a Mingo leader living at the mouth of Yellow Creek (Steubenville, Ohio). Logan waged a personal war to avenge the murders of his family, which Dunmore then used as a pretext for an open war against the Mingo and Shawnee nations. Virginia forces were raised and marched into the backcountry later that year. Following an indecisive battle at Point Pleasant (Point Pleasant, West Virginia) on October 10, the Shawnee were forced into a temporary peace agreement, as their home-lands were threatened with destruction. The temporary peace was followed by a formal treaty at Pittsburgh the following year.[3]

In 1775 the struggle between Virginia and Pennsylvania was put on hold, not through the diplomatic efforts of governors Penn or Dunmore but in a manner neither side could have imagined. Around May 1, news of the battles of Lexington and Concord reached Pittsburgh. As a result, even though there had been no previous agitation in the region against Britain's policies, Virginia and Pennsylvania settlers called an emergency meeting on May 16 at Fort Pitt, out of which came a committee of correspondence for West Augusta, Virginia. The committee began mobilizing a militia, securing ammunition, and cultivating a "friendship with the Indians." The same day, residents of Westmoreland County met at Hannastown, the Pennsylvania county seat, to declare their support for the American cause.[4]

The Virginians and Pennsylvanians had thus put aside their land disputes and joined together by pledging to fight for liberty. Virginian support for Dunmore disappeared, although only a few weeks earlier many Virginians had sent an address thanking him for his help against the Shawnee and repudiating a rumor that the governor had deliberately incited them to war. Their resolves of May 16 to create a revolutionary committee reversed this position and instead blamed the "wicked minions of power to execute our ruin, added to the menaces of an Indian War, likewise said to be in contemplation, thereby thinking to gain our attention, and divert it from that still more interesting object of liberty and freedom."[5]

The majority of frontier inhabitants appeared to favor the American cause. The English traveler Nicholas Cresswell, a young aristocrat in search of wealth through land speculation, often found himself in trouble and was even threatened with tarring and feathering. Cresswell noted that the frontier population was "Liberty mad," thinking of nothing but war, and that "the best riflemen" were prepared to go to Boston "for the humane purpose of killing the English officers." Pittsburgh patriots showed their solidarity and support in August 1775 by confiscating and burning tea at a liberty pole in a local version of Boston's Tea Party. Some, however, were troubled by the prospect of war. Arthur St. Clair, who would later become a major general in the Continental army and Pennsylvania's highest-ranking soldier during the war, wrote in the days after his region's mobilization that he was "as much afraid of success in this contest as of being vanquished."[6]

In May 1775, when most of the inhabitants of Pittsburgh had agreed to favor the patriots, John Connolly had already decided whom he would support. In reply to a letter from Connolly, George Washington informed him that matters between the colonies and Great Britain "wear a disagreeable aspect" and that the "minds of men are exceedingly disturbed at the measures of the British government." Washington ended with the ominous thought that "a little time must now unfold the mystery, as matters are drawing to a point." Connolly now "resolved to exert every faculty in defense of the royal cause." He feared his land grants would be worthless if the Americans won the struggle. At the start of 1775 Pittsburgh had seemed to be firmly under Virginia's control, and it appeared to be only a matter of time before he would reap a substantial profit from his land at the falls of the Ohio River. Without Lord Dunmore, Connolly's claim to the falls was tenuous at best. All of the other land grants Virginia had issued between the Fort Stanwix purchase in 1768 and Lord Dunmore's arrival in 1772 had been dismissed by the Privy Council, including those held by Patrick Henry, Thomas Jefferson, and George Washington. Dunmore's grant to Connolly, which had not been dismissed, was an anomaly. William Preston, the surveyor for Fincastle County, Virginia, informed George Washington that it was "the Opinion of many good Judges [that Connolly's] Patents [were] altogether illegal."[7]

The Revolution posed a serious threat to Connolly's land claims, which would survive only if Dunmore and the British government survived in America. Knowing this, he would do whatever it took to maintain the stability of the existing government. In 1775 he led the negotiations with the Native Americans in Dunmore's absence; his mission was to enlist their support for the royal cause. The negotiations held at Fort Pitt in 1775 had major implications for the war developing in the east. Connolly also took it upon himself secretly to find out who else in Pittsburgh would remain loyal to the king.[8]

Between May 19 and 21, 1775, Connolly issued invitations to the Shawnee, Mingo, and Delaware to attend a conference in Pittsburgh on June 20. Pittsburgh patriots sent word to the Continental Congress about the forthcoming negotiations, asking that it send a representative. Congress responded by creating three Indian departments. The central department, headquartered at Pittsburgh, was governed by a committee of commissioners that included Benjamin Franklin, Patrick Henry, and James Wilson, who appointed Richard Butler, a Pennsylvania trader at Pittsburgh, as their agent at Fort Pitt. Whig leaders in Virginia appointed a committee to attend the conference as well. James Wood, chairman of this Virginia committee, set out for Pittsburgh on June 25. Virginia also recognized the importance of garrisoning Fort Pitt with an armed body and resolved on August 7 to send John Neville—later the tax collector in the Whiskey Rebellion whose house was destroyed—to command there with one hundred men.[9]

Absent from any official role in these talks were the two men who had conducted Indian affairs at Fort Pitt since the first British occupation at Pittsburgh in 1758, George Croghan and Alexander McKee. Croghan had retired from the position of British deputy Indian agent in 1771 to pursue the lucrative field of land speculation with Samuel Wharton's Vandalia venture. The position was then handed to Alexander McKee, but Croghan remained on call in Pittsburgh. McKee was the son of a powerful trader and a Shawnee woman, and had been raised in the Shawnee culture and had a Shawnee wife and child living in the Shawnee villages along the Scioto River at the outbreak of war. While Croghan and McKee had both supported the Virginians during the boundary dispute, Croghan had signed the Virginia resolves of May 16, supporting the American cause, and McKee had not. Croghan was an active patriot in the early days of the Revolution in Pittsburgh; his name led the list of the Virginia resolves of May 16 and his home was the site of the initial negotiations of the 1775 conference. Perhaps his past ties with the British government had led the Continental Congress to bypass him for Richard Butler as Indian agent for the Americans. Nevertheless, Croghan continued to help the American cause by assisting Butler in his duties and asking the Indian nations of the region to remain neutral and ignore the British propaganda coming from Detroit and Niagara.[10]

Pennsylvania officials arrested Connolly on the evening of June 21 and moved him fifty miles east to Ligonier. In captivity, Connolly was informed that he had been imprisoned because he was a "dangerous person and a Tory, an appellation lately revived," as well as being "suspected of an intention to raise a body of men to act against the liberties of America." The Virginia officials of West Augusta suspected that his arrest was actually another maneuver in the boundary dispute, not a preventive measure in the war with Great Britain. Consequently, they arrested three Pennsylvania magistrates and sent a "spirited" letter to the Westmoreland County committee demanding Connolly's release. St. Clair avoided any potential violence by releasing Connolly.[11]

Meanwhile, the council with the Ohio Indians had already begun without Connolly. Upon his release, Connolly joined the conference and took an active role until its close on July 6. The conference was productive, and all of the attending Native American nations, as well as all of the whites, left satisfied, desiring peace. While Connolly was supposed to win the allegiance of the Indians present, the presence of patriot officials prevented him from doing so. Even the committee appointed by Virginia's revolutionary government to oversee the conference was pleased with Connolly's performance. On July 9, James Wood, the Virginia commissioner appointed to the conference, commended Connolly on his "most open and candid manner."[12]

Now that negotiations were over, Connolly was free to leave Pittsburgh to join Lord Dunmore, who had been in exile since July 25 aboard a British warship stationed off the Virginia coast. While making preparations to leave, Connolly carefully sought out the men in Pittsburgh who remained loyal to the king. He composed a list of their names, including Alexander McKee and Alexander Ross, a wealthy land speculator and merchant who had purchased Fort Pitt in 1772, which he later submitted to Lord Dunmore. After disbanding the militia under his command, Connolly left Pittsburgh on July 25 under the pretext of delivering the results of the negotiations to Williamsburg, but actually intending to visit Lord Dunmore on his warship off Norfolk. After avoiding arrest on several occasions, he met with Dunmore.[13]

In their consultation, Connolly proposed a plan to cut the American colonies in half. He requested that he be given a commission and the power to offer three hundred acres to raise an armed group of men and lead an expedition from Detroit to capture Fort Pitt. Connolly understood the power of offering land and felt sure that supporters would flock to his standard. With his army, he intended to march eastward to Alexandria, Virginia, gathering loyalist supporters along the way, where he would meet with Lord Dunmore, who was to march westward from the Atlantic coast, thus successfully cutting the American colonies in half. On August 9 Connolly sent a letter to John Gibson in Pittsburgh, who Dunmore thought was a loyal subject but whose loyalty Connolly questioned, cautioning him to "avoid an over zealous exertion of what is now ridiculously called patriotic spirit" and deliver a message to White Eyes, a leader of the Delaware Indian nation. Dunmore's message to White Eyes and his people reminded them of their friendship with the king and asked them to ignore pleas for assistance from the Americans. In return for their neutrality the king would protect their lands, as well as those of the Mingo, Shawnee, and Iroquois. In sending this letter Connolly "gave up suspicions that afterwards appeared to be too well founded." He was right about Gibson, who turned the correspondence over to the West Augusta committee on September 24.[14]

Next, Connolly proceeded to Boston, where he gained approval of his plan from General Thomas Gage and soon left to implement it. Unbeknownst to Connolly, that plan was leaked to George Washington, in charge of the troops at Boston, who immediately informed the Continental Congress, which issued notices asking for Connolly's capture. As Connolly's party left Hagerstown, Maryland, on November 23, they were arrested and eventually sent to Philadelphia to be jailed. While in jail, Connolly managed to write several warnings about the failure to the western posts and leaders, including Alexander McKee, the British deputy Indian agent at Fort Pitt. This letter was intercepted by American authorities in January 1776 and officials were ordered to arrest McKee. But before he could be arrested, he had other troubles to deal with. In late February Colonel John Butler, an Indian agent at British-held Fort Niagara, wrote to McKee asking him to come to Niagara to join the British service and report on the activity of the Americans at Pittsburgh. Knowledge of the letter's arrival was communicated to the Pittsburgh Committee of Correspondence by its chairman, George Croghan. While McKee had done nothing concrete against America, the Americans took no chances and placed him on restrictive parole and ordered him to refrain from his duties as a British Indian agent.[15]

McKee was not the only one who felt that the sanctions imposed upon him were harsh. American Indian agent Richard Butler felt they were unwarranted, as they had "not seen one act that discovered an inimical intention to this country." Despite his patriotic actions, the Americans did not want Croghan. When Richard Butler resigned his post of Indian agent in April 1776, Croghan lobbied for the position but was denied, and the post was given to George Morgan, an old competitor in the fur trade and land speculation. Morgan shunned Croghan and sought assistance from Alexander McKee when needed. Prerevolutionary friendships and animosities mattered as much to these western frontier traders as their wartime allegiances did, or more so.[16]

Despite the British government's suspicion of McKee, George Morgan enlisted McKee to accompany him on a tour of the Ohio country to visit the

Settlements in the Ohio country during the Revolutionary War. From Detroit and Niagara, British agents directed attacks from their Indian allies against American settlements east of the Ohio River, as well as inciting loyalist sentiments. Courtesy of Fred Threlfall.

Indian nations and counter British overtures. A friendship developed between Morgan and McKee, perhaps through their common dislike of Croghan. McKee's influence with the Indians was not lost on Morgan, and he used it to convince the Indian nations of the sincerity of the Americans. This mission was successful in promoting peace among the many Indian tribes of the Ohio country, and they were invited to Pittsburgh later that year to reaffirm the treaty of 1775. By the time members of the Shawnee and Delaware began to arrive at Fort Pitt in October, British propaganda and promises had begun to take effect. Rumors of attacks and warfare reached both Indians and Americans. Many Indian bands had declined to attend the treaty negotiations, while others joined the British. Despite the attacks and loss of neutrality with several bands of Indians, the treaty talks held in Pittsburgh ended in November 1776 with several groups, including the Shawnee under Cornstalk and the Delaware under White Eyes, pledging continued peace. On November 9 Morgan reported to Congress that although there were attacks in the area, they were isolated, and he had concluded a successful treaty through which "the cloud which threatened to break over this part of the country appears to be nearly dissipated."[17]

Morgan may have spoken too soon. While he explained to Congress that the attacks occurring in the region in the fall of 1776 were isolated, the beginning of 1777 would prove that war had returned to western Pennsylvania for the duration and would last, with only short intervals of peace, through 1794, when Anthony Wayne finally defeated the Ohio Valley Indians at the Battle of Fallen Timbers. In mid-February, Chippewa and Iroquois warriors, along with two white men, attacked the Munsey Town (near Kittanning, Pennsylvania), capturing a trader. In March, Iroquois warriors attacked a settlement near Twelve-mile Run in Westmoreland County, killing two and leaving a note, written by Colonel John Butler of Niagara for the Iroquois, that decried the Americans' illegal possession of the land, as "the lands are ours and we insist on your quitting them immediately . . . or blame yourselves for whatever may happen." Morgan knew that the British agents had the advantage in swaying the Indian nations, especially the Iroquois, who were angered over "the encroachments we have undeniably made on their lands."[18]

In light of these attacks and others, the Continental Congress ordered that Fort Pitt be placed under its supervision, with detachments of the Continental army under Brigadier General Edward Hand, who arrived there on June 1, 1777. This was a relief to the inhabitants, who "were in the utmost consternation," and it was "hoped that the arrival of Brigadier General Hand will dissipate their fears, and add life and vigour to their undertakings." As Hand was "universally loved on the Ohio, the people will no doubt flock to his standard and cheerfully go forth and chastise the savage foe." The results could not have been further from these predictions. While Colonel Henry Hamilton, British commander at

Detroit, was successful in supplying an increasing number of raids along the American frontier, Hand failed to mount a single successful expedition.[19]

Although the Americans won the Revolution, they did poorly in western Pennsylvania. Hamilton issued a proclamation to the settlers near Pittsburgh offering protection in Detroit from the "Tyranny and oppression of the rebel Committees" as well as a bounty of land for those who would take up arms against "Rebels and Traytors, 'till the extinction of this rebellion." Hamilton felt that the appeal to land would sway the residents of the frontier. Additionally, rumors of an attack on Pittsburgh by an army of ten to sixteen thousand Indian warriors, Canadians, and British soldiers led to a great panic among settlers in the region. Hand's plan to destroy the Indian villages along the Scioto River was abandoned after feuding Virginia and Pennsylvania militia refused to assemble for the expedition. To make matters worse, Cornstalk, a leader of the Shawnee and one of the few friends the Americans had among the Indian nations, was murdered by Virginia troops at Fort Randolph in November, leading all neutral Shawnee to join the British. An expedition to destroy a British powder magazine along the Cuyahoga River in February and March 1778 resulted in the murder of an old man, a few women, and a boy at a Delaware settlement along the Mahoning River before troops returned home, derisively calling it the "Squaw Campaign."[20]

The indiscriminate killing that characterized the Squaw Campaign escalated the atrocities committed by the Americans along the middle frontier. The killing of civilians, men and women, young and old, by Indian warriors had fueled a hatred of Indian peoples that predated the Revolution. Most recently, atrocities had been exchanged between settlers and Indians in 1774, leading to Dunmore's War. Once hostilities recommenced with the Revolution, hatred between the races flared into violence once again. British agents in Detroit would tell the Indian warriors to "kill all Rebels" and "put them all to death." When one Wyandot warrior asked if they meant women and children as well, he was answered with "kill all, destroy all; nits breed lice!" As the war continued and the casualties mounted, so did the hatred. By 1782 the residents of western Pennsylvania, failing to secure the frontier, talked "of nothing but killing Indians and taking possession of their lands." Following a raid by hostile warriors, this hatred led to the murder of ninety Christian Indians at the Moravian mission town of Gnadenhütten. Acts like massacre went unpunished, since the belief was, as the Moravian missionary John Heckewelder wrote, that "no man should be put to death for killing an Indian; for it was the same thing as killing a wild beast."[21]

Hand's tenure at Fort Pitt also witnessed severe problems with loyalists. When recounting his youth and his father's life in the Monongahela River valley south of Pittsburgh during the Revolution, John Crawford recalled 1777 as the "Tory Year," in that so many of his neighbors "found a conspiracy against the government, and secretly took an oath to be true to the government of George the Third, in pointed violation of the Declaration of Independence." News of the defeats of the Continental army elsewhere, and the increase of Indian attacks, which were "indiscriminate of all ages and sexes," wore hard on the minds of the people of living south of Pittsburgh. "In this state of suspense, the stoutest hearts trembled for the fate of America." Few "sucked in the love of his King with his mother's milk" early in 1777, but British agents arrived in the area, spreading word of the hopelessness of the American cause and passing on rumors that if British government returned to the area, the property of the patriots would be confiscated. The British agents knew the power of threatening the lands of the settlers, and it had tremendous effects. Many of the settlers came to the frontier because they could not afford land east of the Appalachian Mountains. The frontier offered good, affordable land and an opportunity to build a life. They were willing to risk their lives defending their land from Indian attacks, and now their land was threatened if they chose the wrong side in the Revolution. Even staunch patriots began to question their commitment to what appeared to be a losing proposition. Along the Monongahela River near Redstone, "a man of the name of Smith," who had previously had an argument with a known loyalist that almost came to blows, had even changed his mind at the prospect of losing his land. To the poor frontiersmen, "the thought of losing their lands and improvements [was] dreadful to them," Crawford recalled. "It was their all." Secret meetings were held, gossip flared, and threats were made, as neighbors began to choose sides.[22]

In late August 1777, as tensions built, William Crawford, John Crawford's father (no relation to Colonel William Crawford, who was killed in 1782), was informed of a rumor that General Burgoyne was to march on Fort Pitt and his Indian allies were to take the fort at Wheeling. After taking the forts, the "Tories was to declare themselves for the King, and those who refused to do so would be put to death."[23] The elder Crawford then notified Colonel Thomas Gaddis and Major Uriah Springer, leaders of the local Virginia militia, who informed General Hand and immediately began to organize at Provence's Fort (near Alicia, Greene County, Pennsylvania) to investigate the matter. Loyalists learned of the patriot assembly and began to assemble near the fort. The patriot militia, numbering nearly forty men, forced the hundred loyalists from the field without firing a shot. Sometime later, the loyalists managed to assemble another large body of men to oppose the militia under Gaddis. Upon hearing of the loyalist force, William Crawford went to Captain Jesse Pigman of the local militia to bring reinforcements. Pigman brought his group of thirty men to Swan's fort (Cumberland, Greene County) to recruit more men to oppose the loyalists, and informed the garrison of the small fort that all of them would be coming with him, either as comrades or as prisoners. "There is at this time a large portion of our fellow citizens in arms against this country," he told them, "and there must be no skulking between the parties. We will take you as friends or enemies, and the choice lies with yourselves." Every man turned out to join Pigman to reinforce Gaddis. When they joined him, "the Tories, poor fellows, scattered to the four winds and no doubt were crying to the rocks and mountains to cover them from the vengeance of the Whigs."[24]

Following these confrontations, the "Whig party had many Tories in irons." Under the direction of Colonel Zackquil Morgan and Gaddis, the militia was determined to "purge the county" of loyalists, and had instructions to drive off their cattle if the men could not be found. When William Crawford captured a loyalist officer, he retrieved his weapon, which the loyalist threw away, and noticed that he had made pewter bullets; "such was the urgency of the times that he had taken the little pewter he had on his shelf to make bullets to kill his neighbors." Crawford also captured a "Tory justice of the peace" who "had administered the oath to more than one hundred men." After being apprehended, "the wretches who have sworn to support the enemy" were interrogated at Miner's Fort (upper Tyrone Township, Fayette County, Pennsylvania), and were asked if they had taken the oath of allegiance to the state. If they had not, they were confined. One suspect, a chair maker identified as "E. W.," did not object to taking the oath and was released after doing so. The next suspect admitted taking the oath to the king with twenty-seven other men, including E. W. Angry patriots then seized E. W. and took him to a tree with a rope around his neck, where he was "suspended between Heaven and earth for a short time, his wife screaming and pulling him down by the feet." E. W. was saved at the last moment when William Crawford cut the rope. Nearly twenty loyalists who were considered the most dangerous were sent to Williamsburg, where they were pardoned and given the oath of loyalty to Virginia. Some loyalists joined the militia to escape punishment, but many ran off as soon as they found an opportunity. Three of these deserters took refuge in an abandoned building but were attacked by an Indian war party, and two of them were killed. Another, identified as "T. H.," deserted three times before finally being captured and executed at Fort Pitt.[25]

The loyalist uprising was put down with only one fatality. After being apprehended in October, "Higginson, a noted tory," fell out of a boat and drowned while in irons under the care of Zackquil Morgan. "Whether he tumbled out, or was thrown out" was uncertain. John Crawford recalled that Higginson surfaced several times and called for help and blamed the death on drunkenness, as "the Whig party had a bottle of whiskey at this time and were handing it round amongst them, drinking health to the United States, to the success of General Washington and the Army of the United States, etc. til poor [Higginson] sunk to rise no more." The coroner ruled Higginson's death a homicide, and Morgan was ordered to stand trial. Morgan's arrest threw the local Virginia militia into confusion, for the majority of the men refused to serve without him. Complaining to General Hand, Major James Chew warned that "the Death of a Vile Tory" would destroy the cooperation of the people of the region, who would direct their anger toward the court that had condemned Morgan. Morgan was tried but acquitted of the crime. Higginson's grave was marked for many years afterward, and for Crawford it stood "as a monument to the folly of men on publick business making too free with the bottle." With the uprising successfully quashed and arrival of news of the victory at Saratoga, General Hand felt optimistic about the future in the west and wishfully wondered "who will henceforth dare to be a Tory even in thought?"[26]

When news of the loyalist uprising first arrived in late August, Zackquil Morgan had also notified General Hand that the loyalists had organized "some of the leading men at Fort Pitt" who were to be leaders, and that they would all join a British invasion that was expected to attack Fort Pitt soon. Those accused in the scheme included Indian agent George Morgan, Alexander McKee, Simon Girty, and even General Edward Hand. Hand placed all the suspects under arrest, except of course himself, while he investigated the charges. By the end of December, all were acquitted except Alexander McKee, who was placed on a new parole while Hand asked the Board of War for further instructions, since McKee was also accused of being a loyalist by a Shawnee woman who held "an implacable hatred to the woman who lived with McKee." Congress had learned of the accusations and decided to investigate George Morgan's loyalty as well as allegations of profiteering in his role supplying the Continental army. The congressional investigation continued through March 1778, when the commission not only acquitted Morgan but noted that he possessed an "uncommon degree of diligence" in performing his duties to the United States.[27]

While George Croghan was not named as a suspected loyalist, he still remained under suspicion for his ties to the suspects, and it was suggested that he remove himself to Philadelphia to avoid retaliation, which he did. His friend and associate William Trent remarked sadly that he was "sorry the people used Col. Croghan so ill," as he was sure that Croghan was not a threat to his country "nor would be, if he had it in his power." Shortly after Croghan's arrival in Philadelphia, the city was occupied by British troops under General Howe. Howe sent for Croghan, castigated him for joining the American committee in Pittsburgh, and kept him under close watch through the end of the British occupation. When American forces reentered the city in June 1778, Croghan was accused of being a traitor to the United States for his ties to Alexander McKee. In November he cleared his name before a court of inquiry, but his associates were still being harassed in Pittsburgh, and he was afraid to go there to manage his affairs. Croghan never returned to Pittsburgh and died nearly a pauper in Philadelphia in 1782, while trying to untangle the legalities of his landholdings, which should have made him a wealthy man.[28]

In late December 1777, Hand ordered McKee to present himself before the Board of War in York, Pennsylvania. Feeling that this was the beginning of the end for him at Fort Pitt, McKee ignored the order and began to liquidate his assets. Hand issued the order again in February 1778, but after returning from the infamous "Squaw Campaign" in March was angered to find McKee still in Pittsburgh. Hand's patience had been exhausted by March 28, and soldiers were sent to arrest McKee, but they were too late. McKee, Simon Girty, Matthew Elliott, and a handful of others had escaped the previous night and were bound for Detroit.[29]

The flight of McKee, Girty, and Elliott had created a panic on the western frontier. The Americans knew that McKee's influence with the Ohio country Indian nations was "capable of doing us extensive mischief." Many settlers of the region abandoned their homes and headed eastward. One home near Pittsburgh bore a previous owner's warning in chalk, which read, "Good people, avoid this road for the Indians are out murdering us." Colonel John Proctor of the Westmoreland County Militia wrote that McKee and "sevin other Vilons is gon to the Indians," and warned, "What may be the fate of this County God only knows, but at Prisent it wears a most dismal aspect."[30]

The fear generated by the flight of McKee, Elliott, and Girty was well founded. The three men had strong ties to the Indian peoples of the Ohio country. Matthew Elliott was an Irish immigrant who went to work as an Indian trader in 1763. Elliott adapted to frontier life and, like McKee, took a Shawnee woman as his wife and was raising a child in her village. The Revolution threatened his business, and the likelihood of a British victory in 1778 had swayed him to remain loyal to the king. Girty had been captured as a child in 1756 and raised by the Seneca. While he returned to live at Fort Pitt as an interpreter and scout, he kept close ties with the Indian peoples of the Ohio country. Although he joined the American cause at the opening of the American Revolution and proved his loyalty on several occasions, he was suspected of disloyalty but acquitted. The violent attitude of the frontier settlers and the disastrous policy toward American Indians was evident in the murder of the Shawnee leader Cornstalk; and the murder of Delaware women and children in the "Squaw Campaign" was surely reprehensible to McKee, Elliott, and Girty, who held such close ties to these people. Distrust of those concerned with Indian affairs had further alienated these influential men. Through the British government, they could find respect for their abilities. As they trekked to Detroit, the trio stirred up hatred toward the Americans in Indian settlements, informing them, with considerable justice, that the Americans were intent on "killing every Indian they should meet, be such, friend or foe." When they arrived in Detroit they were immediately employed in the Indian department and put into action to raid the American frontiers and win over the Indian nations.[31]

The influence of these men helped to divert Indian support from American general Lachlan McIntosh's expedition to build a chain of forts across the Ohio country to attack Detroit in late 1778 and early 1779. They also assisted a British attack in the Illinois country against American forces under George Rogers Clark. As McIntosh's campaign bogged down, they assisted in directing attacks against the American fortifications of Fort Laurens (Bolivar, Ohio) and Fort McIntosh (Beaver, Pennsylvania). Girty and McKee directed an attack on an American force ascending the Ohio River from New Orleans with gunpowder destined for Fort Pitt, killing the majority of the men, capturing the supplies, and gaining valuable intelligence. Throughout the course of the war, they remained active in assaulting the American frontier, agitating hatred against the Americans, and leading Indian war parties. They were present at the destruction of the expedition under Colonel William Crawford at Sandusky, the Battle of Blue Licks, and the assault on Fort Henry in 1782. The British frontier strategy of raiding the western American settlements to divert American troops from the campaigns along the eastern seaboard was successful largely thanks to the assistance of McKee, Girty, and Elliott. The alliance of American Indian nations assembled with the British during the Revolution was, as historian Gregory Dowd puts it, "the largest, most unified Native American effort the continent would ever see."[32]

McKee, Girty, and Elliott gained notoriety as they led Indian war parties against the American frontier. Historian C. Hale Sipe describes them as "inveterate and unnatural enemies of the Americans . . . [who] far outdid the Indians in cruelty." The most infamous incident tying loyalists to cruelty was the torture and killing of Colonel William Crawford. Following the defeat of his army in June 1782, Crawford had been captured and made to suffer in retaliation for the murder of the ninety Christian Indians slaughtered by American troops at Gnadenhütten earlier that year. As Crawford was tortured and burned at the stake, Girty reportedly delighted in his torment. When Crawford could stand the pain no longer and begged Girty to shoot him, Girty allegedly laughed and said that he had no gun. The story of Crawford's torture and Girty's conduct reached the Americans, further inflaming their hatred of the Indians and loyalists on the frontier. Girty, who had joined the Americans at the beginning of the war but had left because of American violence against the Indians he knew and respected, now stood as the image of British and Indian cruelty.[33]

By the spring of 1778 the failed expeditions against the Indian towns and the continuing devastation of the Indian raids had demoralized the soldiers and civilians of the region. The bleakness of the Revolution, and especially the situation on the frontier, caused many to long for better days under the British flag. Bounty money for recruiting went unspent, and many soldiers had already deserted. Those who remained were sent after them, and it seemed as if "all the men woud Desert" Fort Pitt and the frontier posts. On April 24 Hand wrote that "the Devil has possessed both the country and the garrison," reporting that nearly fifty men had deserted since January. The problem grew worse over the next month. With morale sinking, a British spy found Pittsburgh ripe for action and spread word that British troops and Indian warriors were on their way and that a number of the townspeople were in on the plan. The loyalists had been meeting at Alexander McKee's home, and the spy had raised the British flag in the king's orchard within sight of Fort Pitt and had a strong following at Redstone (Brownsville, Pennsylvania), not far from Pittsburgh. The loyalists claimed to have scaling ladders hidden in the woods "for their intended enterprize against Fort Pitt: that it was their intention to relieve the Prisoners and seize the General & the heads of the Town, & put the Irons on them that are now on the Prisoners." On April 20 soldiers of the Thirteenth Virginia Regiment stationed at Fort Pitt concocted a plan to blow up the fort, but the plan was detected before they could carry it out, and they fled down the Ohio River headed for Detroit, though most were caught and the ringleaders were tried. Hand sent a party after settlers who had fled Turtle Creek, nine miles from Fort Pitt, destined for Detroit. The miserable situation on the frontier was too much for Hand. On April 21 he learned that his request to be recalled had made progress, and there was discussion of his successor, of whom Hand wished "from my soul he was come." On May 2 Congress agreed to recall Hand, but there would be more problems before his replacement arrived.[34]

British agents were also busy along the frontier in Sinking Valley, Bedford County (near Altoona, Pennsylvania). Agents promised land to anyone willing to join their ranks, and commissions of equal rank for officers who would desert the American forces. The loyalists raised here were to attack Fort Pitt and Frankstown (Altoona) and "kill the male inhabitants capable of bearing arms, who were in any kind of fort or place of defense and all others of any sex or age who attempted to escape or elude their search." In mid-April more than thirty men found the offer of land too good to pass up and began marching to a supposed rendezvous with a force of British troops and Indian warriors at Kittanning. As they arrived, they were met by a band of Iroquois who did not trust them and attacked, killing several of the loyalists. The remainder fled, but most were soon captured by the Americans. While this loyalist venture did not go as planned, Fort Wallace (near Ligonier, Pennsylvania) was attacked in early May. The attack was a carried out by a mixture of "Indians and the still more savage Tories." Although unsuccessful, it was reportedly larger than any previously seen in the area. The strength and frequency of the loyalist uprisings led General Hand to ask for more troops to be sent immediately to the frontier to "overawe the Tory faction" and encourage the settlers. If they were not sent, Hand believed, "this whole country will be absorbed or overrun by the enemy in a short time."[35]

While many of the soldiers of the Thirteenth Virginia Regiment would join the loyalist plot against Fort Pitt in April 1778, others were staunch patriots and carried their war against the loyalists down the Mississippi River to British West Florida. The idea to raid West Florida from Fort Pitt was born out of an earlier expedition down the Mississippi. In July 1776 a group known as "Gibson's Lambs," under the command of George Gibson and William Linn, left Pittsburgh for Spanish-held New Orleans to buy gunpowder. The mission was successful, and they delivered three thousand pounds of much-needed gunpowder to Philadelphia and nine thousand pounds to Fort Pitt, after returning to the region in May 1777. Another trip was launched in January 1778, under the command of Captain James Willing, but this time the object was to attack British West Florida and destroy British government property and that of the loyalists living in the region. Willing and his party, consisting mainly of volunteers from the Thirteenth Virginia at Fort Pitt, descended the Ohio and Mississippi rivers in an armed boat named the *Rattletrap,* arriving at the settlements of West Florida in late February. The Americans immediately set about capturing loyalists and plundering their property. Willing had even drawn up a list of his intended victims, which included many of his creditors. After seizing Natchez, Willing claimed it for the United States and placed his prisoners on parole after they took an oath of neutrality. The Americans continued to pillage the settlements, targeting loyalists and carefully avoiding anyone sympathetic to the United States.[36]

One of the loyalists the Americans targeted was Alexander Ross. Prior to the Revolution, Ross had begun building a successful financial empire along the Ohio and Mississippi valleys and had purchased Fort Pitt from the British government when it was abandoned in 1772. Many residents in Pittsburgh, future loyalists and patriots alike, had fallen into debt to him. He had tried to resurrect John Connolly's 1775 plot to attack the backcountry, but his plans were uncovered after he tried to meet with Lord Dunmore in 1776. Taking refuge in West Florida, he narrowly escaped capture, which could have meant death, and fled to safety under the Spanish in New Orleans with other loyalists. As one witness reported, the Americans threatened that "Alexander Ross will be flayed alive if they catch him," and another loyalist named Alexander was "to be cut into a hundred pieces." By May, the British responded to Willing's raid and restored control of the region, as many Americans fled on their own and others, including Willing, were captured.[37]

Back at Fort Pitt, May 16 turned out to be a day full of good news for General Hand, who oversaw the trials of the loyalists caught in the plot against the fort. Three had been condemned to death. Two of the ringleaders had been hanged already and the third, Alexander Ballantine, for whom Hand had a particular dislike, was also executed. Corporal punishment was dealt out to the rest. George Morgan wrote that day, informing Hand that the alliance with France was certain. He also told Hand that General Washington had named his replacement, General Lachlan McIntosh, who was already on his way to Fort Pitt. The severe penalties imposed on the loyalists at Fort Pitt, the news of the attack on the loyalists who fled Sinking Spring, the alliance with the French, and the flight of McKee, Elliott, and Girty had dealt a crippling blow to the loyalists and would-be loyalists near Pittsburgh. The British offers of land were not so attractive when they appeared to be losing. While regional morale would sink again and desertions would continue, the few loyalists who occasionally surfaced in the area could not take Fort Pitt but would base their operations in Niagara and Detroit.[38]

Concerns about loyalist activity in Pittsburgh resurfaced in 1780. Colonel Daniel Brodhead had replaced the frustrated McIntosh, who asked to be transferred after the failure of his campaign against Detroit in 1779. The frontier had become a refuge for loyalists from other areas, and it was believed that if the "English go there and offer Protection from the Indians, the greatest part will join." Throughout late 1780 Brodhead found that there were a "great number of disaffected inhabitants on this side of the mountain that wish for nothing more than a fair opportunity to submit to the British Government." Loyalist gatherings occurred in the region at which "the King of Britain's health is often drunk in companies." In September, loyalists near Redstone had even joined together in arms, as they had in 1778, but were put down the following month, when American military forces descended on the area in a show of force.[39]

The loyalist uprising in late 1780 may have gained momentum from the news of a proposed plan to invade Fort Pitt, to be led by the newly released John Connolly. Connolly had been held prisoner since 1775 but had been released in 1780. Following his release, he proceeded to visit Sir Henry Clinton, commander of the British forces in North America, in New York, and proposed a revision of his original scheme to cut the colonies in half by attacking Fort Pitt from Detroit and marching eastward. But again the Americans intercepted intelligence regarding the plan and prepared Fort Pitt by rebuilding and reinforcing the crumbling garrison. The plan never came to fruition, as Connolly was captured in September 1781, but repairs continued under the new commander, Brigadier General William Irvine, who arrived in November 1781.[40]

While Connolly was unable to carry out his plan, a force of Iroquois warriors and loyalists from Niagara, under the command of Colonel John Butler and known as Butler's Rangers, had decided to take up the plan early in the summer of 1782. Butler's Rangers were a group composed of loyalists from central and upstate New York who were responsible for the massacres at Cherry Valley, New York, and the Wyoming Valley in Pennsylvania. As they descended the Allegheny River to attack Fort Pitt, they learned of the repairs and reinforcements and decided to change their objective to the weakly defended settlement of Hannastown, the Westmoreland County seat of government, where they attacked on July 13, 1782. Most of the inhabitants were able to escape into a fortification and survive the attack, but the town was decimated. Hannastown would never recover from the attack, and the county seat was moved to Greensburg five years later. Today it exists only as an archaeological site.[41]

The cost of war for the loyalists in western Pennsylvania had been high. In June 1778 the Commonwealth of Pennsylvania had published the names of those accused of high treason and directed that their estates be confiscated. The loyalists, who had taken up arms against their countrymen to preserve their property and gain additional lands, and had joined Indian war parties to protect the Indian rights to their lands, had now lost the very thing they most wanted. The two hundred named traitors included Westmoreland County's George Croghan, Alexander McKee, Matthew Elliott, Simon Girty, and James Girty, Simon's brother, who had also joined the British at Detroit. The following month, John Proctor and Thomas Galbraith were appointed agents to seize the forfeited estates of traitors in Westmoreland County. Permission was granted in April 1781 to sell the confiscated estates, and the first sales occurred in early 1782. The estates of six loyalists were sold, with Alexander Ross and Alexander McKee losing the most. John Connolly lost his claim to the land at the falls of the Ohio River to settlers of western Virginia, who transformed it into Louisville. The largest landholders in Pennsylvania to lose their property were the Penn family, who lost nearly twenty-four million acres of unsold land. In 1779 they were divested of their land but were allowed to retain lands that had been surveyed before July 4, 1776, which included the "Manor of Pittsburgh." In 1784 the Penn family had the town of Pittsburgh laid out and began selling lots, the first of which were sold to Isaac Craig and Stephen Bayard, who purchased the location of Fort Pitt. The sale of the land on which Fort Pitt stood sparked a legal battle for ownership of the structure itself, but one thing was certain: its former loyalist owners would not retain ownership. When Alexander Ross bought Fort Pitt in 1772, he sold one of the redoubts to Alexander McKee, who used it as a home until his flight from Pittsburgh in 1778. When Craig and Bayard bought the land of the fort, they obtained the buildings as well. McKee's redoubt, built by the British in 1764 and then owned by a succession of two loyalists, survives today as the Fort Pitt Blockhouse, the only surviving building of Fort Pitt, and is now owned by the Daughters of the American Revolution. The sale of lots in Pittsburgh transformed the settlement from a collection of landless "Indian Traders" to a growing metropolis of tradesmen and shopkeepers, eventually transforming the town into a major city.[42]

While a few loyalists stayed in western Pennsylvania, most were forced out, many finding a new life in Canada. Those who did not lose their lands were forced to sell them, unable to face their neighbors after taking up arms against them. McKee, Elliott, and Girty remained with the British Indian Department at Detroit and were even joined briefly by John Connolly. They would continue to work with the Ohio country Indian nations against the United States. With their assistance, the Ohio country Indians successfully destroyed two major American military expeditions, under Josiah Harmar in 1790 and Arthur St. Clair in 1791. Their success over St. Clair would be the greatest victory the American Indians ever achieved against the U.S. Army. St. Clair's expedition, nearly seventeen hundred strong, was sent to destroy the military capabilities of the Ohio country Indian nations but instead was destroyed itself, as half the troops were killed or wounded. Following the battle, as the Indian victors forced dirt into the mouths of American corpses to "satisfy in death their lust for Indian land," Simon Girty pointed out the body of Major General Richard Butler, his former neighbor and the American Indian agent at Pittsburgh. The victorious warriors then mutilated the corpse for grisly trophies. McKee, Girty, and Elliott would spend the rest of their lives with the British Indian Department, fighting for the Ohio country Indian tribes.[43]

While the loyalists of western Pennsylvania were forced from their homes, the memory of their deeds remained. According to William H. Nelson, American folktales remembered two kinds of loyalists, the rich elite who feared the loss of their wealthy lifestyle, and the frontier outlaws who joined the Indians. Tales of Simon Girty and his infamous deeds lived on in the threats of frontier mothers to misbehaving children that Simon Girty would get them if they did not listen. But as the frontier vanished from American memory, the outlaw loyalist vanished with it.[44]

Attempts to account for the motivations of loyalists have focused on the eastern seaboard. William H. Nelson briefly explained the motivation of frontier loyalists, as well as of Indians, as a longing to have the British government remain an impediment to settlement of the frontier, fearing "economic and political subjugation by richer adjoining areas." They feared the collapse of their frontier economy with the advance of settlement. Those fears would eventually be realized by the frontiersman who remained in western Pennsylvania. Matters would come to a head in 1794 during the Whiskey Rebellion, as the frontier economy gave way to a new era. Wallace Brown avoided drawing conclusions about the loyalists of the frontier but agreed that Indian peoples favored the British government as an obstacle to western expansion. Brown also showed that the choice to remain loyal to Britain was a personal decision that was different for different groups of people. While the individual choice to remain loyal in western Pennsylvania may have differed from loyalist to loyalist, the common link that motivated them was land. Retaining land, acquiring more, and the contest between the United States and the Indian peoples over possession would guide the loyalties of the various parties.[45]

In his memoir, John Crawford claimed that the loyalists were "with a very few exceptions . . . very ignorant" and that this ignorance was their only excuse for what they had done. But it was land that made them choose. They had come to the frontier because they were poor and could not afford land east of the mountains. Settlers in western Pennsylvania were drawn there by the cheap, fertile land that was available following the French and Indian War. Despite the ravages of war, the population of western Pennsylvania had grown from nearly fifty thousand prior to the Revolution to seventy-five thousand in 1790. Settlers in the area were willing to risk their lives to own land and build lives for their families. Many of them arrived on the frontier as immigrants from Europe. The frontier lands offered them an opportunity unavailable in their home countries. On the frontier, they had small parcels of land and made improvements by which they were able to survive. The lives of these settlers became entwined with their land. They were willing to kill Indians and die defending it in times of war, and the Revolution forced a decision in which loyalists were willing to kill their patriot neighbors to keep it. Crawford concluded that "the thought of losing their lands and improvements [was] dreadful to them. It was their all."[46]

As settlers began building lives on the frontier, the Revolution presented a gamble that involved very serious consequences and could result in the loss of "their all." While most settlers favored the American cause at the outbreak of war, John Connolly chose to be a loyalist, for his claim to land at the falls of the Ohio River was valid only if Lord Dunmore and the British government remained in power. The British understood the power of land, of offering it and of threatening to take it away, and they used it to their advantage. By offering three hundred acres, Connolly believed that he would have no problem gathering recruits to assist him in his plan to cut the colonies in half. In 1777 Henry Hamilton promised land to those who would join the British at Detroit and dispatched agents to threaten those who did not join with the loss of their land. The offer of gaining land and the threat of losing it had been enough to win nearly one hundred men to the British side near Redstone in 1777, inducing one of them to "take the little pewter he had on his shelf to make bullets to kill his neighbors." In Sinking Valley the loyalists were enticed by land as well when they volunteered to attack their neighbors and kill all those who stood in their way, male and female alike.

The rise and decline of loyalism correlated with the prospects of victory. When threats of an invasion of Fort Pitt circulated, the loyalists gained momentum, but when American victory seemed likely, it evaporated with the fleeing loyalists themselves. For loyalists like Alexander McKee, Simon Girty, and Matthew Elliott, loyalism was a way to protect the lands of the Indian peoples to whom they had strong attachments. The anti-Indian sentiment of the Americans led to suspicion of those who dealt with the Indian nations and it drove them away. Atrocities committed by Indians and settlers alike escalated to the level of genocide on the frontier, genocide that would outlast the Revolution. Loyalists on the frontier joined the British by leading Indian war parties against the American settlements. As Eric Hinderaker has shown, the Revolution transformed the feuding colonists competing for their own interests into two groups, "defined by race and driven to violence in the defense of their interests." Gregory T. Knouff explains that this racial divide grew out of the warfare of the decades before the Revolution, but during this conflict race would emerge as "central to the definition of American-ness." Prior to the Revolution, men like McKee, Girty, and Elliott acted as "cultural mediators" who were equally comfortable in both European and American Indian society, but the Revolution forced them to choose sides. The loyalists who joined the British in leading the Indian attacks crossed the established divide. Disloyalty to their country was joined with disloyalty to their race. For this double dishonor, Simon Girty, representative of the worst of the frontier loyalists, would have his body banished to Canada and his memory to hell.[47]

NOTES

1. Stephen Vincent Benet, *The Devil and Daniel Webster and Other Stories* (1936; reprint, New York: Simon and Schuster, 1967), 28.

2. See John W. Huston, "The British Evacuation of Fort Pitt, 1772," *Western Pennsylvania Historical Magazine* 48 (1965): 317–29; Donna Bingham Munger, *Pennsylvania Land Records: A History and Guide to Research* (Wilmington, Del.: Scholarly Resources, 1991), 63; Woody Holton, "The Ohio Indians and the Coming of the American Revolution," *Journal of Southern History* 60 (1994): 457–71; Thomas P. Abernathy, *Western Lands and the American Revolution* (New York: Russell and Russell, 1937), 94; William Henry Smith, ed., *The St. Clair Papers*, 2 vols. (Cincinnati: Robert Clarke and Co., 1882), 1:272, 279; Boyd Crumrine, ed., *Virginia Court Records in Southwestern Pennsylvania* (Baltimore: Clearfield, 1974), 18.

3. "Letters of Thomas Wharton, 1773–1783," *Pennsylvania Magazine of History and Biography* 33 (1909): 445–46; C. Hale Sipe, *Fort Ligonier and Its Times* (Harrisburg: Telegraph Press, 1932), 287–90, 295–98, 321–24; Virgil A. Lewis, *History of the Battle of Point Pleasant* (1909; reprint, Westminster, Md.: Willow Bend Books, 2005), 56.

4. Edward G. Williams, "Fort Pitt and the Revolution on the Western Frontier," *Western Pennsylvania Historical Magazine* 59 (1976): 131, 133–35; Peter Force, ed., *American Archives*, ser. 4, 6 vols. (Washington, D.C.: M. St. Clair and Peter Force, 1837–44), 2:612–15.

5. Anne M. Ousterhout, *A State Divided: Opposition in Pennsylvania to the American Revolution* (New York: Greenwood Press, 1987), 253; Force, *American Archives* ser. 4, 2:612–15.

6. Nicholas Cresswell, *The Journal of Nicholas Cresswell, 1774–1777* (New York: Dial Press, 1924), 74, 97–99; "The Pittsburgh Tea Party," *Pennsylvania Magazine of History and Biography* 39 (1915): 230–31; Smith, *St. Clair Papers*, 1:353–54.

7. John Connolly, "A Narrative of the Transactions, Imprisonment, and Sufferings of John Connolly, an American Loyalist and Lieut.-Col. in His Majesty's Service," *Pennsylvania Magazine of History and Biography* 12 (1888): 314–15; Stanislaus M. Hamilton, ed., *Letters to Washington and Accompanying Papers,* 5 vols. (New York: Colonial Dames of America, 1901–2), 4:345–47. See also Patricia Johnson, *William Preston and the Allegheny Patriots* (Pulaski, Va.: B. D. Smith & Bros., 1976), 114.

8. Connolly, "Narrative of Connolly," 315.

9. Force, *American Archives,* ser. 4, 2:1879, 1883, quoted in Williams, "Fort Pitt and the Revolution," 141; Robert L. Scribner and Brent Tartar, eds., *Revolutionary Virginia: The Road to Independence,* 7 vols. (Charlottesville: University Press of Virginia, 1983), 3:148–55; *Pennsylvania Archives,* 1st ser., ed. Samuel Hazard, 12 vols. (Philadelphia: Joseph Severns, 1851–62), 4:629; "Virginia Legislative Papers," *Virginia Magazine of History and Biography* 14 (1907): 56; Force, *American Archives,* ser. 4, 3:365, 376, also quoted in Williams, "Fort Pitt and the Revolution," 139.

10. Nicholas B. Wainwright, *George Croghan: Wilderness Diplomat* (Chapel Hill: University of North Carolina Press, 1959), 282, 295, 298; Larry L. Nelson, *A Man of Distinction: Alexander McKee and British-Indian Affairs Along the Ohio Country* (Kent: Kent State University Press, 1999), 24–27, 63, 101–2, 106–9; Reginald Horsman, *Matthew Elliott: British Indian Agent* (Detroit: Wayne State University Press, 1964), 18–19, 26; Williams, "Fort Pitt and the Revolution," 133.

11. "Virginia Legislative Papers," 60–61; Connolly, "Narrative of Connolly," 318, 320, 356–57.

12. Connolly, "Narrative of Connolly," 315; Scribner and Tartar, *Revolutionary Virginia,* 3:272.

13. Charles A. Hanna, *The Wilderness Trail,* 2 vols. (New York: G. P. Putnam's Sons, 1911), 2:79–80; Connolly, "Narrative of Connolly," 316–24.

14. Reuben Gold Thwaites and Louise Phelps Kellogg, eds., *The Revolution on the Upper Ohio, 1775–1777* (Madison: Wisconsin Historical Society, 1908), 140–42; Connolly, "Narrative of Connolly," 71, 407–9; Force, *American Archives,* ser. 4, 3:72–73, 1048.

15. Connolly, "Narrative of Connolly," 410, 413–14, 419; George Washington, *The Writings of George Washington, from the Original Manuscript Sources,* ed. John C. Fitzpatrick, 39 vols. (Washington, D.C.: U.S. Government Printing Office, 1931), 4:25; Scribner and Tartar, *Revolutionary Virginia,* 4:262; Force, *American Archives,* ser. 4, 4:617–18; Wainwright, *George Croghan,* 298–99.

16. Wainwright, *George Croghan,* 299; Nelson, *Man of Distinction,* 94–95.

17. Nelson, *Man of Distinction,* 97; Gregory Schaff, *Wampum Belts and Peace Trees: George Morgan, Native Americans, and Revolutionary Diplomacy* (Golden, Colo.: Fulcrum Press, 1990), 111–62, 165–96; Wainwright, *George Croghan,* 279; Nelson, *Man of Distinction,* 75–76; Force, *American Archives,* ser. 5, 3:599–600.

18. Sipe, *Fort Ligonier and Its Times,* 360–63; Samuel Moorehead to George Morgan, March 24, 1777, and George Morgan to John Hancock, March 24, 1777, Letterbook 2, 66–68, Morgan Papers, Carnegie Library of Pittsburgh, Pittsburgh, Pennsylvania.

19. "Council at Detroit, June 17, 1777," in Reuben Gold Thwaites and Louise Phelps Kellogg, eds., *Frontier Defense on the Upper Ohio* (Madison: Wisconsin Historical Society, 1912), 7–14, quoted in Ousterhout, *State Divided,* 255.

20. Ibid.; E. W. Hassler, *Old Westmoreland* (Pittsburgh: J. R. Weldin and Co., 1900), 37–43; Thwaites and Kellogg, *Revolution on the Upper Ohio,* 255–56; George M. Waller, *The American Revolution in the West* (Chicago: Burnham, 1976), 39–40; Reuben Gold Thwaites and Louise Phelps Kellogg, eds., *Documentary History of Dunmore's War* (Madison: Wisconsin Historical Society, 1905), 15–20, 26–37; C. W. Butterfield, ed., *Washington-Irvine Correspondence: The official letters which passed between Washington and Brig-Gen. William Irvine and between Irvine and others concerning military affairs in the West from 1781 to 1783; arranged and annotated, with an introduction containing an outline of events occurring previously in the Trans-Alleghany country* (Madison, Wis.: D. Atwood, 1882), 236–42.

21. John Heckewelder, *History, Manners, and Customs of the Indian Nations who once Inhabited Pennsylvania and the Neighboring States* (1867; reprint, New York: Arno Press, 1971), 337–38; William Croghan to Michael Gratz, April 20, 1782, in William Vincent Byars, ed., *B. and M. Gratz, Merchants in Philadelphia, 1754–1798* (Jefferson City, Mo.: Hugh Stephens Printing, 1916), 208.

22. "Deposition of John Crawford," Draper Manuscripts, series NN, Pittsburgh and Northwest Virginia Papers, 10 vols., Wisconsin Historical Society, Madison, Wisconsin (hereafter Draper MSS), 6:87–88, transcribed in *Indian Warfare in Western Pennsylvania and North West Virginia at the Time of the American Revolution,* ed. Jared C. Lobdell (Bowie, Md.: Heritage Books, 1992), 42–44, 60–61.

23. Lobdell, *Indian Warfare,* 45.

24. Thomas Gaddis to Thomas Brown, August 26, 1777, and Thomas Brown to Edward Hand, August 29, 1777, in Thwaites and Kellogg, *Frontier Defense on the Upper Ohio,* 51–52; Lobdell, *Indian Warfare,* 46–48.

25. Zackquil Morgan to Edward Hand, August 29, 1777, in Thwaites and Kellogg, *Frontier Defense on the Upper Ohio,* 52–53; Edward Hand to Jasper Yeates, September 16, 1777, Draper MSS, 3:15–16; Lobdell, *Indian Warfare,* 50–58.

26. John Gibson to Edward Hand, October 22, 1777, and James Chew to Edward Hand, October 23, 1777, in Thwaites and Kellogg, *Frontier Defense on the Upper Ohio,* 142–45; Edward Hand to George Morgan, November 2, 1777, Draper MSS, 3:59; Lobdell, *Indian Warfare,* 61.

27. Zackquil Morgan to Edward Hand, August 29, 1777, Edward Hand to a Committee of Congress, December 21, 1777, and John Gibson to Edward Hand, September 4, 1777, in Thwaites and Kellogg, *Frontier Defense on the Upper Ohio,* 52–53, 184–87; *Pennsylvania Packet,* December 24, 1777, April, 11, 1778; "Commission acting for Congress . . . against George Morgan, March 27, 1778," Draper MSS, 3:20.

28. William Trent to Barnard Gratz, November 10, 1777, in Byars, *B. and M. Gratz,* 166–67; Wainwright, *George Croghan,* 300–307; "A Proclamation by the Supreme Executive Council of the Commonwealth of Pennsylvania," *Pennsylvania Packet,* June 17, 1778.

29. Nelson, *Man of Distinction,* 101–2.

30. Paul Wallace, ed., *Thirty Thousand Miles with John Heckewelder* (Pittsburgh: University of Pittsburgh Press, 1958), 146; Commissioners at Pittsburgh to Henry Laurens, March 31, 1778, Papers of Continental Congress, National Archives and Records Administration, Washington, D.C., quoted in Nelson, *Man of Distinction,*105; John Proctor to Thomas Wharton, April 26, 1778, *Pennsylvania Archives,* 1st ser., 6:445.

31. Horsman, *Matthew Elliott,* 18–19, 26; T. L. Rogers, "Simon Girty and Some of His Contemporaries," *Western Pennsylvania Historical Magazine* 8 (1925): 150; C. W. Butterfield, ed., *History of the Girtys* (Cincinnati: Robert Clarke and Co., 1877), 38, 46; Edward Hand to a Committee of Congress, December 21, 1777, in Thwaites and Kellogg, *Frontier Defense on the Upper Ohio,* 184–85, quoted in Ousterhout, *State Divided,* 256; Wallace, *Thirty Thousand Miles,* 148. For more on interracial violence, see Gregory T. Knouff, *The Soldiers' Revolution: Pennsylvanians in Arms and the Forging of Early American Identity* (University Park: Pennsylvania State University Press, 2004), 155–93; Knouff, "Soldiers and Violence on the Pennsylvania Frontier," in *Beyond Philadelphia: The American Revolution in the Pennsylvania Hinterland,* ed. John B. Frantz and William Pencak (University Park: Pennsylvania State University Press, 1998), 171–93; and Richard White, *The Middle Ground: Indians, Empires, and Republics in the Great Lakes Region, 1650–1815* (Cambridge: Cambridge University Press, 1991), 396–412.

32. Nelson, *Man of Distinction,* 110, 127–29; Sipe, *Fort Ligonier and Its Times,* 424–25; Butterfield, *History of the Girtys,* 148–50; Robert S. Allen, "The British Indian Department and the Frontier in North America, 1755–1830," in *Occasional Papers in Archaeology and History,* ed. Research Division, National Historic Parks and Sites Branch, Parks Canada (Ottawa: Canadian Government Publishing Centre, 1975), 24–25; Gregory Dowd, *A Spirited Resistance: The North American Indian Struggle for Unity* (Baltimore: Johns Hopkins University Press, 1991), 46, quoted in Colin Calloway, *The American Revolution in Indian Country: Crises and Diversity in Native American Communities* (Cambridge: Cambridge University Press, 1995), 63.

33. Sipe, *Fort Ligonier and Its Times,* 420; Butterfield, *History of the Girtys,* 133–36; Hugh Henry Brackenridge, ed., *Indian Atrocities* (1782; reprint, Cincinnati: U. P. James, 1867), 22–24.

34. William McKee to Edward Hand, March 29, 1778, and Edward Hand to Horatio Gates, April 24, 1778, in Thwaites and Kellogg, *Frontier Defense on the Upper Ohio,* 246–48, 278–79; Edward Hand to Horatio Gates, May 14, 1778, in Reuben Gold Thwaites and Louise Phelps Kellogg, eds., *Frontier Advance on the Upper Ohio, 1778–1779* (Madison: Wisconsin Historical Society, 1916), 49–51; Edward Hand to Jasper Yeates, April 21, 1778, and Edward Hand to Catherine Hand, April 28, 1778, Draper MSS, 3:24–25, 51; "Treachery at Fort Pitt," Affidavit of John Green, May 4, 1778, in *Notes and Queries: Historical, Biographical, and Genealogical, Relating Chiefly to Pennsylvania,* ed. William H. Egle, 3 vols. (c. 1894; reprint, Baltimore: Genealogical Publishing Company, 1970), 4th ser., 1:116–17; John Proctor to Thomas Wharton, May 15, 1778, *Pennsylvania Archives,* 1st ser., 6:506–7, quoted in Ousterhout, *State Divided,* 262–64; Hassler, *Old Westmoreland,* 43.

35. Hassler, *Old Westmoreland,* 49; "Examination of Richard Weston, 1778," April 27, 1778, *Pennsylvania Archives,* 1st ser., 6:542–43; John Piper to Thomas Wharton, May 4, 1778, and Archibald Lochry

to Thomas Wharton, May 13, 1778, Draper MSS, 1:4–6; Edward Hand to Horatio Gates, May 14, 1778, in Thwaites and Kellogg, *Frontier Advance on the Upper Ohio*, 49–51.

36. Hassler, *Old Westmoreland*, 32–35; Robert England, "Willing's Raid," *American History Illustrated* 19 (1984): 19–20; J. Barton Starr, *Tories, Dons, and Rebels: The American Revolution in British West Florida* (Gainesville: University Press of Florida, 1976), 86–90.

37. Scribner and Tartar, *Revolutionary Virginia*, 6:138–39, 345; *Pennsylvania Archives*, 6th ser., ed. Thomas L. Montgomery, 15 vols. (Harrisburg: State Printer, 1906–7), 13:5–35; Starr, *Tories, Dons, and Rebels*, 90; England, "Willing's Raid," 24–26.

38. Edward Hand to Horatio Gates, May 14, 1778, in Thwaites and Kellogg, *Frontier Advance on the Upper Ohio*, 49–51; Edward Hand to Catherine Hand, May 15, 1778, and George Morgan to Edward Hand, May 16, 1778, in Thwaites and Kellogg, *Frontier Defense on the Upper Ohio*, 297–98; Edward Hand to Richard Peters, July 10, 1778, Draper MSS, 3:123.

39. Harvey H. Jackson, *Lachlan McIntosh and the Politics of Revolutionary Georgia* (Athens: University of Georgia Press, 1979), 91–93; Daniel Brodhead to Uriah Springer, October 20, 1780, Daniel Brodhead to Richard Peters, December 7, 1780, and Daniel Brodhead to George Washington, March 27, 1781, all in Reuben Gold Thwaites and Louise Phelps Kellogg, eds., *Frontier Retreat on the Upper Ohio, 1779–1781* (Madison: Wisconsin Historical Society, 1917), 22–23, 277, 285, 302–3, 352–53; Waller, *American Revolution in the West*, 96; Daniel Brodhead to Richard Peters, September 23, 1780, *Pennsylvania Archives*, 1st ser., 12:274.

40. Connolly, "Narrative of Connolly," 167, 283–84; Williams, "Fort Pitt and the Revolution," 436–39; Richard Peters to George Washington, March 4, 1780, and George Washington to Daniel Brodhead, March 14, 1780, in Thwaites and Kellogg, *Frontier Retreat on the Upper Ohio*, 146–47; William Irvine to George Washington, December 2, 1781, in Butterfield, *Washington-Irvine Correspondence*, 72.

41. Glenn F. Williams, *Year of the Hangman: George Washington's Campaign Against the Iroquois* (Yardley, Pa.: Westholme, 2005), 131–33, 144–45, 178–82; W. Stewart Wallace, *The United Empire Loyalists* (Toronto: Glasgow, Brook, 1920), 16; Hassler, *Old Westmoreland*, 177–79, 181.

42. *Pennsylvania Packet*, June 17, 1778, July 9, 1778; *Pennsylvania Gazette*, May 16, 1781, March 27, 1782; *Pennsylvania Archives*, 6th ser., 13:31–35; Neal O. Hammon and Richard Taylor, *Virginia's Western War, 1775–1786* (Mechanicsburg, Pa.: Stackpole Books, 2002), 125; Lorett Treese, *The Storm Gathering: The Penn Family and the American Revolution* (Mechanicsburg, Pa.: Stackpole Books, 2002), 188–89; Charles W. Dahlinger, "Fort Pitt," *Western Pennsylvania Historical Magazine* 5, no. 2 (1922): 99–103, 119; "Claim of Alexr. McKee, Esq., late of Pensilva.," and "Further Evidence in Case of Alexr. McKee," in Alexander Fraser, ed., *United Empire Loyalists Enquiry into the Losses and Services in Consequence of Their Loyalty: Second Report of the Bureau of Archives for the Province of Ontario* (Toronto: L. K. Cameron, 1905), part 2, 987–88, 1082–83; R. Eugene Harper, *The Transformation of Western Pennsylvania, 1770–1800* (Pittsburgh: University of Pittsburgh Press, 1992), 25–26, 90.

43. Lobdell, *Indian Warfare*, 62; Rogers, "Simon Girty," 156–58; Robert Allen, *His Majesty's Indian Allies: British Indian Policy in the Defence of Canada, 1774–1815* (Toronto: Dundurn Press, 1992), 65, 73, 82, 88; J. Leitch Wright, *Britain and the American Frontier, 1783–1815* (Athens: University of Georgia Press, 1975), 125; James Alexander Thom, "Little Turtle, Destroyer of Armies," in *St. Clair's Defeat*, ed. Floyd A. Barmann and J. Martin West (n.p.: Ohio Historical Society and Fort Recovery Bicentennial Commission, 1991), 4; White, *Middle Ground*, 454; Alan D. Gaff, *Bayonets in the Wilderness: Anthony Wayne's Legion in the Old Northwest* (Norman: University of Oklahoma Press, 2004), 9, 57.

44. Nelson, *Man of Distinction*, 85; R. Douglas Hurt, *The Ohio Frontier: Crucible of the Old Northwest, 1720–1830* (Bloomington: Indiana University Press, 1998), 73.

45. William H. Nelson, *The American Tory* (Boston: Beacon Press, 1964), 87; Wallace Brown, *The Good Americans: The Loyalists in the American Revolution* (New York: William Morrow, 1969), 44, 48, 78; Thomas P. Slaughter, *The Whiskey Rebellion: Frontier Epilogue to the American Revolution* (New York: Oxford University Press, 1986), 87–88, 187.

46. Lobdell, *Indian Warfare*, 60–61; Russell J. Ferguson, *Early Western Pennsylvania Politics* (Pittsburgh: University of Pittsburgh Press, 1938), 8–13; Harper, *Transformation of Western Pennsylvania*, 13–15.

47. Eric Hinderaker, *Elusive Empires: Constructing Colonialism in the Ohio Valley, 1673–1800* (Cambridge: Cambridge University Press, 1997), 189, 212–16; Knouff, *Soldiers' Revolution*, 158; Nelson, *Man of Distinction*, 1–2. For more on the development of racial attitudes, see Nancy Shoemaker, *A Strange Likeness: Becoming Red and White in Eighteenth-Century North America* (New York: Oxford University Press, 2004).

8

ESTHER DeBERDT REED AND FEMALE POLITICAL SUBJECTIVITY IN REVOLUTIONARY PENNSYLVANIA: IDENTITY, AGENCY, AND ALIENATION IN 1775

Owen S. Ireland

Late in 1775, Mrs. Esther DeBerdt Reed chose America over England. Her decision, her progress toward that decision, and her understanding of its implications suggest a female political subjectivity that contrasts sharply with the thinking of contemporary public men. Male political decision makers generally acted on the assumption that married women exercised no independent political will. In 1805 the highest court in Massachusetts articulated that view. The government had erred, it ruled, in punishing Mrs. Anna Gordon Martin for leaving with her loyalist husband in 1776. Married women played no autonomous political role and made no autonomous political decisions. Mrs. Martin had had no choice and therefore had incurred no legal liabilities.[1]

Some married women in revolutionary America, however, acted like free and responsible adults making their own political choices. Jane Bartram, for example, a native of Pennsylvania, asserted her right to take a personal stand in opposition to that of her husband, who had gone over to the British. In the eyes of the men who governed Pennsylvania, a loyalist's wife was a loyalist, and they ordered her to leave. Bartram resisted. She claimed that she, a patriot, had always "maintained a friendly and warm desire for the Liberties and rights" of America, and that her husband had "used her grossly ill for her attachment to the cause of American liberty." Pennsylvania officials rejected her claim and exiled her to

I would like to thank those who have encouraged, supported, or facilitated research on this project as well as those who have read and criticized earlier versions of this essay: Dr. Paul Yu, president of SUNY College at Brockport; Colleen Donaldson, grants development director, SUNY College at Brockport; the Research Foundation at SUNY; the Gilder Lehrman Institute of American History; Dr. Ursula Masson, West of England and South Wales Women's History Network, University of Glamorgan, Pontypridd, Wales; Dr. Susan Branson, University of Texas at Dallas; Dr. Lee Ann Caldwell, Georgia College and State University; Dr. Susan Klepp, Temple University; Dr. Elsa Nystrom, Kennesaw State University in Georgia; Dr. Jean Soderlund, Lehigh University; Dr. Patricia Veasey, curator of the Museum of York County, in Rock Hill, South Carolina; and my colleagues in the Rochester United States Historians (RUSH) working-paper group, Dr. Alison Parker, SUNY Brockport, coordinator.

New York. From there, Bartram badgered Pennsylvania officials for permission to return, claiming that they had punished her "for a fault of her husband." In 1782 Pennsylvania relented. Bartram had successfully resisted efforts by the male authorities to impose an identity on her. She had "acted to control her own destiny" and "asserted her own political identity."[2]

Esther DeBerdt Reed, a fellow resident of Philadelphia, also made an independent commitment to the patriot cause. In Reed's case, however, her recent arrival in America, her deep personal attachment to London, and her sense of herself as a traitor to her homeland distinguish her from Bartram. Moreover, a substantial collection of family letters provides us with the opportunity to probe her understanding of these experiences, her subjectivity.[3]

Reed is best known for events that occurred near the end of her life. In the summer of 1780 she organized a women's fund-raising campaign to support the Continental troops, published a broadside that exhorted women to act like the "heroines of antiquity,"[4] supervised a door-to-door solicitation for money, and then argued with General Washington about how best to use the funds.[5] Shortly before her sudden death in September of that year, she accepted Washington's decision that his troops would make better use of shirts than of the cash she had planned to give them.[6]

Reed's decision for America in 1775 reflects the same sense of political efficacy. Increasingly alienated by the intransigence of the people at home, she reconstructed her political identity and made public choices for which she felt she could be held accountable. Her behavior and her thinking reinforce and expand our image of women in late eighteenth-century America as self-conscious political actors and heighten our appreciation of how politically active women understood their participation in the American Revolution.

Identity

When Esther DeBerdt of London fell in love with Joseph Reed of Trenton, New Jersey, in 1764, she had no intention of traveling to America and could not have imagined herself as an American patriot. She was sixteen, the daughter of a prominent and politically connected import-export merchant trading with the American colonies. Joseph was twenty-two and had recently arrived in London to continue his legal studies. Within a few months of their first meeting, she pressed Joseph to ask her father for her hand. DeBerdt refused and forbade her to see Joseph again. Esther complied with her father's wishes for two months and then, in direct defiance of his explicit command, she initiated a clandestine correspondence with Joseph. From the beginning, however, she made it clear to him, "As to my going to America, it cannot be." Joseph agreed. When they married, they would settle in London.[7]

In February 1765 financial difficulties in Joseph's family forced him to return to New Jersey. For most of the next five years, the two lovers continued their secret courtship by transatlantic mail. Then, early in 1770, Joseph returned to London. Esther, with her father's tacit approval, had worked out a scheme. DeBerdt would make Joseph his business partner, and Joseph, now age twenty-eight and with serious prospects in London, could begin his formal courtship of Esther, now twenty-two.

Before Joseph could arrive in London, however, tragedy struck the DeBerdt family. Esther's father died, the family fortune went to his creditors, and the DeBerdt political influence evaporated. Joseph and Esther married in a hurried ceremony at St. Luke's. Both wanted to live permanently in London, and for three months they struggled to salvage something from this disaster. They failed, however, and Esther, with her widowed mother, accompanied Joseph to New Jersey. She saw the trip as a necessary but temporary exile. She expected to return home soon to live her life with the man she loved in the city she loved.[8]

By November 1770 the new Mrs. Reed was an unhappy woman: twenty-three years old, seven months married, four months pregnant, and exiled among pleasant but boring provincials. "America," she wrote on December 12 to her brother, Dennis, still in London, could not "compare to England in any respect."[9] Burlington, New Jersey, her first home in America, bored her. She found it "remarkable for nothing." "Governor [William] Franklin tells me," she told her brother, "that a person may sleep there for a month, without any danger of being disturbed." Only the promise of an early return to "dear England" made bearable this sojourn in a strange and primitive land. For the sake of her husband, and "with the hope of returning," she wrote, "I can spend some time here without repining" (168, 158–59).

A move to Philadelphia in December changed little. The capital of Pennsylvania dwarfed Burlington but shrank into parochial insignificance in comparison with cosmopolitan London. The city did not, she wrote to Dennis, "answer my expectations . . . the houses are low, and in general, paltry in comparison to what I had heard" (158–60).

The women of Philadelphia also disappointed her. Invited to "The Assembly," the apex of social pretension in the city, she saw some "American belles" whom she considered pretty, but no real beauties. American women, she wrote, "stoop like country girls." In addition, their pettiness earned her scorn: "my ladyship opened the ball," she wrote Dennis on November 14, "much to the satisfaction of the company, as something new to criticize on" (158–59).

She missed the amenities she had taken for granted at home and asked Dennis in London to send her some things she could not find in America—"a fine damask table-cloth . . . a very neat fan . . . [a] set of dressing boxes . . . needles from number 5 to number 11"—interrupting herself to lament, "I would give something to be in Price's or Mr. Anybody's shop in London, even in Thames Street" (163–64). Two years later, still struggling to dress in London fashions, she ordered a "half-dressed handkerchief or tippet, or whatever is fashionable. . . . Also a handsome spring silk [dress] fit for summer and new fashion" (176).

The incessant gossip drove her to distraction. "We meet with much civility," she reported in mid-January 1771, "but I can't say the place suits me very well; the people must either talk of their neighbors, of whom they know every particular . . .—or else of marketing, two subjects I am very little acquainted with" (166). She did not see herself as a gossiper or a shopper, at least not in Philadelphia. But she cautioned Dennis to keep her comments to himself, "for we hardly dare tell one another our thoughts, lest it should spread and be told again all over the town" (166).

Time did not ease her dissatisfaction. The birth of a sickly daughter, Martha, in May 1771, added a new reason to return home. "I think," she wrote to her brother a month after the delivery, "I shall like my little girl very well by and by. If she lives, it will make me more anxious than ever to return . . . as the education of girls is very indifferent indeed here" (168).[10] The birth of her second child, Joseph, in July 1772, did not improve her attitude. Three months after his birth, she wrote that she enjoyed fine health and wanted nothing "but clearer prospects of returning to dear England" (172).

She and Joseph continued to look for opportunities to live permanently to London. In January 1771 she urged Dennis to help Joseph become the agent for Massachusetts, a position that her father had held until his death and one that would require that they move to London (165). The post went to Benjamin Franklin. In 1772 they learned that Lord Dartmouth, a previous family patron, had replaced Lord Hillsborough as colonial secretary. Esther told Dennis, "I wish some use could be made of him to advance that foremost wish of our hearts to spend the remainder of our lives together [in London]" (179). Nothing came of the effort, however.

The Tea Act of 1773 reignited the conflict between Great Britain and her North American colonies and complicated Esther's life. Joseph, entering politics for the first time, emerged as a leader of Philadelphia's opposition, but Esther reiterated her desire to return to London and her belief that Joseph wanted this, too (185–86).

Her reaction to the growing imperial crisis suggests some ambivalence, however. She sympathized with the colonials but did not identify with them. "News of . . . [the closing of the port of Boston] distresses every thinking person," she wrote in May 1774, reporting, "the Provinces are determined to . . . make a common cause" (193). Here, as throughout her correspondence for the next year and a half, her choice of words suggests much that she does not explicitly say: she wrote, "every thinking person" rather than "I," "the Provinces," not "we."

In the fall of 1774, visits by New Englanders attending the Continental Congress encouraged Esther to see the conflict through their eyes, but once they departed, her enthusiasm declined. She understood that a hostile response by the British to the actions of the Congress could precipitate violence. Pennsylvania residents, she reported, remained optimistic about a peaceful settlement, but "the people of New England have no such expectations." New Englanders, she wrote her brother, were ready to die for liberty. "These dreadful events," as she described them, made her "wish for a safe retreat in Old England." Still, she admitted, "I hardly know in which country the safest retreat could be found" (203–4). She had delivered a new baby in July 1774 and now had three young children: Martha, still frail at age three and a half, Joseph, healthy and rambunctious at two and a half, and Esther, four months old and still at the breast. As she told Dennis in November, "my hands are pretty full" (202).

In December 1774 Joseph won election to the Philadelphia committee charged with enforcing the congressional nonimportation agreement, and in January 1775 he presided over a province-wide convention that added military preparedness to the economic boycott. By February 1775 Esther could report that Joseph's "engagements in business are so numerous and extensive that his head is almost overcharged . . . his late attention to politics has engrossed him more than common" (206).

Despite Joseph's increasing leadership of the resistance, Esther remained conflicted, as her comments on the Quakers and on Franklin reveal. The Quakers, she wrote her brother in London, "are endeavouring to steer a middle course and make perhaps a merit of it to Government at home. How far their conduct will answer, I don't know, but it is despised here" (207). Two features of her word choice stand out. First, Esther still considered England "home." Second, she writes in the passive voice about the Quakers (their conduct "is despised") allowing herself to describe without taking sides. In contrast, she explicitly criticized Franklin for his equivocation. "Tell us," she wrote Dennis, "whether he has the openness to declare his sentiments before he sees which way affairs will terminate," adding that she herself had "a share in both countries and am interested in the welfare of both more than the common run of the people here" (209–10).

Esther worried that her sentiments differed from those of her neighbors. "I love to think of England and of old times," she wrote, "perhaps I may see it again. It is surely a noble country, but such wishes and hopes I must keep concealed." Here, shortly before the outbreak of war, she first reveals a conscious effort to restructure her thinking. "Perhaps they [such wishes and hopes] had better not arise at all" (207–8).

Between April and October 1775, DeBerdt resolved her conflict. News of Lexington and Concord arrived in Philadelphia on April 24. Within days, Joseph dashed off a letter of support for the people of Massachusetts and then devoted most of his time to mobilizing military and financial support for the eastern provinces. In June, Congress appointed George Washington commander-in-chief, and when Washington left to take up his new responsibilities near Boston, he persuaded Joseph to ride with him as far as New York. On the way, the young planter from Virginia persuaded the young lawyer from Philadelphia to accompany him to Cambridge to serve as his secretary.

When Joseph left with Washington, Esther anticipated a new military role for him, and she understood, as she wrote her brother on June 24, 1775, that this made their "return to England at present totally improper" (218). Her use of the phrase "at present," suggests that returning to England remained her preference.

Esther found Joseph's absence difficult. She had become the head of her growing family, with a household to manage and increased responsibilities in overseeing the law office.[11] "I confess it is a trial I never thought I should have experienced" she wrote Dennis on July 22, 1775, "and am the less prepared to bear it" (218–19).[12] She missed Joseph. Since their marriage, they had seldom been apart for more than a few days. As Dennis later wrote, undoubtedly expressing feelings Esther had conveyed to him, "Alas, my dear Hitty, what dreadful times. . . . War in the country where you reside. Your dearest friend taking an active part [and] . . . friendship's sweet channel stopped up."[13]

The war frightened her. Twenty-six years old, the mother of three small children, and living among a people she still saw as "the other," she needed comfort, support, and familiar faces. She implored Dennis, in a letter of June 24, 1775, to come to America to "protect and take care of us if my dear Mr. Reed should be called to act in defense of his country" (218).

Family and friends, in their concern, added to her burdens. Her brother-in-law, Charles Pettit, pressed her to come and live with his family in Perth Amboy, New Jersey, but the tone of his letter implied some hesitation. He would come to get her, he said, but he was "tied up here for a few days," and he suggested that he and his wife might not easily accommodate all of Esther's family.[14] John Cox, and old friend of Joseph's and the husband of one of Esther's closest American friends, urged Esther to send some of her family to live with Joseph's married younger brother, Bowes Reed, in Burlington, New Jersey, and take the rest to live with Mrs. Cox at their summer place by the river.[15]

Given Esther's independent spirit, having others plan her life was undoubtedly discomfiting. Moreover, no adult woman, mistress in her own home, happily accepted the implicit subordination involved in living in another's woman's home. For most of July Esther tried to solve the problem by herself. She and

Joseph usually took a place outside the city for the summer, especially for the benefit of their eldest child, Martha, whose health improved away from the city in the hot months. Joseph encouraged her to do the same again in his absence, but she could find nothing that suited her purposes either near Philadelphia or in New Jersey (234). Finally, in late July or early August, she gave in and divided her family between Burlington and Perth Amboy.

By the time she returned to the city in October, she had made America's cause her own. She understood the risks. She anticipated that supporting the American cause would brand her as a traitor. She continued to hope that the king would consider the American petitions and thereby "lay the foundations for negotiations," she wrote her brother, so that "we may again be reconciled," but she anticipated that the British would remain intransigent. The temporary stranger in this strange land now identified with her new countrymen, and joined a small but growing cadre ready to declare "our" independence and defend "ourselves" to the utmost against what had been, not long ago, "Dear England" (227).[16]

Agency

Esther DeBerdt Reed had long concerned herself with public affairs, had a sophisticated understanding of both British and American politics, and saw herself as capable of making political decisions and acting to implement them in the public arena. A strong-willed young woman living in a love-based companionate marriage, she felt that she could and did help mold her family's private and public decisions.

Reed usually got her way, both before and after her migration to America. In direct defiance of tradition and of her father's expressed wishes, she had secretly pursued and finally married the man she had chosen for herself at age sixteen. A decade and a half later, in the summer of 1780, she challenged General George Washington over the use of money she had raised for his troops. In the intervening years she had not altered her character, lost her confidence, or abandoned her sense of personal efficacy.

Esther and Joseph had married for love. Romance, affection, respect, and admiration had drawn them to each other and then held them together through six complicated years of courtship (1764–70), but they differed somewhat in how they expressed their feelings to each other. In his letters, Joseph expressed his love explicitly. He addressed her as "my beloved." Her absence, he wrote, "endear[s] you to me the more and if possible I love you more." He needed her love to support him "under these Strokes of adverse Fortune." "It will be the sweet Employment of [my] life," he pledged, "to make every part of yours delightful and agreeable," and he begged her to "tell me that you still love."[17]

Esther wrote with a bit more constraint. She emphasized Joseph's "particular Esteem" and spoke of the couple's "Tenderest Friendship." She wanted, she told him, a "companion who would make it his endeavours to be both friend and Lover to me whom he chose for life." She expected that "Esteem" and "Friendship" would continue to be the unshaken "foundation of our Love." She was not, however, "fond of promising or making great professions," and she illustrated that point in her response to his request for reassurance: "Do you want to hear that I still love? It's [a] truth which I am not ashamed to own to you and one time or another to make it appear to all the world forever." She did not write "I love you," but she assured him, "A heart once gone is not easily called back."[18]

Esther and Joseph had both demonstrated their love through dramatic economic sacrifice. Esther, waiting for Joseph in London, had spurned approaches by men of far greater wealth and higher status. Samuel Powell of Philadelphia, for example, pursued her vigorously in the months after Joseph returned to America in February 1765. Powell, in London completing a seven-year tour of the continent, would shortly return to Philadelphia, marry into a family whose wealth matched his own, build a mansion on Market Street, and serve as a city alderman. While he had accompanied Esther and her mother to Bath and had devoted himself to her company, Esther made it clear to him that she had given her heart to another. After Powell, other desirable young men indicated their interest, but Esther chased them away. For five lonely years she waited, steadfast in her devotion to her American who struggled in faraway New Jersey to repair his family's broken fortunes.[19]

Joseph demonstrated his own commitment in 1770. He arrived in London from the provinces expecting to play public court to a wealthy and well-connected young woman. He found a family in crisis: the father dead, the family's resources and influence gone, the grieving widow spending money she did not have, and creditors threatening to take the family's furniture. Joseph, shocked and shaken, faced a personal crisis. His extended family in New Jersey (approximately fifteen adults and children) depended upon him. To come to London to live, he had suspended a lucrative law practice and invested substantial amounts of his scarce capital, expecting the DeBerdt connection to repay the losses. Now, with no prospects of success in London, his family would reasonably advise him to return home unencumbered. Assuming responsibility for Esther, her mother, and her brother could only further complicate the Reed family's precarious financial situation. Joseph knew all this. He admitted to his family that his actions would seem irrational and dangerous to them. But he also explained that he loved this woman who had waited so long for him and he intended to marry her and bring her home with him. Furthermore, he told his family, he expected them to receive her warmly and to treat her with respect and affection.[20]

For much of her adult life, Esther's political awareness and sophistication probably exceeded Joseph's. A year after Joseph had left her in London, she and her mother begun to attend parliamentary debates, a relatively new activity for women in the British capital. She went seeking information and connections that could help Joseph while he remained in America and speed his return to her in London. In the early spring of 1766, at age eighteen, she followed closely the debates in the House of Commons on the repeal of the Stamp Act and informed Joseph early on that the ministry intended repeal. The next year she became secretary to her father, Dennys DeBerdt, immersing herself in the day-to-day politics of the commercial empire and the political intrigue of London. She schemed to use Lord Dartmouth to obtain a patronage appointment for Joseph in London, and when that failed, she urged Joseph himself to explore patronage opportunities in America. With the help of her family he secured a major sinecure in New Jersey, and Esther discussed with him the possibilities of the New York agency. Between February and July 1767, while her father negotiated for the Massachusetts agency for himself, Esther, with increasing urgency, pressed Joseph to visit Boston, and advised him on the internal politics of the Puritan province.[21] Although Joseph did not immediately benefit from this particular scheme, it paved the way for his return to Esther. Encouraged by reports from America, Dennys DeBerdt invited Joseph to come to London to work with him, a plan largely conceived by Esther that ultimately failed only because of her father's sudden death.

In America, Esther exhibited the same interest in public life. She arrived four months pregnant and exhausted by morning sickness aggravated by three months on the Atlantic. Within days, however, she had met and charmed the royal governor of New Jersey, and within weeks she had persuaded Joseph to abandon his ancestral home and move to Philadelphia, as she wrote her brother in mid-November 1770 (155–59). There she and her mother read the London papers avidly, and after the Tea Act reignited the conflict, she engaged public men in discussion of political matters (193–94). When the Continental Congress met in her city in the fall of 1774, a few weeks after she had delivered her third baby in three years, she joined Joseph in greeting, entertaining, and interrogating the delegates, especially those from New England. For a month she provided room, board, and conversation for her old family friend Richard Cary, down from Massachusetts to observe the Congress, and after he left, she commented, "I never entertained any person more affectionately or with greater pleasure" (204).

She also organized dinners in her home for delegates, and she participated in these typically all-male occasions in much the same way that she had mixed freely with the male guests at her father's regular Sunday dinners in London during the 1760s (204).[22] John Adams and Silas Deane attested to her presence and participation on these occasions. Adams attended a number of dinners in Philadelphia's private homes in September and October 1774 and usually recorded details of the setting and the servings. He less often mentioned the presence of women. When he dined at the Reeds', however, he explicitly noted that Esther and her mother dined with the men. Silas Deane, a delegate from Connecticut, seldom mentioned women in his letters to his wife, but after dining with Esther and Joseph he described for his wife not only Esther's physical appearance but also his impression of her political beliefs. She is, he wrote, "small . . . [with] a most elegant figure and countenance. She is a Daughter of Liberty zealously affected in a good cause."[23]

Between the adjournment of Congress in late October 1774 and the outbreak of war in April 1775, Esther badgered her brother in London for news. She wanted to know about the evolution of public opinion in the capital, about the political activities of the merchants on whose support she and many Americans relied to pressure Parliament, and about the divisions in Parliament itself. "Write us every piece of intelligence concerning American affairs," she implored Dennis, "especially what is said in the House and who is on *our* side and who against," a significant but temporary shift in pronouns (203, 209–10, 207–8, emphasis added).

During the same six months, she analyzed for Dennis the political developments in America. She believed that in New England no "power on earth could take . . . liberty . . . from them but with their lives" (203). But she denied British accusations that America sought independence and articulated a brief but powerful summary of America's position that would have resonated well with the thinking of many of the men most actively engaged in the resistance. "This country," she wrote, "wishes for nothing so much as dependency on the Mother State on proper terms, [and] to be secure in their liberties" (209–10).[24]

After Lexington and Concord, Esther and Joseph entertained George Washington and a small number of men from New England, Philadelphia, and Virginia. The group, including Esther and her mother, stayed up past midnight discussing "the most feasible and prudent method of stopping up the channel of the Delaware, to prevent the coming up of any large ships to the city." One of the New England visitors, an admiralty court judge from Salem, Massachusetts, on his way to becoming a loyalist, noted, "I could not perceive the least disposition to accommodate matters."[25]

Throughout these years of accelerating crisis, Esther knew Joseph's doings and opinions. For much of this period she served as "private secretary to Mr. Reed," as she had earlier to her father (171). Her brother understood that she had access to Joseph's personal and business correspondence. Although Dennis wrote separate letters to Esther, to his mother, and to Joseph, and emphasized different facets of his life in each, he did so knowing that each read the letters he sent to the others: "I have now wrote you pretty fully on my intimate affairs, Mr. Reed on Public ones, and my dear Mother on Matrimonial matters that from them all you may collect what is my plans and intentions." In late May 1775 he wrote directly to Esther about business he had undertaken in London for the Reeds. Joseph, diverted by his political activities, had failed to respond to letters from Dennis, and Dennis turned to Esther, knowing that she had both the information and the understanding to guide him.[26]

Esther not only knew about Joseph's political activities and understood his thinking; she also believed that she could influence his decisions. That had been the case between 1765 and 1770, when he had relied on her counsel and her London connections as he struggled in New Jersey. It also seems to have been the case in their abrupt departure from Burlington shortly after their arrival. She hated that tiny and remote village, she told her brother in late October 1773, and within a few weeks Joseph had found a house for them in Philadelphia, a move he had not planned before their arrival in America and one that involved increased financial risks (185–86).

Two years later, in 1775, she expressed much the same sense of efficacy. For some months they had discussed returning to England. Esther, Dennis, and Joseph had all mentioned it at one point or another in their correspondence, and by 1775 Dennis expected it to happen. In his mind, only the timing remained uncertain.[27] In the end, Esther and Joseph chose to stay, but Esther felt she had been part of the decision. In June 1775, she wrote her brother, "For much as I wish him free of danger yet I could not ask him to act so cowardly a part as to fly when his country so eminently needs his assistance" (216–18). She had not asked him, but she felt she could have asked, and she also felt that such a request on her part would not have been unreasonable, inappropriate, or futile. She believed that Joseph would respond to her needs, should she express them strongly.

Alienation

An intelligent, articulate, charming, ambitious, cosmopolitan, strong-willed, well-educated, and politically aware young woman, Esther DeBerdt Reed cared about public affairs, took pains to inform herself, engaged prominent men in serious discussions of weighty public matters, and felt capable of influencing her family's political choices. In the summer of 1775, she understood the implications of the decisions that she and Joseph faced. Late that fall she chose America over England and took a conspicuous stand on the matter. The crucial question of why, however, remains to be answered.

Family considerations pushed her both ways. Her brother was in London and her mother with her in America (214–15), but mostly she worried about the safety of her children, and for a time, as she confided to Dennis, she could not decide where "the safest retreat could be found" (203, 207).

Friends also played a role. Over time, Esther's letters mention her English friends less, her American friends more. The New England men who first visited her home in the fall of 1774 and intermittently thereafter also had an effect. Esther had known some of them in London, where the "Boston men," as she called them, had congregated at her father's house, and Esther had regularly mingled with them at her father's Sunday dinners. Esther had also corresponded with many of them when she served as secretary to her father. Mr. Cary, who had worked with great diligence in support of DeBerdt's appointment as colonial agency for Massachusetts, had a warm place in Esther's heart (204–5).[28]

Esther's religious beliefs and affiliation contributed as well. Esther's parents had raised her as a religious dissenter, a Calvinist in Anglican England, and her father had maintained close and supportive relations with at least two of America's Presbyterian colleges. Esther took her religion seriously, possibly more so than her husband did.[29] A fragment of her youthful diary suggests a rather intense and introspective spirituality.[30] When she and Joseph had moved to Philadelphia, they both joined the Presbyterian Church.[31]

Esther's Calvinist background linked her to the Congregationalists from New England, and her father's religion had played a part in his selection as the agent for Massachusetts in London. In addition, Calvinist theology made it possible to see resistance to established authority as morally acceptable.[32] Finally, Presbyterians resisted Parliamentary encroachments with a greater degree of unanimity than most other denominations in the city, and Presbyterian ministers in Philadelphia urged their flocks to resist.[33] Thus, Esther's Calvinist background provided her with a moral justification for resistance, and her interaction with Presbyterians and Congregationalists in America would have strengthened and reinforced her transformation.

The family's financial situation also exerted pressure on their political decisions. The Reeds had prospered in Philadelphia. Joseph, in Esther's estimation, was at the top of the city's legal hierarchy. Three of the four eminent lawyers had retired, and the younger men in the profession posed no threat to the more experienced and London-trained Joseph. His "situation here is pretty certain with respect to income, and it rather increases than otherwise," Esther explained in a letter to her brother (179). The Reeds lived in relative affluence. They rented a home in the city, owned property in New Jersey, spent summers in the country, and asserted their rising status by owning four horses, three carriages, and two male slaves, who cared for the animals and drove the vehicles in livered uniforms. The Reeds also owned a wine cellar worth about twice the expected annual earnings of an industrious Philadelphia craftsman.[34]

If they fled to England, they would take little of their wealth or status with them. On the other hand, by the summer of 1775 the Reeds' financial situation in America had grown less secure. Disruption of the courts could restrict Joseph's legal income. The trade boycotts had already reduced his commercial profits, and if, as most expected, the British tried to close American ports, those profits would decline further. Then, early in June, Joseph learned that he had lost his major patronage appointment in New Jersey, a post that constituted the principal support of his brother-in-law's family.[35]

Indeed, the Reeds by then might have had better prospects in London. Although their wealth and status would not travel well, Joseph and Esther would bring with them their industry, their skill, and the rudiments of some important connections. With an additional year of training at the Inns of Court, Joseph could practice law in England, and he had already done legal work in America for both English and Irish clients. Joseph himself had started over in 1765, when he was called home from London to care for a family suddenly plunged into financial crisis. Esther and Joseph together had made a near miraculous economic recovery between 1770 and 1775, after their hasty retreat from London to New Jersey. Esther's brother had developed important connections in London,[36] and until 1775, Joseph had corresponded regularly with Lord Dartmouth. As late as the summer of 1775, Dartmouth had continued to express his interest in hearing from Joseph.[37] Had the Reeds chosen England over America, they would have faced another financial crisis, but given their past accomplishments, their London connections, and the possibility of support from the ministry, they could have reasonably expected a third recovery. The cost of returning to England would have been high, but not impossibly so, while the costs of remaining in America, already high in 1775, promised to grow.

Other factors, equally difficult to calculate, also shaped their thinking. The war itself changed things. Beneath the city's apparent calm during the winter and early spring of 1775, its people had waited with growing apprehension. Then, in April, news of bloodshed in Massachusetts broke the emotional logjam, and the city exploded with martial spirit.

Four days before the city learned of Lexington and Concord, Dr. Robert Honyman had toured the city, staying at the Indian Queen, walking the streets, shopping, eating in public places. He observed no military preparations: no drilling, no marching, and no uniforms.[38]

By the first week in May, Honyman would not have recognized the city. News of war disrupted most normal activities and emotions intensified almost daily.[39] For example, Friday, May 5, saw "drums beating, colors flying, and detachments of newly raised militia parading the streets." On Saturday, "the ringing of bells to the great joy of the city" announced Franklin's return home.[40] The same day, the city "turned out over 4,000 men, 300 of whom are Quakers," in what one observer described as "The Rage Militaire."[41] By Monday, May 8, "almost every man that can produce a firelock [was] . . . learning the military discipline."[42] The New England delegation to Congress arrived on Tuesday, May 9, in a magnificent "cavalcade" escorted through the city by "two or three hundred gentlemen on horseback, preceded . . . by the newly chosen city militia officers, two by two, with drawn swords . . . [while] the rear was brought up by a hundred carriages, the streets crowded with people of all ages, sexes and ranks, . . . [and] all the bells set to ringing and chiming."[43] That night Esther and Joseph stayed up past midnight, debating military tactics with newly arrived congressmen.[44] In the heat of such public frenzy, both Esther and Joseph might understandably have made decisions without carefully assessing their ultimate costs.

The Virginians added a new ingredient to the mix. Esther knew Philadelphia men, and she had sympathized with New England men, but Virginians were different. Men of authority with stature, grace, and power, masters of thousands of acres and hundreds of lives, showmen of the first order, they cut a fine figure among the rather dowdy Philadelphians and the plain New Englanders.[45] These Virginia planters came as close as anyone in America to replicating the English landed gentry to whom even wealthy merchants and successful lawyers in England paid deference. In May 1775 Esther entertained at least three of them in her home: the solemn, forceful, and flammable Richard Henry Lee; the six-foot-four James River Grandee, Benjamin Harrison, grandson of Robert "King" Carter and now speaker of the Virginia House of Burgesses; and the most charismatic of them all, George Washington, red haired, well over six feet tall, a horseman, a dancer, an eloquent "presence" with an "animal vitality" and "an air of power reined in."[46]

Washington's impact on people is hard to exaggerate. "There is not a king in Europe," one man noted, "but would look like a valet de chambre by his side."[47] Women responded with similar hyperbole. Abigail Adams, shortly after meeting the new general, wrote to her husband of his modesty, dignity, ease, and complacence: "the gentleman and soldier . . . agreeably blend in him." Then she turned to the poet Dryden for help: "Mark his majestic fabric; he's a temple / Sacred by birth and built by hands divine."[48]

Esther herself has left us no description of Washington, but she understood and probably shared Joseph's attraction to this handsome, imposing, charming man of military bearing and vitality. He dined at Esther's table, where they discussed political and military matters. He invited Joseph to ride with him to

New York, and on the way he persuaded Joseph to risk his life and the security and prosperity of his family by taking up arms against his sovereign.[49]

Esther had long been sensitive to subtle social distinctions. She had informed Joseph early in their courtship that she wanted him to be a lawyer, not a merchant like her father. In her social world, professional men trumped commercial men. When she and Joseph arrived in America they had tarried only a short time in New Jersey, and in Philadelphia she took much pride in their growing wealth and increased status, as Joseph moved quickly to the top ranks of the legal community. Despite their success, however, the Reeds ranked significantly below the top of Philadelphia's non-Quaker economic elite. But, at least in Esther's traditional English scale of values, landed gentry like the Virginia planters trumped even professional men. Close association with such men would have been a new and probably enticing experience for her. By the summer of 1775 she may well have understood that in marching with Virginia rebels, she and Joseph stood shoulder to shoulder with men who overshadowed anyone in Philadelphia, including her spurned suitor, Samuel Powell.

But none of this would have made much difference had British intransigence and condescension not driven both Esther and Joseph away. Both had started with a predilection in favor of reconciliation. They assumed that the problem lay with a small group of myopic and arrogant British officials, possibly advised by malicious appointees in the colonies, who had initiated and then perpetuated the conflict. Over time, however, the Reeds grew increasingly impatient with the entire English nation. Joseph's letters throughout 1774–75 convey his concern about British ministers who "despise the good will of this country," about "the scandalous treatment of Dr. Franklin," about a "spirit of domination in the Mother Country," and about English "contempt" for America's petitions against the "absolute uncontrolled power of Parliament."[50] His letters also reflect the erosion of his affection for "Great Britain, a country wherein I have spent many happy hours," as he saw her begin "to play the tyrant over America."[51]

Esther, too, had come to appreciate, and possibly to share, colonial resentment at the arrogance and insensitivity of her visiting English countrymen. Charles Pettit, Esther's brother-in-law and Joseph's close business associate, expressed this resentment in a letter to Joseph in January 1774, when he complained about Englishmen who "come . . . intoxicated with the absurd Prejudice . . . that they are of an order of Beings superior to the rest of their species."[52] The young and cosmopolitan Esther had herself exhibited many of the same feelings toward provincial Americans when she first arrived, and she later conceded to her brother that her attitude might have made her transition to this new country difficult (185–86). Relying on her own experience, in the fall of 1774 she cautioned Dennis that if he came to America, he would need to take care not to fall "into the many errors, which almost every Englishman does on his arrival here, and very much to their prejudice" (206).

During the winter and early spring of 1774–75, Esther and Joseph saw America's efforts at economic coercion and military preparation as political vehicles for mobilizing powerful forces in England, especially merchants and manufacturers, to oppose the policy of the ministry. From late December 1774 through early 1775, letters from their British correspondents encouraged the Reeds.[53] Late in January, Joseph reported to Charles Pettit that the "tide is certainly turning towards America," and that "on the whole we have more reason to hope than to fear."[54] In mid-February, Joseph, writing to Dennis but aware that his message would probably reach Dartmouth, said, "all parties are not so far from reconciliation as may be imagined." "The proceedings of Congress," he conceded, "have been pitched in too high a key for some of these middle provinces." He insisted that all Americans, with the possible exception of officeholders under the Crown, remained united on the question of the tax, but he outlined plans to defuse this immediate crisis and build toward structural changes that would prevent future conflicts.[55] Esther, as late as March 14, told Dennis, "If the popular and mercantile voices [in England] are in our favour, I think there is great reason for our hopes" (209).[56]

Letters arriving in the late winter and early spring of 1775, however, suggested that the ministry intended to take a hard line and that the expected support from key economic interests in England had failed to materialize. The Reeds had had hints of ministerial intransigency late in 1774 in an unsigned letter from London, presumably from Lord Dartmouth. Although the author remained cordial to the Reeds, he took a decided stance against Americans, who, he charged, "totally forget the nature of that connexion by which they are held to the Mother Country. . . . The Supreme Legislature of the whole British Empire has laid a Duty." If Americans refused to submit, they were saying "in effect that they will no longer be a part of the British Empire."[57] If Dartmouth was indeed the author of this letter, then the Reeds had reason to worry. They had long thought of Dartmouth as a family ally, and as one of the more moderate members of the current ministry.

Letters from Dennis that spring heightened the Reeds' concerns. Dennis felt that "the inflamed zeal of a few [in America] will destroy the mild measures of the Congress," and he reported British preparations for war. He explained that the London merchants trading with America, while concerned for their business, had not united in support of America's position or its principles, and he expected the British to prevent the meeting of Congress scheduled for May 10.[58]

Josiah Quincy, visiting London, confirmed Dennis DeBerdt's analysis. Quincy found the commercial world in London "ill-disposed" and predicted that neither the economic consequences nor the "religion of the British ministers will . . . restrain them." The "threat of arms in our hands," he wrote, would do more to advance the American cause than petitions from the British merchants could, and he asked, "Hath not blood and treasure in all ages been the price of civil liberty?"[59] Thus, in the month or so before Lexington and Concord, Esther had reason to feel abandoned by her English kinsmen, including the merchants' lobby, probably Dartmouth, and even her brother Dennis, who hinted at his own disquiet over the conduct of the Americans.[60]

On April 19, much to Esther's frustration, the British resort to arms placed new and powerful obstacles in the path to reconciliation, postponing, if not actually precluding, a compromise. Joseph had stated that any effort by the British to use force would unite the colonies, "change those now questioning Congress," and lead to widespread bloodshed. Esther expressed much the same concern: "Whatever our fellow subjects may think, *the people here* are determined to die free," she wrote Dennis in June.[61] By the time Joseph left her to ride north with Washington, Esther had begun to do in earnest what she had hinted at some months earlier: to suppress her feelings of attachment to England and strengthen her commitment to this "glorious" cause (228).

Four letters she wrote to Dennis between June and October show her moving, in fits and starts, toward new commitments, new loyalties, and a new political identity.[62] She began in fear and progressed through anger, frustration, and increasing idealization of the American cause and disillusionment with her people, to the understanding that the British were driving Americans, including herself, toward the unthinkable: separation from their English countrymen and the creation of a new people.

On the day after Joseph's departure, Esther expressed her anxieties to Dennis. She did not know precisely what Joseph would do, but she understood that they were stepping into murky and treacherous waters. "What melancholy scenes we have lived to be engaged in; civil war, with all its horrors, stains this land," she wrote. She worried about Joseph's health. He had been "very unwell this summer with an intermitting fever." She also knew that "the part which my dear Mr. Reed has taken in the civil and military affairs of his country" now prevented them from returning to London. She may even have criticized Joseph's recent behavior indirectly when she described the intensity of popular feeling in Philadelphia. "The people here are determined to die or be free," she told Dennis. "They are now raised to a pitch it was thought they never could arrive at; but so it is, and they shrink not at anything that appears before them" (216).

But if the emotions of the American people frightened her, she accepted the legitimacy of their position, and she prayed that "a kind Providence will interpose yet in our favour and find out some way for our relief." She tried to be brave, but felt increasingly vulnerable (218).

A month later she wrote to her brother again. By now she knew that Joseph would not return soon. Martha's poor health concerned her, she could not find accommodations in the country, and she faced the division of her family and a protracted stay in another woman's home. In a rare instance of complaint, she asserted that Joseph's unexpected absence had left her poorly prepared to deal with the consequences. But she also expressed her growing determination to valorize the American cause. She still hoped for the sympathy and understanding of the British people. "What do you think—what do the people in general think of our distresses and conduct?" she asked Dennis. For the first time, she explicitly praised the American position. "Certainly, my dear brother," she wrote, "it is a glorious . . . [cause]. . . . Virtue, honour, unanimity, bravery,—all conspire to carry it on." And then, half hoping, half declaring, she concluded, "and sure it [the cause] has at least a chance to be victorious. I believe it *will*, at last, whatever difficulties and discouragements it may meet with at first" (219).

Early in September, about ten weeks after Joseph's departure, she again wrote to Dennis, explaining how difficult it was to put a good face on things. By now she was living in the Pettits' home in Perth Amboy, where she had taken Martha; her mother had taken the other two children to Burlington. Joseph's law business in Philadelphia had languished, despite the effort of his clerks, and Joseph remained vague about the time of his return. Those who reported on Esther's condition emphasized both the strain she was under and her courage in bearing it. "The good Mrs. Reed," John Cox told Joseph, "bears your absence with a degree of heroism that does her inexpressible credit yet the good soul at times cannot help showing an anxiety for your return which sensibly affects us, her friends." He assured Joseph that he himself had tried to "keep up the good Mrs. Reed's spirits during your long absence," but despite his best efforts, "she begins now to be rather uneasy."[63]

Esther painted a rather more sanguine picture of her immediate living circumstances. She informed Dennis that their mother, living with two of Esther's children in Burlington, had recovered from a mild illness, and that Esther had taken Martha with her to Amboy. The air and the food there agreed with the child, and Esther was enjoying the visit (228).

The broader political situation, however, bedeviled her, she wrote to her brother in early September. She worried about Joseph at camp "admidst all the confusion and horrors of war." She admitted that the continued disruption "sometimes shakes my firmness and resolution," but she also acknowledged that one can get used to almost anything. Moreover, she now knew that Joseph was relatively safe, serving in the councils rather than in the field, and said she would therefore more "cheerfully give up his profits . . . and . . . acquiesce without repining at his being so long absent from me." She also continued to praise "the cause in which he is engaged, so just, so glorious," but she backed off a bit from her judgment of six weeks earlier. "I hope," she wrote, instead of the earlier "believe," that it "will be so victorious" (228).

By "victorious," she meant that the American effort would produce political change in England. She thought that the colonists' demonstration of military prowess might convince the ministry of America's determination, and she asked Dennis "what effect the Battle of Bunker Hill [June 1775] has both on our friends and our enemies." At the same time, she felt disillusioned and betrayed by those at home, asking, "Where sleep all our friends in England? . . . Where sleep the virtue and justice of the English nation? Will nothing rouse them, or are they so few in number and small in consequence, that though awake, their voice cannot be heard in the multitude of our enemies?" (228).

She allowed herself a moment of regret. "Could we have foreseen it, when we [Esther and Dennis] parted in England, it would probably have prevented that separation," she told Dennis, but then righted herself and reasserted her will. "[But] I believe it is right we should not, for though our private happiness might have been promoted, yet our country would not have been benefited" (228–29).[64] She ended her letter on a revealing note: "I hope it is no treason to say I wish well to the Cause of America." Here, as earlier, she maintained a distance between herself and this "Cause." Although she wished it well, it remained their cause, not hers. More significantly, she revealed that she thought of herself as close to committing treason. She assumed that government officials opened and read her letters. She thought of herself as an English citizen supporting rebellion against her country. She had an interest in both countries, and their divergence compelled her toward a choice; while she saw the justice of the one, she continued to feel an identity with the other. Equally important for our understanding of her mental world, Esther here assumed that she was a free agent capable of making an independent, and therefore punishable, political decision.[65]

Late in October, Esther again wrote to Dennis. She had recently returned to Philadelphia and expected Joseph's return within the week. She sent this letter by private hands, not via the postal system, and thus felt freer of "any prying intruder." She worried a bit about her earlier indiscretions but then reaffirmed her position. "If I have committed treason, it must remain," she declared (232). She had acted and now must follow it through.

Esther defined the issue as "the cause of liberty and virtue" (233), but, as Joseph himself wrote to Charles Pettit at about the same time, she still saw the struggle as one for policy or ministerial change, as a "return to the old ground of 1763."[66] She hoped that the recent petitions from Congress might modify British policy and thus "lay the foundation for negotiations . . . [so that] we may be again reconciled." She wrote to Dennis on October 28, 1775, however, that should that fail, "WE SHALL DECLARE FOR INDEPENDENCE, and exert our

utmost to
to it, we
become '

Esthe
but her
mouth,
"all ou

In
Wayn
thoug
tial d
cons
Ame
indi

vs

of American History 69 (June 1982): 21–41; and the Joseph Reed Papers, ... New York, New York (hereafter Joseph Reed Papers).

5. Reed, Sentiments of an American Woman; Reed, Joseph Reed Papers, 178–86; Roche, Joseph Reed, 179.

6. Esther DeBerdt Reed to George Washington, Banks of ... DeBerdt, 322–24; Roche, Joseph Reed, 179; Norton, Liberty's ...

7. Olson, "London Mercantile Lobby." Olson des... respected merchants" trading with America. She ind... prominent London merchants lobbying on Americ... Deputies, and as active in the committee that ... Esther DeBerdt to Joseph Reed, November 15...

8. Reed, Esther DeBerdt, 156–58.

9. Esther DeBerdt Reed to Denn... DeBerdt, 160 (hereafter cited parenth...

10. Reed did not elaborate on ...

11. Joseph wrote, "You wil... you to give me the earliest i... the city in mid-August. J... Hodge to Joseph Reed...

12. Esther shou... Washington had ... mander-in-chi... to their hom... with the ... men ... inv...

Determina...
(April 1991): 201, 195, 200, 215–10.

3. The work of four historians in particular—Jean Sou...
and Wayne Bodle—has done much to shape my thinking here. Soderlund has urged ...
scend the long-standing emphasis on New England and the emphasis on the female Quaker experience
when we do look at the mid-Atlantic region, and to see women as central to the Revolution. See Soderlund, "Women in Eighteenth-Century Pennsylvania: Toward a Model of Diversity," *Pennsylvania Magazine of History and Biography* 115 (April 1991): 163–83. Brown argues that we need to move beyond
assumptions of essentialism and declension and see the world through the eyes of particular women
(subjectivity) building meaningful lives for themselves (agency) in particular contexts. See Kathleen M.
Brown, "Brave New Worlds: Women's and Gender History," *William and Mary Quarterly* 50 (April
1993), 311–28; and "Beyond the Great Debates: Gender and Race in Early America," *Reviews in American
History* 26 (March 1998): 96–123. Susan Klepp has heightened our awareness of female subjectivity and
female agency in revolutionary America. See her "Revolutionary Bodies: Women and the Fertility Transition in the Mid-Atlantic Region, 1760–1820," *Journal of American History* 85 (December 1998): 910–45.
Bodle's study of Jane Bartram, "Jane Bartram's 'Application,'" serves as the starting point and, in part,
the inspiration for this study.

4. Esther DeBerdt Reed, *The Sentiments of an American Woman* (Philadelphia: John Dunlap, 1780).
For a description of Esther DeBerdt Reed's public role in the later stages of the Revolution, see Mary
Beth Norton, *Liberty's Daughters: The Revolutionary Experience of American Women, 1750–1800* (Boston:
Little, Brown, 1980), 178–86. Biographical information on Esther DeBerdt Reed and her husband, Joseph
Reed, comes principally from William B. Reed, *Esther DeBerdt afterwards Esther Reed* (Philadelphia: C.
Sherman, 1853); William B. Reed, *Life and Correspondence of Joseph Reed,* 2 vols. (Philadelphia: Lindsay
and Blakiston, 1847); John F. Roche, *Joseph Reed: A Moderate in the American Revolution* (New York:
Columbia University Press, 1957); Dennys DeBerdt, *Letters of Dennys DeBerdt, 1757–1770,* ed. Albert
Matthews, reprinted from the publications of the Colonial Society of Massachusetts, vol. 13 (Cambridge:
John Wilson and Sons, 1911); Michael Kammen, *A Rope of Sand* (Ithaca: Cornell University Press, 1968);
Alison G. Olson, "The London Mercantile Lobby and the Coming of the American Revolution," *Journal*

New York Historical Society,

2:263–69; Norton, *Liberty's Daugh-*

the Schuylkill, July 31, 1780, Reed, *Esther
Daughters*, 179–85.

cribes DeBerdt as one of the "wealthy, highly
udes him in a short list of the seventeen most
questions, a member of the Protestant Dissenting
worked for repeal of the Stamp Act (26, 29). See also
1764, Joseph Reed Papers.

s DeBerdt, Philadelphia, December 12, 1770, in Reed, *Esther
tically in the text by page number).

er perception of the inadequacies of female education in the colonies.
hear and know what is to be done on the law business of which I beg
timations." Joseph's law clerk took over this responsibility after Esther left
seph Reed to Esther DeBerdt Reed, Cambridge, July 26, 1775, and Andrew
Philadelphia, August 28, 1775, Joseph Reed Papers.

d not have been too surprised. She must have known it was possible, even probable.
een pressing Joseph to join his "family." Washington accepted the position of com-
on June 16 and spent the evening of June 19 with the Reeds. This was his second visit
e since his arrival from Virginia on May 9. Indeed, he spent his first evening in Philadelphia
eeds. Moreover, this was a highly coveted position actively sought by a number of other young
th far better political connections. It placed Joseph close to power and near the action, and it
lved no great sacrifice, as Congress intended to pay a respectable salary for the position, whereas
seph's income in Philadelphia promised to suffer as hostilities intensified. Esther's words in June and
Joseph's in August suggest that they had discussed the matter before he left the city.

13. Dennis DeBerdt to Esther DeBerdt Reed, London, October 6, 1775, Joseph Reed Papers.

14. He invited not all of them but "as many of your family as you think proper." Charles Pettit to
Esther DeBerdt Reed, Perth Amboy, New Jersey, July 24, 1775, ibid.

15. John Cox to Joseph Reed, Philadelphia, July 26, 1775, and September 9, 1775, ibid.

16. Joseph Reed to Esther DeBerdt Reed, Cambridge, July 26, 1775, ibid.

17. Joseph Reed to Esther DeBerdt, March 4, June 17, February 26, and February 27, 1765, ibid.

18. Esther DeBerdt to Joseph Reed, London, July 8, May 11, July 20, April 13, May 10, and March
17, 1765, ibid.

19. Esther DeBerdt to Joseph Reed, London, December 8, 1764, and February 8, March 17, and
March 27, 1765; Joseph Reed to Esther DeBerdt, Philadelphia, June 17, 1765, ibid.; George B. Tatum,
Philadelphia Georgian: The City House of Samuel Powell (Middletown: Wesleyan University Press, 1976),
9; *Pennsylvania Evening Post*, February 23, 1775.

20. Joseph Reed to Charles Pettit, London, May 7, June 8, July 3, and July 13, and June 25, 1777,
Joseph Reed Papers.

21. Esther DeBerdt to Joseph Reed, London, April 25, 1766; February 19, March 17 and 28, 1767;
July 7, January 30, and March 28, 1768; February 28, June 13, and July 4 and 7, 1767, ibid.

22. For her participation in her father's Sunday dinners, see Esther DeBerdt to Joseph Reed, London, November 9, 1765, ibid.

23. For a sample of John Adams's descriptions of the various dinners he attended in private homes
in the fall of 1774, see Adams's diary entries for August 30, September 7, 8, 11, and 14, 1774, in Paul H.
Smith et al., eds., *Letters of Delegates to Congress, 1774–1789*, 25 vols. (Washington, D.C.: Library of
Congress, 1976–93), 1:4, 33–34, 45, 64, 69. For Esther's participation in the discussions at her own dinners
in Philadelphia, see Silas Deane to E. Dean, Philadelphia, September 1774, ibid., 1:92.

24. Thomas Rodney of Dover, Delaware, expressed much the same sentiment in a letter to Congressman Caesar Rodney on May 10, 1775: "never had anything in view but reconciliation between
England and the colonies upon the full establishment of all American rights and privileges." Caesar
Rodney, *Letters to and from Caesar Rodney, 1756–1784*, ed. George Herbert Ryden (Philadelphia: University of Pennsylvania Press, for the Historical Society of Delaware, 1933), 57–58.

25. Samuel Curwen, *The Journal and Letters of Samuel Curwen, 1775–1783,* ed. George Atkinson Ward (Boston: Little Brown, 1864), journal entry for May 9, 1775, 28.

26. Dennis DeBerdt to Esther DeBerdt Reed, London, January 26 and June 1, 1775, Joseph Reed Papers.

27. Joseph Reed to Dennis DeBerdt, Philadelphia, September 26, 1774, ibid.

28. Esther DeBerdt to Joseph Reed, London, November 11, 1764, and July 7, 1767, ibid.

29. In response to a question from Dennis DeBerdt about his courtship of a woman who did not share his religious attachments, Joseph assured Dennis that he should not hesitate to marry her on those grounds. His own Presbyterian father, Reed pointed out, had married "three Episcopal wives," and "such matters are so frequent here and no fatal misunderstanding arises from them." Thus, if "in all other respects she will make you happy . . . the difference among Protestants is not so essential as that a man do violence to his inclination on that account." Joseph Reed to Dennis DeBerdt, Philadelphia, February 13, 1775, letterbook, ibid.

30. I base this claim on fragments of Esther's early writings in the Joseph Reed Papers. Her father's people had migrated to England from Flanders "for the sake of Religion." In 1758 DeBerdt had arranged for the publication in London of a sermon by the Reverend Samuel Davies, later president of Princeton. Shortly thereafter he helped organize a campaign for funds in England in support of Dartmouth College, and in 1766 he worked (unsuccessfully) with Dr. William Smith of New York to obtain support for a charter for the Presbyterian Church in New York City. See DeBerdt, *Letters of Dennys DeBerdt,* 294, 297, 298–99, 316–17, 445.

31. The Reeds belonged to the Second Presbyterian Church at Arch and Third streets. Roche, *Joseph Reed,* 32.

32. For a discussion of Presbyterian theology and revolution, see Joseph Tiedemann, "Presbyterianism and the American Revolution in the Middle Colonies," *Church History* 74 (June 2005): 306–44, esp. 322–26; and Rosemary Keller, *Patriotism and the Female Sex: Abigail Adams and the American Revolution* (Brooklyn, N.Y.: Carlson Publishing, 1994), 67–69.

33. Tiedemann, "Presbyterianism and the American Revolution." On Sunday, May 7, 1775, Esther's minister, Mr. Sproat, had "entertained [them] . . . with a truly American patriotic sermon." Curwen, *Journals and Letters,* entry for Sunday, May 7, 1775, 28.

34. A document Joseph prepared in July 1774 estimated their total worth at £7,335, with furniture worth £300, a wine cellar worth £70, and their nonlegal library worth £40. An industrious craftsman working in Philadelphia in the early 1770s could expect to earn about £35–40 pounds a year, about half the value of the Reeds' wine cellar. Moreover, the Reeds owned speculative land in Orange County, New York, and in western Pennsylvania, as well as shares worth £1,300 in a London syndicate with extensive land holdings in New Jersey. Roche, *Joseph Reed,* 30–32. According to Gary B. Nash, "Artisans and Politics in Eighteenth-Century Philadelphia," in *The Origins of Anglo-American Radicalism,* ed. James R. Jacobs and Margaret C. Jacobs (London: Allen & Unwin, 1984), craftsmen earned five shillings per day, laborers three shillings a day (164).

35. Joseph Reed to Samuel Spraggs, Philadelphia, May 30, 1775, and Joseph Reed to John Antill[e], Philadelphia, June 5, 1775, Joseph Reed Papers.

36. Joseph had worked closely with Dennis between 1770 and 1775 to help the inexperienced young man enter the business of international trade, and by 1775 Dennis had regained some of the income and stature his father had enjoyed at the time of his death in 1770. In 1775 Joseph used his connections in New Jersey to get Dennis an appointment as London agent for that province. Joseph Reed to Dennis DeBerdt, Philadelphia, December 5, 1775, ibid. For Joseph's role in nurturing Dennis, see their extensive correspondence between 1770 and 1775, ibid. Olson, in "London Mercantile Lobby," 26, identifies Dennis as part of the small cadre of well-to-do and politically connected London merchants trading with America.

37. Roche, *Joseph Reed,* 34; Dennis DeBerdt to Esther DeBerdt Reed, London, June 1, 1775, Joseph Reed Papers.

38. Dr. Robert Honyman, *The Colonial Panorama, 1775: Dr. Robert Honyman's Journal for Mar. and April,* ed. Philip Padel Ford (San Marino, Calif.: Huntington Library, 1939), 71–72.

39. Joseph Reed reported that the court was sitting when the news arrived. The court "immediately closed." Joseph Reed to Samuel Spraggs, Philadelphia, May 20, 1775, letterbook, Joseph Reed Papers.

40. Curwen, *Journals and Letters,* Philadelphia, May 5 and 7, 1775, 27–28.

41. Margaret Wheeler Willard, ed., *Letters on the American Revolution, 1774–1776* (Boston: Houghton Mifflin, 1925), 102.

42. Ibid., 103.

43. Curwen, *Journals and Letters,* May 10, 1775, 28–29; Caesar Rodney to Thomas Rodney, Philadelphia, May 11, 1775, in Smith et al., *Letters of Delegates,* 1:58.

44. Curwen, *Journals and Letters,* May 9, 1774, 28.

45. As Joseph wrote in September 1774, "there are some fine fellows come from Virginia. . . . The Bostonians are mere Milksops to them. They are the capital men of the colony both in fortune and understanding." Joseph Reed to Charles Pettit, Philadelphia, September 4, 1774, Joseph Reed Papers.

46. Gary Wills, *Inventing America: Jefferson's Declaration of Independence* (Garden City, N.Y.: Doubleday, 1978), 3–4, 10–12.

47. "Extract from a Letter from Philadelphia, PA in the Morning Post and Daily Advertiser [London] Jan. 16, 1776," in Willard, *Letters on the American Revolution,* 228.

48. Abigail Adams to John Adams, Braintree, Massachusetts, July 16, 1775, in *Familiar Letters of John Adams and His Wife, Abigail Adams, During the Revolution,* ed. Charles Francis Adams (Boston: Houghton Mifflin, 1876), 79.

49. For Washington's attachment to Joseph Reed, see his letters to Joseph in the winter of 1775–76, after Joseph had returned home to Philadelphia. Washington to Reed, Cambridge, Massachusetts, January 23 and 31, February 10 and 26, and March 9, 1776, in George Washington, *The Papers of George Washington,* Revolutionary War Series, ed. Philander Chase, 18 vols. to date (Charlottesville: University of Virginia Press, 1985–), 3:172–73, 225, 286–91, 369–79.

50. Joseph Reed to Dennis DeBerdt, Philadelphia, May 4 and December 24, 1774, and February 13, 1775, Joseph Reed Papers.

51. Joseph Reed to Josiah Quincy, Philadelphia, October 25, 1774, ibid.

52. Charles Pettit to Joseph Reed, Burlington, New Jersey, January 18, 1774, ibid. Pettit was referring here to a recent male English visitor but might well have had in mind the attitude expressed by Esther herself during her first few years in America.

53. Between May and the end of September 1774, Hugh Baillie wrote from London at least five times. The last of these letters could not have reached the Reeds before early November. Baillie urged them to unite and predicted that a boycott of trade would ruin English manufacturers and thus the current ministry, and would produce a new government at the next election. Hugh Baillie to Joseph Reed, London, May 1, August 2, August 20, September 9, and September 29, 1774, ibid.

54. Joseph Reed to Charles Pettit, January 31, 1775, ibid.

55. Joseph Reed to Dennis DeBerdt, Philadelphia, February 13, 1775, ibid.

56. Esther and Joseph believed that there was indeed a middle ground. Joseph himself had proposed at least two ways "to prevent apprehended extremities." One was for the mother country to "temporize" with respect to "the acts lately passed, leave the question of rights undiscussed," and have the colonies pay for the tea in deference to the "dignity of the Mother Country." A second approach, which he preferred, would be to suspend the present acts and then call together representatives of the Assembly to negotiate a new constitution for America that would provide for "those restraints necessary for the interests of the whole." Joseph Reed to Dennis DeBerdt, Philadelphia, February 13, 1775, letterbook, ibid. Reed undoubtedly expected his proposals to find their way to the ministry. He knew that DeBerdt was in close contact with Dartmouth, and he suspected that the government was opening and reading his mail.

57. Unsigned letter dated July 11, 1774, ibid. Internal evidence suggests that it came from Dartmouth.

58. Dennis DeBerdt to Joseph Reed, London, October 8 1774, January 4, 1775, ibid.

59. Josiah Quincy to Joseph Reed, London, December 17, 1774, ibid.

60. In 1775 the London merchants trading with America disintegrated as an effective lobbying force. By March they had divided over whether to focus their efforts on protecting their "interests" or to expand their concerns to the broad questions of liberty and the constitution, i.e., whether to "espouse a cause rather than explain an interest." Then strong ministerial hostility to them as a group left them in disarray. Olson, "London Mercantile Lobby," 39. Esther's brother, Dennis, was a part of this group and undoubtedly conveyed news of its division and disintegration to Esther in the late spring or early summer of 1775. In February 1775 Joseph had cautioned Dennis and then chided him slightly: "I suspect you . . .

have fallen off a bit from the old principles of your family with respect to this country." Joseph Reed to Dennis DeBerdt, Philadelphia, February 13, 1775, letterbook, Joseph Reed Papers.

61. Esther DeBerdt Reed to Dennis DeBerdt, Philadelphia, June 24, 1775, Joseph Reed Papers.

62. In complex questions like these, probably no particular moment can be singled out in which fundamental change occurred. One's thoughts move first one way and then another. External circumstances of the moment, as well as the accumulation of experiences over time, shape and reshape feelings. One is seldom absolutely convinced, and rarely so transformed as to resist looking back. Nonetheless, there can be little doubt that these four months were decisive for Esther.

63. John Cox to Joseph Reed, Philadelphia, September 9, 1775, Joseph Reed Papers.

64. Her use of the term "country" here is confusing but probably applies to the English-speaking nation threatened by ministerial tyranny.

65. For an extended discussion of whether, under late eighteenth-century coverture and English common law, a married woman could be charged with treason for failing to separate herself from her husband's treasonable acts, see Linda Kerber, *No Constitutional Right to Be Ladies: Women and the Obligations of Citizenship* (New York: Hill and Wang, 1998), 3–46, esp. 27–33. Kerber argues that in the postrevolutionary era Americans divided on this question, with conservatives denying the civic capacity of women and asserting that "a married woman 'cannot commit . . . this species of treason by obeying her husband'" (33). During the war, however, some states had not distinguished between husbands and wives and had given no protection to the dower rights of loyalist wives who fled with their husbands. The court cases Kerber cites for the postwar period, however, favored the older, more traditional view that a married woman lacked the power to separate herself from her husband's political acts and could therefore not be held accountable for failing to do so.

66. Joseph Reed to Charles Pettit, Camp, October 8, 1775, Joseph Reed Papers.

67. See Bodle's discussion of the significance of Bartram's case. "Jane Bartram's 'Application,'" 211–20.

68. For a discussion of the degree to which the legal and social constraints of coverture conceal from historians the political behavior of women and thus "impede the scholarly recovery of their experience," see ibid., 212. Linda Kerber made much the same point when she urged historians to rethink the narrative of the Revolution in such a way as to reveal the "women who live in the interstices of institutions that we once understood as wholly segregated by gender." Kerber, *Toward an Intellectual History of Women: Essays by Linda K. Kerber* (Chapel Hill: University of North Carolina Press, 1997), 98.

9

REDCOAT THEATER:
NEGOTIATING IDENTITY IN OCCUPIED PHILADELPHIA, 1777–1778

Meredith H. Lair

On the evening of January 19, 1778, a new act in the ongoing drama of the American Revolution began amid the twinkling houselights and handcrafted finery of Philadelphia's Southwark Theatre. At seven o'clock the stage curtains swung back to reveal an exquisitely painted drop, a few carefully placed set pieces, and a costumed actor, who delivered, as was the custom of the times, a rhyming prologue specifically written for the event:

> Once more ambitious of Theatric Glory
> *Howe's* strolling Company appears before ye.
> O'er hill & dale & bogs, thro wind & weather,
> With many a hair-breadth scape we've scrambled hither.[1]

The "hair-breadth scapes" endured by the troupe were not the typical mishaps of a touring company but the narrow British military victories under General William Howe at Brandywine and Germantown. Now safely quartered in the American capital for the winter, the officers of the Royal Army and Navy were determined to enjoy the theatrical delights of North America's largest city, even if they had to play all the roles themselves.

Within days of completing fortifications for the city, some of Howe's officers began preparing for a theater season, advertising in the *Pennsylvania Ledger* for a scribe, a clerk, and experienced carpenters and scene shifters to help at the "Play-House."[2] Because a few officers had already participated in theater productions in occupied New York the previous winter, preparations ran smoothly, with officers' wives, Philadelphia belles, and at least one professional actress playing the female roles. Comedies and farces dominated the season, but David Garrick's dramatic satire *Lethe,* John Home's *Douglas: A Tragedy,* and Shakespeare's historical play *The First Part of King Henry IV* were also featured.[3] After each performance, usually on Monday but becoming more erratic after the Easter holidays, the actors and audience streamed into local taverns or graced the dance floors of private balls. Perhaps to celebrate the coming spring, an early March performance even included a "beautiful Exhibition of Fire-Works" after the show.[4] Indeed, one Hessian soldier found enough "assemblies, concerts, comedies, clubs, and the like" available in Philadelphia to "make us forget there is any war, save that it is a capital joke."[5]

In the meantime, the rebel forces were sick and hungry at Valley Forge twenty miles away, where the winter of 1777–78 was hardening the Continental army and refining distinctions between American and English identity. If the proscenium of the Southwark stage is expanded to include the sufferings of war so close at hand, the British theatricals in Philadelphia appear particularly incongruous, providing an opportunity to examine how these disparate groups regarded each other. As an actor on the American stage, the British military aimed to please its colonial following while subduing rebellious hecklers in the gallery. To succeed, this *coup de théâtre* demanded a precise understanding of the American audience, loyalist and patriot alike. But Americans themselves were still sorting out who they were. The pen strokes that severed the colonies from Great Britain did not necessarily transform British subjects into American citizens, for many Pennsylvanians considered themselves both and were loath to choose. As the redcoat theater of Philadelphia demonstrates, the British seriously misread the complex and evolving patterns of American identity, ultimately rendering their exploits in the American Revolution a tragic farce.

For General Howe, the occupation of Philadelphia was an integral component of a political strategy designed to rouse the colonists in support of the Crown. As early as 1776 Howe expressed in correspondence his belief that circumstances had "much changed in Pennsylvania, and their [the citizenry's] minds [are], in general, from the late progress of the army, disposed to peace, in which sentiment they would be confirmed, by our getting possession of Philadelphia." The following year, colonial secretary Lord Germain agreed, anticipating that the "enthusiastic assistance of the Philadelphia Loyalists" would free up valuable manpower to be dispatched to General Burgoyne as he made his way southward from Lake Champlain. In fact, Pennsylvania loyalists were not so much loyal as they were "disaffected" by local circumstances that alienated them from the patriot cause. Accordingly, Howe had difficulty pacifying Philadelphia and its environs in the fall of 1777, so he was unable to send reinforcements to Burgoyne. Thus British misconceptions about the breadth and character of loyalist support in Philadelphia inadvertently contributed to Burgoyne's defeat at Saratoga in October, one of the most decisive engagements of the war.[6]

According to historian Paul Smith, the British misunderstood the "typical American loyalist," whose conservatism, caution, and pacifism were perceived as signs of military weakness. In the first three years of the war, this lack of respect translated into lower pay and housing shortages for the ten thousand loyalists who did take up arms. When British policy shifted in 1778 to encourage loyalist enlistment, long-standing grievances against the British army prevented any new reliance on loyalist manpower.[7] By not providing for the material needs of its subjects, then, Britain expressed unfounded confidence that loyalists would choose to risk the tangibles of home and hearth—indeed, of life and limb—for the abstractions of king and country.

General Howe seemed to sense the precarious nature of loyalist support in the summer of 1777, when he tried to win over the populace with the good behavior of his troops. En route to Philadelphia in July, Howe issued orders against plundering and authorized his provost marshal to execute any soldier in violation. He made a more direct appeal for public support a month later, offering protection to colonists who remained at home and blanket amnesty to anyone, save rebel officeholders, who surrendered arms to the British army. Upon reaching the city in September, however, Howe discarded the role of benevolent liberator and assumed the mantle of martial authority. New requirements for proof of loyalty made it impossible for many wavering loyalists to remain safely at home, and the active recruitment of loyalist troops to occupy the city further divided neighbors against one another.[8]

While quartered in Philadelphia, striking inconsistencies in British occupation policy further alienated the public, as British officers and troops took liberties with curfews and rations not afforded civilians. The plays produced by the British officers at the Southwark Theatre were extremely well publicized, providing constant reminders of the incongruity of theatricals and balls amid martial law.[9] For example, the February 25 issue of the *Pennsylvania Ledger* juxtaposed an announcement from General Howe promising "severest punishment" for black marketeers with a notice of the postponement of an upcoming play. Likewise, the March 25 issue offered a warning against looting on the same page as an advertisement for productions of *The First Part of King Henry IV* and *The Mock Doctor*. Most egregious was the January 10 notice from General Howe imposing a curfew, from 8:30 P.M. until dawn, printed during a desperate advertising blitz to find a copy of Susanna Cent Livre's play *The Wonder*. Given the officers' intention to offer two plays and the customary musical interludes each Monday evening—with tickets ranging from 50¢ to $1 apiece—it seems unlikely that they intended any of their wealthy patrons to be off the streets in time to obey General Howe's orders.[10]

Despite these inconsistencies, the British did not intend to alienate sympathetic Philadelphians during the occupation. Contributing to British misperceptions of loyalists was the evolving nature of their common identity. According to William H. Nelson, the "Tory rank and file" were members of groups with little in common—religious pacifists, southern backcountry farmers, and unassimilated ethnic minorities—who viewed British authority as a benevolent level-ing force.[11] A more cohesive loyalist identity was slow to develop because many people identified with both sides in the struggle. In occupied New York, Judith van Buskirk has found that clear boundaries drawn by political and military authorities on both sides of the struggle were rendered "permeable" by the bonds of family, friendship, and commerce.[12] And in Philadelphia, women who expressed strong personal opposition to independence frequently referred in diary entries to "our Whigs" and "our American army." Only after the Conti-nentals took their husbands captive did these women grudgingly direct their rhetorical support toward the British.[13] By the end of the war, loyalists felt victimized by patriots and redcoats alike. As Robert Calhoon notes, this ambiva-lence coalesced into a self-conscious identity characterized by a "common para-noia at the apparent injustices visited on them by American cruelty and British incompetence."[14]

Economic and commercial factors also influenced the development of dis-tinct loyalist and patriot identities in America. In *The Loyalist Perception,* Cal-hoon argues that the influx of "British styles, products, and national hubris"[15] into America blurred distinctions between colonists and Englishmen. In fact, many Americans bristled at British cultural imports, and at the theater in partic-ular. In response to the nonimportation movement of the 1760s, actor-director David Douglass—who later founded the Southwark Theatre in Philadelphia—changed the name of his "London Company of Players" to the "American Company" the better to reflect the tastes of his colonial audiences. By 1775 Douglass and the American Company had left the northern colonies for Jamaica, in part because of the anti-theater legislation passed by the Continental Congress the previous year. This legislation depicted theater as a threat to Amer-ican values and commerce, and it imposed a ban to "encourage frugality, econ-omy, and industry, and promote agriculture, art and the manufactures of *this* country" (emphasis added).[16] Still, the American Company might have contin-ued performing in the thirteen colonies under euphemisms like "lectures" or "concerts," except that theater itself "was now seen as a British manufactured product, expressly suited to royalist tastes,"[17] and so it had lost some of its common appeal.

Thousands of residents fled Philadelphia when the British arrived in the city in September 1777, but thousands more flocked to the city to winter under British protection. When British officers revived the theater there a few months later, they had no trouble finding an audience to fill the boxes and galleries of the Southwark. Would-be patrons of the arts found a variety of ways to gain entry to the sold-out shows. A notice for the second performance printed in the *Pennsylvania Ledger* requested that the "Foreign Gentleman who flipped . . . a Guinea and a Half into the Hand of the Box-keeper, and forced his Way into the House" come to the theater office to retrieve his unwanted money. Thereafter, every notice included the request that gentlemen not try to bribe the doorkeepers for admittance and that individuals wanting to reserve seats should dispatch a servant to the theater three hours before the curtain—which implies that most of those who attended were wealthy enough to employ servants.[18] In light of the earlier opposition to the theater, then, this level of support for the Southwark performances indicates just how isolated and divided occupied Philadelphia had become, stuffed as it was full of wealthy loyalists and patriots too poor to flee the British lines.

Even so, Philadelphians' desire to partake of the cultural fare of the British occupation did not necessarily represent a desire to see the rebels defeated. Correspondence from Philadelphia belle Rebecca Franks to the wife of a delegate to the Continental Congress suggests how superficial the political struggles and cultural differences seemed to some.

> I spent Tuesday evening at Sir Wm Howes where we had a concert and Dance. I asked his leave to send you a Handkerchief to show the fashions. He very politely gave me permission to send anything you wanted, tho' I told him you were a Delegate's Lady.
>
> Oh how I wish Mr. P. wou'd let you come in for a week or two—tell him I'll answer for your being let to return. I know you are as fond of a gay life as myself—you'd have an opportunity of rakeing as much as you choose either at Plays, Balls Concerts or Assemblys.[19]

Not everyone appreciated the British military as an arbiter of fashion, however. Many of the loyalist faithful found their devotion to the Crown challenged by the frivolous lifestyle being enjoyed in a war zone. References to the "do-nothing army" pepper many loyalist diaries, including that of Grace Galloway, whose husband, Joseph, was the nominal chief of the Philadelphia constabulary. Comparing Whigs with Tories, she concluded that the "greatest rebels was in the king's army," because they took the king's shilling but did not serve the empire in return.[20] Other critics focused their ire on what might have been, one armchair strategist hypothesizing in 1780 that "it was in the Power of the infamous Howe to have finished this rebellion more than four times to my own knowledge."[21]

No single event drew more criticism than the Meschianza, a lavish fete to honor General Howe upon his recall to England in May 1778. Replete with armored knights, jousts, costumed nymphs, fireworks, a regatta on the Delaware River, musical performances, and a lavish feast in a specially built banquet hall on the estate of Joseph Wharton, the Meschianza celebrated with victorious spirit General Howe's dubious exit from the American stage. Philadelphia diarist Elizabeth Drinker described the "Scenes of Folly and Vanity" at length, concluding, "How insensible do these people appear, while our Land is so greatly desolated, and Death and sore destruction has overtaken and impends over so many." Loyalist and former prisoner of the Continental army James Parker shared Drinker's dismay, particularly given France's recent entry into the fray. "Had the Rebels got such a correction as they deserved, restored to their senses, and this been the feast of peace, it would have been very proper. But there are [those] who think it ill-timed, our Country by procrastination being involved in a french War." And Ambrose Serle worried about the propaganda opportunity the Meschianza afforded the resolute Continentals wintering nearby. "It cost a great sum of money. Our enemies will dwell upon the folly and extravagance of it with pleasure."[22]

The Meschianza aside, British indulgence in Philadelphia offered a striking contrast to the American experience at Valley Forge. British soldiers and officers, numbering some sixteen thousand, could stroll paved, lamp-lit streets, reside in well-appointed brick homes, and pursue the base pleasures of drinking, cards, cockfights, horse races, and women. By many accounts, life in occupied Philadelphia was, for the city's elite, "as lively, even livelier than in peace-time."[23] In contrast, Valley Forge, while not quite the crucible of American martial spirit that the foundation myth purports—the infamous "bloody footprints in the snow" do not appear in contemporaneous accounts—was nonetheless muddy and austere. Washington's forces were in rough shape even before arriving at their winter quarters, as evidenced by a surgeon's miserable account from December 1777:

> I am sick, discontented, and out of humor. Poor food, hard lodging, cold weather, fatigue, nasty clothes, nasty cookery, vomit half my time, smoked out of my senses, the devil in it, I can't endure it, why are we sent here to starve and freeze? There comes a soldier, bare feet are seen through his worn out shoes, his legs nearly naked from the tattered remains of an only pair of stockings, his breeches not sufficient to cover his nakedness, his shirt hanging in strings, his hair disheveled, his face meager, his whole appearance pictures a person forsaken and discouraged.[24]

For the next three months, some twelve thousand American soldiers huddled in log huts, often wanting for firewood, proper clothing, and food. They suffered frostbite, lice, and typhus; they grumbled their discontent to their officers; hundreds deserted to the British lines; some plundered food and fuel from local civilians; and two thousand perished from hunger, exposure, disease, and exhaustion. While snowball fights, games, alcohol, and religious services tempered the desperate conditions, life was hard, and the soldiers' morale—indeed, the entire project of American independence—seemed on the brink of collapse.[25]

Just as Ambrose Serle predicted, the gaiety of the British occupation in Philadelphia provided facile propaganda for American writers seeking to maintain soldier morale and to sway wavering loyalists to the patriot cause. On December 10, 1777, both the *Pennsylvania Packet* and the *Pennsylvania Gazette* published a letter that exposed the frivolous behavior of the British officer corps in the city. Titled "From a Gentleman Within to a Gentleman Without," the anonymous writer excoriated General Howe for his lavish appetites. "His debauchery and the immorality of his character is disgusting to those who wish to befriend him," wrote "L. L.," who encouraged active and wavering loyalists to reform, as he had done, and support the frugal patriots at Valley Forge.[26]

Although the theater was not a specific target of the gentleman's diatribe, patriotic resentment of this expensive British entertainment found expression in other forms. Officers in the Continental army actually produced a play of their own while at Valley Forge in early 1778, a production that scholar Jason Shaffer regards as a "counter-performance" that projected to British scouts and spies "the image of a distressed but unbroken army."[27] In striking contrast to British theatricals at the Southwark, the Continentals' austere production of Joseph Addison's *Cato* was mounted outdoors near the banks of the Schuylkill River and performed not just for other officers but for a large crowd of ordinary soldiers. The play tells the story of "a virtuous republican [of ancient Rome] willing to fall on his sword rather than surrender to oppression" and offers what scholar Randall Fuller describes as "a salient version of national destiny characterized by self-sacrifice, republican virtue, and an almost boundless devotion to the principle of liberty." General Washington himself attended, signaling the importance of the production as a morale booster for American troops but also as a timely critique of enemy practice.[28]

Theater's role in negotiating American identity continued even after the British withdrew from Philadelphia. When the Continentals tried to reopen the Southwark Theatre under American military direction in the summer of 1778, swift official condemnation restored the requisite divisions between American and British culture. After an initial performance, congressional delegate Samuel Adams sarcastically accused the would-be thespians of behaving "in humble Imitation . . . of the example of the British army." Legislation passed on October 12, 1778, banned the theater and other spectacles anew. Just as in 1774, the measure had no teeth and was violated the same night with a play at the Southwark and, more egregiously, a ball hosted by the governor of Pennsylvania. Four days later, Congress passed legislation to enforce the ban: "Whereas frequenting Play Houses and theatrical entertainments, has a fatal tendency to divert the minds of the people from a due attention to the means necessary for the defence of their country and preservation of their liberties: *Resolved* that any person holding an office under the United States who shall act, promote, encourage or attend such plays, shall be deemed unworthy to hold such office, and shall be accordingly dismissed."[29] Though producers circumvented the ban by using the usual euphemisms of "lectures" or "concerts" until its repeal in 1789, the law's text did represent an official delineation of American culture and character predicated on simple tastes, hard work, and singular devotion to cause.

In the winter of 1777–78, the Americans cultivated their image as a worthy if disadvantaged David at Valley Forge, while the British army in Philadelphia appeared more like a debauched, lumbering Goliath. Continued plundering and rising crime in 1778 made a mockery of General Howe's earlier promises of civilian protection,[30] and his own officers made light of Provost Marshal William Cunningham's ghoulish reputation for mistreating prisoners in their opening night prologue at the Southwark. The prologue lauds Cunningham's skill at hanging people: "In lofty Terms, old vaunting Sadler's wells / Of her Tight Rope & Ladder-dancing tells / But *Cunningham* in both by far excels."[31] With Washington's army so close at hand, the British could not forage with impunity for food and supplies in the surrounding countryside. And with the Delaware River frozen over or under American guard for part of the occupation, merchant ships had difficulty reaching the city. As a result, the citizens of Philadelphia, including Howe's own loyalist constituency, were forced to take up the slack. Elizabeth Drinker describes in her diary numerous instances of British seizure of private goods; items like blankets, hay, and cattle were commonly taken with no hope of recompense. Like many citizens, Drinker was forced to share her home with a British officer at a time when her family had moved into the front parlor to conserve heat. Two diary entries just days apart also illustrate the double standard at work with the curfew laws: "9 January 1778—there is orders given out that no person shall be out after 8 o'clock. . . . 14 January 1778—I am all out of patience with our Major he stays out so late almost every Night." Drinker and other loyalists surrendered meekly to British will, but they might have been willing to give much more had they perceived the British army as doing all it could to end the war.

It is not surprising that the British army ignored the needs and desires of the loyalists, given that it often failed to care for the needs of its own. Only the income of a country laborer ranked below that of a common British soldier, leaving the dependents of soldiers in the field to fend for themselves. An estimated five thousand women and as many as twelve thousand children were with the British army in America, but British military policy made few provisions for their care and scarcely afforded widows passage back to England. Children of soldiers who lost both parents in America received some private charity from

England in the early years of the war, but after 1777 public interest waned, making relief for widows and orphans a private affair.[32]

Even before American independence was declared, theater was used as a fund-raising mechanism for the British army—for example, a September 1775 production of *The Tragedy of Zara* at Faneuil Hall in Boston to benefit "Widows & Children of the Soldiers."[33] This trend continued in occupied New York throughout the war, with weekly plays and concerts—with subscription series—benefiting needy military dependents. In occupied Philadelphia, however, general poverty proved a more serious problem. The army's presence actually exacerbated the disparity between rich and poor. Shortages of essentials like food and fuel led to price spikes at the same time that British merchants set up shop with imported luxury goods like cricket bats, velvet fabrics, combs, lip salve, and Italian shaving powder, items not only beyond the reach of Philadelphia's poor but beyond their comprehension.[34]

At the Southwark Theatre's opening night in 1778, the tailored prologue expressed the actors' noble intentions for playacting in the midst of a war.

> Benevolence first urg'd us to engage,
> And boldly venture on a public Stage.
> To guard the helpless Orphan's tender years,
> To wipe away th'afflicted Parents' Tears,
> To sooth the Sorrows of the widow's Breast,
> To lull the friendless bosom's Care to Rest,
> This our Design—& sure in such a Cause,
> E'en Error's self may challenge some applause.
> With Candour, then, our imperfections scan,
> And where the *Actor* fails, absolve the *Man*.[35]

Absolution for British feasting in the midst of famine became particularly necessary just weeks later, when public relief for Philadelphia's poor dried up. With an announcement in the February 14 edition of the *Pennsylvania Ledger*, Joseph Galloway issued a proclamation in General Howe's name seeking private donations for the poor. By all appearances, the British military was not taking responsibility for its own actions, for weeks earlier Howe had turned the local almshouse into an army hospital, sending the poor into the streets. Private citizens did try to address the situation; the Quakers opened the Fourth Street Meeting House as a shelter, and other groups organized sales of subscription papers to benefit the poor. In response to the new crisis of need, but still determined to have their entertainment, Howe's thespians quickly directed their proceeds away from British widows and orphans to general "public charity," at once assuaging guilty consciences and legitimizing the energy and expense of the theater season.[36]

Although the financial accounts of the Southwark under British military direction are not available, statistics for similar British military theatricals in New York City demonstrate just how thin the pretense of public charity really was. For example, the 1778–79 theater season in New York cost £3,169 plus the rental of the theater. In 1778, £29 was paid for costumes in just two productions, compared with a total of £140 directed to charity. Likewise, in 1779, £179 went to charity, but £100 was laid out for headdresses and wigs in just two months' time.[37] With more than four thousand square feet of space on the ground floor, plus boxes and a gallery in the rear, the Southwark Theatre could seat several hundred patrons each evening, yielding a likely gross of $300 to $400 a week. Given the lavish nature of the productions, it is unlikely that Philadelphia charities ever received more than token donations from the British thespians.[38]

Situating redcoat theater in the grave context of war clearly demonstrates how British military authorities misread the economic and political situation in Philadelphia that winter, for they alienated many loyalists with their high living, scant charity, and no improvement in the Crown's strategic position. When the sweep of this drama is narrowed to the interaction between actor, text, and audience, the complex dynamics of identity formation are made equally manifest. What words did the soldier-actors speak each night? What kinds of stories did they tell? Examining the plays themselves provides some sense of how the performances resonated in the lives of the audiences—both the literal audience in the gallery and the figurative audience in greater Philadelphia—as they negotiated who they were in relation to one another.

The officers who trod the boards at the Southwark Theatre spoke directly to their wealthy patrons through the texts they performed. Given the war and the attendant problems of trade, it is tempting to assume that the British theater season was dictated by necessity. In fact, two series of advertisements seeking copies of three specific texts—Cent Livre's *The Wonder,* Home's *Douglas,* and Murphy's *The Citizen*[39]—suggest that the plays were chosen with care and consideration of both the actors' and audiences' tastes and prejudices. Adding to the deliberate quality of the performances was the acting style of the day. In the eighteenth century, British acting styles were in transition from a "declamatory" approach borrowed from rhetoric to a more realistic approach that strove for emotional authenticity. The newer mode required time to analyze the text and formulate each moment on stage, time the British soldier-actors did not have. Given the swift pace of the season and the limits of their creative abilities, it is likely that they embraced the declamatory style, barking each line directly to the audience as one would give a speech.[40] Since the texts were chosen with care and the actors spoke directly to their audiences, the words of the plays themselves have meaning beyond the stories they tell.

Several of the plays the British army performed that winter incorporate humorous perspectives on soldiering, suggesting the actors' sense of identification with the characters or, at the very least, their willingness to take a good-natured ribbing. In George Colman's *The Deuce Is in Him,* Colonel Tamper tests his betrothed's love for him by feigning a battery of wounds, including an amputated leg and the loss of one eye. When she refers to his "misfortunes," Tamper protests in a speech that at once honors and ridicules the wounded veteran: "Misfortunes! no misfortunes at all—none at all to a soldier—nothing but the ordinary incidents and common casualties of his life—marks of honour—and tokens of valour—I declare I am about with me as the most honourable badges of my profession—I am proud of them—I would not part with this wooden leg for the best flesh and blood in Christendom."[41] Cent Livre's *The Wonder* offers a similar contradiction, as one British soldier celebrates Britain while another mocks her military strength. Upon arriving in Spain, Frederick waxes sentimental about the English national character in a speech with deliberate connotations for an audience trying to decide where to place its loyalties: "the English are by Nature, what the ancient Romans were by Discipline, courageous, bold, hardy, and in love with Liberty. Liberty is the Idol of the English, under whose Banner all the Nation Lifts; give but the Word for Liberty, and straight more armed Legions wou'd appear, than France, and Philip keep in constant Pay."[42] The significance of the passage is even more acute when recent French assistance to the American cause is factored in. Elsewhere in the play, however, Colonel Britton fleshes out the English national character with a description of the perks of foreign campaigning, something many British officers in America had no doubt discovered: "to behold such Troops of soft, plump, tender, melting, wishing, nay willing Girls too, thro' a damn'd Grate, gives us Brittons strong Temptation to Plunder."[43] George Farquhar's *The Constant Couple* includes the pithiest satire of British soldiers, with one character remarking upon a regiment's arrival in London, "Oh Lord! I shall have a son within these nine months with a leading staff in his hand." And yet, at the end of the play, the British soldier is redeemed in the person of stalwart Colonel Standard, who, it is revealed, had remained faithful to his first love for twelve long years.[44] Loyalty and constancy—virtues much prized amid the confusion of war—reigned supreme as the curtain closed, suggesting a winking plea that American colonists forgive the naughty excesses of their British protectors.

By January 1778, when the redcoat theater season began, Philadelphia audiences certainly had enough experience with British soldiers to gain a special appreciation of both a play's humor and of the life-imitating-art-imitating-life quality of soldiers playing soldiers upon the stage. Because much of the comedy of the day satirized elites, these audiences were also asked to laugh at themselves from time to time. *The Constant Couple* includes two attacks on the upper class. One character likened gentlewomen to whores:

> CLINCHER: Oh, lord! Oh, lord! a whore! Why, are there many in this town?
> DICKY: Ha! ha! ha! many! there's a question, indeed!—Harkye, sir; do you see that woman there, in the pink cloak and white feathers?
> CLINCHER: Ay, sir! what then?
> DICKY: Why, she shall be at your service in three minutes, as I'm a pimp.
> CLINCHER: Oh, Jupiter Ammon! Why, she's a gentlewoman.
> DICKY: A gentlewoman! Why so they all are in town, sir.

Another compared gentlemen to murderers and thieves:

> WIFE: Oh Mr. Constable, here's a rogue that has murdered my husband, and robbed him of his clothes.
> CONSTABLE: Murder and robbery!—Then he must be a gentleman.[45]

David Garrick's *Lethe* is more specific, with lengthy, unflattering descriptions of the idle rich. When a "Fine Gentleman" enters, Aesop describes the fop as "neither Man nor Woman, and yet an odd Mixture of both." After the Fine Gentleman describes his behavior at the theater each night, Aesop protests, "I am afraid, Sir, for all this, that you are oblig'd to your own Imagination, for more than three Fourths of your Importance."[46] And Mrs. Tatoo's explanation of a "Fine Lady" may also have seemed embarrassingly familiar to some members of the audience:

> She lies in Bed all Morning, rattles about all Day, and sits up all Night; she goes every where, and sees every thing; knows every body, and loves no body; ridicules her Friends, coquets with her Lovers, sets 'em together by the Ears, tells Fibs, makes Mischief, buys China, cheats at Cards, keeps a Pug-dog, and hates the Parsons; she laughs much, talks aloud, never blushes, says what she will, does what she will, goes where she will, marries whom she pleases, hates her Husband in a Month, breaks his Heart in four, becomes a Widow, slips from her Gallants, and begins the World again.[47]

Samuel Foote's *The Minor* goes further, soundly repudiating those who might ridicule their own humble roots. "Traduce a trader in a country of commerce," Richard Wealthy blasts his insolent nephew. "It is treason against the community; and for your punishment, I would have you restored to the sordid condition from whence we drew you."[48]

Though these tirades may have hit close to home for privileged Philadelphia audiences, the settings of the plays—Spain, Elysium, but usually London—enabled American audiences to laugh at the slap but not feel the sting, for such behavior occurred *over there,* very far from *here,* America, where the wealthy shared the piety and industriousness of the "common man." Since the austere beginnings of Plymouth and Jamestown, America's bounty was promised to men of virtue, or so the rebels claimed. The patriots—themselves led by social and economic elites—tapped into class antagonisms in the rhetoric of revolution, lumping American Tories with the English aristocracy, hating and ridiculing them as one. In making fun of the elite, then, some of the plays selected by the British officers implicitly celebrated the nobility of the common man and may be seen, in the wider context of the war, as an effort to take the moral high ground away from the beleaguered Continentals. In the end, the British soldier-actors' efforts to appeal to the humility of their wealthy Philadelphia constituents, and to claim the ethos of the common man as their own, fell short. After the Revolution, American dramatists nationalized a "heretofore conventionally English conflict between foppish decadence and austere virtue" in their own plays. The creation of the archetypal Yankee character—strong yet humble, plainspoken, and independent—marked an important milestone in the development of a uniquely American drama and of a distinct American identity.[49]

Although honesty and toil are represented favorably in the British army's repertoire, two other works appear to hold noble birth in even higher esteem. The right to rule and its attendant obligations are addressed in Shakespeare's *The First Part of King Henry IV,* the Bard's only play chosen for the Philadelphia season. Given the availability of other plays—especially other works by Shakespeare—the British military's production of *I Henry IV* suggests a particular desire to engage the audience in a silent discussion of its themes. Henry IV is depicted as a strong ruler who is politically astute and intolerant of insubordination, but his successor, young Prince Hal, seems unlikely to follow in his father's path. The action of the play swings between the irreverent debauchery of Hal's tavern days and his father's life-threatening affairs of state—in striking symmetry with the British military's frivolous exploits in Philadelphia amid a grave challenge to the Crown's authority. Early in the play, Hal promises to fulfill his destiny eventually, but only when he is good and ready:

> So, when this loose behaviour I throw off
> And pay the debt I never promised,
> By how much better than my word I am,
> By so much shall I falsify men's hopes;

And, like bright metal on a sullen ground,
My reformation, glitt'ring o'er my fault,
Shall show more goodly and attract more eyes
Than that which hath no foil to set it off.
I'll so offend to make offence a skill
Redeeming time when men think least I will.[50]

For nervous loyalists wondering when a British military victory might let them venture beyond the confines of Philadelphia, Hal's self-indulgent wanderings may have seemed particularly dangerous, adding an uncomfortable layer of meaning to the evening's performance.

Like *I Henry IV*, John Home's *Douglas: A Tragedy* was specifically chosen for production at the Southwark, opening just ten days after notices requesting copies of it appeared in the *Pennsylvania Ledger.* The haste of the production—along with Arthur Murphy's *The Citizen,* the last to be performed by the British in Philadelphia—suggests the depth of appreciation for the play and its lofty themes, since other works already in production could have been recycled. When Lady Randolph recognizes the handsome commoner who saved her from marauders as her long-lost son, she expresses wonder at the hereditary nature of his courage and valor: "How soon he gaz'd on bright and burning arms, / Spurn'd the low dunghill where his fate had thrown him. And tower'd up to the region of his fire!"[51] For Philadelphia audiences in May 1778, *Douglas* seemed a reassuring fable about the legitimacy of kings, an idea challenged directly by Enlightenment thinkers and rebellious American patriots. The message was particularly timely, as rumors of an impending British withdrawal swirled through the city, leaving loyalists in fear of American reprisals and with serious doubts about the Crown's commitment to its American faithful.

The many associations of identity within these plays—bawdy but constant soldiers, wealthy but deserving elites, commoners of noble birth, nobles with common tastes—reflect the confusing nature of identity in revolutionary America. Loyalists, patriots, and British alike seemed aware of the confusion, but they may have misinterpreted its meaning. In his preface to *The Minor,* Samuel Foote noted, "Whoever affects to be what he is not, or strives to be what he cannot, is an object worthy of the poet's pen, and your mirth."[52] As if to prove the veracity of this statement, twelve of thirteen plays produced by the British military in Philadelphia involve some form of subterfuge.[53] Impersonations are a factor in eight of these plays, woven between numerous other plots: Lady Lurewell in *The Constant Couple* pitting her lovers against one another to exact revenge on all men; Violante keeping secrets from her lover in *The Wonder;* Oriana feigning madness to catch a husband in *The Inconstant;* palace intrigue by Janus-faced nobles in *Douglas* and *I Henry IV;* and Young Wilding just plain lying to meet women in *The Lyar.*

The prevalence of lying in these dramatic works both reflected and legitimized the climate of suspicion that existed among former neighbors and friends living in the tumult of civil war. James Parker's 1780 letter to Sir Alexander Elmsley in London expressed the loyalists' belief that "ninety-nine in the one-hundred of all the rebel chiefs" were of the same infamous personal character as the "Scoundrel" Benedict Arnold.[54] The patriot editorialist "Machiavel" described the British in similar terms in the *Pennsylvania Gazette* in February 1778. In a single column he spoke of "lying pamphlets and papers" from royal authorities, of General Howe's sending "a lie to Congress by General Sullivan," and of General Howe and his brother, Admiral Richard Howe, appointing a "Liar General" in New York. He concluded with the suggestion that the Continental army also advertise for a "Liar General," particularly among the Tories.[55] Given the complex and evolving patterns of identity during the Revolution, then, it seems likely that loyalists and patriots misconstrued their misperceptions as misrepresentations—and called each other liars.

When the British army evacuated Philadelphia in June 1778, the lights of the Southwark Theatre went dark, if only for a few months. Loyalists who remained behind were forced to light their lamps on the Fourth of July for fear that marauding patriots would smash their windows and loot their homes. When the scraggly Continentals entered the city, they found the leavings of a great feast enjoyed by the British officers and their belles, solidifying their belief that these people were indeed decadent and undeserving of power. During the festive months of the British occupation, loyalists negotiated a conflicting identity for themselves in opposition both to the British, who betrayed them, and to the Americans, who threatened their way of life. At the same time, the Americans made good use of British excesses, mobilizing them rhetorically as a low standard of virtue against which the wholesome, stalwart patriots could define themselves. The British, for their part, were willing to sacrifice the confusion of Philadelphia to save New York, where loyalists and patriots could be distinguished more easily. British authorities continued to overestimate loyalist support as the war dragged on, never appreciating how the conduct of their army in the field was making the choice between independence and empire increasingly easy. Of those loyalists who witnessed the British military's foray onto the American stage, many chose the patriot cause and thousands more fled to England, but most sat quietly in the gallery, waiting for the houselights to come up again.

Appendix

A. This prologue was presented at the opening of the British military theater season at the Southwark Theatre, January 19, 1778. It may have been written by the Reverend Jonathan O'Dell and spoken by Major Robert Crewe.[56] It was reprinted in the February 11, 1778, edition of the *Pennsylvania Ledger*.

Once more ambitious of Theatric Glory
Howe's strolling Company appears before ye.
O'er hill & dale & bogs, thro wind & weather,
With many a hair-breadth scape we've scrambled hither.—
For *we,* true Vagrants of the Thespian Race,
While Summer lasts ne'er know a settled place.
Anxious to prove the merit of our Band,
A chosen Squadron wand'ring thro' the land,
How beats each Yankee Bosom at our drum:
"Hark *Jonathan,* Zounds here the Stroller's come."
Spruc'd up with Top Knots & their Sunday dress,
With eager Looks the maidens round us press:
"*Jemima* see—A'nt this a charming sight?"
"Look *Tabitha*—Oh! Lord, I wish 'twas night."
Wing'd with Variety our Minutes fly,
Each minute tinctur'd with a diff'rent dye.
Balls we have plenty and *al-Fresco* too,
Such as Soho & King Street never knew.
Did you see how sometimes we're arrayed
You'd fancy we designed a masquerade.
'Twould tire your Patience were I to relate here
Our Routs, Drums, Hurricanes & *Fete Champetres.*
Let Ranelagh still boast her ample dome
While Heaven's our Canopy, the world our room.
Still let Vauxhall her martial'd lamps display
And gild her shades with artificial day.
In lofty Terms, old vaunting Sadler's wells
Of her Tight Rope & Ladder-dancing tells,
But *Cunningham* in both by far excels.
Now winter—[bell rings] Hark! & I must not say no;
"But soft—A Word or two before I go."
Benevolence first urg'd us to engage,
And boldly venture on a public Stage.
To guard the helpless Orphan's tender years,
To wipe away th'afflicted Parents' Tears,
To sooth the Sorrows of the widow's Breast
To lull the friendless bosom's Care to Rest,
This our Design—& sure in such a Cause,
E'en Error's self may challenge some applause.

With Candour, then, our imperfections scan,
And where the *Actor* fails, absolve the *Man.*

B. British army officers presented the following plays at the Southwark Theatre during the British occupation of Philadelphia, which lasted from September 1777 to June 1778.

January 19	*No One's Enemy But His Own,* by Arthur Murphy
	The Deuce Is in Him, by George Colman
January 26	*The Minor,* by Samuel Foote
	The Deuce Is in Him
February 9	*The Minor*
	A Duke and No Duke, by Nahum Tate
February 16	*The Constant Couple,* by George Farquhar
	A Duke and No Duke
March 9	*The Inconstant,* by George Farquhar
	The Mock Doctor, by Henry Fielding
March 16	*The Inconstant*
	Lethe, by David Garrick
March 25	*The First Part of King Henry IV,* by William Shakespeare
	The Mock Doctor
March 30	*The First Part of King Henry IV*
	Lethe
April 20	*The Wonder,* by Susanna Cent Livre
	A Trip to Scotland, by Paul Whitehead
April 24	*The Wonder*
	The Mock Doctor
May 1	*The Lyar,* by Samuel Foote
	A Trip to Scotland
May 6	*The Lyar*
	A Duke and No Duke
May 19	*Douglas,* by John Home
	The Citizen, by Arthur Murphy

NOTES

1. Reprinted in the *Pennsylvania Ledger,* February 11, 1778. See the appendix at the end of this chapter for the complete text.

2. *Pennsylvania Ledger,* December 31, 1777.

3. The British officers presented fourteen different plays in thirteen performances (two plays each night) between January 19 and May 19, 1778. See the appendix for a calendar of the theatrical season.

4. *Pennsylvania Ledger,* March 7, 1778.

5. Quoted in Kenneth Silverman, *A Cultural History of the American Revolution* (New York: Thomas Y. Crowell, 1976), 334.

6. Paul Smith, *Loyalists and Redcoats: A Study in British Revolutionary Policy* (Chapel Hill: University of North Carolina Press, 1964), 45–46, 51–52; Anne M. Ousterhout, *A State Divided: Opposition in Pennsylvania to the American Revolution* (New York: Greenwood Press, 1987), 2–3.

7. Smith, *Loyalists and Redcoats,* 58, 66.

8. Ira D. Gruber, *The Howe Brothers and the American Revolution* (New York: Atheneum, 1972), 243–44.

9. Twenty-one quarter-page advertisements for the plays appeared in the biweekly *Pennsylvania Ledger* between January 3 and May 16, 1778. Overall, twenty-nine of forty-two issues included some notice about the theater. In addition, hundreds of broadsides advertising the productions were plastered about town every week. *Pennsylvania Ledger,* January 1 to June 1, 1778.

10. Ibid., January 3, 7, 10, and 17, February 25, and March 25, 1778.

11. William H. Nelson, *The American Tory* (Oxford: Oxford University Press, 1961), chapter 5.

12. Judith L. van Buskirk, *Generous Enemies: Patriots and Loyalists in Revolutionary New York* (Philadelphia: University of Pennsylvania Press, 2002), 1–7.

13. Judith L. van Buskirk, "'They Didn't Join the Band': Disaffected Women in Revolutionary Philadelphia," *Pennsylvania History* 62 (Summer 1995): 313–14.

14. Robert McClure Calhoon, *The Loyalists in Revolutionary America, 1760–1781* (New York: Harcourt Brace Jovanovich, 1973), 503. See also Calhoon, *The Loyalist Perception and Other Essays* (Columbia: University of South Carolina Press, 1989).

15. Calhoon, *Loyalist Perception,* xiii.

16. Quoted in Peter A. Davis, "Puritan Mercantilism and the Politics of Anti-Theatrical Legislation in Colonial America," in *The American Stage: Social and Economic Issues from the Colonial Period to the Present,* ed. Ron Engle and Tice L. Miller (Cambridge: Cambridge University Press, 1993), 25.

17. Ibid., 26.

18. *Pennsylvania Ledger,* January 24 and February 14, 1778.

19. Rebecca Franks, Philadelphia, to Mrs. Anne Paca, Maryland, February 26, 1778, reprinted in Catherine S. Crary, ed., *The Price of Loyalty: Tory Writings from the Revolutionary Era* (New York: McGraw-Hill, 1973), 312–13.

20. Van Buskirk, "'They Didn't Join the Band,'" 317.

21. Sylvester Gardiner, England, to his daughter in America, 1780, reprinted in Crary, *Price of Loyalty,* 337.

22. Elizabeth Drinker, diary entry dated May 18, 1778, in *The Diary of Elizabeth Drinker,* vol. 1, ed. Elaine Forman Crane (Boston: Northeastern University Press, 1991), 306; James Parker, Philadelphia, to Charles Stuart, London, reprinted in Crary, *Price of Loyalty,* 317; Ambrose Serle, diary entry dated May 18, 1778, in *The American Journal of Ambrose Serle, Secretary to Lord Howe,* ed. Edward H. Tatum, quoted in Stephen R. Taaffe, *The Philadelphia Campaign, 1777–1778* (Lawrence: University Press of Kansas, 2003), 187.

23. Darlene Emmert Fisher, "Social Life in Philadelphia During the British Occupation," *Pennsylvania History* 37, no. 3 (1970): 243–46; Taaffe, *Philadelphia Campaign,* 169–70. See also John W. Jackson, "Convivial Interludes," in his *With the British Army in Philadelphia, 1777–1778* (New York: Presidio, 1979), 209–18.

24. Diary of Albigence Waldo, December 11–14, 1777, quoted in Taaffe, *Philadelphia Campaign,* 151.

25. Ibid., 148–56, 170. See also Wayne K. Bodle, *The Valley Forge Winter: Civilians and Soldiers in War* (University Park: Pennsylvania State University Press, 2002).

26. *Pennsylvania Gazette,* January 10, 1778, and *Pennsylvania Packet,* January 7, 1778.

27. Jason Shaffer, *Performing Patriotism: National Identity in the Colonial and Revolutionary American Theater* (Philadelphia: University of Pennsylvania Press, 2007), 62.

28. Randall Fuller, "Theaters of the American Revolution: The Valley Forge *Cato* and the Meschianza in Their Transcultural Contexts," *Early American Literature* 34, no. 2 (1999): 128–31. See also Albert Furtwangler, *American Silhouettes: Rhetorical Identities of the Founders* (New Haven: Yale University Press, 1987), 64–84; and Thomas Clark Pollock, *The Philadelphia Theatre in the Eighteenth Century* (Philadelphia: University of Pennsylvania Press, 1933), 36–37.

29. Quoted in Pollock, *Philadelphia Theatre,* 38–39.

30. Gruber, *Howe Brothers,* 244; Jackson, "Convivial Interludes," 192–93.

31. Prologue printed in the *Pennsylvania Ledger*, February 11, 1778. For a discussion of Cunningham's handiwork, see Jackson, "Prisoners of War," in his *British Army in Philadelphia*, 117–45.

32. Sylvia R. Frey, *The British Soldier in America: A Social History of Military Life in the Revolutionary Period* (Austin: University of Texas Press, 1981), 20, 54, 57–60.

33. Broadside, printed in September 1775, Early American Imprints, series 1, Evans (1639–1800), microfilm, no. 13841.

34. Silverman, *Cultural History of the American Revolution*, 333.

35. Prologue printed in the *Pennsylvania Ledger*, February 11, 1778.

36. *Pennsylvania Ledger*, February 14 and 16, 1778; Drinker, *Diary of Elizabeth Drinker*, 267, 288–89.

37. Silverman, *Cultural History of the American Revolution*, 374–76.

38. Ibid., 104; Crary, *Price of Loyalty*, 315.

39. *Pennsylvania Ledger*, January 3, 7, and 17, and May 2 and 6, 1778.

40. Jared Brown, *The Theatre in America During the Revolution* (Cambridge: Cambridge University Press, 1995), 36–39.

41. George Colman, *The Deuce Is in Him: A Farce in Two Acts* (London, 1763), act 1, p. 16.

42. Susanna Cent Livre, *The Wonder: A Woman Keeps a Secret, a Comedy* (London, 1734), act 1, scene 1, p. 2.

43. Ibid., p. 4.

44. George Farquhar, *The Constant Couple*, in *The Recruiting Officer and Other Plays*, ed. William Myers (Oxford: Clarendon Press, 1995), act 1, scene 1, p. 9; act 5, scene 3, p. 74.

45. Ibid., act 2, scene 1, p. 20; act 4, scene 1, p. 49.

46. David Garrick, *Lethe: A Dramatic Satire* (London, 1757), 14, 18.

47. Ibid., 30.

48. Samuel Foote, *The Minor* (London, 1798), act 2, pp. 46–47.

49. Stephen Watt and Gary A. Richardson, eds., *American Drama: Colonial to Contemporary* (New York: Harcourt Brace, 1995), 12.

50. William Shakespeare, *The First Part of King Henry the Fourth*, ed. George Lyman Kittredge (Boston: Ginn and Co., 1940), act 1, scene 2, lines 196–205.

51. John Home, *Douglas: A Tragedy* (London, 1771), act 3, pp. 30–31.

52. Foote, preface to *The Minor*, 7.

53. The only play of those read that did not deal with lying is Garrick's satire *Lethe*. The fourteenth play, Paul Whitehead's elopement farce *A Trip to Scotland*, was not available for my perusal. However, secondary sources reveal that it was first performed in London in 1770 and depicts the elopement of a London heiress and her lover, a city apprentice, who are pursued by her uncle and his housemaid along the London-Edinburgh road. Subterfuge and class tensions are not difficult to imagine as elements of the plot. See Lisa O'Connell, "Dislocating Literature: The Novel and the Gretna Green Romance, 1770–1850," *Novel: A Forum on Fiction* (Fall 2001): 5–23.

54. James Parker to Sir Alexander Elmsley, 1780, in Crary, *Price of Loyalty*, 342–43.

55. *Pennsylvania Gazette*, February 21, 1778.

56. Jackson, "Convivial Interludes," 202 and 324n7.

10

WILLIAM THOMPSON AND THE PENNSYLVANIA RIFLEMEN

Robert J. Guy Jr.

Tensions were mounting in the spring of 1775, and the members of the Continental Congress were faced with a monumental dilemma. How could they expect to mount an armed resistance against the greatest army in the world? They had no army! To whom could they turn to construct one? Though many in the colonies might be willing to fight, who would be equipped for such a task?

There was but one place to turn. On June 14, 1775, Congress took decisive action, approving the raising of ten companies of riflemen, six of them to come from Pennsylvania and two each from Maryland and Virginia. It was, admittedly, a small step, and the numbers far from adequate, for each of these companies consisted of only eighty men. But the Congress viewed this rifle battalion as an essential first step, and rightly so.

Pennsylvania's response to the call for riflemen was so enthusiastic that two counties raised additional companies the following week, and a third was added shortly afterward. William Thompson, a member of the Pennsylvania Assembly, was given a commission as colonel and placed in command. Within a matter of weeks these riflemen, known as Thompson's Rifle Battalion, were on the march toward Boston. They were the first soldiers recruited, organized, and provided for by Congress, thus making up the very beginning of what would eventually become the United States Army.[1]

It is somewhat ironic that such a large majority of the army's first soldiers came from "the Quaker State," which for much of its early history legislated against any military provision. For decades, Penn's vision of a peaceable kingdom had gone untested. But the hostilities of the French and Indian War suddenly transformed Pennsylvanian soil into a bloodied battlefield, and the province found itself poorly prepared to face it.

The British military had always ensured a backdrop of security, but the dramatic defeat of General Braddock near Fort Duquesne in 1755 led to the withdrawal of British troops, leaving the western settlements unprotected. The colonists in these counties learned to provide for the defense of their homes and communities. By 1775 their former protectors had become the enemy.

The frontier conditions in Pennsylvania gave rise not only to a generation of men seasoned in defense but to the development of the most advanced weapon in the world—the Pennsylvania rifle. French Huguenot, German, and Swiss immigrants, who had poured into the counties north and west of Philadelphia, collectively drew on their gun-making skills and gradually developed a new type of firearm. The frontier setting, along with the necessity of hunting and protection in the wilderness, created the demand for a weapon capable of shooting a longer distance with greater accuracy than had previously been available. Also, the high cost of imported powder and lead created the desire to maximize their effectiveness. Soon the *Jaeger,* which the immigrants had brought to America, evolved into a longer-barreled and more efficient firearm that used a minimal amount of powder and lead for each shot. It was much more accurate and deadly than the standard musket, at four times the distance. And many of those who carried this rifle perfected the skill of using it.[2]

The man chosen to lead the revolutionary riflemen, William Thompson, in many ways represented the progressive development of this unique generation. Though relatively unknown to modern readers, at the outset of the American Revolution William Thompson was among the most prominent men in Pennsylvania. Having immigrated from Coleraine in the north of Ireland, the Thompsons were among the earliest settlers of the Cumberland Valley. The organizational records of the Meetinghouse Springs Presbyterian Church, near Carlisle, include several on the Thompson family, dating back to the 1730s. Samuel Thomson, William's uncle, served as pastor there in the 1740s, and the grave of his wife, Janet Thomson, is the oldest known Anglo-American grave west of the Susquehanna River. William was related by marriage to members of the proprietary gentry, including Thomas Cookson, the surveyor instrumental in laying out Cumberland County and the town of Carlisle, and George Stevenson, the chief ranger of York County.[3]

William Thompson immigrated to this region with his father as a young teen. While there are few records of his early education and training, his handwriting clearly demonstrates a significant measure of learning. His certification in surveying would have required a solid training in mathematics. It is also fair to surmise that he benefited from his family associations, especially in connection with Stevenson and Colonel John Armstrong, his first commander during the French and Indian War, who probably had a hand in his military commission and surveying appointments, which would play so prominent a role in his career.[4]

William was nineteen in the summer of 1755, when the Indians began their ruthless attacks on the Pennsylvania backcountry. As militia companies were being organized, Thompson was commissioned a lieutenant in the company commanded by Hans Hamilton, an associate of George Stevenson's from York County. Although these provincial companies saw little engagement with the Indians, Thompson accumulated valuable leadership experience. He received his first taste of command at Fort Lyttleton. While his superior, Hamilton, was away securing necessary supplies, Thompson successfully defended the post against a nighttime attack.[5] He also accompanied Colonel Armstrong on his stealthy preemptive strike in September 1756 on Kittanning, whence many of the French and Indian raids against the Pennsylvania frontier were launched. There Thompson experienced his initiation in the heat of battle. Although it fell short of an overwhelming victory over the hostile Indians, the offensive maneuver against Kittanning marked a new level of maturity for the provincial troops and was the only important successful engagement for either the British or the Americans on the North American continent in the first half of the French and Indian War. Though the raids would continue, even intensify, the killing of Delaware chief Captain Jacobs, and the destruction of a massive store of French-supplied gunpowder, demonstrated a military initiative and effectiveness hitherto unknown in Pennsylvania. To the chagrin of the disapproving Quakers, the "City of Brotherly Love" struck the first medallion made in America to commemorate this event, featuring on one side the seal of Philadelphia. The hero status conferred on the soldiers involved propelled Thompson to the forefront of Pennsylvania's defenders.[6]

As General John Forbes's campaign against Fort Duquesne commenced in 1758, Thompson played an even more significant role. Initially he was named to command Fort Loudon, a post central to the construction of Forbes's road to Fort Duquesne. In May 1758, having already been promoted to captain, Thompson was chosen to command the mounted light horse troops created to patrol the road from Carlisle westward. These troops escorted General Forbes himself on his journey west and were the first to reach the burning embers of Fort Duquesne at the campaign's climax. This high-profile position elevated Thompson's prominence, and his frequent travel along the Forbes Road put him in contact with soldiers and civilians across the whole region.[7]

As the war wound down in Pennsylvania in 1759, Thompson resigned his commission and established a business supplying the rapidly growing post of Fort Pitt, which was being erected near the site of Fort Duquesne. Colonel Henry Bouquet, who had taken over for the deceased Forbes as the British commander in western Pennsylvania, and who seldom gave compliments, praised Thompson for his delivery of high-quality livestock. Thompson acquired a residence in Pittsburgh and entered into partnership with George Croghan and other well-known traders. He also established a trading post outside the fort, which was later burned by the Indians during Pontiac's uprising.

These labors likewise served to distinguish Thompson as an energetic public figure with a good understanding of developments to the west.[8]

Thompson's home remained in Carlisle, however, where he built a small plantation outside the town, which he fondly named "Soldier's Retreat." There he raised his family. Thompson's sphere of influence had been greatly expanded through his marriage, in 1762, to Catherine Ross, whose family circle included many of the province's leading figures. Most notable was her brother, Lancaster attorney George Ross, a member of the Pennsylvania Assembly. In 1762 Thompson partnered with Ross and Stevenson in founding Maryann Furnace, near York, the first Pennsylvania ironworks located west of the Susquehanna River.[9]

While Thompson continued to be involved in westward trade throughout the 1760s, he became increasingly active in surveying as well, and was named deputy surveyor of Cumberland County. When the Treaty of Fort Stanwix, signed in 1768, opened up the settlement of more lands, the Penn family enlisted Thompson to survey several large manors for them, one of which included the forks of the Ohio, which proved to be the first survey of Pittsburgh.[10] Thompson was one of the westernmost surveyors in Pennsylvania, and his surveys were included in Gibson's map of 1771, which extended the Mason Dixon line five degrees latitude from the Delaware River to the eightieth parallel and traced that line directly north across the Ohio River. This survey provided fodder for an impending conflict, controversially distinguishing the area from Virginia and fixing the western border of Pennsylvania well past the area around Pittsburgh. When the Pennsylvania Assembly authorized the creation of two new western counties, Bedford in 1771 and Westmoreland in 1773, Thompson's surveys were instrumental in establishing those boundaries. His multiple roles in the development of these counties demonstrate the influence of his leadership.[11]

Even more significantly, Thompson was able to earn the westerners' respect. One significant occasion on which Thompson demonstrated his keen defense of provincial rights was his involvement in the "Black Boys" affair at Bedford. Though sometimes dismissed as merely another instance of vigilante justice on the frontier, the capture of the British Fort Bedford in 1769 is more accurately understood as an early episode in colonial resistance to British arbitrary rule.

A load of weapons intended for the Indians had been destroyed out of fear they would be used against the settlers. The British soldiers had arrested a number of men, including some who were uninvolved, and were holding them at the fort. James Smith, the son of a local magistrate, spoke out against these arrests. While not condoning the culprits' conduct, he asserted that it was entirely inappropriate that Pennsylvania's justice system was being usurped by the British military, stating that these men should not "lie in irons in the guardhouse, or remain in confinement, by arbitrary or military power." Smith resolved to set the men free so that the matter might be pursued within the proper jurisdiction of Pennsylvania's civil courts rather than arbitrarily dictated by the military. Collecting eighteen friends and traveling several miles from Bedford, Smith spread the news of his intentions to everyone he met along the road; the group then set up camp a number of miles away. Creeping back to Bedford after dark, they blackened their faces and prepared to surprise the fort at dawn.[12]

Smith enlisted William Thompson, whom he described as "a man whom I could trust," as a spy. After providing the necessary reconnaissance, Thompson played a central role in the fort's capture, leading the party into the fort and taking control of the British arms. The fort was taken without incident, and when the prisoners were released, the fort was delivered again into British hands. This retaliatory gesture, clearly demonstrating the colonists' defiance of inappropriate British interference, took place four years before the Boston Tea Party, an incident that likewise would be conducted in blackface. Smith later described this incident as "the first British fort captured by American rebels."[13]

Thompson's involvement in this intervention deepened the admiration that he enjoyed among the western settlements. In 1770 the Pennsylvania Assembly passed an act, directed toward the "Black Boys," to punish "wicked and evil-disposed persons from going armed in disguise and doing injuries and violences to the persons and properties of his Majesty's subjects within the province."[14] The following year, when newly formed Bedford County was given a vote in the Assembly, the people elected William Thompson as their representative. They recognized both his solidarity with them and his unique position as a link between themselves and the provincial elite; Thompson was reelected in 1772. When Westmoreland County was created the following year, the voters likewise elected Thompson as their representative, reelecting him again in 1774 and 1775. Thus every year that the colonial settlers west of the mountains had their own representative in the assembly, William Thompson received their vote.[15]

Thompson's vision seemed to extend ever westward, and as promising opportunities presented themselves, he readily pursued them. By the late 1760s many of his trading associates had established significant businesses as far west as Fort Chartres in the Illinois country. Several chiefs of the Kaskaskia, Cahokia, and Peoria tribes there were seeking to relocate, and they expressed an interest in selling their lands around the town of Kaskaskia. The recent Camden-Yorke opinion in London, in connection with the East India Company, had decreed that land titles "acquired by Treaty or Grant from any of the Indian Princes or Governments" were vested with the purchasers.[16]

Seizing on this decision, Thompson was among a group of men who reorganized the Illinois-Wabash Land Company, purchasing large tracts of land on the Ohio, Mississippi, and Illinois rivers. One potential glitch in the plan was that Britain's proclamation of 1763 had specified that Virginia held jurisdiction over any land transactions in the west. This requirement led the company to petition Virginia's governor, Lord Dunmore, renowned for his thirst for land, to offer his influence in securing the titles for these lands. He consented to help—in exchange for some large tracts for himself.[17]

Also in 1773, Thompson embarked on a second venture involving western lands, overseeing it himself. The 1763 proclamation also provided that tracts of land be given to veterans of the French and Indian War. Once Colonel Donelson settled the boundary between Virginia and the Cherokee lands in 1771, the way was paved for some of these lands to be surveyed and title given to the veterans. Several teams from Virginia ventured down the Ohio River to claim these lands, but Virginia allowed that Pennsylvanian veterans were likewise entitled to their own claims, as long as they were rightly secured through Virginia. At a meeting in Lancaster in 1773, William Thompson was selected to represent the interests of the Pennsylvanian veterans, and to oversee the surveying of their lands in Kentucky. After securing a commission from Virginia in May 1773, appointing him "assistant surveyor of William Preston, surveyor of Fincastle County," Thompson made the necessary preparations for his own expedition to Kentucky.[18]

Thompson arranged to meet with Virginia surveyor Thomas Bullitt at the mouth of the Scioto River. Along with sixty men, including James Smith and John Finlay as guides, Thompson's party left Pittsburgh on flatboats, sending a pack train of supplies by land. Upon arriving at the Scioto, however, Thompson discovered that Bullitt was not there to meet him. Whether by his own authority or by other instructions, he had reneged on his commitment and gone downstream to pursue his own surveys. He thus sabotaged from the outset the validation of the claims of the Pennsylvanian veterans.[19]

To add to his disappointment, Thompson learned that his supply train had been ambushed and some of his men killed by the Shawnee. Undeterred, he and his men continued on their mission throughout the summer and were able to manage without supplies from the east. Thompson organized his party into three teams and surveyed nearly two hundred thousand acres, after which Indians destroyed his canoes, leaving his men to return to Pittsburgh on foot. Once there, they held a lottery to assign plots. Thompson set to work to get their surveys validated, contacting Hugh Mercer, who had served with them in the Pennsylvania regiment during the French and Indian War, requesting that he exert some influence with his Virginia friends. The success of this expedition not only demonstrated the capability of Thompson and his men, it also garnered a great deal of publicity, heavily influencing the flood of migration into Kentucky after the Revolution.[20]

This quest for western lands, with their potential for tremendous wealth, set the stage for conflict between Virginians, Pennsylvanians, and Native Americans, which eventually erupted in Dunmore's War. Though it appears on the surface merely a competition for land between Virginia and Pennsylvania, there were people from both provinces on both sides. More precisely, it was a conflict over competing motivations and loyalties.

Thompson and business partner Alexander Ross, with the assistance of Edward Hand, had purchased the property of Fort Pitt in 1772 when it was decommissioned.[21] Early in 1774 John Connolly arrived in Pittsburgh on the authority of Dunmore and seized control of the town. Though jailed by Pennsylvania's Westmoreland County magistrate, Arthur St. Clair, he was soon released, and he renewed his intentions with a vengeance. He instigated frequent harassments and imprisonments aimed at asserting Virginian authority and provoking unrest among Pennsylvanian settlers. Most significant among the Virginia outrages was the massacre of the Indians at Yellow Creek, which included members of Shawnee chief Captain Logan's family. This provocative action threatened open war with the Shawnee and spread unrest across the Pennsylvania settlements, leading many in Westmoreland County to consider moving back east. St. Clair, in conjunction with other leading Pennsylvanians, established a company of rangers in the hope of providing a measure of security for the wary settlers. These rangers were supplied and salaried by the province, though Thompson occasionally forwarded their wages out of his own pocket, to the tune of a couple thousand pounds.[22]

A committee representing residents of Augusta County, Virginia, as that province called Westmoreland County, sent a petition to the Continental Congress "intimating fears of a rupture with the Indians on acco't of Ld Dunmore's imprudent conduct," though the word "imprudent" was struck from the official record.[23] The delegates in Congress from both Virginia and Pennsylvania, including Benjamin Franklin, John Dickinson, Thomas Jefferson, and Patrick Henry, wrote an eloquent appeal to their patriotic countrymen, requesting "that all animosities, which heretofore subsisted among you, as inhabitants of distinct colonies may now give place to generous and concurring efforts for the preservation of everything that can make our common country dear to us."[24]

As war broke out between Britain and the colonies, Dunmore, Connolly, and many of their supporters showed their true colors, pursuing their own agendas and actively assisting the British. The members of the Pennsylvania Assembly were sifting through their own conflicting loyalties, as the province's inhabitants urged them to oppose England's colonial policies more firmly. Feeling the heat, Assembly president and soon-to-be loyalist Joseph Galloway resigned, and Thompson's brother-in-law, Edward Biddle, assumed the presidency.

It is perfectly understandable, then, that in 1775, when the riflemen of Pennsylvania needed a commander, they turned to William Thompson. His intimate circle included some of the most influential men in Pennsylvania. In addition to Biddle and Ross, Thompson was related by marriage to assemblyman Mark Bird of Berks County and to Continental Congress members James Wilson of Cumberland County and George Read of Delaware, all of whom played pivotal roles in the patriotic cause. His involvement in the Committees of Safety and Correspondence placed him in connection with other patriotic leaders, such as Benjamin Franklin and Anthony Wayne. Thompson's circle of friends in Cumberland County comprised another impressive list of powerful patriots. As early as July 1774 Thompson had met in Carlisle with John Armstrong, John Montgomery, Robert Magaw, William Irvine, and others to express their dissatisfaction with British policies in the colonies and to demonstrate their support for their brothers and sisters in Boston.[25]

When Congress designated the raising of companies of riflemen, it was not simply looking for men carrying rifles but for a particular type of man. Congress was well aware that Thompson's men were already equipped with many of the skills necessary for this calling. They were acclimated to rugged conditions and familiar with deprivation. Their previous clashes with the unpredictable Indians had seasoned them in innovation and adaptability. These riflemen were dressed and equipped to travel lightly and quickly.[26]

The Pennsylvania companies met their quotas of riflemen quickly, there being no shortage of men both willing and qualified, and some even held competitions to enlist only the best marksmen. They enlisted men for a period of twelve months. The call for men drew on some of the more prominent families on the frontier, including the family of William Hendricks, son of Tobias Hendricks, and of James Chambers, son of Benjamin Chambers, who founded Chambersburg. Jesse Lukens, son of John Lukens, Pennsylvania's surveyor-general, tagged along as one of the volunteers. Several of the men's wives went along to help in the camp, and sometimes in the fighting. On June 27, 1775, Thompson informed Congressman James Wilson that most of the companies were complete, and that he believed that "the Spirit of the People is such that nine will be ready to march by the end of next week." He also conveyed the instructions that he had received from generals Washington and Charles Lee to provision any volunteers who wished to join, employing horses and wagons to "take every method to forward the Troops." Thompson's major annoyance was that his own Cumberland County presented some difficulties in getting its companies organized, apparently as the result of a delay in communication.[27]

As the details were marked out for the journey to Boston, Thompson appointed Reading as the point of rendezvous, where several roads converged and supplies could be easily replenished. Thompson was entrusted by Congress with £5,000 for the troops' expenses. Washington instructed Thompson to make provisions for companies coming from Virginia and Maryland as well, which would travel along the same route. Thompson and Edward Hand trailed behind the companies, settling their accounts as they went.[28]

Emotions were high as the riflemen marched toward Boston. There was excitement at the prospect of seeing action and a strong desire to distinguish themselves for both their patriotism and their skill. Many of the riflemen had purchased new frock coats for the journey and adorned themselves with distinctive décor, carrying decorated tomahawks and elaborately inscribed powder horns. The journey to Boston presented opportunities for amusement along the way. One man's journal described the men's crossing of the Delaware, "to the log gaol, where we tarr'd and feather'd one of the ministerial tools, who refused to comply with the resolves of our Continental Congress."[29]

The riflemen made no small stir when they arrived outside Boston. Washington's review of the troops provided them with a long-desired opportunity to demonstrate their marksmanship. The amusement of the onlookers quickly turned amazement as these riflemen consistently splintered seven-inch posts at a distance of 250 yards.[30]

The riflemen have sometimes been portrayed as uncouth and uncontrollable, and as uneducated, undisciplined, and unruly. This was certainly true of some of them. Many were drawn from a region where survival was the highest priority and pragmatism was a greater concern than propriety. Several of the riflemen, however, especially the leaders, were quite learned. Thompson was a Pennsylvania assemblyman. Edward Hand, lieutenant colonel, was a medical doctor educated at Trinity College in Dublin, who had served in the British navy. Robert Magaw, third in command, was a well-established attorney from Carlisle who, along with Thompson, represented the newly formed counties in the Assembly. Many of the riflemen were gentlemen farmers, magistrates, and well-respected leaders in their developing communities.[31]

To be sure, the riflemen were guilty on a few occasions of disruptive and unruly behavior. They were unaccustomed to military procedure and a regimented chain of command. As the first enlisted men in the Continental army, there were no precedents, no regulations, no military code. A man simply signed on as a soldier and pledged to "conform in all instances to such rules and regulations as are or shall be established for the government of the said army."[32]

The army's commander, General George Washington, had the unenviable task of organizing a unified whole out of the varied troops contributed by the diverse colonies. Steeped in the orderly and hierarchical ethos of the English military, Washington initially had little respect for these riflemen, including his fellow Virginians. He railed against them on occasion, obviously frustrated by the additional attention they required and the unnecessary distraction they presented. Thompson, as their commander, naturally bore responsibility for his men's irregularities, and more than once he caught the ire of the commander-in-chief. Within a matter of months, however, these issues were ironed out and ceased to be a distraction. Thereafter the riflemen repeatedly demonstrated that their contributions far outweighed their shortcomings.[33]

The British very quickly recognized the implications of the Americans' possessing such a capability. The ever-present threat of sniper fire forced them to take an unfamiliar degree of caution and ultimately led them to alter the way they fought. Regulars on guard duty learned simply to keep their heads down; as one observer noted, the riflemen had "grown so terrible to the regulars that nothing is to be seen over the breastwork but a hat."[34] The riflemen became a symbol of the American army. The British, hoping to inspire new recruits, transported a captured rifleman to London to demonstrate the remarkable marksmanship of which their opponents were capable. Instead, this ploy discouraged further enlistments.

The Americans, anxious to maximize their every advantage, allowed the mystique of the riflemen to swell to mythic proportions. Charles Lee, well aware of the edge provided by this fear factor, instructed Thompson to restrain the riflemen from shooting when they were uncertain of their aim, as "nothing can contribute to diminish this apprehension so infallibly as frequent ineffectual fire."[35]

This propaganda element has led later historians to believe that the capabilities of the riflemen were overrated, and that their impact on the war was insignificant. Most Continental soldiers used muskets rather than rifles. They fought European-style battles against similarly mustered ranks of British soldiers. But this by no means diminished the crucial role the riflemen played in the Americans' war effort. It simply demonstrated that the riflemen were used as special forces and that their unique skills were employed to complement and enhance the efforts of the regular army.[36]

Thompson's riflemen were given a critical role in the first offensive operation conducted by the American forces. Congress felt that the control of Canada was of the utmost importance, for it was certain that the British would invade the northern colonies from Montreal and Quebec.[37] In early September 1775 Washington ordered three rifle companies to accompany the army's march to Quebec, the captains casting lots to determine who would go. Matthew Smith and William Hendricks of Cumberland County were chosen, along with Daniel Morgan of Virginia. This trip involved a trek of several hundred miles through nearly impassable terrain during the early winter months.

The troops were poorly supplied and unprepared for the conditions they would face. The weather turned cold early in October. Their provisions dwindled to nothing, and the men became sick and hungry. Hendricks wrote in his journal about "some of the musket-men eating two dogs, which they had roasted skins, guts and all." "Many of us were so weak," he wrote, "that we could scarce stand. I myself staggered about like a drunken man."[38] Another rifleman, John Joseph Henry, later reflected, "Tears many years since, have often wetted my cheeks, when recollecting the disasters of that unfortunate campaign. . . . Seven died sheerly from famine; and many others by disorders arising from hard service in the wilderness."[39]

The expedition ended in disaster. Commanding general Richard Montgomery was killed, second-in-command Benedict Arnold wounded, and Daniel Morgan captured. Rifle captain Hendricks was also killed, Captain Smith was incapacitated by illness, and two of the accompanying wives died. The army lost its cannons and abandoned other equipment in the fields, as the disillusioned troops prepared to winter in Canada.

The riflemen who remained with the principal force near Boston were faced with a very different challenge. While sufficiently experienced and prepared for action, they had little experience in waiting. They had left their work, their families, and their farms to fight, not to sit. The enforced idleness and boredom became intolerable. In recognition of their exceptional abilities, the riflemen were exempted from routine work details, an honor that all too often led to mischief on their part and resentment on the part of the regulars. On a couple of occasions riflemen nearly resorted to violence to free their friends from jail, greatly upsetting General Washington, who was forced to intervene. This tainted the reputation of the riflemen as a whole and led to the removal of their special exemptions.[40]

The Pennsylvania riflemen as a unit had only one opportunity to shine during the siege of Boston, at Lechmere Point, where they were called upon to prevent the British from acquiring a herd of cattle to replenish their meat supply. As Washington described it, "Colonel Thompson marched down with his Regiment of Riflemen and was joined by Colonel Woodbridge with a part of his and a part of Patterson's regiment, who gallantly waded through the water and soon obliged the Enemy to embark under cover of a Man of War, a Floating Battery and the Fire of a Battery on Charles Town Neck."[41]

Despite this success, Thompson felt that the prejudice against his riflemen, coupled with Congress's political preferences, might prevent him from receiving the recognition that he rightfully deserved. He voiced concern about his promotion in a letter to Wilson, noting "that Lord Sterling [William Alexander of New Jersey] is talked of, and his Tittle may have its weight in getting him prefer'd before me" to the rank of general.[42] That winter, Pennsylvania's Joseph Reed, the president of Congress, recommended that Thompson be promoted to the rank of brigadier general and sent to Virginia. Washington demurred strongly, charging that such a promotion "would throw everything into the utmost confusion." Washington was well aware that many of his Virginian officers would protest being commanded by an Irishman, especially the very man who represented their rivals in the land controversy. At the same time, however, Washington betrayed his own appreciation of the riflemen's importance to his army, commenting, "I hope more regard will be paid to the service, than to send him to Virginia."[43]

Yet Thompson did receive his promotion, on March 1, 1776, and was sent to relieve Lord Sterling and take charge of the defense of New York City. He was accompanied by the recommendations of New York's congressmen, who said, "General Thompson is a gallant officer and very much respected in this Province: and we doubt not of your Endeavours to make his Command as agreeable to himself, and as salutary to the Country, as possible; to which nothing can contribute more essentially than Harmony and mutual Confidence between him and the civil Power."[44] This promotion, however, meant that Thompson was separated from his riflemen, as he was placed in charge of other Continental troops.

Thompson's command in New York City proved to be the high-water mark of his career. Unfortunately, it did not last long. Thompson was soon ordered to Canada to reinforce General Thomas and the dispirited troops who had wintered there following the Quebec debacle. Informing Congressman James Wilson of this appointment, Thompson demonstrated his patriotic sentiment: "I was very happy here, but I shall always be most pleased where I can best serve my country."[45] Both his happiness and his service to his country, however, were near their end. Within months he would be permanently sidelined for the remainder of the war.

Thompson was shocked by what he found in Canada. Winter had not been kind to the troops who had retreated from Quebec in January. Lacking food and adequate clothing, they had succumbed to sickness, especially smallpox, a devastating foe. General Thomas was himself ill with the pox and therefore incapacitated, though still in command.[46]

Thompson wanted to strike the more weakly supported British posts to the west, cutting off St. Lawrence River traffic from east to west. In April 1776 he proposed to James Wilson the need for a campaign against Detroit, which would provide the Continentals with a hub in the heart of the northwest and effectively neutralize British efforts to strike Fort Pitt from the west.[47] Congress, however, never approved this measure, and the west continued to remain under British control for another two years, when George Rogers Clark led his successful expedition against Detroit for this very purpose.

As it was, Thompson was left to attempt to salvage something from the Quebec fiasco. He recognized that his troops lacked entrenching tools, leaving them unable to construct a solid defensible position. They had no certain accounting of their opposing forces, no reliable reconnaissance, and no accurate conception of their situation. Thompson sent Arthur St. Clair to the town of Three Rivers, an approach to Quebec, to ascertain what he could.[48]

General John Sullivan then arrived with supporting troops and, as the senior officer, assumed the command. Despite Thompson's doubts, Sullivan optimistically ordered an attack upon the post at Three Rivers to commence on June 6. Thompson prepared to lead the force across the river and attack at daybreak.[49] Without reliable information, the entire campaign was placed at the mercy of a Canadian guide, Antoine Gautier, who proved to be one of many treacherous Canadians the Americans dealt with in the coming days. As Colonel William Irvine, who commanded the Seventh Pennsylvania, described it, "The pilot deceived us for his orders were to steer to within four miles of Tro Rivier." "Here our misfortune only began," Irvine continued. "Our guide led us quite out of our way into a Swamp which was sufficient to drown 1000 men."[50]

By the time the American forces found their way out of that "most dreadful place," daylight had come, and they realized that they were still several miles away from Three Rivers. As they continued to march in that direction, just fifty yards from the St. Lawrence River, they were soon discovered by British men-of-war, which "fired incessantly while we marched about three quarters of a mile," Irvine wrote. They entered into the woods to escape the guns, but as Irvine described it, "by avoiding one evil we fell into a greater—for we now enter'd into a Swamp which I suppose to be at least four miles over—Nature perhaps never formed a place better calculated for the destruction of an army."

As the Americans emerged from this swamp, they encountered a main force of British troops, well entrenched, who met them with relentless fire. The lines broke rapidly and were impossible to repair. The majority of the men retreated, cutting the officers off from communication with them. Thompson, William Bird, William Irvine, and a handful of others managed to evade their pursuers for the remainder of the day, though they were "fired upon from all quarters by the Canadians, who were in ambush and skulking in the bushes." They were without food and drank freely from the stagnant water. They built a fire at night and got an hour of sleep.

The following day they sent a guide to scope out their situation. He reported that they were fully surrounded. Exhausted, they consulted together and reasoned that "it would be better to deliver ourselves up to British officers, than to risk being murdered in the woods by Canadians." The officers marched up to a house occupied by the British and surrendered themselves "prisoners at discretion." They were initially treated quite disrespectfully before they were taken to the commanding British generals Guy Carleton and John Burgoyne, who ordered refreshments for them.[51]

Although the Americans' best reconnaissance had led them to estimate the enemy's strength at Three Rivers at between five hundred and fifteen hundred, they had been severely uninformed. Carleton's troops were in the process of being reinforced and had swelled to more than ten thousand men. An American prisoner, Francis Nichols of Hendricks's company, lamented that a British troop ship had just landed when Thompson came into sight, and "if the General had been one hour sooner, he would have carried the post."[52]

Colonels St. Clair and Anthony Wayne were both mildly injured in the battle but were able to escape and to round up and organize the scattered troops and return safely to the south. Thompson and his fellow captured officers were initially separated, Thompson and Bird being placed on the prison ship *Blond* and Irvine upon the *Triton,* and sent to Quebec. They were later reunited on the *Union* and carried to New York.[53]

Thompson's return to New York a few months later reflected the dramatic turn his life had taken. After being granted parole in August 1776, he went back to Pennsylvania, where he was greeted by a letter from Anthony Wayne, who wrote, "Welcome, Welcome once again to freedom and command." Wayne clearly aimed to encourage Thompson, and he expressed the desire to "take ample Revenge for the Unfortunate affair of Three Rivers." But the letter's conclusion proved more accurate: "Fortune to us has hitherto been a fickle Goddess and like many other femails changed for the first new face they saw."[54]

Thompson would spend the next couple of years impatiently awaiting news of his exchange, without which, under the laws of war, he could not return to active service. He battled growing frustration and disappointment at the mounting number of his subordinates who were promoted ahead of him, and at being continually denied the privilege of further serving the cause of his country. Thompson's name arose occasionally in exchange negotiations, but without result. Washington suggested exchanging him for a British general named Prescott, but General Sullivan was exchanged instead. Sullivan, whose military blunders continued to mount, had been at liberty for only four days when he was captured again at the Battle of Long Island, and was exchanged again a few months later. Deeply discouraged at being passed over for release, and reasonably so, Thompson confided to James Wilson that "Gen'ls Sullivan and Sterling being Exchanged and not a word of my release Must operate much against me in the Public—Neglect and reflection will always attend a Defeated Gen'l And the Partiality shown to those Gentm will point me out to the world as a person unfit for the Service of my Country, unless a proper inquiry is made into my Conduct in Canada—and I shall wait on the Honble Congress for that purpose."[55]

While Thompson remained sidelined, and despite the failure of the Americans to hold New York, the riflemen consistently demonstrated their worth elsewhere. At the time of Thompson's promotion, the army had been reorganized. Edward Hand was promoted to command the riflemen, who were honored by being designated the First Continental Regiment, in recognition of their status as the army's first enlisted men.[56] It also became common practice to detach these rifle companies, assigning them to accompany other regiments as special operations troops. Thus they were often sent to do reconnaissance, strategically placed to protect the flanks or rear lines, and used to guard transports of equipment.

While many of the colonies' enlistments dipped dramatically, the riflemen maintained a high level of reenlistment. Many of them appeared later in Daniel Morgan's renowned rifle company, which was composed of many of the army's best scouts and marksmen, more than half of whom were from Pennsylvania.[57] Members of Thompson's Rifle Battalion were involved in every major campaign in the war, fought in every colony and in Canada, and served throughout the entire duration of the war, long after the surrender at Yorktown. The flexibility and durability of the riflemen throughout the whole of the Continental army is illustrated in the account of one rifleman, John Youse, who, in his own words, "first enlisted in the county of Northumberland, under Captain Lowdon, in 1775, and marched to Boston in the first campaign in the Revolutionary war with Great Britain."

> Was in a slight engagement there, at Ploughed Hill, and in several battles and scrimmages on Long Island, and at the taking of the Hessians at the battle of Trenton. At the Battle of Brunswick, where I received a wound in the left hip, and was at the taking of Burgoyne, in the rifle corps commanded by Col. Morgan and Major Parr, my captain then. I was one of the party of the corps in the expedition against the Indians at Genessee, Seneca &c., and was one of the party of five who survived out of twenty-four in a scouting party, and forty-one days of that campaign was on half rations. I was at the taking of Stony Point, and at the attack on the Block House, Gen Wayne our commander. I was one of the eight hundred at Green Springs, in Virginia, in that hard engagement. My last service was on James Island, in South Carolina.[58]

As the war proceeded, Washington gained increasing respect for the riflemen. At some of the most critical points in the war, the riflemen's commanders performed admirably, saving the army and Washington himself on multiple occasions. During the Battle of Long Island in 1776, Edward Hand and his troops demonstrated their tenacity at Brooklyn Heights by returning to the front lines, allowing the rest of the army to escape disaster by crossing the river to Manhattan. Robert Magaw did likewise at Fort Washington in upper Manhattan, enabling the army to retreat to the mainland successfully. Magaw was captured in the process. Refusing at first to surrender to overwhelming British forces, he wrote, "actuated by the most glorious cause that mankind ever fought in, I am determined to defend this post to the very last extremity."[59] He ultimately surrendered, but only to avoid a massacre. Like Thompson, as an officer in command of the rifleman, he was not exchanged for four years.

It was not just the officers who made such heroic contributions to the army. Many of the riflemen repeatedly distinguished themselves by their extraordinary demonstrations of skill and bravery. Timothy Murphy, for example, demonstrated that a sniper can change the entire complexion of a battle, killing General Simon Fraser from a distance of three hundred yards. Fraser's death contributed to the defeat of a disheartened General Burgoyne at Saratoga, a major turning point in the war. Samuel Brady, whom Thompson called "a very fine young fellow," had mastered the mode of "Indian-style" warfare and kept a relentless check on the western threat. Brady and his hand-picked rangers kept the hostile Indians in western Pennsylvania on the defensive and repeatedly recovered women and children held hostage. The army itself, as it incorporated many frontier tactics, met with increasing successes, most notably in the surprise Christmas attack at Trenton and the strategic trap set by Morgan at Cowpens.[60]

The riflemen's many displays of courage, conviction, and commitment were rewarded by commendation and promotion. James Chambers eventually was promoted to command the First Pennsylvania. Richard Butler, having distinguished himself in battle on numerous occasions, was praised by Lafayette, who commented famously, "When I wanted a thing well done, I had a Butler do it."[61] By the war's end, some of Thompson's friends had risen to the top posts in the United States Army. Edward Hand, as the army's adjutant general, accompanied Washington to the surrender at Yorktown. Arthur St. Clair and Anthony Wayne both advanced to the rank of major general, and after the war were placed in command of the new nation's movement into the northwest.[62]

Thompson, meanwhile, waited for his exchange and remained formally in British hands. Deprived of the privilege of an active role in military affairs, he was left to attend to such matters as keeping count of prisoners and reporting on prison conditions. Although a deal was finally arranged in 1779 for Thompson's exchange, it would take another year for the wrinkles to be worked out. At last, in the fall of 1780, Thompson was set free. Having made his promotion to general a condition of his return to service, Congress tabled his paperwork. But it would be his health, and not the Congress, that had the final word. As early as 1778 Thompson had written to George Read, asking him to purchase a grassy farm near the Delaware River on which he could relocate, "as I intend leaving this part of the country, would wish to fix on some healthy spot near you."[63] He wrote to Read again in March 1781, providing a deeper glimpse into his failing health. "I have been laid up with the rheumatism for upwards of a year, and have for this six weeks or two months past been very ill, with a pain in my breast and a bad cough."[64]

By the summer of 1781, as the American forces converged on Cornwallis's depleted army at Yorktown, Thompson was encouraged to set his affairs in order and write a will, which he did in late August. He died on September 3, 1781. What Thompson had written to James Wilson about the American cause could well have served as his own epitaph: "Is there no Possibility to have peace and Liberty without making such a Sacrifice?"[65] As her countrymen celebrated the surrender at Yorktown and the joy of victory, Thompson's widow, Catherine, having exhausted "almost the entire products of a large and well cultivated plantation" and overwhelmed with debt, was forced to forfeit Soldier's Retreat in a sheriff's sale and move in with her daughters. Land poor and virtually penniless, with many of her prominent relatives now gone as well, she lived out her final days in Chambersburg, where she was buried in an unmarked grave.[66]

As the rising sun of the new nation dawned, the heroic tales of the previous years were told by those who lived and survived them. Many of Thompson's friends, promoted to high ranks after the war, have been immortalized in schools, towns, counties throughout America—men like Butler, Wayne, and Mercer. William Thompson, their original commander, was remembered only

The Death of General Montgomery in the Attack on Quebec, 1786, by John Trumbull. Engraving by W. Ketterlinus, 1807. Library of Congress Prints and Photographs Division, Washington, D.C.

briefly by those who had served under him, who had known, trusted, and loved him.

One of those who remembered him was the artist Jonathan Trumbull, the artist from Connecticut who had witnessed firsthand the tragedy of the Quebec campaign and had seen the fearfully vulnerable state of the army during that first year of the war. Trumbull immortalized forever the noble sacrifices of these early struggles, seeking to pay "a just tribute of gratitude to the memory of eminent men, who had given their lives for their country," in his painting *The Death of Montgomery*. Trumbull lamented that the new American government had "omitted to show the gratitude of the nation to those eminent patriots," and hoped that his own works would help to "preserve the remembrance of the great and good men of that memorable period."[67] Included in the painting is an image of William Thompson in his brigadier's uniform, standing boldly at the right, rifle in hand. An engraving of this painting hangs in both the House and Senate chambers in Independence Hall in Philadelphia, where the face of the forgotten first colonel of the U.S. Army remains forever on display, though it is seldom recognized by the thousands who parade past it every year.

NOTES

1. Thompson's colonel's commission is on display at the Hamilton Library of the Cumberland County Historical Society in Carlisle, Pennsylvania.

2. For more information on the development of the Pennsylvania rifle, see George Shumway, *Rifles of Colonial America* (York, Pa.: George Shumway, 1980); Henry J. Kauffman, *The Kentucky Pennsylvania Rifle* (New York: Bonanza, 1980); and John G. W. Dillin, *The Kentucky Rifle* (Birmingham, Ala.: Palladium Press, 1998).

3. The earliest records of the Carlisle First Presbyterian Church, including those pertaining to the Meetinghouse Springs Church, are located in the archives and special collections of the Dickinson College Library, Carlisle, Pennsylvania.

4. For an overview of the life of George Stevenson, see Roland M. Baumann, *George Stevenson (1718–1783)* (Carlisle, Pa.: Cumberland County Historical Society, 1976).

5. *Pennsylvania Archives*, 1st ser., ed. Samuel Hazard, 12 vols. (Philadelphia: Joseph Severns, 1851–62), 2:752. See also William A. Hunter, *Forts on the Pennsylvania Frontier, 1753–1758* (Harrisburg: Pennsylvania Historical and Museum Commission, 1960).

6. For more on the Kittanning medal, see Robert J. Hudson's essays "The Kittanning Medal," *American Journal of Numismatics* 6, no. 1 (1872): 17, and "Old Medals Found in Philadelphia," ibid., 14, no. 2 (1879): 91.

7. For references to Thompson as captain of the light horse troops, see Henry Bouquet, *Papers of Henry Bouquet*, ed. Louis Waddell et al., 6 vols. (Harrisburg: Pennsylvania Historical and Museum Commission, 1984), 2:449, 617. On Forbes's escort, see William A. Hunter, "Thomas Barton and the Forbes Expedition," *Pennsylvania Magazine of History and Biography* 95, no. 4 (1971): 473.

8. For references to Thompson's supply of Fort Pitt, see Bouquet, *Papers of Henry Bouquet*, 3:160–61 and 260–61, 5:700, 765.

9. Soldier's Retreat still stands three miles west of Carlisle, Pennsylvania. For more on Maryann Furnace, see Pennsylvania Society of Colonial Dames, *Forges and Furnaces of the Province of Pennsylvania* (Lancaster, Pa.: New Era Printing, 1914), 160–69.

10. The original copies of the Penn family manor surveys are held in the Pennsylvania State Archives, RG 17 Land Office, series 5, Harrisburg.

11. For additional information on the creation of these counties, see James T. Mitchell and Henry Flanders, eds., *The Statutes at Large of Pennsylvania, from 1682 to 1801* 18 vols. (Harrisburg: State of Pennsylvania, 1896–1911), 8:46–54 and 314–22.

12. For James Smith's account of the attack on Fort Bedford, see Archibald Loudon, *Selection of Some of the Most Interesting Indian Narratives* (New York: Arno Press, 1971), 216–26.

13. Ibid., 218.

14. Mitchell and Flanders, *Statutes at Large of Pennsylvania,* 7:350.

15. For a good overview of Thompson's political career, see Craig Horle, Joseph Foster, and Laurie Wolfe, eds., *Lawmaking and Legislators in Pennsylvania: A Biographical Dictionary,* 3 vols. (Philadelphia: University of Pennsylvania Press, 2005), 3:1358–60.

16. Clarence W. Alvord, *Illinois Country, 1673–1818* (Chicago: Loyola University Press, 1965), 300–301.

17. The original minutes of the Illinois and Wabash Land Company are held in the Gratz Collection, Historical Society of Pennsylvania, Philadelphia (hereafter HSP).

18. A copy of Thompson's commission is in the Read Collection, HSP.

19. For an overview of Thompson's surveys in Kentucky, including the depositions of participants, see R. S. Cotterill, "The Thompson Expedition of 1773," *Filson Society Historical Quarterly* 20, no. 3 (1946): 179–206.

20. William Thompson Read, *The Life and Correspondence of George Read* (Philadelphia: Lippincott, 1870), 124–27.

21. The original receipt for the purchase of Fort Pitt is displayed in the Fort Pitt Museum in Pittsburgh.

22. For correspondence related to Dunmore's War, see William Henry Smith, ed., *The St. Clair Papers,* 2 vols. (Freeport, N.Y.: Books for Libraries Press, 1970), vol. 1; and Reuben Gold Thwaites and Louise Phelps Kellogg, eds., *Documentary History of Dunmore's War* (Madison: Wisconsin Historical Society, 1905).

23. *Journals of the Continental Congress, 1774–1789,* ed. Worthington C. Ford et al., 34 vols. (Washington, D.C.: Library of Congress, 1904–37), 2:76.

24. "A Century of Lawmaking for a New Nation," in ed. Paul H. Smith et al., eds., *Letters of Delegates to Congress, 1774–1789,* 25 vols. (Washington, D.C.: Library of Congress, 1976–93), 1:666.

25. For biographical overviews of many of these men, see Horle, *Lawmaking and Legislators.*

26. For an overview of Thompson's Rifle Battalion, see Oscar Stroh, *Thompson's Battalion* (Harrisburg: Graphic Services, 1976).

27. William Thompson to James Wilson, June 27, 1775, Generals of the Revolution, Gratz Collection, HSP.

28. Ibid.

29. William Hendricks's journal entry is reprinted in Stroh, *Thompson's Battalion,* 48.

30. Thatcher refers to this incident in an August 1775 entry in his *Military Journal during the American revolutionary war, from 1775 to 1783* . . . (Boston: Richardson and Lord, 1823).

31. Hand and Magaw both await worthy biographers. For additional insight into Edward Hand's life, see Michael Craig, *General Edward Hand: Winter's Doctor* (Lancaster, Pa.: Rock Ford Foundation, 1984). For more about Robert Magaw, see Charles F. Himes, *Col. Robert Magaw—Defender of Fort Washington* (1915), manuscript, Hamilton Library, Cumberland County Historical Society, Carlisle.

32. *Journals of the Continental Congress,* 2:90.

33. George Washington, *Papers of George Washington,* Revolutionary War Series, ed. Philander Chase, 18 vols. to date (Charlottesville: University of Virginia Press, 1985–), 1:445–46.

34. Dr. Joseph Reed quoted in Richard Lacrosse, *The Frontier Rifleman* (Union City, Tenn.: Pioneer Press, 1987), 82.

35. Quoted in ibid., 81.

36. Ibid.

37. For a thorough overview of the campaign for Canada, see Justin H. Smith, *Our Struggle for the Fourteenth Colony,* 2 vols. (New York: Knickerbocker, 1907).

38. Quoted in ibid., 2:50.

39. John Joseph Henry, *Account of Arnold's Campaign Against Quebec* (New York: Arno Press, 1968), 66n.

40. See letter of Jesse Lukens, reprinted in Stroh, *Thompson's Battalion,* 27.

41. *Papers of George Washington,* Revolutionary War Series, 2:350.

42. William Thompson to James Wilson, November 14, 1775, Generals of the Revolution, Gratz Collection, HSP.

43. Washington to Joseph Reed, March 7, 1776, *The Writings of George Washington, from the Original Manuscript Sources, 1745–1799,* ed. John C. Fitzpatrick, 39 vols. (Washington, D.C.: U.S. Government Printing Office, 1931), 4:382.

44. New York Delegates to New York Provincial Convention, March 15, 1776, in Smith et al., *Letters of Delegates to Congress, 1774–1789,* 3:382.

45. William Thompson to James Wilson, April 15, 1776, Generals of the Revolution, Gratz Collection, HSP.

46. For an eyewitness account of the state of the troops in Canada, see John Trumbull, *Autobiography of John Trumbull* (New Haven: Hamlin, 1840), 299–302.

47. William Thompson to James Wilson, April 19, 1776, Generals of the Revolution, Gratz Collection, HSP.

48. *Papers of George Washington,* Revolutionary War Series, 4:427–29.

49. For an overview of the attack at Trois Rivières, see Smith, *Our Struggle for the Fourteenth Colony,* 2:388–417.

50. Handwritten account of Colonel William Irvine, Generals of the Revolution, Gratz Collection, HSP.

51. Ibid.

52. Quoted in Allen Crist, *William Thompson—A Shooting Star* (Carlisle, Pa.: Cumberland County Historical Society, 1976), 35.

53. See note 50.

54. Anthony Wayne to William Thompson, September 6, 1776, Wayne Papers, HSP.

55. William Thompson to James Wilson, October 25, 1776, Generals of the Revolution, Gratz Collection, HSP.

56. For more on the reorganization of the Pennsylvania troops, see John B. B. Trussell Jr., *The Pennsylvania Line: Regimental Organization and Operations, 1776–1783* (Harrisburg: Pennsylvania Historical and Museum Commission, 1977).

57. See ibid. for further detail on detachments and reenlistments.

58. *Pennsylvania Archives,* 2d ser., ed. J. B. Linn and W. H. Egle, 19 vols. (Harrisburg: E. K. Myers, 1874–90), 10:31–32.

59. *Papers of George Washington,* Revolutionary War Series, 7:162.

60. For more on Timothy Murphy, see Herbert C. Bell, *History of Northumberland County, Pennsylvania* (Chicago: Brown, Runk & Co., 1891), 101. For many of the famous encounters of Sam Brady, see William Young Brady, *Captain Sam Brady* (Washington, D.C.: Brady Publishing, 1950); and Allan Eckert, *That Dark and Bloody River* (New York: Bantam Books, 1995). For more on these particular battles, see David Hackett Fischer, *Washington's Crossing* (New York: Oxford University Press, 2004); and Dan L. Morrill, *Southern Campaigns of the American Revolution* (Baltimore: Nautical and Aviation Publishing, 1999).

61. Richard Butler also awaits a worthy biography. For more on him, see William D. Butler, *The Butler Family in America* (St. Louis, Mo., 1909), 111. For more on James Chambers, see Lewis H. Garrard, *Memoirs of Charlotte Chambers* (Philadelphia: printed for author, 1856).

62. For a detailed overview of St. Clair, Butler, and Wayne in the northwestern Indian conflicts, see Alan D. Gaff, *Bayonets in the Wilderness: Anthony Wayne's Legion in the Old Northwest* (Norman: University of Oklahoma Press, 2004).

63. William Thompson to George Read, September 26, 1778, Read Collection, HSP.

64. William Thompson to George Read, March 13, 1781, ibid.

65. William Thompson to James Wilson, April 14, 1777, Generals of the Revolution, Gratz Collection, HSP.

66. For a brief overview of Catherine Thompson's life, see William Henry Egle, *Pennsylvania Women in the American Revolution* (Cottonport, La.: Polyanthos, 1972), 189–91.

67. Trumbull, *Autobiography of John Trumbull,* 93, 288.

$$11$$

AGENCY AND OPPORTUNITY:
ISAAC CRAIG, THE CRAFTSMAN WHO BECAME A GENTLEMAN

Melissah J. Pawlikowski

The revolutionary era in the United States created new opportunities for significant social and economic mobility. A combination of open trade, land settlement, and the War of Independence offered economic prospects for working-class men who previously had little chance for social improvement. Furthermore, the success and independence that directly followed the war created an additional surge of opportunities. Isaac Craig, a Scots-Irish migrant who became a prosperous entrepreneur and land speculator, took advantage of these opportunities. Although he deserves credit for his initiative, intelligence, and hard work, Craig's rise to success also illustrates that the process of mobility was multilayered and dynamic. In addition to an environment that promoted economic and social development, the opening of the frontier, family networks, and connections to the highest levels of business and government also assisted Craig. While historians have often explored social and economic mobility in the revolutionary era by following aggregate groups, Craig's story shows how both personal agency and social opportunity intertwined to produce not only a case study but a fascinating story.[1]

In contrast to the circumstances that were opening doors in eighteenth-century America, economic disaster in Ireland was closing doors. Ireland witnessed rampant famine, economic hardship, and heightened political disorder. Formerly, subsistence farming had allowed families to produce what they needed. Families were able to sell or trade what was left over in nearby markets for goods they could not produce themselves. As Great Britain became dependent on Irish wool and linen, large Irish landowners began to shift tracts of land, previously designated for agriculture, to the pasturing of sheep. The result was great economic prosperity for landowners who were in a position to abandon agricultural production. Most of the laboring and landless class, whose economic position was not flexible enough to allow for sudden new ventures, went into an economic freefall.[2]

Isaac Craig was born in 1742 to Protestant parents in Ballykeel Artifinny, of the Hillsborough Parish in the County Down, Ireland.[3] Although Craig's Presbyterian family struggled in poverty, relatives secured him the position of a carpenter's apprentice. During his apprenticeship Isaac probably earned meager wages, if any at all, while living under the same roof as his employer. In exchange for seven years of work, he was furnished with skills that could not be taken away, regardless of where he went. Directly after he completed his apprenticeship, he worked as a house joiner and ship's carpenter, earning wages that enabled him not only to migrate to Philadelphia but to make the passage, unlike most immigrants, free of a sponsor or indenture.[4] Armed with hope and following in the steps of his siblings, James, John, and Jane, Isaac made the monthlong voyage across the Atlantic Ocean.[5] With a letter of introduction in hand, the twenty-three-year-old Craig arrived in the British North America's largest port, Philadelphia.

The year was 1765, and there was no better place for a carpenter; sheer demand placed them in the upper echelons of artisan craftsmen. Carpenters who specialized in home construction, as Craig did, were especially needed in a city where the number of houses grew by 50 percent during the 1770s.[6] Furthermore, carpenters had greater control over their wages than other artisans did, as they had created guild associations, the most important being the Carpenters' Company. In the economically volatile circumstances of colonial life, however, success was never guaranteed, not even for artisans in high demand.[7]

The aftermath of the Seven Years' War had left Philadelphia in an economic depression. A handful of families emerged with new wealth, while the majority of artisans returned to their regular lives. For the majority of middle- and lower-class people residing in Philadelphia, death by accident, disease, and malnutrition were constant realities of life. According to historian Simon Newman, while carpenters may have engaged in substantial contracts and earned equally substantial wages, they lacked access to resources that allowed them to safeguard or invest their money. There were, however, opportunities for employment as the elite built new houses and businesses.[8]

Little is known about Craig's early years in Philadelphia. He quickly found work as a journeyman, possibly under his brother's mentor, Robert Smith, or under Smith's erstwhile partner and his own future partner, Robert Allison. Whoever the master craftsman was who employed Craig, he became a close mentor and opened doors that would otherwise have remained closed to him. Under his direction, Craig honed his carpentry skills and learned to manage business affairs.[9] Later in life, he expressed reverence for his master.

In addition to wages, and because Craig was not married, his mentor provided him with a workshop and tools, as well as food and housing.[10] Craig would have spent five to seven years working as a journeyman before he finally became a master craftsman himself. As a journeyman, Craig probably earned a little more than £38 a month.[11] During this time, however, Craig's economic position was considered below the norm, as he was not required to pay taxes based on his occupation, nor was he responsible for the property tax.[12] While many other journeymen may have struggled to make ends meet on a journeymen's salary, Craig had life somewhat easier, in that he had no wife or child to support. Married or not, Craig was stifled politically by his economic status, as he was also among the majority of Philadelphia residents who were not eligible to vote.[13]

Craig did not have to wait long before finding a promising opportunity to invest his savings and procure his first piece of the American dream. When the opportunity to purchase land presented itself, Craig seized it. Chance, however, played a significant role in Craig's ability to participate in one of the colonies' first large-scale land sales. In 1768 Sir William Johnston purchased property from the Mohawk, Onondaga, Seneca, Oneida, Cajuga, and Tuscarora Nations in the Treaty of Fort Stanwix.[14] This land strip extended from the northeastern corner of Pennsylvania to the bottom southwestern corner. It was made available for purchase and settlement for only £5 per hundred acres and one penny per acre in what was then called the New Purchase. Though there were limitations regarding how much land one could buy and when he or she could buy it, more than two thousand applications flooded the Pennsylvania Land Office before the sale even began. As a result, applicants' names were drawn from a box in a blind lottery.[15]

Owing to of the volume of applications sent in, and because Craig's application was one of the last received, Craig would not have been able to secure his first piece of property had the Land Office not used a lottery system. As it was, Craig was chosen toward the end of the process.[16] What may have made the purchase of this land even possible for Craig was that he had up to a year to pay for it in full.

Another condition of the New Purchase was that the land bought had to be surveyed within the first six months of ownership or the sale would become null and void. Craig, however, did not have his land surveyed for more than ten years.[17] Why Craig had chosen a plot of land in Indian country, more than three hundred miles west of Philadelphia, and in a town with a potential population of fewer than two hundred, was as much a matter of chance as the way in which he gained the land.[18] Like other New Purchase land buyers, Craig saw that small frontier towns had exceptional room for growth. While Craig's purchase may have been a long shot, it was an excellent investment. Eighteen years later, when Craig made his next land purchase, the cost of the same amount of land was eight times higher.

At the end of the year, when full payment was due, the Land Office extended the deadline. The Land Office was also unable to track which lots had actually been surveyed, enabling Craig to postpone surveying until twelve years later, when he also claimed an additional seventeen perches he had not actually paid for. As Craig and numerous other 1768 purchasers illustrated, western land speculation was not reserved for the elite.[19]

Around 1774, Craig became a master carpenter, a feat of upward mobility that only 25 percent of journeymen managed between 1767 and 1780.[20] In this way Craig gained greater independence. He could now take on apprentices and journeymen and share in a portion of their earnings. His own earning potential had grown from around £38 a month to more than £68, a 75 percent increase.[21] Craig attempted to set up a carpentry shop of his own on a water lot at 130 Water Street, along the Delaware River in Southwark, with two older, more established master carpenters, Robert Allison and James Bringhurst. Allison was a Scots-Irish immigrant to Philadelphia in the early 1760s and a successful master carpenter and aspiring architect. Bringhurst, by contrast, had been born to a wealthy Philadelphia Quaker family and was a master carpenter and a member of the Carpenters' Company as well as a registered ironmonger.[22] Although the enterprise was interrupted by war, it continued to operate. As late as 1780 Craig remained a partner, possibly employing journeymen and apprentices to work in his place as the war took him elsewhere.

Regardless of Craig's physical location, his carpentry business was affected by the war itself. Much like the Seven Years' War, the Revolutionary War created new demand for laborers across the board. It also created a labor shortage, as many men left their jobs to serve in the armed forces. The wages of those who remained behind generally increased. Craig's partner Allison had a frustrating time maintaining a full crew, to the point that he was investigated by the Philadelphia Committee of Safety for "enticing workmen from public works" by offering them higher wages.[23] Ironically, Allison was able to use his own government contracts to lure workers away from public employment.[24] Regardless of his success, in 1780 Allison physically left the partnership and joined the Continental army for a short stint, returning as a lieutenant in the Eleventh Pennsylvania Regiment.[25]

Craig had joined earlier. In October 1775 the Continental navy was established, and Craig immediately stepped forward and received an officer's commission in the marines. One month later he was named lieutenant captain and assigned to the navy's first fleet. A letter Craig later wrote to President George Washington stated his motives for joining the military: "I took up arms in defense of the rights of my country determined to lay them down with only my life or the establishment of our freedom."[26] While patriotic, this statement seems less than fully true, as Craig joined the military well before independence was declared. Craig's desire for economic and social advancement probably influenced his decision.[27] Together, these were things that, at the time, only the armed services were likely to produce for a young man not connected to an affluent and respected family.[28] Further, as historian Gregory T. Knouff maintains, lower-class men in particular understood Whig rhetoric as promising them exactly the sort of country that would offer them equality and social mobility.[29] Finally, as a Scots-Irishman, and one whose family had to disperse because of British economic rule over Ireland, Craig probably shared his compatriots' historical dislike for the British.

As a member of the marines, Craig could look forward to high wages and also "interest pay" to offset the drastic inflation that took place during his service. Craig's peers in carpentry could not expect such an adjustment. Craig also came to expect a bounty for any enemy crew member he seized, as well as a share in prize money from the sale of cargo from captured British vessels.[30] During Craig's commission, a ship's company shared, according to rank, one-third of all proceeds from such sales. With this extra compensation to supplement his standard officer's pay, Craig could save money for life after the war.

Craig was placed in command because craftsmen were most likely to be made lieutenants and captains, especially in local militias, owing to their experience managing large groups of men on the job.[31] With an officer's commission also came a title deserving both deference and honor from men who otherwise would have seen Craig as their equal. Craig's drive to gain an officer's commission may have been so substantial that he lied or forged documents to gain one. Beginning in 1775, Craig's military documents and papers listed his name and title as "Isaac Craig, Esq."[32] For all intents and purposes, there is nothing in all of Craig's personal or business papers that authenticate him as an educated man, let alone a man of elite standing or a landed squire. The letter of introduction he carried from Ireland to verify his identity and document his apprenticeship makes no claim of his having formal education or superior breeding.[33] Aside from his military documents, Craig did not use the title "esquire" on any of his documents again until 1791, when he became a notary public.[34] It does not seem that the socially and economically more privileged men in Craig's life, such as James Craig or Robert Allison, who were also members of the Carpenters' Company and thus had greater social standing, had been socially confirmed as esquires. Finally, Craig's military papers said that he came from County Antrim, not the slightly less prosperous County Down.[35] Whether this was purposely deceptive or accidental, joining the new military as an officer played a critical role in Craig's earnings as well as in establishing his social and professional network.

Craig's first ship assignment placed him aboard the *Andrew Doria*. It was through this assignment that Craig began meeting socially prominent military men such as the future secretary of war, Henry Knox, and the leading Virginia inhabitant of western Pennsylvania, John Neville, who remained important "connexions" for Craig, to use the eighteenth-century spelling, for the rest of their life.[36] This first fleet was essential, not for fighting campaigns against the British navy in the traditional manner, but as commissioned privateers. The navy's main objective was to capture munitions for use on the battlefield.[37] This was especially important as it was one of the only sources the country had of building its military stores. On the *Doria*, Craig was the eldest lieutenant, a chance position that ensured his reaching the rank of captain before any other marine aboard that ship. The *Doria* was lucky. On its first voyage it captured two forts, Montague and Nassau, on the Island of New Providence in the West Indies. With these victories the ship retrieved large surpluses of military stores, which resulted in abundant prize money for the crew.[38]

Craig's role in these captures paid off, and he collected a larger portion of the $1,060 bounty than men of lower rank.[39] He also caught the attention of superior officers, who were sent frequent updates on the ship's progress, which included fourteen successful attacks in eleven months.[40] Furthermore, when Craig needed to petition the government for an increase in his pay or reimbursement for expenses, these men granted his requests. In one instance he had participated in a siege that recovered large amounts of "hard money" from the enemy. Under navy regulations, Craig and the other crew members were entitled to split one-third of these funds among themselves. The Continental treasury, however, needed the funds more, and John Hancock appealed to the men to make a gift of it. When they did, he praised their "[public] spirit." Fewer than four months later Hancock played a significant role in promoting Craig to captain, this time in the army, to which he and many of his company were transferred when they reenlisted in Philadelphia.[41] Craig's reputation for honest service appears in the fact that his superior, Captain (later General) Roberdeau, placed substantial sums of money in his charge.[42]

Although Craig's army troops were listed as a "state regiment," they in fact functioned as a Continental unit and were renamed as such on September 3, 1778.[43] As a captain, Craig received a monthly salary increase of more than ten pounds, but the army also offered men who joined a wide range of additional benefits, such as land, goods, clothing, bounties, signing bonuses, tax forgiveness, and in some cases slaves. In truth, the revolutionary military was usually paid late. When soldiers were paid, however, they were paid better than any other military in the world at that time.[44] When their pay came late, at least during the early stages of the war, American soldiers received interest by way of compensation. Receiving pay late may have been a means of forced savings for some of the lower-class men that historian Billy G. Smith has described as unable to save or invest their high wages.

While Craig did not collect his pay regularly throughout the war, he did not need to.[45] As long as he served, the army provided his necessities. He had no family to support, so that in 1784, when Craig finally collected all of his back pay in a single lump sum with interest, he was able to use it to set up a business. Like many Revolutionary War officers, Craig was given "5 [years'] Full Pay in Lieu Of $\frac{1}{2}$ Pay For Life" originally promised by Congress.[46]

While there is no evidence of exactly when General Washington and Craig's paths first crossed, Craig was among the men who crossed the Delaware River into New Jersey in December 1776. Not only was Craig able to capture Washington's attention, he managed to impress him enough for the general to recommend him for a special training program the following year.[47] In February 1777 Craig was assigned to train men in the use of weapons, an assignment in which he proved to be quite talented. As historian Wayne Bodle has pointed out, drillmaster "Baron" von Steuben's work at Valley Forge the following winter built on fine work done by Continental army officers earlier in the year.[48]

In September 1777, six months after his promotion to captain, Craig was wounded at the Battle of Brandywine. He recovered sufficiently to fight in the Battle of Germantown the following month. Throughout the bitter winter of 1777–78, Craig was among the troops at Valley Forge. Although an officer, Craig contended that the conditions he faced were almost as bad as those endured by enlisted men, stating that he had gone days without so much as bread to eat.[49]

The following spring General Washington selected Craig as one of three men to run the army's first training course in "laboratory."[50] This entailed the "scientific" production and stockpiling of munitions, and was the pet project of both Knox and Washington for improving the efficiency of the Continental army.[51] For the first time, large quantities of weapons, mostly manufactured in Pennsylvania, were available to the army. Previously, the army had been dependent on British munitions left over from colonial days, supplies seized during the early stages of the Revolution by privateers such as the *Doria*, and weapons imported from abroad.[52]

When Craig and a handful of other men arrived in Carlisle for laboratory training, it quickly became apparent that he had been well chosen.[53] For the most part, the other men assigned to training refused to perform arduous and dirty work they considered beneath them.[54] But Craig rolled up his sleeves, earning the praise of General Horatio Gates, who remarked that willingness to go above and beyond the call of duty was a trait commonly found in great men.[55] Craig then led a company of skilled artificers, which maintained the army's artillery park.[56] Laboratory was in such demand, but had so few men willing to do it, that thirty-two years later Craig was pulled out of retirement at the age of seventy to build up munitions stores for the War of 1812.[57]

As the war pressed on, Craig continued to be moved where he was needed most. In January 1780 he arrived in Morristown, New Jersey, where the Continental army endured the coldest winter in American history. Not far from the troops was a large British encampment, seemingly cut off from all communications and orders, on Staten Island, New York. Tired, cold, and hungry, the army waited for the right moment to launch an attack against the British. For this campaign Craig was chosen to command the artillery against the British. While this assignment ended in failure, it was through no fault of his own. Strategically the attack fell through because of inaccurate information, as well as low morale and outright mutiny. In the first mutiny by men of the Pennsylvania line, frostbitten and unpaid troops refused to continue fighting until an agreement was reached with regard to their pay.[58]

After the disappointing defeat at Morristown, Craig's superior officer, Colonel Proctor, resigned. During the short phase of reorganization that followed, Craig led his battle-tested men west to Fort Pitt. As none of them had participated in the mutiny—probably a testament to his good leadership—they enjoyed a short furlough. That, however, was not the only reason they were ordered to Fort Pitt. Although substantial battles were being fought along the seaboard, the western frontier also became a major theater of war. Men like Craig, who had a strong foundation in artillery, were in demand to assist in fending off the brutal British-sponsored Native American attacks.[59]

Although he could not foresee how much longer the war would last, at that point Craig decided that when it did end, he would not return to Philadelphia but would remain in Pittsburgh.[60] During his stay at Fort Pitt, Craig began working directly with Lieutenant Colonel Stephen Bayard, a man who later became his business partner. Craig's stationing in western Pennsylvania had also placed him near the small tract of land, Clover Hill, that he had purchased almost eleven years earlier. Whether thanks to profits from his carpentry business in Philadelphia or to military bonuses, Craig had been able to save £1,040. When he closed out his bank account in Philadelphia, Craig finally had both the opportunity and the ability to commission the long overdue land survey of Clover Hill. This was his first real step toward cultivating his prospects on the frontier.[61]

Surveyor Robert Dull's treatment of Craig's land was probably no different from the majority of his other surveys. He drew up two surveys, sending one to the state surveyor, John Lukens, at the Land Office and the other to Craig's proxy, a Mr. Bentley.[62] In Craig's absences, Bentley supervised the sale, rent, and early development of Craig's property. Bentley explained Dull's findings in a letter to Craig. The surveyor described the land as overgrown with brush and awaiting development. He had located a small spring and a few other natural landmarks, and used them to describe the boundaries of Craig's tract. He suggested where roads should be laid down and informed Craig that Jonathan Lane owned the only adjoining property. Finally, Bentley, in a tone similar to that of a modern-day home inspector who has found termites, reported that Dull had found a small infestation of squatters residing on Craig's land.[63]

Craig could have simply attempted to have the squatters thrown off, but instead he resolved the issue in a way that benefited at least one of the squatters as well as himself. Craig had his attorney draw up a mutually binding indenture that was then offered to all of the men who had been living on his land, though only a man named Hamilton accepted. Through this agreement Hamilton gained use of 250 acres of the land for five years, where he was to grow corn. While most of his harvest went to Craig, Hamilton was free to do as he wished with the rest. In lieu of rent, Hamilton cleared and fenced off a section of land that was to be rented to John Williams. During the off season, Hamilton also agreed to work for another of Craig's tenants, Timothy Meadows, who resided on a separate tract of land. With what free time he had, Hamilton could use the rest of his land as he wished. If he failed to meet his obligations, he was legally bound to leave the land, along with all of his improvements, to Craig. If Hamilton met his obligations, at the end of five years he would receive 150 acres, with the option to buy an additional fifty acres at a discounted rate.[64]

This act benefited Craig, for it ensured the land's development while he remained engaged in the war. Most probably, neither man viewed this indenture as an act of exploitation. Craig, like other frontier entrepreneurs, used the work-force that was regionally available to him. Like that of other prominent men, Craig's wealth depended on the work of his labor force. The corn Hamilton supplied allowed Craig to begin perfecting his recipes for whiskey and gin. This arrangement was a small step that eventually enabled Craig to open a distillery. Although it is unclear whether Hamilton successfully completed his indenture, a decade later he was still working for Craig.[65]

While Hamilton worked the farm, General Washington made continued use of Craig's abilities. In March 1781 he sent Craig to Carlisle to restock Fort Pitt's depleted munitions.[66] Upon his return, Washington selected him to accompany General George Rogers Clark on a projected expedition from Pittsburgh to Detroit. Had this expedition been successful it would have been a critical victory, as the goal was to capture Detroit, the British hub for arming and supplying the Indians, who then attacked frontier settlements.[67] Craig led his artillery company, now about sixty men, as well as men from the Pennsylvania militia and Joseph Crockett's Virginia militia, which included the Greenbrier Militia, to Louisville. The artillery's main objective was to protect the expedition from the British-paid Indian scouts who stalked them during their journey.[68] But Craig was able to keep them at bay only as far as the Miami River in southern Ohio. There, he and Clark found that provisions and reinforcements had not yet arrived, and they were forced to change their plans. Meanwhile, the reinforcements, led by Colonel Archibald Lochry, were not far behind Clark. Yet

Lochry and his men traveled without the protection of a band of artillery. Although the men quickly surrendered, more than one hundred of them were savagely slaughtered and scalped alive.[69]

Craig returned from his expedition to Fort Pitt to find that he had been promoted to major in October 1781. According to bimonthly payrolls, this promotion meant that Craig was making about £63 per month, an increase of more than 200 percent from the income he could have expected as a master carpenter. Thanks to this promotion, Craig was also entitled to six hundred acres of land, twice as much as he would have received as a captain.[70]

Craig's stay at Fort Pitt was short, as he was sent once more on an expedition to see if the British had taken up occupancy near the Cuyahoga River. On his return from this mission he learned that a peace treaty had been signed. The year was 1783, Craig was forty-one years old, and the War of Independence had ended in victory for the Americans. A new chapter in Craig's life began. Having joined the army as a young working-class carpenter, Craig was leaving it as an officer who had won the admiration of General Washington and other national leaders. Craig confirmed his upward social mobility by being the third man to join the Society of the Cincinnati, an organization formed by low-ranking revolutionary officers. But when the roll was finished, the original members read like a who's who of the War of Independence, although except for Henry Knox (a friend of Craig's), few of the high-ranking officers were active in the organization. It was far more important to the working-class officers who hoped to use the Cincinnati as a means to social respectability and to create a legacy for their male children, who were entitled to hereditary membership. This explains why 80 percent of the original members of the Pennsylvania chapter of the society, such as Craig, were junior officers.[71]

At the end of the war, Craig abandoned both the carpentry business and Philadelphia. While stationed at Fort Pitt, he recognized the three rivers outlining Pittsburgh as a future hub for trade and industry.[72] Once the peace treaty became official, Craig closed another of his bank accounts in Philadelphia and withdrew $5,124.26.[73] One month later he withdrew all of his pension money, totaling more then $6,154.00.[74] At first Craig attempted to purchase a small distillery already in production. When the owner refused to sell, Craig's plan took a new direction.[75]

With money in hand, Craig formed a business partnership with Lieutenant Colonel Stephen Bayard.[76] Together the two men formed Craig, Bayard & Company. In correspondence with future business partners William Turnbull and Pierre, or Peter, Marmié, the men discussed their predictions for the post-revolution market and how they could make the most of it. Their first move was to build a sawmill, the justification being that the frontier population was about to explode and lumber would be in great demand. The second was to "secure" any high-quality brick or firestone that Craig might come across, especially at forts, including Fort Pitt, that might soon be torn down. Finally, the correspondence focused on the location of natural deposits where high-quality clay, useful for the construction of a new distillery, could be found.[77]

When Craig looked out over the lush landscape of western Pennsylvania, he envisioned grain and corn growing under his direction as far as the eye could see. He recorded in his journal the vast quantity of fertile land available for purchase and development. He knew that prime real estate would not stay available for long. Craig and Bayard's first major goal was to purchase lots quickly.[78] They not only were the first purchasers of land in postwar Pittsburgh, but in January 1784 they strategically bought the riverbanks at the intersection of the Monongahela, Allegheny, and Ohio rivers for about £400. It was not just corn, grain, or alcohol that Craig wanted to sell. He also wanted to import from Philadelphia many of the products settlers needed to build the infant city and occupy the frontier. Craig understood that the two rivers wrapped around the heart of Pittsburgh and the third, the Ohio, formed an eighteenth-century superhighway that—with a transportation network from Pittsburgh to Philadelphia—could connect people with goods from across the Atlantic Ocean to the Gulf of Mexico or north into Canada.[79] By January 1784 Craig was employing at least eleven people for wages that totaled more than what Craig himself had made per month in the military.[80]

Craig's purchases had the potential to monopolize the waterways and the transportation of goods on them. At the same time, however, Colonel George Woods was surveying the town for the Penn family, some of whose members remained in the United States, having stayed neutral during the Revolution and retained their unsettled lands under an agreement with the state. Woods's plan directly conflicted with Craig and Bayard's. A compromise was reached; Craig and Bayard were jointly given thirty lots, which included most of the original thirty acres they had purchased. Additionally, some of their lands had to be used for roads. All in all, Craig and Bayard did well.[81]

Craig soon realized that whiskey was his best economic bet; because of high transportation costs, it was the only agricultural product that was cost effective and profitable to transport across the state.[82] Later he began to make cordials, gin, and rum along with other types of spirits. Craig reasoned that he could sell whiskey for six cents a gallon, and that by producing grain, its main ingredient, he could reduce production costs dramatically. Craig was suggesting an efficient and cost-cutting means of production: vertical integration. He extended this practice when he used his sawmill to provide timber for the construction of boats, both to sell and to use for the transport of his whiskey and other goods that he sold. Craig calculated that his primary expense would be payroll, which he estimated at about £3 per person per week.[83] The cost of labor was negligible, in that by 1785 labor rates had fluctuated little if at all, yet whiskey that had formerly sold for six cents a gallon now cost a dollar.[84]

In 1785 the well-established Philadelphia Company went into partnership with Craig, persuaded by a well-reasoned letter from Craig and the 140 gallons of whiskey he had delivered to William Turnbull and Pierre Marmié.[85] Turnbull, Marmié, and a man named John Holker had formed a mercantile business, Turnbull Marmié and Company, which had the highest tax assessment in Philadelphia and may have been the city's largest mercantile business. Turnbull was a Scottish immigrant who had come to North America in 1770. By 1779 he was purchasing flour for the Pennsylvania Commissary.[86] Turnbull had also found postrevolutionary western Pennsylvania a place ripe for business opportunities. Holker had come to Philadelphia as the French consul and later lent large sums of money to Pennsylvania's superintendent of finance, Robert Morris.[87] Marmié had arrived during the Revolutionary War as the secretary to Marquis de Lafayette. Acting quickly, Craig, Turnbull, Holker, and Marmié began to look at business opportunities in Pittsburgh.

While family historian Archibald Turnbull has written that a long fight to buy Craig out had transpired before Craig joined the Turnbull Marmié and Company partnership, this is not so. Correspondence and legal documents confirm that an eager and healthy relationship had developed between all parties from the outset. Craig and Bayard's location in Pittsburgh provided local contacts that none of the other Turnbull Company members had at that time. Turnbull, Holker, and Marmié provided the bulk of the capital investment.[88]

By joining forces with Turnbull Marmié and Company, Craig was able to increase his profits dramatically. Craig and Bayard built a large distillery and store located on the Monongahela, specializing in the sale of "Dry goods, Hardware and Groceries."[89] They soon had established stores in at least five additional locations—Venango, Deer Creek, Salt Springs, French Creek, and Fall Lick—and had received a state license that enabled them to trade with Native Americans.[90] In one letter, Craig explained that for just "three barrels of whisky and one of rum," he was able to get all the skins and furs he needed.[91] Craig's alcohol was not only useful for bartering but was also quite popular among settlers, and was thus in constant demand. Craig and Bayard also built a gristmill, saltworks, and sawmill, and later, with the Turnbull and Marmié partners, invested in an ironworks.[92] Finally, the company gained a military contract, providing the army stationed nearby with local foodstuffs, clothing, munitions made at their ironworks, and other essentials.[93] The Philadelphia partnership also allowed Craig to sell luxury items, imported to Philadelphia from abroad and then brought into the interior of Pennsylvania.[94]

In setting up these specific enterprises, Craig and his partners were right on the money. The average cost of building a sawmill was about $1,000, yet once put into production its output was around a thousand feet of lumber a day, at about a dollar per hundred feet.[95] Less than two years later there was a shortage of lumber in eastern Pennsylvania; it was in such high demand that Craig's correspondents outside Pittsburgh were ordering planks and nails from him.[96] In the following eleven years Craig watched as thirty-seven manufactures opened in Pittsburgh, seven of which he had been a part of. Over the course of this period, 10,032 people had settled in Allegheny County, all of them potential consumers.[97]

The ironworks was a great asset and helped Craig win the military contract. It also produced many essentials of frontier life, including "nails, spikes, brads, tacks, and wire; shovels, spades, hammers, and hoes; horseshoes, bits, and stirrups; edged tools (axes, chisels, handsaws, knives, scythes, mill saws); anvils, anchors, and cannons; stoves, skillets, kettles, and other hollow ware; and the iron parts of mill machinery, engines, firearms, wagons, harrows, and plows."[98] The ironworks produced an almost endless supply of things both for local use and for export to other settlements farther into the country's interior.

Craig had good business acumen and was industrious and innovative as well. His ownership of prime land wedged between the three important rivers allowed Craig to harness the waterpower to generate energy for the operation of his grist- and sawmills. A water mill worked well during the warm months but was useless when the rivers froze during the winter. Craig had learned from his military campaigns in the West Indies that wind could be used to generate energy, and he wanted to harness it as well. Had his partners allowed Craig to commission the windmills he designed for Pittsburgh, they might have led to far greater profits.[99]

By 1785 Craig and Bayard's store in Venango was doing very well in trading with the Seneca from Buffalo Creek, as well as polities from other regions, while also maintaining its profitable customer base of white settlers. Craig traded clothing, alcohol, tobacco, flour, sugar, and other goods for furs and skins. He sold the same items, along with household goods, furnishings, cloth, shoes, and some luxury items to families who had come to settle in western Pennsylvania. Craig's customer base grew quickly, from fewer than twenty people in 1784 to more than 230 a year later. Like most merchants in this era of currency shortages, he allowed these customers to pay with Continental dollars, British pounds, and merchandise, and he occasionally let regular customers buy on credit. Using the business skills he had learned from his first employer in Philadelphia, Craig kept meticulous records of every exchange.[100]

Although Craig had probably contributed less start-up money than any of his partners, he was responsible for most of the day-to-day supervision of their affairs. He also employed a Native American to assist Marmié in trading with surrounding tribes.[101] In a letter from his vendor at Fall Lick to Craig, he was asked to send as much merchandise as he could as quickly as possible, because the Venango post was selling out rapidly. Craig was diligent in making sure that products were distributed efficiently. Goods such as silver and keg powder did not make a profit at the Salt Spring location, but he maintained the post because it was a prime location for indigenous tribes from whom he received ample deer, otter, raccoon, beaver, bear, and wolf skins and furs for shipment elsewhere.[102] Maintaining locations that served settlers of European ancestry as well as Native Americans was profitable not only for Craig but for the community at large. Craig's stores and trading posts, and others like them, assisted in the circulation of goods and the creation of a frontier consumer culture. It was, after all, these types of stores that brought Native Americans to purchase things they could not, or did not, produce, as well as settlers who found Native American goods useful. During volatile times, stores and trading posts acted as the middle ground between the two groups, making the continued dispersal of goods possible.[103]

In addition to Craig's business sense, he never lost his carpentry skills, and he designed the mills and distillery his company built.[104] He also designed and constructed boats from his own lumber, which were prized by his customers.[105] While Craig did not have the final say in many of the large business decisions, he was in charge of setting prices for goods sold locally or transported. Not only did he secure the government contracts for ammunition that allowed him and his partners to assist in the establishment of western Pennsylvania's first blast furnace, he also helped run the furnace.[106]

In 1785, at age forty-three, Craig entered a different kind of legal partnership when he married the "beautiful and talented" Amelia Neville, the twenty-three-year-old daughter of wealthy landowner General John Neville.[107] Neville was a Virginian of relatively old money who had come to Pittsburgh as a British solider only to turn coat at the beginning of the Revolution and besiege Fort Pitt for the rebels. After the war he became Pittsburgh's largest and wealthiest landholder, and later, as a federal excise collector, he became the prime target of farmers during the Whiskey Rebellion of 1794. While Craig and Neville never formally entered a business partnership, the tone of their correspondence suggests that they had an informal commercial relationship that supported Craig's enterprises. Marriage served as a form of networking and consolidation of economic and social power. In addition, because the practice of bequeathing the bulk of an estate to the eldest son had never been popular in the United States, when Neville died in 1812, half of his substantial landholdings were transferred to Craig and his wife.[108] Later in life, as Craig confronted the ongoing economic instability of the early national period, he was able to turn to this bond of kinship for support and opportunity, and was also able to sell off bits of the thousand-acre lot inherited from Neville.[109]

By 1787, just as Craig had foreseen, a city was sprouting up around him. In an article describing Pittsburgh as blessed with an abundance of natural resources and ready for "quick establishment," a group of speculators to which Craig belonged explained their plan to civilize the outlying area around Pittsburgh. Seven hundred and fifty plots had been laid out, to be sold for $10 each.[110] Lots in Pittsburgh Town were 60 x 240 feet, while outlying lots were five to ten square acres. James O'Hara, a future business partner of Craig's, was the largest purchaser, buying 312 acres.[111] The original plan for Pittsburgh Town was presented for public view in Craig's home. Anyone wishing to purchase land had to meet with either Craig or a small handful of other men who had first pick of these parcels.[112]

Craig soon ran into trouble with his partners. Bayard moved south of Pittsburgh in order to woo and then marry Elizabeth Mackay.[113] After he left the company, in 1787, Bayard pursued a successful career building boats and purchasing land. He later owned the majority of a town on the Allegheny, dubbed Bayard's Town and later Elizabeth Township.[114] Although Craig's mercantile business continued after Bayard's departure, letters to Craig reveal that the managers of at least two stores were dissatisfied with the slow delivery and insufficient quantities of goods, which were cutting into their profits. It seems unlikely that Craig, a calculating man bent on efficiency and improvement, would have remained idle after receiving these letters. These same mangers complained that Marmié himself had become a menacing drunkard. In one instance, store manager Wilkins informed Craig that Marmié had grown combative, fighting with local Native Americans and with at least one settler, Elijah Mathews. In another instance, Marmié and a group of men had piloted several boatloads of goods to the French Creek store, arriving drunk after consuming half a gallon of "good spirit . . . and a keg and a half of whiskey."[115] These problems were beyond Craig's control and may have been contributing factors in the dissolution of his partnership with Turnbull Marmié and Company.

Marmié was not the only problem the partnership faced. Although Craig and Bayard owned the land on which Fort Pitt stood, they did not have rights to the fort itself. Turnbull wanted to disassemble the fort, use whatever building supplies he could, and sell off the rest. This went against everything Craig, as a patriot, stood for, but to Craig the businessman it made perfect sense. After a long legal battle to remove a small band of military men, led by Captain David Luckett, from the fort, the partners were able to gain only one section for their own use and were quite displeased. Craig's next problem was that he needed large quantities of coal for his company's ironworks on Jacob Creek. Craig had found the coal, as well as clay for bricks, at Coal Hill, and Turnbull wanted to purchase the land so as to secure the resources. While Craig purchased lots on Coal Hill later, he was unable to secure them when the iron was needed, upsetting Turnbull immensely. The final break in their tenuous partnership occurred when the army fell behind in its payments for food.[116]

Throughout the early 1790s, the company held contracts to supply food to the military. The army, however, was actively engaged in war with several Native American nations and thus constantly on the move, which made food deliveries quite difficult. Food thus spoiled, and Craig, as well as the company as a whole, took a loss. This did not stop the patriotic Craig from continuing to contract the company's services to the army, but Turnbull accused Craig of making "unwarranted advances" and sued him, claiming that Craig owed him more than $2,000.[117]

Struggling with the turn his life had begun to take, Craig became a public servant. In April 1791 he became a notary public at the appointment of Thomas Mifflin, the first governor of Pennsylvania, and on the recommendation of his father-in-law, John Neville, a member of the Pennsylvania General Assembly.[118] At about the same time, the first secretary of war, General Henry Knox, asked Craig to assume the position of deputy quartermaster and keeper of the military stores for troops throughout the western frontier.[119] Craig's actions in this capacity justified Knox's choice. He maintained records as detailed of those he had kept for his own business. In theory, not so much as one nail was used without Craig's documenting its cost or use.[120]

In addition, Craig's background in both building and the military made him a likely candidate to superintend the building of many western forts and similar military projects under General Anthony Wayne. The same men he had pleased during the war sought out their favorite carpenter to help build the nation's security on the frontier. In addition to designing these structures, Craig also chose and purchased the land on which these military bases operated. The largest construction project Craig supervised was Fort Fayette, a short distance from Pittsburgh. He also oversaw the creation of an army supply line along the Ohio River.[121]

By 1793 Turnbull Marmié and Company was dissolving all business ties with Craig. In the meantime Craig maintained control of the land he had owned jointly with his former partners, including the land at the forks of the Ohio River and the buildings there. Craig could work both the public and the private sphere for his personal advantage. Craig the deputy quartermaster needed warehouse space for the military stores as well as waterway access to ship provisions in and around Pittsburgh. Craig the businessman had land, buildings, and boats, all for rent. Craig was his own best resource on both sides of the arrangement and used his warehouse, land, and boats for the housing and transportation of soldiers and goods.[122] He collected additional payments for the military's use of his property until the company took legal action against Craig for the property.[123] The lawsuit was successful, and Turnbull was able to seize some of

Craig's land and business properties.[124] It took the partners another five years to complete the legal separation.[125] After a long and bitter legal battle, Craig paid the original settlement. He got only about $47 from the seizure of his property, substantially less than he had contributed for the original purchase and a far cry from what his subsequent labor and investments had added to its value.[126] It was a devastating financial loss.

Leaving the partnership behind, Craig settled on an extensive farm in Allegheny County, where he was the second-largest slave owner in the county.[127] Surviving documentation regarding Craig's ownership of slaves is limited, probably owing to the deliberate destruction of documents relating to this aspect of his life. But slaves were of great value to Craig. When one of his slaves, Toby, ran away, Craig posted a $15 reward for his capture and return. Craig also offered to pay for any expenses incurred for Toby's maintenance and delivery. Craig's advertised description of Toby related that he had only one eye, was knock-kneed, and was slow from an illness.[128]

Craig continued to keep himself busy throughout the 1790s. With permission from Knox, he sold to the general public any extra supplies that the army had received.[129] He maintained the post of deputy quartermaster until, as a Federalist, President Jefferson removed him. While holding this position he oversaw the building of more than 150 keel boats for General Anthony Wayne in preparation for the Battle of Fallen Timbers, which in 1794 successfully ended the Indian threat in western Pennsylvania, Craig was also the project manager for the construction of two armed galleys, the *President Adams* and the *Senator* [George] *Ross,* named for the Federalist U.S. senator from western Pennsylvania.[130] Craig also took over the biweekly mail route that extended from Pittsburgh to Louisville between 1794 and 1798. And he acted the part of the benevolent entrepreneur in contributing to the welfare of those beneath him. In 1793 he helped raise money for relief during the great yellow fever outbreak in Philadelphia.[131] In 1798 he directed a project to build piers on the Allegheny River. While he received some government funding, the city raised $12,000 through the sale of lottery tickets, at $5 a ticket.[132]

Eventually Craig gained another partner, General James O'Hara. In real estate investments alone, O'Hara had spent more than $58,000 on land and developments. His businesses included the "salt trade, tanning and milling, brewing, shipbuilding, and iron manufacturing."[133] O'Hara had been Craig's superior as quartermaster-general from 1792 to 1796. While stationed in the Presque Isle area as O'Hara's deputy, Craig recognized another great region of opportunity and wrote to O'Hara that it would "soon become a place of great importance[,] the situation is so delightful."[134] He added that there was potential for a highly profitable government contract for someone who could provide better supplies to the army stationed in Pittsburgh and the surrounding area.

With nearby Canadian salt only $3 a bushel, flour at $7 a barrel, and substantial waterways to transport the goods, O'Hara would not even have to own the salt but could make a profit by purchasing it and then distributing it to both settlers and the military. Just as Pittsburgh had grown from settlement to borough, Craig believed Presque Isle could do the same.[135]

Despite these allurements, Craig and O'Hara did not go into business at Presque Isle. Instead, between 1796 and 1798 they began to build the first glass manufacture in western Pennsylvania, the Pittsburgh Glass Works, offering $100 to anyone who could locate high-quality clay able to withstand the heat of a glass furnace.[136] The glass works was much more costly than Craig's ventures of the 1780s. The start-up money alone, necessary to get the project off the ground, came to $23,078.48. Of this initial investment, Craig contributed about $11,250.[137] O'Hara had considerably more wealth than Craig and owned such a vast amount of land, buildings, and businesses, that his obituary read that he had "almost created a city himself."[138]

The day the Pittsburgh Glass Works finally went into operation, O'Hara wrote in one of his accounting books, "To-day we made the first bottle, at a cost of $30,000.00."[139] The total investment had been huge for the era. By January 29, 1798, the glassworks was in full production of a standard size and quality green glass. Craig and O'Hara accepted orders for window glass in person or through a store, Prather & Smilie, located in the busy downtown area. "Hollow ware, bottles, vases," and the like were distributed in both local stores and at the factory itself.[140] The glassworks used eight clay pots to produce an average of three hundred square feet of window glass a day.[141]

Following the electoral triumph of Thomas Jefferson and the Republican Party in 1800, Craig decided to enter politics. He ended his partnership with O'Hara, and in 1802, as a member of the Federalist Party, was elected "by a large majority" chief burgess of the borough of Pittsburgh. This was an important position, roughly equivalent to a present-day mayoralty. Pittsburgh was beholden to the Federalists for eliminating the Indian menace at the Battle of Fallen Timbers in 1794 and for negotiating Pinckney's Treaty with Spain in 1795, which opened New Orleans to American commerce. Craig was elected to a second term in 1807. He was also elected president of the Board of Trustees of the First Presbyterian Church in Pittsburgh and served on the Board of Trustees of the Pittsburgh Academy, later renamed the University of Pittsburgh.[142] Serving the public was one of Craig's passions. After finishing his term as chief burgess, he was appointed at least twice to serve on the city council under the men who succeeded him, James Ross in 1808 and William Steele in 1810.[143] Although a subordinate office, this was an important one. The chief burgess oversaw all aspects of law, development, and economic activity within the borough of Pittsburgh and therefore required four reliable and knowledgeable men to assist him. By serving as both burgess and city councilor, Craig gained valuable inside information that guided his private investments.

From this advantageous position, Craig began restructuring his business ventures from private industry and trade to money lending and purchasing interest in joint-stock companies. The closing of the First Bank of the United States in 1811 had allowed for the creation of new, unregulated banks in the cities. They concentrated their efforts on generating large investments for expensive projects rather than serving the common man. For this reason, especially in smaller cities, established men took to lending money individually or formed joint-stock corporations that funded smaller, community-focused projects.[144] In 1810, even before the national bank closed, Craig and a sizable group of men received a charter from the governor of Pennsylvania to help develop Pittsburgh. They built two bridges, one over the Allegheny River, the other over the Monongahela, and a road extending from Harrisburg through Lewistown and Huntingdon to Pittsburgh.[145] The War of 1812 was imminent, and Craig had won several military contracts during the country's prewar buildup. As the United States became fully engaged in war, so too did Craig, applying successfully to the Bank of Pennsylvania for a loan in the amount of $10,443.[146] He used this money to pay the private military contractor's bond and to buy the materials he required for the large-scale production of gun carriages, a contract that remained his until the end of the war. This was a very lucrative venture, yielding Craig $1,000 to $4,000 per order.[147]

The year 1812 also marked a turning point in Craig's land transactions. Between 1786 and 1812 he had, on his own and with partners, purchased more than 831 lots of land in western Pennsylvania, Ohio, and New York.[148] Thereafter, Craig sold off his land rather than buy more. The land's value had increased dramatically over time, and Craig was able by selling it to create a substantial financial safety net for his retirement. In 1796 Craig had purchased six hundred acres called Mingo Bottom for $1,200; now he sold this parcel to a Mr. Henderson for $9,000.[149] Between 1811 and 1813 Craig sold two small but well-developed lots, numbered 256 and 150, before selling seven hundred acres of land on Chartiers Creek. Craig had inherited one of these lots, and so its sale was pure profit. The other lot had increased substantially in value thanks to its development, the result of Craig's practice of rental indenture, which required that tenants improve the land in addition to making other forms of payment.[150] Craig by no means sold off all of his property, and he continued to make a substantial income renting the land he still owned.[151]

After the War of 1812, Craig's finances began to take a downward turn. His troubles probably arose from his attempt to pay off the debts of his brother-in-law, Presley Neville, which amounted to more than $50,000. This financial black hole may have become a substantial burden and near social disaster. In

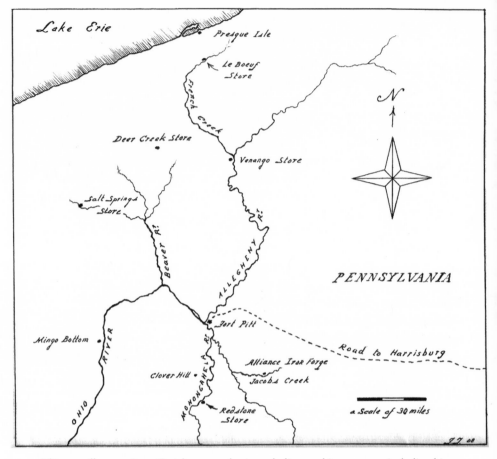

This map illustrates Isaac Craig's western business dealings and investments, including his first land purchase, Mingo Bottom, joint-stock investments, and many of his first stores and trading posts. Note that Craig's stores and trading posts were established on abandoned trade routes and centers of the French fur trade. Courtesy of Fred Threlfall.

1816 Presley fell behind in the tax due on land he owned.[152] Because of their connection, both Neville's and Craig's names were printed in the *Pittsburgh Gazette* in a list of residents who owed back taxes. Two years later the taxes remained unpaid. Although Craig's own ventures had thrived, Neville's need for assistance may have damaged Craig's financial standing irreparably. A younger man might have rebounded or at least tried to, but Craig had reached his seventy-sixth year. Maintaining his position as notary was work enough. The service-pension act of 1818 brought the last of the Revolutionary War generation to Craig's office to collect what they were owed.[153]

In September 1819 in the midst of the national Panic of 1819, Craig sold off some of his smaller lots in order to pay debts the Craig family had inherited

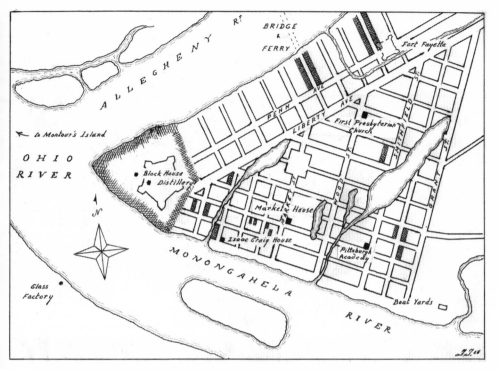

This map of downtown Pittsburgh features some of Isaac Craig's real estate investments, business ventures, military projects, and philanthropic activities. These dealings were essential in order for Craig to complete his social and economic transformation and to maintain his upward mobility. Note the diversity of Craig's involvement in the early founding and development of Pittsburgh. Real estate properties of significance are indicated with shading. Courtesy of Fred Threlfall.

when Presley Neville died. He was unable or unwilling, however, to pay debts owed to one Arthur Brown, and Brown sued and confiscated a lot from Craig. Three months later Craig may have looked on as his nephew, Morgan Neville, Presley's son and the local sheriff, auctioned off a piece of his land at a sheriff's sale.[154] Two years later Craig resigned from the position of notary public and left public life, moving to Montour, which he affectionately had dubbed Farm Island. Craig passed away seven years later, in 1826, at the age of eighty-four. He did not die in poverty or shame. He still had revenue from the thousand-acre estate he had inherited as a young man, along with the rents he continued to receive from his properties in western Pennsylvania, Ohio, and New York.[155]

Isaac Craig's story is a fascinating case study in the opportunities for economic and social mobility in the revolutionary era and early Republic. Had Craig not seized the opportunity to navigate the new social and economic climate by changing careers and domiciles, upward mobility might have eluded him. Craig's success was due to his flexibility and his willingness to take chances. These traits were common in men whom the historian Joyce Appleby calls "the first generation of Americans." They found prosperity after taking substantial risks, changing occupations to meet the changing needs of the new nation.[156] Most men never rose to Craig's status or even came remotely close. Craig's initiative and drive were crucial factors in his rise, but chance, networking, and timing also played important roles, and in other circumstances these factors could just as easily have worked against him. Craig's extraordinary success was the exception to the rule, and additional research into his experience can help us further understand the dynamic of class and rank in this period, and give us a greater understanding of the process of social and economic mobility.

Craig succeeded because he was able to get in on the ground floor, when the western Pennsylvania frontier opened up after the Revolution. Yet, like so many of his contemporaries, including Robert Morris, in the end Craig lost much of his wealth through financial misfortune and speculation, the direct results of an open and expanding frontier. Craig's experiences and earnings during the Revolution laid the groundwork for his significant role in the development of Pittsburgh and the surrounding region. As a builder of stores, forts, factories, roads, and bridges, and as one of the men who helped to redefine American industry, Craig should be remembered as one of the founding fathers of western Pennsylvania.

NOTES

1. A great many thanks are owed to Jay Dwyer for the conception of this essay. Doug MacGregor, Gregory Priore, Art Louderback, and the entire staff at the Historical Society of Western Pennsylvania were a wonderful and endless source of assistance and inspiration. A substantial portion of this project stems from data collected in the underused Craig Collection, 1768–1868, housed in the Carnegie Library in Pittsburgh. This collection boasts an astounding sixteen thousand items, including personal papers, letters, receipts, deeds, military certificates, legal documents, journals, newspaper clippings, business ledgers, land warrants, indentures, business contracts, muster rolls, military orders, tax documents, and business papers. Similar papers from the Papers of the Craig-Neville Family, 1773–1865, held by the Historical Society of Western Pennsylvania, have also proved valuable. Because of Neville B. Craig's biases, I used his papers and sketches with great caution. Other primary sources include government transcripts, newspaper ads, census data, the personal papers of many men, daybooks, and military and other legal documents.

2. D. A. Chart, *An Economic History of Ireland* (Dublin: Talbot Press, 1920), 59, 72.

3. C. W. Butterfield, ed., *Washington-Irvine Correspondence: The official letters which passed between Washington and Brig-Gen. William Irvine and between Irvine and others concerning military affairs in the West from 1781 to 1783; arranged and annotated, with an introduction containing an outline of events occurring previously in the Trans-Alleghany country* (Madison, Wis.: D. Atwood, 1882), 406.

4. Isaac Craig Family Papers, folder 2 (loose paper), Historical Society of Pennsylvania, Philadelphia (hereafter Craig Family Papers, HSP).

5. John W. Jordan, ed., *Colonial and Revolutionary Families of Pennsylvania: Genealogical and Personal Memoirs*, vol. 2 (New York: Lewis Publishing, 1911), 1163.

6. Billy G. Smith, *The "Lower Sort": Philadelphia's Laboring People, 1750–1800* (Ithaca: Cornell University Press, 1990), 82.

7. David Brody, *In Labor's Cause: Main Themes on the History of the American Worker* (New York: Oxford University Press, 1993), 5.

8. Simon Newman, "Dead Bodies: Poverty and Death in Early National Philadelphia," in *Down and Out in Early America,* ed. Billy G. Smith (University Park: Pennsylvania State University Press, 2004), 43.

9. Neville B. Craig, ed., "Sketch of the Life and Services of Major Isaac Craig," Papers of the Craig-Neville Family, 1773–1865, Historical Society of Western Pennsylvania, Pittsburgh (hereafter Craig-Neville Papers).

10. Brody, *In Labor's Cause,* 12.

11. Carl Bridenbaugh, *Cities in Revolt: Urban Life in America, 1743–1776* (New York: Oxford University Press, 1955), 28; Billy G. Smith, "Philadelphia: The Athens of America," in *Life in Early Philadelphia: Documents from the Revolutionary and Early National Periods,* ed. Billy G. Smith (University Park: Pennsylvania State University Press, 1995), 9.

12. Philadelphia Tax Lists, March 13, 1772, Tax Assessment for Philadelphia, microfilm box 26, City of Philadelphia, 1774, ser. 3, vol. 14, 203; Records of the Office of the Comptroller General, Record Group 4, ser. 4.61; Tax and Exoneration Lists for Philadelphia County, 1769, 1774, 1779, 1780, Pennsylvania Historical and Museum Commission (hereafter PHMC).

13. Billy G. Smith, "The Vicissitudes of Fortune: The Careers of Laboring Men in Philadelphia, 1750–1800," in *Work and Labor in Early America,* ed. Stephen Innes (Chapel Hill: University of North Carolina Press, 1988), 225–26.

14. Treaty of Fort Stanwix, 1768, reprinted in E. B. O'Callaghan, ed., *Documents Relative to the Colonial History of the State of New York,* 19 vols. (Albany: Weed, Parsons, and Co., 1857), 8:111–37.

15. Kenneth D. McCrea, *Pennsylvania Land Applications,* vol. 2, *New Purchase Applications, 1769–1773* (Philadelphia: Genealogical Society of Pennsylvania, 2003).

16. Donna Bingham Munger, *Pennsylvania Land Records: A History and Guide to Research* (Wilmington, Del.: Scholarly Resources, 1991), 82.

17. Clover Hill Land Survey, October 1781, Land Deeds folder, Craig-Neville Papers.

18. Clara E. Duer, ed., *The People and Times of Western Pennsylvania: Pittsburgh Gazette Abstracts,* 5 vols. (Pittsburgh: Western Pennsylvania Genealogical Society, 1988–95), 5:405.

19. Munger, *Pennsylvania Land Records,* 83.

20. Smith, *"Lower Sort,"* 142.

21. Carl Bridenbaugh, *The Colonial Craftsman* (Chicago: University of Chicago Press, 1974), 28.

22. Effective Supply Tax, 1780, in *Pennsylvania Archives* 3d ser., ed. William H. Egle and George Edward Reed, 30 vols. (Harrisburg: State Printer, 1894–99), 15:252; Harwood A. Johnson and Diana Edwards, "Ornamental Wedgwood Wares in Philadelphia in 1793," *Magazine Antiques,* January 1994, 9; *Pittsburgh Gazette,* October 15, 1792; *Prime Directory of Craftsmen, 1785–1800,* Phoebe Phillips Prime and Alfred Coke Collection, American Philosophical Society, Philadelphia.

23. Steven Rosswurm, *Arms, Culture, and Class: The Philadelphia Militia and the "Lower Sort" During the American Revolution, 1775–1783* (New Brunswick: Rutgers University Press, 1987), 342.

24. Robert Allison to Craig, October 19, 1780, Craig Collection, 1768–1868, Carnegie Library, Pittsburgh, Pennsylvania (hereafter Craig Collection).

25. Revolutionary War Military Abstract Card File, indexed items 43–60, between Allison, John, and Allman, Lawrence, Pennsylvania Digital Archive, PHMC, http://www.digitalarchives.state.pa.us (hereafter PDA).

26. Craig to George Washington, February 23, 1782, in *The Writings of George Washington, from the Original Manuscript Sources,* ed. John C. Fitzpatrick, 39 vols. (Washington, D.C.: U.S. Government Printing Office, 1931), vol. 18. That Craig refers to the "rights of my country," rather than to his own individual rights or those of men in general, suggests that he was talking about actual separation from the Crown rather than the philosophical rights of man or other popular concepts with which he would have been familiar before the Declaration of Independence.

27. Philadelphia Tax Assessment, March 13, 1772, microfilm box 26, PHMC; Smith, *"Lower Sort,"* 224–29; Gary B. Nash, "Urban Wealth and Poverty in Pre-Revolutionary America," *Journal of Interdisciplinary History* 6, no. 4 (1976): 552.

28. Melissah J. Pawlikowski, "From the Bottom Up: Isaac Craig and the Process of Social and Economic Mobility During the Revolutionary Era" (master's thesis, Duquesne University, 2007), 6–8, 71–73.

29. Gregory T. Knouff, *The Soldiers' Revolution: Pennsylvanians in Arms and the Forging of Early American Identity* (University Park: Pennsylvania State University Press, 2004), 38.

30. Kenneth R. Bowling, William Charles DiGiacomantonio, and Charlene Bangs Bickford, eds., *Documentary History of the First Federal Congress*, 17 vols. (Baltimore: Johns Hopkins University Press, 1974–2004), 7:164, 435.

31. Bridenbaugh, *Colonial Craftsman*, 174.

32. Military papers B-G, box 56, Craig-Neville Papers.

33. Letter of introduction from Trevor Benson for Isaac Craig, 1765, ibid.

34. Notary Public contract, April 13, 1791, record group 8 B, Craig Collection.

35. General return of Pennsylvania state regiments of artillery commanded by Colonel Thomas Proctor, Esq., taken April 3, 1779, *Pennsylvania Archives*, 5th ser., ed. Thomas L. Montgomery, 8 vols. (Harrisburg: State Printer, 1906), 3:978.

36. Bowling, DiGiacomantonio, and Bickford, *Documentary History of the First Federal Congress*, 7:436–37; Kenneth Gordon Davis, ed., *Documents of the American Revolution, 1770–1783*, Colonial Office Series, vol. 13 (Shannon: Irish University Press, 1976), March 14 1782, 233; William Noel Sainsbury et al., eds., *Calendar of State Public Papers*, Colonial Office Series, vol. 14 (Ann Arbor: University of Michigan Press, 1908), minutes, April 16, 1785, 406.

37. "Intelligence Regarding the Naval Force at Philadelphia, February 16, 1777," in William Bell Clark, ed., *Naval Documents of the American Revolution, 1775–1783*, 3 vols. (Washington, D.C.: U.S. Government Printing Office, 1964–2005), 3:1322; Jack Coggins, *Ships and Seamen of the American Revolution: Vessels, Crews, Weapons, Gear, Naval Tactics, and Actions of the War of Independence* (Harrisburg: Stackpole Books, 1969), 26; Gardner W. Allan, *A Naval History of the American Revolution*, 2 vols. (New York: Russell and Russell, 1962), 1:52–53.

38. J. Mattock to Craig, March 7, 1780, box 56, Craig-Neville Papers.

39. *Journals of the Continental Congress, 1774–1789*, ed. Worthington C. Ford et al., 34 vols. (Washington, D.C.: Library of Congress, 1904–37), 7:288–87 (April, 23, 1777).

40. Committee of Secret Correspondence, minutes of proceedings, May 25, 1776, and September 20, 1776, *Letter of Delegates to Congress*, vol. 4, *May 16, 1776–August 15, 1776*, available at http://memory.loc.gov/ammem/index.html; James L. Mooney, ed., *History of American Naval Fighting Ships*, vol. 1, *Andrew Doria* (Washington, D.C.: Naval History Division, 1959).

41. Document D, October 22, 1776, Craig-Neville Papers; Moore to Isaac Craig, February 21, 1782, *Pennsylvania Archives*, 1st ser., ed. Samuel Hazard, 12 vols. (Philadelphia: Joseph Severns, 1851–62), 9:497.

42. President of Congress to agents for prizes at Philadelphia, June 13, 1776, *Pennsylvania Archives*, 1st ser., 5:846.

43. John B. B. Trussell Jr., *The Pennsylvania Line: Regimental Organization and Operations, 1776–1783* (Harrisburg: Pennsylvania Historical and Museum Commission, 1977), 205.

44. Bowling, DiGiacomantonio, and Bickford, *Documentary History of the First Federal Congress*, 7:164–65.

45. Revolutionary War Military Abstract Card File, indexed items 51–66, between Craft, Peter, and Craig, Jared, PDA.

46. Item 66, ibid.

47. Journal, 2, Craig-Neville Papers.

48. Ibid., 3; Wayne K. Bodle, *The Valley Forge Winter: Civilians and Soldiers in War* (University Park: Pennsylvania State University Press, 2002).

49. Journal, 3, Craig-Neville Papers. See also the essay by James Bailey in this volume.

50. Henry Knox Correspondence, 1791–92, folder 3, Craig-Neville Papers.

51. John Newton Boucher, ed., *A Century and a Half of Pittsburgh and Her People*, vol. 1 (New York: Lewis Publishing Company, 1908), 10.

52. Robert K. Wright, *The Continental Army* (Washington, D.C.: U.S. Government Printing Office, 1983), 103–5.

53. *Pennsylvania Archives*, 1st ser., 5:209–10.

54. John Blair Linn and William H Egle, ed., *Pennsylvania in the War of the Revolution, Battalions and Line, 1775–1783*, vol. 2 (Harrisburg: Lane S. Hart, 1880), 231.

55. Document K, Craig-Neville Papers.

56. Wright, *Continental Army,* 104.

57. Jordan, *Colonial and Revolutionary Families of Pennsylvania,* 2:1163.

58. Journal, 7, Craig-Neville Papers. See also James Bailey's essay in this volume.

59. Trussell, *Pennsylvania Line,* 209.

60. Journal, Craig-Neville Papers.

61. Craig to Charles Levit, January 15, 1779, Craig Collection.

62. Mr. Bentley to Craig, August 2, 1783, Craig-Neville Papers.

63. 1782 land survey by Richard Dull, Clover Hill, property folder 2, ibid.

64. Indenture, April 1781, folder 4, ibid.

65. List of Residents on Rope Place, Craig Collection.

66. Order of the Supreme Executive Council, April 24, 1780, in Linn and Egle, *Pennsylvania in the War of the Revolution,* 2:197.

67. General Clark to Craig, March 23, 1781, Craig Collection.

68. Alan Fitzpatrick, *Wilderness War on the Ohio: The Untold Story of the Savage Battle for British and Indian Control of the Ohio Country During the American Revolution* (Benwood, W.Va.: Fort Henry Publications, 2003), 420–22.

69. Journal, 8–10, Craig-Neville Papers.

70. Document G, Certificate from the United States of America in Congress Assembled, ibid.

71. W. T. R. Saffell, ed., *Records of the Revolutionary War* (Baltimore: Charles Saffell, 1894), 468–70.

72. Jon Kukla, *A Wilderness So Immense: The Louisiana Purchase and the Destiny of America* (New York: Knopf, 2003), 96.

73. Notarized bank withdrawal, Craig Collection.

74. Register of depreciation certificates, PDA.

75. Archibald Douglas Turnbull, *William Turnbull, 1751–1822, with Some Account of Those Coming After* (Binghamton, N.Y: Vail-ballou Press, 1933).

76. Journal, 12, Craig-Neville Papers.

77. Turnbull and Marmié to Craig and Bayard, September 23, 1784, and Craig to Edward Smith, October 8 1784, Craig Collection.

78. Boucher, *Century and a Half of Pittsburg and Her People,*1:11.

79. Land agreement of January 4, 1985, RG-47, records of county government, Allegheny County, record of deeds, 1788–1851, PHMC.

80. Receipt for payment, miscellaneous, 1773–1868, and undated folder 9, Craig-Neville Papers.

81. Charles W. Dahlinger, "Fort Pitt," *Western Pennsylvania Historical Magazine* 5, no. 2 (1922): 100–108.

82. Curtis Nettels, *The Emergence of a National Economy, 1775–1815* (New York: Harper and Row, 1969), 177.

83. Craig to Trumbull and Marmié, July 28, 1784, Craig Collection.

84. Mr. Wilkins to Craig and Bayard, April 23, 1785, ibid.

85. Craig to Trumbull and Marmié, September 1, 1784, ibid.

86. Robert Abraham East, *Business Enterprise in the American Revolutionary Era* (New York: AMS Press, 1969), 136.

87. John Holker Papers, loose papers, folder 1, HSP.

88. Turnbull, *William Turnbull,* 20–30.

89. *Pittsburgh Gazette,* April 12, 1788, *Pittsburgh Gazette* Collection, reel 1, July 29, 1786–May 8, 1790, University of Pittsburgh, Hillman Library (hereafter *Pittsburgh Gazette* Collection).

90. Craig to [illegible], 884, Craig Collection.

91. Dahlinger, "Fort Pitt," 100.

92. Journal, 12, Craig Neville Papers.

93. Turnbull, *William Turnbull, 1751–1822,* 18–25.

94. List of goods to be purchased by Turnbull, Craig Collection.

95. Nettels, *Emergence of a National Economy,* 277–78.

96. D. Bradford to Isaac Craig, May 2, 1787, Craig Collection.

97. Raeone Christensen Steuart, ed., *Pennsylvania 1800 Census* (Utah: Heritage Quest, 2000).

98. Nettels, *Emergence of a National Economy,* 270.

99. Craig to Trumbull and Marmié, July 29, 1784, Craig Collection.

100. General merchandise accounts, July 1785, ibid.

101. Wilkins to Craig, July 21, 1785, ibid.

102. Fall Lick to Craig, July 24, 1795, ibid.

103. Wilkins to Craig and Bayard, April 23, 1785, ibid.

104. Mill blueprint sketch and dimensions, ibid.

105. J. Clark to Craig, July 31, 1781; Mr. Lacassagne to Craig, 1794; receipt, all in ibid.

106. Turnbull, *William Turnbull*, 16–20.

107. James Hodgdon to Craig, August 16, 1785, Craig Collection.

108. Land transfer from John Neville to Isaac and Amelia Craig, August 3, 1812, box 56, property folder 2, Craig-Neville Papers.

109. Duer, *Pittsburgh Gazette Abstracts,* 4:210.

110. *Pittsburgh Gazette,* February 20, 1788, *Pittsburgh Gazette* Collection, reel 1.111. Munger, *Pennsylvania Land Records,* 168.

112. *Pittsburgh Gazette,* February 20, 1788, *Pittsburgh Gazette* Collection, reel 1.

113. Hodgdon to Craig, August 16, 1785, Craig Collection.

114. *Pittsburgh Gazette,* February 16, 1819, in Duer, *Pittsburgh Gazette Abstracts,* 5:401.

115. French Creek to Craig and Bayard, April 23, 1785, and Venango to Craig, September 19, 1785, Craig Collection.

116. William Stiles to David Luckett, May 28, 1785, and William Stiles to David Luckett, May 28, 1785, Papers of the Continental Congress, Library of Congress, Washington, D.C.

117. Turnbull, *William Turnbull*, 18–25.

118. *Pennsylvania Archives,* 9th ser., ed. Gertrude MacKinney, 10 vols. (Philadelphia: Pennsylvania Bureau of Publications, 1931–35), 1:67.

119. Journal, Craig-Neville Papers, 15; Venango to Craig, 1788, Craig Collection.

120. Memorandum book, Craig-Neville Papers.

121. Supply purchase request, "New Fort," Fort Fayette, Fort Washington, Craig Collection.

122. Journal, 14, Craig-Neville Papers.

123. *Pittsburgh Gazette,* August 16, 1794, *Pittsburgh Gazette* Collection, reel 2, January 19, 1793–February 25, 1797.

124. See note 79.

125. *Pittsburgh Gazette,* February 20, 1788, *Pittsburgh Gazette* Collection, reel 5, April 19, 1809–October 9, 1812.

126. Turnbull and Marmié to Craig, October 9, 1787, Craig Collection; Turnbull and Marmié to Craig, February 10, 1791, Craig-Neville Papers.

127. *Heads of Families at the First Census of the United States Taken in the Year 1790, Pennsylvania* (Baltimore: Genealogical Publishing Company, 1966), 15.

128. *Pittsburgh Gazette,* May 21, 1802, *Pittsburgh Gazette* Collection, reel 4, December 11, 1801–April 12, 1809.

129. *Pittsburgh Gazette,* September 26, 1796, ibid., reel 2.

130. Jordan, *Colonial and Revolutionary Families of Pennsylvania,* 2:1163.

131. Undated loose papers, folder 2, record group 1451, Craig Family Papers, HSP.

132. Craig Family Papers, HSP; *Pittsburgh Gazette,* July 1801, *Pittsburgh Gazette* Collection, reel 4.

133. Charles Shetler, "James O'Hara's Landholdings in Allegheny County," *Western Pennsylvania Historical Magazine* 34 (1951): 23.

134. Craig to James O'Hara, August 16, 1795, record group 699, Anthony Wayne Papers, HSP.

135. Craig to James O'Hara, July 4, 1795, and Craig to James O'Hara, September 24, 1795, ibid.

136. *Pittsburgh Gazette,* May 21, 1802, *Pittsburgh Gazette* Collection, reel 4.

137. Records of deeds, 1799–1851, vol. 9L, PHMC; Shetler, "James O'Hara's Landholdings," 23; Dorothy Daniel, "The First Glass House West of the Alleghenies," *Western Pennsylvania Historical Magazine* 32, nos. 3–4 (1949): 106.

138. Shetler, "James O'Hara's Landholdings," 24.

139. Jordan, *Colonial and Revolutionary Families of Pennsylvania,* 2:882.

140. *Pittsburgh Gazette,* February 29, 1800, *Pittsburgh Gazette* Collection, reel 3, March 4, 1797–December 4, 1801, and reel 5, March 1810.

141. Jordan, *Colonial and Revolutionary Families of Pennsylvania,* 2:882.

142. *Pittsburgh Gazette,* April 5, 1811, *Pittsburgh Gazette* Collection, reel 5.

143. *Pittsburgh Gazette,* March 8 and 16, 1810, ibid.

144. Elisha P. Douglass, *The Coming of Age of American Business: Three Centuries of Enterprise, 1600–1900* (Chapel Hill: University of North Carolina Press), 52.

145. Executive minutes, March 20, 1810, *Pennsylvania Archives.,* 1st ser., 9:4506–7, 5502; Duer, *Pittsburgh Gazette Abstracts,* 4:212.

146. Loan documents, land valuation, March 10, 1786, and Craig to Bank of Pennsylvania, July 1812, Craig Collection.

147. Articles of Agreement Commissioned Between United States and Craig, February 5, 1805; Craig to William Timmons, Esq., March 1813; Isaac Craig in A/C with the United States, July 1815, all in ibid.

148. *Pittsburgh Gazette,* February 20, 1788, *Pittsburgh Gazette* Collection, reel 1; land warrants of October 1, March 10, and April 10, 1786, all in Craig Collection; and land warrants of September 11, 1795 (vol. 4D), March 7, 1794 (vol. 10K), December 4, 1796 (vol. 8H), December 12, 1796 (vol. 10K), July 17, 1799, and May 17, 1800 (vol. 9I), June 15, 1802 (vol. 10K), June 1800 (vol. 11L), September 23, 1801 (vol. 10K), January 15, 1803 (vol. 11L), and June 22, 1806 (vol. 10K), all in Lukens-Lenox Papers, PHMC.

149. *Pittsburgh Gazette,* June 24, 1811, *Pittsburgh Gazette* Collection, reel 5; Peter Wilson to Craig, June 1809, Craig Collection.

150. Duer, *Pittsburgh Gazette Abstracts,* 4:190.

151. *Pittsburgh Gazette,* February 16, 1810, *Pittsburgh Gazette* Collection, reel 5; Duer, *Pittsburgh Gazette Abstracts,* 4:282, 359 (July 1815 and May 18, 1816).

152. J. Bernard Hogg, "Presley Neville" (master's thesis, Slippery Rock University, 1931).

153. Duer, *Pittsburgh Gazette Abstracts,* 4:126–28 (March 10 and July 31, 1818).

154. Ibid., 4:314, 341 (September 1, 1819).

155. Executive minutes, May 14, 1821, *Pennsylvania Archives,* 1st ser., 9:5505; Boucher, *Century and a Half of Pittsburgh and Her People,* 1:13.

156. Joyce Appleby, *Inheriting the Revolution: The First Generation of Americans* (Cambridge: Belknap Press of Harvard University Press), 81.

12

CONSTRUCTING COMMUNITY AND THE DIVERSITY DILEMMA: RATIFICATION IN PENNSYLVANIA

Elizabeth Lewis Pardoe

In 1787, Pennsylvanian politicians, who lived daily with diversity and faced the task of turning the many American republics into one federal nation, sought to integrate Euro-American political concepts while drafting their own definitions of pluralism. Recalling classical political theory, Anti-Federalists feared that a large republic like the proposed federation would threaten this diversity and corrupt the virtue of the fragile new Republic. Pennsylvanian Federalists, on the other hand, had to show the compatibility of diversity with both a large republic and a strong central government. To do so, the Federalists reframed the question of where sovereignty lay—in the state or the national government—and asked to what form of government the people granted which aspects of *their* innate sovereignty. This imaginative shift from state sovereignty to popular sovereignty allowed the Federalists to concentrate on what community meant in the new Republic. James Wilson took the lead among Pennsylvania Federalists in reworking European definitions of community and republic to suit a heterogeneous society. This immigrant statesman focused on an individual's ability to belong to many communities and to form many contracts, at the national, state, and local levels, each governing a different aspect of his life. Scottish philosopher David Hume's threatening factions could be transformed into useful constituent communities in a new nation defined by its diversity. Although James Madison usually receives the credit, Wilson had already defended the value of a multifaceted government for a multifaceted people and had used this very pluralism as the basis for a national identity. This kind of federal republic would not threaten other cultural allegiances; it was a nation that presupposed pluralism.

The core of this paper began as an MPhil essay under the supervision of Quentin Skinner. It has since benefited from comments by John Dunn, the late Mark Kaplanoff, John Murrin, Seth Cotlar, Albrecht Koschnik, Anthony Grafton, James Merrill, Sean Wilentz, James Sidbury, Bernard Bailyn, Timothy Breen, and participants in sessions of the 2004 annual meeting of the OAH and the tenth anniversary conference of the Harvard Atlantic History Seminar.

The project of drafting a federal constitution confronted American political thinkers with the problem of diversity. Nowhere was diversity a greater issue than in Pennsylvania, with its large non-English-speaking population and its divided English-speaking religious, ethnic, and political constituencies. Once it located the debate over Federalism within this pluralist context, the ratifying convention's discussions about the nature of sovereignty and political contracts acquired new meaning.

Throughout the eighteenth century, European philosophers and American politicians grappled with a common language of rights, republics, factions, and federations. Today, historians divide this discourse into classical republicanism and liberalism in terms closely aligned with debates in political philosophy between "communitarians," who willingly yield their rights and lives to the greater good of the community and defend "positive liberty," on the one hand, and "individualists," who place greater value on the freedom of acquisition and expression, or "negative liberty."[1] In 1787, Pennsylvanians attempted to integrate these contradictory Euro-American concepts into their own definitions of political pluralism. Each side struggled with these opposing concepts. The Anti-Federalists found themselves pretending that the diverse and fractious population of Pennsylvania could sustain a peaceful and united republic at the state level, and that a diverse, loosely united confederacy could survive.[2] The Federalists could not avoid tripping over the fact that a central government would promote some interests and shortchange others, not to mention that it would exclude the interests of the indigenous and enslaved altogether, while accommodating some types of American diversity and freedom.

The Anti-Federalist Argument

The Pennsylvania Anti-Federalists faced a major obstacle in presenting their case. The Commonwealth of Pennsylvania had recently, and barely, emerged from a series of contested boundary disputes. The border with Maryland, contested since the arrival of William Penn in 1682, was not settled until the establishment of the Mason-Dixon Line in 1767. Virginia's desire to assert control over the Ohio Valley along Pennsylvania's western border led to conflicting jurisdictions in the Pittsburgh area until 1781. Connecticut Yankees continued to dispute land claims with their Pennsylvania neighbors in the northeastern Wyoming Valley until the early nineteenth century, although Congress had made the region part of Pennsylvania in 1786.

Within the commonwealth, loyalty to local, religious, and ethnic groups competed with and often overshadowed devotion to Pennsylvania as a whole. The Anti-Federalists nevertheless theoretically defined pluralism in terms of communities and states, which entered into political agreements as preexisting sociopolitical wholes. Therefore, the original states were the sole repositories of sovereignty upon entering into a confederation. In the eyes of Anti-Federalists, the Lockean contract between individual and state was irrelevant to the federal government, because every American citizen had already entered into a social compact with his state during the Revolution. For them, the state of nature was a historical artifact with little bearing on contemporary political decisions. Rather than reconstruct social compacts, Anti-Federalists turned for guidance to the French political philosopher Montesquieu's idea of a federal republic of culturally homogenous geographical communities allied for the purpose of common defense.

Pennsylvania Anti-Federalists insisted that the state was the most important community, the appropriate site for the merger of individual and local interests into a homogeneous entity. When Irish-born Anti-Federalist John Smilie quoted the state constitution of 1776, he chose a passage that focused on the integrity of community rights, claiming "that government is, or ought to be, instituted for the common benefit, protection and security of the people, nation or community." The state constitution protected the interests of the community as a whole as opposed to "the particular emolument or advantage of any single man, family, or set of men, who are only part of that community." Although this Anti-Federalist defense argued against the perceived elitism of the proposed federal Constitution, the underlying concept of government by community, not individuals, remained clear. According to Smilie, "the community hath an indubitable, unalienable and indefeasible right to reform, alter or abolish government," and these changes were to be made "in such a manner as shall be by that community judged most conducive to the public weal."[3]

At the heart of Anti-Federalists' argument lay the inviolable sovereignty of the state government. Many of the same political elements that now opposed the federal Constitution had designed the radical state constitution in 1776. In enforcing it, however, their own exercise of sovereignty and effort to build community failed. They managed only to achieve the appearance of homogeneity for the new Commonwealth of Pennsylvania by administering test oaths, which banned large segments of the population (including Quakers) from political participation. Having fabricated one community, they were loath to disassemble it in order to construct an even larger, more diverse national one. When Pennsylvania-born Robert Whitehill began his attack on the Constitution, he objected foremost to the use of the phrase "We the people of the United States," which he called "a sentence that evidently shows the old foundation of the Union is destroyed." Because "the people" as a whole were assenting to a national government, Whitehill believed, "the principle of confederation [was] excluded," and the alternative was "a new unwieldy system of consolidated empire" built "upon the ruins of the present compact between the states." For Whitehill, the coexistence of state and national communities seemed an impossibility. If a nation were to be created, the states must cease to exist. As a result, Whitehill understood the Constitution as "incontravertibly designed to abolish the independence and sovereignty of the states individually" (393).

Although Ulster-born William Findley insisted that he shared the Federalist view that "sovereignty essentially resides in the people," he believed that the new government, for all intents and purposes, "vested [sovereignty] in a senate or a monarch [the president]." As a result, the transfer of sovereign power to a national government concerned Findley. States had "already parted with a portion of their sovereignty" under the Articles of Confederation, and the Constitution asked them to yield yet more. The people, he claimed in a speech before the Pennsylvania convention on December 5, 1787, never intended that all sovereignty be "given up to the general government." Findley agreed that "states were made for the people and not the people for the states." Nevertheless, once the people had established a state, "they may vest what portion" of sovereignty "they please in the state legislatures."[4] Findley, like Whitehill, envisioned the Constitution as "consolidating government for all purposes of sovereignty," because it "puts all the thirteen states into one" (502–4).

Pennsylvania's two most vocal Anti-Federalists considered the Federalist notion of a sovereign people a fiction. John Smilie defined a "consolidating government" as "one that will transfer the sovereignty from the states to the general government" (508). "Why is the sovereignty of the people always brought into view?" asked Robert Whitehill in his remarks to the convention on December 7. For Whitehill there existed "13 sovereignties in the United States; and 13 different governments." Even to discuss the sovereignty of the people already compromised the integrity of the states more than Whitehill could allow. "Why," he asked, "knock down all distinction of different governments?" (513).

William Findley's Anti-Federalist thought developed from the belief that in 1787 Americans no longer lived in a state of nature but were already members of states and thus not at liberty to construct a new government. The Articles of Confederation secured the sovereignty of the states by having each state vote as a unit. According to Findley, "a state can speak but one voice." Like Whitehill, Findley objected to the use of "We the people," but Findley relied on a Lockean argument against its usage. The phrase assumed Americans to be "in a state of nature"; "to a stranger it would appear that no states were in existence" (446). The example of taxation made plain the Anti-Federalists' objection to the entire governmental structure. Assuming monolithic definitions of community and sovereignty, Findley wrote, "there cannot exist two independent sovereign taxing powers in the same community" (448). When the dissenting representatives in Pennsylvania wrote their opinion of the Constitution, they focused again on "the words 'We the people of the United States,' which is the style of a compact between individuals entering into a state of society, and not that of a confederation of states" (630).

A "confederation," as the Pennsylvania Anti-Federalists imagined it, shared a great deal with the kind of federal republic that Montesquieu outlined in *The Spirit of the Laws*. Indeed, Federalists and Anti-Federalists alike cited Montesquieu, but they offered opposing interpretations.[5] The location of sovereignty determines the nature of government, according to Montesquieu's analysis, and "republican government is that in which the people as a body, or only part of the people, have sovereign power."[6] The people of a republic must possess virtue if the system is to survive, and the nature of that virtue is selfless devotion to the well-being of the community as a whole. Education is a prerequisite for republican government, because "political virtue is a renunciation of oneself, which is always a very painful thing" and requires tutelage (1.4.5.35).

An understanding of classical *virtú* informed the Anti-Federalists' view that a single person could not possibly renounce his individual interests for the sake of both a republic and a strong federation. If renunciation of selfish gain in favor of the common good is complete, then this first state possesses the collective sovereignty of all living within it and speaks for all, as a unit, in relation to the outside world. Montesquieu defines political virtue "as love of the laws and the homeland." The stress on the homeland as an organic unit complemented the Anti-Federalists' understanding of diversity as spread among the states, and their implicit denial that diverse communities and individuals lived within each state (1.4.5.36).

In the eighteenth-century understanding of a republic, the public whole completely absorbed the individual self and left no room for the multiple "publics" proposed in the federal Constitution. Community, by Montesquieu's and the Anti-Federalists' definition, is organic, characterized by geography, not by negotiated cultural choice. For the people to love the communal good, the community must be a spiritual entity capable of inspiring love. In essence, the community represents a culture defined in the limited sense of shared values and experiences. Montesquieu understands the "spirit" of nations in these terms. The things that "govern men" and create a "general spirit," Montesquieu holds, are "climate, religion, laws, the maxims of the government, examples of past things, mores, and manners" (3.19.4.310).

Foremost among these influences is the shared experience of a nation's climate and physical environment; Montesquieu devotes five entire books in *The Spirit of the Laws* to the subject. Both people and their governments should be shaped to fit their surroundings, for "the character of the spirit and the passions of the heart are extremely different in the various climates." Thus "laws should be related to the differences in these passions and to the differences in these characters" (3.14.1.231). Applied to the American confederation in 1787, this analysis would rule out the proposed federal Constitution. If the nature of the states is determined by their geography and climate, it would be completely unreasonable to ask the people of Georgia to empathize with the problems of people in New Hampshire. The two states' "spirits" would be fundamentally different and incapable of mutual understanding.

Despite their many borrowings from Montesquieu, Pennsylvania Anti-Federalists left out two key elements of his thought that pointed to the weaknesses of their case. The Anti-Federalists mention neither religion nor "examples of past things," which would imply a shared history as critical to their state-based concept of community. America's religious diversity undermined Montesquieu's argument about the interaction between religion, environment, and politics. Although Montesquieu accepted Christianity as the one true religion, he saw religion the world over, and even the distinction between Catholicism and Protestantism, as a function of climate. Southern climates led to laziness, servitude, and increased "sensitivity to pleasures." Catholicism, a southern religion in Montesquieu's view, "better suits a monarchy" than a republic (3.14.2.233–34; 5.24.5.463). By contrast, northern Europeans became Protestants because the climate had already led them to "a spirit of independence and liberty," which inclined them to prefer a religion without a "visible leader" (5.24.5.463). According to Montesquieu, princes should not try to change their subjects' religion, because the "former religion is linked with the Constitution" and is "in accord with the climate," while its replacement is not. In Pennsylvania, however, a large number of religions, which had developed in different climates, coexisted in one geographical region.

Similarly, Montesquieu's notion of a shared state history had little relevance in a state whose boundaries had been arbitrarily defined in the very recent past. Thomas Paine developed an effective shared historical past for the Federalists when he proclaimed in *Common Sense* that "Europe, not England, is the parent country of America. This new world hath been the asylum for persecuted lovers of civil and religious liberty from *every* part of Europe." To support his argument that the common American experience was persecution and migration, Paine stressed that larger identities resulted from individuals' coming together across narrow geographic boundaries. "In this extensive quarter of the globe, we forget the narrow limits [of England] . . . and carry our friendship on a larger scale; we claim brotherhood with every European Christian and triumph in the generosity of the sentiment." Just as an Englishman's home parish paled in importance to his nation when traveling in Europe, "by a parity of reasoning, all Europeans meeting in America . . . are *countrymen*." Pointing to Pennsylvania, Paine observed that "not one third of the inhabitants, even of this province, are of

English descent." To use "the phrase of parent or mother country applied to England only" was thus "false, selfish, narrow, and ungenerous."[7] Aimed at dislodging colonists' allegiance to the king, Paine's argument also undermined Anti-Federalist claims to the significance of Pennsylvania as a cultural unit. Paine asserted the sole sovereignty of the United States under the Articles of Confederation before removing himself and his revolutionary quill to Paris in May 1787.[8]

The Anti-Federalists claimed that the states were essentially different from one another and thus rendered the shared American experiences of immigration and revolution culturally impotent. William Findley asserted that it would be unfair and unwise to allow "a citizen of Pennsylvania to be taxed by a Representative of Georgia."[9] As Paine had shown, however, migration and revolution were capable of providing a common history for the disparate cultures within Pennsylvania. Thus, a German Moravian in Georgia might represent a Pennsylvanian German Moravian's interests far better than an Ulster-Irish Presbyterian in Pennsylvania could. By denying the possibility of American cultural and political unity while insisting on such unity at the state level, the Anti-Federalists undermined their claim to the cultural and political legitimacy of their own state.

Anti-Federalists thus found themselves in a paradoxical position. They argued for the primacy of the states rather than individuals as units of political power, while at the same time demanding that the Constitution enshrine individual rights. The argument that no one state could ever represent a cohesive cultural whole was the foundation of the Anti-Federalist argument. Findley acknowledged this paradox, confessing, "When I was proposed as a member of the late [Federal] Convention, I declined it as I thought it too great an undertaking *for me* to *represent* and *guard* all the rights and liberties of the people of Pennsylvania." When Findley had declared at the state ratifying convention that "there cannot exist two sovereign powers to tax," both James Wilson and Anthony Wayne remained silent but expressed their skepticism in marginalia on their copies of the Constitution. Wilson merely identified "County Taxes," which clearly contradicted Findley's point. Wayne noted that "the objection as to taxation is as absurd, when the present Constitution is in operation as it would be for any one county in the state to object to being taxed by the other counties because the people of that county had not the app[ointmen]t, etc."[10]

The distinction between the regulatory realms of the state and federal government was another critical issue for Montesquieu and the Anti-Federalists. The constitution of a federal republic, according to Montesquieu, "has all the internal advantages of republican government and the external force of monarchy" (2.9.1.31). The proposed system, according to Findley, "increased the difficulty of drawing the line between general and state governments by encroaching into *internal* objects," internal objects being those powers that ought to be reserved to the separate states. In Findley's opinion, commerce between states was the only activity that the federal government could legitimately control. "The federal head" was to have no hand in legislation or its accompanying taxation, because that would destroy the state legislature.[11] Since Montesquieu wrote, and Anti-Federalists believed, that a federal republic was "a society of societies" in "which many political bodies consent to become citizens of the larger state that they want to form," the larger federal state could not regulate the internal affairs of the smaller member republics (2.9.1.131–32).

Whereas Montesquieu provided Anti-Federalists with a model for ideal government, David Hume's "Idea of a Perfect Commonwealth" raised their awareness of the dangers to liberty lurking within governmental systems. The Anti-Federalists' fear that the federal government would be a "consolidated" government followed Hume's political analysis. Hume envisioned free government as being threatened by consolidated power from above and factional chaos from below.[12] Like Montesquieu, Hume advocated a federal model of government, but his model was less sensitive to the issues of pluralism than Montesquieu's.

As opposed to Montesquieu's model of a federal republic formed by smaller republics, Hume focused on the structurally less complicated notion of one nation divided into ever smaller local units, a model that would facilitate representation and the electoral process. Hume called his ideal government a commonwealth rather than a federal republic. Reflecting the different premise of the structure, Hume proposed that "Great Britain and Ireland, or any territory of equal extent be divided into 100 counties," a model opposed to Montesquieu's federal republic, which was formed by agreement between preexisting states and could continually accept "new associates" (2.9.1.131).[13] Hume wished to treat "every county as a kind of republic within itself," but the distinction between internal and external matters is not as clear as Montesquieu's. The general government, or any county, may annul the by-laws of another county.[14] The ability of counties or republics to interfere in the governance of one another suggests the similarity in social circumstances that Hume took for granted, in contrast to the differences among internal societies that both Montesquieu and the Anti-Federalists assumed.

Anti-Federalist thought ran parallel to Hume's treatment of the senate in his ideal commonwealth. In Hume's commonwealth, the hundred counties are subdivided into one hundred parishes, with one freeholder representing each parish. This representative, in turn, meets with the other ninety-nine parish representatives from the county to elect ten county magistrates and one senator. These hundred senators possess the full executive power of the commonwealth but none of the legislative power. According to Hume, two inherent dangers accompany every such senate, "its combination and its division," combination being the greater of the two dangers.[15]

The Anti-Federalists' critique of the Constitution echoed two aspects of Humean analysis. First, a senate should be an executive power, and the Constitution undermined this premise by permitting the federal Senate broad legislative powers. Second, the federal government encouraged the combination of powers, which Anti-Federalists called "consolidating government." Both of these Humean issues returned to the perception of diversity between rather than within the states. The federal government's ability to exercise legislative power over the constitutive states implied the loss of the states' power to pursue their particular interests. These more expansive powers led directly to consolidated government and to the dangerous possibility that uniform policies would be imposed on the states from above, against the states' wishes and needs.

The Senate's influence on the House and on the presidency caused the Anti-Federalists great unease. John Smilie objected to the Senate's power to check presidential power. He worried that the Senate's "share in the executive department" would "corrupt the legislature" and would drain "the proper power of the President," making him merely "a tool of the Senate." The combination of legislative and executive power possessed by the Senate was Smilie's greatest concern; he claimed that the Senate would "overset the balance of government by having the purse and the sword." The president, he feared, would not limit the senators but would "act in concert with them." The joined powers of "the purse and the sword" were irrefutable evidence, in Smilie's view, that the ratifying convention never intended the new government to be free. There needed to be "three branches of government in every society," he argued, and "the executive ought to have a negative on the legislature."[16] While attacking the federal plan, the Anti-Federalists again compromised their ability to defend the Pennsylvania constitution. The executive veto that Smilie demanded was missing from the radical Pennsylvania government. Indeed, he and Findley changed their minds and supported the new constitution of 1789, which restored a legislative state senate and a governor with a veto power.[17]

The Anti-Federalists not only employed Humean rhetoric for their own purposes but feared the Federalists' use of Humean logic against their cause. They worried that both branches of the federal Congress would extend the limits of their power by delaying elections and appointments or by changing the location of polling to influence electoral results. They expected Federalists to manipulate election statutes "under various pretences," including "an apprehension of invasion," or the Humean claim of "the factious disposition of the people."[18]

Hume feared not only a combination in the Senate but also faction among the masses.[19] Like most of his contemporaries, he considered "the people," when assembled in large groups, incapable of rational debate; "absurdity" guided the "mob."[20] Federalists took seriously Hume's warnings of chaos from below, and Anti-Federalists heeded Hume's counsel to expect, in response, heavy-handed action from above. While Federalists wished to bring order to pluralistic chaos by broadening the voting base so that no one faction could gain a disproportionate voice,[21] the Anti-Federalists treasured the range of options left open to the states in the factiousness that reigned between revolution and ratification. Paradoxically, the Anti-Federalists were truer to Hume's plan to eliminate faction; they insisted on small electoral districts. And they thought that voters must be familiar with their local candidates if they were to be capable of judging each man's virtue.

The struggle to define the nature of the bond between Americans runs from the colonial period to the present day, but the years between 1776 and 1787 were critical in the process that Edmund Morgan has aptly called "inventing an American people."[22] Linda Colley's work on the creation of a British identity emphasizes the particular difficulty of this process in America. Britons, according to Colley, found a common identity as non-French throughout a century of war with their continental adversary.[23] Americans lacked such simple methods of self-definition. During the Revolution they could claim to be the non-English, but their institutions were largely English, and English was the common language of their commerce and government. English colonial control was one of the few common bonds among all residents of the continent, whether they were ethnically English or not. The cohesive power of a heritage had just been overthrown. The Anti-Federalists in Pennsylvania wanted no part of an "American" identity based on Englishness, a particularly weak bond in a state populated overwhelmingly by migrants from Germany and the Celtic fringe. Mutual distrust permeated the Scots-Irish population's relationship to both England and the elite Anglophiles of Philadelphia.[24]

In this context of conflicting interests and disintegrating bonds, the Anti-Federalists thought the foundation of an American political system for an American people a ludicrous but dangerous imposition upon several different peoples. As William Findley noted, "The general government is farther removed from the people than the state governments."[25] Pennsylvania could barely limp along as a political unit with its diverse population. How, then, could the federal Constitution create a nation of thirteen disparate entities? From the standpoint of the Anti-Federalists, the only meaningful political units were the preexisting states. These political constructs lacked a shared history or a shared faith, but at least each one possessed its own organic similarities of climate and geography, which made it possible to think of each as a small republic.

In Pennsylvania, the pacifist monks of the Ephrata Cloister and the rabble-rousing Paxton Boys shared a landscape but not a *mentalité*. The Philadelphia radicals and their Quaker adversaries struggled with the same conundrum. Nevertheless, the Anti-Federalists' concept of pluralism still thrives in American historiography. Many historians continue to divide early America into New England, the middle colonies, the Chesapeake, and the lower South, despite similarities and differences across regions.[26] Within limits, this regionalism, based on environment, with correlated agricultural and trade patterns, provided a useful delineation of cultural boundaries for politicians in the eighteenth century just as it provides convenient guidelines for historians today.[27]

The Anti-Federalists, like Montesquieu and many historians, saw commerce as a key unifying influence on the colonies. Jack P. Greene focuses on the individual "pursuit of happiness," which he believes provided a common link across colonial boundaries. T. H. Breen stresses a fascination with English goods, which drew all colonists into a transatlantic commercial society.[28] The clash between commerce and idealized republicanism colored Anti-Federalists' interpretation of the diversity surrounding them. Federalists encouraged the forces described by Greene and Breen as the means to American unity and national greatness. Anti-Federalists reiterated Montesquieu's warning that corrupt politicians who lost interest in the virtue necessary for a republic turned instead to "manufacturing, commerce, finance, wealth, and even luxury" (1.3.3.22–23). Despite this anxiety, Anti-Federalists realized that commerce was necessary and agreed with the Federalists in considering its interstate and international regulation the acceptable province of the federal government. As a result, even a limited federal government would constantly threaten the virtue of citizens and the integrity of the individual state republics.

At a time when Anti-Federalists hoped to draw Pennsylvania's citizens together, Montesquieu informed them that while commerce "unites nations, it does not unite individuals in the same way." Commerce is a dangerous game for a republic. Without commerce, society is reduced to "banditry." With "the spirit of commerce, there is traffic in all human activities and all moral virtues; the smallest things, those required by humanity, are done or given for money." Although commerce "polishes and refines barbarous mores," it "corrupts pure mores" (4.20.1.338–39). The Anti-Federalists wanted to limit federal commerce to a refining influence rather than a destructive force. If social historians are correct that connections to European and particularly English commerce forged the most solid bonds between the individuals of the early American states, then Anti-Federalists—following Montesquieu's logic—were justifiably frightened that the commerce, though bringing the nation together, would tear the tentative identities of the state republics apart.

John Smilie recognized that the people would devote themselves to the common good only if the state reciprocated their efforts. If a federal government were established, he argued, "the people themselves will become indifferent" to the state governments, "and at least, indifferent to the continuance of an expensive form, from which they derive no advantages." In a wonderful overlapping of Lockean contract and republican theory, Smilie declared, "the attachment of citizens to their government and its laws is founded upon the benefits which they derive from them and it will last no longer than the duration of the power to confer those benefits."[29] For Smilie, attachment to the government—defined as virtue—was the necessary prerequisite for a functional republic, but the maintenance of virtue required that the state government remain capable of providing for the common good. If the federal government were perceived to provide for all aspects of the public interest and the state government for none, citizens' attachment to and love for the state republic would disappear. This integrated contract nurtured virtue in return for public benefit. The citizenry would not maintain its attachment if its private interests were infringed upon without compensation.

John Smilie was not alone in his attempt to reconcile Montesquieu's virtuous republican and Locke's contracting individual. Thomas Jefferson also employed a combination of republican and Lockean arguments to justify the American Revolution. Jefferson relied on the ancient constitution and republican principles to prove that the people of America had passed their sovereignty to the colonies. The colonies were no longer willing to be members of the British Empire, which had violated their sovereign rights, but chose to be independent states. But Jefferson used Lockean rhetoric to exclude American Indians from the new confederation. If the former colonies were truly sovereign states and distinct cultural communities within a confederation, then the American Indian nations could be incorporated into this pluralistic structure with ease. Sidestepping the choice between inclusion or hypocritical exclusion, Jefferson depicted the Indians as savages in a state of war and prohibited them from claiming any right to join a Lockean confederation of consenting, sovereign, civilized republics.[30] Nor did Virginians permit the diversity of the Shenandoah Valley to unseat the Anglican hegemony of the Tidewater.[31] Jefferson used political theory to enforce his homogeneous dream of white yeoman farmers tilling the soil unburdened by the complications of cultural and racial difference. In Jefferson's agrarian utopia, Africans would return to Africa or move to Haiti,[32] the indigenous tribes would move west, and religious liberty would eliminate the principal impulse for fractious disputation.[33]

Pennsylvania Anti-Federalists attempted to define pluralism but found themselves caught in a contradiction. The sovereignty of the states allowed Pennsylvanians to maintain their autonomy within a varied confederation and work toward the common bonds of virtue and public good aspired to in republican theory. But part of this common good emerged from the liberal tradition. Anti-Federalists hoped to make Pennsylvania a republican community, but they also wanted to preserve the individual rights of citizens in their heterogeneous state.

The diversity of individuals, ethnicities, and faiths that anchored communities in Pennsylvania and the state-based pluralism of Montesquieu's federal republic were mutually exclusive. Caught between homogeneous republican theory and heterogeneous reality, Pennsylvania Anti-Federalists struggled to protect the sovereignty and define the nature of their fractious society within a diverse "confederation." The powder keg of feuding ethnic and religious communities barely contained by the political fiction known as "Pennsylvania" might explode if the new federal Constitution took any power away from their fragile state. Thus, the Pennsylvania Anti-Federalists fought to defend the rights of their fictionally unified republic from the new fiction outlined in the federal Constitution.

The Federalists' Perspective

Pennsylvania Federalists' desire to reconcile virtuous republics with commercial federations required a shift in focus. Whereas the Anti-Federalists based their thinking on Locke's concept of sovereignty—which held that people can enter only one social contract and have one government—Scottish immigrant James Wilson took the lead among Federalists in reworking European definitions of community and nation for a heterogeneous society. Reflecting his own immigrant experience, Wilson focused on the ability of an individual to belong to different communities and to form different contracts, each governing a different aspect of his life. Even Hume's factions became constituent communities in a nation defined by its internal diversity.

Wilson reinterpreted Montesquieu in a manner conducive to the Federalist argument, granting the existence of thirteen "mutually independent" governments and their diversity in all of Montesquieu's categories. "Those governments present to the Atlantic a front of fifteen hundred miles in extent," and across that expanse, "their soil, climates, their production, their dimension, their numbers are different." Between the thirteen states, "in many instances a difference and even an opposition subsists among their interests." Beyond real difference, Wilson argued, "a difference and even an opposition is imagined to subsist in many more," for "an apparent interest produces the same attachment as a real one; and is often pursued with no less perseverance and vigour." The product of "such a diversity of things" was "a proportionate diversity of sentiment." Amazingly, however, rather than discord, "such a diversity of sentiment rendered a spirit of mutual forbearance and conciliation," and "mutual concessions and sacrifice were the consequences of mutual forbearance and conciliation."[34] Wilson created his own fiction, peaceable pluralism, in defiance of Pennsylvania's recent past.

Turning to the type of government appropriate for the different territories,

Wilson followed Montesquieu's logic to the conclusion of a federal republic. Wilson joined Montesquieu in answering the "dilemma" of adapting democracy to a large territory in proposing a system that "secured all the internal advantages of a republic" and "maintained the external dignity of a monarchy." Before focusing on the system's ability to assemble "distinct societies," Wilson highlighted the shared values and experiences Americans had gained during the Revolution. Unity within the existing states came from the high value they all put on "freedom and independence, which has been manifested in their united and successful opposition to one of the most powerful kingdoms of the world."[35]

Wilson relied on Lockean rhetoric to explain the functions and nature of the federal republic. Human "want, imperfections, and weakness" make us tend toward society, "but it is certain; society cannot exist without some restraints." Individuals have unrestrained rights in the state of nature, but "by the interfering claims and the consequent animosities of men," these rights are "rendered insupportable." As a result, "the aggregate of liberty is more in society, than it is in a state of nature." From this Lockean principle Wilson returned to the concept of a common public interest and declared it to be "a fundamental principle of society, that the welfare of the whole shall be pursued and not of a part." This principle, Wilson insisted, "is universally allowed to be just with respect to single governments" as well as in "instances in which it applies with equal force to independent communities." In all governments, "private and individual rights are subservient to the public and general happiness of the nation." Wilson chose his words carefully. His "nation" fit Paine's definition of America, while states, like individuals, yield their rights for the good of the nation.[36]

This integration of Montesquieu and Locke inspired Wilson to define a new type of liberty for the new nation: "federal liberty," which "consists in the aggregate of the civil liberty which is surrendered by each state to the national government." Further, "the same principles that operate in the establishment of a single society, with respect to the rights reserved or resigned by the individuals that compose it," would "justly apply in the case of a confederation of distinct and independent states."[37] He argued that such a democracy would encourage a combination of republican, Lockean, and Humean values: "liberty, caution, industry, fidelity, and an opportunity of bringing forward the talents and abilities of the citizens without regard to birth or fortune." The "disadvantages" of diverse democracy, however, "are dissension and imbecility." These Humean problems result from "the assent of many being required," as "their exertions will be feeble, and their councils too soon discovered."[38]

Hume's fear of faction found an even more direct route into Federalist rhetoric in Wilson's argument that Congress should have "power, in the dernier resort" over "any state in the Union whose measures might at any time be influenced by faction and caprice."[39] Hume's understanding of faction put a heterogeneous free society, like the thirteen states, at constant risk of dissolution. Hume warned against the "founders of sects and factions," who were "to be hated" for being "directly contrary to the laws," subversive, and able to "render laws impotent." Most important, faction could "beget the fiercest animosities among men of the same nation, who ought to give mutual assistance and protection to each other." The essential problem underlying faction is a diversity of "real" interests, principles, and affections—"personal" factions, which are most likely to occur in a small republic and emerge from each "domestic quarrel" as "an affair of state." The "richest soil" for factions is "free government, where they always infect the legislature itself" and where the only antidote is "the steady application of rewards and punishments."[40]

Wilson's fellow Pennsylvania Federalist and son of Ulster immigrants, Thomas McKean, employed Hume's metaphor for political faction, Christian sectarianism. The nature of biblical disputation led to the "split into new divisions and heresies," which spawned "mutual hatred and antipathy." These "parties of religion are more furious and enraged than the most cruel factions that ever arose from interest and ambition."[41] McKean began his comments to the Philadelphia convention with a call for conciliation and a commentary on American religious factions, which subtly used Hume's analysis as justification for the Constitution. "Even in religion, we disagree to confine ourselves to one sect—how various are the doctrines, church discipline, and worship of Christians." Nevertheless, McKean claimed, "we have but one rule, the New Testament—the new Constitution (if you please)." The ability of "men to think so differently on the most important subject which can interest society" proved to McKean, and thus should prove to the Anti-Federalists, "how silly, how extremely narrow it is, that we should quarrel, because we cannot altogether agree on the subject before us."[42] In short, if all Pennsylvanians could find a place under the umbrella of Christianity, they could do the same under the umbrella of federal government. Pennsylvania's diverse religious landscape made McKean's argument particularly compelling.

Hume addressed the problem of faction by dividing "the people into many separate bodies" so that "they may debate with safety."[43] Anti-Federalists found the Constitution's provision of only one representative for every thirty thousand people inadequate; they agreed with Hume that smaller districts selected better men and eliminated faction.[44] Ironically, Virginian James Madison suggested a less lofty goal: functional factionalism. In *The Federalist* No. 14, Madison refers to the Union as "our bulwark against foreign danger, as the conservator of peace among ourselves, as the guardian of our commerce and common interest," as well as "the proper antidote for the diseases of faction, which have proved fatal to other popular governments, and of which alarming symptoms have been betrayed by our own."[45] The contagion of faction was not fatal in a large federation, because the broad range of factions would deny any one undue influence. Thomas McKean hoped that ratification would "have a tendency to break our parties and divisions, and by that means, lay a firm and solid foundation for the future tranquility and happiness of the United States in general" and for "this state [Pennsylvania] in particular."[46]

Madison, writing under the pseudonym Publius, reverted to his Chesapeake roots and strained to prove that Americans were a legitimate, organic nation in *The Federalist* No. 14. Americans, according to Publius, are "knit together by so many cords of affection" that their "kindred blood" has "mingled," having been "shed in defense of their sacred rights."[47] Although Americans certainly did not share the same ancestral bloodline, the various ethnicities had "mingled" to a greater or lesser degree through intermarriage and in bloodshed on the battlefield. James Wilson also aspired to create a sense of nationalism, but he took a more realistic view. For Wilson, "national character" would be developed in the American people after ratification of the Constitution; he felt no need to concoct a shared ethnic or blood nationalism from a recently united and undeniably diverse population.[48] His forward-looking interpretation of national identity may well have been the product of his own immigrant experience and his personal knowledge that American identity was not grounded in myths of a shared past but in aspirations for a shared future.

Wilson explicitly acknowledged that it was only through ratification that "we shall become a nation" and "also form a national character." This character would "be adapted to the principles and genius of our system of government," he wrote, but he admitted that "as yet we possess none."[49] Wilson acknowledged the multiple influences acting on American society: "our language, manners, customs, habits, and dress depend too much upon those of other countries." "Every nation," he asserted, "in these respects should possess originality." Rather than choose national traits dependent on religion or culture, the Pennsylvanian charged Americans with constructing a shared identity out of their "activity, perseverance, industry, laudable emulation, docility in acquiring information, firmness in adversity, and patience and magnanimity under the greatest hardships."[50] All of these "national" traits are free of any ties to ethnicity, faith, or particular state or geographic region. Wilson proposed an identity with no apparent barriers to assimilation, one that could be assumed without violating other cultural allegiances, a nationalism presupposing pluralism. Wilson used his oratorical skill to defend the definition of the American nation that Thomas Paine drafted in *Common Sense* and that James Madison institutionalized in the federal Constitution.[51]

Wilson also conceived of the Constitution itself as pluralist. The fundamental principle of Wilson's political understanding was that "the supreme, absolute, and uncontrollable authority remains with the people." Americans were the first people to be given the "honor" of recognizing "this truth" in practice. "The great and penetrating mind of Locke" seemed to Wilson "the only one that pointed towards even the theory of this great truth." Although the supreme power "resides in the PEOPLE," they "can delegate it in such proportions, to such bodies, on such terms, and under such limitations as they think proper." By this logic, Wilson agreed with the Anti-Federalists that "there cannot be two sovereign powers on the same subject," merely different levels of delegation.[52] Wilson's fellow Federalist, the second-generation Pennsylvanian and war hero "Mad" Anthony Wayne, highlighted the multiple levels of delegation already in existence within each state. While taking notes on one of William Findley's speeches against federal taxation, Wayne wrote in the margin, "The State of Pennsylvania has the power of taxing, etc. yet the counties also exercise the right of laying and collecting taxes." Responding specifically to Findley's claim that "there cannot exist two sovereign powers to tax," Wayne drew a direct parallel between "county taxes and counties" within an individual state and "the 13 United States" within the federation.[53] Wayne wisely omitted mention of counties' dependence on state approval for their creation and dissolution.

Wilson revealed his sensitivity to the issue of ethnic and religious diversity in Pennsylvania through his approach to popular sovereignty and the role of "community" in the proposed federal government. "Community" is a broad term that can be defined in many ways, but in Pennsylvania community was fundamentally linked to the varying ethnic and religious origins of immigrant groups. As Paine pointed out in *Common Sense,* fewer than one-third of Pennsylvanians were of English ancestry. The French immigrant Hector St. John de Crèvecoeur's famous description of the German Lutheran and the Dutch Calvinist living and worshipping side by side noted the distinctions while denying the complications such diverse communities created.[54] Wilson recognized the diversity of interests within each state, born of community variation, and across state lines as well. He explained federation as a means of meeting heterogeneous needs. The Pennsylvania Federalist described "the people of the United States, as forming one great community," and "the people of the different states, as forming communities again on a lesser scale." The subdivision "of the people into distinct communities" justified the need to give their governments "different proportions of legislative powers . . . according to the nature, number, and magnitude of their objects."[55]

Wilson constructed a philosophy of American identity built in layers. Once national and state identity are understood as constituent parts of personal identity, community and ethnic-religious identity can be integrated within this same structure at a substate level. Wilson used the model of the solar system to describe the workings of the state and national governments. He believed that the line between state and national control was well drawn, and he envisioned state-federal interaction as like "the planetary system, where each part moves harmoniously within its proper sphere, and no injury arises by interference or opposition."[56] When read in concert with the broader statement that people may delegate aspects of their sovereignty to whatever political bodies they choose, Wilson's solar system model also accommodates local, ethnic, and religious moons rotating in their smaller spheres around state planets. This structure allows for multiple levels of cultural affiliation, from the local or ethnic, through the state or geographical, to the creation of a new nationalism.

Just as Jefferson locked Native and African Americans out of his definition of American community, so too did Wilson. The Virginian and the Pennsylvanian concurred that Indians fell outside the new federation. Wilson argued that Americans had a particular responsibility to follow God's command "to increase and multiply" because they formed a country, "the smaller part of whose territory is yet inhabited." Part of Wilson's proposed national character rested on Euro-Americans' role as "representatives . . . not merely of the present age, but of future times." This expansionist vision included the conquest of Indian lands, "not merely of the territory along the seacoast" but also "of regions immensely extended westward."

Wilson mixed his openness to European heterogeneity with a profound lack of respect for indigenous culture and land rights. An undefined "we," Wilson argued, "should fill, as fast as possible, this extensive country, with men who shall live happy, free, and secure." The "we," of course, was European, since there were already other men and women living "happy, free, and secure" in the country described. Wilson saw this expansionist goal as "the great end" and "leading view of all our patriots and statesmen." The Constitution and immigration remained the two prerequisites to this proto–Manifest Destiny. Americans, "by establishing peace and harmony among" themselves and "dignity and respectability among foreign nations," would "draw numbers from the other side of the Atlantic, in addition to the natural sources of population," and together rise to the challenge of settling a continent.[57]

Wilson's willingness to construct sovereignty as popularly delegated to different levels of government was not universal among Pennsylvanian Federalists. Benjamin Rush was more interested in Lockean thought regarding property and "pre-occupancy" as grounds for the existence of unwritten natural rights, as opposed to a written bill of rights. Rush disliked pluralism in either practical or theoretical form. The Pennsylvania-born delegate argued that a bill of rights would make sense only if "this government was immediately to be administered by foreigners, strangers to our habits and opinions and unconnected with our interests and prosperity." Beyond assuming that Americans already shared sufficient habits and opinions to make themselves incomprehensible to "foreigners and strangers"—a fact that his colleague Wilson denied when he urged that foreign immigration be encouraged—Rush insulted both Amerindians and Anti-Federalists by claiming that opposition arguments were "better calculated for an Indian council fire than the meridian of this refined and enlightened convention."[58]

Compared to Wilson, Rush was taciturn at the convention. His silence seems wise when we contrast Rush's few xenophobic comments with the friendlier message Wilson sent to a heterogeneous population. Wilson's consistent emphasis on the delegation of sovereign powers to different governments was a far more palatable version of the Anti-Federalist interpretation of the states as republican communities than Rush's image of a truly "consolidating" government. Pennsylvania's immigrants, including the many gathered at the convention, understood the nature of an individual identity as a Scot, an Ulsterman, and a Presbyterian—or as a Swabian, a Württemberger, and a Lutheran—with no one aspect of identity prohibiting the existence of the others.[59]

Rush's and Wilson's differences stand out when their positions are compared to John Locke's *Second Treatise of Government*. Rush focused on the devolution of rights from property, by which Rush clearly meant material property and land gained through occupation. Wilson focused instead on the nature of the social contract. The people "choose to indulge a part of their sovereign power to be exercised by the state governments." Should the people decide that the state no longer merited the sovereignty they had delegated to it, they would "resume it, or make a new distribution, more likely to be productive of that good which ought to be our constant aim." Wilson allowed each individual multiple contracts. "The power both of the general government, and the state governments, under this system, are acknowledged to be so many emanations of power from the people."[60]

Wilson used Locke's "strange Doctrine," which claimed "that in the State of Nature, every one has the Executive Power of the Law of Nature," as the basis for his plural delegation of sovereignty.[61] Men continue in the state of nature "till by their own Consents they make themselves Members of some Politick Society." The crux of the transformation from the state of nature to "Political, or Civil Society" is the resignation of individual executive power "to the publick," thus authorizing "the Society" and therefore "the Legislative thereof to make Laws for him as the publick good of the Society shall require."[62] This analysis justifies the individual's transfer of certain executive powers to the state society and other executive powers to a federal society. Such a transfer prohibits conflict between the two layers of government, because the individual has granted each a different set of executive powers.

The definition of "Community" Locke put forward in the *Second Treatise* helps to explain Wilson's intent. According to Locke, every individual must exercise "his own Consent" in order to be "subjected to the Political Power of another." An individual may accept "the bonds of Civil society," but only by an independent decision, "agreeing with other men to joyn and unite into a Community." The role of such a freely formed community is to guarantee to members "their comfortable, safe, and peaceable living one amongst another, in a secure Enjoyment of their Properties, and a greater Security against any that are not of it." Once "Men have so consented to make one Community," they constitute "one Body Politick, wherein the Majority have a Right to act and conclude the rest."[63]

To allay the Humean fear of faction, Wilson had found in Locke a contextualized individualism that pacified pluralism. Because the federation would constitute a different and larger community, with interests different from and larger than those of each state, the residents of any of the thirteen states could consent to participate in two separate "communities" or "bodies politic." For the preservation of state interests, a particular Pennsylvanian could consent to a civil society, or community, with other residents of Pennsylvania. For the preservation of federal interests, the same individual could consent to the formation of a community with all other Americans. Having established the concept of multiple contracts and communities, neither state nor federal civil societies would prevent an individual from consenting to additional local, ethnic, or religious communities that govern other interests.

Fellow Federalists in the Pennsylvania convention joined Wilson in struggling to balance Hume's factions and Locke's communities. Jasper Yeates shared Rush's fear of faction but supported Wilson's Lockean analysis of community. "The objects of state legislation," Yeates argued, "are different from those of the Federal Constitution." State laws "are confined to matters within ourselves." Federal laws "embrace the general interest of the United States and conduct them into one common channel to enrich and render happy the citizens of the whole community."[64] To use Lockean terminology, the "peaceable living" of each state requires consent and organization from a smaller group of individuals than the consent required for the "peaceable living" of all thirteen states. Those "not of" a particular state's community include people within the national community. The "peaceable living" of the federation demands that the governance of the two communities remain within their separate spheres, despite their overlapping membership.

The Pennsylvania Federalists proposed a national spirit for the future that could exist without the foundation of a common past. They offered a national identity born of a process of ongoing consent rather than of a body of tradition. Notoriously, this process of consent omitted large segments of the American population. James Tully argues convincingly that both Federalists and Anti-Federalists turned to John Locke's work on the origins of property as a means of divesting indigenous tribes of their historical lands and traditions.[65] Locke opened the door to individual development and political pluralism with his Enlightenment view of contractual government, but his Reformation sociology of men sent by God to "subdue the Earth" simultaneously slammed that door on women and non-Christians.[66]

Federalists also stewed over the issue of the African American slaves in their midst. In 1773 Benjamin Rush lambasted defenders of slavery and demanded that the nefarious institution be brought to an end in the "British Settlements in America," but he did not mean that enslaved men and women had the right to a political voice, although Rush was happy to educate "young Negroes" in reading, writing, and business, while inculcating "the principles of virtue and religion." Adults already possessed of "all the low vices of slavery," and those whose "age or infirmity" rendered them "unfit to be set at liberty," were to live out their lives as "the property of those . . . from whom they contracted those vices and infirmities."[67] African Americans' forcible removal to the New World was hardly compatible with Paine's image of refugees fleeing oppression. Their migration *was* oppression and therefore un-American. They arrived on American shores not in search of asylum but to confront a living hell.[68]

During the ratification debate in Philadelphia, the Federalists lauded the Constitution's ability to accept a type of pluralism already thriving in eighteenth-century Pennsylvania. The Federalists won the competition to place pluralism within peaceful government when they won the argument for ratification. They proposed an American identity derived from shared experience, a present and predicted future rather than a shared past, and they devised a multifaceted government for a multifaceted people. Their intellectual triumph was the creation of a political concept that Europeans thought an oxymoron: a virtuous federal republic. The Constitution was not only a republican remedy for a republican disease—it was a Pennsylvanian one.

NOTES

1. In the most reductionist terms, this is an extension of a philosophical debate about positive versus negative liberty, best articulated by Isaiah Berlin and now pursued by Charles Taylor and John Rawls, and a historical debate between Gordon Wood and Jack Greene.

2. In *The Myth of American Individualism: The Protestant Origins of American Political Thought* (Princeton: Princeton University Press, 1994), Barry Shain argues that the Anti-Federalists were not really "democratic" but communitarian and that they defined the community as both local and state. They regarded individuals who were against local and state communities as elitist. I argue here that Pennsylvania Anti-Federalists failed to acknowledge the existence of local and ethnic communities at odds within the state, thus finding themselves trapped in a contradictory argument.

3. Quoted in Merrill Jensen, ed., *The Documentary History of the Ratification of the Constitution*, vol. 2, *Ratification of the Constitution by the States: Pennsylvania* (Madison: State Historical Society of Wisconsin, 1976), 385. Hereafter cited parenthetically in the text.

4. Note that the eighteenth-century definition of "state" implied a nation-state such as France or Spain (although these too absorbed a variety of cultural subgroups).

5. James Wilson and William Findley seemed to be competing over who could cite Montesquieu and Locke more prolifically (compare Wilson's 11 citations to Findley's 6). Anti-Federalists John Smilie (1), Robert Whitehill (1), and Thomas McKean (2) dabbled in the game as well. Strikingly, the Swiss philosopher Emmerich de Vattel also came in for frequent citation. See Jensen, *Ratification of the Constitution: Pennsylvania,* 459, 465–66, 469, 492–93, 502–4, 543, 545, and 586. Vattel, like Montesquieu, with whom the Pennsylvanians tended to pair him, wrote on international law in his *Law of Nations* (1758). While his political philosophy was similar to that of the French Montesquieu, Vattel, being Swiss, built upon the work of the German philosophers Gottfried Leibniz, Christian von Wolff, and Samuel Pufendorf.

6. Montesquieu, *The Spirit of the Laws,* trans. and ed. Anne M. Cohler, Basia Carolyn Miller, and Harold Samuel Stone (Cambridge: Cambridge University Press, 1989; reprint, 1992), part 1, book 2, chap. 1, p. 10. Hereafter cited parenthetically in the text by part, book, chapter, and page numbers.

7. Thomas Paine, *Common Sense* (London: Penguin, 1988), 84–85.

8. A. J. Ayer, *Thomas Paine* (Chicago: University of Chicago Press, 1988), 51–52.

9. Jensen, *Ratification of the Constitution: Pennsylvania,* 503.

10. Ibid., 504, 446–47.

11. Ibid., 506, 504.

12. See David Hume, "Idea of a Perfect Commonwealth," in *Utopias of the British Enlightenment,* ed. Gregory Claeys (Cambridge: Cambridge University Press, 1994), 64–65. Hume's essay was first published in 1752 and is generally considered to have had a great influence on James Madison. See Stanley Elkins and Eric McKitrick, *The Age of Federalism* (Oxford: Oxford University Press, 1993), 86–87. Early American Imprints, series 1, Evans (1639–1800), microfilm, nos. 28867 and 30602, include various editions of Hume's *History of England, from the Invasion of Julius Caesar to the Revolution in MDCLXXXVIII,* but colonial intellectuals surely had access to Hume's essays via friends in Britain. For example, Alexander Hamilton cites Hume's *Essays* in Federalist No. 85, in Alexander Hamilton, James Madison, and John Jay, *The Federalist Papers,* ed. Clinton Rossiter (New York: Menton, 1999), 495.

13. Hume, "Idea of a Perfect Commonwealth," 59.

14. Ibid., 62.

15. Ibid., 59–60, 65.

16. Jensen, *Ratification of the Constitution: Pennsylvania,* 508, 511.

17. Douglas M. Arnold, *A Republican Revolution: Ideology and Politics in Pennsylvania, 1776–1790* (New York: Garland, 1989), 300–301; Owen S. Ireland, *Religion, Ethnicity, and Politics: Ratifying the Constitution in Pennsylvania* (University Park: Pennsylvania State University Press, 1995), 276.

18. "The Dissent of the Minority of the Convention," in Jensen, *Ratification of the Constitution: Pennsylvania,* 628–29.

19. See J. G. A. Pocock, *Virtue, Commerce, and History: Essays on Political Thought and History, Chiefly in the Eighteenth Century* (Cambridge: Cambridge University Press, 1985), 135–36.

20. Hume, "Idea of a Perfect Commonwealth," 64–65.

21. Edmund S. Morgan, "Safety in Numbers: Madison, Hume, and the Tenth Federalist," *Huntingdon Library Quarterly* 49 (Spring 1986): 110.

22. Edmund S. Morgan, *Inventing the People: The Rise of Popular Sovereignty in England and America* (New York: W. W. Norton, 1988), 263. Timothy Breen argues that Americans began to create their own identity in opposition to xenophobic English nationalism as early as the 1760s; see his "Ideology and Nationalism on the Eve of the American Revolution: Revisions Once More in Need of Revising," *Journal of American History* 84, no. 1 (1997): 13–39.

23. See Linda Colley's argument throughout her book *Britons: Forging the Nation, 1707–1837* (New Haven: Yale University Press, 1992), esp. 1–54.

24. Ireland, *Religion, Ethnicity, and Politics,* 39–40, 260; Richard A. Ryerson, "Republican Theory and Partisan Reality in Revolutionary Pennsylvania: Toward a New View of the Constitutionalist Party," in *Sovereign States in an Age of Uncertainty,* ed. Ronald Hoffman and Peter J. Albert (Charlottesville: University Press of Virginia, 1981), 120.

25. Jensen, *Ratification of the Constitution: Pennsylvania,* 502.

26. Bernard Bailyn, *The Peopling of British North America: An Introduction* (New York: Knopf, 1986), 91–111.

27. See ibid., esp. 112; and Bernard Bailyn, *Voyagers to the West: A Passage in the Peopling of America on the Eve of the Revolution* (New York: Knopf, 1986).

28. See Jack P. Greene, *Pursuits of Happiness: The Social Development of Early Modern British Colonies and the Formation of American Culture* (Chapel Hill: University of North Carolina Press, 1988); T. H. Breen, "'Baubles of Britain': The American and Consumer Revolutions of the Eighteenth Century," *Past and Present* 119 (1988): 73–104.

29. Jensen, *Ratification of the Constitution: Pennsylvania,* 409.

30. I am relying here on James Tully's analysis in *Strange Multiplicity: Constitutionalism in an Age of Diversity* (Cambridge: Cambridge University Press, 1995), 152–56.

31. For the similar demographics of western Pennsylvania and Virginia, see John B. Frantz, "The Religious Development of the Early German Settlers in 'Greater Pennsylvania': The Shenandoah Valley of Virginia," *Pennsylvania History* 68 (January 2001): 66–100.

32. Ari Helo and Peter S. Onuf, "Jefferson, Morality, and the Problem of Slavery," *William and Mary Quarterly* 60, no. 3 (2003): 583–614.

33. For the different political responses of Pennsylvanians and Virginians to their diverse populations, see Eric Hinderaker, *Elusive Empires: Constructing Colonialism in the Ohio Valley, 1673–1800* (Cambridge: Cambridge University Press, 1997); Woody Holton, *Forced Founders: Indians, Debtors, Slaves, and the Making of the American Revolution in Virginia* (Chapel Hill: University of North Carolina Press, 1999); and Owen S. Ireland, "The Invention of American Democracy: The Pennsylvania Federalists and the New Republic," *Pennsylvania History* 67 (Winter 2000): 161–71. Ireland argues that New Englanders' and Virginians' inability to grasp pluralist politics led to the tightening of immigration policy and intolerance toward foreigners that Marilyn C. Baseler finds at the turn of the century in *"Asylum for Mankind": America, 1607–1800* (Ithaca: Cornell University Press, 1998).

34. Jensen, *Ratification of the Constitution: Pennsylvania,* 351.

35. Ibid., 341–42. Stanley Elkins and Eric McKitrick have determined that the leading Federalists were younger than the Anti-Federalists and had developed continental reputations during the War of Independence, whereas the political influence of the leading Anti-Federalists was confined to their localities. See Elkins and McKitrick, "The Founding Fathers: Young Men of the Revolution," *Political Science Quarterly* 46, no. 2 (1961): 181–216, esp. 202–3.

36. Wilson paraphrased Montesquieu, "who says, I believe, that it [a federal republic] consists in assembling distinct societies, which are consolidated into a new body capable of being increased by the addition of other members; and expanding quality peculiarly fitted to the circumstances of America." Jensen, *Ratification of the Constitution: Pennsylvania,* 342–46.

37. Ibid., 347.

38. Wilson uses the adjective form "democratical" to describe the federal system. "In its principles, sir, it is purely democratical; varying indeed, in its form, in order to admit all the advantages and to exclude all the disadvantages which are incidental to the known and established constitutions of government. But when we take . . . view of the streams of power . . . however diversified and remote the blessings they diffuse, we shall be able to trace them all to one great and noble source, THE PEOPLE" (ibid., 349). Later he is even more explicit. He first declares, "I had occasion to describe what I mean by a democracy" (ibid., 493). He then says that the new federal government fits this definition, because "all authority of every kind *is derived by* REPRESENTATION *from the* PEOPLE, *and the* DEMOCRATIC *principle is carried into every part of the government.*" He says that "Montesquieu, book 2d, ch. 2d [1.11–18], speaking of laws relative to democracy, says 'when the body of the people is possessed of the SUPREME POWER, this is called a *democracy*'" (497).

39. Ibid., 406.

40. David Hume, *Political Essays,* ed. Knud Haakonssen (Cambridge: Cambridge University Press, 1994), no. 7, "Of Parties in General," 33–36.

41. Ibid., 37–39.

42. Jensen, *Ratification of the Constitution: Pennsylvania,* 380.

43. Hume, "Idea of a Perfect Commonwealth," 64.

44. Hamilton, Madison, and Jay, *Federalist Papers;* U.S. Constitution, art. 1, sec. 2.

45. Madison, *The Federalist* No. 14, *Federalist Papers,* 67.

46. Jensen, *Ratification of the Constitution: Pennsylvania,* 543. See also Edmund S. Morgan's examination of the ways in which Madison turn's Hume on his head in "Safety in Numbers," 110.

47. Madison, *The Federalist* No. 14, *Federalist Papers,* 71–72.

48. Jensen, *Ratification of the Constitution: Pennsylvania,* 582.

49. Compare Wilson's language (ibid.) to Benedict Anderson's definition of nation in *Imagined Communities: Reflections on the Origin and Spread of Nationalism* (London: Verso, 1995), 5–7.

50. Jensen, *Ratification of the Constitution: Pennsylvania,* 582.

51. Again, see Elkins and McKitrick's analysis of Wilson's and Madison's arrival on the Continental stage during the Revolution.

52. Jensen, *Ratification of the Constitution: Pennsylvania,* 471–72.

53. Ibid., 446–47, 733.

54. Paine, *Common Sense,* 85; J. Hector St. John de Crèvecoeur, *Letters from an American Farmer* (New York: Penguin Books, 1986), 74–75.

55. Jensen, *Ratification of the Constitution: Pennsylvania,* 472.

56. Ibid., 496.

57. Ibid., 477.

58. Ibid., 433–34.

59. For an excellent history of the Ulstermen in Pennsylvania, see Patrick Griffin's *People with No Name: Ireland's Ulster Scots, America's Scots Irish, and the Creation of a British Atlantic World, 1689–1764* (Princeton: Princeton University Press, 2001). The different cultural outlooks of German Lutheran pietists from Prussia versus those from Württemberg pervade Roeber's study of German immigrants. See A. G. Roeber, *Palatines, Liberty, and Property: German Lutherans in Colonial British America* (Baltimore: Johns Hopkins University Press, 1993), esp. 27–94, 243–82.

60. Jensen, *Ratification of the Constitution: Pennsylvania,* 559.

61. Locke writes, "I doubt not but this will seem a very strange doctrine to some men." John Locke, *Two Treatises of Government,* ed. Peter Laslett (Cambridge: Cambridge University Press, 1960; reprint, 1989), book 2, chap. 2, par. 9.

62. Ibid., chap. 2, par. 15; chap. 7, par. 89.

63. Ibid., chap. 8, par. 95.

64. Jensen, *Ratification of the Constitution: Pennsylvania,* 435.

65. See James Tully, "Placing the Two Treatises," in *Political Discourse in Early Modern Britain,* ed. Nicholas Phillipson and Quentin Skinner (Cambridge: Cambridge University Press, 1993), 253–80.

66. Locke, *Two Treatises of Government,* book 2, chap. 5, par. 32.

67. Benjamin Rush, "An Address to the Inhabitants of the British Settlements in American upon Slave-Keeping" (Philadelphia, 1773), reprinted in *The Making of the Modern World,* ed. Thomson Gale (2007), available at http://www.galeuk.com/trials/mome/.

68. Paine, *Common Sense,* 84–85.

13

THE DECLINE OF THE CHEERFUL TAXPAYER:
TAXATION IN PENNSYLVANIA, C. 1776–1815

Anthony M. Joseph

Pennsylvanians of the early Republic paid few taxes. At first glance this fact seems unremarkable. Many Pennsylvanians not only opposed parliamentary taxation in the years leading up to the Revolutionary War but also blocked the efforts of their own state government to collect taxes in the 1780s. Later, back-country farmers in western Pennsylvania launched the Whiskey Rebellion (1794), and disaffected German Americans in the east participated in Fries's Rebellion (1799). Both rebellions directly challenged the federal government's power to tax. And what open tax resistance could not achieve in the minds of Pennsylvania's political leaders, the anti-statist beliefs of voters presumably could. First radical "Constitutionalists," then Anti-Federalists, and finally Jeffersonian Republicans gave voice to such beliefs among Pennsylvania's farmers and mechanics, many of whom looked warily upon a government apparatus that appeared to them all too prone to domination by a mercantile elite. By 1800, indeed, the Jeffersonians were well on their way to controlling the state government and fulfilling by peaceful means goals similar to those that had animated the tax resisters all along.

Unquestionably, tax resistance in Pennsylvania tapped into reserves of social discontent and ideological hostility to taxation that ultimately influenced state tax policy. But this essay suggests a broader ideological, fiscal, and political context in which to view the tax resistance. It does not seek to explain away that resistance but rather to give due weight to the evidence for tax compliance in Pennsylvania and to see both resistance and compliance as part of a single intelligible whole. Pennsylvania's movement away from taxation was not the result of a pervasive popular contempt for taxation. Most Pennsylvanians throughout the period were ideologically primed to pay taxes. They acknowledged the ideal of the "cheerful taxpayer" who willingly submitted to taxation as a mark of civic allegiance. Most, too, actually paid the taxes levied upon them, and in unprecedented amounts during the Revolutionary War. Nor was the largely tax-free state the result of a desire among Pennsylvania's political leaders to pacify its most aggressive tax resisters. Pennsylvania's policy was substantially in place before the outbreak of the rebellions of the 1790s. Revolutionary-era Pennsylvanians were pushed along a rapid current of war, nation building, and fiscal innovation that finally left them gently rowing toward a tax-free shore. They had entered the period as cheerful taxpayers. They ended the period as hardly taxpayers at all.

Perhaps the most difficult part of this account to accept is the notion that the ideal of the cheerful taxpayer had ever had any prominence at all in America. Historians have focused so much on tax resistance in the revolutionary era that they have paid relatively little attention to tax compliance and its accompanying ideological supports. Yet the ideal of the cheerful taxpayer expressed a basic American posture toward taxation in the eighteenth century. The cheerful taxpayer was an early modern ideal: a subject or citizen who paid taxes willingly, promptly, and completely. Appearing in eighteenth-century European sources such as Montesquieu and Thomas Gordon (of *Cato's Letters*), the ideal traveled effortlessly across the Atlantic.[1] Americans employed it in a variety of circumstances. During the Seven Years' War, the Pennsylvania Assembly "cheerfully and voluntarily" granted the king £100,000 in funds.[2] In the 1770s, when the colonies' quarrel with parliamentary taxation was at its rhetorical height, the Continental Congress used the ideal to express America's willingness to pay taxes that met the key constitutional requirement of representative consent. In its address to the people of Great Britain, in its memorial to the inhabitants of the colonies, and in its petition to the king, the Congress claimed that the colonies had cheerfully contributed their share of taxes during the Seven Years' War and stood ready to do so again.[3] Later, when Congress began to make tax requisitions on the states, its delegates expressed their hope and expectation that the people would pay "with a cheerful heart."[4]

The ideal of the cheerful taxpayer suffered no diminution in rhetorical force with the coming of republican government in 1776, for in a republican context the ideal could take on deeply consensual and even self-interested tones. The influential French philosopher Montesquieu asserted that taxes were generally heavier in republican governments than in despotic ones "because the citizen, who thinks he is paying himself, cheerfully submits to them."[5] Thus even during the young American Republic's fiscally dark days of 1783, when the Continental Congress debated the levying of an impost tax, Pennsylvanian James Wilson attributed shortcomings in the "cheerful payment of taxes" to structural defects in federal finance, not the people themselves.[6] Later, western Pennsylvanians petitioning Congress against the federal excise tax on stills and spirits insisted that they had paid previous taxes "punctually and cheerfully." And in 1802, petitioners from Chester County, Pennsylvania, implored the state legislature to tax rather than take on new debt, pledging "cheerfully to meet the just and necessary expences of Government."[7]

Granted, Americans often spoke of cheerful tax paying in the middle of objecting to a particular tax. But the ideal of the cheerful taxpayer never implied soft acquiescence in taxation. The cheerful taxpayer was an informed taxpayer, freely consenting to the tax and intelligently acknowledging its necessity; he was not a cheerful *pushover*. Close consideration of the fiscal and political circumstances of a tax, of its equity, of the mechanism of collection—such concerns were entirely consistent with the ideal and could shape its meaning and implications in any particular circumstance. The government was obligated to structure its tax regime so as to ensure that citizens could pay the taxes cheerfully. Thus employed, the ideal suggests that Americans considered a basic willingness to pay taxes the discursive point of departure in any debate over the justness or necessity of a particular tax. The ideal of the cheerful taxpayer constituted an important part of the ideology of taxation in late colonial America, and with this ideological heritage Pennsylvanians entered and endured the Revolutionary War.

But Pennsylvania's heritage was fiscal as well as ideological. By 1776 Pennsylvanians had been paying provincial property taxes for some twenty years. At the outbreak of the Seven Years' War, the Pennsylvania Assembly began to print paper money to fund the Anglo-American war effort. To ensure that this fiat currency did not produce inflation, the Assembly provided for the retirement of the money through taxation. In 1755 the Assembly emitted £55,000 in bills of credit, to be retired through an annual tax on real and personal property at the rate of sixpence per pound value and a poll tax of ten shillings on single freemen. The Crown soon had need of additional funds, and so in 1757 and 1758 the Assembly authorized the printing of an additional £200,000 and increased the tax rates to eighteen pence per pound on property and twenty shillings on freemen. From 1755 to 1775 the Assembly enacted five emissions of paper money backed by the property tax.[8] The province also collected excise taxes, imposts, and fees for marriage and tavern licenses, but for the remainder of the colonial period the "eighteen-penny tax" was Pennsylvania's most substantial levy on the people.

Pennsylvanians were far from quiescent about the charge. They complained about inequities in valuations and assessments. The Assembly pressed the Penn family to accept taxation of its vast landholdings; after an eight-year dispute, Thomas Penn finally gave up the claim to exemption.[9] Taxpayers in eastern counties argued that the government overcharged them in comparison to the western counties. Taxpayers in western counties sometimes claimed that they were Virginians. Even so, Pennsylvanians paid the tax quite regularly. Annual revenues from the eighteen-penny tax ranged from roughly £18,000 to

£28,000.[10] Counties typically fell in arrears on each annual levy but made up the arrearages within a year or two, as payments passed first from taxpayers to local collectors, then from the collectors to county treasurers, and finally to the provincial treasurer. Records of annual arrearages are misleading unless read in light of this process. The eighteen-penny tax for 1772, for example, remained 34 percent unpaid in September of that year, but by September 1773 only 3 percent was still outstanding. In any given year, few counties were in arrears for taxes beyond the previous year's levy. Altogether, Pennsylvania's counties by September 1775 owed only some £2,000 on all the property taxes levied since 1758.[11] By contemporary British standards, of course, Pennsylvania's tax system was small and rudimentary; the eighteen-penny tax amounted to only 7.5 percent of assessed value. Nonetheless, Pennsylvania's tax system was operating without fundamental opposition during the twenty years preceding the Revolutionary War. The regularity of tax collection provided a strong cultural and political precedent for a taxpaying citizenry once the Revolutionary War began.

It is not surprising, then, that the Pennsylvania Assembly responded to the fiscal imperatives of the Revolutionary War according to the practice of the last decades of the colonial period. Even before independence, the Assembly approved four emissions of paper money totaling £222,000.[12] The contrasts were great between this Assembly, slow to support independence, and the radical Assemblies that immediately followed under the commonwealth.[13] Yet with respect to war finance, the radicals proved to be traditionalists. They busily passed state paper emissions with accompanying taxes to fund the state's war effort, and enacted additional taxes to retire the paper money emitted by the Continental Congress. In March 1777, for example, the Assembly approved a £200,000 emission, to be retired by a new eighteen-penny tax on property and a ten-shilling tax on single freemen. The manner of collection was to follow that of the paper emission law of 1764, which itself referred to the emission law of 1755. In October 1777 the pressure of inflation induced the Assembly to raise the tax rates to five shillings on property and thirty shillings on single freemen. This tax was renewed the following year.[14] Between March 1778 and March 1783 the Assembly enacted an additional £367,281 in state paper taxes. To retire Congress's money, meanwhile, the Assembly levied roughly $56 million in Continental money during the same period.[15]

Much remains to be learned regarding public response to these taxes during the war. Certainly the state's Quaker and German pacifists protested militia fines as well as the additional property taxes charged upon "nonassociators," while supporters of the war effort pressed the Assembly to preserve or even toughen these penalties. And Indian raids and the British army made tax collection in many counties, including eastern ones, difficult or virtually impossible.[16] The dislocations of war had only a modest impact on the collection of taxes owed in ever-depreciating Continental currency; some 85 percent of those levies were paid by August 1784. The impact on collection of state money taxes was more visible, as only 62 percent of these had been deposited with the state by the same date. Cumberland, Bedford, Northumberland, and Westmoreland counties contributed very little of their quotas. The eastern counties paid substantially more but fell short of their colonial rates.[17] In the crucible of war, the relatively stable colonial system of public finance based on paper money and property taxes had foundered.

Tax paying in Pennsylvania was even more profoundly shaken by the introduction in 1781 of taxation in coin, or specie. By this time, the Continental Congress was in earnest need of specie, particularly to make payments on its foreign loans. In response to a congressional requisition, the Assembly passed the first of three "specific supplies" acts, levying a £200,000 tax. In the following year, the second supplies act levied a further £420,297. The third and final act, of 1783, charged another £225,000.[18] The passage of these extraordinary measures has been attributed to the nationalist majority in the Assembly, a faction then known as "Republicans." The strongest opposition to specie taxation, meanwhile, undoubtedly came from their opponents, the defenders of local autonomy called "Constitutionalists" for their support of Pennsylvania's radical constitution of 1776.[19] Both factions, however, took seriously the Continental government's need for specie, and the closest students of the assemblies of these years have found that other issues were more controversial.[20] Indeed, although disagreement arose during the consideration of each supply bill, all three finally passed without a roll call vote. Tightly contested measures could sometimes pass the Assembly without being put to such a test, but in all likelihood neither faction would have declined to put these bills to final roll call votes if it had opposed them in their final form.

A brief glance at each measure will confirm the point. The supply bill of 1781 permitted persons who had professed allegiance to the state and fulfilled their militia duty to pay half their tax in state paper money. Some twenty-one assemblymen, a majority of them identifiably Republican,[21] objected to this concession. They pointed out that the clause was inconsistent with another in the bill that allowed *all* taxpayers to pay half their taxes in wheat or flour. Furthermore, the provision was "totally repugnant" to the supply bill's purpose, "frequently mentioned in debate," of raising specie for Congress. With both the wheat/flour clause and the paper payment clause in effect, many Pennsylvanians would be able to pay half their tax in paper and half in produce—avoiding specie payment altogether. The wheat/flour clause was subsequently stricken, leaving in place the provision for half-payment in paper. In the end, the mix of paper and specie payment proved acceptable to both factions, and neither insisted on a roll call vote on final passage.[22] A year later, the supply bill of 1782 called for payment of the congressional requisition entirely in specie. Constitutionalists preferred to furnish only half the amount by means of a specie tax collected in two quarterly payments, with the remainder to be raised within the year "by such other means as may be in the power of the House." Republicans, by contrast, wanted to supply the full amount by an immediate tax payable quarterly throughout the year. Speaker Frederick A. Muhlenberg, a Republican, broke the tie in favor of full payment. Subsequently the apportionment of the tax among the counties was controversial, but in the end this supply bill also passed without a roll call vote.[23] Finally, the supply act of 1783 repeated the feature of half-payment in paper found in the 1781 law, this time extending the privilege to all citizens. Republicans did not bother to bring the provision up for a roll call vote. How to apportion the tax among the counties was the touchiest question addressed before the Assembly finally passed the measure without a roll call vote.[24]

Enacting the levies, of course, was not the same as collecting them. After half a decade during which the state had been awash in paper currency, both state and federal, the taxes of 1781–83 now demanded coin that could not easily be squeezed out of the specie-poor Pennsylvania countryside. What followed was perhaps the most pervasive tax resistance Pennsylvania has ever seen. Taxpayers forcibly opposed the assessment of their property or distraint for nonpayment. Tax assessors quietly neglected to submit returns and collectors declined to file suit against delinquents. Where suits and foreclosures did occur, communities arranged not to bid at auction, or sheriff's sales went without bidders on account of the same shortage of money that had led to the sales to begin with. When sales did occur, goods typically went for only a fraction of their value.[25] By 1784, the state's tax collection system had virtually collapsed. In April, state treasurer David Rittenhouse reported "almost a total stop in the Collecting of Taxes." By August, some 64 percent of the levies of 1781–83 were still in arrears. Only Bucks, Chester, and the city and county of Philadelphia had paid even half of their assessed amounts. In five of six central and western counties, at least 95 percent of the county quotas remained outstanding.[26]

It is tempting to interpret the resistance of 1781–84 as part of a continuous tradition in Pennsylvania of radical agrarian protest against dominance by political elites.[27] That view, however, overstates the degree of class antagonism behind the resistance. Tax resisters did appeal to long-standing ideological traditions and made use of widely recognized means of avoiding payment. But the resistance of taxpayers and the acquiescence of local officials were too pervasive and open to be attributable to a distinct model of agrarian protest against elite control. Many local officials quickly realized that specie taxation was an unworkable system given the shortage of specie. They were not so much part of a radical anti-elitist/ anti-statist tradition as lukewarm or disaffected agents of a bad policy.

Even if we reduce the elite to the Assembly in Philadelphia, the conflict fails to materialize into a full-blown battle of classes. The 1780s were a period of enormous expansion in popular access to the Assembly. Representation doubled, and the number of petitions submitted to the Assembly skyrocketed to five times the colonial level. In this setting, the fragile revolutionary regime proved responsive to the crisis it had created. In March 1785, the Constitutionalists, who had regained control of the Assembly in the annual elections of the preceding October, put an end to the experiment in specie taxation. They provided for the emission of £150,000 in new paper money and enacted an annual "funding" tax on real and personal property, payable in the new paper money or specie. They also made all back taxes, including the specie taxes, payable in paper and required collectors to obtain a special warrant from a justice of the peace before seizing the goods of delinquents.[28]

The new policy, however, was not a complete abandonment of the hard money approach that had been so starkly expressed in specie taxation. Pennsylvanians did not return to the soft money years of the war, when the Continental Congress and the Pennsylvania Assembly flooded the state with paper currency. At £150,000, the emission of 1785 could not be expected to easily cover the funding tax, which amounted to nearly £77,000 annually. This was especially the case given that two-thirds of the new emission, or £100,000, went directly into the hands of the state's public creditors as interest payments; only the remaining £50,000 would be available for broader immediate distribution in the form of loans by a new state loan office. The statute appropriately spoke of the emission as a "moderate sum."[29]

Even so, the paper money policy of 1785 ended the state specie crisis.[30] When Republicans regained control of the Assembly in October 1786, many of them considered specie taxes no longer necessary or politically unfeasible, and so the controversial levies were never renewed. In the Assembly session of 1786–87, the most vigorous criticism of the funding tax came from nonresident landholders in Bedford, Northumberland, and Westmoreland counties, who complained of unfair assessments. The only serious calls of distress came from Wyoming Township, in Northumberland County, and from sixty-six inhabitants of Dauphin County, who asked for a "short period of years" to pay their taxes on account of hardship caused by the flooding of the Susquehanna River.[31]

Despite the political retreat from specie taxation and the low collection rate on the taxes of 1781–83, revolutionary Pennsylvania was far from a tax-resistant republic. On the contrary, its political elites had demonstrated a striking willingness to levy taxes, so much so that a forceful modern argument for a tax-resistant popular culture in the state must view those elites as fundamentally alienated from their constituencies.[32] Both political factions supported specie taxation in some amount and mode during 1781–83. Their policy proved harsh, and clearly they overestimated the tax burden their constituents were able and willing to bear. Even so, over the course of the revolutionary era the Pennsylvania citizenry demonstrated a willingness to pay taxes that approached the intentions of the legislators. By August 1784 Pennsylvanians had contributed £269,058 ($718,385) in specie since 1781. Although only some 43 percent of the total amount of specie requested, this was an unprecedented contribution from a population accustomed to supplying less than £30,000 annually—and that in paper money—during the last years of the colonial era. From a civic point of view, the revenues were embarrassingly concentrated in the southeastern counties, particularly Philadelphia, Bucks, and Chester.[33] But given the chronic shortage of specie in the Pennsylvania countryside, the low collection rate is not a reliable indicator of basic dispositions regarding taxation.

Indeed, ultimately the rate of collection was substantially higher. Even in periods of monetary stability, eighteenth-century tax collection was a machine of multiple slow-moving cogs. Thus 1784 is too early a cut-off date for assessing the efficiency of a tax levied in 1783, or even 1781. Throughout the 1780s county treasurers deposited with the state treasurer sizable sums owed on the taxes of 1781–83. By November 1787 some 62 percent had been paid in; by 1792, the collection rate had risen to 88 percent.[34] Collection on the annual funding tax introduced in 1785 was quicker. The funding tax for 1785 was 87 percent paid within three years of its first coming due (see table 1). The taxes for 1786 and 1787 were collected at comparable rates.[35] The funding tax continued to be levied through 1789, and by the end of 1792 roughly 85 percent of the entire amount, £384,729, had been paid in.

This is not to say that tax resistance ceased entirely after 1784. In York, Cumberland, Bedford, Northumberland, and Westmoreland counties, representing one-quarter of the state's taxable inhabitants and 18 percent of the total funding tax due annually, collection rates on the funding tax of 1785 remained below 50 percent through 1788 (see table 1). The list of low-paying counties is similar for the funding tax of 1786. In these jurisdictions, the testimony of the state fiscal records correlates with the stories of officials' nonenforcement, no-bid covenants at auctions, and physical resistance to the taxes. The correlation applies especially well in the case of Westmoreland County, where countless foreclosures and hundreds of bidderless auctions help contextualize and explain the county's low collection rate. But for other counties, anecdotal evidence can be misleading. In December 1786 tax officials in Chester County reported to the Supreme Executive Council that the shortage of money made it impossible for them to send any more tax payments. Yet Chester County's funding tax for 1785 was 99 percent paid by that point, and its tax for 1786 would be 87 percent paid within a year. In Northampton County, the future scene of Fries's Rebellion, a tax official reported in February 1786 that he was having great difficulty securing witnesses against delinquent taxpayers; yet by the end of the year the county had paid 84 percent of its 1785 tax. For at least part of 1787, no prosecutions against delinquent taxpayers were conducted in the county, yet by the end of that year some 68 percent of its 1786 tax had been paid in, and by end of 1788 the proportion had risen to 99 percent. In Dauphin County, officials refused to sue delinquents who were unable to pay, and farmers refused to bid on foreclosed property, yet by the end of 1788 the county had paid its first two funding taxes in full.[36] The generally high collection rates on the funding tax suggest that the road closings in various Pennsylvania counties during the late 1780s and early 1790s were not typically motivated by opposition to state taxes.[37]

Payments into the state treasury, of course, are far from indisputable evidence of cheerful tax paying. But bidderless auctions and officials' reluctance to sue delinquents cast doubt on the notion that high collection rates owed much to the coercive mechanism of foreclosures. Indeed, despite *all* the coercive mechanisms of the law, there was simply no way to achieve high collection rates without liberal quantities of genuine consent lubricating the entire system. The crisis years of the early 1780s show easily enough what happens when the people charged with employing those mechanisms refuse to employ them. Pennsylva-

Table 1   County Receipts on the Funding Tax of 1785 (£)

County	1785	1786	1787	1788	Total Paid	Tax Quota	Total Paid (%)
EASTERN COUNTIES							
Philadelphia	1,112	18,380	0	0	19,492	19,492	100
Bucks	2,059	1,907	219	0	4,185	5,042	83
Chester	0	7,694	351	0	8,045	8,094	99
Montgomery	0	5,221	632	115	5,968	6,000	99
Lancaster	0	8,864	*	*	8,864	8,194	108
Berks	0	5,105	299	51	5,455	5,510	99
Northampton	0	2,662	269	37	2,968	3,172	94
CENTRAL AND WESTERN COUNTIES							
York	0	0	1,000	550	1,550	6,103	25
Cumberland	0	0	755	312	1,067	3,384	32
Bedford	0	314	400	0	714	1,739	41
Northumberland	0	327	234	159	720	2,148	34
Westmoreland	0	232	0	13	245	700	35
Washington	0	1,178	300	0	1,478	1,479	100
Dauphin	0	1,723	1,867	0	3,590	2,759	130
Fayette	0	779	0	0	779	779	100
Franklin	0	749	740	100	1,589	2,353	68
TOTAL	3,171	55,135	7,066	1,337	66,709	76,948	87

* Lancaster's deposits in 1787 and 1788, totaling £11,152, were mistakenly credited toward its quota on the tax of 1785, and so have been omitted here.

Source: See note 35.

nia's consent to taxation was neither unanimous nor unequivocal, but it was of such a kind and degree that most taxes were paid. This consent appears to have been characteristic of most Pennsylvania counties, including the most populous ones, after 1784. And when all factors are considered—the dislocations of war, the vicissitudes of state and federal public finance, the lack of specie— revolutionary Pennsylvanians hardly appear to have been inveterate tax avoiders. They paid vastly more in taxes after independence than before and came as close to the ideal of the cheerful taxpayer as their economic circumstances and the state's sometimes overly demanding fiscal policy allowed.

Were Pennsylvanians any different with respect to federal taxation? We feel almost inexorably drawn to the conclusion that they must have been. To the Whiskey Rebellion and Fries's Rebellion, two obvious departures from cheerful tax paying, we can add the Anti-Federalist/Jeffersonian tradition and the even more radical political variations that inspired the rebellions. Yet, as with state taxation, the story is not as straightforward as it first appears.

The abundant scholarship on the Whiskey Rebellion demonstrates that the backcountry farmers who opposed the federal excise tax on distilled spirits artic- ulated their grievances from within the Anglo-American opposition tradition that had fueled the Revolution. In that tradition excise taxes were the most odious form of taxation because they required exceptionally intrusive methods of assessment and collection. The backcountry farmers also complained of the shortage of money in the west.[38] Beyond these grievances, however, the Whiskey Rebellion exposed Pennsylvanians' concern not for mere tax avoidance but for tax *equity*. Opponents of the excises made positive statements about other forms of federal taxation and even proposed a direct tax on land to make the federal tax system more equitable. This part of the story deserves close attention, as the regard for tax equity imposed an important limit on anti-tax sentiment in eighteenth-century Pennsylvania.

In 1791 Congress introduced an excise tax on the domestic manufacture of distilled spirits. Three years later came a string of additional excises—on refined sugar, manufactured tobacco and snuff, carriages, wines and foreign spirits sold at retail, and sales at auction.[39] Excise taxes by their very nature raised questions of distributive equity. Conceivably, almost anything made, used, or consumed in the United States could be subject to an excise. But short of a complete system, what justified the imposition of taxes on some items but not others? In Congress, advocates of the excise relied on the argument that the costs of excises were ultimately passed on to the consumer. Indeed, one congressman asserted that any tax, if made permanent, would "soon be equal," as its costs were quietly distributed throughout the community. The only difference between an excise and a direct tax was that the former distributed the burden over time while the latter did so immediately. Why not then impose a direct tax? In 1794, while the additional excises were under consideration, a resolution for a $750,000 direct tax on land was also on the table. But after a brief debate Congress shied away from it as a tax of last resort best reserved for times of war.[40]

Objections to the excise taxes arose soon after they were enacted. In the case of the tax on distilled spirits, the so-called "whiskey excise," the lack of distributive equity seemed especially acute. Payment was to be made according to gallons produced, not gallons sold; thus spirits consumed by the producer would be taxed without benefit of passing on the cost. The excise also burdened western farmers who converted their grain to alcohol rather than undertake the expensive work of transporting it to eastern markets for sale. The distributive inequity of the whiskey excise was an important factor in the resistance to the tax in western Pennsylvania in 1794. Western Pennsylvanians who petitioned Congress against the excise insisted that in the past they had paid taxes "punctually and cheerfully . . . because they were proportioned to our real wealth." They even left open the possibility of an amendment to the tax as an alternative to outright repeal. The text of the petition, attributed to Albert Gallatin, undoubtedly did not represent the most radical wing of the resistance, which advocated open disobedience of the law. But the petition gives us a better idea than sheer violence alone of the ideology of taxation in Pennsylvania during the early Republic.[41]

In the mid-1790s, in fact, Jeffersonians would take the lead in proposing direct taxation as a more equitable alternative to the excises. To historians accustomed to viewing the Jeffersonians as opponents of taxation, the debate of 1796–97 on a proposed permanent annual direct tax on land and slaves, amounting to $1,484,000, must appear shocking, for Jeffersonians were among the strongest advocates of the measure.[42] In several respects, the Republican case for a direct tax was all cool fiscal reasonableness. At a time when the federal treasury seemed in immediate need of additional revenue, Republicans argued that increasing customs duties would only encourage smuggling, that the disruptions to America's foreign commerce made diversifying the tax base an urgent necessity, and that excise taxes cost too much to collect, making them "unproductive." Inserted among these purely fiscal considerations, however, was the belief that distributive equity demanded a direct tax. Pennsylvania Jeffersonians were among the most prominent advocates of this view. According to Albert Gallatin, direct as well as indirect taxes ought to be laid "in order that property of every kind might contribute its due proportion." William Findley, who represented Pennsylvania counties involved in the Whiskey Rebellion, asserted that a direct tax was necessary "to equalize the taxes." John Swanwick, a Philadelphia representative who had won election to Congress as an opponent of excise taxation, now not only pointed out "how unproductive it had been" but also insisted that landed property should "no longer escape from paying its due proportion towards the public burdens." Indeed, Swanwick believed that "it would have been better for this country if [a direct tax] had been adopted sooner."[43] Amazingly, the Jeffersonians in the House carried the day when the direct tax resolution passed, 49–39. Overall, Republicans supported the tax, 26–18. The Pennsylvania delegation voted in favor, 8–2, with each party voting 4–1 in support. The heart of the resistance came from Federalists, who were about evenly split, 23–21, and in particular from the Federalists of New England, who complained that the apportionment of the states' quotas according to the population figures of the 1790 census would leave their states overtaxed.[44]

The measure languished in 1797, as federal revenues for 1796 proved greater than expected, but that development should not obscure the fact that Republicans had argued and voted for the tax and Pennsylvania congressmen of both parties had firmly supported it. Oliver Wolcott, then secretary of the treasury, would later theorize that the Republicans' direct tax proposal was merely a political ruse to draw the majority Federalists into passing a measure that would be deeply unpopular with their constituencies around the nation. But neither the record of congressional debate nor the roll call vote substantiates Wolcott's view. Federalists, whom one would expect to be sufficiently keen to detect such a ploy, did not accuse the Republicans of such a stratagem, and half of them voted in favor of the measure. Wolcott, it appears, had an ideological tin ear when it came to Republicans and taxation. We should take care to hear them better than he did. Both the Jeffersonians' argument and their votes leave little doubt of their authentic political and ideological investment in direct taxation during this period. They would not go so far as to promote a direct tax in the absence of a clear fiscal need—hence the demise of the measure—but their concern for tax equity did propel them to support additional taxation. And in Pennsylvania, Federalists as well as Republicans were clearly cut from this same ideological cloth.

By 1798 relations with France had deteriorated, and House Federalists, insisting on war, now unanimously supported a one-year direct tax on houses, slaves, and land; Republicans were about evenly divided on the measure. The Pennsylvania delegation was representative of both these trends, with the state's Federalists voting 4–0 and its Republicans 3–3.[45] Predictably, Albert Gallatin was accused of inconsistency for opposing the 1798 measure after supporting a direct tax in 1796. Gallatin explained, plainly enough, that additional revenues were needed two years earlier, but not now. For Gallatin the Federalist argument in favor of the tax—"invasion, the fate of Venice, divisions at home, weakness, &c."—would apply to "everything and nothing."[46]

His doubts were representative of Republican skepticism. Hence the direct tax of 1798, wrapped up in the packaging of a war with France, an expansive military program, and the Alien and Sedition Acts, became as closely attached to the Federalist Party as those other policies and statutes were. Already criticized for the excises, the Federalists were now more decisively branded as the party of oppressive taxation. No one who knew the legislative history of 1796 and 1797 could reasonably accept that portrait. Against the Federalists' one-year tax of 1798, levied in war, was the *permanent* tax, to be levied in peacetime, supported by a majority of House Republicans eighteen months before. But the political value of the portrait was too great to pass up. Jefferson himself, as vice president, had recognized the need for a direct tax and even proposed one. But once the direct tax of 1798 passed, he relished the prospect that it would excite "the public mind" against the whole Federalist program of that year. The Jeffersonians won in 1800 partly because the tax did just that.[47] Nonetheless, the whole episode demonstrates that Pennsylvania congressmen, and particularly the Republicans, were capable of supporting federal direct taxation in the 1790s.

Republican constituencies are not known to have advocated direct taxation with the same fervor as their congressmen, but their protests of the direct tax of 1798 were just as politically contextualized and were far from being bare expressions of hostility to taxation. Petitions to Congress appear to have focused more on the Alien and Sedition Acts than on the direct tax; congressional debate certainly reflected that emphasis.[48] Fries's Rebellion, which broke out in early 1799, reflected how deeply the resistance to the tax was embedded in the broader political configuration of Northampton, Bucks, and Montgomery counties in southeastern Pennsylvania. Certainly the German American "Kirchenleute" at the heart of the rebellion believed the tax was inequitable and unconstitutional—of a piece with the parliamentary taxes that had justified the American Revolution. But they also had just secured the election of a Republican to Congress and chafed at the prospect of seeing their property valued by Federalist assessors, one English and the other Moravian. Insult was added to injury when twenty resisters were arrested and scheduled for trial fifty miles away in Philadelphia. The central act of rebellion became Fries's forcible release of the resisters after the federal marshal repeatedly refused to accept his offer to post bail for them.[49] Ultimately, we cannot view the rebellion through the relatively narrow lens of the resisters' ideology of taxation. That Fries himself had marched westward against the whiskey rebels five years earlier should discourage us from doing so.

But even if viewed solely as a tax revolt, Fries's Rebellion was too localized to be taken as representative of Pennsylvanians' attitudes toward the direct tax of 1798 or taxation generally. Indeed, most Pennsylvanians paid the direct tax without violent protest. At the end of 1799, Oliver Wolcott stated privately that the tax had received "as little opposition as I expected"[50]—he got this right, at least—and in 1800, the first full year of collection, more than $700,000 in revenues was deposited into the federal treasury. Another $700,000 came in during the next two years. By November 1803 some 83 percent of the levy had been paid in—a figure comparable to the compliance rate on federal income taxes today. Pennsylvania's shortfall as of March 1803 was only $21,430, or 9 percent of its quota. In Northampton County, a center of the rebellion, some $1,930 remained in arrears, one of the largest shortfalls among Pennsylvania's thirty-two collection districts. Elsewhere in the region and state the rebellion appears to have had little impact on tax collection. One could argue that the five hundred federal troops who marched to the scene of the resistance in April 1799 effectively suppressed all opposition to payment.[51] But the much larger army of fifteen thousand dispatched against the whiskey rebels in 1794 had not had that effect among these German Americans five years later. If the Kirchen-leute had not been cowed by the whiskey precedent of 1794, it is hard to see how they or anyone else could have been cowed by five hundred troops in 1799. The more likely explanation for compliance is that few Pennsylvanians ardently opposed collection of the direct tax of 1798, especially after election results in 1799 and 1800 put the future direction of the state and nation in the hands of Republicans.

Given Pennsylvania's tax history in the latter half of the eighteenth century, one could credibly project a more or less seamless transition to a peacetime taxing state as the nineteenth century approached. Instead, Pennsylvanians quietly disengaged themselves from the ideal of the cheerful taxpayer. They did so without explicitly rejecting the ideal or consciously severing themselves from their own past—making the discontinuity harder for historians to detect. Yet there can be little doubt that the largely tax-free polity of the nineteenth century was a break from Pennsylvania's colonial and revolutionary heritage rather than an elaboration of it.

The disengagement from federal taxation is already well known, but it proceeded more slowly than generally has been supposed. The Republicans who took power under Jefferson repealed the excise taxes in 1802 but let stand the direct tax of 1798 and even passed two laws strengthening its enforcement. During the War of 1812 Republicans vindicated their concern for tax equity by levying both direct taxes and a great variety of excise taxes. The coming of the war brought the ideal of cheerful tax paying to the rhetorical foreground. In December 1810 Pennsylvania's Republican governor, Simon Snyder, reminded his fellow citizens that "Pennsylvania will ever be ready, cheerfully to embark her fortunes and resources" in defending the rights of the nation. After the war had begun, Georgia governor Peter Early explained that a free people "will with cheerfulness contribute whatever may be necessary" for the defense of their rights. Near the end of the conflict, President Madison encouraged Congress to trust that the people would "cheerfully and proudly bear every burden of every kind which the safety and honor of the nation demand. We have seen them every where paying their taxes, direct and indirect, with the greatest promptness and alacrity."[52]

But peace rather than war proved determinative of American public finance. When the guns were silent, the federal government relied heavily on customs duties for revenue. Fittingly, Jefferson asked in his second inaugural address, "what farmer, what mechanic, what laborer, ever sees a tax-gatherer of the United States?" The customs duties, according to Jefferson, were being paid mainly by Americans "who can afford to add foreign luxuries to domestic comforts." For Jefferson, the typical American taxpayer was a prosperous (even wealthy) consumer enjoying luxuries—a characterization very far from the ideal of the cheerful taxpayer. The relative ease with which the customs duties were collected (the Embargo of 1808 still lay in the future) seemed to transcend the collection problems that the ideal had always been called upon to address. With taxes like these, who needed cheerful taxpayers?

Pennsylvania's disengagement from state taxation, meanwhile, is a story with its own curious lesson to teach. Conceivably the withdrawal of the federal government from most sources of revenue could have made those sources available for state taxation. And, as at the federal level, Pennsylvania politicians well into the 1800s considered state taxation more seriously than has generally been recognized. But ultimately they too abandoned the cheerful taxpayer.

Within just a few years of the adoption of the U.S. Constitution, Pennsylvania repealed its annual funding tax. The state would remain without a tax on real or personal property for the next four decades. The positioning of the state within the new federal framework had much to do with this outcome. During the debate on ratification of the Constitution, Pennsylvania Federalist James Wilson had predicted that Pennsylvania's funding tax "must naturally expire" when a "competent and energetic fœderal system shall be substituted."[53] Far from rejoicing at such a prospect, Anti-Federalists feared what the end of state taxation portended for the balance of power: Wilson's "energetic federal system" would reduce Pennsylvania state government to a shadow of its former self. The dissenting minority in Pennsylvania's ratifying convention summed up the line of argument: "As there is no one article of taxation reserved to the state governments, the Congress may monopolise every source of revenue, and thus indirectly demolish the state governments, for . . . the taxes, duties, and excises imposed by Congress may be so high as to render it impracticable to levy further sums on the same articles."[54] The assumption of state debts by the federal government would of course render federal taxes necessary; the states, thus crowded out, would be less able to retain their authority through taxes of their own.

Wilson and other Federalists did not accept the notion that one taxing sovereign necessarily dislodged another in this way.[55] But in 1790 Wilson's prediction, and Anti-Federalists' fears, did begin to be fulfilled. Congress passed Alexander

Hamilton's fiscal program, whereby the federal government refinanced its war debt and assumed the war debts of the states. At this time the Pennsylvania legislature was controlled by Federalists who were determined to see Hamilton's program succeed. To give federal taxation the widest possible range of application, the Federalists in 1791 repealed the state's annual funding tax, first enacted in 1785 by the Constitutionalists.[56] The Anti-Federalist minority in the legislature opposed the repeal. Their burst of pro-tax sentiment was an aftershock of the massive transfer of power that had occurred over the previous two years. It revealed an important truth: even the most localist and anti-statist Pennsylvania politicians could embrace state taxation when it appeared to be a necessary counterpoise to federal power.

The federal assumption brought an enormous windfall to the Pennsylvania treasury, leaving the state fiscally strengthened. The federal government took responsibility not only for the federal debt that Pennsylvania had assumed in the 1780s but also for more than $1 million in Pennsylvania's state debt proper.[57] Moreover, Pennsylvania in 1790 possessed $1.2 million in Continental certificates that it had accepted as payment on the purchase of its public lands. These depreciated securities were now accepted under the federal funding scheme at face value, providing the state with an enormous capital asset out of what might have otherwise proved to be worthless paper.[58] The sale of these holdings in 1792 allowed the state to pay off most of the remaining state debt not covered under the federal assumption. By the end of 1792 the state owed only about $100,000 and held a tidy $300,000 in the stock of the U.S. debt.[59] Meanwhile, the legislature adroitly turned to the sale of public lands for additional revenues. From 1792 through 1794 land sales brought in nearly $1.6 million.[60] The state treasury was heavily in the black by 1793. Pennsylvania moved into a new stage of public finance—the challenge of managing a surplus.

A financial settlement approved in the spring of that year became the cornerstone of a legislative policy that was to persist well into the nineteenth century. Its chief advocate was none other than Albert Gallatin, then a member of the Pennsylvania House of Representatives. His proposed "permanent financial establishment" was simple: invest nearly all the state's available funds in the stock of the soon-to-be-incorporated Bank of Pennsylvania, and then let the state be supported, as much as possible, by the dividends that resulted.[61] The dividend revenues "perhaps would be sufficient for the regular expences of government," Gallatin explained, and would "greatly lighten the burden of public taxes."[62] The plan's objective of avoiding taxes was evident to all, and neither Federalists nor Republicans appear to have objected to that goal. Some did question the prudence of investing all the public funds in a single institution. Others thought the state had a duty to support the federal government by retaining the U.S. stock the state held. Supporters of the existing Bank of North

America pitched for placing funds in that institution. But in the crucial House vote on section 1 of the bill of incorporation, the tally was 44–18 in favor, and the measure passed easily in the Senate, 11–3.[63]

The investment worked just about as Gallatin had predicted. The state sank $1 million into the Bank of Pennsylvania, and dividends began immediately to be paid.[64] The investment forecast the state's dependence on banks as its largest and most consistent source of revenue at least through 1820. Additional revenues came from land sales, auction duties, licenses, and taxes on writs, but bank revenues soon became the bedrock of the state's finances. With little in the way of public spending beyond the basic expenses of government, annual bank dividend revenues alone invariably amounted to at least 50 percent of annual expenditures, and during the 1810s typically exceeded them.[65] Later investments in the Bank of Pennsylvania, investment in the Bank of Philadelphia, incorporated in 1804, gratuities charged to banks in exchange for the granting of their charters, and ultimately a tax on banks enacted in 1814 all enabled the treasury to reach into the deepest pockets in the commonwealth, leaving most Pennsylvanians largely untouched.

The policy begun in the 1790s proved of long duration, but then and later Pennsylvanians considered a return to state taxation. During the French crisis of 1797–99 the legislature considered a $500,000 loan-and-tax plan, partly to fund the state militia, but dropped it when Congress passed the direct tax. More explicitly than in 1791, the Federalists again deferred to the federal government. The property affected by the federal tax could not also be taxed by the state; one or the other polity had to give way. In 1799 Governor Thomas Mifflin regretfully acknowledged that adding a state land tax to the federal levy would cause "considerable inconvenience."[66]

Indeed, Pennsylvania's first two governors, whose annual addresses to the legislature form a distinct corpus of republican thought, repeatedly put forth taxation as the remedy for expected shortfalls in revenues. In 1797 Thomas Mifflin argued that "in a free country, under a Republican system, nothing can be more desirable, than that the citizens should be called upon for such pecuniary contributions, as will constantly excite their vigilance, in scrutinizing the administration and the expences of their government." It was "a favourite maxim in my theory of the administration of a republican system," Mifflin added in 1798, "that, whatever may be the wealth of a state, the charge of supporting its government should fall directly and individually on its citizens. The imposition of an adequate tax for that specific purpose is calculated to produce vigilance in the people, and œconomy in the magistrates." In 1799, finally, Mifflin recommended that a "small, but certain contribution" be levied, because of both fiscal need and the "republican principle" that estates be taxed to support government. Mifflin's Republican successor, Thomas McKean, was no less favorably disposed toward taxation. In 1800, 1802, and 1803 McKean recommended that some sort of tax be enacted, especially as the frugality of the Jefferson administration had "released from taxation" a "variety of objects." The prospect of popular opposition was gently swept from view. McKean was confident that Pennsylvanians would prefer to fund the government by "an immediate application to the people" rather than "a constant and unlimited recourse to the credit of the state."[67]

The governors were not alone in believing that taxation was the best means of sustaining a republican government. In 1802 petitioners from Chester County argued along familiar republican lines that "no bounds can be set to [public debt] when once admitted, but Governmental insolvency, and all its attendant horrors." But their means of avoiding debt was to tax. Would the people object? Taxation to avoid debt was an act of patriotism, and the petitioners "pledge themselves, and rely on the support of their fellow citizens throughout the State, cheerfully to meet the just and necessary expences of Government."[68]

Had the reasoning of Pennsylvania's governor and the Chester County petitioners prevailed, the whole ideology and practice of taxation in Pennsylvania would have turned out differently. But that reasoning did not prevail, and its fiscal superficiality was partly why. Shortly after the *Philadelphia Aurora* published the Chester County petition, a rival address from Republicans in the same county appeared in the same newspaper. The Republicans stated their preference for taxes over loans but argued that the legislature should levy no tax until some effort was made to reduce state expenses. And the Republicans had just the plan for doing so—shorten the legislative session, reduce legislators' wages, and abolish two positions in the land office. In all, these economies could save the state precisely $33,086.70 per year. Still greater savings, they asserted, might be achieved by legislators truly intent on achieving them. With costs pared, the state's bank dividend earnings would be sufficient to cover the expenses of government, while remaining revenues could be applied toward the purchase of additional stock or even to fund internal improvements. By a "safe and judicious arrangement of our present revenue," the Republicans suggested, "an half a century might elapse before it would be necessary to lay a tax."[69]

That statement proved prophetic. Banks continued to be the key financial resource upholding the state, and for the next three decades Pennsylvania managed to avoid imposition of a property tax. In 1809 Governor Simon Snyder happily concluded that the need for taxation had been bypassed, making him the first Pennsylvania governor to say so. In 1811 the Pennsylvania House Ways and Means Committee was similarly upbeat: "Such is found to be the situation of the finances of the state, that what have sometimes been considered almost the sole duties of a committee of ways and means, namely, to devise modes of taxation, and to find new sources of supply for the wants of government, have been superseded and are out of use."[70]

Coming as it did on the eve of the War of 1812, such a rosy report now seems odd. For if any fiscal imperative could propel the legislature into taxation, it was war. Pennsylvania legislators of every political stripe had at one point or another consented to taxes for which war was the justification. This was true of the Constitutionalists in the first several years of the Revolutionary War. It was true of both Constitutionalists and Republicans during 1781–83, when taxes in specie, the most demanding form of exaction, were thought necessary. It was true of Federalists in 1797, who considered a state property tax to provide funds for the state militia before deferring to the federal direct tax passed the following year. Nor were the fiscal demands of war square pegs to be awkwardly fitted into the round holes of ideology. As we have seen, the ideal of the cheerful taxpayer had a home in Anglo-American political thought and was frequently employed by Americans before, during, and after the Revolution. Never was its use more fitting in the Republic than during a war fought to preserve the Republic.

Yet the war taxation that Pennsylvania had thus far acceded to was not to be repeated during the War of 1812. When Congress in 1813 imposed a direct tax quota of $310,657 on the state, the sum was paid with an existing surplus in the state treasury. Later war expenses were financed through borrowing, with no taxes levied to pay the loans back. In the end, the federal government helped pay Pennsylvania's war expenses, allowing the state to avoid new taxes throughout the conflict and long after.[71]

The willingness and capacity of the Pennsylvania legislature to avoid direct taxation even in the War of 1812 is strong evidence of the state's disengagement of civic values from public finance. The personal sacrifice expected of a true republican involved the cheerful relinquishment of one's "fortune," if necessary, in order to preserve liberty. But where was the sacrifice in using surpluses and drawing loans? Even in peace, how could liberty be preserved without some form of general exaction, be it ever so small?

Pennsylvanians of the early Republic did not reassert a colonial anti-tax heritage that Parliament had pressed them to forget or that their own tax resisters had pressed them to recall. Rather, they discovered that the essential structure of government could be preserved without regular recourse to the wealth of all the citizens of the state. This realization precipitated the decline in the ideal of the cheerful taxpayer. After all, that ideal belonged first to an early modern world in which taxes were considered inescapable pledges of allegiance to governments whose very existence depended on them. During the Revolutionary War, Pennsylvania was still part of that world: fledgling state and federal governments struggled to engage in war and simultaneously retain and increase the allegiance of the people. Despite extreme monetary instability and demanding taxes, the old ideal of the cheerful taxpayer did not then lose its hold. Only after the war did Pennsylvania enter a distinctively modern, or at least "post–early modern" world. In this world, state taxation was optional to an extent scarcely imaginable to sovereign governments before 1776. Federal largesse, financed by customs duties, allowed the Pennsylvania government to forego taxing most of its citizens. This model pervaded the states of the Union and even stretched to Britain's minimally taxed, heavily subsidized new province of Upper Canada.[72] Banks, too, reshaped the landscape of public finance, providing the state with the bulk of its annual revenues, making taxes that much less necessary. Hence the decline of the cheerful taxpayer owed much both to the buoyancy of the federal regime and to the key institutions of early American capitalism. This decline was far from complete by the end of the War of 1812, but it was well under way, and despite the subsequent introduction of numerous taxes both state and federal, it has never been reversed.

NOTES

1. Charles de Secondat, Baron de Montesquieu, *The Spirit of the Laws,* ed. Franz Neumann, trans. Thomas Nugent, 2 vols. (New York: Hafner, 1949), 1:214–15; Thomas Gordon, *The Nature and Weight of the National Taxes Consider'd* (London, 1722), 10, 18.

2. James T. Mitchell and Henry Flanders, eds., *The Statutes at Large of Pennsylvania, from 1682 to 1801,* 18 vols. (Harrisburg: State of Pennsylvania, 1896–1911), 6:7.

3. *Journals of the Continental Congress, 1774–1789,* ed. Worthington C. Ford et al., 34 vols. (Washington, D.C.: Library of Congress, 1904–37), 1:84–85, 96, 2:168.

4. Ibid., 9:954. For similar expressions from delegates, see ibid., 12:493; and Paul H. Smith et al., eds., *Letters of Delegates to Congress, 1774–1789,* 25 vols. (Washington, D.C.: Library of Congress, 1976–93) (also available on Historical Database CD-ROM, 1995), 12:503–4, 537, 13:584, 14:343.

5. Montesquieu, *Spirit of the Laws,* 1:214–15.

6. Quoted in Smith et al., *Letters to Delegates of Congress,* 19:618–19.

7. Albert Gallatin, *Selected Writings of Albert Gallatin,* ed. E. James Ferguson (Indianapolis: Bobbs-Merrill, 1967), 20; "Petition from sundry inhabitants on the subject of Finance, Economy, and Frugality," folder 3, 1801–2, House File, House of Representatives, RG-7, Records of the General Assembly, Historical Society of Pennsylvania, Philadelphia.

8. Mitchell and Flanders, *Statutes at Large,* 5:201, 294, 303, 337; 6:7, 344. Three smaller emissions, in 1756, 1767, and 1769, were backed by a provincial excise tax (ibid., 5:243; 7:100, 204).

9. Alan Tully, *Forming American Politics: Ideals, Interests, and Institutions in Colonial New York and Pennsylvania* (Baltimore: Johns Hopkins University Press, 1994), 83–84; see also Nathan Kozuskanich's essay in this volume.

10. Robert A. Becker, *Revolution, Reform, and the Politics of American Taxation, 1763–1783* (Baton Rouge: Louisiana State University Press, 1980), 49–59, 237.

11. *Votes and Proceedings of the House of Representatives of the Province of Pennsylvania* (Philadelphia, 1772), Early American Imprints, series 1, Evans (1639–1800), microfilm, no. 12507, 394–400; *Votes and Proceedings of the House of Representatives of the Province of Pennsylvania* (Philadelphia, 1773), 478–84; *Votes and Proceedings of the House of Representatives of the Province of Pennsylvania* (Philadelphia, 1775), Evans, no. 14373, 663–70.

12. Becker, *Revolution, Reform,* 178–79; Lemuel Molovinsky, "Pennsylvania's Legislative Efforts to Finance the War for Independence: A Study of the Continuity of Colonial Finance, 1775–83" (PhD diss., Temple University, 1975), 34–35, 257. For a discussion of Pennsylvania German pacifist responses to war taxes, see John B. Frantz's essay in this volume.

13. See the discussion in Richard A. Ryerson, *The Revolution Is Now Begun: The Radical Committees of Philadelphia, 1765–1776* (Philadelphia: University of Pennsylvania Press, 1978), chapter 7.

14. Mitchell and Flanders, *Statutes at Large*, 10:102, 52, 183, 301, 305; 5:345–46.

15. Roger H. Brown, *Redeeming the Republic: Federalists, Taxation, and the Origins of the Constitution* (Baltimore: Johns Hopkins University Press, 1993), 57.

16. Becker, *Revolution, Reform*, 178–81.

17. Brown, *Redeeming the Republic*, 57–58.

18. Mitchell and Flanders, *Statutes at Large*, 10:326, 385; 11:82.

19. Brown, *Redeeming the Republic*, 53; Robert Morris, *The Papers of Robert Morris, 1781–1784*, ed. E. James Ferguson, 8 vols. (Pittsburgh: University of Pittsburgh Press, 1973–95), 1:153.

20. E. James Ferguson, *The Power of the Purse: A History of American Public Finance, 1776–1790* (Chapel Hill: University of North Carolina Press, 1961), 113; James Mott Aldrich, "The Revolutionary Legislature in Pennsylvania: A Roll Call Analysis" (PhD diss., University of Maine, 1969); Owen S. Ireland, "The Crux of Politics: Religion and Party in Pennsylvania, 1778–1789," *William and Mary Quarterly*, 3d ser., 42 (1985): 453–75.

21. Owen S. Ireland, "The Ratification of the Federal Constitution in Pennsylvania" (PhD diss., University of Pittsburgh, 1966), 254–56; Aldrich, "Revolutionary Legislature in Pennsylvania," 179–83.

22. *Minutes of the Third Session of the Fifth General Assembly of the Commonwealth of Pennsylvania* (1780–81) (Philadelphia, 1780–81), Evans, no. 17293, 448–51, 462, 465.

23. *Minutes of the First Session of the Sixth General Assembly of the Commonwealth of Pennsylvania* (1781–82) (Philadelphia, 1781 [1782]), Evans, no. 17295, 553–54; Aldrich, "Revolutionary Legislature in Pennsylvania," 179–82; Ireland, "Ratification of the Constitution," 254–56; *Minutes of the First Session of the Seventh General Assembly of the Commonwealth of Pennsylvania* (1782–83) (Philadelphia, [1783]), Evans, no. 17663, 867; Morris, *Papers of Robert Morris*, 4:336–38.

24. Mitchell and Flanders, *Statutes at Large*, 10:81, 87; *Minutes of the Seventh General Assembly* (1782–83), 867.

25. Brown, *Redeeming the Republic*, 60–63; Terry Bouton, "A Road Closed: Rural Insurgency in Post-Independence Pennsylvania, *Journal of American History* 87 (December 2000): 855–87.

26. Brown, *Redeeming the Republic*, 55–68.

27. Bouton's "Road Closed" is a full exposition of this view.

28. Brown, *Redeeming the Republic*, 64–65.

29. Mitchell and Flanders, *Statutes at Large*, 11:454, 480.

30. As Roger H. Brown has so ably shown, other states also returned to paper taxation after similar experiments with levies in specie (*Redeeming the Republic*, 53–138).

31. *Minutes of the First Session of the Eleventh General Assembly of the Commonwealth of Pennsylvania* (1786–87) (Philadelphia, 1787), Evans, no. 44947, 9, 16–18, 28, 33, 139, 167, 184.

32. See Bouton, "Road Closed," 855–87.

33. Brown, *Redeeming the Republic*, 57; Molovinsky, "Pennsylvania's Legislative Efforts," 267; Becker, *Revolution, Reform*, 237. My collection rate figure is somewhat higher than Brown's (36 percent), to account for the half-payment in paper allowed under the taxes of 1781 and 1783. It is not known what percentage of taxpayers qualified under the allowance for the 1781 tax.

34. *A State of the Finances of the Commonwealth of Pennsylvania* (Philadelphia, [1787?]); *Report of the Register-General of the State of the Finances of Pennsylvania, For the Year 1792* (Philadelphia, 1793), Evans, no. 49691, schedule no. 26. The 1787 report indicated that £324,659 was still in arrears, out of a total £845,297 levied. The 1792 report listed £105,752 in arrears.

35. *State of the Accounts of David Rittenhouse, Esq., Treasurer of Pennsylvania, From January 1785, till January 1786* (Philadelphia, 1790); *State of the Accounts of David Rittenhouse, Esq., Treasurer of the Commonwealth of Pennsylvania: From January, 1786, till January, 1787* (Philadelphia, 1790), Evans, no. 22769; *State of the Accounts of David Rittenhouse, Esq., Treasurer of Pennsylvania, From 1st January till 1st November 1787* (Philadelphia, 1790), Evans, no. 22770; *State of the Accounts of David Rittenhouse, Esq., Treasurer of Pennsylvania, For the Year 1788* (Philadelphia, 1791), Evans, no. 23680; *State of the Accounts of David Rittenhouse, Esq., Treasurer of Pennsylvania, From September 1788, till September 1st, 1789* (Philadelphia, 1791), Evans, no. 23681. Missing are Bucks County receipts on the 1786 funding tax during 1788 and the Philadelphia City and County receipts for the funding taxes of 1786 and 1787 during the same year.

36. *Report of the Register-General . . . 1792*, schedule no. 26.

37. For collection figures, see Rittenhouse accounts cited in note 35. Bouton provides no direct evidence that any of the road closings were acts of resistance to state taxes ("Road Closed," 878–79). Two of the four closings he specifically describes occurred in Dauphin (1788) and Lancaster (1792), counties where tax compliance was generally high. A third, Huntingdon County's in 1792, is hard to interpret, as Huntingdon was a new county and its tax burden was fairly minimal. Only the Northumberland County closing (1792) involves a county in which tax collection was typically low. It should also be noted that the funding tax was repealed in 1791. Closings in subsequent years, if related to state taxes at all, would have concerned arrearages rather than new levies.

38. The literature on the Whiskey Rebellion is extensive. See Thomas P. Slaughter, *The Whiskey Rebellion: Frontier Epilogue to the American Revolution* (New York: Oxford University Press, 1986); Steven R. Boyd, ed., *The Whiskey Rebellion: Past and Present Perspectives* (Westport, Conn.: Greenwood Press, 1985); and William Hogeland, *The Whiskey Rebellion: George Washington, Alexander Hamilton, and the Frontier Rebels Who Challenged America's Newfound Sovereignty* (New York: Scribner, 2006).

39. "An Act repealing, after the last day of June next, the duties heretofore laid upon Distilled Spirits imported from abroad, and laying others in their stead; and also upon Spirits distilled within the United States, and for appropriating the same" (March 3, 1791), *The Public Statutes at Large of the United States of America*, ed. Richard Peters, 18 vols. (Boston: Charles C. Little and James Brown, 1845), 1:199; "An Act laying certain duties upon Snuff and Refined Sugar" (June 5, 1794), ibid., 1:384–90; "An Act laying duties upon Carriages for the conveyance of Persons" (June 5, 1794), ibid., 1:373–76; "An Act laying duties on licenses for selling Wines and foreign distilled spirituous liquors by retail" (June 5, 1794), ibid., 1:376–78; "An Act laying duties on property sold at Auction" (June 9, 1794), ibid., 1:397–400.

40. U.S. Congress, *Annals of the Congress of the United States, 1789–1824*, 42 vols. (Washington, D.C.: Gales and Seaton, 1834–56), 3d Cong., 1st sess., 643–47.

41. Gallatin, *Selected Writings of Gallatin*, 20; Roland M. Baumann, "Philadelphia's Manufacturers and the Excise Taxes of 1794: The Forging of the Jeffersonian Coalition," *Pennsylvania Magazine of History and Biography* (January 1982): 34, 35, 36.

42. *Annals of Congress*, 4th Cong., 2d sess., 865, 1843.

43. Mark Cachia-Riedl, "Albert Gallatin and the Politics of the New Nation" (PhD diss., University of California, Berkeley, 1998), 76; *Annals of Congress*, 4th Cong., 1st sess., 841–56; 2d sess., 1853, 1854, 1909.

44. *Annals of Congress*, 4th Cong., 2d sess., January 19, 1797, 1917, 1918.

45. Ibid., January 19, 1797, 1920, and January 20, 1797, 1941; *House Journal*, 5th Cong., 2d sess., July 2, 1798, 362–63. Congressional party affiliations are taken from Rudolph M. Bell, *Party and Faction in American Politics: The House of Representatives, 1789–1801* (Westport, Conn.: Greenwood Press, 1973), 255–57.

46. *Annals of Congress*, 5th Cong., 2d sess., May 7, 1798, 1617, 1619.

47. Thomas Jefferson to Peregrine Fitzhugh, June 4, 1797; Jefferson to John Taylor, November 26, 1798; Jefferson to James Madison, January 3, 1799; Jefferson to Madison, January 16, 1799; Jefferson to James Monroe, January 23, 1799; Jefferson to Elbridge Gerry, January 26, 1799, all in Thomas Jefferson, *The Works of Thomas Jefferson*, ed. Paul Leicester Ford, 12 vols. (New York: G. P. Putnam's Sons, 1904–5) (also available at the online Library of Liberty, http://oll.libertyfund.org/); Herbert E. Sloan, "Hamilton's Second Thoughts: Federalist Finance Revisited," in *Federalists Reconsidered*, ed. Doron Ben-Atar and Barbara Oberg (Charlottesville: University Press of Virginia, 1998), 74, 75.

48. *Annals of Congress*, 5th Cong., 3d sess., 2985–3016. Neither the *Annals* nor the legislative journals print the texts of the petitions; their content is thus known mainly through committee reports and speeches.

49. Paul Douglas Newman, "Fries's Rebellion and American Political Culture, 1798–1800," *Pennsylvania Magazine of History and Biography* 119 (January–April 1995): 47–56.

50. Oliver Wolcott to Fisher Ames, December 29, 1799, in Fisher Ames, *Works of Fisher Ames, as Published by Seth Ames*, ed. W. B. Allen, 2 vols. (Indianapolis: Liberty Classics, 1983), 2:1341.

51. U.S. Congress, *American State Papers*, 38 vols. (1789–1838), 3, *Finance* 2:66–67, 70, 919; Newman, "Fries's Rebellion," 65; Kenneth W. Keller, *Rural Politics and the Collapse of Pennsylvania Federalism* (Philadelphia: American Philosophical Society, 1982), 26. In the mid-1980s the Internal Revenue Service estimated that close to 20 percent of federal personal income taxes went unpaid. Jeffrey A. Roth et al., eds., *Taxpayer Compliance*, 2 vols. (Philadelphia: University of Pennsylvania Press, 1989), 1:1, 47–48.

52. *Journal of the House of Representatives of the Commonwealth of Pennsylvania* (1810–11) (Lancaster,

1811), 16; *Journal of the House of Representatives of the State of Georgia* (October–November 1814 session) (1815), 6 (Early State Records microfilm); U.S. Congress, *Senate Journal*, 13th Cong., 2d sess., September 20, 1814, 526–27.

53. Quoted in Bernard Bailyn, ed., *The Debate on the Constitution: Federalist and Antifederalist Speeches, Articles, and Letters During the Struggle over Ratification*, 2 vols., Part One, *September 1787 to February 1788* (New York: Library of America, 1993), 1:68.

54. Ibid., 1:537.

55. See Elizabeth Lewis Pardoe's essay in this volume.

56. *Journal of the First [–Second] Session of the House of Representatives of the Commonwealth of Pennsylvania* (1790–91) (Philadelphia, 1790 [1791]), 230–31, 335; *Journal of the Senate of the Commonwealth of Pennsylvania* (1790–91) (Philadelphia, 1791), 195, 199.

57. Roland M. Baumann, "Heads I Win, Tails You Lose: The Public Creditors and the Assumption Issue in Pennsylvania, 1790–1802," *Pennsylvania History* 44 (July 1977): 198, 203; "Report of the Register-General Relative to the Revenue and Expenditures of the Commonwealth of Pennsylvania 1790," in *Pennsylvania Archives*, 3d ser., ed. William H. Egle and George Edward Reed, 30 vols. (Harrisburg: State Printer, 1894–99), 7:511–12; Ferguson, *Power of the Purse*, 228–31.

58. "Report of the Register-General . . . 1790," 495.

59. Mitchell and Flanders, *Statutes at Large*, 14:305; *Journal of the First Session of the Third House of Representatives of the Commonwealth of Pennsylvania* (1792–93) (Philadelphia, 1792 [1793]), Evans, no. 25974, 13–14; *Report of the Register-General . . . 1792*, schedule no. 11. The state debt not covered under federal assumption was enlarged significantly by the legislature's decision in 1791 to make up the difference between what the federal government would pay in interest and what Pennsylvania had paid before the assumption scheme was enacted. Baumann, "Heads I Win," 220; Mitchell and Flanders, *Statutes at Large*, 14:76.

60. *Report of the Register-General . . . 1792;* "Report of the Register-General of the State of the Finances of Pennsylvania, For the Year 1793," in *Journal of the First Session of the Fourth House of Representatives of the Commonwealth of Pennsylvania* (Philadelphia, 1793 [1794]), Evans, no. 27480; *Report of the Register-General of the State of the Finances of Pennsylvania, For the Year MDCCXCIV* (Philadelphia, 1795), Evans, no. 29293.

61. *Journal of the Third House of Representatives of Pennsylvania*, 156; *General Advertiser*, February 14, 1793.

62. *General Advertiser*, February 14 and 18, 1793.

63. Ibid., February 14, 15, 16, and 18, 1793; *Journal of the Senate of the Commonwealth of Pennsylvania* (1792–93) (Philadelphia, 1793), Evans, no. 25975, 194; *Journal of the Third House of Representatives of Pennsylvania*, 254–55.

64. Mitchell and Flanders, *Statutes at Large*, 14:365.

65. Anthony M. Joseph, "The Pennsylvania Legislature, 1776–1820," (PhD diss., Princeton University, 1999), 177.

66. *Journal of the Second Session of the Seventh House of Representatives of the Commonwealth of Pennsylvania* (1797) (Philadelphia, 1797), Evans, no. 48218, 5; Mitchell and Flanders, *Statutes at Large*, 15:524; *Journal of the First Session of the Seventh House of Representatives of the Commonwealth of Pennsylvania* (1796–97) (Philadelphia, 1797), 372–74; Alexander Hamilton, *The Papers of Alexander Hamilton*, ed. Harold C. Syrett, 27 vols. (New York: Columbia University Press, 1961–87), 20:469n, 483–84, 487; Peters, *Public Statutes at Large*, 1:522, 580, 597; *Annals of Congress*, 5th Cong., 2d sess., 1925, 2066; *Journal of the First Session of the Tenth House of Representatives of the Commonwealth of Pennsylvania* (1799–1800) (Philadelphia, 1800), Evans, no. 38218, 17.

67. *Journal of the First Session of the Eighth House of Representatives of the Commonwealth of Pennsylvania* (1797–98) (Philadelphia, 1798), Evans, no. 34326, 17; *Journal of the First Session of the Ninth House of Representatives of the Commonwealth of Pennsylvania* (1798–99) (Philadelphia, 1799), Evans, no. 36062, 18; *Journal of the Tenth House of Representatives of Pennsylvania*, 14, 16, 17; *Journal of the First Session of the Eleventh House of Representatives of the Commonwealth of Pennsylvania* (1800–1801) (Lancaster, 1800 [1801]), 66; *Journal of the Thirteenth House of Representatives of the Commonwealth of Pennsylvania* (1802–3) (Lancaster, 1803), 26; *Journal of the Fourteenth House of Representatives of the Commonwealth of Pennsylvania* (1803–4) (Lancaster, 1804), 31.

68. "Petition from sundry inhabitants."

69. *Philadelphia Aurora*, December 31, 1802, and January 7, 1803.

70. *Report on the Finances of the Commonwealth of Pennsylvania, For the Year 1810* (Lancaster, 1810), 14. The Bank of Pennsylvania's charter was extended in February 1810. *Acts of the General Assembly of the Commonwealth of Pennsylvania* (1809–10) (Philadelphia, 1810), 27; *Journal of the Twentieth House of Representatives of the Commonwealth of Pennsylvania* (1809–10) (Lancaster, 1810), 28; *Journal of the Twenty-First House of Representatives of the Commonwealth of Pennsylvania* (1810–11) (Lancaster, 1811), 692.

71. *Report on the Finances of the Commonwealth of Pennsylvania, For the Year 1813 . . . by the Auditor-General* (Harrisburg, 1814), 3; *Journal of the Twenty-Fourth House of Representatives of the Commonwealth of Pennsylvania* (1813–14) (Harrisburg, 1814), 1; *Journal of the Twenty-Fifth House of Representatives of the Commonwealth of Pennsylvania* (1814–15) (Harrisburg, 1815), 33–34, 357–59, 440–41, 548–49; *Acts of the General Assembly of the Commonwealth of Pennsylvania* (1814–15) (Harrisburg, 1815), 128.

72. Alan Taylor, "The Late Loyalists: Northern Reflections of the Early American Republic," *Journal of the Early Republic* 27, no. 1 (2007): 7–8.

14

TWO WINTERS OF DISCONTENT:
A COMPARATIVE LOOK AT THE CONTINENTAL ARMY'S
ENCAMPMENTS AT VALLEY FORGE AND JOCKEY HOLLOW

James S. Bailey

A Continental soldier sat huddled in his crude quarters fighting the bitter winter cold that penetrated the rags that passed for clothing. His mind was numbed by cold and dulled by the hunger that by now had become commonplace. The cruel January wind howled through the chinking in the crude hut he called home, matched in ferocity only by the growling of his pitifully empty stomach. Perhaps, he thought, he would venture outside to scour the war-ravaged countryside for some victuals, but he quickly thought better of it. The snow and savage cold made any outdoor activity both difficult and dangerous. No, he would remain in his cramped quarters with his comrades, but they provided little diversion from the suffering. Each man sat sullenly pondering his own private misery and seemed in no mood to talk. Our Continental soldier remained alone with his thoughts. He wondered which would kill him first: hunger, cold, or boredom. Fortunately for historians, the young soldier survived that awful winter, and after the war he recorded his experiences for posterity. Private Joseph Plumb Martin later wrote of the winter in question:

> At one time it snowed the greater part of four days successively, and there fell nearly as many feet of snow. We were absolutely, literally starved. I do solemnly declare that I did not put a single morsel of victuals into my mouth for four days and as many nights, except a little black birch bark which I gnawed off a stick of wood, if that can be called victuals. I saw several of the men roast their old shoes and eat them, and I was afterwards informed by one of the officers' waiters, that some of the officers killed and ate a favorite little dog that belonged to one of them. If this was not "suffering" I request to be informed what can pass under that name. If "suffering" like this did not "try men's souls," I confess that I do not know what could.[1]

Joseph Martin very ably captured a moment frozen in time. His words have offered a testament to the fortitude and suffering of the Continental army. Yet, if asked, most Americans would guess that Martin was describing the horrible winter of 1777–78 at Valley Forge, Pennsylvania. At that hallowed site the Continental army was tested by cold, hunger, and disease and emerged in the spring newly forged, inured to hardship, and freshly trained under the watchful eyes of Baron von Steuben. But the brutal winter that Joseph Plumb Martin recalled so vividly was the winter of 1779–80, spent at Jockey Hollow, near Morristown, New Jersey.

This was the "other" hard winter of the war. Little remembered by modern Americans, the winter encampment of 1779–80 has been even more ignored by historians. Most monographs on the war tell the familiar story of Valley Forge, the lack of clothing, the paucity of food, the brutal cold and snow, the rampant disease. The remarkable resilience of the soldiers and their miraculous transformation into European-style regulars under the steady hand of Baron von Steuben are the stuff of American legend. Washington kneeling in prayer in the snow, the bloody footprints trailing across the moonlike landscape—these images have been seared into the national consciousness. Told and retold through the generations, the stories have taken on a life of their own, and for many Americans they have become history.

Why is Valley Forge the stuff of legend, while Jockey Hollow is all but forgotten? A comparative look at both winters reveals that the physical conditions endured by the soldiers near Morristown were far worse than those at Valley Forge, and the shortages of food and clothing far more dire there. Indeed, a careful survey of primary sources confirms that contemporaries were well aware of this. Why, then, does Valley Forge remain the classic tale of suffering and endurance? Two factors—physical geography and a desire to bury the memory of the breakdown in army discipline and waning civilian support for the war—largely relegated the winter of 1779–80 to the dustbin of history. In essence, the proximity of Valley Forge to Philadelphia and Morristown's relative isolation helped determine why one site of heroism would become immortalized and the other all but forgotten.

Background and Weather at Valley Forge

In December 1777 George Washington arrived at a political arrangement with the flagging revolutionary government of Pennsylvania; the main body of the Continental army would go into winter quarters in the hills to the west of Philadelphia to protect that valuable farmland from British pillaging, prop up the sagging morale of the populace, and maintain surveillance on Lord Howe and his victorious army. The troops began to arrive in mid-December and immediately set to work erecting the log encampment that served as their home for the duration of the winter. Washington, with a characteristic flair for the dramatic and a will to hold his fragile army together by personal example, lived in his tent while the first huts were being built. Few other general officers followed suit. Almost immediately, Washington began to assess the state of his army and to beg the Continental Congress and the various state governments for material aid.

Washington desperately sought the means to provide his soldiers with adequate food, clothing, and housing, to protect them from the ravages of winter. But what of the weather? David Ludlum provides the answers. His work, compiled from primary source documents, provides a solid basis from which to objectively assess the weather conditions at Valley Forge.

Ludlum described the winter of 1777–78 as a moderate one.[2] Only two periods of severe cold occurred, one at the end of December, which saw a low of six degrees Fahrenheit, and one in early March, which had a low of eight degrees. Two periods of what Ludlum termed "moderate cold" also occurred, one in January (a low of twelve degrees) and one in February (a low of sixteen degrees). He also discerned only three snowstorms for the entire winter, all of the "moderate-to-heavy" category. The area received four inches on December 28, 1777, a "deep snow" on February 8, 1778, which was washed away by rain on February 10, and "enough snow for sleighing" on March 2–3. The winter seemed to be characterized by frequents thaws, for Ludlum noted that the ground was covered by snow for most of January but was bare more often than not in March.

The area received its first snowfall on December 12, while the army was encamped at Whitemarsh, but Ludlum cites December 27 as the real start of the winter season. This day saw the heaviest single snowfall of the winter, and severe cold followed. Spring came close to the normal time of early to mid-March, specifically March 12.[3] Weather observations made by a Philadelphia lawyer by the name of Phineas Pemberton, from his home two miles west of the city, support Ludlum's data. Pemberton, an amateur meteorologist, kept a detailed weather log throughout the winter of 1777–78. His log reveals that temperature readings taken at 8:00 A.M. for the month of December averaged 32.7 degrees, cold but not excessively so.[4] The temperature at 3:00 P.M. averaged 37.9 degrees. He further noted that "a little" snow fell on December 11 and 14, and that it snowed on December 19, 20, 26, and 28. But none of these storms seemed unusual or severe enough to warrant any descriptive comment. The log further reveals a rather wet but mild December. Any snowfall in this month would have been transitory and would have melted quickly, as temperatures routinely remained above freezing.

January saw a similar weather picture. The average daily temperature at 8:00

A.M. was twenty-seven degrees. Although colder than December, this was not out of the ordinary. Pemberton recorded snowfalls on January 16, 26, and 29, but again made no descriptive comments. The data support firsthand accounts indicating that small amounts of snow remained on the ground for much of January but that the weather was not excessively cold. January 1777 was rainy and invariably muddy, but it was not abnormally cold or snowy. By all objective accounts, then, the winter at Valley Forge seems to have been a fairly typical one.

Despite the relatively mild weather of 1777–78, the historical record abounds with firsthand accounts that portray that winter in the harshest of terms. The writings of notables such as Nathanael Greene, James Varnum, and George Washington are filled with references to the ravages of the weather. For instance, Brigadier General Varnum noted in a letter of March 7, 1778, "Here there is no distinction of seasons. The weather frequently changes five times in twenty four hours. The coldest I have perceived has been this month. Snow falls, but falls only to produce mire and dirt. . . . Sometimes the weather is moderate, but that season gives time only to reflect upon gentle breases [sic] and cooling zephers, that the immediate extremes may excite greater pain."[5]

On the surface, this seems to contradict the observed weather data. In *The Valley Forge Winter: Civilians and Soldiers in War,* Wayne Bodle suggests that Washington deliberately exaggerated in his reports to the Continental Congress and Pennsylvania's revolutionary government in an effort to prod the civilian authorities to provide adequate supplies, to increase manpower, and to end political debate over the disposition of the army for the winter.[6] Bodle's argument is convincing. It must also be noted that the Valley Forge winter was essentially the first winter that the army remained intact as a unit and built its own winter quarters. Thus officers used to wintering in the substantial wood and brick homes of local civilians now had to deal with the weather in much cruder quarters than they were used to.

On December 23, Washington sent one his most famous missives of that winter to Henry Laurens, recounting a litany of shortcomings in supplies and the suffering of his men and concluding that if government authorities did not respond promptly, "the army must starve, disperse, or dissolve."[7] Even as the ink was drying on this letter, Washington received information that Lord Howe was preparing a large foraging expedition into the Pennsylvania countryside. Washington acted decisively. He instructed each brigade in his army to detail fifty men and eight officers to join some local militiamen in a reinforced screen line to harass the British. This screen line proved effective and curtailed British efforts in the area. Perhaps emboldened by this small success, Washington discreetly asked his trusted subordinate Nathanael Greene to sound out some of the other generals on the feasibility on attacking the British garrison at Philadelphia.

Despite Washington's often chilling portrayals of the harsh weather, weather conditions were in fact relatively mild, as noted above. Washington's aggressive military actions at times gave the lie to his communications, especially the December 23 letter to Laurens. As we will see, it was only in the late twentieth century that a historian offered a possible explanation for this incongruity. This is not to suggest that the soldiers at Valley Forge did not suffer, or that the weather was pleasant. The men at Valley Forge clearly suffered from the weather and inadequate supplies, but not nearly so much as the Continental army would suffer during the "hard winter" of 1779–80.

Logistics at Valley Forge

The Continental army endured three principal "starving times" during the winter of 1777–78. The first occurred from October through November, when the army was encamped at Whitemarsh about thirteen miles south of Valley Forge. The second was occasioned by the move to Valley Forge itself, and the third occurred in February 1778.

Beginning in October 1777, the logistical support structure of the Continentals began to come apart. Although the army was encamped in the area of Whitemarsh and received supplies from the relatively close depot at Wilmington, Delaware, maintaining an adequate amount of food, clothing, and medicine became exceedingly difficult. Structural defects in the Quartermaster and Commissary departments, lack of money, and shortages of wagons and drivers all combined to hamper efforts to supply Washington and his men. As the fall gave way to winter, intermittent light snowfall combined with generally warm temperatures to produce a quagmire of mud of epic proportions. A supply situation that was already bad became even worse.

The logistical situation was so dire that it affected all operational and strategic planning. As Wayne Bodle has pointed out, "It was rare enough that the commissaries could even assure the army of its next day's victuals, much less provide it with a three days' margin sufficient, at a minimum, to risk a general engagement."[8] Hamstrung by an inefficient organization foisted upon the army by a meddlesome Congress, and crippled by lack of leadership and possible internal corruption, the Commissary and Quartermaster departments were simply not up to the tasks at hand. The increasingly desperate situation was clearly reflected in a letter from commissary agent Colonel Thomas Jones to his superior, Charles Stewart, on October 29. Jones told Stewart that supplying the army was a day-to-day affair and that his men were at the mercy of the weather. "If the weather should continue much longer our army will be ruined."[9] Jones wrote the same day to commissary agent Gustavus Riesbig at Trenton, informing him that he had sent him seven empty wagons, which were to be loaded with salt and returned. "For Gods sake," Jones implored Riesbig, "send this article or we shall be undone." He also asked Riesbig to send bread, flour, soap, and spirits.[10] Clearly, these were lean times indeed. As Bodle put it, "In the camp of the American Army, the winter of discontent had begun early."[11]

The second crisis began in mid-December, when the first of Washington's approximately eleven thousand regular soldiers began the move from White-marsh to Valley Forge, a journey of some thirteen miles that weather, mud, and fatigue would prolong for a week. The exasperated Thomas Jones continued to struggle valiantly to forward foodstuffs and supplies to the army, but his words reflected his foreboding. He wrote in a December 19 letter to commissary agent Thomas Wharton that there was an "approaching calamity that threatens our Army for want of provisions," and he grimly predicted that the army would "not be able to Exist one week longer" without 200 to 230 barrels of flour per day.[12]

This second supply crisis caused consternation not only with Washington. As Washington formulated his response to Howe's foraging expedition, Brigadier General Jedediah Huntingdon wrote sardonically to Timothy Pickering that "fighting will be far more pref[erable] to starving," adding that his brigade was entirely out of provisions and that the commissary could not provide meat.[13] Brigadier General James Varnum voiced his frustrations to the commander-in-chief himself when he wrote that "the men must be supplied or they cannot be commanded."[14]

Although this lack of meat was undoubtedly bad, the soldiers did have flour. During later winter "starving times," this would not be the case. Little could these hungry and wet soldiers know that the situation would be worse in the future. In late December 1777, however, the supply crisis and the British forag-ing expedition were the immediate crises that had to be dealt with.

In fact, Howe's foraging raid had unexpected consequences for the Continen-tal army. Even as Washington's detachments reported to Brigadier General Dan-iel Morgan near Darby, Pennsylvania, they began to realize that Howe's movement had actually opened more of the countryside to foraging. Major General William Alexander (Lord Stirling) quickly capitalized on this boon and began to round up wagons to ferry foraged supplies back to Valley Forge. This action, combined with Washington's creation of advanced foraging parties, helped end the second supply crisis of the winter.

By December 28 Howe had begun his retreat back to Philadelphia, lumbering wagonloads of confiscated booty in tow. Morgan, Stirling, and the Pennsylvania militia harassed the British all the way to the Schuylkill River before finally retiring themselves. With this act of the drama concluded, the business of fin-ishing the construction of winter quarters began in earnest. The advance foraging parties that Washington had sent out on December 24 also began to spread throughout the countryside and to forward a constant stream of supplies to the main cantonments. These supplies were probably not abundant and at times were of dubious quality, but they nonetheless provided sustenance to the hungry soldiers. This was more than can be said of many periods during the Jockey Hollow encampment two years later.

Although the foraging parties eased the food situation, they did little to ease the shortage of clothes. The soldiers were by all accounts in great need of serviceable clothing. Major General Nathanael Greene lamented this shortage in a January 5 letter to his brother, Christopher Greene: "the troops are worn out with fatigue, badly fed and almost naked. There are and have been some thousands of the army without shoes for months past."[15] Greene, perhaps anticipating his coming role as quartermaster-general, worked particularly hard that winter to acquire clothing for his Rhode Island troops and for the army as a whole. He continued to write letters to Rhode Island politicians, begging for shoes, clothing, and socks. At one point he claimed that "the present mode of clothing the army is ruinous. We have had 3,000 soldiers unfit for want of clothing, this fall and winter."[16] It appears that Greene's efforts did meet with some success, as Rhode Island governor Nicholas Cooke replied to Greene on January 13, "We have done everything in our power to cloath them comfortably, we have now obtained a considerable quantity."[17] He went on to report that two wagonloads of clothing, containing 1,000 stockings, 600 pair of shoes, 300 shirts, 120 breeches, 50 coats, and other assorted articles, would be dispatched for Valley Forge the next day.

Rhode Island was not the only state that responded to the desperate clothing needs of its troops. But an exasperated George Washington wrote to the Board of War on January 2 about a new, and paradoxical, problem with the supply system: "The Connecticut troops now here have received more necessaries of an essential nature then their present wants require."[18] The army was in great need of three to four thousand blankets, Washington told the board, but because individual states sent supplies directly to their own troops, this bypassed the central army supply system and caused great inequities. The Connecticut troops received more clothing than they could reasonably use, while some of their less fortunate countrymen were dressed in rags. Thus, as Washington, inspired by his vision of national solidarity and civic virtue, struggled to build a cohesive and effective force out of the troops from thirteen diverse states, the political leadership of these fractious and parochial states undermined his efforts.

Heavy rain in late February and early March wreaked havoc upon an already precarious supply situation and inaugurated the third "starving time" of the winter. The precipitation presented a twofold problem. The rain not only turned the primitive roads into almost impassable quagmires but also caused the

Schuylkill River to flood, creating yet another obstacle to wagons attempting to reach Valley Forge with badly needed foodstuffs. The irregular flow of food now slowed to a crawl.

Washington once again reacted with a decisiveness that belied the charges of indecision and timidity that were then circulating in Congress, taking quill in hand and pleading for assistance from civilian leaders. He also directed his commissary agents to take extreme measures. On February 7 Washington wrote an extraordinary letter to commissary agent Peter Colt, in which he stated that "the present situation of the army is the most melancholy that can be conceived. Our provisions of the flesh kind for some time past have been very deficient and irregular—a prospect now opens of absolute want, such as will make it impossible to keep the army much longer from dissolving, unless the most vigorous and effectual measures be persued to prevent it."[19]

These vigorous measures included transporting salted meat from magazines in Virginia that were intended for the summer campaign. In essence, Washington mortgaged the future logistical health of the army to meet its current needs. He also ordered Greene and Wayne to strip the area between the Schuylkill and the Brandywine clean of any provisions. Wayne took fifteen hundred to two thousand of the remaining Continentals out of camp and proceeded on a large foraging expedition. Although these measures eased the immediate crisis, they must be seen as extraordinary. Washington was always reluctant to seize civilian property out of fear of alienating the population, whose support was critical to the success of the Revolution. Furthermore, he jeopardized the ability of the army to fight in the coming summer by using carefully stockpiled stores. The want in February must have been great. In any event, the measures Washington took proved successful, and by late February the immediate crisis was over.

Health and Disease at Valley Forge

Eighteenth-century armies were beset with a host of diseases that the medical science of the day could readily prevent or cure. Chief among these was smallpox, all but extinct now; this disease frightened soldiers and civilians above all others. It was extremely virulent, highly infectious, and very lethal. The cramped conditions, poor food, scanty clothing, and lax hygiene practices at Valley Forge provided ideal conditions for epidemic breakouts. In order to forestall this, Washington took the step of inoculating every Continental soldier at Valley Forge against the disease. This involved injecting a live strain of smallpox into the patient, in essence giving him a mild case of the disease. Once recovered, the patient would be immune to future infection. Although Washington had inaugurated the inoculation campaign during the previous winter of 1776–77, spent at Morristown, New Jersey, the army was not yet fully immunized.

Although sound in theory, the procedure was not without its dangers. Soldiers did become sick with smallpox, and despite the best efforts of army surgeons, a small percentage of them died. The patients were also extremely contagious and likely to infect any uninoculated persons they came into contact with. Add the inadequacies of diet, clothing, and hygiene, and you had a recipe for disaster. The smallpox situation added to the army's already strained hospital system.

The Continental army had a fairly extensive system of hospitals, magazines, armies, and depots that dotted the American countryside, of which Valley Forge was just a part. Far from being an isolated camp in a desolate wilderness, Valley Forge lay at the heart of a thriving rural economy that helped serve the needs of the metropolis of Philadelphia, and was just a part of the military establishment. The system of hospitals was another branch of this extensive system.

Three types of hospitals were in use during the winter of 1777–78. The first were large outlying hospitals called general hospitals that served the needs of the seriously ill and convalescent. The nearest general hospital to Valley Forge was in Yellow Springs, ten miles to the west. The second type, located closer to the main encampment, were emergency hospitals, generally barns, Quaker meeting-houses, and other large structures pressed into service as needed. The extent of this practice at Valley Forge belied the tragically high number of illnesses among the soldiers. Sadly, these first two types of hospital did not prove adequate to handling the flow of patients, so Washington directed the construction of hospital huts, or "flying hospitals," at Valley Forge itself. In a general order issued by his headquarters on January 13, 1778, Washington directed that "the flying hospitals are to be fifteen feet wide and twenty-five feet long, in the clear and the storey at least nine feet high; to be covered with boards or shingles only, without any dirt. A window made in each side and a chimney at one end."[20] Despite Washington's attempts to prevent the accumulation of foul air and miasmas in the hospital huts, disease continued to be a problem throughout the army's stay at Valley Forge.

The flying hospitals were much in use that winter, as Washington's inoculation program got into full swing. It is estimated that by March 22 approximately three to four thousand soldiers had been inoculated in these hospital huts.[21] The soldiers could do little but suffer in silent agony in these cold, crowded huts, and suffer they did. Smallpox, however, was not the only scourge ravaging the ranks. Dysentery, or "the bloody flux," typhus, scabies, pneumonia, and typhoid also stalked the camp and claimed the lives of soldiers.

The army that arrived at Valley Forge that winter was a sick one. Muster returns for the month of December 1777 indicate that of a total reported strength of 14,122 soldiers, 2,087 were "sick present" (unable to perform normal duty but still in camp; some of these men were probably healthy but lacked adequate clothing) and 5,008 "sick absent" (sick enough to have been evacuated to a general or emergency hospital).[22] Thus, in the month of December 1777, 50.2 percent of the Continental army was incapable of performing duty owing to illness. This was truly a desperate situation, one that the inadequate medical department and inefficient and overwhelmed Quartermaster and Commissary departments simply were not equipped to deal with.

Dr. Benjamin Rush, surgeon general of the Middle Department, wrote Washington a rather desperate letter on December 26, 1777, in which he described the sickness pervading the army and the great difficulties faced by the army surgeons who were trying to stem the tide. "We now have upwards of 5,000 Sick in our hospitals," he wrote, adding, "I am safe when I assert that a *great majority* of those who die under our hands perish with diseases caught in our hospitals." Rush outlined the major difficulties facing the hospitals: overcrowding, a lack of proper nutritious food and of clean sheets, blankets, and shirts, an inadequate number of guards and officers, the assignment of ill-trained soldiers and officers to hospital duty, and faulty organization of the "medical establishment." These substandard conditions resulted in an alarmingly high mortality rate. "Every day deprives us of four or five patients out of 500 in the hospital under my care in this place," Rush lamented.[23] The Continental army clearly faced a crisis of epic proportions.

The monthly returns revealed the sad state of the army and alarmed Washington, who continued his letter-writing campaign, exhorting state governments and the Continental Congress to alleviate the suffering of his army. On December 27 he wrote Patrick Henry, the governor of Virginia, thanking him for his exertions in procuring clothes for the Virginia troops. But he also described the condition of the army and told Henry, "I fear I shall wound your feelings by telling you that a Feild [sic] return on the 23rd Inst. had in Camp not less than 2898 Men unfit for duty by reason of their being bare foot and otherwise naked."[24] As if this was not distressing enough, Washington continued, "Besides these, there are many Others detained at Hospitals & in Farmers Houses for the same causes."

Army surgeons struggled valiantly to alleviate the suffering, but the lack of adequate clothing and blankets, poor diet, deficient medicines, and medical ignorance hampered them at every turn. A. Chapman was one of the heroic surgeons who labored unceasingly amid scenes of horrific suffering and death. Chapman wrote of his arrival at the hospital at Ephrata, Pennsylvania, "after arrival at this place I received orders to Superintend the Hospitals and found them all in confusion."[25] "Forty or so" soldiers had died in Ephrata, and the supply situation was so confused that no account of clothes was possible. Surgeons like Chapman did the best they could, but soldiers continued to sicken and die throughout the winter, as the scourge of smallpox ravaged the army.

In January 1778 the army's total assigned strength was 8,095 men; of these, 1,455 were sick present and 3,598 were sick absent. Thus 62.4 percent of the army was incapacitated owing to illness, injury, or lack of clothing. As the winter progressed, the sickness continued unabated. February saw a remarkable 91 percent of the army listed as sick present or sick absent. If ever the army was in danger of succumbing completely to disease, it was now. The muster returns for March, which saw some improvement in the health of the army, listed 84 percent of the assigned 7,316 soldiers as sick. As spring came to muddy slopes of Valley Forge, the situation began to improve slightly. In April only 39.9 percent of the soldiers were listed as sick, although this figure is misleading, as the overall number of sick soldiers decreased very little. In fact 3,798 soldiers were sick present and 2,311 sick absent, but Washington had received substantial reinforcements that swelled his total assigned strength. Despite Washington's attempts at "spring cleaning"—he ordered soldiers to cut windows in the huts and remove chinking—the warmer weather brought no significant relief from disease. In fact, in June 1778, the beginning of the active campaigning season, Washington still listed 902 soldiers as sick present and an astonishing 5,066 soldiers as sick absent. The debilitating effects of epidemic diseases made their presence felt far past the end of winter.

The ravages of disease at Valley Forge took a heavy toll on Washington's army. Many soldiers experienced the horrors of the cramped and unsanitary hospitals, and all who needed it received inoculation against smallpox in a desperate attempt to stave off disaster. Unfortunately, many soldiers never returned from these army hospitals. The muster returns again tell a harrowing tale. According to the returns, 1,162 soldiers assigned to Washington's army died between December 1777 and June 1778, for an average monthly death rate of approximately 194 soldiers for this six-month period. Compare this with the relatively low casualties sustained by the army in pitched battles (approximately 300 killed at Brandywine, the second-largest engagement of the war). The danger of succumbing to disease far outweighed that of being destroyed on the battlefield.

Background and Weather at Jockey Hollow

David Ludlum has categorized the Morristown winter of 1779–80 as one of two severe winters of the Revolution (the other being 1781–82). By any standard, this winter was exceedingly brutal. "There has only been one winter in recorded American history during which the waters surrounding New York City have frozen over and remained closed to all navigation for weeks to come," Ludlum writes. "This occurred during the Hard Winter of 1780."[26] This fact alone indicates the depth, severity, and persistence of the cold that swept over the barren lands during that long winter.

Ludlum's temperature data for the month of January reveal an average temperature at sunrise of 4.1 degrees. These measurements were for the Hartford, Connecticut, area and therefore cannot be taken as completely accurate for the Morristown area, but they do give a general idea of the extent of the cold. Thermometers in Philadelphia recorded only one reading above freezing in January, and this lasted for only a short time. It is little wonder, then, that Ludlum calls January 1780 "the most persistently cold calendar month in the history of the eastern United States."

Unfortunately for the Continental troops, it was also an uncommonly wet winter. The beginning of the winter was marked by a series of heavy snowstorms followed by gale-force winds that caused massive drifting problems. Snow began to fall on the East Coast in early November and continued throughout the winter. The greatest snowfall occurred in the ten-day period between December 28, 1779, and January 7, 1780, in which three separate large storms ravaged the East Coast. "The three major snowstorms at the turn of the year 1779–80 rank with the greatest such combinations in our meteorological history," according to Ludlum. These conditions would be brutal for people ensconced in comfortable permanent dwellings; for soldiers in crude huts or tents, they would be horrific.

The first major storm commenced in eastern Pennsylvania early on December 28 and progressed east. A Tory editor in New York City by the name of Hugh Gaine reported a mix of snow and rain during the day. By 6:00 P.M. "a most violent storm of rain and wind set in from the N.E. and continued at least six hours; it did little or no damage in the harbor, but many are uneasy about the fleet, I hope it is safe," wrote Gaine. Although the British fleet rode out the first storm in relative calm, the British were not so lucky with the second storm, a savage northeaster that battered the coast. The combination of wind, high tides, and snow caused at least three British ships in the New York area to run aground. Reverend Henry Mühlenberg, writing from Trappe in eastern Pennsylvania, noted in his journal on January 2, "After service it began to snow heavily again accompanied by stormy northeast wind." His entry for January 3 read, "Since yesterday afternoon and throughout the night, there was such a snowstorm that the house and yard are so circumvallated that one can scarcely get out or in, and the snow is still falling." The third storm, another northeaster, came hard on the heels of the second and began lashing the Morristown area on January 6. Washington noted in his weather diary that the sixth saw "snowing and sunshine alternately—cold with the wind west and northwest and increasing—night very stormy." January 7 saw much of the same, strong winds and intermittent snow. Although this storm did not produce prodigious amounts of snowfall, the high winds caused massive drifts that all but closed land transportation routes.

The cumulative effects of these storms devastated the East Coast. Exact snowfall measurements for the Morristown area do not exist, but measurements taken near Yale College indicate a total snowfall of ninety-five inches, as compared to twenty-five inches for the following winter of 1780–81.[27] The frigid cold exacerbated the ill effects of each snowstorm, preventing one snowfall from melting before another hit. Continental army surgeon James Thatcher noted that by early January the snow was three or four feet deep.

The bitter cold of January led to a general freeze of both the Hudson and East rivers, such that by January 20, 1780, both could be crossed on foot. Although this was not uncommon in that era, what happened next was unique in the recorded weather history of North America. By January 29 the freeze had become so severe and sustained that New York Harbor froze solid—so solid that pedestrian and sled traffic was possible between Staten Island and Manhattan. This did not go unnoticed by patriot forces.

The freezing of New York Harbor led to one of the most bizarre chapters in American military history: Major General William Alexander (Lord Stirling) sought and received permission in mid-January to take advantage of the frozen harbor and launch a raid on Staten Island by sled. Undoubtedly, an important goal was to seize badly needed food and supplies from the British. During the planning process, Elizabethtown militia learned of the proposed raid and gained permission from Washington to join Stirling's men on January 14, one day before the raid was to occur. Stirling and his men, riding on sleds, set out the next day in the frigid cold and headed for Staten Island. After landing there and scouring the area for military stores, Stirling's men pulled back to a defensible hill and spent a long, cold night before retiring to Morristown the next morning, pursued by British forces. The raid itself accomplished little, as the British, probably alerted by Tory sympathizers, reacted quickly and shifted reinforcements from Manhattan Island. Although little fighting occurred, patriot forces, especially local militia, engaged in an orgy of looting of Tory homes. This not only embarrassed Washington deeply but also provoked retaliatory raids on Elizabethtown and Newark.

In addition to achieving little of military value, the raid exposed the Continental troops to the full fury of the record cold. Joseph Plumb Martin of the Connecticut line had the misfortune of accompanying the raid and experienced the ravages of the weather firsthand. "We then fell back a little distance," he wrote later, "and took up our abode for the night upon a bare bleak hill, in full rake of the northwest wind, with no other covering or shelter than the canopy of the heavens, and no fuel but some old rotten rails which we dug up through the snow, which was two or three feet deep. The weather was cold enough to cut a man in two." As if to add insult to injury, the weather continued to worsen after the raid. "Soon after this there came several severe snowstorms," Martin wrote. "At one time it snowed the greater part of four days successively, and there fell nearly as many feet deep of snow."[28]

The weather generally remained below freezing until February 15, when a rainstorm brought the first significant melting of the accumulated snow. A general warming trend continued through the first half of March, but then winter returned. Yet another northeaster hit the coast on March 31, dumping ankle-deep accumulations. Although this was the last appreciable snowfall of the year, it was not the end of the cold. To the dismay of soldiers and farmers alike, spring came very late in 1780. Frosts as late as June 4, 5, and 6 indicated the persistence of winter. The "hard winter" was made even harder by its long duration.

Although the objective data on the winter of 1779–80 clearly place it in a class by itself in terms of its length, cold, and amount of snowfall, the question remains, how did those who experienced it perceive it? Of special interest are those hardy individuals who experienced both winters. Did they feel that the winter at Jockey Hollow was exceptional, or that the winter at Valley Forge was abnormally mild?

The primary sources are revealing in this respect. At Valley Forge, Washington, Greene, and others routinely complained of the lack of clothing, food, and shelter, and occasionally of the lack of shoes, which caused some soldiers to leave bloody footprints in the snow; and although they surely commented on the effects of the weather on the soldiers, no one seemed overly impressed with an *unusual severity* of the weather. This is not the case when we look at the "hard winter" of 1779–80. All who lived through that winter noted the extremes of temperature and the suffering it produced in both man and beast.

Major General Johann DeKalb lived through both winters, and he wrote of 1779–80:

> The roads are piled high with snow until, in some place they are elevated twelve feet above their ordinary level. The present winter is especially remarkable for its uninterrupted and unvarying cold. The ice in the rivers is six feet thick. Since this part of North America has been settled by Europeans, the North River at New York, where it is a mile and a half wide near its mouth, and subject to the ebb and flow of a strong tide, has not been frozen over so fast as to be passable by wagons. Unfortunately our camp will suffer even more from the thaw than the frost, for it is too much exposed to inundation. Those who have only been in Valley Forge

and Middlebrook during the last two winters, but have not tasted the cruelties of this one, know not what it is to suffer.[29]

How extraordinary a winter it must have been to bury roads under twelve feet of snow. Not only was the snowfall remarkable, but so was the "uninterrupted and unvarying cold," which could only have compounded the effects of each individual snowfall and made life an unceasing battle for survival against the cruel elements.

Surgeon James Thatcher also noted the extraordinary nature of the winter weather at Morristown. The fierce blizzard of January 3, 1780, with its howling winds, blinding snow, and bone-chilling cold, caused Thatcher to remark, "On the 3d instant, we experienced one of the most tremendous snowstorms ever remembered; no man could endure its violence many minutes without the danger of his life. Several marquees were torn asunder . . . and some of the soldiers were actually covered while in their tents."[30] Thatcher, DeKalb, and other officers were used to the rigors of military campaigns and to dealing with the vagaries of the weather. Yet the severity of the winter of 1779–80 astonished them.

Logistics at Jockey Hollow

In the autumn of 1779 George Washington turned to his most trusted subordinate, Quartermaster-General Nathanael Greene, to find a suitable site at which to encamp the Continental army. With customary diligence, Greene and his staff scoured the northern New Jersey countryside and ultimately choose an area very familiar to the army—Jockey Hollow, near Morristown. On November 14, 1779, Greene formalized his recommendation in a letter to Washington. Greene recounted the primary considerations he had used in selecting the cantonment area, primary among which were its security from British attacks, foraging opportunities, ease of transporting provisions, abundance of wood, and sources of potable water. But Greene's missive also revealed apprehensions among the high command about concentrating the army for another bleak New Jersey winter. Greene discussed the relative merits and disadvantages of both concentration and dispersal and ultimately concluded that "dispersing the Troops should be avoided at all events."[31] Washington stated that he chose the site for "the double purpose of security and subsistence."[32] Security Washington would get; subsistence would be another matter altogether.

Unfortunately for the Continental soldiers, the always shaky Quartermaster and Commissary departments were experiencing an acute crisis. The supply situation during the hard winter would not be episodic but would be exacerbated by a long, bitterly cold winter of deprivation and starvation brought about by a general collapse of the American economy.

Quartermaster-General Greene's correspondence with his harried subordinates reveals the problems caused by lack of funds and monetary inflation. On November 14, 1779, the deputy quartermaster, Colonel John Mitchell, informed Greene of the dearth of money. "Depreciation of the money is not yet stopped," he wrote, "and I fear will not soon, as there has been some deficiency (where I will not say) in not making proper provision for stopping it. I wish it may not be too late." Mitchell also lamented that he not only lacked funds to purchase additional supplies but could not pay for provisions already provided, and concluded with the warning, "It is impossible to proceed in our preparations without money."[33] Colonel Thomas Chase revealed the extent of the inflation in letter to Greene dated December 1, 1779: "The money depreciates so fast no body will trust the Continental One day."[34]

November communications within the Quartermaster Department revealed yet another recurring problem, the lack of fodder for horses and cattle. Moore Furman, a civilian purchasing agent, wrote Greene on November 15 that "as few Horse as possible should be kept in this state [New Jersey] as there is no supplies coming in that I hear from the Southward, and what can be spared here will not be sufficient to keep those that *must* remain with the Army well."[35] Furman's prediction was all too accurate, as lack of fodder for draft animals further compounded logistical and transportation problems for the army during the winter.

The relative isolation of Morristown, a small farming community ensconced in the Watchung Mountains, which made it relatively safe from British attack, also made it difficult to supply, unlike Valley Forge, which was well integrated into Philadelphia transportation routes and possessed a well-connected series of farms, forges, and small manufacturers. In fact, almost no supplies reached the cantonment area of Jockey Hollow for three weeks, as wagons were either snowed in at warehouses or abandoned en route. At one point Washington sent local militia to open a route from Hackettstown to Princeton. These militiamen reported that fences and even buildings were buried in snow. On December 5, 1779, a second severe snowstorm (the first had occurred in late November) hit the area and added to the misery to the masses of troops still living in tents. Supplies did manage to trickle into Morristown over the frozen landscape until a ferocious storm on January 3 brought movement to a complete halt.

By January 7, four feet of snow carpeted the ground, with drifts many times as high. Morristown, for all intents and purposes, was cut off from the rest of the world. With no supplies coming in, the soldiers could only sit in their huts and starve. It is of this period that Joseph Plumb Martin wrote, "I did not put a single morsel of victuals into my mouth for four days and as many nights, except for a little black birch bark." In a winter of starving, the first week of January represented the absolute nadir for the Continental soldiers.

As he had done at Valley Forge, Washington issued urgent appeals to the governors of the mid-Atlantic states, beseeching them to rush food, fodder, blankets, clothes, and medicine to Morristown as quickly as possible or face the possibility of the army's dissolution. On December 19 he revealed the depth of the supply crisis, stating that his soldiers had been for "five or six weeks past on half-allowance."[36] Even this meager half-ration ran out by January 1, 1780, and the soldiers had nothing to eat for several days. On the fifth and sixth days of this starving week, a trickle of food began to arrive, but by all accounts it was not enough to feed one regiment, let alone an entire army. Faced with the prospect of starvation, the desperate soldiers resorted to robbing the local population, which Washington deplored but to which he was forced to turn a blind eye.

The bitter month of January was quite possibly the closest the Continental army came to dissolution. Washington took the drastic and desperate step of forcing a levy for supplies on each county in New Jersey, enacted through the local magistrates. Perhaps more than any other revolutionary leader, Washington was loath to jeopardize the cause by forcing heavy-handed requisitions or levies on the people on whose support the fate of the army rested. But he had no choice. While Washington tried to force supplies out of the reluctant New Jersey countryside, Nathanael Greene waged his battles from within the Quartermaster Department, forwarding supplies to Morristown from distant magazines. Greene's January 6 letter to New Jersey militia colonel Benoni Hathaway reflected not the only the desperate state of the army but also the devastating impact of the weather on supply operations.

> The Army is upon the eve of disbanding for want of Provisions, the poor soldiers having been several days without, and there not being more than a sufficiency to serve one Regiment in the Magazine. Provision is scarce at best; but the late terrible storm and the depth of the Snow and the drifts in the Roads, prevent the little stock coming forward which is in readiness at the distant Magazines. This is therefore to request you to call upon the Militia Officers and people of your Battallion to turn out their teams and break the Roads between this and Hacketstown, there being a small quantity of provision there that cannot come on until this is done. The Roads must be kept open by the Inhabitants or the Army cannot be subsisted. And unless the good people lend their assistance to foreward supplies the Army must disband.[37]

Washington and Greene continued their frantic efforts to keep the army alive and intact throughout the seemingly endless winter. Congress was also aware of the plight of the army at Morristown and dispatched one of its own, Congressman Richard Peters, to observe and investigate. Peters arrived in camp on March 3, 1780, and immediately saw the army's great distress. "Unless the speediest relief is afforded," he told Congress, "it is by no Means improbable that the Army will be obliged to disband."[38] Despite Peters's firsthand report, supplies continued to trickle in at a rate insufficient to feed and clothe the army. Only the coming of the summer campaign would bring relief to the suffering soldiers.

Lack of food, clothes, and medicine was not the only logistical issue to vex Washington during this hard winter. Washington once again faced a loss of manpower, as enlisted men finished their service and left the army. He wrote of this exodus in a letter of March 27, in which he stated that the "force at this post [Jockey Hollow] amounts to 7,000 rank and file, thirteen hundred of whom will have completed their term of service this last of May."[39] The brutal conditions at Morristown and the shortage of food made retaining experienced soldiers, and recruiting new ones, especially difficult.

As winter gave way to spring, the weather continued cold and wet, and material conditions improved little. Brigadier General Huntingdon complained to Washington in late April that he was losing two to three soldiers a day as their terms expired, and that many of his soldiers could not perform their duties because they had no shoes. Even more telling on the logistical health of the army was Nathanael Greene's letter to Washington on April 2, in which he bemoaned the lack of funds and provisions. "Circumstances oblige me to confess myself unable, for want of sufficient support," he told Washington, "either to make the proper provision in my department necessary for marching the troops to the Southward, or for putting the Army in motion in these Northern States. There would be no difficulty either in the one case or the other, could the treasury furnish the proper supplies of cash. But in its present exhausted state, with the enormous demands upon the Department, the agents have neither credit nor influence equal to the business."[40]

Thus the unusually cold, wet spring provided little relief from the privations of winter. In fact, the same general pattern prevailed—an overall period of insufficient supply punctuated by episodes of total deprivation. Unlike Valley Forge, where the periods of greatest want were limited to three "starving times," the encampment of 1779–80 at Jockey Hollow is better characterized as one long period of general starvation. The soldiers who had the misfortune of being at Jockey Hollow suffered as perhaps no other American soldiers before or since. These men had tremendous fortitude, but even they had a breaking point. In May 1780 troops of the Connecticut line, including the intrepid Joseph Plumb Martin, reached theirs.

Martin and his brigade surely got their fill of the New Jersey countryside that fateful winter. These troops had the dubious honor of being included in the sled-borne raid on Staten Island of January 14–15, which froze them nearly to death and accomplished little beyond arousing the ire of the British, who retaliated with raids on Newark and Elizabethtown. After the raid, the Connecticut Continentals returned to the main cantonment area at Jockey Hollow. Martin stated of this time period that "we continued here, starving and freezing, until I think sometime in February, when the two Connecticut Brigades were ordered to lines near Staten Island."[41]

Apparently, duty near Staten Island did not improve the supply situation for the soldiers. In a statement that typifies their experience that winter, Martin wrote later, "we sometimes got a little beef, but no bread, we however, once in a while got a little rice, but as to flour or bread, I do not recollect that I saw a morsel of either during the winter." This presents a stark contrast to Valley Forge, where flour was available almost the entire winter and where the soldiers rarely went entirely without food. Martin and his comrades suffered and starved in the lines near Staten Island and, to their dismay, found conditions no better in Jockey Hollow when they returned to the cantonment on May 25. It was with some bitterness that Martin recalled, "we had entertained some hopes that when we had left the line and joined the main army, we should fare a little better, but we found there was no betterment in the case. For several days after we rejoined the army, we got a little musty bread and a little beef, about every other day, but this lasted only a short time and then we got nothing at all. The men were exasperated beyond endurance. They could not stand it any longer. They saw no alternative but to starve to death, or break up the army give all up and go home."[42]

These Connecticut men had reached the breaking point. After several days without food, they threatened to go into the local countryside and procure food on their own volition, an act expressly forbidden by Washington and army regulations. At evening roll call, the exasperated Eighth Connecticut Regiment refused to disperse and again threatened to go into the countryside in search of food from the populace. Officers who were desperately trying to control the situation exchanged words with the angry soldiers, and tempers began to flare. The men of the Eighth attempted to recruit nearby units to join in the mutiny. The alarmed officers raced to quash the mutiny before it could grow and rushed uniformed troops of the Pennsylvania line to the parade ground in an attempt to quell the budding rebellion. When the Pennsylvania troops found out that their Connecticut comrades were threatening to mutiny because of a lack of food, however, they refused to obey their superior officers, and the terrified officers sent them back to their barracks before they could join the mutiny. At this point a minor scuffle ensued between some of the mutineers and their officers, which resulted in the wounding of Colonel Jonathan Meigs. Some of the Connecticut officers were finally able to persuade the men to follow orders and go back to their barracks. Although the officers had restored order, the breakdown in discipline was ominous.

The mutiny in May did not lead to widespread chaos or to dispersal of the army, but it did reveal the dreadful extent of deprivation among the soldiers and the very fragile and tenuous nature of the Revolution. More important, the mutiny also helps explain the relative lack of attention that scholars and historians have paid to the hard winter encampment of 1779–80. Valley Forge can boast of the improvements wrought by Baron von Steuben's modified drill, while Morristown/Jockey Hollow can only exhibit a lack of revolutionary resolve by the populace and mutiny by the army. These are not events to memorialize or build foundational myths upon. While the Valley Forge experience easily lent itself to the myth of rebirth through hardship, the Morristown mutiny made the hard winter encampment difficult to reconcile with patriotic virtues and thus became, in a word, forgettable.

Health and Disease at Jockey Hollow

The story of health and sickness at Jockey Hollow during the hard winter of 1779–80 stands in stark contrast to that of Valley Forge. Valley Forge saw the scourge of smallpox and other highly infectious and virulent diseases sweep through the camp and claim many lives. Although the human suffering at Jockey Hollow due to weather and lack of food far surpassed that which occurred at Valley Forge, the death toll due to disease was significantly lower. A thorough review of the muster returns for the Continental army from December 1779 to June 1780 reveals that the army recorded only 124 soldier deaths in all of the units assigned to stations in New Jersey. This would include not only units in the Morristown area but units assigned to detached duty throughout north and central New Jersey. As incredibly low as this number is, it does correspond to the National Park Service's claim that only eighty-six soldiers actually died in the cantonment area at Jockey Hollow near Morristown.[43]

Two significant factors contributed heavily to this very low mortality rate. One was Washington's adoption of the forced smallpox inoculation program for all soldiers, begun in the winter of 1776–77 and continued during the Valley Forge winter of 1777–78, when smallpox began to break out among the soldiers. Although the inoculation program at Valley Forge did contribute mightily to the disease and suffering of the soldiers at that encampment, it paid dividends during the "hard winter" at Jockey Hollow by drastically reducing the occurrence of smallpox. The second factor was the changes that surgeon James Tilton made to the design and layout of hospitals. Tilton discontinued the use of tents and civilian dwellings as hospitals and instead designed log structures, much like the "flying hospitals" constructed at Valley Forge. Significantly, Tilton's design called for a central structure from which two long wings or wards would radiate. This allowed patients with similar symptoms to be grouped together and thus helped prevent cross-contamination. Tilton also directed that the cabins be built with very loose chinking in order to allow proper ventilation.[44]

The army's muster returns reveal that the inoculation program and Tilton's reforms improved the health of the army significantly. Washington began the encampment with approximately 11,053 men assigned to Morristown and New Jersey; of these, 14 percent (1,542) were either sick present or sick absent (and, as in the Valley Forge case, soldiers who had inadequate clothing to perform outside duty may very well have been listed as sick present). This figure climbed to 23 percent during the month of January, not surprisingly, for January was by far the most brutally cold month of that winter. From that point, the percentage of Washington's troops listed as sick declined slowly until May and June 1780, when it stabilized at 15 percent. Although modern military observers may cringe at the thought of 15 percent of their combat power unavailable because of illness, this was vastly better than the 91 percent of the army at Valley Forge listed as sick present or sick absent during the month of February 1778. In terms of suffering due to disease, the Jockey Hollow encampment pales in comparison with Valley Forge.

Myth and Historical Memory

The objective comparison between the Valley Forge and Jockey Hollow encampments reveals some interesting facts. As we have seen, and contrary to popular opinion, the weather conditions at Valley Forge were relatively mild, nothing like the record winter that brutalized soldiers at Jockey Hollow. In addition, food, although never abundant, was available in adequate quantities at Valley Forge except for three acute shortages. By contrast, the entire winter at Jockey Hollow may be accurately described as a starving time. Only in terms in sickness and disease was Valley Forge truly exceptional. It was the ravages of smallpox and other infectious diseases that decimated the ranks and caused so much human misery and suffering, making the winter at Valley Forge a true test of resolve and patriotic spirit.

Despite the availability of these objective data, the myths surrounding Valley Forge continue to reverberate across the American landscape and through the American psyche. Special programs on the History Channel, prints, popular stories, and countless books portray the Valley Forge winter as exceedingly cold and snowy and as marked by an almost total absence of food. Iconic images of soldiers dressed in rags, bloody footprints in the snow, miraculous shad runs,

and Washington kneeling in the snow in prayer have become staples of revolutionary lore.[45] In documenting Valley Forge, historians have long painted the
story with the broad brushstrokes of romanticism and mysticism. One need
only examine the titles of monographs on Valley Forge to get a sense of where
Americans have lodged Valley Forge in their collective memory. Such titles as
Valley Forge: A Chronicle of Heroism, Ordeal at Valley Forge, and *Valley Forge:
Crucible of Victory* are common. Libraries are full of monographs, novels, plays,
and documentaries that focus on the themes of suffering and rebirth at Valley
Forge.

Clues to how the myth of Valley Forge evolved can be found in the earliest
attempts to document that winter of 1777–78. One of the earliest monographs
on the Valley Forge encampment is Henry Woodman's *The History of Valley
Forge,* which Woodman wrote in 1850 in the form of weekly letters published
serially in the *Doylestown (PA) Intelligencer.* In 1920 Woodman's descendants
published his work in book form and claimed that it was the first history of
Valley Forge. Woodman, a native of the Valley Forge area, based his narrative
on information from his father, a veteran of Washington's army who served at
Valley Forge, and other surviving veterans. Woodman's book helped further the
process of mythmaking that had begun nearly as soon as the Revolution itself
was over.

Woodman's account, drawn from the fading memories of participants many
years after the fact, began the tradition of overdramatizing the weather conditions at Valley Forge. Woodman described Valley Forge as the place where
Washington and his army "suffered for a period of seven months, the most
severe privations and hardships" during a "severe and protracted winter."
Woodman's soldiers were "almost destitute of clothing and provisions, sustained
by the principles of purest patriotism."[46]

Woodman also recounted two stories about George Washington that continue to generate controversy to this day. The first concerns Washington's supposed habit at Valley Forge of praying aloud in solitary places. We see this in
many famous prints and paintings of Washington praying fervently alone in the
woods. According to Woodman, a man named Isaac Potts (an inhabitant of
Valley Forge?), a friend of Washington's, supposedly discovered Washington
during one of his solitary prayer sessions. Woodman admitted that he had no
way to verify this story, but he recounted a second apocryphal tale involving the
commander-in-chief that he claimed was true.

According to Woodman, his father was planting a field on the site of the
encampment one day in the spring of 1796. His father's plowing was interrupted
by the arrival of "an elderly person of a very dignified appearance, dressed in
plain black, on horseback."[47] This elderly gentleman inquired about the owners
of various houses and about farming techniques of the region. Only after Wood-

man's father told the stranger that he was not a native of the region but had been a soldier at Valley Forge did the gentleman reveal himself as George Washington. Although modern researchers have found substantive errors in this account, the story contributed to the making of the Valley Forge myth.

Frank Taylor's 1846 *Valley Forge: A Chronicle of American Heroism* was another such early account. This work, which helped establish the centrality of Valley Forge in the victorious outcome of the Revolutionary War and highlighted the extreme weather and inadequate food and clothing, began a long tradition of eulogizing the Valley Forge experience. Many other prominent authors followed Taylor's lead.

Henry Emerson Wildes's 1938 *Valley Forge* continued in the tradition begun by Taylor and Woodman. According to Wildes, "the country was preserved through the inspiration of the Valley Forge winter." Wildes lamented that Henry Woodman's *History of Valley Forge* was the last work on the subject for eighty years, and he sought to improve upon the amateur historian's collection of reminiscences. He did improve upon Woodman's story in terms of sources and historical methodology, but Wildes told essentially the same tale that Woodman had. "The Revolution was won at Valley Forge," Wildes wrote. "A defeated, dispirited, and tattered array came here hungry, cold and broken; Washington led away the same men, drilled and disciplined into a confident army, in pride to victory." Wildes also perpetuated the myth of the "bitter" winter of 1777–78, and he alluded to barefoot troops when he wrote of "Washington's bleeding soldiers."[48] Wildes reinforced myths such as the famous shad run, which he characterized as lasting for days and attested had helped end the last great period of need. No modern researcher has found any firsthand accounts of this event.

John F. Reed's *Valley Forge: Crucible of Victory* tells a familiar tale of "bitter" weather conditions and starving soldiers.[49] Perhaps most telling is Reed's choice of titles. Indeed, Reed's choice reflects a long historical tradition that made Valley Forge the seminal event of the Revolution, and works like his, published in 1969, show the lasting power of this myth.

John Joseph Stoudt's 1963 *Ordeal at Valley Forge* began slowly to move away from the melodramatic accounts of Wildes and the other early historians. Although Stoudt's winter was "intensely cold," the primary sources on which he relied painted a less dramatic portrait of the Valley Forge winter, and his depiction was correspondingly toned down, including less emphatic statements such as "Clothing was scarce, and food was short for a time. There was much sickness, especially smallpox."[50] Stoudt did not directly challenge such myths as Washington praying in the snow or the shad run, but their absence from his story is telling.

John B. B. Trussel's 1976 *Birthplace of an Army* continued to mine the vein that Stoudt had opened and began to depart from some of the loftier hyperbole of the nineteenth and early twentieth centuries. Trussel described the winter at Valley Forge as "marked . . . by cold weather, recurrent starvation, rampant disease, near nakedness."[51] But he also acknowledged that, in terms of weather and shortages of supplies, the winter of 1777–78 was not the worst winter of the war. Like most other historians, however, he neglected to mention which winters, and therefore which encampments, were worse. Trussel made no mention of Jockey Hollow or Morristown.

It is only recently that historians have begun to pry open the cracks in the face of the Valley Forge myth. As noted above, Wayne K. Bodle directly challenged many of the supposed historic facts of the encampment and reassessed its importance to the Revolution in his *Valley Forge Winter.* Most significantly, Bodle advanced the theory that Washington's horrific descriptions of an army on the precipice of dissolution were intentionally exaggerated for the purpose of goading the Supreme Executive Council of Pennsylvania and the Continental Congress into action. Bodle also reevaluated the effect of Baron von Steuben's training and concluded that the army did not fight enough after June 1778 to make it possible to evaluate the winter training fully.

Bodle also offered a striking reinterpretation of the health and general condition of the army. He dismissed Washington's famous "starve, dissolve, or disperse" letter to Henry Laurens as more exaggeration than fact. This prophecy of doom was simply incompatible with the vigorous response to British excursions then in progress, and with the operational planning for a proposed assault on Philadelphia that was in the works. Bodle pointed out this was not at all in keeping with the picture of an army on the verge of starvation and dissolution. He argued compellingly that Washington's letters during the Valley Forge winter must be seen in the context of the political situation he faced.

Bodle's analysis of the encampment represents perhaps the most balanced and objective assessment of the data to date, and marks a significant departure from the myth-filled histories of the past. But even given his exemplary treatment of the historical record with respect to Valley Forge, Bodle makes no mention of the hard winter at Jockey Hollow, apart from one explanatory note of the extreme hardships the Continental army faced outside Morristown during the winter of 1779–80.

Historians are beginning to focus some attention on other encampments of the Revolutionary War, albeit very slowly. In marked contrast to the rich history of laudatory and heroic tomes on Valley Forge, scant attention has been paid to these other encampments, and to the winter of 1779–80 in particular. What images immediately come to mind when we think of Jockey Hollow? Sadly, the answer for most of us is none.

The existing literature on the winter encampment at Jockey Hollow consists mainly of National Park Service material such as *Morristown: Official National Park Service Handbook,* published by Russell F. Weigley and George F. Scheer in 1983, Ricardo Torres Reyes's *The 1779–1780 Encampment: A Study of Medical Services; Morristown National Historical Park* (1971), and small local interest works like Samuel Stelle Smith's *Winter at Morristown, 1779–1780: The Darkest Hour* (1979). Although these works contain valuable information for researchers, none of them is a comprehensive examination of the Continental army's encampments near Morristown, and none is comparative in nature. This dearth of research has further dimmed the historical memory of that extraordinary winter of suffering.

Despite the lack of lack of scholarly research, local residents of the Morristown area have long used the Jockey Hollow location as a commemorative site. The last two owners of the Ford mansion (the site of Washington's headquarters) turned the house into an informal museum that they sometimes opened to unscheduled visitors.[52] Despite this informal use of the mansion, the property was put up for sale at public auction in June 1873, and its continued existence was thrown into doubt. A group of four prominent New Jersey citizens understood the historical value of the property and bought it at auction. This group of men formed the Washington Association of New Jersey on March 20, 1874, in order to maintain and preserve the historic building for public use. This acquisition marked the beginning of the process that would ultimately result, in 1933, in the establishment of the first National Historical Park in the United States.

As early as 1895, local residents made attempts to expand the scope of the preservation by purchasing the site of Fort Nonsense, so called because the fort was said to have made no sense and was built essentially to keep soldiers busy and out of trouble. Despite this early interest, the state commission formed to create a public park on the site failed in its mission, and the town of Morristown eventually purchased the ground. The push to create a national park in Morristown essentially began with the efforts of Morristown mayor Clyde Potts in 1929. Potts's collaboration with wealthy resident Lloyd Smith and with the second director of the National Park System, Horace M. Albright, and its chief historian, Verne E. Chatelain, culminated in the creation of the Morristown National Historical Park in 1933. The legislation transferred control of the Jockey Hollow site (bought privately by Lloyd Smith and donated to the town of Morristown), the Fort Nonsense site (owned by the town), and the Ford mansion (owned by the Washington Association of New Jersey, which today serves in an advisory capacity to the National Park System). After the formal dedication of the park on July 4, 1933, Charles McAlpin donated land that contained the camp site of the Connecticut brigade.[53] In 1969 another area resident donated the area that encompassed the cantonment area for the New Jersey brigade, establishing the park's present-day configuration.

The objective data on the Valley Forge and Jockey Hollow encampments demonstrate that both locations were scenes of human misery, despair, sickness, sacrifice, and ultimately triumph in the face of the great obstacles. Both places speak to us today of the sacrifices that must be made periodically to sustain the liberties that we cherish. It is also clear that Valley Forge holds a preeminent spot in the hearts and minds of Americans, while Jockey Hollow has been generally neglected by historians and the public alike.

No single explanation accounts for this discrepancy; rather, it is a result of many factors. Valley Forge's physical proximity to the thriving city of Philadelphia, the transformative effects (both actual and imagined) of von Steuben's training, the large number of soldiers present there, and the extreme suffering due to disease all played a role in shaping the image of Valley Forge.

Valley Forge's proximity to Philadelphia is perhaps the single greatest factor in ensuring its fame. This thriving capital city was the premier colonial city at the time of the Revolution. Valley Forge's location on the Schuylkill River, approximately twenty miles west of the city, gave it access to a large population base that discovered early on both the patriotic symbolism and the recreational value of its rolling hills. From its earliest colonial days, Valley Forge was tied into the greater Philadelphia economy. Its network of farms, forges, and small workshops regularly sent their surplus production to the city, thus inextricably linking the two areas. In fact, it was Philadelphia's position as capital of the new Republic that makes Henry Woodman's story of Washington's 1796 visit to Valley Forge plausible. The veracity of this story is not as important as its illustration that Valley Forge was within easy traveling distance of Philadelphia, and that the throngs of people attracted to Philadelphia by government jobs could easily visit the site. Furthermore, Philadelphia was central to many famous revolutionary sites, including Independence Hall, the Liberty Bell, Germantown, Paoli, and Brandywine, in addition to Valley Forge. Philadelphia was home to many iconic displays of revolutionary history; Independence Hall, for example, served as an art gallery from 1783 to 1785, and portraits of Washington were prominently displayed there. In 1794 Charles Wilson Peale, one of the most prolific painters of the American Revolution (among his paintings is a famous portrait of Washington at Valley Forge), moved his museum of Revolutionary War art and natural history exhibits to Philadelphia's Philosophical Hall.[54] In short, any citizen interested in touring sites associated with the American Revolution would be drawn to Philadelphia, and thus to Valley Forge by association.

Two other primary factors make Valley Forge memorable. It was there that Baron von Steuben trained the Continental army and made it a more effective fighting force. For the rest of the war the army performed admirably; the mauling of the British army rearguard at Monmouth, New Jersey, in the spring of 1778, as it retreated from Philadelphia to New York, was the first battle it fought after Valley Forge. Finally, the high death rate at Valley Forge made it a worthy site of remembrance.

Just as a confluence of factors combined to create an aura around Valley Forge, others have conspired to obscure the importance of Morristown and Jockey Hollow. Perhaps chief among these is the relative geographic isolation of the area. Throughout the nineteenth century, farming remained the main occupation in Morris County, just as it had been in colonial days. It was only in the early twentieth century that the town became the center of local business that it remains today. The area that contains the actual cantonment location of Jockey Hollow did not witness this commercial development, and although New York businessmen built grand estates in Morris County, the local economy was not significantly tied into the greater New York metropolitan economy. Morristown's location in the Watchung Mountains made access from the city difficult. No tales were told of return visits by President Washington, and unlike Valley Forge, no event such as Daniel Webster's 1824 political rally focused nationwide attention on the Morristown area.

Moreover, the mutiny by parts of the Connecticut line in May 1780 cast a dark shadow over the encampment and made the entire episode more likely to be forgotten than eulogized. No notable military action, such as the Battle of Monmouth, followed, either; the main force of the Continental army remained inactive until the Battle of Yorktown in September 1781. The total breakdown in the supply system and the flourishing of trade between the British and local civilians pointed to a lack of revolutionary resolve on the part of the populace. This flagging of public support, and Congress's inability to provide for even the basic needs of Washington's army there, were embarrassments to be buried in the dim recesses of the historical past, not tales to be celebrated in story and song. The dark side of the Morristown story made the Valley Forge story, by comparison, even more appealing to a young nation that needed to forge an identity and a set of shared cultural values as it made its way in the world. This helped ensure that the story of the "hard winter" encampment would become a footnote in American history, while Valley Forge would be remembered as one of the central dramas in the birth of a nation.

NOTES

1. Joseph Plumb Martin, *Joseph Plumb Martin, Yankee Doodle Boy: A Young Soldier's Experiences in the American Revolution Told by Himself* (1830), ed. George F. Scheer III (1962; reprint, New York: Holiday House, 1995), 119–20.

2. David M. Ludlum, *Early American Winters, 1604–1820* (Boston: American Meteorological Society, 1966), 101.

3. Ibid.

4. Phineas Pemberton, weather diary, December 1776–January 1777, American Philosophical Society. A copy of this document was accessed at the archives of the Valley Forge National Military Park, Valley Forge, Pennsylvania.

5. James Varnum to (Mrs.?) William Greene, March 7, 1778, John Reed Collection, quoted in Wayne K. Bodle, *Valley Forge Historical Research Project, 1980,* vol. 1 (Washington, D.C.: National Park Service, 1980), 314.

6. Wayne K. Bodle, *The Valley Forge Winter: Civilians and Soldiers in War* (University Park: Pennsylvania State University Press, 2002), 113–25.

7. George Washington to Henry Laurens, December 23, 1777, in *George Washington: Writings,* ed. John Rhodehamel (New York: Penguin Books, 1997), 282.

8. Bodle, *Valley Forge Historical Research Project, 1980,* 42.

9. Thomas Jones to Charles Stewart, October 29, 1777, Charles Stewart Collection, New York State Historical Archives, accessed at Valley Forge National Military Park archives.

10. Thomas Jones to Gustavus Riesbig, October 29, 1777, ibid.

11. Bodle, *Valley Forge Historical Research Project, 1980,* 51.

12. Thomas Jones to Thomas Wharton, December 19, 1777, ibid., 80.

13. Jedediah Huntingdon to Timothy Pickering, December 22, 1777, Henry Laurens Papers, accessed at Valley Forge National Military Park archives.

14. James Varnum to George Washington, December 22, 1777, ibid.

15. Nathanael Greene to Christopher Greene, January 5, 1778, in *Papers of Nathanael Greene,* ed. Richard K. Showman, 5 vols. (Chapel Hill: University of North Carolina Press, 1976–89), 2:248.

16. Nathanael Greene to Jacob Greene, January 3, 1778, ibid., 2:244.

17. Nicholas Cooke to Nathanael Greene, January 13, 1778, ibid., 2:256.

18. George Washington to Board of War, January 2, 1778, in *The Papers of George Washington,* Revolutionary War Series, ed. Philander Chase, 18 vols. to date (Charlottesville: University of Virginia Press, 1985–), 13:111.

19. George Washington to Peter Colt, February 7, 1778, ibid., 13:467.

20. *The Writings of George Washington, from the Original Manuscript Sources,* ed. John C. Fitzpatrick, 39 vols. (Washington, D.C.: U.S. Government Printing Office, 1931), 10:300.

21. Ibid., 10:39.

22. Charles H. Lesser, ed., *The Sinews of Independence: Monthly Strength Reports of the Continental Army* (Chicago: University of Chicago Press, 1976), 55. All figures on assigned strength and numbers of reported sick in this chapter are taken from Lesser's compilation of monthly strength reports.

23. Benjamin Rush to George Washington, Princeton, N.J., December 26, 1777, *Papers of George Washington,* Revolutionary War Series, 7:7.

24. George Washington to Governor Patrick Henry, December 27, 1777, ibid., 7:17–18.

25. A. Chapman to Theo Woodbridge, February 1, 1778, Woodbridge Papers, Connecticut Historical Society, accessed at Valley Forge National Military Park archives.

26. This and the quotations and weather data in the following three paragraphs are from Ludlum, *Early American Winters,* 111–14.

27. Ibid., 112–14.

28. Martin, *Joseph Plumb Martin, Yankee Doodle Boy,* 119.

29. DeKalb quoted in A. E. Zucker, *General DeKalb, Lafayette's Mentor* (Chapel Hill: University of North Carolina Press, 1966), 190.

30. James Thatcher, *The American Revolution from the Commencement of the American Army Given in the Form of a Daily Journal with the Exact Dates of all Important Events: Also, a Biographical Sketch of all the Most Prominent Generals* (New York: American Subscription Publishing House, 1860), 185.

31. Nathanael Greene to George Washington, November 14, 1779, *Papers of Nathanael Greene,* 5:59–60.

32. Quoted in Samuel Stelle Smith, *Winter at Morristown, 1779–1780: The Darkest Hour* (Monmouth Beach, N.J.: Philip Freneau Press, 1979), 5.

33. John Mitchell to Nathanael Greene, November 14, 1779, *Papers of Nathanael Greene,* 5:70.

34. Thomas Chase to Nathanael Greene, Boston, December 1, 1779, ibid., 5:138.

35. Moore Furman to Nathanael Greene, November 15, 1779, ibid., 5:83.

36. Quoted in Smith, *Winter at Morristown*, 14.

37. Nathanael Greene to Benoni Hathaway, January 6, 1780, *Papers of Nathanael Greene*, 5:243.

38. Quoted in Smith, *Winter at Morristown*, 15.

39. Quoted in ibid.

40. Nathanael Greene to George Washington, April 2, 1780, *Papers of Nathanael Greene*, 5:494.

41. Martin, *Joseph Plumb Martin, Yankee Doodle Boy*, 121.

42. Ibid., 122, 125.

43. Russell F. Weigley and George F. Scheer, *Morristown: Official National Park Service Handbook* (Washington, D.C.: National Park Service, 1983), 61.

44. Ibid.

45. Legend has it that the starving soldiers at Valley Forge were sustained by an unexpectedly large and early run of shad up nearby streams. The hungry soldiers supposedly scooped thousands of fish out of the water. Despite the dramatic nature of this story, no primary evidence has been found to substantiate the claim.

46. Henry Woodman, *The History of Valley Forge* (Oaks, Pa.: John U. Francis, Sr., 1920), 24.

47. Ibid., 126.

48. Henry Emerson Wildes, *Valley Forge* (New York: Macmillan, 1938), vii, 1, 5.

49. John F. Reed, *Valley Forge: Crucible of Victory* (Monmouth Beach, N.J.: Philip Freneau Press, 1969).

50. John Joseph Stoudt, *Ordeal at Valley Forge: A Day by Day Chronicle from December 17, 1777 to June 18, 1778 Compiled from the Sources* (Philadelphia: University of Pennsylvania Press, 1963), 8.

51. John B. B. Trussel Jr., *Birthplace of an Army: A Study of the Valley Forge Encampment* (Harrisburg: Pennsylvania Historical and Museum Commission, 1976), iii.

52. Larry Lowenthal, *Morristown National Historical Park: Morristown, New Jersey Administrative History*, draft copy, June 2005, accessed at Morristown National Historical Park Archives, 30.

53. Ibid., 33, 67.

54. Gary B. Nash, *First City: Philadelphia and the Forging of Historical Memory* (Philadelphia: University of Pennsylvania Press, 2002), 95.

15

MUSIC, MAYHEM, AND MELODRAMA:
THE PORTRAYAL OF THE AMERICAN REVOLUTION IN
PENNSYLVANIA ON FILM

Karen Guenther

*For twenty-five years the screen has made its patrons living participants in
their country's history. . . . Dramatization of episodes in American history
has made us conscious of a common heritage.*

—WILL H. HAYS (1940)

Historians, when they evaluate film portrayals of historical events, assess both
the historical accuracy of the medium and the films' roles in transforming myth
into popular historical memory.[1] Producers, writers, and directors take dramatic
license when making a movie; unfortunately, what historians perceive as
"truth," based on information recorded in primary sources, is often embellished
or misrepresented to move the plot along. Historical accuracy, as viewed by
historians, generally loses out when the purpose of the medium is to entertain
rather than educate.[2]

The 1986 film *Sweet Liberty* took a satirical approach to this subject that in
many ways demonstrates the conflict between historical accuracy and entertainment. History professor Michael Burgess (Alan Alda), upon finding out that
director Bo Hodges (Saul Rubinek) is turning his monograph on the Battle of
Cowpens into a romantic comedy, laments, "I just wrote the book from which
the movie has *not* been taken." Hodges, meanwhile, justifies the revisionism by
informing Burgess that changes must be made in order to satisfy teenage audiences, who expect three things in a movie: defiance of authority, destruction of
property, and nudity—and that the American Revolution clearly meets two out
of these three goals. Hodges's cynicism about history films is relatively accurate,
as movies about the American Revolution do not portray the rebellion as merely
a war for independence, a social and political upheaval, or a story of great men,
but also add bloodshed and sexual innuendo to enhance the story.[3]

Occasionally, these films also perpetuate stereotypes. The Indians in John Ford's *Drums Along the Mohawk,* for instance, including Blue Back (Chief Big Tree) as a proverbial cigar store Indian, could have been transplanted from any of his westerns. Film portrayals thus challenge the historiography of the era—in the case of the films discussed in this chapter, of the American Revolution—and, because of the visual imagery, are often more memorable than the written accounts.[4]

Even though many historical films focus to some degree on warfare, whether the Civil War in *Gone with the Wind* or World War II in *A League of Their Own,* the American Revolution has not been a popular subject of movies. Abigail Adams and Martha Washington are not as charismatic as Scarlett O'Hara, and George Washington was a less successful military leader than George S. Patton. There is no equal to *Glory* that examines the role of minorities during the conflict (other than the "savage" natives of *Drums Along the Mohawk*), or to *Letters from Iwo Jima* that views the Revolution from the British perspective. Nevertheless, feature films and television movies and miniseries have depicted the War of Independence, and particularly Pennsylvania's role in it, in ways that have enlightened, entertained, and contradicted the popular understanding of the past.[5]

The American Revolution on Film: The Silent Era

The American Revolution was a popular subject during the first two decades of the twentieth century, as the nation reflected on its own history while becoming a global empire. Between 1907 and 1912 more than sixty one- and two-reelers depicting the American Revolution were produced by the Champion Film Company, Edison Company, Kalem Company, Lubin Manufacturing Company, Republic Motion Picture Manufacturing Company, Thanhouser Film Corporation, Universal Film Manufacturing Company, and Vitagraph Company of America. Of these, nine related to the American Revolution in Pennsylvania. Unfortunately, none of the films produced between 1908 and 1917 discussed here has survived for viewing in the twenty-first century.[6]

The Kalem Company produced two films on the Revolution, *Washington at Valley Forge* (1908) and *Molly Pitcher* (1911). The former was a ten-minute short that focused on the Continental army's encampment during the winter of 1777–78. The latter told the story of Mary Ludwig Hays, whose husband had enlisted in the Seventh Pennsylvania Artillery Regiment during the war. This movie concentrated in particular on action at the Battle of Monmouth, although it erroneously portrayed Molly as a heroine for rescuing her husband from Hessian soldiers.[7]

In 1909 the Vitagraph Company of America distributed two short films about George Washington: *Washington Under the British Flag* and *Washington Under the American Flag*. In both films Broadway actor Joseph Kilgour played the title role. *Washington Under the British Flag* included scenes depicting Washington's experiences in the French and Indian War in western Pennsylvania, while *Washington Under the American Flag* covered the period from his service in the Continental Congress through his retirement.[8]

D. W. Griffith, whose most famous films include *The Birth of a Nation* (1915) and *Intolerance* (1916), also made movies related to the Revolution. In 1909 Griffith directed *1776, or the Hessian Renegades,* for Biograph. Two years earlier Griffith had spent countless hours at the New York Public Library reading everything he could find on the American Revolution as research for his play *War*. Griffith used this knowledge when making both *1776* and his subsequent feature-length film *America*. He took particular care to use authentic period structures for *1776*, an adventure story about farmers detaining Hessian soldiers who are attempting to capture an army messenger. Mary Pickford, who co-starred as one of the farmers' daughters, disguises herself in a British army uniform to distract the troops and give her father time to alert the countryside and liberate her brother, the messenger in danger.[9]

Thomas Edison produced two films that focused on the Revolution in Pennsylvania, *The Declaration of Independence* (1911) and *How Washington Crossed the Delaware* (1912). The latter was a slapstick comedy with period costumes rather than a serious treatment of a subject that would appear in several films about the Revolution in Pennsylvania. Other silent shorts of the 1910s with scenes of the Revolution in Pennsylvania include Thanhouser Film Corporation's *Declaration of Independence* (1911), Universal Film Manufacturing Company's *Washington at Valley Forge* (1914), and World Film Corporation's *Betsy Ross* (1917).[10]

Feature-length films on the American Revolution began to appear in 1917 with George Siegmann's *The Spirit of '76*. A stinging anti-British portrayal of the Revolution, this film tells the story of the colonists' revolt through the character of Catherine Montour, queen of the Iroquois Nation. Montour was also known as Hannah Lightfoot, having been raised by a Quaker sea captain and his wife. Hannah Lightfoot has a morganatic marriage with George III, and she disappears after the British ministry arranges for the king to wed German princess Charlotte and annuls her marriage. The film attempts to show the true "spirit of 1776," from the courts of England to the trans-Appalachian frontier, and in the process starkly compares the characters of King George III and George Washington.[11]

The Spirit of '76 proved to be an extremely controversial film because of its anti-British sentiment. Contrary to producer Robert Goldstein's wishes, the picture, which included several portrayals of the Revolution in Pennsylvania, was perceived as un-American. The U.S. Department of Justice and local censorship boards forbade the film's distribution out of fear it would provoke opposition to England after U.S. entry in World War I. On April 15, 1918, a jury found Goldstein guilty on two counts of violating the Espionage Act, and U.S. district judge Benjamin F. Bledsoe fined him $5,000 and sentenced him to ten years in the federal penitentiary at McNeil Island. Following Goldstein's conviction, *Photoplay* described the picture as "a fifty-fifty libel of the Colonies and Mother England" and "German propaganda, impure and simple."[12]

Interest in the War of Independence increased during the 1920s in anticipation of the nation's sesquicentennial. Another silent film, *Cardigan* (1922), focused on prerevolutionary upstate New York; its protagonist, Michael Cardigan (William Collier Jr.) participated in the battles of Lexington and Concord.[13]

D. W. Griffith again addressed the American Revolution in *America* (1924). Occasionally considered "the definitive motion picture about the American Revolution," this picture was Griffith's epic attempt to commemorate the Revolution, just as *The Birth of a Nation* depicted the Civil War and Reconstruction.[14] *America* was primarily a narrative of the Revolution told through the perspective of Nathan Holden, a Boston patriot, and Nancy Montague, daughter of a Virginia Tory. The War Department supplied cavalry for the picture, and the Daughters of the American Revolution provided historical advice. In fact, according to Iris Barry, through the efforts of the DAR, "*America* was seen as an ideal vehicle to teach school children about their heritage and the winning of freedom from oppression." The film was neither a critical nor a popular success, however, "possibly because its historical detail and educational spirit were at odds with the Jazz Age in which it was produced," according to Barry.[15] The producer's Anglophilia prevented him from portraying the British as the true enemy in the film. Instead, a loyalist, Captain Walter Butler (Lionel Barrymore), led the attacks at Cherry Valley and embodied all of the evil portrayed in the film.[16]

Also in 1924, Marion Davies—who became William Randolph Hearst's wife—starred in Hearst's production *Janice Meredith*. Based on Paul Leicester Ford's *Janice Meredith, a Story of the American Revolution* (1899) and directed by E. Mason Hopper, the film is a historical romance about the daughter of a Tory who is pursued by Charles Fownes (Harrison Ford), an indentured servant belonging to her father and an aide to George Washington (Joseph Kilgour, who had also played Washington in the two Vitagraph films in 1909). To stifle Janice's attraction to Fownes, Squire Meredith (Macklyn Arbuckle) sends his daughter to Boston. Janice manages to leave Boston and by 1776 is in Trenton, just in time for Washington to cross the Delaware and defeat the Hessians at the Battle of Trenton. Historical characters in the film include George and Martha Washington (Joseph Kilgour and Mrs. Macklyn Arbuckle), Sir William Howe

(George Nash), General Charles Lee (Walter Law), and Benjamin Franklin (Lee Beggs). W. C. Fields plays a British sergeant smitten with Janice.[17]

The American Revolution on Film:
From "Talkies," to Technicolor, to Television

Aware of the controversy surrounding *The Spirit of '76* prior to U.S. entry into World War I, filmmakers took care to ensure that Revolutionary War–themed films of the 1930s and 1940s did not portray the British as the enemy. *Drums Along the Mohawk* (1939), based on Walter D. Edmonds's novel, focused on the impact of the Revolution on settlers in the Mohawk Valley. As in *America,* American Tories, not the British, are the enemies who incite native resistance to frontier settlements. *The Howards of Virginia* (1940), based on Elizabeth Page's novel *The Tree of Liberty,* tells the story of Virginia backwoodsman Matt Howard (Cary Grant), who marries into an aristocratic Tidewater family. Filmed on location in Williamsburg, Virginia, the movie takes place during the Revolutionary War but lacks much action. Again, Tory loyalists are the enemy, with Fleetwood Peyton (Sir Cedric Hardwicke), Matt Howard's brother-in-law, playing the chief villain. *Where Do We Go from Here?* (1945) stars Fred MacMurray as a man who receives a 4F classification during World War II and seeks the assistance of a wizard who can make him fit for military service. The confused wizard instead transports MacMurray's character back in time to the Revolutionary War, where he serves as a soldier in the Continental army. Another film of the 1940s, *The Time of Their Lives* (1946), provides an Abbott and Costello version of the Revolution. Of these four films, only *The Howards of Virginia* includes any action relating to the Revolution in Pennsylvania.[18]

In the 1950s four more films addressed the American Revolution. *The Scarlet Coat* (1955) used a spy to provide a pseudo-explanation of Benedict Arnold's treason, introducing a cold war approach to the conflict. *Johnny Tremain* (1957) reinforced the Disney concept of history in its interpretation of Esther Forbes's novel. George Bernard Shaw's play *The Devil's Disciple* was made into a film in 1959, taking a satirical approach to the Revolution. Another 1959 film, *John Paul Jones,* was a biographical portrayal of the naval hero, with Robert Stack in the title role. Of these films, only *John Paul Jones* contained anything about the Revolution in Pennsylvania.[19]

Surprisingly, the War of Independence got no attention during the turbulent 1960s. The next film portrayal was 1972's big-screen production of the Tony Award–winning Broadway musical *1776*. This film tells the story of the drafting of the Declaration of Independence, congressional debates on the document, and the final adoption of Richard Henry Lee's resolution on independence.[20]

The bicentennial of the Revolution saw no feature films on the subject, and not until 1985 was another Revolutionary War movie produced, this one called simply *Revolution*. Al Pacino stars as Tom Dobb, a New York fur trapper who joins the army in search of his son, who has been drafted. *Revolution* portrays the conflict as one between lower-class laborers and elitists and incorporates social history, with the result that it is probably more realistic in its depiction of early American life than most films. Echoing *America* and *The Howards of Virginia,* Dobb's love interest is Daisy McConnahay (Nastassja Kinski), daughter of a loyalist.[21]

Most recently, *The Patriot* (2000) has supplied a depiction of the southern theater of the conflict. French and Indian War hero Benjamin Martin (Mel Gibson) wants no part of the War of Independence until his son Thomas (Gregory Smith) is killed by the dastardly Colonel William Tavington (Jason Isaacs). Seeking revenge for his son's death—and trying to save his eldest son, Gabriel (Heath Ledger), who has been taken captive, from the hangman's noose— Benjamin joins the local militia and uses the same frontier tactics that brought him success during the earlier conflict. This film reportedly is based on the military escapades of guerrilla Francis Marion, but Gibson turns the fictionalized Benjamin Martin into a sympathetic figure. Loaded with special effects, *The Patriot* depicts the British as the enemy, although American loyalists also commit evil deeds.[22]

The American Revolution on Television: Movies and Miniseries

Television movies and miniseries have also examined the American Revolution, with mixed results. Two episodes of the Kent Family Chronicles (based on John Jakes's novels), *The Bastard* (1978) and *The Rebels* (1979), cover the prerevolutionary era and the War of Independence. *George Washington* (1984), starring Barry Bostwick in the title role, explores the life of the great general from his teen years through the Newburgh Conspiracy. Two Howard Fast novels, *April Morning* (1988) and *The Crossing* (1999), have been turned into television movies. *April Morning* tells the story of the battles of Lexington and Concord, showing that colonial patriotism, rather than British atrocities, was responsible for the conflict. *The Crossing* focuses solely on the planning, implementation, and consequences of Washington's invasion of New Jersey in December 1776 and the surprise attack on Trenton. *Mary Silliman's War* (1993) is a made-for-television movie that brings to life Richard Buel Jr. and Joy Day Buel's *The Way of Duty,* which focused on the impact of the Revolution on a small town in Connecticut. Mary Silliman's husband had been captured by Tories, and the film examines the impact of his absence on household operations and her efforts to liberate him. Most recently, the A&E network, which produced *The Crossing,* made *Benedict Arnold: A Question of Honor* (2003), a picture that attempts to shed light on the most infamous traitor of the Revolution, the military commander of Philadelphia in 1777–78.[23]

Prologue to Revolution in Pennsylvania: *Allegheny Uprising*

Although technically not a film that focuses on the Revolution, *Allegheny Uprising* (1939) depicts some of the issues that spurred Pennsylvanians to support separation from England. Set during the latter stages of the French and Indian War, *Allegheny Uprising* tells the story of James Smith (John Wayne), leader of the Black Boys of the Conococheague. Based on Neil Swanson's novel *The First Rebel* (and released in England under that title), the film shows British and colonial officials colluding to incite native rebellions along the frontier. British troops commanded by Captain Swanson (George Sanders) at Fort Loudon ostensibly are stationed there to protect the frontier settlers from the marauding natives. At the same time, British and colonial officials assist Ralph Callendar (Brian Donlevy), a trader who supplies liquor and weapons to the Indians. Ultimately, Smith and the settlers attack the fort, hoping to have Callendar arrested for vandalism, illegal trading, and murder. *Allegheny Uprising* provides a relatively entertaining depiction of frontier life in Pennsylvania during the 1760s, yet its historical accuracy is marred by a forced love story between James Smith and a tavernkeeper's daughter, Janie MacDougall (Claire Trevor, who actually receives top billing).[24]

Allegheny Uprising provides a justification for the colonists to rebel against British authority (while also including a forced romance, often a staple of historical films). When examining the historiophoty of feature films and television miniseries and movies that have portrayed the American Revolution in Pennsylvania, four topics emerge: the actions of the First and Second Continental Congresses, including the drafting of the Declaration of Independence; Washington crossing the Delaware River prior to the Battle of Trenton; the Continental army encampment at Valley Forge; and Philadelphia during the Revolution, including the British occupation and the military governorship of Benedict Arnold.[25]

The First and Second Continental Congresses on Film

Debates in the First and Second Continental Congresses are vividly portrayed in the television miniseries *George Washington.* Based on James Thomas Flexner's

Pulitzer Prize–winning multivolume biography, *George Washington* begins in Pennsylvania on the eve of the French and Indian War, when the young Washington is surveying land owned by the Fairfax family in the western part of the colony. The miniseries also recounts Washington's activity during this conflict, from Fort Necessity, to Braddock's March, to the fall of Fort Duquesne. Washington arrives in Philadelphia in 1774 as a delegate to the First Continental Congress, meeting with John Adams, Samuel Adams, and Patrick Henry at City Tavern to discuss Joseph Galloway's proposed Plan of Union.

Washington returns to Philadelphia the following year, when the Second Continental Congress convenes in May. The two Adamses and Richard Henry Lee meet outside Independence Hall and discuss the potential appointment of Washington as commander-in-chief of the Continental army. Lee presses John Adams for an explanation as to why Virginia should be dragged into Massachusetts's fight. When asked whether he thinks Washington would accept the post, John Adams responds, "If not, then why is he always wearing that uniform?" Congress appoints Washington commander-in-chief. As Washington modestly accepts the appointment, the entire body stands and applauds.[26]

One of the earliest scenes, chronologically speaking, in D. W. Griffith's *America* (1924) depicts the Second Congress's selection of George Washington as commander-in-chief of the Continental army. Just as in the television miniseries, Washington is in full dress uniform when he accepts the appointment.

Declaring Independence on Film

The Declaration of Independence was a popular topic during the silent era, with no fewer than two shorts and two feature-length films addressing this document. In 1911 both the Edison Company and Thanhouser Film Corporation distributed film shorts entitled *The Declaration of Independence*.[27] Robert Goldstein's *Spirit of '76* was the first full-length feature film to portray this event; one of the historical tableaux in the film depicts the ringing of the Liberty Bell following its adoption. According to reviewer Oma Moody Lawrence of the *Chicago Evening Post,* "The climax of the picture is reached when the waiting populace is made aware that the Declaration of Independence is signed and the huge Liberty Bell starts to ring." Genevieve Harris wrote in *Motography,* "the signing of the Declaration of Independence and the ringing of the Liberty Bell was spontaneous and the audience was genuinely stirred."[28]

D. W. Griffith also reenacts the signing of the Declaration in *America*. Delegates watch as John Hancock signs the document, a reverse image of John Trumbull's 1817 painting in the U.S. Capitol rotunda. The Liberty Bell subsequently tolls, announcing the great accomplishment. Caesar Rodney's ride from Delaware to Philadelphia to approve the Declaration is the main focus of the Vita-phone Corporation's *Declaration of Independence* (1938). Directed by Crane Wilbur, this film received the Academy Award for Best Short Subject–Two Reel in 1939, the only film relating to the Revolution to win an Oscar.

The drafting of the Declaration of Independence is a minor point in *The Howards of Virginia* (1940). Matt Howard (Cary Grant) is a childhood friend of Thomas Jefferson (Richard Carlson), and the two men share a pro-revolutionary spirit. Before enlisting in the army, Howard asks his wife to move the family to Philadelphia so that they will be closer to where he will be fighting. His wife, Jane (Martha Scott), refuses; instead, she and the children move in with her Tory brother Fleetwood Peyton (Sir Cedric Hardwicke). Over Jane's objections, Matt Howard joins the army and goes to Philadelphia, asking his good friend Thomas Jefferson to check on his family when Jefferson returns to Virginia. Jefferson agrees, informing Howard that he is planning to return home to Monticello as soon as he finishes writing the Declaration. Howard's sons, against their mother's and uncle's wishes, later join the army and meet up with their father at the Morristown encampment.

The best-known (and most entertaining) portrayal of the Declaration of Independence is without a doubt the musical *1776* (1972). The sexual revolution of the 1960s and 1970s clearly plays a role in this representation of the founding fathers. The film concludes with a true rendering of Trumbull's portrait (in contrast to the reverse image presented in *America*), but that is the only similarity to other film portrayals of the event. For instance, instead of telling Matt Howard that he is writing the document, Thomas Jefferson (Ken Howard) is unable to prepare a draft until his wife, Martha (Blythe Danner), makes a conjugal visit. The military aspects of the war receive scant mention; only periodic dreary dispatches from George Washington, read aloud to Congress by secretary Charles Thomson (Ralston Hill), and a visit by John Adams (William Daniels) and Samuel Chase (Patrick Hines) of the War Committee to an army camp in New Jersey indicate that there is more to the story than a bunch of fancily dressed men singing and dancing in Congress. The fact that Continental troops had successfully driven the British out of Boston a few months earlier and would not confront the enemy for another seven weeks did not deter the film's writers from depicting the dismay that set in later that year.

Historically, *1776* does an outstanding job of conveying the chaos of the congressional debate over independence and the sectional discord that threatened to destroy the new nation before it could even be established. The film even succeeds in portraying the bustle—along with the heat and humidity—of Philadelphia during this era. Its credibility suffers, however, every time a member of Congress breaks out in song, whether to attack the character of the "obnoxious and disliked" John Adams, determine who will draft the Declaration, establish blame for the institution of slavery, or choose a national bird.

The film shows anything but reverence for the founding fathers. Thomas Jefferson comes off as someone who is incapable of writing a coherent sentence until his wife visits. Benjamin Franklin (Howard Da Silva), meanwhile, dances quite well for a seventy-year-old man plagued with gout and is quite sexually active for his age. Richard Henry Lee (Ron Holgate) is a buffoon who makes puns about his last name and is hardly a staunch advocate of independence. Delegates from New York, including Lewis Morris (Howard Caine) and Robert Livingston (John Myhers), appear to be idiots because they "abstain courteously" on every vote. Moderate John Dickinson (Donald Madden) is the villain who opposes independence, not the patriotic author of *Letters from a Farmer in Pennsylvania.* Judge James Wilson (Emory Bass) indecisively echoes Dickinson, whom Franklin finally persuades to follow his conscience and support independence. Edward Rutledge (John Cullum), by contrast, ably represents the concerns of southern planters and their disdain for New Englanders; his operatic "Molasses to Rum" is perhaps the most effective description on film of the triangular trade. Caesar Rodney (William Hansen), meanwhile, goes home to Delaware to die of cancer but is dragged back to Philadelphia by bombastic fellow delegate Thomas McKean (Ray Middleton). In spite of these caricatures, the film's climax—when the delegates agree to declare independence and approve Jefferson's draft with revisions—is quite compelling, and inevitably some of the tunes will linger in the mind long after the movie has ended.[29]

Washington Crossing the Delaware

Edison's *How Washington Crossed the Delaware* (1912), although a comedy, was the first film to depict the attack on Trenton.[30] Neither *The Spirit of '76* nor *America* provided a film portrayal of Emanuel Gottlieb Leutze's 1851 painting. William Randolph Hearst, in fact, even persuaded Griffith to omit Washington's crossing in return for a positive review of *America* in Hearst newspapers.[31] The first movie to include this event in its plot was *Janice Meredith* (1924).[32]

As noted above, Janice Meredith, daughter of a Tory, is in Trenton in 1776. According to one description of the plot, her beau, Charles Fownes, "appears, disguised as a Hessian, and he is given papers which reveal the disposition of British troops. He is unmasked and ordered shot, but slips the papers to Janice who delivers them to Washington, who then makes his heroic crossing of the Delaware."[33] In other words, without Janice Meredith, Washington would not have attempted the attack on Trenton.

Produced by William Randolph Hearst as a vehicle for his mistress, the film provides a memorable depiction of the crossing and the attack on Trenton. Kenneth M. Cameron describes the scene as follows: "After much to-ing and fro-ing about spying and being caught and court-martialed, Davies rides, trudges, and crawls through the snow to give Washington a paper that apparently tells him that attacking Trenton would be a swell idea. . . . The crossing of the Delaware is stunning, a careful re-staging of the Leutze painting."[34] The *New York Times* reviewer noted that director E. Mason Hopper took "full advantage of an opening left to him by Mr. Griffith" by including this event in the film.

> It is something in moving picture photography which will be remembered for years by all those who see it, even if they behold it but once. . . . There is a picture of Washington in a familiar pose, inspiring his men, who with oars, boathooks, sticks and bayonets are pushing, pulling, and shoving to get their craft to the other side, making woefully slow progress in their short but hazardous journey. One sees men in the water being rescued from the great cakes of ice. Slowly, very slowly, the boats made progress, and in this film it all seems as if life had suddenly been given to the well-known oil painting. There is eight hundred feet of this stretch, without a dull second.[35]

George Washington (1984) also depicts this momentous event. The scene begins with Washington (Barry Bostwick), General Henry Knox (Farnham Scott), General Nathanael Greene (Scott Hylands), and General John Stark (Robert Stack) sitting outside a tent and discussing the problem of enlistments expiring at the end of the year. John Laurens (Kevin Conroy), who has recently volunteered for service, reads *Common Sense* to the troops at the winter camp in Bucks County, encouraging them to reenlist for six more weeks.

At this encampment, Washington lays out his plan to boost the army's morale with a Christmas evening attack on the Hessian camp at Trenton. General Horatio Gates (Jeremy Kemp) expresses opposition to the reckless plan, but Washington points out that the Hessians will not be expecting an attack during the winter, let alone on Christmas. Washington and the other officers stand in the boats as they cross the Delaware River, and their last-gasp effort indeed succeeds and saves the army.

The Crossing (1999) provides a different interpretation of this event. Once again, Bucks County serves as the location for the army's winter camp, but the distinction between officers (particularly Washington) and enlisted men is clearly evident, as Washington accepts the use of a stone farmhouse as his headquarters while the troops sleep in canvas tents. Jeff Daniels ably assumes the persona of Washington, touring the camp on horseback.

Because *The Crossing* focuses on only one aspect of the Revolution, greater detail is given on the planning and execution of the attack on Trenton. Washington argues the urgent need for a victory, even pointing out that Congress has fled Philadelphia for Baltimore in anticipation of a British attack. Colonel John Glover (Sebastian Roché) and his mariners use Durham boats to carry troops across the ice-packed river from McConkey's Ferry to New Jersey, with McConkey's inn serving as a guard post. *The Crossing* pays particular attention to the Pennsylvania German troops in the Continental army and has Captain Heineman (Kristen Holden-Reid) ask permission to give his regiment early notice of the attack, because these soldiers view the Hessian troops as the devil incarnate. Washington's troops march through snow to the icy river, and the general sits on the boat along with the troops and officers. Following the victory at Trenton, Washington asks the Pennsylvania German troops to accompany the Hessian prisoners back to Pennsylvania.

The Encampment at Valley Forge

The army's encampment at Valley Forge probably has received more attention than any other aspect of the Revolution in Pennsylvania. Several films use Henry Brueckner's *The Prayer at Valley Forge* (1866) as their model. Two early silent films, the Kalem Company's *Washington at Valley Forge* (1908) and Universal's 1914 film of the same name focus on this crucial encampment.[36] *The Spirit of '76* (1917) includes a historical tableau of Washington at Valley Forge. Lionel Esmond (Howard Gaye), a former military aide to George III and the brother of Catherine Montour, supports the patriot cause, and he and sharpshooter Tim Murphy (Jack McCready) are serving in the Continental army under the command of George Washington (William Beery). One description of the film reads in part, "Here, Washington is discouraged with his starving troops and kneels in the snow to pray, with Lafayette at his side, and sees a vision of the United States as they are about to be. He becomes inspired and encourages the downhearted troops so that they cheer and regain their enthusiasm."[37]

D. W. Griffith's *America* repeats the scene in *The Spirit of '76*. In a scene called "At Valley Forge—The Sacrifice," Griffith has the Continental army marching through the snow to their winter camp. Then George Washington (Arthur Dewey) is shown kneeling in prayer. The soldiers live in log huts and wrap their feet with strips of cloth. The hero, Nathan Holden, still remembers his beloved Nancy Montague, despite the hardships. Washington sends Holden north with Morgan's Raiders to defend the Mohawk Valley.[38]

The winter at Valley Forge figures in *Janice Meredith* as well. One of the historical tableaux includes Washington and his troops suffering there. Charles

Fownes is one of the Continental soldiers; he manages to sneak through the British defenses to visit Janice, who has moved to Philadelphia with her family.[39]

Several biographical films also feature the Valley Forge encampment. In *John Paul Jones* (1959), the title character, played by Robert Stack, meets with Washington (John Crawford) at Valley Forge to resign his commission. *New York Times* reviewer Bosley Crowther noted that this scene "permits not only a tableau of Continental soldiers huddling drearily in the snow but a chance to hear Washington dictating his famous description of conditions among his men." After chastising Jones, Washington persuades the captain to go to France and notify Benjamin Franklin of Burgoyne's defeat at Saratoga. Stack's acting certainly did not merit rave reviews; in Crowther's words, Stack "performs the knotty little Scotsman as though he were a slightly dull but talkative member of a conservative gentlemen's club."[40]

George Washington provides the most complete depiction of the Continental army's suffering at Valley Forge. The scene opens with Washington visiting Congress and advocating a promotion for Benedict Arnold. Members of Congress rebuff Washington, citing the abundance of high-ranking officers from New England in general and from Connecticut in particular (setting the stage for Arnold's future betrayal). Congress then discusses replacing Philip Schuyler with Horatio Gates as the commander of the northern theater. The Marquis de Lafayette (Philip Casnoff) arrives and volunteers to serve in the Continental army without pay; Washington eagerly accepts the French volunteer. Soon thereafter Washington learns of the impending British presence in the Delaware Bay, and following the Continental defeat at Brandywine, Congress leaves Philadelphia.

As the army retreats after the Battle of Germantown, word spreads among the officers that Philadelphia merchants hid goods rather than supply the army, contributing to the soldiers' suffering. During the withdrawal, the brave Continental troops sing "Yankee Doodle" as they march across the countryside. Upon arriving at the encampment, the troops build drafty log huts with sod roofs, while Washington enjoys the luxury of Isaac Potts's stone home. While the poorly dressed troops complain about the conditions and the need for more foraging parties, the discovery of the Conway Cabal diverts Washington's attention. Meanwhile, Martha Washington (Patty Duke Astin) arrives to visit her husband and comforts a soldier whose frostbitten feet require amputation. General Washington demonstrates his concern by riding through the camp and meeting with militia officers, who express their support for his leadership.

George Washington (1984) gives an effective portrayal of both sides of the encampment, especially when it depicts Washington's compassion and the troops' excitement at receiving food. Particularly entertaining is a scene in which soldiers go on a foraging expedition to acquire food and transportation from a local Quaker farmer who prefers to trade with the British (who pay in cash) rather than accept the worthless Continental script. When the foraging party encounters British troops, a skirmish ensues, and the victorious troops are particularly excited about their acquisitions—a live goose, a wagon, food, and boots. The fortune of the army brightens further with the arrival of Baron Friedrich Wilhelm Augustus von Steuben (Kurt Knudsen), who drills the troops in new techniques of warfare.

The Valley Forge encampment also merits notice in *Revolution* (1985). Unlike previous films about the war, *Revolution* incorporates no historical characters. The main character, fur trapper Tom Dobb (Al Pacino), and his son Ned (Sid Owen) become army scouts at Valley Forge. However, the Valley Forge of *Revolution*, a British production, is vastly different from previous depictions. There is a minimal amount of snow on the ground, and the soldiers are relatively well dressed. In addition, supplies do not appear to be much of a problem, as Daisy McConnahay (Nastassja Kinski), a loyalist's daughter who is also Tom Dobb's love interest, brings food, medicine, and supplies to the encampment. Daisy, however, remains at the camp when her wagon is temporarily confiscated to take sick troops to the hospital. Ultimately, Daisy regains her wagon and carries infirm soldiers to the hospital in Philadelphia. British troops attack the hospital convoy, and Tom tries unsuccessfully to save her. Daisy and Tom finally get back together at Yorktown.[41]

Valley Forge also serves as a setting in *The Patriot* (2000). Gabriel Martin (Heath Ledger), son of Benjamin Martin (Mel Gibson), joins the Continental army and serves as a courier. When Gabriel is at Valley Forge, he writes a letter to his brother Thomas describing the conditions at the winter quarters. The typical scenes of George Washington (Terry Layman) riding through the soldiers' camp and of snow falling reinforce the traditional depiction of Valley Forge, and Gabriel's presence at the encampment demonstrates that even though most of the action in *The Patriot* occurs in South Carolina, the conflict is national.

Benedict Arnold: A Question of Honor (2003) features Valley Forge as well. It is at the winter encampment that George Washington (Kelsey Grammer) offers a wounded Benedict Arnold (Aidan Quinn), hero of Saratoga, the position of military governor of Philadelphia. Washington warns Arnold about Joseph Reed, president of Pennsylvania, whom Washington perceives as an extremist.

Philadelphia During the Revolution: The British Occupation and Arnold's Governorship

Philadelphia during the Revolution has also received attention in the same movies discussed above. In *The Spirit of '76* (1917), Catherine Montour and her friends "go to the Mischianza, a feast given in Philadelphia to Lord Howe" at the same time that her love interest, Lionel Esmond (who she does not realize is her brother), is starving at Valley Forge. At this farewell party for Howe, Catherine persuades Peggy Shippen to convince her husband, Benedict Arnold, to join the British side. Lionel later returns to Philadelphia following Cornwallis's surrender, and he reunites with Cecile Stewart (Jane Novak), his childhood sweetheart.[42]

Janice Meredith also includes action during the British occupation of Philadelphia. Squire Meredith has arranged for his daughter, Janice, to marry Philemon Hennion (Olin Howard), but Charles Fownes and some Continental troops arrive from Valley Forge to interrupt the nuptials. Janice flees to Philadelphia, and Charles follows her. The British army arrests Fownes for treason, but British general Sir William Howe recognizes his old friend Lord Brereton (who had changed his name to Charles Fownes) and releases him.[43]

George Washington (1984) also portrays the British occupation of the city. General Charles Lee (John Glover), whom the British had captured in December 1776, accompanies General William Howe (Patrick Horgan) and General Charles Cornwallis (John Horton) to a Punch and Judy puppet show. Peggy Shippen (Megan Gallagher), daughter of loyalist Edward Shippen, and Major John André (Randy Anderson) handle the puppets, and their performance shows George Washington as weak and indecisive and Martha Washington as a domineering and controlling wife. While chatting with Howe and Cornwallis, Lee hatches a plan to provide a swift end to the war. The British generals dismiss Lee's proposal as the ramblings of a traitorous colonial.

Upon learning about the French alliance, British troops evacuate Philadelphia and plan to consolidate their forces in New York under the command of General Henry Clinton (Barrie Ingham). Hearing the news, Washington sends a small detachment led by General Benedict Arnold (Stephen Macht) to secure the city. John Laurens and the Marquis de Lafayette observe the British withdrawal and report back to Washington, who suggests that the Continental army next attack the British at Monmouth.

Benedict Arnold: A Question of Honor (2003) also depicts the British occupation of the city. Edward Shippen (John Kavanagh) is a particularly active loyalist and enjoys watching British troops hang suspected patriot spies; only when one of the victims is his chimney sweep does he express any objections to the execution of innocent citizens. His daughter Peggy (Flora Montgomery), meanwhile, is smitten with Major John André (John Light), and as André departs for New York, he gives her a lock of his hair. Peggy's father watches the exchange with great interest from an upstairs window, apparently approving of the British officer's courtship of his daughter.

The British evacuation of Philadelphia in 1778 spurs an equally vicious response from the patriots. Joseph Reed (Stephen Hogan), the president of Pennsylvania, incites a mob to confiscate loyalist property. The group's first stop is the home of Joseph Galloway. As Benedict Arnold arrives to begin his stint at military governor, Reed announces that Philadelphia had recently experienced five hundred days of British occupation. As a consequence, each day for the next five hundred days, a loyalist will be hanged.

As we know, however, Arnold is dishonest, and he actively engages in extortion and bribery to finance a lavish lifestyle. The high living introduced by the British continues under Arnold's watch, and he buys Mount Pleasant in Fairmount Park as a summer home—one he would share with Peggy Shippen. His nemesis is Joseph Reed, who objects to Arnold's activities and pledges to make Arnold's life difficult.

Revolution (1985), by contrast, focuses on the destruction in Philadelphia following the British evacuation of the city. Tom Dobb searches for Daisy, whom he fears the British army has killed. Tom accompanies a Continental soldier and surveys the damage to the assembly room at Independence Hall. Broken furniture and torn window coverings reveal the British demolition of the hallowed site. The last scene in Pennsylvania shows Continental army troops parading through Philadelphia on their way to engage the British regulars in New Jersey.

With the exception of *Benedict Arnold: A Question of Honor,* the action in these films does not return to Pennsylvania until 1780. That year, *George Washington* returns to Philadelphia, and the commander-in-chief meets with Thomas Mifflin (Peter Evans) to request more supplies for the troops. Mifflin alerts Washington to suspicions that Arnold has been associating with Tory speculators while serving as military governor. Washington meets with Arnold at a dinner party and confronts Arnold about the accusations. Arnold blames Mifflin and Joseph Reed and insists the charges are false. He pronounces himself fit for combat and requests reassignment to West Point, which Washington promises to consider. Washington, who has a starving army in Morristown, New Jersey, is disgusted by the display of roast pig and other delicacies at the reception held in his honor, especially when Peggy Shippen offers to load his plate with food.

George Washington does not blatantly blame Arnold's treason on Peggy Shippen Arnold but concentrates on Washington's reaction to a trusted officer's betrayal. *Benedict Arnold: A Question of Honor,* however, clearly identifies Peggy Shippen as the force behind Arnold's treason. Peggy, in fact, initiates the contact with her former paramour, John André, that ultimately leads to Arnold's defection. The title character in this movie is obviously upset by the persistent attacks on his character, and the plot to hand West Point to the British originates in Philadelphia.

Historical Inaccuracies and Contradictions

Films that portray historical events or the lives of historical characters are notorious for providing revisionist interpretations of the past, and the films discussed in this essay certainly bear this out. It is highly unlikely that the Continental Congress debated Richard Henry Lee's resolution for independence, or Thomas Jefferson's draft of the Declaration of Independence, between choruses. Loyalists, not the British, are the enemies in *America* and *Drums Along the Mohawk*, while *Benedict Arnold: A Question of Honor* almost reveres the Tories and has Arnold enjoying the company of Tory ladies while military governor of Philadelphia. Meanwhile, *Revolution* views the War of Independence as primarily a class conflict between poor colonials and well-to-do British regulars.[44]

Representations of Washington crossing the Delaware provide contrasting interpretations. Washington is the architect of the Christmas Day crossing and attack on Trenton in *George Washington* and *The Crossing*, while *Janice Meredith* has the lead character playing a pivotal role in the decision. Both *Janice Meredith* and *George Washington* have the commander standing during the trip, while in *The Crossing* he is safely seated alongside Henry Knox. *The Crossing*, however, exaggerates the influence of Alexander Hamilton, who did not become a trusted aide to Washington until after the Battle of Trenton.

The winter encampment at Valley Forge is also depicted in a variety of ways. Virtually every feature-length film or miniseries that portrays the Revolution in Pennsylvania (the only exceptions are *The Howards of Virginia*, *1776*, and *The Crossing*) includes Valley Forge as one of its "stops" on the cinematic history tour. *The Spirit of '76*, *America*, and *Janice Meredith* all include historical tableaux showing bedraggled troops struggling to survive. *The Spirit of '76* and *America* both have Washington kneeling in the snow to pray. Major and minor fictional characters—Lionel Esmond in *The Spirit of '76*, Nathan Holden in *America*, Charles Fownes in *Janice Meredith*, Tom and Ned Dobb in *Revolution*, and Gabriel Martin in *The Patriot*—all take part in the encampment.

George Washington provides the most complete depiction of the winter camp, but it does not include a scene in which Washington kneels and prays. Instead, Washington seems more preoccupied with Congress's interference in the prosecution of the war, at least until his wife visits. Martha's concern for a wounded soldier, incidentally, is one scene in which *George Washington* strays from James Thomas Flexner's biography. Flexner remarked to the producer, Richard Fielder, that no evidence exists of such an incident, but because Martha Washington was known for her compassion, it conceivably could have occurred—an example of a historian consenting to the Hollywood version of history.[45]

Sometimes the action at Valley Forge stretches credulity. In *Benedict Arnold:*

A Question of Honor, the title character meets with Washington, and the two discuss the virtues of the ladies of Philadelphia. Given that Arnold was recuperating at a hospital in Albany from wounds suffered at the Battles of Saratoga during the Valley Forge encampment, and that Martha Washington visited George that winter, it is extremely unlikely that this conversation occurred.[46]

Benedict Arnold: A Question of Honor, in fact, is rife with factual inaccuracies about Pennsylvania during the Revolution. For instance, Joseph Reed vows to hang a Tory for each of the five hundred days Philadelphia suffered British occupation; in actuality, British control of the city lasted less than nine months. Furthermore, while Edward Shippen was a loyalist and a former vice-admiralty court judge, he also became chief justice of the Pennsylvania Supreme Court in the 1790s and really was not that ardent a loyalist.[47]

Romance, too, characterizes these films. Lionel Esmond and Cecile Stewart in *The Spirit of '76,* Nathan Holden and Nancy Montague in *America,* Janice Meredith and Charles Fownes in *Janice Meredith,* Matt Howard and Jane Peyton in *The Howards of Virginia,* Thomas and Martha Jefferson in *1776,* John and Abigail Adams in *1776,* George and Martha Washington in *George Washington,* Tom Dobb and Daisy McConnahay in *Revolution,* and Benedict Arnold and Peggy Shippen in *Benedict Arnold: A Question of Honor* all join James Smith and Janie MacDougall of *Allegheny Uprising* as fictional and historical characters whose romances were affected by the War of Independence. *George Washington* even includes a soldier who, in the depths of despair at Valley Forge, comments that he dreams more of eating a good meal than of "tupping his wife"—certainly demonstrating the desperate times at the encampment.

Contemporary Criticisms of Films

Most of these films, despite their historical inaccuracies, achieved critical acclaim when they initially appeared in theaters or on television, mainly because their purpose was to entertain, not to educate. Silent films in particular got relatively positive reviews. *The Spirit of '76* received favorable praise upon its first showing in Chicago and decidedly unfavorable criticism following Goldstein's conviction. O. L. Hall wrote in the *Chicago Daily Journal,* "*The Spirit of '76* is, as its title indicates, the filming of the very story of the Revolutionary War. It undertakes to do for that period of our history what *The Birth of a Nation* does for the Civil War." Mae Tinne of the *Chicago Tribune* commented, "the acting, costumes, sets, photography, and direction are all excellent." Following Goldstein's conviction, however, *Photoplay* noted that "*The Spirit of '76* was first designed as German propaganda. But the Germans, after seeing the film, evidently disowned it. So now it is called Irish propaganda. . . . If this is a specimen of the real Spirit of '76, how did we ever manage to win the Revolution?"[48]

According to the *New York Times* reviewer, one of the high points in *America* came at Valley Forge; "Mr. Griffith obtains real drama out of the episode of pulling a wagon. The players' feet slip, the difficulty of moving the vehicle is brought out in the different photographs and the unswerving determination of the men is stressed in the sub-titles." The reviewer noted, though, that too many scenes played out too slowly.[49] The *New York Times* review of *Janice Meredith* praised the performance of Marion Davies in the title role and observed that director E. Mason Hopper had developed a more inspiring love story than the one in *America*. But, while the *New York Times* lauded the film—"No more brilliant achievement in ambitious motion pictures dealing with historical romances has ever been exhibited than Marion Davies's latest production, 'Janice Meredith' "—both *Variety* and *Photoplay* panned it as inferior overall to *America*.[50]

"Talkies" also received mixed reviews. *The Howards of Virginia,* according to *New York Times* reviewer Bosley Crowther, was "a stern and sobering reminder of our liberal tradition." Cary Grant seemed out of place as a Continental soldier, although Crowther noted, "he looks like the genuine article in the buff-and-blue of a Continental officer"[51]—an interesting description considering that *The Howards of Virginia* was filmed in black-and-white. Vincent Canby panned *1776,* remarking, "The lyrics sound as if they'd been written by someone high on root beer. . . . '1776' is far from being a landmark of musical cinema, but it is the first film in memory that comes close to treating seriously a magnificent chapter in the American history."[52] Canby attacked *Revolution* as "a mess, but one that's so giddily misguided that it's sometimes a good deal of fun for all of the wrong reasons. . . . There's an underlying wrong-headedness about it that, like senility, is universal in its effects."[53]

Television movies and miniseries also have merited comment. *George Washington* received praise from *New York Times* reviewer John J. O'Connor for filming many of the famous battles at the original locations and for focusing on Washington the man. O'Connor lauded the miniseries, noting, "Trying to depict the past as accurately as possible, the production does not go out of its way to suggest parallels with the present."[54] Barry Bostwick received positive reviews for his performance in the title role; Bostwick himself noted that the two shared physical characteristics (except that Washington's "nose was bigger").[55]

In contrast, Jeff Daniels's performance as George Washington in *The Crossing* got mixed reviews. William McDonald wrote in the *New York Times,* "Mr. Daniels offers a sympathetic portrait, but his expression generally remains as impenetrable as the one on the dollar bill." Brian Taves, however, considered Daniels "an ideal Washington in perhaps the best performance ever achieved in this difficult role." McDonald praised the television movie's supporting characters, observing that "the crossing itself is vividly depicted and evocatively photographed—the boats ferrying their huddled cargo cut across the screen in silhouette through a blue mist—without the patriotic bombast that a schmaltzier film would drum up." Taves, concurred, noting that "*The Crossing* is unprecedented as a dramatically engaging yet primarily factual filmic treatment of the Revolution."[56]

Benedict Arnold: A Question of Honor fared poorly with both historians and film critics. Suzanne Broderick poked fun at the casting choice of Kelsey Grammer for George Washington, once referring to the character as Frasier, and noted that Grammer had played a minor aide to Washington in *George Washington* and had now received a promotion. Aidan Quinn, who plays Benedict Arnold, she said, "draws upon an Irish charm that the strictly Puritan-raised Arnold may not have had at his disposal."[57] Meanwhile, James Kirby Martin, author of a recent Arnold biography, observed, "Apparently, Benedict Arnold will never have to stop paying for his treason. His latest punishment comes in the form of the docudrama, hyped by A&E television network as an authentic re-creation of Arnold's life during the American Revolution as well as an exploration of the reasons for his treason." "This production does not do well in regard to other tests of historical reality," Martin continued, "including maintaining a semblance of factual accuracy." Fictional scenes, conversations, and events all made this film an outstanding example of bad history, according to Martin.[58]

One hundred years have passed since the earliest attempts to depict the American Revolution in Pennsylvania on film. Silent films focused on specific themes, such as the winter encampment at Valley Forge, or included historical tableaux that provided snapshots of the war and its political, social, and military impact. Depending on the era in which the film appeared, the enemy changed; loyalists and Native Americans, rather than the British, were the enemy in *America* and *Drums Along the Mohawk*, reflecting the state of U.S.-British relations in the post–World War I and pre–World War II era. The cold war clearly influenced the tale of Benedict Arnold's treason in *The Scarlet Coat*. Occasionally Pennsylvania served as the location for a single scene, such as Matt Howard's meeting with Thomas Jefferson in Philadelphia in *The Howards of Virginia*, or Gabriel Martin's description of conditions at Valley Forge in *The Patriot*. In other films, Pennsylvania was the sole historical scene, yet the films were actually shot in Canada (*The Crossing*), England (*Revolution*), or Ireland (*Benedict Arnold: A Question of Honor*).

Like Michael Burgess in *Sweet Liberty*, historians complain that movie producers and directors neglect the historiography of the Revolution (*The Patriot*—also known among critics as "Braveheart Does the Revolution"—is a good example of Hollywood not considering what historians were writing in the 1990s). Overall, the portrayal of the American Revolution in Pennsylvania on film has provided some entertaining and enlightening depictions of life in revolutionary America, although some of the entertainment, as far as historians and film critics are concerned, is unintentional. Perhaps in the future a film will be produced that presents a more accurate visual representation of the Revolution in Pennsylvania—a "Mary Wanner's War" to accompany *Mary Silliman's War*—and provide a more complete picture of the impact of the Revolution on the commonwealth.

NOTES

1. The epigraph by Hays is quoted in Bosley Crowther, "The American Ideal: How Profound Is the Effect of Filmed History upon the Popular Mind," *New York Times,* September 29, 1940.

2. Steven Mintz, "Recent Books on History and Films: Some Reflections," *Film and History* 25 (1995): 68–69. For additional information on the relationship between film and history, see Tony Barta, ed., *Screening the Past: Film and the Representation of History* (Westport, Conn.: Praeger, 1998); Natalie Zemon Davis, "'Any Resemblance to Persons Living or Dead': Film and the Challenge of Authenticity," *Historical Journal of Film, Radio, and Television* 8 (1988): 269–83; Natalie Zemon Davis, "Film as Historical Narrative," *Phi Kappa Phi Journal* 81 (Spring 2001): 16–21; Marcia Lundy, ed., *The Historical Film: History and Memory in Media* (New Brunswick: Rutgers University Press, 2000); R. C. Raack, "Historiography as Cinematography: A Prolegomenon to Film Work for Historians," *Journal of Contemporary History* 18 (July 1983): 411–38; Robert Rosenstone, "*AHR Forum*—History in Images/History in Words: Reflections on the Possibility of Really Putting History onto Film," *American Historical Review* 93 (December 1988): 1173–85; Robert Rosenstone, ed., *Revisioning History: Contemporary Filmmakers and the Construction of a New Past* (Princeton: Princeton University Press, 1995); Robert Rosenstone, *Visions of the Past: The Challenge of Film to Our Idea of History* (Cambridge: Harvard University Press, 1995); Vivian C. Sobchack, "Beyond Visual Aids: American Film as American Culture," *American Quarterly* 32 (1980): 280–300; Vivian C. Sobchack, "The Insistent Fringe: Moving Images and Historical Consciousness," *History and Theory* 36 (December 1997): 4–20; Paul Smith, ed., *The Historian and Film* (New York: Cambridge University Press, 1976); Pierre Sorlin, *The Film in History: Restaging the Past* (Oxford: Blackwell, 1980); Robert Brent Toplin, "*AHR Forum*—The Filmmaker as Historian," *American Historical Review* 93 (December 1988): 1210–27; Robert Brent Toplin, *History by Hollywood: The Use and Abuse of the American Past* (Urbana: University of Illinois Press, 1996); and Hayden C. White, *The Content of the Form: Narrative Discourse and Historical Representation* (Baltimore: Johns Hopkins University Press, 1987).

3. *Sweet Liberty* (Universal Pictures, 1986), produced by Martin Bregman and directed by Alan Alda; and Kenneth M. Cameron, *America on Film: Hollywood and American History* (New York: Continuum, 1997), 7, 9.

4. Additional studies of the relationship between film and history include Cameron, *America on Film;* Mark C. Carnes, "Shooting (Down) the Past: Historians and Hollywood," *Cineaste* 29 (Spring 2004): 45–49; David Eldridge, *Hollywood's History Films* (London: I. B. Taurus, 2006); George Macdonald Fraser, *The Hollywood History of the World: From One Million Years B.C. to Apocalypse Now* (New York: Beech Tree Books, 1988); Marnie Hughes-Warrington, *History Goes to the Movies: Studying History and Film* (New York: Routledge, 2007); David Herlihy, "*AHR Forum*—Am I a Camera? Other Reflections on Films and History," *American Historical Review* 93 (December 1988): 1186–92; Caryn James, "They're Movies, Not Schoolbooks," *New York Times,* May 21, 1995; Trevor B. McCrisken and Andrew Pepper, *American History and Contemporary Hollywood Film* (New Brunswick: Rutgers University Press, 2005); Steven Mintz and Randy Roberts, eds., *Hollywood's America: United States History Through Its Films,* 3d ed. (St. James, N.Y.: Brandywine Press, 2001); John E. O'Connor, "*AHR Forum*—History in Images/Images in History: Reflections on the Importance of Film and Television Study for an Under-

standing of the Past," *American Historical Review* 93 (December 1988): 1200–1209; John E. O'Connor, ed., *Image as Artifact: The Historical Analysis of Film and Television* (Malabar, Fla.: R. E. Krieger, 1990); John E. O'Connor and Martin A. Jackson, eds., *American History/American Film: Interpreting the Hollywood Image* (New York: Ungar, 1979); Peter C. Rollins, *Hollywood as Historian: American Film in a Cultural Context*, rev. ed. (Lexington: University Press of Kentucky, 1998); and Joseph Roquemore, *History Goes to the Movies: A Viewer's Guide to the Best (and Some of the Worst) Historical Films Ever Made* (Garden City, N.Y.: Doubleday, 1999).

5. Surveys of the portrayal of the American Revolution on film include Mark Glancy, "The War of Independence in Feature Films: *The Patriot* (2000) and the 'Special Relationship' Between Hollywood and Britain," *Historical Journal of Film, Radio, and Television* 25 (October 2005): 523–45; Lawrence L. Murphy, "Feature Films and the American Revolution: A Bicentennial Reappraisal," *Film and History* 5 (1975): 1–6; Bertil O. Österberg, *Colonial America on Film and Television: A Filmography* (Jefferson, N.C.: McFarland, 2001), 22–32; Nancy L. Rhoden, "Patriots, Villains, and the Quest for Liberty: How American Film Has Depicted the American Revolution," *Canadian Review of American Studies/Revue Canadienne d'Études Américaines* 37 (2007): 205–38; Cotton Seiler, "The American Revolution," in *The Columbia Companion to American History on Film: How the Movies Have Portrayed the American Past*, ed. Peter C. Rollins (New York: Columbia University Press, 2003), 49–57; Jack Spears, "The American Revolution in Films," *Films in Review* 28 (January 1977): 1–22; and Brian Taves, Review of *The Crossing* and *The Patriot*, *American Historical Review* 105 (October 2000): 1439–40. For more on historical films as adventure films, see Brian Taves, *The Romance of Adventure: The Genre of Historical Adventure Movies* (Jackson: University Press of Mississippi, 1993). Histories of the American Revolution from the British perspective include Christopher Hibbert, *Redcoats and Rebels: The American Revolution Through British Eyes* (New York: W. W. Norton, 2002); and Michael Pearson, *Those Damned Rebels: The American Revolution as Seen Through British Eyes* (New York: DaCapo Press, 2000).

6. Spears, "American Revolution in Films," 6.

7. *Washington at Valley Forge* (Kalem Company, 1908); *Molly Pitcher* (Kalem Company, 1911), directed by Sidney Olcott; Österberg, *Colonial America on Film*, 237; and Spears, "American Revolution in Films," 8, 12. Champion Film Company also distributed a film entitled *Molly Pitcher* in 1911.

8. *Washington Under the British Flag* (Vitagraph Company of America, 1909), directed by J. Stuart Blackton; *Washington Under the American Flag* (Vitagraph Company of America, 1909), directed by J. Stuart Blackton; Cameron, *America on Film*, 16, 18–19, 34, 54; Österberg, *Colonial America on Film*, 237; and Spears, "American Revolution in Films," 8.

9. *1776, or the Hessian Renegades* (Biograph Company, 1909), directed by D. W. Griffith; Robert M. Henderson, *D. W. Griffith: The Years at Biograph* (New York: Farrar, Straus and Giroux, 1970), 81–82, 201; Robert M. Henderson, *D. W. Griffith: His Life and Work* (New York: Oxford University Press, 1972), 6, 11 (quotations), 83, 295; Kemp R. Niver, *Motion Pictures from the Library of Congress Paper Print Collection, 1894–1912* (Berkeley and Los Angeles: University of California Press, 1967), 216; and Spears, "American Revolution in Films," 2.

10. *The Declaration of Independence* (Edison Company, 1911), directed by J. Searle Dawley; *How Washington Crossed the Delaware* (Edison Company, 1914), directed by J. Searle Dawley; *The Declaration of Independence* (Thanhouser Film Corporation, 1911); *Washington at Valley Forge* (Universal Film Manufacturing Company, 1914), directed by Francis Ford; *Betsy Ross* (World Film Corporation, 1917), directed by George Cowl and Travers Vale; Cameron, *America on Film*, 16; Österberg, *Colonial America on Film*, 22, 237; and Spears, "American Revolution in Films," 6.

11. *The Spirit of '76* (Continental Producing Company, 1917), produced by Robert Goldstein and directed by George Siegmann; Cameron, *America on Film*, 20–21, 57, 224; Glancy, "War of Independence in Feature Films," 526–27; Österberg, *Colonial America on Film*, 32, 230–31; Anthony Slide, ed. and comp., *Robert Goldstein and "The Spirit of '76"* (Metuchen, N.J.: Scarecrow Press, 1993). The story of Catherine Montour/Hannah Lightfoot and the future George III is also explored in Jan Bondeson, *The Great Pretenders: The True Stories Behind Famous Historical Mysteries* (New York: W. W. Norton, 2004), 158–87.

12. Alan Pell Crawford, "A Movie on Trial," *American History* 36 (April 2001): 58–64; Michael Selig, "United States v. Motion Picture Film 'The Spirit of '76': The Espionage Case of Producer Robert Goldstein," *Journal of Popular Film and Television* 10 (1983): 168–74; Slide, *Robert Goldstein*, 223; Dawn B. Sova, *Forbidden Films: Censorship Histories of 125 Motion Pictures* (New York: Checkmark Books, 2001), 279–81; and *Photoplay* 20 (October 1921): 93–94, quoted in Slide, *Robert Goldstein*, 233.

13. *Cardigan* (American Releasing Corporation, 1922), produced by Messmore Kendell and directed by John W. Noble; and Österberg, *Colonial America on Film*, 28, 66–67.

14. Spears, "American Revolution in Films," 2.

15. Iris Barry, *D. W. Griffith: American Film Maker* (Garden City, N.Y.: Doubleday, 1965), 71, 73.

16. *America* (United Artists, 1924), produced and directed by D. W. Griffith; Cameron, *America on Film*, 35–38, 52, 56, 57, 224, 232, 233, 234; Rob Edelman, "America," in *Magill's Survey of Cinema: Silent Films*, ed. Frank N. Magill, 3 vols. (Englewood Cliffs, N.J.: Salem Press, 1982), 1:246–49; Glancy, "War of Independence in Feature Films," 527–29, 246–50; Henderson, *D. W. Griffith: His Life*, 246–50, 306; Lawrence L. Murray, "History at the Movies During the Sesquicentennial: D. W. Griffith's *America*," *Historian* 41 (1979): 450–66; Österberg, *Colonial America on Film*, 23, 28, 32, 45–51; Seiler, "American Revolution," 50–51, 52–53, 56, 159; Spears, "American Revolution in Films," 2–4 (quotation on 2); and John D. Thomas, "George Washington," in Rollins, *Columbia Companion to American History on Film*, 199–200. An edited version of this film, entitled *Love and Sacrifice*, was released in England to mixed reviews.

17. *Janice Meredith* (MGM, 1924), produced by Cosmopolitan Pictures and directed by E. Mason Hopper; Cameron, *America on Film*, 35–38, 52, 54, 57, 224, 232, 233, 234, 235; Rob Edelman, "Janice Meredith," in *Magill's Survey of Cinema*, 2:597–600; Österberg, *Colonial America on Film*, 141–45; Seiler, "American Revolution," 50–51, 56; Cotton Seiler, "The Founding Fathers," in Rollins, *Columbia Companion to American History on Film*, 159; and Spears, "American Revolution in Films," 4–6. Hearst retitled the British release of the film *The Beautiful Rebel*.

18. *Drums Along the Mohawk* (Twentieth Century-Fox, 1939), produced by Raymond Griffith and Darryl F. Zanuck and directed by John Ford; *The Howards of Virginia* (Columbia Pictures, 1940), produced and directed by Frank Lloyd; *Where Do We Go from Here?* (Twentieth Century-Fox, 1945), directed by George Ratoff; *The Time of Their Lives* (Universal Pictures, 1946), directed by Charles Barton; Cameron, *America on Film*, 55–58, 70, 77, 110; Edward Countryman, "John Ford's *Drums Along the Mohawk*: The Making of an American Myth," *Radical History Review* 24 (Fall 1980): 93–112; Fraser, *Hollywood History of the World*, 178–79; Glancy, "War of Independence in Feature Films," 529–30; Österberg, *Colonial America on Film*, 25, 28, 103–6, 134–36; Rhoden, "Patriots, Villains, and the Quest for Liberty," 207, 210, 214, 218, 221, 223, 226–29; Roquemore, *History Goes to the Movies*, 49–51; K. R. M. Short, "Colonial History and Anglo-American Tension in 1939: 'Allegheny Uprising' and 'Drums Along the Mohawk,'" *Film-Historia* 6 (1996): 3–4, 9–16; Seiler, "American Revolution," 51, 56; Seiler, "Founding Fathers," 159; Spears, "American Revolution in Films," 10, 14–15; and Anthony F. C. Wallace, "Drums Along the Mohawk," in *Past Imperfect: History According to the Movies*, ed. Mark C. Carnes (New York: Henry Holt, 1995), 94–97.

19. *The Scarlet Coat* (MGM, 1955), produced by Nicholas Naytack and directed by John Sturges; *Johnny Tremain* (Buena Vista, 1957), produced by Walt Disney and directed by Robert Stevenson; *The Devil's Disciple* (United Artists, 1959), produced by Hal Hecht and directed by Guy Hamilton; *John Paul Jones* (Warner Brothers, 1959), produced by Samuel Bronston and directed by John Farrow; Cameron, *America on Film*, 100–102, 120, 226; Glancy, "War of Independence in Feature Films," 530; Österberg, *Colonial America on Film*, 23, 25–27, 103, 145–48, 218–19; Rhoden, "Patriots, Villains, and the Quest for Liberty," 208–10, 213–15, 218, 221; Roquemore, *History Goes to the Movies*, 51; Seiler, "American Revolution," 51, 53–54, 56; Seiler, "Founding Fathers," 159; Spears, "American Revolution in Films," 15–18; and Thomas, "George Washington," 199, 201.

20. *1776* (Columbia, 1972), produced by Jack L. Warner and directed by Peter Hunt; Cameron, *America on Film*, 164; Thomas Fleming, "1776," in Carnes, *Past Imperfect*, 90–93; Glancy, "War of Independence in Feature Films," 530–31; Österberg, *Colonial America on Film*, 23–24; Rhoden, "Patriots, Villains, and the Quest for Liberty," 207, 209, 219, 221, 224, 227, 229; Seiler, "American Revolution," 51, 56; Seiler, "Founding Fathers," 154, 159; Spears, "American Revolution in Films," 18.

21. *Revolution* (Goldcrest-Viking/Warner Brothers, 1985), produced by Irwin Winkler and directed by Hugh Hudson; Fraser, *Hollywood History of the World*, 179; Glancy, "War of Independence in Feature Films," 531; McCrisken and Pepper, *American History and Contemporary Hollywood Film*, 18–24; Österberg, *Colonial America on Film*, 213–16; Rhoden, "Patriots, Villains, and the Quest for Liberty," 207, 210–11, 213, 215, 218, 222, 224, 227, 229; and Seiler, "American Revolution," 51, 54–56.

22. *The Patriot* (Columbia Pictures, 2000), produced by Dean Devlin, Mark Gordon, and Gary Levinsohn and directed by Roland Emmerich; Owen W. Gilman Jr., "The South," in Rollins, *Columbia Companion to American History on Film*, 465, 472; Glancy, "War of Independence in Feature Films,"

524–25, 531–40; McCrisken and Pepper, *American History and Contemporary Hollywood Film*, 24–36; Rhoden, "Patriots, Villains, and the Quest for Liberty," 207, 213, 215–16, 221–22, 225, 229–30; and Seiler, "American Revolution," 56.

23. *The Bastard* (Universal, 1978), produced by Joe Byrne and directed by Lee H. Katzin; *The Rebels* (Universal, 1979), produced by Gian R. Grimaldi and Hannah L. Shearer and directed by Russ Mayberry; *George Washington* (MGM/United Artists, 1984), produced by Richard Fielder and directed by Buzz Kulik; *April Morning* (Samuel Goldwyn, 1988), produced by Samuel Goldwyn Jr. and directed by Delbert Mann; *Mary Silliman's War* (Citadel Films, 1994), directed by Stephen Surjik; *The Crossing* (Arts and Entertainment Network, 1999), produced by David Coatsworth and directed by Robert Harmon; *Benedict Arnold: A Question of Honor* (A&E Television Networks, 2003), directed by Mikael Salomon; Virginia K. Bartlett and Irving J. Bartlett, Review of *Mary Silliman's War, William and Mary Quarterly*, 3d ser., 52 (January 1995): 194–96; Carol Berkin, Review of *Mary Silliman's War, Journal of American History* 81 (December 1994): 1396–98; Joy Day Buel and Richard Buel Jr., *The Way of Duty: A Woman and Her Family in Revolutionary America* (New York: W. W. Norton, 1995); Alvin H. Marill, *Movies Made for Television: The Telefeature and the Mini-Series, 1964–1986* (New York: New York Zoetrope, 1987), 157–58, 342; Österberg, *Colonial America on Film*, 23–24, 26–28, 32, 51–52, 115–20, 149–52; Rhoden, "Patriots, Villains, and the Quest for Liberty," 207, 209, 211–12, 217, 220–22, 225, 229; Seiler, "American Revolution," 51, 56; and Seiler, "Founding Fathers," 159.

24. *Allegheny Uprising* (RKO, 1939), directed by William Seiter and produced by P. J. Wolfson; Cameron, *American History on Film*, 54–55, 69, 222; Fraser, *Hollywood History of the World*, 177; Österberg, *Colonial America on Film*, 43–45; and Short, "Colonial History and Anglo-American Tension," 3–9. The exploits of James Smith and the Black Boys are discussed in Robert G. Crist, "Cumberland County," in *Beyond Philadelphia: The American Revolution in the Pennsylvania Hinterland*, ed. John B. Frantz and William Pencak (University Park: Pennsylvania State University Press, 1998), 112–16. Additional explanations of the impact of frontier violence on the coming of the Revolution include Nicole Eustace, "The Sentimental Paradox: Humanity and Violence on the Pennsylvania Frontier," *William and Mary Quarterly* 65 (January 2008): 29–64; Nathan Kozuskanich's essay in this volume; James Kirby Martin, "The Return of the Paxton Boys and the Historical State of the Pennsylvania Frontier, 1764–1774," *Pennsylvania History* 38 (April 1971): 117–33; and Alden T. Vaughan, "Frontier Banditti and the Indians: The Paxton Boys' Legacy, 1763–1775," *Pennsylvania History* 51 (January 1984): 1–29.

25. For a definition of historiophoty, see Hayden White, "*AHR Forum*—Historiography and Historiophoty," *American Historical Review* 93 (December 1988): 1193–99. Historical studies of the American Revolution in Pennsylvania include Frantz and Pencak, *Beyond Philadelphia*; Gregory T. Knouff, *The Soldiers' Revolution: Pennsylvanians in Arms and the Forging of Early American Identity* (University Park: Pennsylvania State University Press, 2004); Thomas J. McGuire, *The Philadelphia Campaign*, vol. 1, *Brandywine and the Fall of Philadelphia* (Mechanicsburg, Pa.: Stackpole Books, 2006); and Stephen R. Taaffe, *The Philadelphia Campaign, 1777–1778* (Lawrence: University Press of Kansas, 2003).

26. *George Washington* (MGM/UA TV miniseries, 1984), produced by Richard Fielder and directed by Buzz Kulik. See also James Thomas Flexner, *George Washington*, 4 vols. (Boston: Little, Brown, 1965–72), and the abridged version, Flexner, *Washington: The Indispensable Man* (Boston: Little, Brown, 1974).

27. For historical accounts of the Declaration of Independence, see Carl Becker, *The Declaration of Independence: A Study in the History of Political Ideas* (New York: Vintage Books, 1958); and Pauline Maier, *American Scripture: Making the Declaration of Independence* (New York: Knopf, 1997).

28. *The Spirit of '76*; Lawrence and Harris quoted in Slide, *Robert Goldstein*, 65, 205.

29. See Vincent Canby, "'1776' Comes to the Music Hall Screen," *New York Times*, November 10, 1972; and Fleming, "1776," 90–93. Rodney's solo ride would later be commemorated on the Delaware quarter.

30. Cameron, *America on Film*, 16. For a historical account of Washington crossing the Delaware, see David Hackett Fischer, *Washington's Crossing* (New York: Oxford University Press, 2004).

31. Edelman, "America," 1:140.

32. Edelman, "Janice Meredith," 2:597–600; and Österberg, *Colonial America on Film*, 144–45.

33. Edelman, "Janice Meredith," 2:598.

34. Cameron, *America on Film*, 39.

35. "The Screen: The Spirit of '76," *New York Times*, August 6, 1924.

36. See Österberg, *Colonial America on Film*, 237. Historical accounts of the Valley Forge encamp-

ment include James S. Bailey's essay in this volume; Wayne K. Bodle, *The Valley Forge Winter: Civilians and Soldiers in War* (University Park: Pennsylvania State University Press, 2002); and John B. B. Trussell Jr., *Birthplace of an Army: A Study of the Valley Forge Encampment* (Harrisburg: Pennsylvania Historical and Museum Commission, 1976).

37. Slide, *Robert Goldstein*, 34.

38. Edelman, "America," 1:138–39. See also "Mr. Griffith's America," *New York Times*, March 2, 1924.

39. Edelman, "Janice Meredith," 2:598.

40. Bosley Crowther, "'John Paul Jones' Opens at Rivoli," *New York Times*, June 17, 1959; see also Alan Gevinson, ed., *Within Our Gates: Ethnicity in American Feature Films, 1911–1960* (Berkeley and Los Angeles: University of California Press, 1997), 530. Samuel Eliot Morison's biography of John Paul Jones appeared the same year as the film and probably was not available for the screenwriter's use. See Samuel Eliot Morison, *John Paul Jones: A Sailor's Biography* (Boston: Little, Brown, 1959).

41. McCrisken and Pepper, *American History and Contemporary Hollywood Film*, 18–24.

42. Cameron, *America on Film*, 21 (quotation); and Slide, *Robert Goldstein*, 34. The Mischianza is discussed in Meredith Lair's essay in this volume.

43. *Janice Meredith* (1924); Edelman, "Janice Meredith," 2:598; and Österberg, *Colonial America on Film*, 142–44.

44. Henderson, *D. W. Griffith: His Life*, 246–49; Fleming, "1776," 90–93; and McCrisken and Pepper, *American History and Contemporary Hollywood Film*, 18–24. See also Jesse Lemisch, "Jack Tar in the Streets: Merchant Seamen in the Politics of Revolutionary America," *William and Mary Quarterly*, 3d ser., 25 (1968): 371–407; Ray Raphael, *A People's History of the American Revolution: How Common People Shaped the Fight for Independence* (New York: New Press, 2001); and Steven Rosswurm, *Arms, Country, and Class: The Philadelphia Militia and the "Lower Sort" During the American Revolution, 1775–1783* (New Brunswick: Rutgers University Press, 1987). Obviously, neither Raphael's book nor Rosswurm's was at Robert Dillon's disposal when he wrote the script.

45. Herbert Mitgang, "TV's Quest for a Man Called Washington," *New York Times*, November 27, 1983.

46. James Kirby Martin, Review of *Benedict Arnold: A Question of Honor, Journal of American History* 90 (2003): 1121–23.

47. See Kenneth Roeland Kimsey, "The Edward Shippen Family: A Search for Stability in Revolutionary Pennsylvania" (PhD diss., University of Arizona, 1973), for more information on Edward Shippen and his family during this era.

48. Hall, Tinne, and *Photoplay* 20 (October 1921): 93–94, quoted in Slide, *Robert Goldstein*, 64, 233.

49. "Mr. Griffith's America."

50. "The Screen: The Spirit of '76," 13; and Österberg, *Colonial America on Film*, 145.

51. Bosley Crowther, "The Screen," *New York Times*, September 27, 1940.

52. Canby, "'1776' Comes to Music Hall Screen," 44.

53. Vincent Canby, "The Screen: 1770's Epic, 'Revolution,'" *New York Times*, December 25, 1985.

54. John J. O'Connor, "'George Washington' Breathes Life into an Icon," *New York Times*, April 8, 1984.

55. Noah James, "Carving Out a Human Washington," *New York Times*, April 1, 1984.

56. William McDonald, "The General, the River, the Famous Boat Ride," *New York Times*, January 10, 2000; Taves, Review of *The Crossing*, 1440.

57. Suzanne Broderick, "Benedict Arnold: A Question of Honor," *Film and History* 33 (2003): 73. See also Ron Wertheimer, "Is That You, Mr. W., or a Dream Sequence from 'Frasier'?" *New York Times*, January 13, 2003.

58. Martin, Review of *Benedict Arnold: A Question of Honor*, 1121. Martin's biography is James Kirby Martin, *Benedict Arnold, Revolutionary Hero: An American Warrior Reconsidered* (New York: New York University Press, 1997).

★ APPENDIX: ★
PUBLICATIONS OF HENRY MILLER

Translated by Jan Logemann
Notes by William Pencak

EDITOR'S NOTES: *The Philadelphia publisher Heinrich Möller, who changed his name to Henry Miller in America, was born in Germany in 1702 but spent his formative years in Switzerland. Miller began his Pennsylvania newspaper,* Die Philadelphische Wöchentliche Staatsbote, *on January 18, 1762, and it displays, his biographer notes, "his high ideals of fair-play, with a keen sense of justice and with an unswerving determination to serve the cause of truth." He hired agents extending from Nova Scotia to Georgia, and from the seaboard to the frontier, to handle its sales.[1] By "truth," Miller meant the cause of patriotism and America, as excerpts from his paper demonstrate.*

Staatsbote, No. 1 (January 18, 1762)

Kind Reader,
since it is customary with new publications for the author or editor to state the motives for their work or to mention their intentions in a preface or introduction, the same will now be expected of me.

I will then in a few words report the motivations for my undertaking; these are the manifold demand for a well-established weekly German newspaper; the frequent encouragement of many benefactors to edit such a weekly paper; and because, I, as an experienced printer, seek to serve God and my neighbor (especially the Germans in this part of the world so distant from their fatherland)— dutifully and to the best of my abilities and without making profit-seeking my true focus. [I seek to serve them] by means of the profession in which divine providence placed me in my youth and which I have since pursued.

As the proverb says: "One man's service is another's gain"; I ask as repayment of my countrymen a kind reception of my future well-intentioned work.

We dedicate this translation and these notes to Professor Hermann Wellenreuther of the University of Göttingen, who kindly called our attention to the song, with thanks for his friendship and great contributions to the study of German Americans in the colonial and revolutionary eras.

Since I mentioned service to God and one's neighbor, it behooves me to touch upon the matter that a Christian (who should do everything in honor of God) can by means of a newspaper not only add to the general benefit, but to the honor of God as well.

And this entails on part of the editor that he will be extremely careful not to incorporate into his paper untruths or aggravating smear which would give occasion to discord and disunity; instead he will in his reports seek the truth and on occasion will make an effort to advertise Christian and civic virtues. As readers of these regularly published papers one can achieve the purpose of honoring God in paying attention to the signs of the times which are made plain therein. And, [the reader can] on the one hand take God's punishments and judgments as a warning and an occasion for penance; but on the other hand [can] contemplate God's kindliness towards his own and his work of grace to spread his kingdom to be awakened to faith and trust in God and obedience to him and to be heartily encouraged to spread his honor and praise.

Concerning the benefit to the common wealth, it could be generally proven—if it would not go beyond the limits set by me for this introduction—in what ways a newspaper can advance it in the best fashion. But since I have to come to an end, I will just say with one word that as long as such a paper is written in an orderly and clean manner, well established and above factions, everyone will not only readily recognize its general usefulness but will be convinced of it by experience.

To never lose sight of the above mentioned main characteristics of the Staatsbote will be [my] constant effort.

Kind reader, your most willing and humble servant, the editor.

Staatsbote, No. 195 (October 7, 1765) [upon news of the Stamp Act]

It is impossible to capture the consternation with which this news spread through the city.—Fury, a deep sensation of pain and grief appeared in every face and the mournful utterances of each and all of our citizens seem to say Good Night, Good Night, oh Liberty!—America, oh you America condemned by premature judgment to slavery!—is it then your loyalty—the childlike obedience—your exhausted treasures—and the streams of blood shed by your sons to spread the glory of the British arms, are they it, I say, which tempted the country which is after all your mother to wrap you in sorrow rather than soft swaddling clothes, by wresting away the cherished rights of your children? Or was this caused by disloyalty?—But, oh! Words escape me—and frightful and painful worries make my quill hesitate,—Oh my fatherland, my fatherland!

Staatsbote, No. 761 (August 10, 1775) [letter from a correspondent in Germany]

All of Germany stands in awe and admiration of the steadfast and heroic spirit of the brave Americans; and it pleases us very much [to see] their intrepid resistance against the various attacks of the awful power of England which is being used to rob them of their true rights and natural liberty to chain them forever in bondage and servility; and this should be the dreadful consequence should they subjugate you with their fleets and armies.

Great numbers of us Germans live in America and experience to a high degree in this happy land the sweetness of liberty which they were unable to enjoy here under their autocratic, dreadful lords; these people will exercise every fiber of their being in support of the just cause that is their sweet liberty. Their many friends and relatives here constantly and fervently pray to the great divine ruler of all things to come into your midst and stand by you with his almighty arm, and to obliterate all godless attempts by your enemies to subjugate you; however they also hope you will not fold and rest your arms and trust in the power of your friend's prayers alone; but that you will use means of defense, and they hope and believe providence will look kindly upon your cause of which you already have a pledge [*Unterpfand*] so that your oppressors may be scattered. We wish that, as England is about to hire foreign mercenaries in the vain hope that it will force you into submission (as their own troops are enervated and without spirit as soon as they step on American soil) it could fall on Germans to be sent on this mission. Because in that case we can already predict that this would be to your advantage, insofar as you have much more extensive land for Germans to build on, because no people loves rewarding work more or is as adept to this purpose, which America has already experienced for a long time, and we know that they will soon throw away their guns and pick up farming instead.

We have the highest regard for the wisdom of your American Congress and for its good facilities throughout this great and expansive Western land; we also cannot admire enough the respectable and devoted yet manly and stout-hearted language of all their petitions to the throne and by contrast we cannot look with enough disgust at how indecent and jeering they have been treated and received by these prideful men which direct the affairs of the nation after their own interest.

Staatsbote, No. 693 (May 2, 1775)

Philadelphia, May 2 1775. A week ago today at 3 o'clock in the afternoon, as publicly announced, there was a gathering of nearly 8000 inhabitants of this town, to consider measures to be followed in face of the current, confused state of American affairs.

This business was opened with several emphatic and patriotic speeches and those gathered there agreed unanimously to enter a covenant with the objective to defend with weapons their property, liberty, and life against all attempts to rob them thereof.

We understand that such covenants were agreed upon in most of the counties of this province.

Staatsbote, No. 695 (May 1775)

Our provincial weapons, powder etc. are all secured. Indeed Mars has established his dominion over this populous city. It cannot be doubted that we will have 4000 well equipped, capable soldiers ready for our own defense and to aid our neighbors within a few weeks of today. . . . An apprentice of the so-called Tories thought it prudent to leave in a haste so as to avoid making the acquaintance of a barrel of tar. . . .

It is nearly impossible to describe the pervasive martial zeal that now reigns in this city. A decent number of Quakers has joined with the militias. There is an entire company consisting of young gentlemen who profess to that religion. And as we understand, in Lancaster County a great number of Mennonites is also not opposed to taking up arms.

Staatsbote, No. 696 (June 2, 1775)

Philadelphia, June 2, 1775. The spirit of resistance against the arbitrary and tyrannical acts of the state officials and the Parliament of Great Britain has generally spread throughout this province, so that the people, reaching to the farthest frontier, tirelessly submit to its disciplining force.

The old as well as the young are marching out daily under the banner of liberty and discover an unwavering resolution to defend liberty to their death.

Three companies have already been formed in the city of Reading in Berks County which are already exercising very skillfully; since then however, as we are informed with certainty, a fourth company has assembled, including the company of old men. It consists of about 80 Hochdeutsche [northern Germans?] of 40 years and older, many of whom had been in military service in Germany. Their leader in the field, after their first assembly, is 97 years old, has been in military service for 40 years and participated in 17 major battles; and their drummer is 84 years old. Instead of a cockade they wear black ribbon [mourning bands] on their hats, to express their sorrow over the lamentable events which caused them to take up their arms against our brothers in the final part of their life, to uphold just that liberty which to enjoy they had left their fatherland.

A correspondent who recently watched them exercise for a few hours, reported that they showed so much steadfastness in their faces and such strength and so much skill in handling their weapons and other military tasks that he was filled with the highest respect and regard for this honorable band.

Staatsbote, No. 700 (June 1775)

The women of Bristol Township have shown prize-worthy regard for the good of their country: at their own expense they equipped the regiment of said county with flags and drums, and now they are collecting money to supply those with guns who are unable to purchase them on their own. We have learned that the woman designated to hand over the flags to the regiment admonished the soldiers never to leave the women's flag behind if they desired the women to enlist in support of their banner.

Staatsbote, No. 702 (June 13, 1775)

Philadelphia, June 13, 1775. A gentleman who recently traveled through Connecticut reported that he met an honorable old woman there who told him she had equipped five sons and eleven grandsons and sent them to Boston after she heard of the skirmishes between provincial and regular troops. . . .

Staatsbote, No. 789 (March/April 1776)

Of all the frauds that are being impressed upon the public, not even the most vicious of persons could come up with a worse one than the one which has come to the attention of the editor of this paper, viz. that people travel for 50 or more miles into the countryside to purchase goods under the pretext that it is for supplying the soldiers and then turn around and sell the same wares for twice the price in the city. To betray the simple country folk through a cursed and phony benevolence they claim to buy linen for soldiers' shirts when they come to Mennonites and others who don't bear arms. They suggest that since they don't fight themselves they should help the poor soldiers get shirts etc., etc.

Staatsbote, No. 782 (March 19, 1776)

Tuesday, March 19. From an English newspaper.

"Americans! Remember the Stamp Act, by which immense sums were to be yearly extorted from you.

Remember the Declaratory Act, by which a power was assumed of binding you, in all cases whatsoever, without your consent.

Remember the broken promise of the Ministry,* never again to attempt a tax on America.

* In Lord Hillsborough's Circular Letter

Remember the Duty Act.

Remember the massacre of Boston, by British soldiers.

Remember the ruin of that once flourishing city, by their means.

Remember, the massacre at Lexington.

Remember the burning of Charlestown.

Remember General Gage's infamous breach of faith with the people of Boston.

Remember the cannonading, bombarding, and burning of Falmouth.

Remember the shrieks and cries of the women and children.

Remember the cannonading of Stonington and Bristol.

Remember the burning of Jamestown, Rhode-Island.

Remember the frequent insults of Newport.

Remember the broken Charters.

Remember the cannonade of Hampton.

Remember the Act for screening and encouraging your murderers.

Remember the cannonade of New-York.

Remember the altering your established Jury Laws.

Remember the hiring foreign Troops against you.

Remember the rejecting of Lord Chatham's, Mr. Hartley's, and Mr. Burke's plans of conciliation.

Remember the rejecting all your numerous humble Petitions.

Remember the contempt with which they spoke of you in both Houses.

Remember the cowardly endeavour to prevent foreign nations supplying you with arms and ammunition, when they themselves knew they intended coming to cut your throats.

Remember their hiring Savages to murder your farmers, with their families.

Remember the bribing Negro slaves to assassinate their masters.

Remember the burning of Norfolk.*

* This, and all the before-mentioned, were open, defenceless towns, which, by the laws of war, should always be spared.

Remember their obliging you to pay treble duties, when you came to trade with the countries you had helped them to conquer.†

† An Act of Parliament, 14 George 3d, laying a duty of three pence per gallon on all spirits imported into Canada from Britain; and nine pence if from any of the North American Colonies.

Remember their depriving you of all trade in the fisheries you had, equally with them, spent your blood and treasure to acquire.

Remember their old restrictions on your woolen manufactures; your hat-making; your iron and steel forges and furnaces.

Remember their arbitrary Admiralty Courts.

Remember the inhuman treatment of the brave Colonel Allen, and the irons he was sent in to England.

Remember the long, habitual, base venality of British Parliaments.

Remember the corrupt, putrefied state of that nation, and the virtuous, sound, healthy state of your own young constitution.

Remember the tyranny of Mezentius, who bound living men face to face with dead ones, and the effect of it.‡

‡ The corruption of the one poisoned the other

Remember the obduracy and unforgiving spirit of the tyrant, evident in the treatment of his own brothers.

Remember that an honourable death is preferable to an ignominious life; and never forget what you owe to yourselves, your families, and your posterity."[2]

A German friend of liberty demands to see the following added to the above list:

Remember your own that you moved to America under great hardship and adversity to escape servitude and to enjoy liberty.

Remember that where serfdom prevails in Germany, no serf may marry without the consent of his lord and that both parents and children are regarded little better than the black slaves in the West Indies.

Remember that under a certain great king, male children are marked with a red collar for future servitude from the cradle, as it were.

Remember the compulsory labor which subjects, especially peasants, are obliged to do in many places. Frequently people have to fulfill these labor obligations at their own expense two to three days a week, while the remainder of the time they can work for themselves.

Remember the heavy and nearly unaffordable payments subjects are making to their Lords so that the former have barely enough to hang on to dear life.

Remember that the peasant in many places has to watch his fields from seed-time to harvest so that the crops are not eaten by the game; and is under harsh penalties forbidden to chase the game away.

Remember that whenever it pleases the lord to enjoy a hunt, the peasant has to corral the game.

Remember that whenever an official clerk needs to send a letter half a days or a full days distance, he only needs to ask whose turn it is to run as messenger. The messenger comes; the secretarial clerk gives him the letter and gives him orders by which time he has to be back. If he is not back by the set time, then he is lucky to get away without a pounding. If he has taken a piece of bread on his journey, then he will have something to eat; if not, he will have to beg or go hungry.

Remember that during times of war, when soldiers are marching through or are quartered in, they almost chase the burgher or peasant out of their homes, they demand the best rooms and beds even if their hosts have to lie on straw or a bench.

Remember that the servants of the English state and their Parliament want to bring down America to exactly that level, perhaps even worse.

Many other thoughts could be added to this.

But, fellow countrymen.

Also remember especially the countless reasons we have to thank God for the land that He has given us. [Remember] to implore him to give us the grace to walk along his path; [remember] to accredit to His undeserved grace and not to our own heroic deeds etc. the advantages we have gained thus far over our enemies; and [remember] to take to heart his word "victory comes from the Lord and not from great numbers." Then we should fight courageously for our dear liberties and hope and trust he will direct everything to our best according to his infinite wisdom.

How important was Miller's work? When the Continental Congress sought reinforcements for George Washington's army, which was assembling outside Boston, it called on Pennsylvania (six companies) and Virginia (two companies) for riflemen. The Pennsylvania counties that contributed these first units of the Continental army were Lancaster, Berks, Northampton, York, and Cumberland, the first four being predominantly German, the last, Scots-Irish.[3] Miller's newspaper went from being weekly to biweekly at this time, and Miller published articles in nearly every issue exhorting his German-speaking countrymen to action. He had a wide network of subscribers and distributers, with agents in Halifax, Nova Scotia; Ebenezer, Georgia (the heart of that province's German community); Fredericktown, Maryland; New Jersey (four agents), and New York (three agents). In Pennsylvania, his agents could be found in Germantown, Lancaster, and York, with seven agents in Philadelphia County, four in Berks, and seven in Northampton. He probably circulated between one and two thousand papers a year, but it must be remembered that in the eighteenth century papers were not only read privately by individuals but also—even more so—aloud at taverns, houses, political meetings, and even churches. Storekeepers, innkeepers, and some clergymen were Miller's principal agents. Furthermore,

Miller published notices of meetings of the committees that organized supplies, recruited troops, and set policy.[4]

Miller's politically charged publications in 1775 and 1776 coincided with the raising of troops and with grassroots political involvement of the Pennsylvania (and other) Germans. It is possible to argue that his fervent support and publicity for the Revolution made him an important agent in the Pennsylvania Germans' transformation at that time into political actors rather than clients of the Quakers,[5] and into the Pennsylvania Riflemen, whose steadfast adherence to the cause until the end of the war, Pennsylvania's mutinies near the end of the war notwithstanding, were a major catalyst of American independence.[6] So was Miller himself, the leading prorevolutionary publisher—the Christopher Saur family, the other major German printers in Germantown, were staunchly pro-British—for the largest non-English-speaking ethnic group in the new nation.

Miller died in 1782 in Bethlehem, where he had fled when the British army occupied Philadelphia in 1782. John Jacob Zubly (on whom see below), for whom resistance made sense but revolution did not, died a loyalist the previous year. The Philadelphische Correspondenz, *which had begun publishing in 1781, printed this obituary (no. 51, April 17, 1782):*

On Sunday, March 31st, Mr. Henrich Miller died in Bethlehem, North-ampton County; a man to whom the public and especially the Germans owe a great deal. He was born in Rheden [Rhoden] in the principality of Waldeck on March 12th 1702. In 1715 at age 13 he came to Basel Switzerland to learn the noble art of printing from Mr. Johann Ludwig Brandmiller. In 1721, after the years of his apprenticeship he traveled to Zurich and then to Leipzig in the fall and from there in the following year to Altona. From here he went to London in 1725 where he stayed until 1728 when he left England to travel to Amsterdam via Rotterdam. In the year 1729 he traveled again to Altona and after a three-and-a-half-year stay there he went on to Switzerland in 1732. There he worked in Basel, Geneva and Zurich in print shops until he went to Hamburg in 1738 and Amsterdam in 1739 and from there in the very same year to Paris via Rotterdam, Antwerp and Brussels. He stayed there 13 months and in November of 1740 traveled to London via Calais and Dover.

In that same year he went by ship to America and arrived here in Philadelphia in November and took work with Mr. Franklin. In 1742 he returned to Europe and traveled from London through Holland to Germany. He spent the years 1747 to 1751 in England, Scotland and Ireland and in 1751 he reached Philadelphia for a second time where he installed a German print shop. He traveled to Europe once again in 1754 and upon returning to England from Germany in 1756, he set up his own press in

London. In June of 1760 he took his print shop on a ship to Philadelphia where he arrived on September 12th.

From this time on he loyally served the public here with his printing until a few years ago when age and frailty forced him to quit this occupation which he otherwise so enjoyed. [He needed to find] some rest after his fortune and press were severely hurt especially during the time when the enemy held this city because he was known as a fervent defender of the liberties of his country.

Two years ago he moved from here to Bethlehem where he ended his pilgrimage through this era after five days of illness. He ended it in Christian submission to the will of God, believing in the atonement of Jesus Christ and in happy anticipation of eternal life. He was 80 years and 19 days of age.[7]

Miller was also the publisher, if not the author, of the song reproduced below. It is most notable for mentioning that pacifist sects and Jews, a tiny minority, were active in the revolutionary cause. Why Jews, who probably numbered no more than a hundred souls and fewer than fifty adult males in prerevolutionary Pennsylvania? Historian A. G. Roeber notes that Miller's position that religious tolerance and the ability of diverse groups to work together came from Switzerland, and extended even to Roman Catholics, who with Protestants constituted the Swiss Confederation.[8] But there was one exception: Switzerland did not admit Jews until 1806, when Napoleon compelled it to do so when it became part of his confederation, and did not give them full citizenship until 1874. But Miller had experienced toleration of Jews on trips to Amsterdam and London, where synagogues existed and Jews lived pretty much as other inhabitants, albeit without the right to vote or hold office.

Miller learned the hard way that a newspaper publisher could be blamed for articles written by others, and that anti-Semitism was not necessarily a selling point for newspapers in Pennsylvania. In 1766 Ludwig Weisz, a notary public, sent the following item to the Staatsbote: *"I have unquestioningly been a declared enemy of the Jew landlords. As long as I saw a group of these terrible people make false claims and purchase land for a small sum of pocket money, then set upon German plantations and not question the resulting ruin of ten or twenty German families, I placed myself in the way of such people." Weisz was referring to Joseph Simon, along with his four sons-in-law and other Jews in the area. Simon was a major purchasing agent for the British army (which continued to maintain border garrisons after the French and Indian War), an Indian trader, and the wealthiest man in Lancaster. Hitherto, Miller had printed items sent him without charge and without question, needing to fill his pages with community news and announcements. But readers responded with so many complaints about Weisz's remarks that within a month*

Miller posted a notice in his paper announcing that he would print similar slurs only as special supplements paid for by the writer, thereby distancing himself and his paper from bigotry. Five years later, he printed without comment a notice reading, "Last Saturday in Cherry Alley in this city [Philadelphia] was opened the first Jews-synagogue."[9]

In what for practical purposes we can assume was his song, Miller called the three major pacifist groups in Pennsylvania—the Moravians, the Mennonites, and the Quakers—to arms. Miller himself was a Moravian, a sect whose principal features were to have men and women live separately, consider every church member, male or female, a missionary, and emphasize sensuality in worship and theology—their beautiful eighteenth-century music is similar to eighteenth-century European classical music, and they regarded the Holy Spirit as the feminine aspect of the Holy Trinity. But Miller strongly supported the Revolution (like the "Fighting Quakers"—now the name of University of Pennsylvania sports teams—who were banished from the Quaker meeting); his calling the three major sects to arms was an extension of his own experience.

But why mention the Jews? One reason may be that Jews were setting a fine example for the severely divided province by their nearly unanimous support for the rebellion. They enlisted in the army or furnished it with supplies almost to a man. Colonel Solomon Bush of Philadelphia was the highest-ranking Jew in the Continental army; he was wounded four times during the war, nearly fatally at the Battle of Germantown. David Salisbury Franks, who came to Philadelphia from Montreal in 1774, rose to the rank of major and, unfortunately for him, came under suspicion as an aide-de-camp to Benedict Arnold at the time he betrayed the cause. Merchant Jonas Phillips, in a letter to Amsterdam merchant Gumpel Sampson, spoke for the Jewish community in general when he reported the signing of the Declaration of Independence: "The war will make all England bankrupt. The Americans have an army of 100,000 fellows and the English only 25,000 and some ships. The Americans have already made themselves like the states of Holland." Philadelphia became a haven for Jewish patriot refugees from all over the continent, beginning with New York and Newport, occupied by the British in 1776, and later Savannah (1778) and Charleston (1779).[10]

Miller's attention to Jews may also have stemmed from his publication of Georgia Presbyterian minister John Jacob Zubly's sermon "The Law of Liberty" at about the same time that he published the song. He advertised the publication several times in the Staatsbote in September and October 1775.[11] The song undoubtedly dates to sometime between the Battle of Bunker Hill in Boston (June 1775) and March 1776, when Gage was cooped up there by patriot forces. Zubly, a Swiss immigrant himself, compared the Jews' struggle for freedom in biblical times with that of the American revolutionaries.

Passages from Zubly's Sermon "The Law of Liberty"

And there was a time when there was a king in Israel, and he also did what was right in his own eyes—a foolish son of a wise father; his own imprudence, the rashness of his young counselors, his unwillingness to redress the grievances of the nation, and the harsh treatment he gave to those who applied for relief, also brought on a civil war, and issued in the separation of the ten tribes from the house of David. He sent his treasurer to gather an odious duty or tribute, but the children of Israel stoned him that he died; and when he gathered one hundred and fourscore thousand men, that he might bring again the kingdom into Roboam, God sent him a message, "Ye shall not go up, nor fight against your brethren; return every man to his house, for this thing is done of me." God disapproved of the oppressive measures and ministry of Roboam, and that king's army appears more ready to obey the command of their God, than slay their brethren by orders of a tyrant. "They obeyed the voice of the Lord, and returned from going against Jeroboam."

The things that happened before are written for our learning. By comparing past times and proceedings with these that are present, prudence will point out many salutary and religious lessons. The conduct of Roboam verifies the lamentation of his father, "Woe to thee, O land, when thy king is a child." A very small degree of justice and moderation might have preserved his kingdom, but he thought weapons of war better than wisdom; he hearkened not, neither to the people, nor to some of his more faithful counselors; and the consequence was, that, instead of enslaving the ten tribes who stood up for their liberty, God gave Judah to be servants to the king of Egypt, that they might learn the difference between his service and the service of the kingdoms of the nations. A people that claim no more than their natural rights, in so doing, do nothing displeasing unto God; and the most powerful monarch that would deprive his subjects of the liberties of man, whatever may be his success, he must not expect the approbation of God, and in due time will be the abhorrence of all men. . . .

. . . When the Jews boasted of their freedom, and that they never were in bondage, our Lord does not reprove them for it, but only observes, that national freedom still admits of improvement: "If the Son shall make you free, then are you free indeed." . . .

As to the Jewish religion, it seems really strange that any should charge it with favoring despotism, when by one of its express rites at certain times it proclaimed "Liberty throughout the land, to the inhabitants thereof." It required their kings "not to be lifted up in their hearts above their brethren." And the whole system of that religion is so replete with laws against injustice and oppression, it pays such an extraordinary regard to property, and gives such a strict charge to rule in justice and the fear of God, and to consider those over whom they judge as their brethren, even when dispensing punishments, and forbids all excess in them, that is really surprising any one acquainted with its precepts should declare it favorable to despotism or oppression.

Going back one step further, Zubly's own interest in the Jews was shaped by more than reading the Bible. In the late 1760s the Jews of Savannah joined with the Protestants who were outside the established Church of England—everyone had to pay a tithe to support that church even if they attended a different one and supported it as well—in opposing Anglican minister Samuel Frink, who insisted on receiving fees for the burial of non-Anglicans even if he did not participate in the ceremony. He also denied them use of the city's burial ground, where there had been separate sections permitting internments for Jews, as well as for other Protestants, since the colony's founding in 1733. Frink died in 1770 at age thirty-five, but the controversy so angered Levi Sheftall that he opened his family's private burial ground to other Jews as well. Zubly joined with the non-Anglican Protestants in protesting Frink's actions, all the way up to province agent Benjamin Franklin in England.[12]

A Song Against the Unjust Conduct of the King Against America

To the tune of "I can live rather carefree" [*Ich kann recht sorglos leben*].

1. Oh King what are you thinking,
That you let us be insulted in this way,
In our North-America,
What reason do you find,
Where do you take the right,
To oppress your servants,
   Who are after all free,
   Of disloyalty.

2. How can you let yourself be dazzled,
By the reasons of Parliament,
Which always only put you
In very great danger;
They are putting the law aside,
[And] In this way you are disgraced,
   Here in this time
   And for eternity.

3. Why do you let it happen,
That it should go this way,

To send here your army
Who would have ever,
Thought this of you,
It has not been through our fault,
    Attacks us,
    With the cannon.

4. Your armies have come,
One has taken them in
With all due deference,
Because one is not longing for a fight with you,
But also one did not expect,
That they should with such fury,
    Attack us,
    As they did.

5. Who will honor you any longer,
Because you allow to be destroyed,
A country in its free right,
Through your tyrannical servants,
Who rudely have already in their fury,
Shed much innocent blood,
    Oh great misery,
    Help Dear Lord.

6. One has not seen it before,
What your people are committing,
They chase women and children from their homes
And plunder entire cities,
And set them on fire thereafter,
Burn them down onto the sand,
    Such a disgrace
    Has not been known.

7. Who can after such misery,
Love the king any longer,
He always puts us at unease,
America has to act,
Even if it fills our hearts with sorrow,

We still now have to go to the fight
 To remain free,
 Of slavery.

8. Now King you will see,
That we will now go,
To fight against your might,
Because you have brought it upon us,
The entire country is already ready
To move against you and fight,
 We risk blood
 For our property.

9. The Quakers and Mennonites,
They are also now arming themselves,
Who never would have thought of it,
They are now taking up weapons:
The spirit of freedom is entirely sealed [verpicht],
Nothing is there to interrupt it any more
 In the fight,
 For our right.

10. We certainly do know it,
The sea cities have to suffer,
As Boston already stands already,
Under the king's cruelty,
But when they come into the country-side
Then the tables will be turned,
 Because our people,
 Already stand ready.

11. Gage, the great hero,
Does not dare to come on the battlefield,
He only sits in his hut [hermitage],
Out of which he does not want to come,
In women, children and old people
He is looking for his prey:
 In battle
 He does not dare to engage.

12. The gates of parliament,
They will have to shake,

Apparently they did not think,
That such a warring force,
America could present,
As it has presented itself to be true:
    But such a quarrel
    Is still regrettable.

13. Because one is forcing us,
To wrestle for our right,
The decision now stands firm,
That we all stand watch;
We already have many thousand men,
Who are ready to get going
    Fully justified,
    To the fight.

14. From all corners
The peoples [pl.!] are continuously converging,
They all jauntily arrive,
Each one being armed,
With a gun and a bayonet,
And [they] do not hesitate
    To travel away
    To the battlefield there.

15. One, in all ends of the land,
Is still associating,
That all the townships in their entirety
Join companies.
One is surprised by the skill,
As all the crews are ready
    To advance,
    In this plan.

16. One is exercising it
Also teaching before use,
So that when the need is there,
We all may be prepared,
Because our freedom is worth it,

That we carry what may burden us
    Because it is the right,
    For which one fights.

17. We no longer miss anything
Which is part of waging war,
We indeed have many a battalion,
Already decided on at this time,
The country-man even leaves the plow behind,
To go to exercise,
    The Jew just like the Christian
    Has armed himself.

18. Now King what do you say,
Will you dare to take us on,
Has then your injustice
Still not given you regrets
Should your people still in such fury
Shed more innocent blood,
    Maybe such a deed,
    You will regret too late.

19. Will you not stop it,
To wage war against us,
Well we are in good spirit,
We wager our property and blood,
We will for our right,
Not let up in the fight,
    As long as one man
    Can still fight.

20. The heavens will show
That after all will have to be silent
The great council of England,
Which has dealt the injustice against us,
It will be the judge of all worlds
(On whom we built our case)
    Show,
    Who has done right.

21. The Lord may make it become so
That quite soon they will regret

The king and the Parliament,
The injustice they dealt out,
For that we want to be thankful,
And all praise your name,
   Here in this time
   And for eternity.

THE END

Printed by John Henry Miller, 1775[13]

NOTES

1. Charles Frederick Dapp, *The Evolution of an America Patriot, Being an Intimate Study of the Patriotic Activities of John Henry Miller, German Printer, Publisher, and Editor of the American Revolution* (PhD diss., University of Pennsylvania, 1922, first published in *Pennsylvania German Society: Proceedings and Addresses* 32 [1922]; reprint, Lancaster, Pa., 1924), 6, 11. The originals of the translations below are found in this source.

2. In this passage Miller translated an English letter, "Mementoes for the Americans," Philadelphia, March 13, 1776. We have reproduced the original text here, which can be accessed at http://www.stan klos.net/index.php?act = para&psname = CORRESPONDENCE%2C%20PROCEEDINGS%2C%20 ETC.&pid = 7684. The text that appears at this site, which we have reproduced exactly, is followed by this citation: "The content of this cite was edited and taken directly from: AMERICAN ARCHIVES: Containing A Documentary History Of The United States Of America Series 4, Six Volumes and Series 5, Three Volumes: *M. St. Clair Clarke and Peter Force under the authority of Acts of Congress; Washington, D.C.: 1848–1851. 9 Volumes Folio—over 12"–15" tall. Containing A Documentary History Of The United States Of America From The Declaration Of Independence, July 4, 1776 To The Definitive Treaty Of Peace With Great Britain, September 3, 1783. Volume II—Edited by Stanley L. Klos, 2005.*"

3. See the essays by Philipp Münch and Patrick Spero in this volume on the importance of popular publications in both German and English, and also the chapters on Berks (Karen Guenther), York (Paul Dautrich), Northampton (Eugene Slaski), and Cumberland (Robert G. Crist) counties, in *Beyond Philadelphia: The American Revolution in the Pennsylvania Hinterland,* ed. John B. Frantz and William Pencak (University Park: Pennsylvania University State Press, 1998). For Lancaster County, see Jerome H. Wood, *Conestoga Crossroads: Lancaster, Pennsylvania, 1730–1790* (Harrisburg: Pennsylvania Historical and Museum Commission, 1979).

4. Willi Paul Adams, "The Colonial German-Language Press and the American Revolution," in *The Press and the American Revolution,* ed. Bernard Bailyn and John B. Hench (Worcester, Mass.: American Antiquarian Society, 1980), 167–68, 205; see Hermann Wellenreuther et al., *The Revolution of the People: Thoughts and Documents on the Revolutionary Process in North America, 1774–1776* (Göttingen: Göttingen University Press, 2006), for grassroots organization.

5. On this point, see A. G. Roeber, *Palatines, Liberty, and Property: German Lutherans in Colonial British America* (Baltimore: Johns Hopkins University Press, 1993).

6. See Robert J. Guy's essay in this volume.

7. See Dapp, *Evolution of an American Patriot,* for the obituary in the original German.

8. A. G. Roeber, "Henry Miller's *Staatsbote:* A Revolutionary Journalist's Use of the Swiss Past," *Yearbook of German-American Studies* 25 (1990): 61, 68–73.

9. *Philadelphische Wöchentliche Staatsbote,* May 12, 1766, and June 9, 1766, discussed in Edwin Wolf II and Maxwell Whiteman, *Philadelphia Jews from the Colonial Period to the Age of Jackson* (Philadelphia:

American Jewish Publication Society, 1956), 45; for the announcement of the synagogue, see *Staatsbote,* July 31, 1771.

10. Sidney M. Fish, *Barnard and Michael Gratz* (Lanham, Md.: University Press of America, 1994), 134; Andres Grob to Barnard Gratz, October 24, 1770, McAlister Collection, Historical Society of Pennsylvania, Philadelphia; Jacob Rader Marcus, *American Jewry: Documents, Eighteenth Century* (Cincinnati: Hebrew Union College Press, 1959), 74, 278; Jonas Phillips to Gumpel Samson, July 28, 1776, and Solomon Bush to Henry Lazarus, November 15, 1775, both in *Publications of the American Jewish Historical Society* 23 (1915): 128–30 and 177, respectively; Hyman Polock Resenbach, *The Jews in Philadelphia Prior to 1800* (Philadelphia: E. Stern, 1883), 38.

11. John J. Zubly, "The Law of Liberty. A Sermon on American Affairs, Preached at the Opening of the Provincial Congress of Georgia. Addressed to the Right Honourable the Earl of Dartmouth. With an Appendix, Giving a Concise Account of the Struggles of Swisserland [*sic*] to Recover Their Liberty" (Savannah and Philadelphia, 1775), Early American Imprints, series 1, Evans (1639–1800), microfilm, nos. 14635 and 14636. Also available at http://www.belcherfoundation.org/law_of_liberty.htm.

12. William Pencak, *Jews and Gentiles in Early America, 1654–1800* (Ann Arbor: University of Michigan Press, 2005), 159–63.

13. "Ein Lied gegen das unrechte Verfahren des Königs, gegen America. Nach der Weis, Ich kann recht sorglos leben," Evans, no. 42861.

JAMES S. BAILEY received a BS in history from the Military Academy at West Point and served for ten years in the U.S. military. He received an MA in history from Penn State in 2007 for a master's thesis on the subject of his essay in this volume. He has worked as an interpretive ranger for the National Park Service at Antietam National Battlefield and currently works for the U.S. State Department.

JOHN B. FRANTZ, associate professor emeritus of history at Penn State, has served as president and business secretary of the Pennsylvania Historical Association. He has published numerous articles on Pennsylvania Germans in the *William and Mary Quarterly, Pennsylvania History,* the *Pennsylvania Magazine of History and Biography,* and other journals.

KAREN GUENTHER received her PhD from the University of Houston and is currently professor of history at Mansfield University and business secretary of the Pennsylvania Historical Association. She is the author of *"Rememb'ring Our Time and Work Is the Lords": The Experiences of Quakers on the Eighteenth-Century Pennsylvania Frontier,* published by Susquehanna University Press in 2006.

ROBERT J. GUY JR. holds several degrees in theology, including a DMin from Pittsburgh Theological Seminary. A co-founder of a traveling museum called William Thompson: Forgotten Patriot, he is currently writing a biography of William Thompson and a history of the Ross family of colonial Pennsylvania. He is also completing an MA degree in American history at Slippery Rock University, and is the current pastor at the Barkeyville Church of God in western Pennsylvania.

OWEN S. IRELAND is distinguished teaching professor emeritus at the State University of New York at Brockport. He received his PhD from the University of Pittsburgh and is the author of numerous articles on revolutionary Pennsylvania and the book *Religion, Ethnicity, and Politics: Ratifying the Constitution in Pennsylvania* (Pennsylvania State University Press, 1995).

ANTHONY M. JOSEPH received his PhD from Princeton University in 1999. *The Pennsylvania Legislature: 1776–1820,* based on his doctoral dissertation, was published by Lexington Books in 2010. A former fellow of the McNeil Center for Early American Studies, he is currently associate professor of history at Houston Baptist University.

NATHAN KOZUSKANICH is assistant professor of American history at Nipissing University in North Bay, Ontario. He holds a PhD (2005) from Ohio State University. He has published articles on Pennsylvania and the right to bear arms in the *Rutgers Law Journal* and the *University of Pennsylvania Journal of Constitutional Law*. He is currently working on a book titled *Pennsylvania, the Militia, and the Creation of the United States*.

MEREDITH LAIR received her PhD from Penn State in 2004 and is currently assistant professor of history at George Mason University. She is completing a book based on her dissertation, "Beauty, Bullets, and Ice Cream: Re-Imagining Daily Life in 'Nam."

JAN LOGEMANN received his PhD from Penn State in 2007. "Different Paths to Mass Consumption: Consumer Credit in the United States and West Germany During the 1950s and '60s," an article based on his dissertation, appeared in the spring 2008 issue of the *Journal of Social History*. He has taught history at Bloomsburg University and is a research fellow at the German Historical Institute in Washington, D.C., in 2009–10.

DOUGLAS MACGREGOR is the museum educator at the Fort Pitt Museum, managed by the Pennsylvania Historical and Museum Commission, in Pittsburgh. He received his BA at Slippery Rock University and his MA at Indiana University of Pennsylvania, completing his thesis on American loyalist John Connolly. His articles on western Pennsylvania and Ohio Valley history have appeared in *Pennsylvania History, Western Pennsylvania History, Westmoreland History,* and the *Dictionary of Virginia Biography*.

PHILIPP MÜNCH is a PhD candidate at the German Institute for International and Security Affairs, Stiftung Wissenschaft und Politik (SWP), Berlin.

ELIZABETH LEWIS PARDOE studied European history at Cambridge University as a Marshall Scholar before earning her doctorate in American history from Princeton in 2000. Her essays have appeared in the *Archive for Reformation History, Common-Place,* and *Pennsylvania History*. She has taught at Valparaiso and at Northwestern University, where she is associate director of the Office of Fellowships.

Melissah J. Pawlikowski received her MA from Duquesne University and is currently completing a PhD at Ohio State University, where she received a Bradley Military Fellowship for her research on Isaac Craig, on whom she is completing a biography. She is co-author of "'This Wretched World': John Michael Lindenmuth, a Common Soldier's Journal During the 1758 Forbes Campaign to Capture Fort Duquesne," *Pennsylvania History: A Journal of Mid-Atlantic Studies* 74 (2007): 374–93.

William Pencak, professor of history at Penn State, received his PhD from Columbia University. This is the sixth book he has edited or co-edited for Penn State Press on Pennsylvania or early American history. He edited *Pennsylvania History* from 1994 to 2002 and was the founding editor of *Explorations in Early American Culture,* now *Early American Studies,* the journal of the McNeil Center for Early American Studies in Philadelphia. His latest book, *Jews and Gentiles in Early America: 1654–1800,* published by the University of Michigan Press in 2005, was a runner-up for the National Book Award in American Jewish history.

Patrick Spero received his BA from James Madison University and his PhD from the University of Pennsylvania in 2009. His thesis is "From Contested Ground to Commonwealth: The Transformation of Pennsylvania, 1730–1800." He is currently the historian of the David Library of the American Revolution in Washington Crossing, Pennsylvania.

Russell Spinney received his BA from Middlebury College and his PhD in 2009 from The Pennsylvania State University. His thesis is "A People in Peril: Rethinking Fear and Ethics in the Weimar Republic." He has been a Corrie ten Boom Fellow at the Shoah Foundation Institute's Visual History Archive in Los Angeles and a Richard M. Hunt Fellow of the American Council on Germany. He is a lecturer at the University of Maryland, Baltimore County.